Rethinking Brahms

Rethinking Brahms

EDITED BY
Nicole Grimes and Reuben Phillips

OXFORD
UNIVERSITY PRESS

Oxford University Press is a department of the University of Oxford. It furthers
the University's objective of excellence in research, scholarship, and education
by publishing worldwide. Oxford is a registered trade mark of Oxford University
Press in the UK and certain other countries.

Published in the United States of America by Oxford University Press
198 Madison Avenue, New York, NY 10016, United States of America.

© Oxford University Press 2022

All rights reserved. No part of this publication may be reproduced, stored in
a retrieval system, or transmitted, in any form or by any means, without the
prior permission in writing of Oxford University Press, or as expressly permitted
by law, by license, or under terms agreed with the appropriate reproduction
rights organization. Inquiries concerning reproduction outside the scope of the
above should be sent to the Rights Department, Oxford University Press, at the
address above.

You must not circulate this work in any other form
and you must impose this same condition on any acquirer.

Library of Congress Cataloging-in-Publication Data
Names: Grimes, Nicole, editor. | Phillips, Reuben (Musicologist) editor.
Title: Rethinking Brahms / edited by Nicole Grimes and Reuben Phillips.
Description: New York, NY : Oxford University Press, 2022. |
Includes bibliographical references and index.
Identifiers: LCCN 2022010890 (print) | LCCN 2022010891 (ebook) |
ISBN 9780197541739 (hardback) | ISBN 9780197541753 (epub)
Subjects: LCSH: Brahms, Johannes, 1833-1897—Criticism and interpretation. |
Brahms, Johannes, 1833-1897—Appreciation. | Music—19th century—History and criticism.
Classification: LCC ML410.B8 R37 2022 (print) | LCC ML410.B8 (ebook) |
DDC 780.92—dc23/eng/20220303
LC record available at https://lccn.loc.gov/2022010890
LC ebook record available at https://lccn.loc.gov/2022010891

DOI: 10.1093/oso/9780197541739.001.0001

9 8 7 6 5 4 3 2 1

Printed by Integrated Books International, United States of America

Contents

Acknowledgments ix
List of Contributors xi
About the Companion Website xvii

    Introduction: Rethinking Brahms 1
    NICOLE GRIMES AND REUBEN PHILLIPS

Part I: Intellectual Contexts

1. Brahms in the Schumann Library 7
   REUBEN PHILLIPS

2. Johannes Brahms, Connoisseur of Graphic Arts 25
   STYRA AVINS

3. Settling for Second Best: Brahms's *Männerchor-Lieder* in Historical Context 56
   DAVID BRODBECK

4. Hearing and Seeing Brahms's Harps 70
   JANE HINES

Part II: Rehearing Brahms

5. Brahms and the Unreliable Narrative 91
   JANET SCHMALFELDT

6. The Transmission and Reception of Courtly Love Poetry in Late Folksong Settings by Johannes Brahms, Friedrich Wilhelm Arnold, and Wilhelm Tappert 110
   LORETTA TERRIGNO

7. Rehearing Brahms's Late Intermezzi: The Eternal Recurrence of Reflection 142
   TEKLA BABYAK

8. Joachim and Brahms in the Spring and Summer of 1853: Formative
   Influences and Performative Identities Reconsidered   156
   KATHARINA UHDE

9. Doesn't Play Well with Others: Performance and Embodiment
   in Brahms's Chamber Music with Piano   177
   ANNA SCOTT

Part III: Analytical Perspectives

10. First-Theme Syntax in Brahms's Sonata Forms   195
    JULIAN HORTON

11. Formal Elision in the Chamber Music of Mendelssohn
    and Brahms: A Case Study in Romantic *Formenlehre*   229
    BENEDICT TAYLOR

12. Compositional Range versus Compositional Ideal Type:
    Some Reflections on Brahms and Dvořák   249
    PETER H. SMITH

13. Intentional Transgressions: Transformation and Prolongation
    in Selected Works by Brahms   278
    FRANK SAMAROTTO

Part IV: Monuments and Memorialization

14. Images, Monuments, Constructs: Johannes Brahms in the
    Culture of Remembrance   301
    WOLFGANG SANDBERGER

15. Templates of Grief: Brahms's Requiem and the Dresdner
    Kreuzchor, 1939–1949   319
    MARTHA SPRIGGE

16. *"Aimez-vous Brahms?"*: The History of a Question   341
    DANIEL BELLER-MCKENNA

Part V: Afterlives of Brahms

17. Brahms's *Serious Songs* in the Orchestral Imagination:
    Two Episodes in the Arrangement History of Op. 121   357
    FRANKIE PERRY

18. Hearing Rihm Hearing Brahms: *Symphonie "Nähe fern"* and
    the Future of Nostalgia   375
    NICOLE GRIMES

19. Specters and "Derangements": Michael Finnissy's Summonings
    of Brahms the Progressive   396
    EDWARD VENN

Notes   *413*
Bibliography   *509*
Index of Compositions by Johannes Brahms   *545*
General Index   *551*

Acknowledgments

Many of the contributions that appear in this volume were presented at the international conference "The Intellectual Worlds of Johannes Brahms" held at the University of California, Irvine (UCI), in February 2019. We are grateful to the Department of Music at the Claire Trevor School of the Arts, UCI, in particular to Haroutune Bedelian, David Brodbeck, Michael Dessen, Lorna Griffitt, Sarah Koo, Nina Scolnik, and Stephen Tucker. Thanks are also due to the Deutscher Akademischer Austauschdienst, the American Brahms Society, and UCI Illuminations for supporting this event.

Suzanne Ryan encouraged this book at its early stages and we express our thanks both to her and to her successor at Oxford University Press, Norm Hirschy, for their assistance in the different stages of the publication process. As editors we are indebted to the various institutions that have enabled our respective contributions to this project: the University of California, Irvine, the University of Oxford, and the British Academy.

Much of the work on this book coincided with the coronavirus lockdowns of 2020 and 2021. At a time of such turmoil we are grateful to have been in regular contact with a friendly community of scholars engaged in thinking about different aspects of Brahms's music, cultural context, and the reception of his legacy. We thank all of our authors warmly for their diligent work on the individual chapters and for the enjoyable and fruitful exchanges we have had over the past eighteen months.

Contributors

Styra Avins was born and educated in New York City. Past Adjunct Professor of Music History at Drew University, she is a professional cellist with an academic degree from the City College of New York. Her involvement with Brahms's music led to authorship of *Johannes Brahms: Life and Letters* (Oxford, 1997), and chapters in *Performing Brahms: Early Evidence of Performing Style* (Cambridge, 2003), *Brahms and His World* (Princeton, 2009), and *Brahms in the Home and the Concert Hall* (Cambridge, 2014). Recent publications include "Myth in Brahms Biography, or What I Learned from Quantum Mechanics," in *Fontes Artis Musicae*, and "Joseph Joachim and His Jewish Dilemma," in *The Creative Worlds of Joseph Joachim* (Boydell & Brewer, 2021). She serves on the Board of Directors of the American Brahms Society.

Tekla Babyak is an independent scholar (PhD, Musicology, Cornell University, 2014) currently based in Davis, California. Her research focuses on hermeneutic approaches to nineteenth-century German and French music. She is especially interested in musical temporalities of regeneration as expressed through tonal and formal processes. Her work has appeared in *Journal of the Royal Musical Association*, *Current Musicology*, and *Historians without Borders: New Studies in Multidisciplinary History* (Routledge). She has also published and presented talks on her disability activism. As an activist with multiple sclerosis, she seeks to advocate for the fuller inclusion of independent and disabled scholars in academic networks.

Daniel Beller-McKenna is Associate Professor of Music at the University of New Hampshire, where he has taught since 1998. His scholarship has focused primarily on cultural issues surrounding the music of Johannes Brahms, including the monograph *Brahms and the German Spirit* (Harvard, 2004) and numerous articles and book chapters. His recent research has focused on nostalgia as an issue in Brahms's works and their reception from the composer's time to the present. He has also published essays on John Lennon and the Rolling Stones, and he is coediting a volume of essays on the songwriter Townes Van Zandt.

David Brodbeck is Professor of Music, History, and European Studies at the University of California, Irvine. His research focuses on Central European music and musical culture in the long nineteenth century. Among his recent publications are "Carl Goldmark and Cosmopolitan Patriotism" (*Music History and Cosmopolitanism*, 2019), "*Heimat* Is Where the Heart Is; or, How

Hungarian Was Goldmark" (*Austrian History Yearbook*, 2017), and the monograph *Defining Deutschtum: Political Ideology, German Identity, and Music-Critical Discourse in Liberal Vienna* (Oxford, 2014), winner of both the Virgil Thomson Award, given by the ASCAP Foundation for the Outstanding Book in the Field of Music Criticism, and the Award for Excellence for a Book on Jewish Studies and Music from the Jewish Studies and Music Group of the American Musicological Society.

Nicole Grimes is Associate Professor of Music at the University of California, Irvine. Her books include *Brahms's Elegies: The Poetics of Loss in Nineteenth-Century German Culture* (Cambridge, 2019), *Rethinking Hanslick: Music, Formalism, and Expression* (coedited with Siobhán Donovan and Wolfgang Marx, Boydell & Brewer, 2012), and *Mendelssohn Perspectives* (coedited with Angela Mace, Ashgate, 2011), as well as numerous articles and chapters on the music of Brahms, Clara Schumann, Schoenberg, Liszt, Wolfgang Rihm, and Donnacha Dennehy. Her research has been funded by a Marie Curie International Fellowship from the European Commission, the Deutscher Akademischer Austauschdienst, and the Irish Research Council for the Humanities and Social Sciences. She serves as the Vice-President of the American Brahms Society.

Jane Hines is a PhD candidate in musicology at Princeton University. Her dissertation explores the faculty of the imagination in Austro-German musical discourse during the long nineteenth century. She holds master's degrees in music theory and music history from Bowling Green State University and has been a visiting PhD student at the University of Vienna supported by a Fulbright-Mach grant. As an active harpsichordist, she directed Princeton University's early music ensemble from 2015 to 2019. She has written and presented on topics including eighteenth-century compositional theory, nineteenth-century musical aesthetics, and improvisational practices.

Julian Horton is Professor of Music Theory and Analysis at Durham University. His work concerns the theory, analysis, and reception of nineteenth-century instrumental music, with foci on the theory of form, the music of Brahms, and the music of Bruckner. He is author of *Bruckner's Symphonies: Analysis, Reception and Cultural Politics* (Cambridge, 2004) and *Brahms' Piano Concerto No. 2, Op. 83: Analytical and Contextual Studies* (Peeters, 2017); editor of *The Cambridge Companion to the Symphony* (2013); and coeditor with Lorraine Byrne Bodley of *Schubert's Late Style* (Cambridge, 2016) and *Rethinking Schubert* (Oxford, 2016), and with Jeremy Dibble of *British Musical Criticism and Intellectual Thought 1850–1950* (Boydell & Brewer, 2017). He is currently writing *The Symphony: A History* for Cambridge University Press.

Frankie Perry was awarded her PhD from Royal Holloway, University of London, in 2021 where her studies were funded by the Arts and Humanities

Research Council. Her research focuses on arrangements and reimaginings of lieder in the twenty-first century, and broader interests include reception histories of nineteenth-century music, completions of unfinished music, transcription and arrangement studies, and song studies. She has presented widely at conferences with papers on reimaginings of Schubert, Schumann, Mahler, and Brahms, and has published reviews of such repertoire in *Nineteenth-Century Music Review* and *Tempo*.

Reuben Phillips is a British Academy Postdoctoral Fellow at the Faculty of Music of the University of Oxford. He received his PhD from Princeton University for a dissertation that explored Brahms's engagement with German Romantic literature during the 1850s and 1860s. His doctoral research was supported by a grant from the Deutscher Akademischer Austauschdienst and the Karl Geiringer Scholarship of the American Brahms Society. He has been the recipient of fellowships from the Staatliches Institut für Musikforschung in Berlin, Edinburgh University's Institute for Advanced Studies in the Humanities, and of an Edison Fellowship from the British Library. His articles have been published in the *Musical Quarterly*, *Music & Letters*, and the *Journal of the Royal Musical Association*.

Frank Samarotto is Associate Professor of Music Theory at Indiana University Bloomington. He led workshops at the Mannes Institute for Advanced Studies in Music Theory Summer Institute in Schenkerian Theory and Analysis in 2002, as well as at the first conferences in Germany devoted to Schenkerian theory and analysis held in Berlin, Sauen, and Mannheim in June 2004. His publications have appeared in *Schenker Studies II*, the *Beethoven Forum*, *Theory and Practice*, *Music Theory Spectrum*, *Music Theory Online*, *Intégral*, the *Rivista di Analisi e Teoria Musicale*, as well as several recent book chapters; two of these collections were recipients of the Society for Music Theory's Outstanding Multi-Author Award. He is coauthor with Allen Cadwallader and David Gagné of *Analysis of Tonal Music: A Schenkerian Approach*.

Wolfgang Sandberger has been Professor of Musicology and Director of the Brahms-Institut at the Musikhochschule Lübeck since 1999. His doctoral dissertation *Das Bach-Bild Philipp Spittas* was published in 1997 and recognized through an award from the Joachim Jungius-Gesellschaft der Wissenschaften. Sandberger is the editor of the *Brahms-Handbuch* (Bärenreiter, 2009) and the author of many essays on music history from the sixteenth to the twenty-first centuries from the perspectives of biography, reception history, and intellectual history. As a journalist in music broadcasting he presents programs on German public radio. He is the Program and Artistic Advisor to the Göttingen Handel Festival and since 2013 has been Project Director of the Brahms Festival at the Musikhochschule Lübeck.

Janet Schmalfeldt has taught music theory at McGill University and at Yale; she is now Professor Emeritus at Tufts University. In recent years she has offered graduate courses as a visiting professor at the University of Chicago, Harvard, Boston University, the University of Pavia, and McGill. She authored a book on Berg's opera *Wozzeck* and has published widely on eighteenth- and nineteenth-century European music. Her book *In the Process of Becoming: Analytic and Philosophical Perspectives on Form in Early Nineteenth-Century Music* received a 2012 ASCAP Deems Taylor Award and the 2012 Wallace Berry Award from the Society for Music Theory. She has served as President of the New England Conference of Music Theorists and of the Society for Music Theory, and she has given numerous lectures in the United States, Brazil, and Europe.

Anna Scott is a Canadian pianist-researcher who specializes in nineteenth-century performance practices, with a broader interest in untangling the historical, cultural, and political underpinnings of how we currently play and understand canonical repertoires. An active pianist renowned for her startling performances of nineteenth-century solo, chamber, lied, and orchestral repertoires ranging from Schubert to Debussy, she is Assistant Professor at Leiden University's Academy of Creative and Performing Arts and on the staff at The Royal Conservatory of The Hague.

Peter H. Smith, author of *Expressive Forms in Brahms's Instrumental Music* and coeditor of *Expressive Intersections in Brahms*, is Professor of Music at the University of Notre Dame. He is a past President and past Vice President of the American Brahms Society and is approaching thirty years of service on the Society's board of directors. In addition to his many articles on Brahms's chamber music and issues of Schenkerian and formal analysis, Smith has written extensively on Schumann's adaptations of traditional instrumental forms. His chapter in this volume continues his current, ongoing exploration of Dvořák's compositional output. Smith began, in 2020, a three-year term as editor-in-chief of *Music Theory Spectrum* and serves on the editorial board of *Theory and Practice*.

Martha Sprigge's research focuses on expressions of mourning and loss in Germany after 1945. She is the author of *Socialist Laments: Musical Mourning in the German Democratic Republic* (Oxford, 2021), as well as several essays on music and German memorial culture. She is an Associate Professor of Musicology at the University of California, Santa Barbara.

Benedict Taylor is Reader in Music at the University of Edinburgh and coeditor of *Music & Letters*. His work focuses on the music of the late eighteenth to twentieth centuries, analysis, and philosophy. Publications include *Mendelssohn, Time and Memory: The Romantic Conception of Cyclic Form* (Cambridge, 2011), *The Melody of Time: Music and Temporality in the Romantic Era* (Oxford, 2016), and *Music, Subjectivity, and Schumann* (Cambridge, 2022). He is the recipient of the Jerome Roche Prize of the Royal Musical Association and has held fellowships from the Institute for Advanced Study Berlin and Alexander von Humboldt and Andrew W. Mellon Foundations. Currently he is working on a study of Hensel's chamber music, and a large-scale collaborative project on sonata form in the nineteenth century.

Loretta Terrigno has been faculty at The Juilliard School and becomes Assistant Professor of Music Theory at the Eastman School of Music in Fall 2022. Her research interests include narrative in the nineteenth-century lied, Schenkerian analysis, and text-music relations in Brahms's folksong settings. Recent publications have appeared in *Music Theory Online, Music Analysis, Music Research Forum, Notes: The Quarterly Journal of the Music Library Association*, and *Nineteenth-Century Music Review*. She is on the editorial board of *The Journal of Music Theory Pedagogy Online* and is a board member of the American Brahms Society. She is also a pianist and holds degrees in performance from the Mannes College of Music and a PhD in music theory and musicology from the Graduate Center, City University of New York.

Katharina Uhde, DMA, PhD, is an Associate Professor of Music at Valparaiso University. She is the author of *The Music of Joseph Joachim* (Boydell & Brewer, 2018) and has edited for Bärenreiter two compositions by Joseph Joachim (2018). She has written chapters, articles, and encyclopedia entries related to Joachim. She is currently under contract with Boydell & Brewer for a coauthored monograph, *Riddles in Sound: Musical Ciphers and Codes across the Centuries*. As a violinist she has won prizes in competitions, released several CDs, and has recorded virtuoso violin works by Joseph Joachim with the Radio Orchestra Warsaw for the Soundset label. She has received grants from the Fulbright Commission, the Andrew W. Mellon Foundation, the Fritz Thyssen Foundation, and the American Brahms Society.

Edward Venn is Professor of Music at the University of Leeds. His research focuses on twentieth-century and contemporary music. Recent publications include articles and book chapters on the music of Thomas Adès, Harrison Birtwistle, Simon Holt, David Matthews, and Michael Tippett; current activity takes in the work of Julian Anderson, Michael Finnissy, Thomas Adès, and the documentaries of composers by the director Barrie Gavin. He is editor of the journal *Music Analysis*. His second monograph, *Thomas Adès: Asyla*, supported by a Leverhulme Research Fellowship, was published in 2017 by Routledge, which has also recently issued his *The Music of Hugh Wood* (Ashgate, 2008) in paperback. He is currently writing his third monograph, *The Operas of Thomas Adès*, supported by an AHRC Leadership Fellowship.

About the Companion Website

www.oup.com/us/rethinkingbrahms

Oxford University Press has created a website to accompany *Rethinking Brahms*. Material that cannot be made available in the book is provided here, namely full color images for Chapter 2, and audio files for Chapter 9. Use of headphones or earbuds is recommended for the best sound for audio files. We encourage you to consult this resource in conjunction with the chapters.

Introduction

Rethinking Brahms

Nicole Grimes and Reuben Phillips

Do we need another book on Brahms? After all, among those figures with an established place in the Western musical canon, Brahms seems particularly notable for the constant outpouring of discourse and discussion that his music has occasioned over the past 170 years. We can observe this in the aftermath of the composer's death in Vienna: in lengthy eulogies that appeared in the Viennese press, and in the range of memoirs and biographical studies that were published in the early decades of the twentieth century.[1] Brahms's music had also been extensively discussed in print during his own lifetime. In 1892 he was the subject of essays by Wilibald Nagel and Philipp Spitta that sought to make sense of his works historically, either by describing the composer as Beethoven's successor or through reference to a larger swathe of music history that stretched back to the seventeenth and eighteenth centuries.[2] From the mid-1850s his published compositions were analysed in detail in a variety of German-language music periodicals.[3] We might trace the start of all this intellectual preoccupation with Brahms's music back to the celebrated and often cited essay "Neue Bahnen" by Robert Schumann that was published in the *Neue Zeitschrift für Musik* at the end of October 1853.

Brahms's music has also long had a significant role with respect to music studies in university and conservatory environments. In the first quarter of the twenty-first century, Brahms remains central, albeit in different ways, to the work of a great many music theorists, scholar-performers, music aestheticians, and music historians. The last ten years have seen a large number of monographs and edited collections in English and German on different Brahmsian themes. These variously explore Brahms's music in relation to aspects of his historical context,[4] examine his engagement with earlier musical repertories,[5] and provide analytical and critical readings of many individual compositions in both vocal and instrumental genres.[6] Recent work on Brahms has notably been shaped by scholars adopting a broad range of approaches; these encompass music theory,[7] reception history,[8] and research into nineteenth-century performance practice.[9]

For all the importance of Brahms in the academy and the concert hall, though, the question of whether we need another book on Brahms seems particularly pressing in light of global events in 2020. One of the dominant narratives about Brahms's music that came into sharp focus in 2020 was its purported universality. Paavi Järvi's 150th anniversary performance of the German Requiem with the Deutsche Kammerphilharmonie Bremen in 2018 was streamed during the Coronavirus lockdown in 2020. The ensuing DVD release was aimed at "untold numbers of people" who "feel loss and seek consolation."[10] This stands in contrast to a 2014 performance of that same work, juxtaposed with the protest song "Which Side Are You On" in an effort to fight for racial justice in the St. Louis suburb of Ferguson, Missouri. The event aimed to "raise awareness peacefully but also to disrupt the blind state of white St. Louis,"[11] and to challenge the predominantly white audience attending that performance.[12] The Black Lives Matter movement has played an integral role in a number of performances and installations held during the Coronavirus lockdown in March 2020. One such initiative came from Nicolas Stemann of the Zurich Schauspielhaus whose subversive and cutting-edge musical the *Conoravirus Passion Play*—a collage of online performances—saw the juxtaposition of Brahms's song "Feldeinsamkeit" with the voice of Kimberly Jones.[13] Recent efforts to bring Brahms into conversation with the Black Lives Matter movement resonate with Langston Hughes's short story "Home" from *The Ways of White Folks* (1933), which brings a disturbing context to the subject of the universality of Brahms's music.[14] For Hughes, "Mr. Brahms" is a synecdoche for Western classical music which, in turn, represents white European tradition and oppression. The trajectory of this tale of homecoming, unlike the "ascending circle" or "spiral" that M. H. Abrams sees as being embedded in such tales, conveys a journey of cultivation that culminates in a descending and disturbing spiral into violence.[15]

The essays presented in this collection certainly do not resolve the complex cultural issues that Brahms, as a lionized European male composer, might occasion us to confront. We do hope, however, that by stimulating critical reflection, including on issues such as Brahms's canonicity, and by drawing on the work of a wide range of writers—some of whom might not agree with one another—we present a model for bringing together a group of diverging scholarly contributions that have arisen from a shared set of musical enthusiasms. The chapters that follow demonstrate some of the imaginative research that is being done on Brahms's music, cultural context, and the reception of his legacy by musicologists, music theorists, and performer-scholars at different career stages; this includes offerings from writers whose first languages are German rather than English, and contributions from academics whose primary occupation to date has been outside of the field of Brahms studies.

The chapters in Part I of *Rethinking Brahms* interrogate the intellectual and artistic contexts of Brahms's creativity, including the composer's close engagement with literature, the visual arts, and the cultural politics of his day. The material presented in Part II draws both on a range of historical evidence and on literary and philosophical concepts to stimulate productive rehearings of familiar works; particularly important for two of the chapters is a consideration of the role of historical and modern performers in shaping established notions of Brahms and of how his music might sound. These essays often bring into focus the productive tension that exists between the perceived fixedness of musical texts and the ephemerality of performance. The chapters in Part III respond to recent developments in music theory on nineteenth-century form and harmony and provide analyses that shed fresh light on Brahms's remarkable harmonic imagination and on the compositional strategies employed in his instrumental music. While Brahms's own works have long been central to the music-theoretical canon, the same is not true of other nineteenth-century composers of chamber music; two of these chapters demonstrate the significant gains that arise from considering Brahms's chamber compositions alongside works by Mendelssohn and Dvořák.

A crucial contention of the editors of this book is that because of Brahms's long-standing canonicity, our thinking about the composer is richest when it is not confined to events up until Brahms's death in 1897. Jonathan Miller's concept of the "Afterlife of Plays" offers an appealing framework for this aspect of rethinking Brahms in 2021. Miller suggests that an artwork "must necessarily undergo change with the passage of time." Such change can come about by works being "translated to places that were unexpected or unforeseen by their makers"; it may be the result of the work itself undergoing "a cognitive transformation," or it may be that artworks "cognitively undergo change because [we] reclassify them."[16] The last two parts of the book engage with these themes by exploring aspects of Brahms's later reception. The trio of essays in Part IV consider topics such as shifting reactions to Brahms's music in twentieth-century French music criticism, the use of his music as an aid to processing grief in postwar Dresden, and the construction of Brahms monuments. Part V explores engagements with Brahms's oeuvre by Michael Finnissy (b. 1946), Wolfgang Rihm (b. 1952), and Detlev Glanert (b. 1960), revealing some of the fascinating ways in which his music continues to been "rethought" and reframed in the field of contemporary composition.

Given the certainties that have often seemed to abound with respect to Brahms's music and wider cultural significance, it is perhaps fitting that this book's cover illustration shows the drawing of an entrance portal by the Swiss architect Carl Zehnder (1859–1938)—a Brahms monument that was sketched but never constructed.[17] The portal in this drawing speaks to notions of fixedness and ephemerality, to imagination and realization, and to the modes of translation, cognitive transformation, and revision that pervade our efforts to rethink Brahms.

PART I
INTELLECTUAL CONTEXTS

Chapter 1

Brahms in the Schumann Library

Reuben Phillips

By mid-July 1854, Robert Schumann had been resident in a private sanatorium at Endenich just outside of Bonn for four and a half months, but to the relief of family and friends his health now showed some sign of improvement.[1] On Monday, 17 July, he had taken a walk, eaten well, and then ventured into the garden to pick flowers intended for his wife, Clara. The twenty-one-year-old Johannes Brahms, who had hurried to Clara Schumann's assistance following reports of Robert's suicide attempt, reported joyously on the composer's improved condition in a letter to Albert Dietrich. At the end of the note, Brahms briefly mentioned his own activities:

> Of myself, only that I am well, and that to my great delight at the Schumanns' I have organized the books and music library and now sit there the whole day studying! I have seldom felt so well as I do now rummaging in this library.[2]

Brahms in fact appears to have spent many a happy hour in the Schumann library in Düsseldorf during the year 1854, and there are several reasons why this rich collection of books and music would have enthralled him. Perhaps most obviously, the Schumann library might have served as a substitute for Robert Schumann the man, providing Brahms with the opportunity to acquaint himself more fully with the older composer's musical-poetic environment and, in so doing, to explore the sources of Robert's extraordinary literary and musical creativity. Given Brahms's own youthful love of reading, though, and his ambition to expand his musical and wider cultural horizons, the abundant collection of books, scores, and musical treatises would probably have delighted him, irrespective of the hallowed hands that had once held them.[3] As a bookworm, a nascent scholar, and a student of Robert Schumann's works, the well-stocked shelves of the bookcases in the Schumann library in Düsseldorf would have provided Brahms with abundant means of entertainment and edification. (See Figure 1.1.)

In this chapter I seek to shed fresh light on Brahms's engagement with Robert and Clara Schumann from the perspective of their shared enthusiasms for literature and reading. Well before his arrival in Düsseldorf, Brahms had developed a passion for the writings of the German Romantics: a devotee of the moonlit, mysterious worlds of Eichendorff's poetry and prose fiction, the young Brahms styled himself after one of E. T. A. Hoffmann's characters as

Figure 1.1 Small bookcase belonging to the teenaged Robert Schumann containing books from the Schumann library. Robert-Schumann-Haus Zwickau; Archiv-Nr.: 2361–B3.

the "young Kreisler."[4] Robert Schumann's overlapping literary and musical activities are more widely known, but it is worth noting that his entries in the Schumann household book reveal that when Brahms came knocking on the door in 1853 he was in the midst of re-reading the novels of his beloved Jean Paul.[5] The extravagant images and turns of phrase of this author can be traced in Robert's essay on Brahms published in the *Neue Zeitschrift für Musik* several weeks later. More generally, the communal pastime of reading aloud, which was practiced in the Schumann household, together with the exchange of books as gifts, would prove central in Brahms's mutually sustaining friendship with Clara Schumann in the aftermath of Robert's hospitalization.

One of the most revealing sources for exploring Brahms's relationship with the Schumanns through the lens of their love of literature is a collection of quotations, aphorisms, and poems assembled by Brahms in the early part of his career known as *Des jungen Kreislers Schatzkästlein* (*The Young Kreisler's Little Treasure Chest*).[6] This collection, comprising four notebooks, was published by the Deutsche Brahms-Gesellschaft in an abridged form in 1909 and it turns out that approximately a quarter of the published entries from the notebooks derived from Robert Schumann's past and projected literary publications. In reflecting on the significance of Brahms's repurposing of these treasures, this investigation suggests the crucially important role played by literature in the development of Brahms's own musical sensibility and provides a fuller understanding of the library as a crucial site for the young Brahms's engagement with the Schumanns' creative and intellectual world.

Living in Literature

Even within Brahms's own lifetime, his visit to the Schumann family home in Düsseldorf in the autumn of 1853 became the stuff of legend. A cornerstone of accounts of the lives of the Schumanns and Brahms, the event was mentioned in Josef von Wasielewski's biography of Robert Schumann that was published in 1858, just two years after the composer's death.[7] Probably the most vivid nineteenth-century description of the encounter was by Adolf Schubring in an essay printed in the *Allgemeine musikalische Zeitung* in 1868. Schubring conjured up an image of Brahms's appearance at the Schumann house in Düsseldorf on a beautiful October morning in "tattered clothes, with heavily worn shoes and few pennies in his pocket," and went on to provide his readers with an imagined script for the ensuing exchange:

> "Have you also tried your hand at composition?" Schumann asked of him, and, on Brahms's affirmative response "do you have your manuscripts with you?" "I can play them without music at the piano." "Then play something—there is the instrument." Brahms seats himself at the piano, Schumann barely lets him finish a piece, and then interrupts with the words "Clara must hear that," fetches his wife, "here darling Clara, you shall hear music as you have not heard it before; now begin the piece again, young man."[8]

Writing in the early twentieth century, Brahms's biographer Max Kalbeck was understandably skeptical about the rampant mythology surrounding Brahms's meeting with the Schumanns, but his account of the episode nonetheless remains indebted to earlier writers.[9] The great significance that Kalbeck accorded to the Düsseldorf encounter is slightly undercut by the suggestion that Brahms might previously have encountered Robert and Clara Schumann in Hamburg in March 1850, but it was the meeting in Düsseldorf that gave rise to enduring friendships, and it seems to have been at this moment that Brahms and the Schumanns sensed their shared artistic values.[10] Robert's diary entry for 1 October 1853 is short but suggestive: "Visit from Brahms (a genius)."[11] More verbose was the language he employed in the essay "Neue Bahnen" for the *Neue Zeitschrift für Musik*. Appearing in the paper that Schumann had founded and edited up until 1844, it was "Neue Bahnen" that effectively launched Brahms's musical career.[12]

Kalbeck rightly stressed the importance of shared literary interests between Brahms and Robert Schumann as being a decisive factor in establishing their friendship. Robert's diary entries around the time of Brahms's visit offer a glimpse of the intertwining of professional activities and social visits with his parallel absorptions in literature and music. In the evenings throughout Brahms's stay in Düsseldorf, he was a frequent guest at the Schumann house for music-making, and on 10 October Robert notes that he read poems aloud to Brahms; five days previously Robert records having heard Brahms's lieder and also reading to the end of Jean Paul's novel *Der Titan* with Clara.[13] Perhaps the most significant result of the literary-musical entanglements in the Schumann house in October 1853 was Robert Schumann's Hölderlin-inspired piano cycle, *Gesänge der Frühe*, completed on 18 October and later published as Op. 133 with a dedication to the *salonnière* and literary celebrity Bettina von Arnim. Two of Brahms's Hamburg friends, Louise and Minna Japtha, were present in Düsseldorf that autumn, and while the latter was recovering from measles Brahms visited them, reading aloud Hoffmann stories borrowed from Schumann's shelves. During this period Hoffmann's novella *Prinzessin Brambilla* (1820) apparently inspired Brahms to write a string quartet.[14]

Tellingly, both Robert Schumann and Brahms took to describing each other with recourse to characters and images borrowed from Romantic fiction. Ulrich Tadday has characterized the famous "Neue Bahnen" essay as a proclamation in which Schumann upheld Brahms as the heir to the aesthetic project of musical Romanticism.[15] What is most striking in terms of the essay's literary style, though, is the use of formulations and ideas that seem inspired by Hoffmann and Jean Paul. Seated at the piano, Schumann informed his readers, Brahms "started to reveal wondrous regions," drawing listeners into "ever more magical circles."[16] Praiseworthy to Schumann was the diversity exhibited by Brahms's musical compositions:

> every one so different from the others, that they each seemed to flow from a different source. And then it appeared as if he united all of them as a roaring current at a waterfall, that bore aloft a peaceful rainbow over the plunging waves, and, by the water's edge, was circled by butterflies and accompanied by the chirping of nightingales.[17]

Such intricate images did not flow from Schumann's pen in a single burst of inspiration. Constantin Floros has observed the extent to which, in writing this essay, Robert made use of ideas about Brahms previously committed to paper in the Schumann household in the form of letters and diary entries.[18] Particularly noteworthy here is Robert's stylized recasting of sentences present in Clara Schumann's diary:

> *Clara*: "He has studied with Marxsen in Hamburg, but what he played for us is so masterful that one feels as if the good Lord had put him into the world already finished like this."
> *Robert*: ". . . one who would bring us mastery, not in stepwise unfolding, but rather would spring, like Minerva, fully armed from the head of Cronus."
> *Clara*: "A beautiful future is ahead of him, for once he starts to write for orchestra he will really have found the right field for his imagination."
> *Robert*: "When he lets his magic wand descend, where the might of the masses, in choir and orchestra, lend him their strength, there awaits us yet more wonderful glimpses into the secrets of the spirit world."[19]

Brahms himself could not match this sophisticated literary style, and when he sought to convey his understanding of Robert's deeply poetic personality he resorted to more straightforward comparisons. In August 1854 he would comment in a letter to one of his benefactors: "I find him [Schumann] best described in several works of E. T. A. Hoffmann (Rath Krespel, Serapion, or even the magnificent Kreisler, etc.)."[20] It is noteworthy that these three Hoffmann protagonists all teeter on the brink of insanity. Given Brahms's employment of literature as a means of making sense of the world around him, it might well be significant that one of the *Schatzkästlein* notebooks he worked on in the Schumann house during Robert's time in Endenich contains quotations from *Die Reiseschatten* (1811) by Justinus Kerner. A theme briefly explored in this work of prose fiction, as in many of Hoffmann's tales, is the relationship between madness and artistic creativity.

While we can only speculate about the topics of the conversations that Brahms had with the Schumanns, it seems very likely that the discussion of literature would have been important to their interaction. Prior to Robert's suicide attempt in February 1854, Brahms encountered both Robert and Clara in Hannover in late January, when the Schumanns traveled to the city to participate in concerts that had been arranged by Joseph Joachim. This appears to have been a merry occasion for all involved; Robert was in especially high spirits, enjoying student pranks and large quantities of champagne. On his return he reminisced to the young violinist:

> Dear Joachim,
> Eight days we have been gone, and we still haven't sent word to you and your companions! But I have often written to you in invisible ink, and also in between these lines there is a secret code that will later break forth.

> And I dreamed of you, dear Joachim; we were together for three days—you had heron feathers in your hands from which champagne flowed—how prosaic! but how true![21]

Schumann's extravagant images in this letter, together with the idea of spirits kept high through alcohol, is particularly suggestive of the writings of Hoffmann, whom both Robert Schumann and Brahms clearly had on their minds that month. Schumann's household book reveals that he was reading the *Kreisleriana* stories in the middle of January; Brahms's copy of Hoffmann's *Fantasiestücke*, the larger literary collection that contains these tales, is inscribed "Johs. Kreisler jun. / Hamburg January 1854."[22]

In the months after Robert's suicide attempt, a shared enjoyment of literature, particularly of writings by Hoffmann and other German Romantics, played a part in Brahms's friendship with Clara. When Brahms relocated to Düsseldorf to assist the Schumann family, he took up lodgings near to the Schumann home in Bilkerstrasse, and the presence of his handwriting in the Schumann household books make clear the type of practical assistance he provided during this period.[23] Extracts from Clara's diary suggest that in July 1854 he also read aloud to her from Hoffmann's works.[24] In October, when back in Hamburg, he encouraged her to read more by this author and enclosed a copy of the *Fantasiestücke*, writing: "I see from your letter that Hoffmann had its effect, you have two 'selfs.'"[25] The extent to which the busy Clara would have had time to direct and support Brahms's investigation of the Schumann library is uncertain, but we can assume that she would have played some role in guiding Brahms's general musical and cultural education. Brahms's developing interests during the period in which he rummaged in the Schumann library included early music and counterpoint, the latter of which Clara had studied in tandem with Robert in earlier decades; in July 1854 she and Brahms together explored Beethoven's Ninth Symphony through Liszt's arrangement of the work for two pianos.[26]

There is much that we don't know about Brahms's friendship with Clara Schumann, but one detail that emerges with clarity is the role of book-giving within it. In August 1855 Brahms wrote admiringly to her: "From you I constantly learn that one acquires vitality (= vigorous creativity) not from books, but rather from one's own soul."[27] In spite of such comments, the exchange of books seems to have been very meaningful for them both. The Schumann-Haus in Zwickau counts among its holdings a volume of Eichendorff poems with an inscription to Clara from Brahms in August 1855;[28] in January 1856 he also presented her with of a copy of Hoffmann's novel *Kater Murr*, "To dear Clara from young Kreisler."[29] Even making allowances for items that were subsequently lost, gifts in the other direction almost certainly outstripped the presents from Brahms. Clara's gift to Brahms at Christmas in 1855 was the first volume of the Bach-Gesellschaft Edition,[30] and this had been preceded by a large number of books, including many multivolume editions, in the previous eighteen months: Robert Schumann's *Collected Writings* (June 1854), *A Thousand and One Nights* and Holtzmann's *Indian Legends* (November 1854), the works of Jean Paul and Carl Maria von Weber (Christmas 1854), Ariosto and Dante (May 1855), Schiller (June 1855), Sophocles and Ossian (July 1855), and Plutarch (August 1855).[31]

Copying Robert Schumann

In August 1854, after several months in Düsseldorf, Brahms and Clara Schumann departed independently for summer holidays: Clara traveled to Ostend, while Brahms headed to the Black Forest for a solitary walking tour. In a letter to her from 15 August, penned at the conclusion of his wanderings along the Neckar River, Brahms records how on his arrival in Heidelberg three days earlier he had sought out the house where Robert had lived while a university student in that city.[32] This action was probably the logical extension of Brahms's own independent studies in the preceding months in Düsseldorf, during which time he had carefully examined Robert's music and writings. Brahms's engagement with Robert's piano compositions notably bore fruit in the Op. 9 Schumann Variations that are based on a theme from the *Bunte Blätter*, Op. 99, and were presented to Clara following the birth of the Schumanns' youngest son, Felix, in mid-June.[33] This composition, which in the manuscript is titled "Short variations on a theme by him/Dedicated to her"[34] was bound up with the creative and musical activities of the Schumann pair in a variety of ways. Brahms's inspiration for writing the variations seems to have been Clara's own set of variations on the same theme that had been presented to Robert on his birthday on 8 June 1853. Brahms's variations also allude to a number of Robert's piano compositions and, emulating Robert's employment of the compositional personae "Florestan" and "Eusebius," in the manuscript version of the work, as shown in Figure 1.2, Brahms variously signed the individual numbers as "B" and "Kr" (for "Brahms" and "Kreisler"). The entries that Brahms made in his *Schatzkästlein* notebook during this same period provide a glimpse of an equivalently deep engagement with Robert's literary activity.

In much the same way that Brahms appears to have been fascinated by Robert's early piano compositions, he took a lively interest in back issues of the *Neue Zeitschrift für Musik*. The first page of Brahms's fourth *Schatzkästlein* notebook presents seven aphorisms on the theme of art, which appeared in issues of Schumann's journal between December 1835 and January 1836. (See

Figure 1.2 Manuscript of Brahms's Op. 9 Schumann Variations, showing the end of Variation 8 (signed "B.") and Variation 9 (signed "Kr."). Archiv, Bibliothek und Sammlungen der Gesellschaft der Musikfreunde in Wien, Signatur: A 145.

Figure 1.3 and Figure 1.4.) The majority of the quotations Brahms extracted from the journal comprise the short poetic mottos that appeared on the front page ahead of the leading essay:

> 1. See that schooling leads you toward life, that you are always on firm ground, that your knowledge doesn't pose itself as a cloudy medium between your art and nature, and that you don't merely learn daily to become a greater mannerist.
>
> Kunstblatt.
>
> 2. A guild system of a noble sort must evolve that expels everything that is unworthy of art.
>
> J. Feski.[35]

The poetic mottos in the *Neue Zeitschrift* were drawn from a wide range of sources, reflecting Schumann's broad reading, and their presence was a constant from the very first issue of the paper that appeared in April 1834.[36] In discussing this use of literary quotations in the context of music criticism, Martin Geck suggests that the poetic mottos allowed Schumann "to throw open a window on those distant landscapes of the mind in which he wanted his

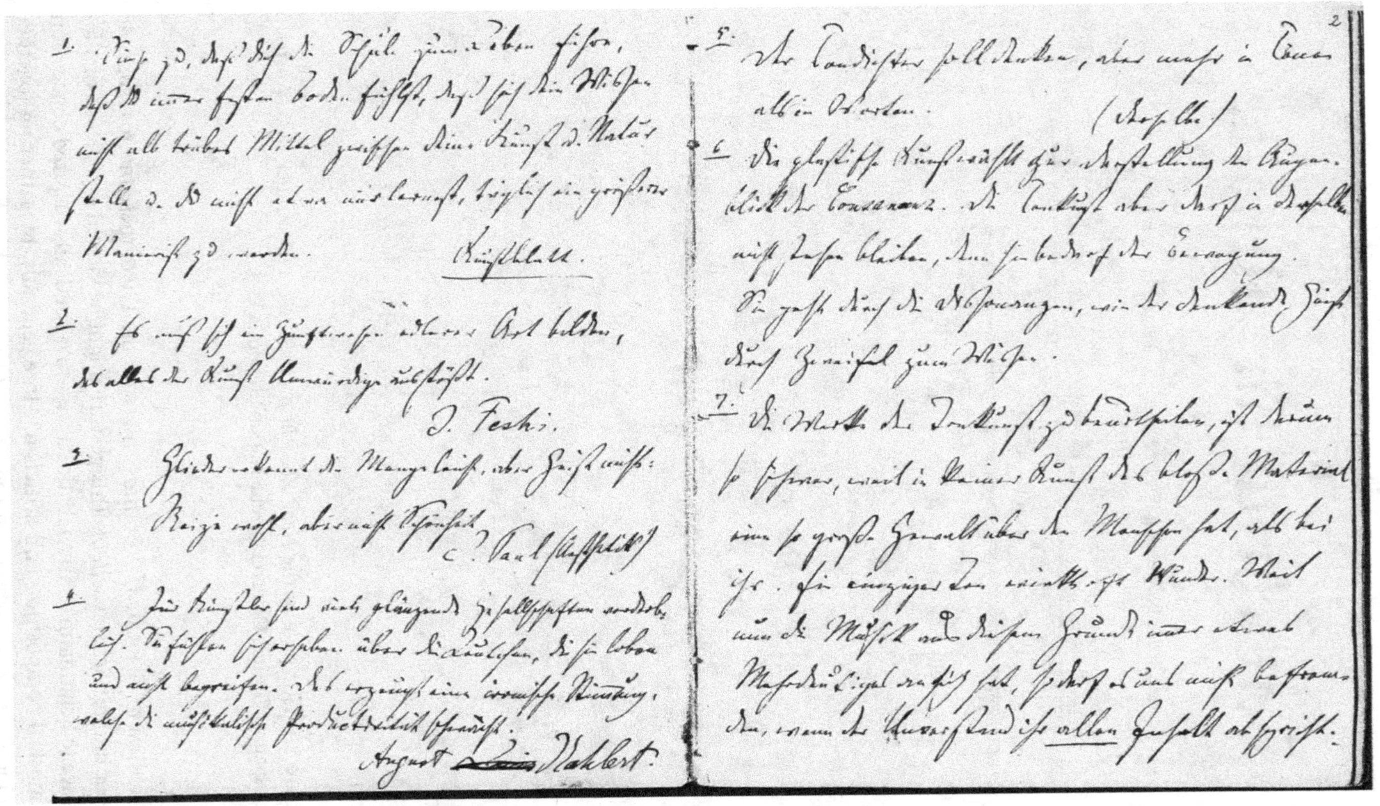

Figure 1.3 Opening pages of Brahms's notebook, "Schöne Gedanken über Musik." Wienbibliothek im Rathaus, Handschriftensammlung Ia 79562, H.I.N.55729.

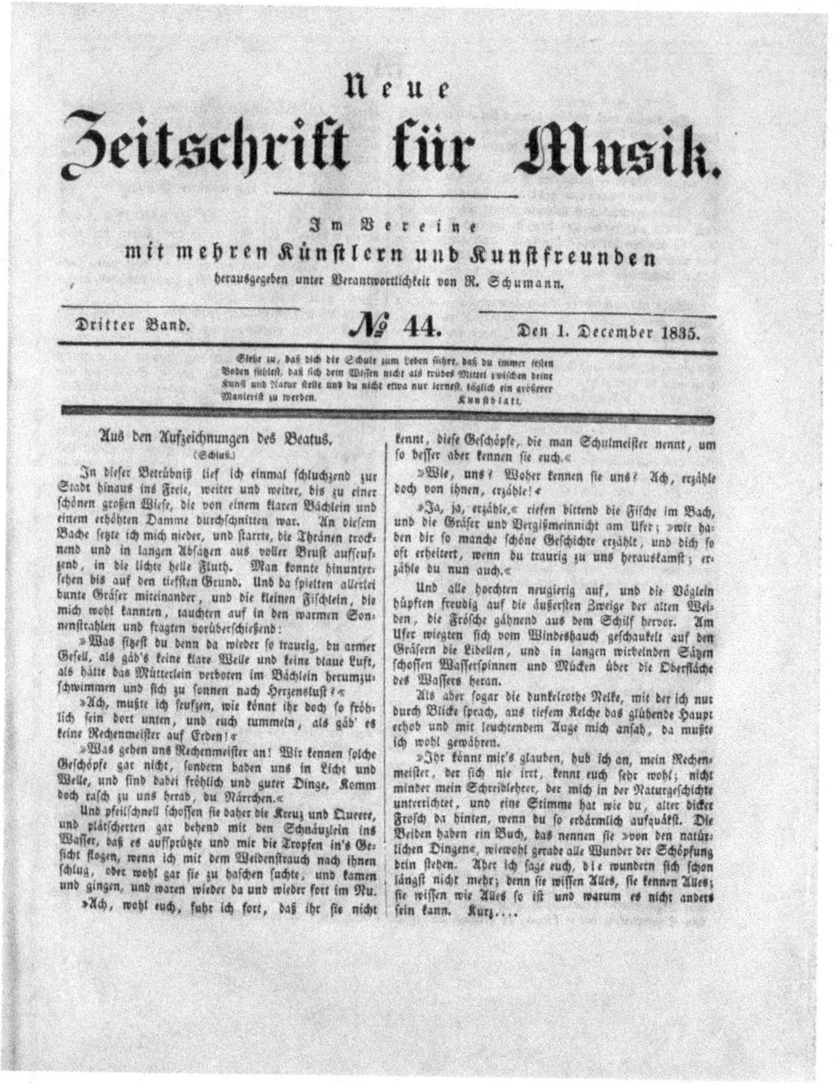

Neue

Zeitschrift für Musik.

Im Vereine

mit mehren Künstlern und Kunstfreunden

herausgegeben unter Verantwortlichkeit von R. Schumann.

Dritter Band. № 44. Den 1. December 1835.

Strebe zu, daß dich die Schule zum Leben führe, daß du immer festen Boden fühlest, daß sich dein Wissen nicht als trübes Mittel zwischen deine Kunst und Natur stelle und du nicht etwa nur lernest, täglich ein größerer Manierist zu werden.
Kunstblatt.

Aus den Aufzeichnungen des Beatus.

(Schluß.)

In dieser Betrübniß lief ich einmal schluchzend zur Stadt hinaus ins Freie, weiter und weiter, bis zu einer schönen großen Wiese, die von einem klaren Bächlein und einem erhöhten Damme durchschnitten war. An diesem Bache setzte ich mich nieder, und starrte, die Thränen trocknend und in langen Absätzen aus voller Brust aufseufzend, in die lichte helle Fluth. Man konnte hinuntersehen bis auf den tiefsten Grund. Und da spielten allerlei bunte Gräser miteinander, und die kleinen Fischlein, die mich wohl kannten, tauchten auf in den warmen Sonnenstrahlen und fragten vorüberschießend:

»Was sitzest du denn da wieder so traurig, du armer Gesell, als gäb's keine klare Welle und keine blaue Luft, als hätte das Mütterlein verboten im Bächlein herumzuschwimmen und sich zu sonnen nach Herzenslust?«

»Ach, mußte ich seufzen, wie könnt ihr doch so fröhlich sein dort unten, und euch tummeln, als gäb' es keine Rechenmeister auf Erden!«

»Was gehen uns Rechenmeister an! Wir kennen solche Geschöpfe gar nicht, sondern baden uns in Licht und Welle, und sind dabei fröhlich und guter Dinge. Komm doch rasch zu uns herab, du Närrchen.«

Und pfeilschnell schossen sie daher die Kreuz und Queere, und plätscherten gar behend mit den Schnäuzlein ins Wasser, daß es aufsprützte und mir die Tropfen in's Gesicht flogen, wenn ich mit dem Weidenstrauch nach ihnen schlug, oder wohl gar sie zu haschen suchte, und kamen und gingen, und waren wieder da und wieder fort im Nu.

»Ach, wohl euch, fuhr ich fort, daß ihr sie nicht kennt, diese Geschöpfe, die man Schulmeister nennt, um so besser aber kennen sie euch.«

»Wie, uns? Woher kennen sie uns? Ach, erzähle doch von ihnen, erzähle!«

»Ja, ja, erzähle,« riefen bittend die Fische im Bach, und die Gräser und Vergißmeinnicht am Ufer; »wir haben dir so manche schöne Geschichte erzählt, und dich so oft erheitert, wenn du traurig zu uns herauskamst; erzähle du nun auch.«

Und alle horchten neugierig auf, und die Vöglein hüpften freudig auf die äußersten Zweige der alten Weiden, die Frösche gähnend aus dem Schilf hervor. Am Ufer wiegten sich vom Windeshauch geschaukelt auf den Gräsern die Libellen, und in langen wirbelnden Sätzen schossen Wasserspinnen und Mücken über die Oberfläche des Wassers heran.

Als aber sogar die dunkelrothe Nelke, mit der ich nur durch Blicke sprach, aus tiefem Kelche das glühende Haupt erhob und mit leuchtendem Auge mich ansah, da mußte ich wohl gewähren.

»Ihr könnt mir's glauben, hub ich an, mein Rechenmeister, der sich nie irrt, kennt euch sehr wohl; nicht minder mein Schreiblehrer, der mich in der Naturgeschichte unterrichtet, und eine Stimme hat wie du, alter dicker Frosch da hinten, wenn du so erbärmlich aufquäkst. Die Beiden haben ein Buch, das nennen sie »von den natürlichen Dingen«, wiewohl gerade alle Wunder der Schöpfung drin stehen. Aber ich sage euch, die wundern sich schon längst nicht mehr; denn sie wissen Alles, sie kennen Alles; sie wissen wie Alles so ist und warum es nicht anders sein kann. Kurz....

Figure 1.4 Title page of the *Neue Zeitschrift für Musik*, 1 December 1835. Austrian Newspapers Online, Österreichische Nationalbibliothek.

periodical to be located."[37] Brahms entered some 120 of these mottos from the paper into his *Schatzkästlein*. This gesture might be viewed as a pledge of allegiance to Schumann's early artistic cause—to a poetically inspired conception of musical composition and criticism. More generally, by gathering together the mottos strewn throughout the pages of the periodical, he reveals a desire to gaze out of those same windows opened up some decades earlier by his now absent mentor.

While Brahms's copying of the poetic mottos reveals his engagement with Robert Schumann's literary activities of earlier decades, it is clear that he also had knowledge of some of Schumann's more recent projects. During his time as music director in Düsseldorf, Schumann had arranged for the publication of his collected writings through the Leipzig firm of Georg Wigand. The four volumes of *Gesammelte Schriften über Musik und Musiker* (*Collected Writings on Music and Musicians*) appeared in May 1854, comprising the essays Schumann had originally penned for the *Neue Zeitschrift*, though with some of the texts now judiciously revised.[38] In the fourth volume of the writings, Schumann had included a few pages of aphorisms of his own devising that take up themes such as the responsibilities of the artist and the philistinism of the general public:

> To send light into the depths of the human heart—the artist's calling!
>
> "It was pleasing" or; "it wasn't pleasing" the people say. As if there were no higher goal than to please people![39]

These aphorisms, together with three others that were printed on the same page, found their way into Brahms's fourth *Schatzkästlein* notebook. As noted above, Brahms would have had access to his own copy of Robert's collected writings from at least as early as June 1854, when he received a copy as a gift from Clara Schumann. That same month, after reading the recently published volumes, Joachim wrote excitedly to Brahms: "what character, what spirit, what rich imagination! the more one knows him the more one must take him into one's heart."[40] In copying out Robert's own aphorisms Brahms, it seems, was doing precisely that.

Perhaps of greatest significance for Brahms's *Schatzkästlein* collection was Schumann's other late literary project—the *Dichtergarten für Musik*, that, unlike the *Gesammelte Schriften*, did not make it into print before his death in 1856.[41] This compendium of quotations about music drawn from world literature occupied Robert in the last years of his life and was clearly known about by Schumann's contemporaries, receiving brief mentions both in an obituary in the *Düsseldorfer Zeitung* and in Wasielewski's biography. Given the very few references to the *Dichtergarten* in English-language scholarship, it is worth reviewing Schumann's ambitions for the publication in some detail.

As Gerd Nauhaus and Ingrid Bodsch note in their foreword to the 2007 edition of the *Dichtergarten* fragment, the *Dichtergarten* project related to Robert's long-standing literary interests and incorporated a notebook containing excerpts from Shakespeare's dramas that Robert had begun in 1841 with the assistance of Clara.[42] Robert's systematic reading for the project seems to have begun in October 1852 with the Shakespeare plays *Richard III* and *A Winter's Tale*, followed by Aeschylus and then more Shakespeare. By May 1853 he had moved on to Jean Paul (it was his comprehensive sweep through this writer's works that occupied him when Brahms visited the Schumann house in the autumn). In early 1854, Robert was particularly interested in classical texts. In the above-cited letter to Joachim from 6 February he referred playfully to his project:

> In the meantime, I have worked again constantly on my garden. It becomes ever more handsome; I've also placed signposts here and there, so that one does not get lost (by which I mean explanatory text). Now I'm on to the ancient past—Homer and the Greeks. Particularly in Plato I've turned up wonderful passages.[43]

Just a few days later, on 11 February in the company of Albert Dietrich, Schumann made a trip to the Königliche Landesbibliothek in Düsseldorf.[44] Clara Schumann's diary entries, however, express her concern about her husband's strenuous engagement with Latin and Greek texts as early 8 February, and two weeks later (just six days before Robert's suicide attempt) she was worried about her husband's reading of scripture:

> Tuesday, the 21st of February, again we didn't sleep all night; he spoke constantly about being a sinner and that he must read passages from the Bible and so on. I observed in general that his condition became more agitated when he read from the Bible and thus came upon the idea that in reading this book, when he was working on his *Dichtergarten*, he possibly immersed himself too deeply in subjects that confused his spirit, for his sufferings were of an almost unceasingly religious nature and were plainly due to overexertion.[45]

That Schumann had not given up on the *Dichtergarten* while at Endenich is suggested by mention of literary texts in the letters to and from family and friends. Brahms visited Schumann at Endenich, as did Bettina von Arnim. It was to her that Schumann wrote one of his last letters, probably in early May 1855—a document that provides the fullest surviving account of the *Dichtergarten* plans:

> In 1853 I had the idea of collecting and forming into a whole, with the title of *Dichtergarten für Musik* [Poets' Garden of Music], what is to be found about music in the best poets and poetesses, how it affects them, affects them wondrously like a heavenly language. The noblest and richest has been furnished by Martin Luther, Shakespeare, Jean Paul, and Rückert. These in particular were to form the first part of the *Dichtergarten*; the second, from the Holy Scriptures up to the present.[46]

The precise nature of Brahms's involvement in Robert's *Dichtergarten* is hard to ascertain. Kalbeck suggested that in his later *Schatzkästlein* notebooks, which were headed "Schöne Gedanken über Musik" (Fair Thoughts about Music), the young Brahms may well have been following the example set by

Schumann with his *Dichtergarten* and speculated that these volumes, begun during the period that Robert was in Endenich, might have been intended as a present for the older composer.[47] Kalbeck's implication that Brahms was helping with the *Dichtergarten* is rendered unlikely by the large number of entries on musical subjects (over fifty) by Shakespeare, Jean Paul, Novalis, Kulmann, Zedlitz, and Menzel's *Kunstblatt* that Brahms appears to have copied directly from the *Dichtergarten* manuscript.[48] As with the poetic mottos of *Neue Zeitschrift*, the full extent of Brahms's borrowing from Robert Schumann is hard to assess as a result of the unavailability of the originals of three of the *Schatzkästlein* notebooks. The third notebook was, however, sold by Sotheby's in London in 1935 and the catalogue description attests to the presence of a large number of Shakespeare quotations.[49] It is likely that some of these together with duplicate entries from other authors may well have been omitted by Carl Krebs, who edited the notebook for the Deutsche Brahms-Gesellschaft publication.

Aesthetic Implications

While the full effect of Brahms's diligent reading and copying in the Schumann library is hard to gauge, we should be cautious about too readily dismissing the Kreisler persona and his literary enthusiasms as youthful infatuations that Brahms quickly outgrew. It is noteworthy that many of Brahms's long-lasting musical interests that can be traced to the early 1850s find support in the writings of the German Romantics: the celebration of folksong (Eichendorff, Arnim, and Brentano), the fascination for early music (Hoffmann and Tieck), and the attachment to a canon of high art music that was appreciated by a relatively small circle of initiates (see, in particular, Hoffmann's veneration of Palestrina, Bach, Mozart, and Beethoven).

Also significant in this context are the references in published memoirs and correspondence to certain musical works produced during the early part of Brahms's career that have not been preserved through publication. John Daverio suggested that for Robert Schumann the act of musical composition might be understood as a type of literary activity,[50] and this characterization also seems apt for certain early compositions by Brahms, several of which were later lost or destroyed. This includes the aforementioned string quartet that Brahms was apparently inspired to write after reading Hoffmann's *Prinzessin Brambilla*, the large number of Eichendorff and Heine settings that he claimed to have written,[51] and a collection of short pieces for piano in different styles and genres that Brahms had originally planned to publish under the title *Leaves from the Diary of a Musician, Edited by the Young Kreisler*.[52] This latter aborted project, which would have included a neo-baroque Sarabande as well as "modern" compositions, including the Op. 9 variations, is particularly significant as it suggests the extension of the Kreisler persona beyond fiery and impetuous piano writing and the use of a playful German Romantic frame for the practice of stylistic composition.[53] Brahms was ultimately persuaded from this elaborate publication by Joseph Joachim, but his initial intention is suggestive: like Hoffmann in many of his literary works, Brahms seemed here to have been engaged in a game of authorship, the conceit of this planned publication being that the pieces presented were "found" by the editor rather than newly composed.[54]

Beyond these immediate projects, though, what was arguably of greater and longer lasting significance with respect to Brahms's time in the Schumann library was his engagement with literature as part of his general cultural education and as a means of reflecting on important artistic themes. In this sense, the *Schatzkästlein* notebooks that he maintained seem extremely revealing, both in the extent to which they document Brahms's engagement with the creative and intellectual world represented by Robert and Clara Schumann, and also for the way in which they show him gathering together and weighing up different, and sometimes contradictory, aesthetic ideas. Given the metaphorical significance of the term "Schatzkästlein" for the writers quoted by Brahms, as not just a little treasure chest, but as a space in which one cultivates an inner life, Brahms's notebooks emerge as integral to his early artistic self-fashioning.

Like Robert Schumann, in gathering entries for his notebooks Brahms seems to have been particularly attracted to quotations that focus on the powers of music and the notion of musical transcendence. In both Brahms's *Schatzkästlein* and Robert Schumann's *Dichtergarten* it is a cluster of Romantic ideas about music that are celebrated above any individual composer or musical work. A commonly recurring theme here is the seemingly unique capacity of pure instrumental music to give voice to the human soul—a notion taken up by Tieck, Wackenroder, and other German Romantics.[55] Probably the most famous formulation of this idea occurred in Hoffmann's celebrated essay on Beethoven's instrumental music. In words marked by Brahms in own his copy of Hoffmann's text (see Figure 1.5), the German writer praises instrumental music as:

> The most romantic of all arts, one might almost say the only truly romantic, for only the infinite is its subject.... Music unlocks an unknown realm for man that has nothing in common with the sensory world that surrounds him, and in which he takes leave of all specific feeling in order to give himself up to inexpressible longing.[56]

Equivalent celebrations of musical transcendence are provided by Jean Paul, the most frequently cited writer by both Robert Schumann and Brahms. For Jean Paul the revelatory capacity of music as an art was often bound up with paradox, as in his exclamation about the way that music seems to offer glimpses of another realm, but does so in an intensely private manner: "O Music! Echo of

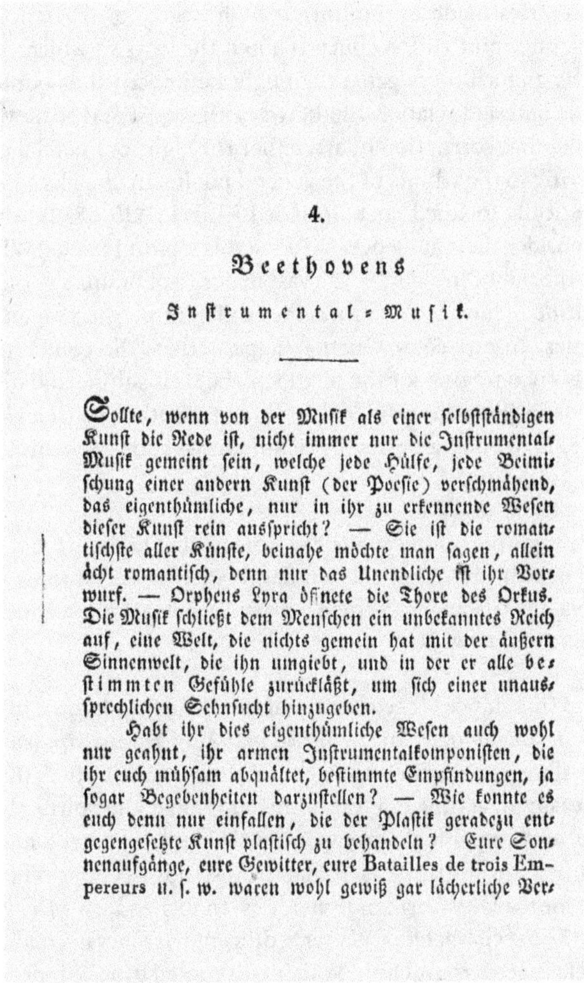

> **4.**
>
> **Beethovens**
>
> **Instrumental-Musik.**
>
> Sollte, wenn von der Musik als einer selbstständigen Kunst die Rede ist, nicht immer nur die Instrumental-Musik gemeint sein, welche jede Hülfe, jede Beimischung einer andern Kunst (der Poesie) verschmähend, das eigenthümliche, nur in ihr zu erkennende Wesen dieser Kunst rein ausspricht? — Sie ist die romantischste aller Künste, beinahe möchte man sagen, allein ächt romantisch, denn nur das Unendliche ist ihr Vorwurf. — Orpheus Lyra öfnete die Thore des Orkus. Die Musik schließt dem Menschen ein unbekanntes Reich auf, eine Welt, die nichts gemein hat mit der äußern Sinnenwelt, die ihn umgiebt, und in der er alle bestimmten Gefühle zurückläßt, um sich einer unaussprechlichen Sehnsucht hinzugeben.
>
> Habt ihr dies eigenthümliche Wesen auch wohl nur geahnt, ihr armen Instrumentalkomponisten, die ihr euch mühsam abquältet, bestimmte Empfindungen, ja sogar Begebenheiten darzustellen? — Wie konnte es euch denn nur einfallen, die der Plastik geradezu entgegengesetzte Kunst plastisch zu behandeln? Eure Sonnenaufgänge, eure Gewitter, eure Batailles de trois Empereurs u. s. w. waren wohl gewiß gar lächerliche Ver-

Figure 1.5 Marginal annotation in Brahms's copy of Hoffmann's *Fantasiestücke*. Archiv, Bibliothek und Sammlungen der Gesellschaft der Musikfreunde in Wien, Signatur: Brahms-Bibliothek 256.

a remote, harmonious world! Sighs of the angels within us!"[57] Jean Paul's obsession with musical culture as a source of metaphor frequently yielded witticisms, as in his likening of proposals and marriage to an appoggiatura (*Vorschlag*) and its resolution.[58] But he also approaches the idea of music with a great deal of profundity: "listening to music," he has one of his characters declare, it is: "as if I hear a sonorous past or future. Music has something sacred about it, it can portray nothing but the good, unlike other arts."[59] Brahms seems to have been attracted to these words, copying them together with a substantial number of Schumann's other Jean Paul quotations from the *Dichtergarten* manuscript.

In other entries made by Brahms, a high degree of reverence for music stands in counterpoint with a concern about the ways in which the integrity of both music and art more generally might be imperiled or tainted. Crucial here was the contested relationship between the artist and society, and a fear about the potential corruption of art, either through commercial exploitation or by pandering to the whims of the general public. In one place Brahms cites the democratically inclined poet Gottfried Kinkel (1815–1882), who enjoined writers to consider their audiences: "To me it is a pitiful poet, / Who does not always keep the public in sight."[60] The vast majority of Brahms's other entries in the *Schatzkästlein*, however, offer a rather different perspective on the artist's responsibilities. In one entry Goethe suggests that "the contentment of the public is only encouraging for the mediocre, but is insulting and discouraging for the genius."[61] For Anton Friedrich Thibaut—author of *Über Reinheit der Tonkunst* (1825), a book admired by Schumann—public taste was also rarely worth taking seriously:

> A significant portion of the public has in general only a mind and constitution for the mediocre. What one can desire, though, is that those who only comprehend the vulgar and the mediocre will avoid making judgments about true and inspired artworks.[62]

Integral to this stance is the concept of the philistine, known in German as the *Philister* or *Spießbürger*. In the prose fiction of Hoffmann, Jean Paul, and Eichendorff, these figures often serve as antipodes against which the true artist might be measured, acting as a foil to the emotional and spiritual energies of these novels' archetypal male protagonists.[63] Goethe's *Sturm und Drang* hero Werther defined the philistine as "a man who stands in public office," and this was also key for the later German Romantics. In Eichendorff's *Dichter und ihre Gesellen* (1833), the character of Walter, a diligent bureaucrat, contrasts sharply with the poets that surround him. Walter is confined to a life indoors, his time is not his own, and he prizes marriage and bourgeois stability over an existence of free exploration and artistic expression. While Eichendorff portrayed Walter as a likable fellow, for other writers and critics there was a strong urge to savage the philistine. In 1835, Robert Schumann had Florestan issue a battle cry in the pages of the *Neue Zeitschrift*: "Assembled *Davidbündler*, youths and men alike, prepare to slay the Philistines, musical and otherwise."[64] Ultimately more effective than violence, though, was humor. In an extract from Jean Paul's novel *Die Flegeljahre* that seems to have appealed to both Schumann and Brahms, Vult, one of the novel's central characters, complains about the desecrated forms of music enjoyed in the bourgeois concert hall:

> If something catches the attention of the philistine, it is one of two or three things at most: 1. When a fortissimo suddenly bursts forth like a

partridge from a half-dead pianissimo; 2. When someone, particularly a violinist on the highest string, dances and slides with the highest pitches and then, with sunken head, swoops down to the lowest; 3. When both occur simultaneously—at such moments the philistine can no longer control himself and overflows [literally "sweats"] with praise.[65]

Behind such expressions of disdain was the fundamental belief that the judgment of art was a matter for artists rather than for their audiences.

Connected to the disdain was also a strongly idealistic notion of the artist's calling and a firm commitment to the personal project of *Bildung*, or self-formation. In a couplet quoted by Brahms, the poet Friedrich Rückert neatly encapsulates the sense of striving that was a key aspect of the idea of *Bildung* in the German intellectual tradition: "In front of every person is an image [*Bild*] of that which he should become / So long as he has not attained it, he is not yet at peace."[66] In addition to this notion of striving towards an ideal, Schiller emphasized the crucial importance of an inner resilience: "The true genius is indeed uplifted by external judgments from time to time, but the developed feeling for his powers soon renders this crutch dispensable."[67] Other quotations included by Brahms consider the issue of how to develop inner confidence such that this external support might be rendered dispensable. Elsewhere Schiller thus states the need for a high level of decisiveness and resolve:

> Going forth from life two paths are opened to you,
> One leads to the ideal, the other to death.
> See that in good time, still free, you head to the first
> Before the Parca forcibly carries you off on the other.[68]

Given the range of writers included within Brahms's collection, there are inevitable conceptional tensions with respect to how *Bildung* was understood and what its ultimate purpose might be. Here, by way of conclusion, it is worth noting the contrast between Brahms's early attraction toward otherworldly Romanticism, and what scholars Margaret Notley and Nicole Grimes have respectively identified as his mature political and artistic outlooks.[69] For many of the German writers who concerned themselves with the issue of education, the dual goals of the project were to inculcate the individual human subject with a sense of independence, and, through this process, to improve society as a whole. Thus Kant famously described the purpose of practical and moral education as: "education of character, the education of a freely acting person, who is self-sustaining and constitutes a member of society, but however retains a sense of his inner worth."[70] For Goethe's protagonist Wilhelm Meister, the sense of both self and society remained important. By contrast, among the German Romantics, the social—often denounced as the worldly—tended to cede its significance to the artistic development, and free expression of the individual protagonist. This latter more aestheticized conception of *Bildung* underlies several novels quoted in Brahms's *Schatzkästlein*, such as Tieck's *Franz Sternbald* (1798) and Novalis's *Heinrich von Ofterdingen* (1802). The dreamy protagonists present in these texts have little ambition to be links within a chain; for them, education is pursued not so much as to allow them to play a role within society, as to develop their own spiritual and artistic inner lives.

Given the extent to which Robert Schumann, much more than Brahms, made his engagement with literature part of his public identity as a musician, there is a strange irony in the fact that Brahms's privately maintained *Schatzkästlein* notebooks were published as early as 1909, almost a full century ahead of the *Dichtergarten* fragment. Both collections remain, in many ways, messy sources: in the nature of their preservation, but also in their conceptual orientation, and what we might infer from the varied ideas about music, art, and society that they bring together. The identification that such a substantial number of Brahms's entries derive from Schumann's collection is a gain, but it also makes clear the range of strategies by which he gathered quotations for his personal literary collection, aside from directly reading the authors in question.

In January 1854, Clara Schumann, observing Brahms's introversion, noted in her diary that he certainly has "his secret inner world . . . that he takes up everything beautiful into himself and feeds on it inwardly."[71] This seems to offer a particularly good way of viewing Brahms's *Schatzkästlein* notebooks, and suggests that Brahms's extensive copying of poetic mottos from the *Neue Zeitschrift* and of materials from Robert Schumann's *Dichtergarten* might be understood as a type of silent self-fashioning: Brahms's rapt absorption, through the library, of a new and exciting intellectual world.

Chapter 2

Johannes Brahms, Connoisseur of Graphic Arts

Styra Avins

At age twenty-four, in the course of writing to Clara Schumann from Detmold, Johannes Brahms advised her on whether to buy William Hogarth (1697–1764) prints, something he apparently felt qualified to do. Unlike his well-known involvement with the literature and poetry of the time, Brahms's interest in the graphic arts has received limited attention, but it is an aspect of his life that began early and remained a lively lifelong interest.[1] That interest is readily discovered by reading Brahms's letters, memoirs written by his friends, and other primary documents. Brahms's engagement with art and artists emerges as a consequence of the path his life took; if he commented on the artistic merits of the works he enjoyed, he did not normally do so for the record, so we have only occasional hints of what appealed to him.

Posterity's first notice of Brahms's interest in the graphic arts comes from his early days in Düsseldorf. "He is chock-full of crazy notions," his friend Julius Grimm wrote of him to their mutual friend, Joseph Joachim in 1854, "—as the Artist-Genius of Düsseldorf, he has painted his apartment full of the most beautiful frescoes in the manner of Callot, i.e. all kinds of grotesque visages and Madonna faces—."[2] Jacques Callot was a French painter and engraver of great skill of the early seventeenth century, an inspiration not only to Brahms but, more importantly, to E. T. A. Hoffmann. The volume containing Hoffmann's influential *Kreisleriana*, a collection of tales and essays, is entitled *Fantasy Pieces in Callot's Manner* in homage to the artist. Brahms's own copy of the work is inscribed "Johns. Kreisler jun. Hamburg Januar 1854," so it is clear Brahms would have been familiar with the stories by the time of Grimm's letter, and had long identified himself with Hoffmann's mad Capellmeister.

Here is Hoffmann:

> Why can I never get enough of your fantastical drawings, you cheeky Master, why can't I get your figures out of my mind, so often indicated merely by a few bold strokes? If I gaze upon your overabundant compositions long enough, made up of the most heterogeneous elements, the thousands and thousands of figures come alive, and each one strides out powerfully from the deepest background and in the most natural, radiant colours, where at first it was difficult even to discover them.

Styra Avins, *Johannes Brahms, Connoisseur of Graphic Arts* In: *Rethinking Brahms*. Edited by: Nicole Grimes and Reuben Phillips, Oxford University Press. © Oxford University Press 2022. DOI: 10.1093/oso/9780197541739.003.0003

No master has known how to pull together in a small space an abundance of objects, close to each other, even stepping upon one another, without confusing one's view, so that the individual stands for itself, yet takes its place in the whole....

Couldn't a poet or a writer, who perceives the manifestations of ordinary life in his innermost romantic spirituality and presents them bathed in the glow they there acquired in strange and wondrous finery, excuse himself by referring to this Master and say: He had wanted to work in the manner of Callot?[3]

"The manner of Callot" is on vivid display in Figures 2.1 and 2.2. *The Temptation of St. Anthony* is one of his most famous works, perhaps the one Hoffmann had in mind. Here is a vast panorama filled with figures, tiny at the back of the scene, more and more detailed as the eye is drawn forward. Here are grotesque forms—a devil whose nose resembles a shotgun, a wind instrument with an unlikely source of air, flying and fire-breathing monsters, a great variety of fanciful figures part human and part animal. On a smaller scale, Callot created dozens of Gobbi (Figure 2.3). A popular genre of the time, they are whimsical depictions of dwarf humans, misshapen, often beggars or street musicians.

Figure 2.1 Jacques Callot, *The Temptation of St. Anthony*, 1635. Author's personal collection.

Figure 2.2 Jacques Callot, *The Temptation of St. Anthony*, detail, 1635. Author's personal collection.

Callot's richness of exact detail and his fantastical imagination is a harbinger of Brahms's future taste in art. The artist was skilled at mixing fantasy and realism, something characteristic of Brahms himself with his combination of down-to-earth practicality, creativity, and the detailed finish of his compositions. Brahms's library was rich in fairy tales; he eventually owned and read all of Ludwig Tieck (1773–1853), as well as Hoffmann's collected works.

Brahms's interest in graphic art may have been kindled while still a teenager in Hamburg, where he would have seen displays of engravings while browsing in the stalls of booksellers, the standard way to market works of art. Once in Düsseldorf, he met a number of artists through the Schumanns including the engraver Julius Allgeyer (1829–1900), and that is probably how he learned to appreciate the skill of good copper engravings, because by 1857 he was writing to Clara Schumann to warn her off purchasing an unnamed collection of Hogarth prints. "Be sure not to buy the Hogarth. Beautiful copper engravings, after all, are the main thing. . . . Perhaps one day I'll find the prints cheaply and in fine condition, then I'll buy them."[4] Apparently it wasn't Hogarth's work he objected to, but the quality of the prints. It is clear that he knew the famous series *High Life, Marriage à la Mode*, with the commentary by Georg Christoph Lichtenberg (1742–1799). (See Figure 2.4.) The six engravings depict the disastrous course of a marriage arranged for money on the one hand, and

Figure 2.3 Jacques Callot, *A Few Gobbi*, 1618–1622. Author's personal collection.

social position on the other. They are in essence scenes from a play depicted in still life, where every detail tells part of the story. Hence the popularity of the "Commentaries," or explications. The six were housed in the University Library of Göttingen, where Brahms could have seen them while visiting Joachim there. Brahms's letter to Clara continued, with a reference to Lichtenberg's famous commentary: "By now it is too late to want to explain Hogarth, we'll probably always have to be satisfied with Lichtenberg's beginning."[5] Eventually Brahms did own what he believed was a Hogarth—a portrait of Handel in a mezzotint of the original painting. (See Figure 2.5.)

It is clear that Brahms was intrigued by the visual arts. Florence May states that he was intimately acquainted with artistic circles in Vienna, knowledge she gained from interviewing his friends and acquaintances as she was writing

Figure 2.4 William Hogarth, *Marriage à la Mode—Betrothal*, the first in the series ca. 1743. Author's personal collection.

Figure 2.5 William Hogarth, *Portrait of George Friedrich Handel*, ca. 1740 The Burghley House Collection.

her biography of him.[6] Arriving in Düsseldorf as a twenty-year-old, thanks to the Schumanns he was able to make contact with Johann Wilhelm Schirmer (1807–1863), perhaps the leading German landscape artist of his time. The acquaintance struck up between the two was friendly enough to allow the young man to stop off in Karlsruhe with the intent to visit with Schirmer in 1855, as he was returning from a two-week excursion along the Rhine with Clara Schumann.[7] Schirmer, now the director of the Art School (the present State Academy of Fine Arts), was away at the time; but during Brahms's next visit to Karlsruhe in 1862 he made a point of renewing his contact not only with Schirmer but with Karl Friedrich Lessing (1808–1880), another acclaimed landscape and historical painter known to Brahms from his early days in Düsseldorf. At this point Lessing was director of the Karlsruhe Gallery, and with his music-loving wife Ida would become an important part of the group of friends that formed during Brahms's longer stays in Karlsruhe in 1865. The group included other prominent artists and their musical wives as well as local intellectuals, the conductor Hermann Levi (1839–1900), Julius Allgeyer with whom he re-established a close friendship, and Anselm Feuerbach (1829–1880).[8] Allgeyer had returned to Germany after spending time in Rome. Although still active as an engraver, he was now exploring the new technology of photography; but while in Rome he had met Feuerbach, a young artist whose visit to the Uffizi Gallery in Florence had aroused in him the calling to becoming a historical painter. This was a kind of art already falling out of favor in general—but not, apparently, for Allgeyer nor for Brahms. Allgeyer had come to admire Feuerbach's work in the course of engraving some of his paintings: it is he who introduced Brahms to the artist who would become one of Brahms's most admired painters. Feuerbach painted scenes from ancient history; his figures were based on classical and Renaissance models, cool and distant (often in profile), the historical paintings laid out on huge canvases.

Brahms's interest in classical art was well-nurtured by the time he met Feuerbach. The years in Hamburg between his return in 1856 and his decision to go to Vienna in 1862 were partly spent in furthering his education; he studied Latin and attended lectures in history and art.[9] In 1860 he received as a present the monumental three-volume survey of art by Franz Kugler (1808–1858), *Handbook of Art History* (*Handbuch der Kunstgeschichte*), "from Constantin to the Present," with many illustrations. Feuerbach's work appealed to Brahms not only because of its subject matter and painterly skill, but in addition he admired the artist's intense dedication to his work. (See Figures 2.6 and 2.7.) Feuerbach—in his own words—strove for greatness, calm, and simplicity [Grösse, Ruhe, Einfachkeit].[10] It is also possible that in the mid-1860s the two friends inspired each other to engage with the orientalist figure of Hafis (Hafez), the fourteenth-century Persian poet much admired and freely translated by the poet Georg Friedrich Daumer (1800–1875). In the mid-1860s Brahms set several of his poems to music and Feuerbach created two important

Figure 2.6 Anselm Feuerbach, *Orpheus and Euridike*, 1868–1869. Author's personal collection.

paintings of the poet.[11] Brahms, who had etchings of two historical paintings hanging on his walls, followed Feuerbach's progress on the work of his historical paintings with great interest, although not always with appreciation.[12]

But Feuerbach was problematic: apart from the high opinion he had of himself (immodest about his abilities as a painter, he was aware of his good looks, was attracted to fine clothes, and to women), he had contracted syphilis in 1855. He was often in bad health and consequently often ill-tempered. In 1866, Allgeyer, who was close to both Anselm and his devoted stepmother Henriette Feuerbach, received this letter from her in response to an incident which had troubled him:

> Anselm very often does not know what he writes and what he speaks, not even what he thinks. He lets off steam like a force of nature that hits where

Figure 2.7 Anselm Feuerbach, *Musikalische Poesie*, ca. 1856. Author's personal collection.

> it hits . . . his spirit and his mind are absorbed in artistic sensation. . . . One must take him, if one wants to deal properly with him, as a good but terribly ill-bred child.[13]

Brahms's own relations with him cooled when Feuerbach came to Vienna as professor of historical painting at the Viennese Academy of Fine Art in 1873. Now the tensions of their contrasting personalities surfaced; while Brahms, ever practical, urged Feuerbach to start modestly, to get a feel for Vienna's politics before exhibiting his work, Feuerbach insisted on showing two enormous paintings. The *Symposium* (Figure 2.8) depicts a rowdy moment described in Plato's text of the same name. Feuerbach spent several years on

Figure 2.8 Anselm Feuerbach, *The Symposium*, 1869. Staatliche Kunsthalle, Karlsruhe.

this monumental painting. Illustrated here is the first of two versions. The second was specifically prepared for display in Vienna. The painting, so large it could not be hung in the World Exhibition Hall for which it was intended, was not well received. *The Battle of the Amazons (Amazonenschlacht)* was the other large painting which the newcomer was anxious to show. Brahms had his doubts, as did a friend he took along to Feuerbach's studio to see it; Klaus Groth (1819–1899), from Kiel, described the visit in a letter to his wife as not being very successful.[14] The critics agreed.

Henriette must have known that Anselm's situation in Vienna was deteriorating and hoped Brahms was the person who could help. She wrote to him: "I beg you to remain a devoted and well-meaning friend to him and to be concerned about his well-being, something your inner harmony and your self-confidence readily allows you to do."[15] Eventually Feuerbach lost his position in Vienna in a quarrel over the ceiling fresco of the new Academy of Art building, and left the city. Brahms's admiration for the artist remained undiminished. The choral work *Nänie*, based on the poem by Friedrich Schiller with opening words "Auch das Schöne muss sterben" (even beauty must die), was dedicated to Feuerbach's devoted stepmother. It was Brahms's response to the painter's death in Venice in 1880.[16] Traveling in Italy with his friend Joseph Widmann in 1888, he made a point of visiting places that had been important to Feuerbach during his student years in Rome, and as inspiration for one of his most important paintings. A later excursion to Karlsruhe included a visit to the Kunsthalle to see some of his friend's paintings.[17] And in a letter to Widmann he named Feuerbach, along with Arnold Böcklin (1827–1901), Max Klinger (1857–1920), and Adolph Menzel (1815–1905), as leading artists whose work "fill[ed] Heart and House," counting himself lucky to live in such a time.[18] Brahms knew all four artists personally and owned works of each.

We return to Julius Allgeyer and the emerging technology of photography. Allgeyer, trained as a lithographer in Karlsruhe, took part in the Revolution of 1848; fled, like Wagner, to Switzerland; and when amnestied came to Düsseldorf to work as an engraver. That is how he met Clara Schumann, and thereby Brahms. Off to Rome in 1856, Allgeyer met Feuerbach, and the triple connection was formed. Upon return to Germany he settled in Karslruhe and founded a photography studio, his real calling. A pioneer in the practice, his specialty was portraiture, the first popular use of the technology: Brahms's letters to his friends are filled with requests for their photographs, and in the end, he had a large collection. Louis Daguerre's invention (the silver-plated thin copper plate) was expensive, and remained so for a long time. That explains the impact of Brahms's present to his father upon Johann Jakob Brahms's remarriage: a splendid portrait of himself by Allgeyer. (See Figure 2.9; see also Figure 2.10 for Allgeyer's portrait of Feuerbach.)

But in deep contrast to the art of Feuerbach and the painters of historical scenes Brahms admired, *another* movement in art was flowering, and would soon arouse his interest—one that occasioned an exploration of the relationship between music and painting and the creation of paintings that are musical.

Figure 2.9 Julius Allgeyer, Photograph, *Portrait of Brahms*, 1866. Author's personal collection.

Figure 2.10 Julius Allgeyer, Photograph, *Portrait of Anselm Feuerbach*, 1865. Author's personal collection.

The "contest" between the two arts has a long history. In 1859 Louis Viardot (1800–1883) published an influential article, "Ut pictora musica" (As with music, so with painting).[19] In it Viardot claimed to address "a very new question for the first time": the parallels between painting and music. The claim was disingenuous, as the issue had been discussed since the Renaissance when Leonardo da Vinci wrote *Il paragone delle arti* (*Comparison of the Arts*), which makes the case that music should be understood as a minor sister of painting; but Viardot's essay awakened interest and led to conversations among the many artists and musicians, both French and from abroad, working in Paris. E. T. A. Hoffmann, Tieck, the early German Romantics, and Schopenhauer had already made a strong case for the superiority of music, based on its perceived abstractness that expresses higher, inner realms located beyond empirical reality. Tieck wrote: "Art is independent and free in instrumental music; it prescribes its own rules all by itself . . . it completely follows its dark drives and expresses . . . what is deepest and most wonderful. . . . Sounds which art has miraculously discovered . . . do not imitate and do not beautify, rather, they constitute a separate world for themselves."[20] Tieck wrote this at a time when instrumental music was coming into its own as the major art, no longer tied to language. Théophile Gautier, writing in 1858, remarked that the smile of Mona Lisa was "vague, infinite, inexpressible, like a musical thought." Although proponents of the "Music of the Future," the powerful musical faction led by Franz Liszt, wished to connect music with a literary program, it would seem that for painters in France the efforts of Liszt and Berlioz to endow music with articulated speech and powers of description apparently went unheeded. Music was vague, infinite, inexpressible, and some painters wanted their paintings to capture those qualities. Baudelaire claimed that the arts aspired to a condition "in which they lent each other new powers."[21]

Brahms would have had occasion to discuss Viardot's ideas with him, as the writer was the husband of the singer Pauline Garcia Viardot (1821–1910), a close friend of Clara Schumann's. The Viardots had an elaborate and hospitable establishment in Baden-Baden, to which Brahms was a frequent visitor during the many summers he spent in the spa town. His dwelling was an old farmhouse close to Clara Schumann, who summered there with her entire family. Brahms's friendly acquaintance with the Viardots suggests abundant opportunity to discuss "Ut pictora musica." For Brahms, who admired Tieck and other German Romantic writers, the idea that music had the possibility of leading one to the edge of the Infinite must have struck a resonance. Inspired by Viardot's essay, there were painters with the same goal.

The chief player in this attempt was the French painter Henri Fantin-Latour (1836–1904). Musical himself, his wife and sister played the piano, including Brahms's works for four hands. At the age of twenty-one he had been introduced to the Parisian artist circle where contemporary German music was enjoyed, above all Brahms and Schumann. His admiration of them was lifelong. "Of everything modern I've heard, it is the work of this very talented young student of Schumann which makes the best impression on me," he exclaimed.[22] In trying to express the feelings aroused by their music, Fantin-Latour, the unparalleled and meticulous painter of flowers, developed his own method of lithography—working directly on stone with pencil and oil crayon. This technique gave him a more subtle variety in texture, a more plastic fluidity—a technique that was adequate to transcribe his feelings about music. Critics have called these his most individual and creative works. Fantin-Latour made a distinction in materials between his naturalistic paintings and the paintings of his imagination. "I don't understand how one can create a poetic subject with reality," he said. Instead, his "reality" became myth and allegory. His chief love was Berlioz, but in several lithographs he honored the *Four Truths: Schumann, Berlioz, Wagner, and Brahms* (1881). Fantin-Latour reacted particularly to the moment in Brahms's *Rinaldo* (Op. 50) when Rinaldo's companions tear him away from Armide. Figure 2.11 is one of several studies of the subject. When Brahms died, he

Connoisseur of Graphic Arts

Figure 2.11 Henri Fantin-Latour, Lithograph, *J. Brahms, Rinaldo*, 1877. Author's personal collection.

produced an image of Music weeping. (See Figure 2.12.) These late nineteenth-century works relied on symbolic forms from the classical world: winged and draped figures, garlands, wreaths, marble tablets, and columns, standard stuff of celebratory painting, sculpture, and art. But Fantin-Latour was not the only artist to turn to classical symbols.

In discussions of those painters whom Brahms admired, Fantin-Latour must play some role because two of these painters, Arnold Böcklin and Max Klinger, were familiar with the influential work of the very well-known Frenchman. I know of no evidence that Brahms himself knew of Fantin-Latour's work, but it would be surprising if, given his keen interest in graphic arts, he was unaware

Figure 2.12 Henri Fantin-Latour, *Hommage à Brahms*, 1900. Author's personal collection.

of the Frenchman who so honored him, above all in the medium of lithography. Klinger was in Paris for a time; his work shows clear evidence that he felt a connection between music and his art. He was himself a notably able pianist, and produced a series of etchings as "Opuses." We will return to him.

Brahms met the Swiss painter Arnold Böcklin in Munich, in 1873, while in company with the conductors Herman Levi and Franz Wüllner (1832–1902), the poet and writer Paul Heyse (1830–1914), and other artists, musicians, and intellectuals. Böcklin had known Heyse in Rome in 1855. He, along with Feuerbach, whom he also met in Rome, had been deeply influenced by Heyse

Figure 2.13 Arnold Böcklin, *Flora*, 1875. Author's personal collection.

who was at that time himself much taken with myth and fairy tale: it was upon meeting Heyse that Böcklin turned to Italian and Greek landscapes with classic and mythical figures. The allure of the sunny Italian landscape is evident in his *Flora* (Figure 2.13), painted while in Rome. The painting was owned by Max Klinger. But at the time Brahms met Böcklin he had just painted his *memento mori*, *Selbstbildnis mit fiedelndem Tod* (*Self-Portrait with Death Fiddling*) (Figure 2.14), a stark addition to his earlier Italian-mythological landscapes—a brooding painting that pointed to his future fame as one of the founders of the German Symbolist school. Böcklin, who indeed played the violin, here shows himself with an instrument lacking all but one string, the darkest-sounding G-string. The early deaths of many of his children might have had a role in

Figure 2.14 Arnold Böcklin, *Self-Portrait with Death Fiddling*, 1872. Author's personal collection.

his transformation from a painter of glowing landscapes concerned with Greek mythology to one that included dark visions of desolation and isolation (Figures 2.15 and 2.16). What remained unchanged was his meticulous skill as a painter.

The most famous of all Böcklin's paintings is *Die Toteninsel* (*The Isle of the Dead*), painted in five versions over a period of several years. (See Figure 2.17.) Max Klinger was commissioned to make an etching of it, which greatly spread its popularity throughout Germany. It provided the inspiration for Sergei Rachmaninoff's Symphonic Poem of the same name. Brahms is reported to have visited Böcklin in his studio in 1885 (although this date is likely a few years too early),[23] and in 1894 received as a gift from the artist the first volume

Figure 2.15 Arnold Böcklin, *Ruine am Meer*, 1880. Author's personal collection.

of *Arnold Böcklin: eine Auswahl der hervorragendsten Werke des Künstlers in Photogravüre* (*Arnold Böcklin: A Selection of the Most Outstanding Works of the Artist in Photogravure*).[24]

Of an utterly different character were the etchings of Daniel Chodowiecki (1726–1801), an artist whose work Brahms cherished. Chodowiecki was born in Poland but lived in Berlin. A Huguenot and champion of the Enlightenment, he was incomparable at depicting above all the life of the lower middle class and family life in northern Germany and, somewhat in the manner of Hogarth, caricaturing the nobility and the plight of commoners. Brahms was enthralled, and started the new year of 1877 by getting in touch with the Leipzig bookseller, publisher, and foremost collector of his etchings, Wilhelm Engelmann (whose

Figure 2.16 Arnold Böcklin, *Bergruine*, ca. 1886. Author's personal collection.

Figure 2.17 Arnold Böcklin, *Isle of the Dead*, 1880. Author's personal collection.

name is familiar to Brahms lovers because he was the father of Theodor, dedicatee of Brahms's String Quartet Op. 67). Luckily for Brahms, Wilhelm was the most outstanding collector and cataloguer of Chodowiecki's work. Upon hearing from the composer, he sent Brahms his catalogue of the complete etchings, the definitive catalogue of his work even today.[25] Engelmann also sent Brahms any etching of which he had duplicates—"I should be ashamed to possess such a treasure," Brahms responded, but added that any artist would be glad to have an admirer as enthusiastic as he was.[26] Engelmann's own appreciation rested on the artist's "inner, philosophical, and dense art content, and with a concept of the knowledge of the common heart and the world which shines forth in it everywhere."[27] Possibly that is what Brahms saw in his work. His estate included over 200 of Chodowiecki's etchings.[28] The artist made many etchings of everyday life, as in *Kitchen Work* (Figure 2.18), which shows details of the work inside the kitchen and guides the eye to activities seen through the open door. Figure 2.19 is an illustration to Shakespeare's *Coriolanus*, Act IV, Scene I, with Coriolanus greeting his mother at the gate.

At age fifty-seven, Brahms met the great illustrator and painter Adolph Menzel. Their friendship was born over Menzel's sketch of the clarinetist Richard Mühlfeld, made during the Berlin premiere of Brahms's Clarinet Quintet. The two had much in common, in addition to the artist's serious

Figure 2.18 Daniel Chodowiecki, *Kitchen Work*. Author's personal collection.

Figure 2.19 Daniel Chodowiecki, *Coriolanus Greeting His Mother at the Gate*. Author's personal collection.

interest in music. Both had received the Prussian Order *Pour le Mérite*, both were confirmed bachelors, both enjoyed late evenings of beer drinking in cafés, lived in a simple fashion well below their incomes, and had a strong work ethic. Brahms's letter to Clara Schumann of 4 February 1896 provides a telling view of his affinity for Menzel the person and the artist:

> I wanted to try to tell you something about Menzel, the great artist (probably the greatest of our time) and the splendid man. . . . *I am particularly pleased that he is the only one of our famous men who lives in the most modest middle-class circumstances.* His rooms are not half as high and large as yours, and you have never seen such an exceedingly unpretentious studio. [emphasis added][29]

And most important, perhaps, they both felt themselves "outsiders." Menzel was the most celebrated illustrator in Germany, yet at four feet six inches in height, numerous scholars have reported that he felt isolated from ordinary social interactions.[30] He achieved fame as a young man for his 400 woodblock engravings for a biography of Frederick the Great, engravings showing in extraordinary fullness every detail of a soldier's uniform including, for example, their buttons. His artistic life spanned seventy-five years; the range of his paintings is therefore exceptional, from his ultra-realistic historical drawings, to broadside illustrations, to illustrations of literary works, to vast historical canvases documenting the reign of his kings, to paintings almost—but not quite—impressionistic, the difference being that every inch of the canvas is there in detail. By the time he met Brahms, Menzel was responding to the new industrial world Germany had entered, and made dozens of detailed sketches of working men before painting one of his most astonishing paintings—one of roiling action and blazing heat. (See Figure 2.20.)

Menzel had another artistic interest that Brahms prized as well: that of genre painting. Menzel's vast output in this area is resolutely secular, focused on the everyday. Eyeglasses, binoculars, the view of an empty lot seen out of his window, street scenes, studies for hands, heads, soldiers in uniform, his worn-out paint brush, an unmade bed—with his insatiable willingness to observe everyday life, everything was material for his stunning skill as a draftsman. He has been called one of the three great realist painters of the nineteenth century.[31] It is not known how much of Menzel's work Brahms actually saw, but

Figure 2.20 Adolph Menzel, *Iron Rolling Mill*, 1872–1875. Author's personal collection.

Figure 2.21 Adolph Menzel, sketch, *Flötenkonzert*, ca. 1848. Author's personal collection.

he did visit the artist's studio at least once. He owned Menzel's illustrations to the life of Frederick the Great with its hundreds of engravings, and at least one smaller book of drawings.

A tiny sample of this extraordinary artist includes a preliminary sketch for the well-known painting *Flute Concert of Frederick the Great at Sanssouci*. The sketch shows C. P. E. Bach at the keyboard performing with Frederick the Great and Crown Prince of Braunschweig. (See Figure 2.21.) Menzel also produced dozens of scenes from everyday life, leading one prominent art historian of the day (Max Jordan, 1837–1906) to comment, upon Menzel's death, that "he was wholly what he was exclusively and always in the present moment."[32] (See Figures 2.22 and 2.23.)

Figure 2.22 Adolph Menzel, *Leipziger Volksszenen*, 1831. Author's personal collection.

For one of his most astonishing paintings, commissioned by the newly crowned king of Prussia Wilhelm I (1861), Menzel declined to highlight the king himself. Instead, the eye is drawn to the brilliant white of the royal women in the center of the painting, perhaps a subtle snub of a very reactionary new king. In preparation for the final painting, over a period of six months every attending dignitary at the coronation sat individually for his portrait. (See Figures 2.24 and 2.25.)

The artist best known for his connection to Brahms is Leipzig-born Max Klinger (1857–1920), who created the *Brahms-Phantasie*, published as a book containing a series of forty-one engravings that accompany, or are accompanied by, five of Brahms's lieder (with both words and music) including

Figure 2.23 Adolph Menzel, *Emilie am Klavier stehend* (*Sister Emilie at the Piano*), 1866. Author's personal collection.

"Alte Liebe," Op. 72, No. 1; "Sehnsucht," Op. 49, No. 3; "Am Sonntag Morgen," Op. 49, No. 1; "Feldeinsamkeit," Op. 86, No. 2; and "Kein Haus, Keine Heimat," Op. 94, No. 5. The series also includes the complete *Schicksalslied* in piano reduction, and a group of independent works based on Greek myths. Klinger's teacher and artistic ideal was Menzel, but his work is very different from that of the older artist. It is steeped in fantasy with images from mythology and classicism, redolent of symbolism. Upon publication the *Phantasie* was celebrated as the most important work in the realm of fantasy art since Dürer, and it is a precursor to the twentieth-century symbolists, some of whom he influenced directly.

Figure 2.24 Adolph Menzel, *Krönung* (Coronation), 1861–1865. Author's personal collection.

Figure 2.25 Adolph Menzel, *Krönung* (Coronation), detail, 1861–1865. Author's personal collection.

Klinger spent time in Paris, knew Fantin-Latour, and can't have failed to know about the French interest in "paintings that sound"—the effort to create paintings that produced the indefinite feelings created by music. In France that led famously to landscape painting, with no narrative, no program, but with color: Impressionism. Klinger took a different route, evoking something mysterious, even bizarre, creating an oeuvre that was infused with romantic but unspecific longing. Rather than color, his etchings and lithographs depend on line and shades of dark and light. Many of his paintings include tiny figures, mythical and otherwise, set in a vast landscape, often with an indefinite horizon, and are meant for an audience with a knowledge of mythology, art, poetry, and music—an educated audience with a common cultural vocabulary. "Accorde," the first of the forty-one etchings (see Figure 4.3 in chapter 4, p. 87), displays some of these qualities: a vast, indistinctly seen horizon and sky and, in the foreground, strange, enigmatic figures, some semi-mythical, referring to music but arrayed as in a dream. As if to situate his drawing in the contemporary world, in the near distance is a visual quote of Böcklin's *Isle of the Dead*, which Klinger's own engraving had helped to popularize. Klinger and Brahms were not unknown to each other when the painter began the *Phantasie*. He had sent Brahms a collection of poetry with his engravings in 1877, and dedicated his cycle of graphics *Amor und Psyche* Op. V to Brahms in 1880. The title pages of Brahms's Opp. 96 and 97 with additional covers—four Klinger etchings in all—were also designed by him. Now, in sending primary proofs and sketches of the *Brahms-Phantasie*, Klinger made his intentions clear:

> Above all, in these things I was not concerned with "illustration" but rather with the feelings to which poetry and above all music blindly draws us, to cast a look at an assemblage of emotions, and from there, leading us further, to connect or to amplify. The last word seems impertinent. But it is hardly that, since the entire work was based on an idea which was likely already present in the poetic mood of your work, but which in this case remained unarticulated.[33]

The opening song of the series is "Alte Liebe," Op. 72, No. 1: "Es kehrt die dunkle Schwalbe aus fernem Land zurück" ("The dark swallow returns from a distant land"). While most of the illustrations in the *Brahms-Phantasie* are symbolic, if not obscure to a modern viewer, this one brings the music and text literally into his drawing; The swallows are flying away across the two pages of the illustration.[34] (See Figure 2.26.)

Upon receiving the early proofs and sketches of the *Brahms-Phantasie*, Brahms wrote to Klinger to express his profound pleasure: "I see the music, along with the lovely words—and then quite imperceptibly your wonderful drawings carry me further; looking at them, it seems as if the music resounded into the infinite and expressed all I could have said, more clearly than the

Figure 2.26 Max Klinger, *Brahms-Phantasie*, "Alte Liebe," 1893–1894. Author's personal collection.

music can but nevertheless just as enigmatically and portentously. . . . I must conclude in the end that all art is the same and speaks the same language."[35] In one succinct utterance Brahms encapsulated the ongoing aesthetic debate over the relationship between music and painting. To his friend Joseph Widmann, he wrote that the folios were "quite wonderful, made as if for forgetting every possible wretchedness and allowing oneself to be carried to the most sublime heights . . . one dives into them with ever wider and deeper vision and thought."[36] Klinger's art stimulated his own fantasy.

Brahms also owned the entire set of Klinger's *12 Intermezzi*. Klinger titled his graphic cycles "Compositions," and gave them opus numbers. The title page of his *Brahms-Phantasie* reads Op. XII, and his set of "Intermezzi" is printed with a title page in imitation of a volume of music, marked "Radierung Op. IV,

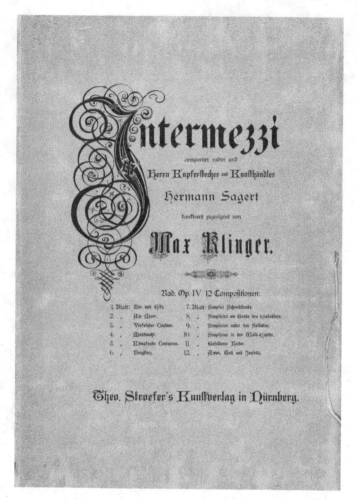

Figure 2.27 Max Klinger, "Radierung Op. IV, 12 Compositions." Author's personal collection.

12 Compositions" (Figures 2.27 and 2.28). The human figures in the Fourth Intermezzo are insignificant in the vast scene.

This chapter has thus far been about Brahms and the *artists* he particularly admired, whose works—largely in the form of etchings—he actively engaged with. But the artworks in his home, the images he saw every day, reveal another side. On his walls were a mix of views depicting important historical moments; likenesses of composers and writers most dear to him; pictures of places important to him; and several etchings of Renaissance or Renaissance-style paintings.[37] The composers are Haydn, a porcelain bust from the estate of C. F. Pohl whose biography of Haydn Brahms supported enthusiastically;

Figure 2.28 Max Klinger, Intermezzo No. 4. Author's personal collection.

Bach, in a lithograph by von Rohrbach, probably after the 1746 painting by Elias Haussmann; Robert and Clara Schumann, an engraving of the double medallion by Ernst Rietschel (1804–1861); Robert Schumann, in a photograph; Cherubini, in an engraving from 1843 of a painting by Jean-Auguste-Dominique Ingres (1780–1867); Beethoven, a life mask by Franz Klein; Handel, a portrait by William Hogarth in a mezzotint (as mentioned above); and the young Mendelssohn at the piano, in the drawing commissioned by Goethe. There was a photograph of *Beethoven Enthroned*—the Beethoven monument on the Beethoven Platz, Vienna, by the noted sculptor Caspar von Zumbusch (1830–1915) that was unveiled in 1880. Also present was a bronze relief of the head of Bismarck, and an engraving of Shakespeare.

A fine etching of the Stephansdom in Vienna by Carl Schütz (1745–1800), the renowned engraver of Viennese city views, was present in Brahms's collection. It dates from 1792, one year after Mozart's death, perhaps the reason for Brahms's particular interest in it. The other building was a little oil sketch of the house Brahms occupied in Ischl during his summers there. Brahms's appreciation of classic art is on full display in several other paintings: not only is Ingres's portrait of Cherubini self-consciously in the already antiquated classic style, Guido Reni's painting of *Apollo in the Sun Chariot* in the engraving by Raphael Morghen (1758–1833) is also in the classical manner (although Reni [1575–1642] is a product of the Baroque).

Raphael's *Sistine Madonna*, which was present in Brahms's collection in the engraving by Steinla, is the painter's most discussed work. Located during Brahms's lifetime in Dresden, the Madonna was particularly well known in Germany. The *Mona Lisa* kept her company in a copper engraving by Luigi Calamatta (1801–1869), another highly regarded engraver. A further example of Brahms's taste in neoclassical Italian Renaissance painting was the photograph he possessed of the cartoon (full-size drawing) of *The Apocalyptic Riders* (*Die apokalyptischen Reiter*) by Peter von Cornelius (1783–1867), one of the Nazarene Brotherhood of young German painters. The large drawing was meant for a cycle of frescoes commissioned by Frederick William IV for a proposed royal mausoleum in Berlin. Brahms owned Hermann Grimm's book about Cornelius's cartoons.[38] There was also a sizable etching by Max Klinger, but no details are available about which particular etching this was and the photographs showing Brahms's apartment in the 1905 *Brahms-Bilderbuch* (the key source for such information) are inconclusive.

Two large historical scenes took up space on Brahms's walls, each reflecting in its own way his sense of identity. *Der Friedensschluß zu Münster* (The Peace Treaty at Münster), etched from a painting by Bartholomeus van der Helst (1613–1670), shows a landmark moment for all of Europe. On 30 January 1648, Spanish and Dutch representatives signed a treaty that not only ended eighty years of war between Spain and the Netherlands, but marked the definitive recognition of the sovereignty of a Protestant nation and included specific religious provisions that altered European history: *cujus regio, ejus religio*, "whose land, his religion." It was the end of the Wars of Reformation. Catholics had to live with the reality that Catholicism was now only one among several possible religions. Brahms's etching depicted the celebration as observed at a banquet at the headquarters of the St. George Guard of Amsterdam in June 1648. Seen are portraits of actual members of the Guard including the drummer, conspicuously displayed front and center. A bit of the city of Amsterdam shows through the window at the back wall. Perhaps Brahms, who had a special affection for that city, acquired the engraving on one of his tours. The second historic etching is *Ziethen sitzend vor seinem Königen* (Ziethen Seated before His King), by Daniel Chodowiecki. Hans Joachim von Ziethen (1699–1786) was a famous

Connoisseur of Graphic Arts

cavalry general in Frederick the Great's army, hero of several important battles of the Seven Years' War, much honored by the king, and renowned for his strength and daring and shown here one year before his death. Even during his lifetime he was celebrated in song. One is reminded of Brahms's appreciation of two other strong men: Bismarck, and Shakespeare's Coriolanus.[39] If Brahms generally preferred etchings of a work of art rather than original oil paintings, those he owned were certainly of the highest quality, whether gathered in folders in his sitting room, or—as in the case of these two scenes—hanging on his walls.

In summarizing Brahms's engagement with the graphic arts, we can observe that his collection was a source of nourishment, to be perused at leisure. A significant number of his favorite artists delved into the fantastic, starting with Callot and ending with Klinger; this was fantasy bordering on the grotesque, encouraging an active mind to boundless imagination and reflection. An attentive listener to Brahms's compositions will encounter innumerable instances of mysterious, even eerie, "unheimliche" passages.[40] Then there are the painters who appealed to that other side of him, the Brahms who loved folksongs, who relished the Wurstelprater, Vienna's amusement park for Everyman, the Brahms who sat on the back stairs chatting with the servants instead of with the hosts who invited him to their elegant parties. Menzel, Hogarth, Chodowiecki, and Callot all detailed the everyday life of their time.[41] His interest in Feuerbach, and the various artworks Brahms had hanging on the walls of his flat, bears witness to his admiration for the classical, rather impersonal beauty of the Renaissance. But almost all of the artworks he prized have several characteristics in common: to start with, they are strikingly secular. There are scenes from mythology, from history, from daily life low and high, or pure fantasy, but there are almost no religious scenes.[42] In addition, whether in the fantastical engravings of Jacques Callot, the classic or historical paintings of Feuerbach, the eerie landscapes of Böcklin, the evocative drawings of Klinger, or the innumerable pictures of everyday life by Menzel and Chodowiecki, there is clarity, technique, great skill, artful detail in every inch of the canvas. We know that Brahms cared for these traits because Widmann describes how moved Brahms was when visiting monuments in Italy as he encountered the care lavished on details even in nooks and crannies where they could not be seen. These are the traits he sought. This is what unifies Brahms's eye for the graphic arts with Brahms's music, and with Brahms the man.

Chapter 3

Settling for Second Best

Brahms's *Männerchor-Lieder* in Historical Context

David Brodbeck

One day in the winter of 1896–1897, Johannes Brahms received a parcel from his old friend Felix Hecht. The package consisted of a number of pamphlets containing short satirical stories written half a century earlier by the journalist Adolf Glassbrenner. Most likely they were from the series *Berlin wie es ist und—trinkt* (Berlin as it is [*ist*]/as it eats [*isst*] and—drinks), which Glassbrenner, using the pseudonym Adolf Brennglas, published in thirty short installments between 1833 and 1849. Hecht purchased the pamphlets from an antiquarian and had them bound together as a present that was surely meant to provide Brahms with a diversion as he suffered at home in Vienna from the liver cancer that would kill him a few months later.[1]

Glassbrenner was a humorist, radical democrat, and champion of the lower classes who had been an opponent of the Prussian state during the *Vormärz*, the years of repression that preceded the revolutions that swept from Paris into cities across the German Confederation in March 1848. Glassbrenner was never taken to be a great writer, but he was a very popular and successful one, and as a political activist he was committed, as Mary Lee Townsend has put it, to using "his literary talent and marketing genius to foster liberal ideas and an oppositional spirit among his readers."[2] As we may gather from the letter the composer wrote to Hecht to acknowledge the gift, among these readers was the young Brahms:

> Then along comes your Berlin pamphlets as a book, and before I devote myself to "cheerful" reading, I must say thank you very much. I wonder if it will be cheerful? I am spoiled in that respect, for right now I'm in the middle of *Tristram Shandy* for the nth time. But if every now and then we must recall that miserable period, we do enjoy remembering our earliest youth, and how we used to devour those pages back then.[3]

Common to all the revolutions of 1848 were liberal demands for constitutional government and the rule of law, suffrage rights, effective parliaments, freedom of the press, and freedom of association. But in Germany, liberalism was only part of the story; the delegates who gathered in the Frankfurt National Assembly (18 May 1848–31 May 1849) also pushed for the creation of a unified constitutional German nation-state. This was a dream that animated liberals following Napoleon's withdrawal from Germany in 1813 but had come to nothing with the conservative restoration imposed by the Congress of Vienna two years later.[4] Widespread unrest in 1848 offered another bite at the apple. Yet this attempt, too, foundered, in part on account of differences between moderate bourgeois and more radical democratic activists, in part on the question of how or even whether to include the multinational Austrian Empire. Was there to be a Greater German solution that would include all the German states and be dominated by Habsburg Austria, or a Lesser German solution that would exclude Austria and be dominated by Hohenzollern Prussia? This so-called German Question would remain unresolved for years to come.

Early on, the liberals at Frankfurt prevailed over their democratic brethren in determining that the new state would be a constitutional monarchy, not a republic, and in June 1848 the Habsburg Archduke Johann accepted appointment as the Imperial Regent of the short-lived German Reich. When, in November, Austria rejected the Assembly's proposal of a modified Greater German solution in which only Austria's predominantly German-speaking lands would be incorporated, the Lesser German solution remained the only viable option. That, too, came to nothing. In April 1849, King Friedrich Wilhelm IV of Prussia refused the imperial crown he was offered, and the delegates to the Assembly soon went home empty-handed.[5]

The liberal nationalists may not have achieved German unity, but their efforts were not entirely ineffectual. For one thing, most German states retained their recently gained parliaments and constitutions in whatever weakened form. Austria became an exception when its short-lived constitution of 1849 was revoked two years later, ushering in a period of neo-Absolutism. Prussia, too, lived under a form of neo-Absolutism for most of the 1850s, but because its constitution and parliament survived, liberals tended to hold it in higher esteem than its rival Austria.[6] "The apparent political slumber of the 1850s was deceptive," writes David Blackbourn, even if "the exuberant mass mobilization and popular politics" of the revolutionary era had now come and gone.[7] The lesson the liberals learned from their sobering experience was to seek to bring about progressive reform, not through revolutionary action, but in incremental steps.

The revolution in Brahms's hometown of Hamburg followed a course different from that, say, in the larger capital cities of Berlin and Vienna and elsewhere in Germany.[8] As a thriving commercial seaport, the Free and Hanseatic City of Hamburg had always looked outward into the world more than it had looked inward toward the rest of Germany. (Hamburg was one of four republican city-states in the German Confederation; the other thirty-five members were monarchies of various kinds.) The Hamburg Senate, dominated by wealthy mercantile oligarchs, was highly protective of the city's autonomy, and its representatives to the Frankfurt National Assembly were concerned primarily with the city's political and economic interests.[9] There was no monarchy in Hamburg to seek to overthrow or reform, although this is not to suggest that no efforts were made from below to liberalize and even democratize the institutions of governance. If street skirmishes in Hamburg were fewer in number and less bloody than in the Prussian and Austrian capitals, they did occasionally occur. And even in proudly independent Hamburg the national question became more present now, primarily as a result of its proximity to the Elbe duchies of Schleswig and Holstein, the status of which was a subject of fierce dispute between Denmark and the German Confederation. (We shall revisit this matter.) Even still, heightened concern in Hamburg about the fate of the duchies had as much to do with market and other economic considerations as it did with the national question per se.[10]

Brahms had been too young to participate in the tumultuous events of 1848 but, as suggested, he was already imbibing liberal ideas. Soon he made himself acquainted with political writings of a higher niveau than those of Glassbrenner. From *Des jungen Kreislers Schatzkästlein* (*The Young Kreisler's Little Treasure Chest*), a handwritten anthology of favorite passages encountered in Brahms's wide range of reading, we can determine that by the early 1850s he knew the work of many notable liberals and democrats.[11] Among the collections of political poetry acquired by Brahms at this time was Ferdinand Freiligrath's *Neuere politische und soziale Gedichte* (Recent political and social poems, 1849–1851).[12] In the first volume of *Des jungen Kreislers Schatzkästlein*, Brahms quotes Freiligrath's wildly popular poem of July 1848, "Die Todten an die Lebenden" (The dead to the living), in which those who had fallen on the barricades in Berlin in March 1848 exhort those who had survived the debacle to be undaunted by the defeat they had endured and to continue the revolution until they had successfully overthrown the repressive Prussian monarchy and replaced it with republican government. For Brahms's biographer Max Kalbeck, this notation and others like it provide evidence of the young musician's penchant for writing down passages from poems that embodied the most revolutionary sentiments of the time.[13] Even many years later, after the founding of the German nation-state in 1870–1871, Brahms made a point of acquiring Georg Herwegh's *Gedichte eines Lebendigen* (Poems of a living man, 1841–1843), which had been banned on political grounds in *Vormärz* Prussia.[14]

No less anathema to the Prussian authorities than Freiligrath and Herwegh was August Heinrich Hoffmann von Fallersleben, author of the iconic "Lied der Deutschen" (Song of the Germans, 1841), with its call to repudiate traditional German particularism (*Kleinstaaterei*) in favor of German unity ("Deutschland über Alles").[15] On 17 July 1853, Brahms met the poet in the home of the Göttingen music director Arnold Wehner, and he immediately set four of his lyric poems to music (Op. 3, Nos. 2–3, and Op. 6, Nos. 5–6). Later that summer, with those new songs in his knapsack, Brahms called on him at his home in Neuwied while on a walking tour of the Rhineland that would take him to Düsseldorf at the end of September for his introduction to Robert and Clara Schumann.[16]

Brahms would spend a good deal of time over the next few years in the company of the many friends he made that fateful summer, not only the Schumanns in Düsseldorf, but also Joseph Joachim in Hannover, Julius Otto Grimm in Göttingen, and Albert Dietrich in Bonn and later Oldenburg. His goal, however, was to base his career at home in Hamburg, where he was forging relationships with the city's leading musicians, including Theodor Avé-Lallement, Carl Georg Peter Grädener, and Georg Dietrich Otten.[17] By the late 1850s and early 1860s Brahms had put the emotional turmoil created by Robert Schumann's tragic end and his own complicated early relationship with Clara Schumann behind him. And following something of a fallow period during those troubled years, he was composing actively again and beginning to publish the works of his first maturity. What is most relevant to this discussion, however, is the composer's immersion in liberal culture in Hamburg during a crucial period in the city-state's history.

In 1858, Hamburg's liberals renewed their demand for constitutional reform. In doing so, they took inspiration from the liberalizing New Era initiated in Prussia that year when Prince Wilhelm assumed the duties of the throne after his brother Friedrich Wilhelm was incapacitated by a series of strokes.[18] Two years later they achieved their goal at last with the adoption of a liberal constitution. The political system they envisioned consisted of a male-dominated discursive space comprising voluntary associations, newspapers, pamphlets, and public speech, what Jürgen Habermas called the "bourgeois public sphere."[19] Rational consensus was to be achieved through a process of ongoing public discussion conducted by self-reliant, mature, and autonomous males able to adjudicate matters of civic importance in accordance with disinterested logic. "The new, liberal government," writes Madeleine Hurd, "would be accountable, transparent, and neutral." It would also, with the notable exception of state-financed public education, be strictly libertarian.[20]

This exception for education was critical, in that education was the foundation on which everything else rested. As Hurd explains:

> Rational debate required a general understanding of the "natural laws" of science, economy, and society, while shared knowledge of the nation's high culture would further the abolition of particularist interest. Secular primary schools—and their sisters, the educational voluntary associations—freed men politically. They taught their pupils to penetrate the lies of the tyrant, the obfuscating superstitions of the church, and the simplistic teachings of communism. The individual was freed from state and corporation in his economic life; education gave him mental autonomy.[21]

It is an easy matter to see traces of Brahms in this account, beginning with the value placed on liberal education as an indispensable means to attain political maturity. To be sure, Brahms's formal schooling ended at age fourteen, but he worked hard thereafter to acquire the liberal hallmark of *Bildung*. In the summer of 1853, for example, he and Joachim became informal students in history of Ludwig Aegidi, an erstwhile student revolutionary who was working as a *Privatdozent* in Göttingen.[22] Studies of this kind continued in Hamburg in 1860–1861, facilitated in part by the composer's friendship with the merchant Johann Gottfried Hallier. Two of Hallier's daughters were members of Brahms's Hamburg Women's Choir; one of his sons, Emil, was a professor at the city's Academic Gymnasium. Brahms attended Emil Hallier's lectures in art history and also received tuition from him in Latin. At the same time, he attended classes in history once more with Aegidi, who was now lecturing on the subject as Hallier's colleague at the Academic Gymnasium. The composer regularly joined in readings of Shakespeare in the home of Avé-Lallement, and he frequented the weekly gatherings in the Halliers' home of artists and artistically inclined persons, where he not only provided entertainment at the piano but was an avid participant in discussions ranging across social, cultural, and political issues. An inveterate reader of newspapers—the daily political press was, of course, a critical component of the bourgeois public sphere—he was given to expressing strong opinions on all such matters of the day. Nor did he make any secret of his religious unorthodoxy, another liberal hallmark. Brahms was, in short, a man of mental autonomy.[23]

Meanwhile in Prussia, the prince regent Wilhelm's initiatives to reform and increase appropriations for the military were stymied by the liberal majority in the Diet.[24] By the summer of 1862 this stalemate had brought Wilhelm I—the regent had acceded to the throne upon his brother's death on 2 January 1861—to the brink of abdication in favor of the liberal Crown Prince Friedrich Wilhelm. At the last minute, however, the king thought the better of things and, on 23 September 1862, put the final nail in the coffin of the New Era by making the conservative Otto von Bismarck his new minister-president. A week later, in one of his most famous speeches—what the liberals could only view as an attack on constitutional parliamentary democracy—Bismarck proclaimed: "The position of Prussia in Germany will not be determined by its liberalism but by its power. . . . The great questions of the time will not be settled by speeches and majority decisions—that was the great mistake of 1848 and 1849—but by iron and blood," that is, by building Prussia's military-industrial base and being willing to resort to a strategic use of war to gain one's ends.[25]

Events would bear Bismarck out. Through a series of three military conflicts won in six years' time—with Denmark, in 1864; with Austria, in 1866; and with France, in 1870—a Smaller German nation-state was delivered by means of a stunning revolution from above.[26] Brahms would eventually come to venerate Bismarck and would celebrate his great achievement in the splendiferous

Triumphlied, Op. 55 (1872). But like his fellow liberals, he initially disdained the Iron Chancellor, not least for resorting to extraconstitutional means to bring about the modernized military that would prosecute the Wars of Unification. Indeed, when given the opportunity to meet Bismarck in Baden in the summer of 1865, the composer declined for what he later remembered to have been "democratic reasons."[27] It was in this early period of German liberal discontent with Bismarck that Brahms composed a work even more explicitly political, if more modestly scaled, than the *Triumphlied*. This is the music to which we now turn.

One War and Four Soldiers' Songs

The Five Songs for Four-Part Male Chorus, Op. 41 (1867), is the only essay Brahms published in a genre that had been a prime medium for the expression of liberal-nationalist sentiment dating back to the years of Napoleonic domination of the German lands. Two songs have drawn particular notice on account of their calls to the German people to defend the fatherland from foreign adversaries. Modern commentators, more apt to think of Hitler's Germany than of the unified constitutional state about which the liberal nationalists dreamt, have struggled to find the right tone in which to discuss Brahms's voicing of such sentiments. That struggle is evident in Siegfried Kross's pioneering survey of the composer's choral music, a product of the early years of Germany's reckoning with its Nazi past. Kross recognized that to the audiences of his time, Brahms's male part-songs could only come off as "unconscionably nationalistic, almost a little chauvinistic" ("hemmungslos nationalistisch, ja beinahe etwas chauvinistisch"), even if, as Kross allowed, such attitudes would have seemed far-off to the composer. Still, Kross was relieved that audiences had grown "deaf to the national and patriotic emotionalism of these songs" ("man [ist] weitgehend taub geworden für das nationale und patriotische Pathos dieser Lieder"), and so had rendered the work, in effect, "completely dead" ("völlig tot"). As if that were indeed its fate, Hans Michael Beuerle gave Op. 41 not so much as a passing mention in his own extensive survey from twenty-five years later.[28]

Even those postwar scholars who have offered commentary on this music have done so only fleetingly, almost sheepishly. Some seem put off by the supposedly "aggressive-chauvinistic tenor" ("aggresiv-chauvinistischer Inhalt") of the "ideologically suspect verse" ("ideologisch fragwürdige . . . Lyrik") and have interpreted Brahms's decision to compose such texts as evidence of "how far toward military enthusiasm [his] youthful patriotism could lean."[29] Like Kross, Daniel Beller-McKenna acknowledges that the music was written in the context of traditional German liberal nationalism, but he never really gives up his charge against the young Brahms of militant and enthusiastic national chauvinism.[30] In my view, it is high time to rethink these assumptions. What has been missing is the careful delineation of the historical context in which the music was written. Only with that established can we hope to hear the songs with the ears of Brahms's contemporaries.

I will for the time being postpone consideration of "Ich schwing' mein Horn in's Jammerthal," Op. 41, No. 1, which is an outlier in several respects and has never been the subject of criticism on political or other ideological grounds. Instead, let us first take up what I consider to be Op. 41's original incarnation as a set of only four songs (Op. 41, Nos. 2–5) whose texts were drawn from a large omnibus collection of *Lieder und Gedichte* (1861) by Carl Lemcke.[31] "Geleit" (Procession), Op. 41, No. 3, was composed first, in the summer of 1863, as a one-off for a newly founded Viennese male choral ensemble. The other three songs—"Freiwillige her!" (Volunteers, come forth!), "Marschieren" (Marching), and "Gebt Acht" (Take heed), Op. 41, Nos. 2, 4, and 5, respectively—use texts chosen from a subgroup of seven *Soldatenlieder* and were evidently set to music somewhat later under an entirely different set of circumstances.[32]

When taken in the order in which they would finally appear in Op. 41, the four Lemcke settings form not only a thematically—each tells of the soldierly life—but also a tonally compatible set in C.[33] "Freiwillige her!" (No. 2), in C minor, exhorts the able-bodied men of all the German lands to come together to defend the fatherland from foreign aggression. The text of "Geleit" (No. 3) is not one of Lemcke's specially designated *Soldatenlieder*, but it fits in easily with those songs, inasmuch as it depicts a battlefield burial of a fallen comrade-in-arms. Brahms's setting is in E♭ major, the closely related major mediant of the prevailing tonic, C. The somewhat comical "Marschieren" (No. 4) tells a timeless, light-hearted generic tale of a bored garrison soldier who is eager to go marching after spending two years confined in the home base (or, as Lemcke put it, using the salty language of a solider, "*in der verdammten Ki, Ko, Ka, in der Kasern[e]*").[34] Each of its five stanzas is in C minor; each one ends with a refrain in C major. And like the opening "Freiwillige her!," the concluding "Gebt Acht" (No. 5) is in C minor and is concerned with guarding the nation's borders against affronts from abroad.

The autograph of "Freiwillige her!" is inscribed "Januar 1864 / Joh. Brahms." Margit McCorkle expressed doubt about the relevance of this inscription to the genesis of the song, but the poetic text and the historical context suggest that we really ought to take Brahms at his word here.[35] This date is significant, in that the song can be convincingly related to a watershed historical event that took place that year. The autographs of "Marschieren" and "Gebt Acht" are undated, but we may reasonably assume that they, too, were composed in 1864 for the same reasons.

"Freiwillige her!" is one of the two songs—"Gebt Acht" is the other—that is most susceptible to being misunderstood today on ideological grounds. I shall focus on it in what follows. Lemcke's summons to German patriots everywhere reads:

Freiwillige her! Freiwillige her!	Volunteers come forth! Volunteers come forth!
Von der Memel bis zum Rhein,	From the Memel to the Rhein,
Von den Alpen bis zum Meer,	From the Alps to the sea,
Freiwillige her!	Volunteers come forth!
Schwarz Roth Gold ist das Panier,	Black, red, gold is our banner,
für dich, Deutschland, kämpfen wir!	For you, Germany, we fight!
Freiwillige her! Freiwillige her!	Volunteers come forth! Volunteers come forth!
Nehmt die Büchsen, zielet gut!	Take your rifles and aim well!
Auf zu Roß mit Schwert und Speer!	Mount your horses with sword and lance!
Freiwillige her!	Volunteers come forth!
Schwarz Roth Gold ist bedroht—	Black, red, and gold is at risk.
Vaterland! Sieg oder Tod!	Fatherland! Victory or death!
Freiwillige her! Freiwillige her!	Volunteers come forth! Volunteers come forth!
Duldet ihr Feinde Spott?	Do you tolerate the enemy's mockery?
Ist der Fluch noch nicht zu schwer?	Is the curse not yet strong enough?
Freiwillige her!	Volunteers come forth!
Dänen, Welsche, wer es sei—	Danes, French, whoever it may be.
Nieder fremde Tyrannei!	Down with foreign tyranny!
Freiwillige her! Freiwillige her!	Volunteers come forth! Volunteers come forth!
Durch das Volk da braust der Sturm:	A storm is brewing among the people:
Einig! Keine Trennung mehr!	United! No more division!
Freiwillige her!	Volunteers come forth!
Einig! Ruft's im Schlachtenroth!	United! It's calling in the blood of battle!
Deutsches Volk, Sieg oder Tod!	German nation, victory or death![36]

This poem is rich in national allusions.[37] Like the members of the Lützow Free Corps in 1813, the only unit among the anti-Napoleonic troops made up of volunteers from all the German lands, and gathering under the same liberal colors of black, red, and gold, Lemcke's volunteers are called from the farthest reaches of Germany to unite as one in defense of the fatherland. The delineation of the geographical borders of the historic German nation recalls Hoffmann von Fallersleben's "Lied der Deutschen": what in that iconic song was the Maas River in the west, Memel River in the east, Etsch River in the south, and Baltic straits in the north now becomes the Memel River in the east, Rhine River in the west, the Alpine region in the south, and the Baltic Sea in the north. Moreover, by its images of a storm of national sentiment let loose among the nation and of the bloodshed of battle called for by the great moment of national awakening (*Schlachtenroth*), Lemcke recalls Theodor Körner's "Männer und Buben" (Men and boys, 1813), one of a large number of songs from a posthumous collection of patriotic poetry by this legendary Lützower that quickly became staples of the liberal-nationalist *Burschenschaften* (student leagues).

Both poems remind us that attachment to *Vaterland*—as opposed to *Heimat*, with its associations with everyday experiences in a specific locale for which one has the warm feelings of home—was something that had to be inculcated in the popular mind. This distinction is important. As Anna Wierzbicka has observed, the "point of reference [of the idea of fatherland] was not experiential but political, with a particular emphasis on the unity of a large abstract entity, seen against the background of a number of smaller, local entities."[38] Poems such as "Freiwillige her!"—and by extension musical settings of them—were designed to do important nation-building work.

At the same time, Lemcke refers to Hoffmann von Fallersleben's "Die Freiwilligen" (The volunteers). That poem, together with Nikolaus Becker's "Rheinlied" (Rhine song), Max Schneckenburger's "Die Wacht am Rhein" (The watch on the Rhine), and countless other similar *Zeit-Gedichte* (topical poems), was born of the Rhine Crisis precipitated in 1840 when France, frustrated by the failure of its attempt to expand its influence in the Levant, sought compensation closer to home by reasserting the claim that its natural eastern border ran to the Rhine River. This French provocation engendered a fervent nationalist response in the German lands, including in poetry and song.[39] Something of that fierce response can be seen in "Die Freiwilligen." In the first of its two stanzas, the poet proudly recalls the decisive defeat of Napoleon in 1813; in the second he calls for the Germans to act once more with similar selflessness and determination to thwart the renewed French threat in 1840. Brahms was only seven at the time of the Rhine Crisis, but, like other schoolboys in the north of Germany in the 1840s, he surely would have heard enough stories told about the deprivations suffered during the Napoleonic era to be wary of French ambitions and military power.[40]

The Wars of Liberation of 1813 and the Rhine Crisis of 1840 were not the only patriotic topics to come within the purview of Lemcke's "Freiwillige her!" In the third stanza, the poet makes an unmistakable reference to the so-called Schleswig-Holstein Question. This complex matter—one "so complicated," as Lord Palmerson famously quipped, that "only three men in Europe ever understood it"—concerned the relations of the Elbe duchies of Schleswig (a Danish fief) and Holstein (a German fief) to the Danish crown, on the one hand, and to the German Confederation, on the other. At the heart of the dispute was the question of whether linguistically and culturally mixed Schleswig was indissolubly united to Holstein and therefore a rightful part of Germany.[41]

James J. Sheehan explains how things stood at the beginning of 1848, when the childless Frederick VII succeeded to the Danish throne:

> The duchies were ruled [in personal union] by the King of Denmark; they were legally inseparable [as set out by charter when the Danish king Christian I was accepted as duke in 1460], but only Holstein belonged to the German Confederation. Moreover, they were governed under Salic Law, which stipulated that their sovereign must be a male. Since the male line of the Danish royal house was about to die out, the duchies' future was in doubt. Although they were linguistically mixed—Germans in the south, heavily Danish in the north—German nationalists hoped to use the impending constitutional crisis to unhitch the duchies from Denmark and turn them into a German state. . . . However, the new Danish government, which had no intention of abandoning the duchies, annexed Schleswig on 21 March [1848]. The Germans in the south rebelled and established their own provisional government [under Prince Christian August II of Augustenburg]. When the Danes sent troops to back up their claims, the Germans [i.e., the Schleswig-Holsteiners] sought support from Prussia and a few smaller states.[42]

Shaken by the revolt that had engulfed Berlin earlier that month, Friedrich Wilhelm reckoned that he could win the support of the liberal and democratic revolutionaries by sending his military to aid the Schleswig-Holsteiners. This intervention did not last long. Prussian troops quickly occupied Schleswig, but by the summer, under international pressure, they had been withdrawn. Fighting continued sporadically thereafter in what was a civil war but led to no conclusive settlement of the underlying issues. The terms of the ensuing London Protocol (1852) simply re-established the *status quo ante bellum*. The Danish king would continue to rule the Elbe duchies in personal union but make no further attempt to annex them. At the same time, the Augustenburg prince renounced his claim to the duchies in exchange for payment, and the right to succession was transferred by the female heirs to Prince Christian of Glücksburg.

We may take it for granted that Brahms's sympathies would have been with the Schleswig-Holsteiners. His father had been born in Holstein, where he remained until moving to Hamburg when he was nineteen. Brahms visited his father's hometown of Heide as a boy and met his relatives there; later he encouraged his father to maintain that family connection.[43] And though Brahms's mother was a native of Hamburg, her father had come from Tondern (now Tønder), in the German-speaking south of Schleswig, and her mother from the town of Itzehoe in Holstein. It is not surprising, then, that when the Schleswig-Holstein Question flared up anew in 1863–1864, Brahms gave clear voice to his sympathies in music.

Again, a brief account of the facts is in order.[44] On 13 November 1863, in violation of the London Protocol, the Danish parliament passed a new constitution that annexed Schleswig once more. Two days later, Christian IX succeeded to the throne upon the death of his father, Frederick VII. Mindful of the legal perils of abrogating the same treaty that had established his right to succession in the duchies, but also of the need not to antagonize his Danish subjects, Christian signed the constitution on 18 November. This set off a clamorous German liberal response, and, under the unusual combined lead of both the pro–Greater Germany *Reformverein* and the pro–Lesser Germany *Nationalverein*, some 900 Schleswig-Holstein associations were quickly established throughout Germany. In late November, over the objections of Prussia and Austria, the Confederal Diet voted to recognize Prince Friedrich of Augustenburg, the eldest son of Christian August II, as Duke of Schleswig-Holstein, envisioning that the united duchies would then join the German Confederation. In December, after Denmark failed to change course in response to this pressure, confederal troops from Hannover and Saxony were dispatched to Holstein.

Ignoring the national question and still offering no support of the liberal-backed Augustenburg candidate, Prussia and Austria now took matters into their own hands. (In the words of Abigail Green, neither appeared to "g[iv]e a damn about German public opinion or the liberal nationalist agenda.")[45] On 16 January 1864, the two major German powers issued an ultimatum to Denmark that gave it forty-eight hours to rescind the November constitution, pledging in exchange to support the Danish king's claims to the duchies. In effect, Prussia and Austria were insisting that all parties continue to honor the terms of the London Protocol. Denmark once again held firm, and on 21 January Austrian and Prussian troops entered Holstein. On 1 February, they crossed the Eider into Schleswig and fighting began. Denmark's defeat in the Battle of Dybbøl/Düppel in April was the decisive engagement in the short war that followed. There were a few remaining skirmishes, but on 1 August the Danes sued for peace. By the terms of the Treaty of Vienna (30 October 1864) Denmark gave up all claims to the duchies, the ultimate fate of which was left to be decided later.

Brahms could not have foreseen the outcome of the war with Denmark or its long-term ramifications when, in January 1864, he composed "Freiwillige her!," but he could certainly rally the troops for the great national cause. Suddenly the reference in Lemcke's poem to the Germans' defense against Danish actions around mid-century acquired new proximate meaning.[46] Marked Allegro con fuoco, the song unfolds a modified strophic form in C minor. Stanzas 1 and 2 share the same music and, with their tonicizations of the mediant, are suggestive of the opening half of a binary form. In Brahms's setting of the first four lines, insistent calls for volunteers to step forward, sounded in urgent, unison triplets, are sandwiched around a homophonic passage written in forceful dotted block chords. In bar 9, as he returns to the chordal texture, Brahms underscores Lemcke's invocation of the liberal-nationalist tricolor with horn calls in triplets and the beginning of the tonal shift to the heroic key of E♭ major. Then in bar 12, he introduces yet another textural change, this time to imitative polyphony, for both stanza's salient final line ("For you, Germany, we fight!" and "Fatherland! Or death!"). Things close, still in E♭ major, with several final outbursts of the cry for volunteers, not in unison but rhythmically augmented in the first tenor, superimposed on repeated iterations in the usual rhythm in the second tenor and first bass, and over a strong cadential line in the second bass.

The third stanza begins once more in the tonic and follows the same general course, except that now the homophonic passage in dotted rhythm is replaced by one marked legato in two-part voice leading that is seemingly intended to cajole the uncertain into fighting ("Do you tolerate the enemy's mockery? / Is the curse not yet strong enough?"). The final stanza presents a louder, faster version (*ff*, animato) of the third until taking its own course at bar 38 with the accented climactic final two lines of text: "United! This calls for bloody battle! German nation, victory or death!" To make the point, Brahms then sets the last line once more, now with the added urgency of a fourfold imitative triadic arpeggiation on the words "German nation." All this is done, not in E♭, but in C, the tonic major. In that key, this dramatic passage initiates a final cadence that is completed by one last iteration of the call for volunteers.

Epilogue: An Old German Text for the New German Reality

In the summer of 1865, tensions between Prussia and Austria were coming to a boil. At issue in the short term was the future of the newly acquired Elbe duchies. Bismarck hoped to absorb them into the Prussian kingdom; Austria preferred that they remain autonomous duchies ruled jointly from Berlin and Vienna. The compromise terms of the ensuing Gastein Convention (14 August 1865) offered the last hope for a peaceful resolution of the German Question. Yet this agreement satisfied no one and only created further tensions that Bismarck would soon be able to exploit to advance his long-term goal of excluding Austria from the German Confederation altogether.

Brahms's correspondence in the spring of 1866 is replete with gloomy comments about the deteriorating situation.[47] This was not unwarranted: on 14 June, the German War (as this civil conflict is known in German historiography) broke out between the two major German powers, each joined by their allies in the Third Germany. Within weeks Prussia had won a surprising victory that gave Bismarck everything he wanted. By the terms of the Peace of Prague (23 August 1866), the German Confederation was dissolved, Austria was forced to give up all its authority in German affairs, and Prussia annexed the German states north of the Main River into the new North German Confederation.

This is the context in which to understand Brahms's early, unsuccessful attempts to publish what would become his Op. 41. In a letter of 6 September 1865, he offered his new soldiers' songs to the publisher P. J. Simrock, characterizing them, in an allusion to the recent war with Denmark, as "a small book of songs for male chorus that might even be called topical" ("ein Heft Männerchor-Lieder, die sogar zeitgemäß nennen können"). Simrock took a pass, as did Breitkopf & Härtel shortly thereafter.[48] Nine months later—and four days after the beginning of the German War—Brahms offered his *Männerchor-Lieder* once more to Simrock, again to no avail, describing them now as "a small book of 5 male choral songs. Quite easy to sing, needless to say rather topical."[49] Obviously, the second of these letters, dated 18 June 1866, establishes the *terminus ante quem* of the five-song gathering of Op. 41, which would finally see print with J. Rieter-Biedermann in 1867. Does it also help us to ascertain its *terminus post quem*? Do we have reason, in other words, to suppose that it was the outbreak of the German War that led Brahms to provide his Lemcke settings with a kind of musical preface? The circumstantial evidence is suggestive.

As noted, "Ich schwing' mein Horn in's Jammerthal," Op. 41, No. 1, has nothing about it that might be considered "ideologically suspect." The Old German text, attributed to Ulrich, Duke of Württemberg (1487-1550), is an allegory of love and resignation. Ulrich loves Elisabeth, Countess of Brandenburg, but is obliged to enter into a marriage with Sabina, Duchess of Bavaria, that has been arranged for political reasons by Emperor Maximilian I. Elisabeth is the lovely doe; Sabina, the less comely hare. The hunter would prefer to eat venison but must resign himself to having rabbit instead. Brahms's beautiful, archaic-sounding setting, a study in what can be done using only root-position harmony, may date to as early as 1847; in any case, it must have been composed by ca. 1859-1860, when Brahms arranged it for his Hamburg Women's Chorus.[50]

It is difficult to imagine what Brahms might have considered topical about Ulrich's poem in 1863-1864, when, at an ascendent moment for liberal nationalism, the four Lemcke texts were set to music. Matters were different when war broke out in June 1866 between Prussia and Austria. Seen in the light of what this conflict meant, the supposition that it was only now that Brahms repurposed his earlier setting of Ulrich's allegorical poem seems compelling. For all practical purposes, the war dashed once and for all the old liberal-nationalist dream of a united, constitutional state comprising all the German lands. Like Ulrich, Brahms could not have what he really wanted. He would have to settle for second best—for a Smaller Germany instead of a Greater Germany, for Sabina instead of Elisabeth.

Somewhat tactlessly, the composer said as much to a Viennese friend in the immediate aftermath of Austria's banishment from the fatherland: "The mood where you are [Vienna] must be so distressing. . . . But the world makes progress slowly and meanwhile we can, I suppose, be grateful to the Prussians for the brouhaha they have caused, for nothing moves forward without that."[51]

Chapter 4

Hearing and Seeing Brahms's Harps

Jane Hines

In January 1890, Johannes Brahms wrote in a letter to his friend, the composer and conductor Franz Wüllner, that he had just "walked through" the score of Wüllner's *Te Deum*. Although his encounter with the score was only in his mind's ear, Brahms spoke of his visceral reaction to Wüllner's orchestration: "I stumbled every time that the harp or muted violins occurred! Might it appear, in such a case, that we are in danger of speaking in two languages?"[1] We can only speculate as to what Brahms meant by the "two languages": was he referring to the difference between text-painting and independent orchestration? Or was this bound up with the question of whether the composition was sacred or secular? Wüllner's response indicates that he interpreted Brahms's "stumble" as a reaction to the sonic and symbolic profiles of the harp in the context of a *Te Deum*:

> But why shouldn't one use the harp in a composition that, like a *Te Deum*, depends on not only giving the greatest possible shimmer to the timbre, but also giving here and there in the more delicate places, if possible, the color of transfiguration (I can think of no other expression); for example, at the *Sanctus* of the angels, or at the mention of the Holy Ghost, the heavenly kingdom, eternity, etc. Schumann did not spurn the use of the harp for similar sentiments in *Faust* (Ariel, Doctor Marianus), and neither did you yourself in the German Requiem (where the harp works so beautifully).[2]

Wüllner's defense reflects his own compositional practice; the harp's first appearance in his *Te Deum* is at the angels' proclamation of "Sanctus" (bars 87–117), a literal sounding of the instrument of the angels at the moment they speak. He goes on to use the harp (along with muted violins) when the Holy Ghost, heaven, and eternity are mentioned.[3] If Brahms responded to Wüllner's defense or his gentle admonition in respect to the Requiem, we do not have record of it.

In this chapter, I consider how this exchange might illuminate Brahms's own use of the harp as a symbol in his scoring of the instrument and in his imitation of its sound. Brahms called for harp in only three compositions: *Vier Gesänge für Frauenchor* with two horns and harp, Op. 17 (1861); *Ein deutsches Requiem*, Op. 45 (1868); and *Nänie* for choir and orchestra, Op. 82 (1881). I argue that in the Requiem, *Nänie*, and his further vocal-orchestral works with texts that index the symbolism of the harp, Brahms more frequently simulates the technical and expressive capacities of the harp, rather than calling upon the instrument itself. Brahms is unlikely to be thought of as an archetypal composer for the harp, yet Max Klinger harnessed the harp's symbolism in his graphic cycle *Brahmsphantasie* (1894), a personal tribute to and commentary on Brahms's music. I suggest that in their invocations of the harp, real or implied, both Brahms and Klinger intersect with two particular facets of its symbolism: transfiguration and monumentality. I conclude that the harps in Brahms's music and Klinger's art are invitations to interpret, inviting the listener's or viewer's active participation in a constellation of allusions, in which the harp acts as a synecdoche for the art of music in general.

The Harp in the Nineteenth-Century Orchestra and in Brahms's Works

The harp plays two parallel roles in the nineteenth century: one to do with performance practice and the other to do with its symbolism in literary, visual, and musical culture.[4] During this century, we see the role of the harp transition from a more selective use in opera, ballet, and programmatic contexts supporting an extramusical narrative, to its establishment as a regular member of the symphony orchestra with growing independence from its symbolic associations. The harp's increased relevance as an orchestral instrument was made possible by Sébastien Érard's invention of the double-action pedal harp (patented in 1810), which allowed for chromatic playing without retuning.[5] Before this development and subsequent introduction into the orchestra, the harp's role was comparable to the piano as both a solo instrument and one suitable for song accompaniment, and the two instruments were often considered interchangeable.[6]

In symphonic repertoire, the harp was the object of special attention by Berlioz and his disciples but remained a rarity in works by Austro-German composers until the last quarter of the nineteenth century. Berlioz advocated for the harp in his orchestration treatise, even describing his ideal orchestra as having no fewer than thirty harps, which could be enhanced by a "full body of strings playing pizzicato (which would make a gigantic harp of 934 strings)" to create a magnificent harmonic effect.[7] Berlioz often used the harp to depict the instrument's presence in the accompanying narrative. In the case of *Lélio* (1831), the sequel to *Symphonie fantastique*, Berlioz used the harp programmatically in the fourth and fifth tableaux, "Chant de bonheur" and "La harpe éolienne—souvenirs," to accompany Lélio's beloved in song and to represent the Aeolian harp monumentalized on the lovers' future grave.[8]

Composers of non-programmatic symphonies were slower to adopt the harp into their orchestras. To my knowledge, the earliest use of harp in a non-programmatic symphonic work is Mily Balakirev's Symphony No. 1, begun in 1864, but not premiered until 1898, following a period of revisions. In the Austro-German symphonic repertoire, the harp remains an outlier until Anton Bruckner's Symphony No. 8 (initially comp. 1887) and Gustav Mahler's Symphony No. 1 from the same period (comp. 1887–1888).[9] By this time, Brahms's works with harp—and indeed, his published orchestral compositions without the harp—were already completed.

Brahms's first composition for harp, *Vier Gesänge für Frauenchor*, Op. 17, belongs to an altogether different tradition of works for accompanied women's chorus. The instrumentation is sui generis among Brahms's compositions and was met with bafflement by his friends. Clara Schumann wrote that she could not imagine the sound of harp and horn together, and Julius Otto Grimm grumbled that he could not make sense of the first three songs, although the final song was "herrlich" (marvelous).[10] Despite their incredulity, the combination of harps and horns was not unprecedented. In his treatise on orchestration, Berlioz wrote that "of all known timbres, it is odd that horns, trombones, and brass instruments in general blend best with harps."[11] By the time Brahms composed Op. 17, there already existed a number of chamber works written exclusively for the duo, thanks in part to the Romantic fascination with the typology of the itinerant poet-musician.[12] James Macpherson's contribution to this tradition, with his invention of the third-century Gaelic bard Ossian, provided a new precedent for the harp and horn pairing. Following in the tradition of Orpheus, Homer, and the troubadour, Ossian's instrument was a harp, and the horn was a natural complement to the questing and hunting tropes that appear in his lore.[13] The preoccupation with Ossian lasted well into the nineteenth century, borne out in literary, visual, and musical depictions of the bard's life and poetic works.[14]

The final song of Op. 17, "Gesang aus Fingal," belongs to the Ossianic tradition and exemplifies two aspects of Brahms's writing for harp: polyrhythm and the manual acceleration and deceleration of surface-level rhythms. It sets a scene from *Fingal*, in which the bard reveals the death of Trenar to his lover, the Maid of Inistore. Beyond their established role in Ossian's mythos, the harp and horn are not mentioned in the text. In contrast to the strophic forms of the preceding three songs, "Gesang aus Fingal" is through-composed, with internal repetitions of text and a modified return of the opening material at the song's conclusion. The harp's role in the song closely follows the drama of the text. It begins with block chords that give the impression of an acceleration as they break into diminutions in eighth notes, triplets, and finally sixteenth notes. At its most frenetic, the harp plays sextuplets against sixteenth notes when the opening two lines of text return: "Wein' an den Felsen der brausenden Winde / Weine, o Mädchen von Inistore!" ("Weep on the rocks of the wuthering winds / Weep, O Maid of Inistore!"). Despite the rhythmic frenzy and the bard's directive, an extreme slowing of the tempo, marked "Poco più

Example 4.1 Brahms, Op. 17, No. 4, "Gesang aus Fingal," harp only, bars 159–66.

lento" (bar 155), accompanies the final statement of this line, unraveling the Maid's grief into a more hopeful C-major conclusion (Example 4.1).

At first glance, "Gesang aus Fingal" is of more formal and harmonic interest than are the first three songs in Op. 17, but in each song, the harp and horn are written in a narrowly conceived idiomatic manner (block or arpeggiated chords and melodies characterized by fifths, respectively), and the voices rarely venture beyond a close, homophonic texture. It is likely that Grimm's unreserved preference for the "herrlich" "Gesang aus Fingal" went beyond its formal and harmonic attributes and also concerned its text-music relationships. The harp occupies different roles in relation to the four song texts in Op. 17. In the first song, "Es tönt ein voller Harfenklang," the harp is named in Friedrich Ruperti's text, which draws an allegory between the harp and the palpitations of a grieving heart, while the subsequent songs, "Lied von Shakespeare" and "Der Gärtner," contain no references to the harp at all. Between these two extremes, the text of "Gesang aus Fingal" does not mention the harp, but both harp and horn are closely related to its Ossianic context. "Gesang aus Fingal" exemplifies Brahms's typical approach to the harp, which avoids placing it in a direct relationship to the text. That is, while Brahms often imitates the harp when it is directly mentioned in poetic text, he generally avoids using real harps at such moments. The degree of literalness we find in "Es tönt ein voller Harfenklang," where the sounding harp relates to the text as an icon or exact likeness is quite unusual within Brahms's oeuvre.

Brahms's remaining two works with harp, *Ein deutsches Requiem* and *Nänie*, confirm this pattern in setting texts that obliquely reference the harp's symbolic contexts. Had Brahms scored for the Requiem's harps following Wüllner's example, he might have evoked the "color of transfiguration" in the fourth movement, "Wie lieblich sind deine Wohnungen, Herr Zebaoth," when the soul longs for heaven. Although this movement comes closest to the heavenly symbolism described by Wüllner and accompanied by harps in his *Te Deum*, Brahms relied only on the imitation of the harp through near-constant arpeggiated chords in the strings and woodwinds. The strings alternate between bowed (slurred and staccato) and pizzicato, and the ascending broken chords are often staggered asynchronously between instruments in the orchestra, characteristic of the effect achieved in the displacement between a harpist's hands (Example 4.2). While it does not call for harp, the sixth movement contains the only moment in the Requiem where instrumentation corresponds in a literal manner to the text: "zu der Zeit der letzten Posaune" ("at the last trump"[15]) coincides with the first entrance of the trombones (*Posaunen*) and tubas at bars 68ff.

Despite calling for at least two harps in the Requiem, Brahms actually used them rather sparingly, and more often evoked the sound of the harp through imitation in other instruments. After the end of the second movement, the harps remain silent until the last nine bars of the final movement. They do not appear until bar 46 in the first movement, at the setting of "Die mit Tränen säen, werden mit Freuden ernten" ("They that sow in tears shall reap in joy"), the first text drawn from the Book of Psalms—perhaps a subtle reference to the harp of King David. This first entrance of the harps also coincides with a deceptive cadence in F major to ♭VI (D♭ major) initiating the movement's first modulation. At this transfiguring moment, already hinted in the preceding bars with stray ♭VI harmonies and here fully realized, the broken arpeggios of the harp ring out. Strikingly, the harp appears in this movement only at tonicizations of ♭VI (bars 46ff and 87ff) and within the movement's closing gestures.

Nänie, the last of Brahms's three works that employ a harp, is also bound up with themes of death and loss. The piece was dedicated to the stepmother of

Example 4.2 Brahms, *Ein deutsches Requiem*, Op. 45, "Wie lieblich sind deine Wohnungen, Herr Zebaoth," bars 115–23, flutes, clarinet, and violas only.

the artist Anselm Feuerbach following Feuerbach's premature death in 1880. Schiller's poem, which Brahms sets here, does not explicitly cite the harp, but it thematizes the idea of sung laments and the first of the many mythological allusions that occur in the text is to Orpheus' loss of Eurydice. In Brahms's work, the harp itself does not enter until bar 65, prefigured in bar 64 by ascending triads in the cellos, violas, bassoons, clarinets, and flutes. The harp's role in bars 67ff was, however, evidently important enough for the composer to write a part for the first violins to be played in its absence (Example 4.3), illustrating a synthesis between the harp and instruments capable of its imitation. Brahms draws on this imitative technique again at the opening of the più sostenuto, in bars 85ff, and at 119ff, where pizzicato strings and harp are in three-against-two rhythmic counterpoint.

Nänie opens with plucked chords, not from the harp but emanating from pizzicato strings, including spread chords in the cellos. There is an illusion of the harp and horn pairing; the simulated, orchestral harp is joined by woodwinds and horns scored in horn fifths. They accompany the opening oboe solo, which begins with $\hat{3}$-$\hat{2}$-$\hat{1}$. This motif and its accompaniment alludes to the leave-taking gesture heard at the opening of Beethoven's Piano Sonata in E♭ Major, "Lebewohl," Op. 81a, likewise voiced with horn fifths.[16] While the harp and horn suggest an Ossianic context, Daniel Beller-McKenna makes a case for their pairing in works by Brahms and Robert Schumann that take a consolatory approach to grief, arguing that in these works the harp and horn are symbolic of the hope of the afterlife and the poignancy of remembrance, sonically capturing the distance opened between loved ones by death.[17]

Brahms's subtle imitation of the harp through other string instruments that we find in the German Requiem and *Nänie* also occurs in several works where real harps are entirely absent from the instrumental ensemble. Noteworthy here is Brahms's setting of the words "Wie die Finger der Künstlerin / Heilige Saiten" ("as the fingers of the harpist / on holy strings") (bars 52–61) in *Schicksalslied* and at the mention of "Psalter" ("Psaltery," a harp-like plucked instrument) in the *Alto Rhapsody* (bars 116ff).[18] In his review of a performance of *Triumphlied*, Op. 55 (1871), critic and music historian August Wilhelm Ambros commented positively on Brahms's choice to imitate the harp rather than score for it directly. Referring to a particular passage (bars 163–84), Ambros wrote:

> The accompaniment has highly original pizzicato—perhaps by that Brahms thought of the harps of the twenty-four elders of the Apocalypse, which he also found in the [Book of Revelation's account of] the Apocalypse?[19] Still, it is well that he spurned [*verschmäht*] the actual harp—it is, undeniably, the specific instrument of the angels in paintings, but not "acceptable" for sacred music; when one thinks of harps (like in Rossini's *Petite messe solennelle*), one thinks of the salon. The high priestess among the instruments is and remains the organ.[20]

Example 4.3 Brahms, *Nänie*, Op. 82, flute, clarinets, bassoon, harp, and strings only, bars 64–70.

Both Ambros and Wüllner use the verb *verschmähen* (to spurn or revile) to describe a composer's opposition to the harp, suggesting that scoring for the instrument was a fraught enterprise. Ambros clearly states that the harp is not "acceptable" for sacred music but, like Wüllner's *Te Deum*, none of the works cited—neither Brahms's *Triumphlied* nor Rossini's *Petite messe solennelle*—was intended for liturgical or sacred performance.[21]

Yet, in the symbolic contexts that I have described in relation to Brahms's music, the harp occupies sacred *and* secular roles. At the beginning of this chapter, I raised the possibility that Brahms's mention of "two languages" in his correspondence with Wüllner could be bound up with the question of whether a work was sacred or secular. Brahms's criticism of Wüllner's *Te Deum* can be understood to have implications for his own Requiem. Brahms scholarship has given much attention to questions of faith as they relate to Brahms. From his correspondence and his various utterances on the matter, we know that Brahms was not dogmatic; instead, his compositional output betrays the cultural influence of German Protestantism, but not an avowal of its precepts.[22] Might we then interpret Brahms's criticism of Wüllner to suggest that he considered his own Requiem more secular than sacred? If this is the case, Brahms is consistent in calling for the harp in an appropriately secular register.

The Symbolism of the Harp I: Transfiguration

The question of the harp's sacred or secular identity is central to Wüllner's identification of the instrument with "the color of transfiguration" ("die Farbe der Verklärung"). His subsequent examples of the Holy Ghost and the heavenly kingdom situate transfiguration in a sacred context, but he also cited a secular example in Robert Schumann's *Szenen aus Goethes Faust*, where Schumann used the harp to accompany Ariel, an earth-bound spirit, and Doctor Marianus, a heaven-drawn theologian. The German *Verklärung* indicates a heightened or intensified state, even in the sense of being infused with literal or metaphorical light, as in the biblical episode of the Transfiguration of Christ, where his human form is infused with light, thus revealing his divine nature to his disciples.[23] Turning to a secular literary context, the figures of Ariel and Doctor Marianus are liminal beings who fully belong to neither one world nor the other. We might understand Wüllner's description of the timbral profile of the harp as the "color of transfiguration," then, not only to represent a transfiguration or change between states (as in the English sense of the word) or the achievement of an elevated state of being, but also to signify the movement between or displacement of those states.

The harp figures metaphorically not only in its symbolism as a heavenly instrument (the afterlife, in the Judeo-Christian sense, being the ultimate transfigured state), but also as the means through which transfiguration is achieved. For example, the harp often appears in myth as a bridge between worlds or as an instrument of power, as in Orpheus' lyre-accompanied performance for Charon, which wins him entry into the underworld to rescue Eurydice. This idea of the harp as facilitating access to another world was taken up in the philosophy, poetry, and prose of the German Romantics. In Wackenroder's *Phantasien über die Künst* (1799), he employed the image of the harp to capture music's transcendent powers:

> It is the same with the mysterious river in the depths of the human soul. Language counts and names and describes its transformations in a foreign medium;—but music allows the river to flow before us by dauntlessly seizing the mysterious harp. It strikes into the void dark miraculous signs in precise succession,—and the strings of our hearts ring out, and we understand their sound.[24]

In this passage, the harp takes over where language fails, mediating between knowledge and the unknowable depths of the human psyche.[25] The Romantics drew on this type of metaphor to describe the possibility of an intuitive grasp of the absolute through art, which formed one of the central tenets for the primacy of art as a philosophical enterprise.[26]

The transfiguring significance of the harp is particularly evident in the aforementioned works by Brahms that deal with grief or loss. Death, of course, entails transfiguration, not only in the passing of the loved one from life into death, but also in the mourners' subsequent emotional journey. John Daverio describes Brahms's consolatory approach to grief in various vocal-orchestral and instrumental works such as the "Requiem idea." "For Brahms," Daverio writes, "the essence of the Requiem idea lay not in maudlin lamentation but in the situation of death in a cycle of dissolution and renewal."[27] More recently, Nicole Grimes has taken up the role of grief in Brahms's works in her study of *Schicksalslied*, *Nänie*, and *Gesang der Parzen*, which she describes as "Brahms's Elegies": a group of works that are especially influenced by German Idealism and the reception of Antiquity and share in "the promise that there is comfort and joy to be found for the living in a stoical acceptance of fate and of death."[28] Brahms's allusions to the symbolic profile of the harp are central to these wider themes of transfiguration and consolation. In the works mentioned above, these allusions are intricately bound up with two other expressive tropes: a tonal trajectory from minor to major, and the use or evocation of the harp within a work's closing gestures.

Several of Brahms's compositions are shaped by a large-scale tonal trajectory of C minor moving to C major, and he would have been keenly aware of earlier compositional precedents. Haydn famously employed the tonal shift in

The Creation as the work moves from chaos to light. Beethoven's Symphony No. 5 in C minor has also been widely understood in relation to this *per aspera ad astra* archetype.[29] James Webster aligns the similar modal shift in Brahms's *Alto Rhapsody, Schicksalslied*, and the German Requiem's sixth movement with the sublime, with psychological resolution, and with climax.[30] In Brahms's works this shift sometimes, though not always, coincides with the imitation or use of the harp. At the end of "Gesang aus Fingal," the concluding C major is heard in the four final bars (one of which is silent!) (Example 4.1).[31] Here the brevity of C major's appearance belies its significance in altering the tone of grief in the song. In a similar manner, but in the context of a larger-scale composition, the implied harp appears at the onset of the C-major tonality in the *Alto Rhapsody*. Significantly, in this setting from Goethe's *Harzreise im Winter*, which contrasts human loss and despair with renewal, the shift to C major coincides with the beginning of the third stanza that sees the protagonist appeal to the father of love to refresh his heart. The opening words of that stanza, "Ist auf deinem Psalter" ("If there is on your psaltery"), are accompanied by pizzicato strings imitating the harp or its distant cousin, the psaltery (bars 116ff).

Christopher Reynolds suggests a close compositional relationship between the *Alto Rhapsody* and *Schicksalslied*, both of which evince a C minor–C major tonal shift, and both of which are concerned with the opposition of "mortal suffering and divine happiness."[32] In the case of Brahms's *Schicksalslied*, however, the hermeneutic possibilities that arise through the work's extraordinary ending are somewhat contested. Here Brahms sets a poem contained within Friedrich Hölderlin's classically influenced epistolary novel, *Hyperion*. Brahms's *Schicksalslied* begins in E♭ major, but modulates to a tortured C minor at the third stanza, concluding with an instrumental postlude based on the opening material, now expressively transformed to C major. Because the C-major postlude follows the despair articulated within Hölderlin's third and final stanza (Figure 4.1), it has been interpreted as Brahms's supplement to, or even subversion of, the poetic text.[33] Grimes has argued, however, that Brahms's instrumental postlude might be understood as being faithful to

Doch uns ist gegeben	But for us it is fated
Auf keiner Stätte zu ruhn,	In no place to rest,
Es schwinden, es fallen	They dwindle, they fall,
Die leidenden Menschen	The suffering mortals
Blindlings von einer	Blindly from one
Stunde zur andern,	Hour to another,
Wie Wasser von Klippe	Like water from rock
Zu Klippe geworfen,	To rock hurled down,
Jahrlang ins Ungewisse hinab.	Years-long down into the Unknown.

Figure 4.1 Third stanza of *Schicksalslied* from Hölderlin's *Hyperion*. Translation from Friedrich Hölderlin, *Hyperion, or the Hermit in Greece*, trans. Howard Gaskill (Open Book Publishers, 2019), with slight modifications.

Hölderlin's words if one considers the position of the poem in the novel as the breaking point before a resolution. The C-major ending does not mark a conclusion but a transformation, a renewed beginning. Grimes suggests the postlude is commensurate with the shape of a *Bildungsroman* like *Hyperion*, both requiring the active participation and interpretation of the listener or reader.[34]

The changes within Brahms's orchestral texture that prepare this momentous tonal transformation are significant to my investigation because they incorporate techniques that I identify with Brahms's imitation of the harp. Before arriving at C major, the C-minor section (encompassing bars 104–379) foreshadows the ending with moments of calm. This section is largely governed by frenetic string tremolos (for example, bars 104–44) that, in the first instance, set the text "Doch uns ist gegeben / Auf keiner Stätte zu ruhn." The string tremolos devolve into harp-like arpeggios (Example 4.4), a manual deceleration that offers one example of Brahms's harp imitation techniques, akin to the figuration found in the "Gesang aus Fingal." The transition facilitates the transformation from the despairing frenzy of the tremolos, to a softer, perhaps more resigned, statement of the text.

There are clear affinities between Brahms's treatment of transfiguration in *Schicksalslied* and in the German Requiem. In particular, the harmonic plan, text, and scoring of *Schicksalslied* bear comparison with the sixth movement of the latter work, "Denn wir haben hie keine bleibende Statt" ("For here we have no continuing city"). Before Brahms added the fifth movement ("Ihr habt nun Traurigkeit") to the Requiem, the tonal succession between the fourth and sixth movements precisely followed that of *Schicksalslied*: E♭ major–C minor–C major. Moreover, the text of the sixth movement describes our displacement on earth, much like Hyperion's lament that there is no resting place.[35] In this movement, hope lies in the fact that, instead of a final sleep, we will be transformed ("Wir werden nicht alle entschlafen, wir werden aber alle verwandelt werden") at the sound of the final trumpet, when we will be victorious over death and the grave in eternal life. The shift from C minor to C major occurs in bar 204 on the word "Sieg" after the final, defiant challenge to death: "Wo ist dein Sieg?" ("Where is thy victory?"). Eighth-note tremolos in the upper strings and straight eighth notes in the lower strings prepare this modal change (bars 76–192), a scoring identical to the string tremolos in *Schicksalslied* that accompany the third stanza (bars 104–44; 274–324).

Arguably the most expressively significant usage of the harp in the German Requiem is at the close of the first and last movements, and these moments also allow for suggestive comparison with closing gestures in *Schicksalslied* and *Nänie*. Whereas rest was the object of distant longing in Brahms's Hölderlin setting, the final movement of the Requiem, "Selig sind die Toten," promises rest to those who die in the Lord ("ruhen von ihrer Arbeit"). The end of the first and seventh movements of the Requiem are identical, comprising ascending

Example 4.4 Brahms, *Schicksalslied*, Op. 54, strings only, bars 162–85.

arpeggiations of an F-major tonic chord in the harp (Example 4.5a). The ending of the seventh movement is, of course, doubly striking, both because of the way it echoes the Requiem's opening movement and because it marks the first time the harp has been heard since the second movement. The conclusion

Example 4.5a *Ein deutsches Requiem*, Op. 45, final movement, harp only, bars 158–66 (identical to the harp part at the end of the first movement, bars 150–58).

Example 4.5b Brahms, *Schicksalslied*, Op. 54, flutes, clarinets, and horns only, bars 406–9.

of *Schicksalslied* involves a similar figuration, though without the presence of a sounding harp: here an arpeggio ascends through the horns, clarinets, and flutes (Example 4.5b). Hanslick described this ending as revealing "the whole transfiguring [*verklärende*] power of music."[36] An ascendant harp is also employed at the conclusion of *Nänie* (Example 4.5c). Here we reach a final point of repose in the work's D-major tonic, set with repetitions of the word "herrlich" (marvelous) (bars 177–81).

In the sense of resounding into the absolute (to return to Wackenroder's harp metaphor), the endings of the Requiem, *Schicksalslied*, and *Nänie* are not endings with a clear sense of finality. Rather they are acts of transfiguration, which can be understood to signify new beginnings. The harp not only signals a mediation between worlds, but also the sense of displacement found in a liminal space that belongs neither to one world nor the other, themes confronted in the texts and settings of *Schicksalslied* and the Requiem. My reading of transfiguration at the endings of these two works is in keeping with interpretations

Example 4.5c Brahms, *Nänie*, Op. 82, strings and harp only, bars 176–81.

that ultimately understand them not to be about despair and hopelessness, but rather to express a form of resolution that goes beyond the perceived "endings" of human life or of temporal works of art.

The Symbolism of the Harp II: Monumentality

In addition to the harp's association with moments of transfiguration, a further crucial aspect of the instrument's symbolism relates more materially to ideas of monumentality and to the ways in which we mark the transition between different states of being.[37] There is perhaps no better illustration of this symbolism than Brahms's chosen city of Vienna, where the instrument is visible at almost every turn. The pedestal supporting the Schubert-Denkmal in the Stadtpark depicts a muse seated on a Sphinx, with kithara in hand,[38] and at the Beethovenplatz a cherub with harp stands at the foot of the Beethoven-Denkmal. Rudolf Weyr's Brahms-Denkmal in the Karlsplatz, unveiled in 1908, places the muse Euterpe bowed over her lyre at the feet of an enthroned Brahms. The harp in these instances participates in the work of classical reception, its presence affording these composers a mythological and godlike status akin to that of Orpheus or Prometheus. This final section briefly considers the harp's symbolic role in the monumentalizing function of art and the musical manifestations of this symbolism in *Nänie*, the Requiem, and Max Klinger's *Brahmsphantasie*.

Auch das Schöne muß sterben! Das Menschen und Götter bezwinget,
　　Nicht die eherne Brust rührt es des stygischen Zeus.
Einmal nur erweichte die Liebe den Schattenbeherrscher,
　　Und an der Schwelle noch, streng, rief er zurück sein Geschenk.
Nicht stillt Aphrodite dem schönen Knaben die Wunde,
　　Die in den zierlichen Leib grausam der Eber geritzt.
Nicht errettet den göttlichen Held die unsterbliche Mutter,
　　Wenn er, am skäischen Tor fallend, sein Schicksal erfüllt.
Aber sie steigt aus dem Meer mit allen Töchtern des Nereus,
　　Und die Klage hebt an um den verherrlichten Sohn.
Siehe, da weinen die Götter, es weinen die Göttinnen alle,
　　Daß das Schöne vergeht, daß das Vollkommene stirbt.
Auch ein Klaglied zu sein im Mund der Geliebten ist herrlich,
　　Denn das Gemeine geht klanglos zum Orkus hinab.

Even the Beautiful dies! It may conquer all gods and all humans,
　　But with a bosom of steel Stygian Zeus is unmoved.
Once and once only did love win over the Lord of the Shadows,
　　Yet on the threshold of life sternly his gift he revoked.
Great Aphrodite cannot heal the wounds of her beautiful lover,
　　Horribly carved by the boar into his delicate flesh.
Even the goddess his mother cannot save the godlike hero,
　　When he at the Scaean Gate falls and fulfills his destiny.
Out of the sea she arises with all of Lord Nereus' daughters,
　　Keening her grievous lament over her glorious son.
Look how the gods shed tears, and the goddesses join them in weeping,
　　Weeping that Beauty must pass, what is most perfect must die.
Yet to be a lament in the mouth of the Beloved is marvellous,
　　Those who are common descend songless to Orcus' domain.

Figure 4.2 Schiller's *Nänie*. Translation from Michael Ferber, "Translating 'Nänie' by Friedrich Schiller (1799)," *Translation Review* 82/1 (2011): 11–12 (with slight modifications to lines 8 and 13).

The idea of monumentality is germane to Brahms's Requiem and his setting of Schiller's *Nänie*, both works that foreground acts of commemoration. In simple generic terms, a requiem and a *nenia* (a funeral song or *Klaglied*[39]) are Christian and pagan musical genres intended to assist the deceased on their journey into the afterlife. Neither Schiller's poem nor Brahms's Requiem, however, fulfills such basic generic expectations. In Schiller's poem (Figure 4.2), the title "Nänie" is actually misleading, as the poem is not a *nenia* in the strict sense of a lament for the deceased but rather it is *about* lamenting. The poem invokes the deaths of Eurydice, Adonis, and Achilles—lamented by Orpheus, Aphrodite, and Thetis, respectively—but it identifies Beauty, and not an individual, as that which is departed. Preceding the closing gestures discussed above, Brahms chose the penultimate line of Schiller's poem to conclude his setting: "Yet to be a lament in the mouth of the beloved is marvelous." With this phrase, Schiller lets the poem speak in its own voice, thus objectifying the form or genre of lament itself.[40] Epitaphs on monuments are often voiced in a similar manner—addressing the reader with a warning or reminder—and there is a self-reflexivity in the way that Schiller's poem and Brahms's setting, as works of art, reify the permanence of beauty through their own aesthetic memorialization (or representation) of transience and death.

Brahms's Requiem performs a similar formal turn as Schiller's poem in its attempt to give permanence to memory through its self-articulation. As has often been noted, Brahms's personal assemblage of biblical texts for this work subverts the generic function of a liturgical requiem. His Requiem is concerned less with the soul(s) of the deceased than their memory in the hearts and minds of the living. Given Brahms's position on matters of faith, this composition would seem to shift focus away from the Judeo-Christian afterlife to the inevitabilities of grief and remembrance among the living. This recalls Brahms's use of the harp in the Requiem and its significance at endings. The ending of the Requiem as a whole is especially poignant, because of the repetition of material between the first and seventh movements. The very first line of the Requiem is "Blessed are they that mourn," while its final line is "Blessed are the dead." At the conclusion of the Requiem, Brahms repeats the word "Blessed" ("Selig"), thereby beginning and ending the work with this same word, a benediction of both the mourners and the deceased.

Unlike *Nänie* and the Requiem, Klinger's *Brahmsphantasie* (1894) was not intended to commemorate the dead, but it nevertheless fulfills a monumentalizing function as Klinger's personal tribute to the music of Brahms. The *Brahmsphantasie* consists of Klinger's assemblage of piano-vocal scores alongside fantastical images rendered in a virtuosic hybrid of intaglio techniques— engraving, etching, aquatint, and mezzotint. Here, Klinger's visual representation of a harp participates in the concepts of transfiguration and monumentality. The cycle opens with a full-page image "Accorde," followed by the scores to five Brahms lieder: "Alte Liebe," Op. 72, No. 1; "Sehnsucht," Op. 49, No. 3; "Am Sonntag Morgen," Op. 49, No. 1; and "Feldeinsamkeit," Op. 86, No. 2, which are embellished with discrete, symbolic vignettes in the margins; and "Kein Haus, keine Heimat," Op. 94, No. 5, which appears on an otherwise blank page. On the page opposite "Kein Haus, keine Heimat," is another allegorical image, "Evocation." This is followed by the first six of seven images depicting the myth of Prometheus: "Titanen" (Titans), "Nacht" (Night), "Raub des Lichtes" (Theft of Fire), "Fest" (Celebration), "Entführung des Prometheus" (The Abduction of Prometheus), and "Opfer" (Sacrifice). Initiating the final sequence of music and image, Klinger placed an image called "Homer," a portrayal of the poet-musician with kithara in hand, alongside the text of Hölderlin's poem "Schicksalslied."[41] The piano-vocal score to Brahms's *Schicksalslied* follows from pages 23 to 36 and, like the first four lieder, is accompanied by vignettes with references to mythology.[42] The seventh image of the Prometheus cycle, "Der befreite Prometheus" (Prometheus Unbound), follows *Schicksalslied* and concludes the graphic cycle.

Klinger did not intend the images in the cycle to represent the selected compositions, but to give his own impression of the "unausgesprochen" (unspoken) essence of Brahms's music.[43] Brahms conveyed this enthusiastically to Clara Schumann: "they are not illustrations in the usual sense, but rather entirely gorgeous, wonderful fantasies about my texts. Offhandedly (or without some clarification), one would be likely to miss some of the sense and the coherence of the text."⁴⁴ Brahms suggests that this is a work that requires the active participation of the viewer. Klinger's treatise on painting and drawing, published in 1891 during the early years of his work on the *Brahmsphantasie*, states the imperative for the viewer to participate in the realization of the work. He asserts that the graphic arts are the most expressive of the visual arts, because in the absence of color, the images require acts of completion from the viewer.⁴⁵ The *Brahmsphantasie* is Klinger's dialogue with Brahms's music, yet it reaches beyond that dialogue and invites the viewer (and, perhaps, the listener) to participate in this exchange.⁴⁶

There is no single, unifying thread or narrative to guide one through a first encounter with Klinger's labyrinthine array of music, images, and text; rather, it is a work that invites continual interpretation. The commentators whom I cite in this study have deciphered, to some extent, the symbolism governing Klinger's images and have revealed the themes common to other cycles in his oeuvre. One such recurrent theme is the opposition between the gods and humanity—a theme that we have already encountered in *Schicksalslied* and Hölderlin's "Song of Fate." Additionally, Klinger was known to subvert well-known classical tropes or mythological endings. In the case of his cycle *Rettungen Ovidische Opfer* ("Rescues of Ovid's Victims"), Klinger rewrites the endings of tragic episodes from Ovid's *Metamorphoses*. As Paul Kühn framed it in 1907, these rescues are not "a travesty based on Ovid's metamorphoses, but rather mischievous, cheerful, fantastic reworkings of the stories of Pyramus and Thisbe, Narcissus and Echo, and Apollo and Daphne."⁴⁷ In the *Brahmsphantasie*, it is especially significant that Klinger positions the myth of Prometheus along with Hölderlin's poem and the piano-vocal score of *Schicksalslied*. Prometheus exemplifies the consequences of the gods' interference in earthly matters and was sentenced to eternal torture for daring to mediate between worlds in order to bring humanity out of darkness and into light with the gift of fire. With what seems to have been calculated rhetorical emphasis, Klinger withheld Prometheus' rescue by Hercules until opposite the final page of the C-major postlude of *Schicksalslied*. In this image, "Der befreite Prometheus," the newly reprieved Titan appears overcome, holding his face in his hands. Just as the ending of *Schicksalslied* invites the listener to interpret the postlude's turn to C major, Prometheus' shielded face leaves his reaction to the imagination of the viewer.

Aside from the interpolated Prometheus cycle, the images "Accorde" (Figure 4.3) and "Evocation" (Figure 4.4) are the only images in the *Brahmsphantasie* directly linked to each other. They complement each other in both content and structure: staging the same triangulation of a pianist, a woman, and a harp, and marking a structural division between the first half, the Brahms lieder, and the second half, comprised of the Prometheus cycle, "Homer," and the score of *Schicksalslied*.⁴⁸ The first image, "Accorde," foregrounds the harp. The seated pianist is in fact a self-portrait of Klinger, who appears oblivious to the harp

Figure 4.3 Max Klinger, *Brahmsphantasie*, "Accorde." © bpk-Bildagentur / Kupferstichkabinett, SMB / Dietmar Katz.

Figure 4.4 Max Klinger, *Brahmsphantasie*, "Evocation." © bpk-Bildagentur / Kupferstichkabinett, SMB / Dietmar Katz.

emerging from behind him as he plays. The woman seated behind him to his left gestures toward the score, but her right arm is outstretched and almost touches a harp emerging from the sea. A Dionysian mask—which Kühn fervently believed to be Brahms's likeness—is rendered on the harp's column, supported by Triton and two nereids.[49] In "Evocation" on page 15, the harp remains foregrounded, but Klinger and the woman are now positioned on opposite sides. Whereas in "Accorde," Klinger is seemingly unaware of the action taking place behind him, "Evocation" captures a moment of revelation. The outstretched hands of both the woman and Klinger at the piano might at first suggest a drawn-out moment of suspense, but the cascading garment and mask, which have just fallen from the woman to reveal her true form, indicate that this is an instant captured as part of an unfolding scene. The unveiled woman is thought to represent Melpomene, the muse of song and tragedy, foreshadowing the tragic elements to follow in the Prometheus cycle and *Schicksalslied*.[50] Klinger contrasts the divide between worlds by casting the conflict of the Titans in hazy aquatint in the background, while dark and velvety mezzotint sculpts the scene in the foreground.

I interpret this scene as a glimpse of, and monument to, the moment of inspiration before it is transformed—or transfigured—into musical or visual form. The harp occupies a mediating role in the image's composition, caught between the inspiration of the muse and the work of the artist at the piano. In a note of thanks to Klinger, Brahms wrote:

> Beholding [your splendid engravings], it is as if the music resounds farther into the infinite [*Unendliche*] and everything expresses what I wanted to say more clearly than would be possible in music, and yet still in a manner full of mystery and foreboding. Sometimes I am inclined to envy you, that you can have such clarity with your pen; at other times I am glad that I don't need to do it. But finally I must conclude that all art is the same and speaks the same language.[51]

Brahms concludes his note by reflecting on the similarities between the languages of different arts, but he does not assert that these languages state the same thing. The real or imitated harp in Brahms's music enjoins the listener to interpret its meaning symbolically and, in a similar manner, Klinger invites the viewer to interpret the meaning of his images by animating them with color, movement, and even sound.

Without having read Brahms's commentary or Klinger's treatise, we might nonetheless respond to their shared call for active participation by attending to the title "Evocation." While the image itself recalls the classical trope of invoking a muse for inspiration, Klinger's choice of *Evocation* rather than *Invocation* suggests a different interpretation: more of an open summons or a calling forth from memory than a specific appeal to a named higher power. In Klinger's image, as in Brahms's music, the work and beauty of art is to be found in the infinite possibilities of evocation, of calling out of that which is in an artwork, implicit in which is an imperative for the listener, and the viewer, to engage in acts of interpretation.

PART II
REHEARING BRAHMS

Chapter 5

Brahms and the Unreliable Narrative

Janet Schmalfeldt

For connoisseurs of the "unreliable narrative" in works of fiction, pleasure and intrigue come from knowing that one must watch for the author's clues that the narrator is on shaky ground. If readers of *The Adventures of Huckleberry Finn* (Twain, 1884) don't immediately wonder about Huck's ungrammatical antebellum Mississippi River dialect, they will discover on page 2 that he is not only unschooled but sorely ignorant of "sivilized" religious traditions: he mistakes his guardian's prayer of grace over supper for her need to "tuck down her head and grumble a little over the victuals, though there warn't really anything the matter with them."[1]

Most commentators about Charles Kinbote, the notoriously unreliable narrator of Vladimir Nabokov's *Pale Fire* (1962), conclude that he is outrageously egotistical, delusional, and probably insane. As *Pale Fire* aficionados know, he is, moreover, one of *two* "authors" of the novel (putting aside the actual Nabokov), the other being his accidental neighbor—the (fictional) poet John Shade, whose 999-line autobiographical poem is presented in full at the beginning of the work, with all but the missing last line. Kinbote believes that he, disguised as a Russian scholar, is the exiled "King Charles II" of the mysterious land of Zembla, and that he has persuaded Shade slyly to incorporate his Zembla story within the poem. Through a bizarre circumstance, Kinbote absconds with the manuscript of the poem at the moment of Shade's death, only to discover that Shade had included not a single hint of the Zembla tale (a shattering disappointment!). So, Kinbote anoints himself the poem's editor, providing a foreword, a book-length commentary, and an index; the paranoid, indignant, defensive tone of the foreword will surely be the first clue that Kinbote is in psychological distress. As a satire on the worst kind of scholarly excess, the commentary utterly dwarfs Shade's modest poem; the novel's innovative form itself underscores the narrator's unreliability. What has confounded critics is the question of how the narrator Charles Kinbote could "write" as brilliantly as Nabokov himself, throwing into relief "[t]he longest-running and the fiercest disagreement in the interpretation of any of Nabokov's works . . . over the internal authorship of *Pale Fire*."[2]

Huckleberry and Kinbote, though vastly different characters inhabiting fictions that are worlds apart, are two of the innumerable unreliable narrator types, usually (but not always) speaking in first person. A fairly widespread unreliable narrative strategy is the case of the "twist ending," or "plot twist." Agatha Christie's first-person narrator in *The Murder of Roger Ackroyd* (1926) reveals at the very end that he is the murderer. In Albert Camus' *La Peste* (1947), the final pages disclose that the third-person narrator is in truth the principal character, Dr. Rieux, telling his own story. A more complex, even controversial case arises in Ian McEwan's much acclaimed *Atonement* (2001), brought to international attention through the 2007 film adaptation.[3] The twist here is the sudden, shocking, eleventh-hour revelation that we have been reading a "novel" within a novel; the "novel" has been written in third person by Briony Tallis, the protagonist who, at the impressionable age of thirteen in 1935, fatally misidentifies a rapist, sending her sister's innocent lover into prison and then, as a soldier, into the retreat at Dunkirk. Fifty-nine years later, Briony, the "real" author and now a distinguished novelist, confesses in first person that she has tried to atone for her tragic misjudgment by fabricating a reunion of the lovers and giving them a happy ending; in fact, neither her sister nor the lover had survived the war.

Stories with twist endings tend to withhold clues, in order to avoid spoiler alerts; McEwan encourages enough sympathy for Briony to reduce our chances of noticing his scant clues, even during a second reading. An ethical question has nonetheless been raised: does Briony really deserve to achieve atonement, when in fact she might have tried to tell the truth much earlier? She herself knows that the answer is no.[4] A similar question might arise as we move now toward the narrative with the twist ending that serves as the focal point of this chapter: what are we to make of a radically unreliable exchange in which we learn, in the final moment, that a mother has advised her son to murder his father? I refer not to a novel, but rather to the folk tale well known as the "Edward" ballad, and to Brahms's reference to it at the head of the first of his Four Ballades for solo piano, Op. 10, composed in 1854 and published in 1856. Departing from earlier writings about this movement, I propose that the mother's advice to her son suggests the presence of *two* unreliable characters in the "Edward" ballad; this interpretation may shed new light on why the form of Brahms's Ballade No. 1 gradually abandons the dialogic poetic structure of the ballad, in favor of a surprise ending of its own.

The term "unreliable narrative" emerged as a literary concept in 1961, when it was introduced by Wayne C. Booth in his seminal study *The Rhetoric of Fiction*.[5] Over the last many decades, the concept has taken hold as central and indispensable for narratologists. In an earlier essay,[6] to which this present one can be regarded as a companion, I survey some of the critiques, debates, and expansions that Booth's work has generated, and I give attention to the proliferation of unreliable narrator-types that has been especially encouraged by narratologist James Phelan, whose widely cited six general categories have greatly broadened the array of possibilities.[7] Studies of narratives ranging from the epistolary novels and early fiction of the late eighteenth century to recent postmodernist experiments have predominated in literary theory, but the "Edward" ballad reminds us that unreliable narration has been around for a much longer time.

Among the many types of unreliable characters and narrators in past and recent fiction that have become regarded as such since Booth, we have the pompous type (the Roman playwright Plautus' comic character *miles gloriosus*, from around 205 BC, who endlessly exaggerates and brags); the deluded type, like Don Quixote (Cervantes, 1605, 1615); the clown, who plays recklessly with narrative conventions (Tristram, of Laurence Sterne's *Tristram Shandy*, is the premier example, 1759–1767); the biased (Nelly Dean, in Emily Brontë's *Wuthering Heights*, 1847); the deceived or benighted, who may unwittingly underreport (John Dowell in Ford Madox Ford's *The Good Soldier*, 1927); the gullible and misinformed, who misinterprets (like Twain's teenager Huck Finn and Salinger's Holden Caulfield, in *The Catcher in the Rye*, from 1951); the postmodernist *je-néant*, or "absent-I" narrator (in Alain Robbe-Grillet's 1957 *La Jalousie*); and of course the insane (Kinbote; or the narrator of Edgar Allan Poe's "The Tell-Tale Heart," 1843; or Dostoevsky's Underground Man, 1864). I draw these labels from a host of analytic essays with analyses of individual narratives.[8] Near the top of the list of unreliable types, there will always be the liar. On this count alone, both Edward and his mother qualify as unreliable.

The Scottish bard—the unidentified narrator who transmitted the "Edward" ballad—will remain forever anonymous, and the poem has survived only because a probably inauthentic version appeared in Thomas Percy's highly influential *Reliques of Ancient English Poetry* (1765). "Edward" resurfaced in Johann Gottfried Herder's German translation of folk poems, from 1778 to 1779, where it became instrumental as one of the many ballads that nurtured the folkloric interests of Germans in search of a national identity. It is to Herder's collection, brought to his attention by his friend Julius Allgeyer, that Brahms refers in his inscription at the head of his first Ballade. As shown in Example 5.1,[9] the inscription reads: "Nach der schottischen Ballade: 'Edward' in Herders *Stimmen der Völker*" ("After the Scottish ballad: 'Edward' in Herder's *Voices of the People*").

Let us first consider the "Edward" ballad itself; the text is shown at Figure 5.1, as presented in the German by Herder and translated by Dillon Parmer,[10] with my annotations. The poem's structure is unusual for folk ballads: it consists entirely of a dialogue—in this case, the gruesome exchange between the mother and the son. As mentioned by Parmer and indicated in the figure, the ballad's seven stanzas, each containing a dialogue, divide into two unequal groups, during the first three of which Edward's mother persists in pressing him for answers about his blood-stained sword. Here is where the mother drives him to commit two lies—first, "Oh I've struck my falcon dead," and then "Oh I've struck my horse dead." Edward expresses remorse about both actions, but the mother questions his veracity. She knows he's lying, and we

Example 5.1 Brahms, Ballade, Op. 10, No. 1, "Nach der schottischen Ballade: 'Edward' in Herders *Stimmen der Völker*," bars 1–26.

do, too: Edward's second explanation invalidates his first. The third stanza concludes with Edward's true confession: "Oh I have struck my father dead."

In the remaining four stanzas, the mother begs Edward to explain what he will do for penance; his answers, as summarized by Parmer—"voluntary exile, abandonment of house, wife, and child"[11]—culminate in a stunning oedipal revelation: in the last lines Edward explosively curses his mother for having counseled him to commit the murder; thus he accuses her of being just as unreliable, and just as guilty, as himself. Moreover, if she has colluded with him, her questions and his answers have been nothing but a charade—a pretense for

Example 5.1 Continued

delaying admission of the truth. The presence of *two* unreliable characters in the "Edward" ballad is an uncommon literary ploy.[12] I shall explore the possibility that Brahms not only recognized the dual deception but also strove to underscore it.

How to interpret Brahms's reference to the "Edward" tale has been under debate over many decades, and this essay will surely not put the debate to rest. No commentator has contested that the first part of Brahms's Ballade represents the dialogue within the first two stanzas of the poem; but parallels between poetic structure and musical form end there. Edward's curse at the end of the ballad is the twist ending, the climax toward which the entire poem has insidiously been headed. Those familiar with Brahms's Ballade already know, however, that his musical climax falls within the middle section of his ternary (A–B–A′) form, rather than at the end; his reprise, the A′ section, features only a much subdued, but maybe also sinister, variant of the music *exclusively* associated with the mother. This disparity has led numerous Brahms scholars to deny a programmatic content, to downplay its role, or to dismiss it as irrelevant. Illustrious contributors to this range of outlooks include, in the early twentieth century, Paul Mies,[13] and, more recently, Michael Musgrave,[14] Walter Frisch,[15] and James Parakilas.[16] In response to these perspectives, Dillon Parmer and Charise Hastings[17] have revisited the question of the ballad-Ballade relationship. I shall refer to their work as I proceed.

Group 1

1. Dein Schwert, wie ist's von Blut so rot? (a)
    Edward, Edward!
Dein Schwert, wie ist's von Blut so rot,
    Und gehst so Traurig da? – O!

O ich hab geschlagen meinen Geier tot, (a)
    Mutter, Mutter!
O ich hab geschlagen meinen Geier tot,
    Und keinen hab ich wie er – O!

2. Dein's Geiers Blut ist nicht so rot,
    Edward, Edward!
Dein's Geiers Blut ist nicht so rot,
    Mein Sohn, bekenn mir frei – O!

O ich hab geschlagen mein Rotroß tot,
    Mutter, Mutter!
O ich hab geschlagen mein Rotroß tot,
    Und war so stolz und treu – O!

3. Dein Roß war alt und hast's nicht not,
    Edward, Edward!
Dein Roß war alt und hast's nicht not,
    Dich drückt ein andrer Schmerz – O!

O ich hab geschlagen meinen Vater tot,
    Mutter, Mutter!
O ich hab geschlagen meinen Vater tot,
    Und weh, weh ist mein Herz – O!

Your sword, why is it so red with blood?
    Edward, Edward!
Your sword, why is it so red with blood?
    And why so sad go thee there? – Oh!

Oh I have struck my falcon dead,
    Mother, Mother!
Oh I have struck my falcon dead,
    and I have no other like him – Oh!

Your falcon's blood is not so red,
    Edward, Edward!
Your falcon's blood is not so red,
    My son, confess it to me freely – Oh!

Oh I have struck my red-roan steed,
    Mother, Mother!
Oh I have struck my red-roan steed,
    and he was so proud and faithful – Oh!

Your horse was old and you've no need of him,
    Edward, Edward!
Your horse was old and you've no need of him,
    another sorrow presses on you – Oh!

Oh I have struck my father dead,
    Mother, Mother!
Oh I have struck my father dead,
    and woe, woe is my heart – Oh!

Group 2

4. Und was für Buße willt du nun tun?
    Edward, Edward!
Und was für Buße willt du nun tun?
    Mein Sohn, bekenn mir mehr – O!

Auf Erden soll mein Fuß nicht ruhn,
    Mutter, Mutter!
Auf Erden soll mein Fuß nicht ruhn,
    Will gehn fern übers Meer – O!

5. Und was soll werden dein Hof und Hall?
    Edward, Edward!
Und was soll werden dein Hof und Hall?
    So herrlich sonst und schön – O!

Ich laß es stehn, bis es sink und fall',
    Mutter, Mutter!
Ich laß es stehn, bis es sink und fall',
    Mag nie es wieder sehn – O!

And what will you now do for penance?
    Edward, Edward!
And what will you now do for penance?
    My son, tell me more – Oh!

My foot shall never rest on earth,
    Mother, Mother!
My foot shall never rest on earth,
    I want to go far over the sea – Oh!

And what will become of your court and hall?
    Edward, Edward!
And what will become of your court and hall?
    otherwise so lordly and beautiful – Oh!

I will let it stand until it sinks and falls,
    Mother, Mother!
I will let it stand until it sinks and falls,
    I want never to see it again – Oh!

Figure 5.1 "Edward" Ballad (from Herder, *Stimmen der Völker*, 1778–1779; 2nd ed. 1807). Translation adapted from Dillon Parmer, "Brahms and the Poetic Motto: A Hermeneutic Aid?," *Journal of Musicology* 15/3 (1997): 380–81.

6. Und was soll werden dein Weib und Kind?
    Edward, Edward!
Und was soll werden dein Weib und Kind?
    Wenn du gehst übers Meer – O!
	And what will become of your wife and child?
	    Edward, Edward!
	And what will become of your wife and child?
	    When you go over the sea? – Oh!

Die Welt ist groß, laß sie betteln drin,
    Mutter, Mutter!
Die Welt ist groß, laß sie betteln drin,
    Ich seh sie nimmermehr – O!
	The world is large, let them beg in it,
	    Mother, Mother!
	The world is large, let them beg in it,
	    Nevermore will I see them – Oh!

7. Und was willt du lassen deiner Mutter teur?
    Edward, Edward!
Und was willt du lassen deiner Mutter teur?
    Mein Sohn, das sage mir – O!
	And what will you leave your dear mother?
	    Edward, Edward!
	And what will you leave your dear mother?
	    My son, tell me – Oh!

Fluch will ich euch lassen und höllisch Feuer,
    Mutter, Mutter!
Fluch will ich euch lassen und höllisch Feuer,
    Den Ihr, Ihr rietet's mir! – O!
	A curse I will leave you and hell's fire,
	    Mother, Mother!
	A curse I will leave you and hell's fire,
	    because you, you counselled me to do it!

Figure 5.1 Continued

The first part of the Ballade, the musical dialogue, is shown at Example 5.1. As should be abundantly clear, the mother's music, in the opening Andante, contrasts in so many ways with Edward's music, at the *poco più mosso*. The mother's theme, with its vast registral expanse, its widely spaced doublings, its archaic open fifths, and its processional character, conjures for me an immensely powerful image—a towering Highlander, austere, forbidding, even regal (we learn that her son possesses a lordly home), yet dressed all in black, as if in mourning. The twenty-one-year-old Brahms has outdone himself here; the effect is of solemn symphonic D-minor grandeur. A fragment of the mother's opening idea sequences into the subdominant, and then a stretching of the phrase concludes with a half cadence—ideal for the reinforcement of her questions.

At the *poco più mosso*, Edward tries to placate his mother. Now the chorale-like close spacing, the mostly conjunct motion, and the rich contrary motion between bass and soprano aim to deflect her questions, with a warmth of sonority that neutralizes the mother's harsh open fifths. And yet, Edward's theme seems harmonically unstable: as shown, it begins as if in B♭, the submediant (VI), but it leads into a cadential gesture in G minor, the subdominant. A sequence in descending thirds feigns a motion into the region of C minor, but the direction instead swerves abruptly toward a home-tonic half cadence. This is the very goal his mother had reached; but now the chordal third is missing, thus echoing the mother's open fifths on the downbeat of bar 2. We might sense that Edward is equivocating, because the music suggests as much. The slightly faster tempo and the harmonic vacillation hint at nervousness, at an overly anxious effort to convince.

There can be no question that Brahms opens his Ballade with the "Edward" ballad directly in mind; he has made an overt effort to portray two distinct musical characters in opposition to one another. Moreover, Max Kalbeck and Paul Mies both argue that the words of the ballad's first stanza neatly fit beneath Brahms's opening melody, as shown at Example 5.2; Mies even surmises that the Ballade began as a song before becoming a solo piano piece.[18] On the other hand, the mother's and her son's themes also share at least one telltale family trait, noted by Günther Wagner, Parmer, and Hastings.[19] As shown with brackets in the score at Example 5.1, the mother's melody abounds with descending perfect fifths, as especially brought to the fore with her repeated descents from E to A, clearly standing in for the textual repetition "Edward, Edward!" I regard these descending fifths as motivic, even when some of them cross the border between the ending of a slur and a new melodic beginning. Perfect fifths appropriately become the more troubling diminished fifths at bars 5–8, where the words "und gehst so traurig da?" ("and why so sad go thee there"?) might be underlaid. Descending perfect fourths, as inversions of the fifths, counterpoint these moments.

Edward moderates his mother's descending fifths by filling them in stepwise, over the span of one-bar units (see the beamed notes within the score). But he also then alludes to his mother's plaintive opening gesture—the neighbor grace-note motion B♭-to-A, $\hat{6}$-to-$\hat{5}$—from her first downbeat: in his approach to the half cadence at bar 13, he reiterates the neighbor $\hat{6}$-to-$\hat{5}$ relationship, expanded through the progression iv-to-V. I propose that these points of motivic commonality are not there just for the purpose of musical and, shall we say, generational continuity; they also hint, below the musical surface, of the mother-son complicity. Edward has already begun to insinuate his mother's guilt, and he will expand upon this soon enough.

Example 5.2 Text underlay from Paul Mies, as shown in Michael Musgrave, *The Music of Brahms* (Oxford: Clarendon Press, 1985), 23.

When the mother now speaks again (bars 14–21), her music is an almost exact repetition of her opening statement. This inspires Hastings to suggest that it is as if "the second theme [the son's theme] never happened," that "the second theme is negated by the lack of change in the first theme's response."[20] I'll go further: the mother has hardly needed to listen to her son's fabrication about killing his falcon; she *knows* the truth, and she only wants Edward to admit to it. Perhaps her one variant—her half cadence now on the dominant of B♭—arises as a clever ploy, ever so gently urging Edward to put away his fruitless lies; her ending now connects smoothly as dominant-to-tonic with the return of Edward's theme. This time the theme entails invertible counterpoint—the original soprano and bass are exchanged; the result is less conjunct motion, with new leaps in both voices. These changes, in combination with the thinner texture, might just suggest a diminishing of confidence: will it really be worth his effort for Edward to pretend that he has killed his beloved horse? But a sign of rising courage emerges with the cadence that marks the end of Edward's second lie. On the surface, this is a half cadence in the subdominant, G minor, but it is about to be heard as a glaring home tonic—a pointed reference to the mother's opening chord, and perhaps a furtive innuendo: here's another triad that lacks its third. As the movement's second part, the Allegro B section, then begins, a chordal third is recovered, but it will be the third of the tonic major.

From this point forward, the musical dialogue ends, and thus the formal parallels between Ballade and ballad also come to their end. If the sense of a narrative account remains in play, it's now apparently all about Edward. As shown at Example 5.3, the predominant melodic idea in this Allegro comes directly from Edward's theme: appearing first in the bass, it consists of the first five tones of his melody from bars 21–22, originally his bass line at bars 8–9. Some have associated the new, all-pervasive eighth-note triplets with the galloping of Edward's steed;[21] for others, Brahms here abandons the dialogue structure of the ballad in order to "back up" chronologically and substitute a musical enactment of the murder itself.[22] As an alternative view, less in conflict with the present tense of the mother-son dialogue, we might imagine that Brahms's B section enacts Edward's *reliving* of the murder, in all its enormity and triumph, its horror and shame. Let's take a closer look at this passage.

If we can agree that the Allegro seems to relate to Edward, then perhaps we might also perceive that his mother hovers over the passage as well. It opens harmonically with a summoning of the mother's initial tonic-to-dominant motion—her opening two-bar idea, but now in the major mode and expanded to encompass a four-bar phrase. The pianist's fingers might also remember the mother's eighth-note gesture in bar 1, when it reappears in the right hand's triplet upbeat at bar 28, rhythmically transformed. The shift to the submediant at bar 31 initiates a common variant of the ascending-step sequence (ii–[V]–iii), arriving on the mediant (F♯ minor) at bar 34. With a *crescendo* now underway, a three-bar unit serves as the model for a sequence that lands triumphantly on

Example 5.3 Brahms, Ballade, Op. 10, No. 1, bars 27–43.

Example 5.3 Continued

Example 5.4 Brahms, Ballade, Op. 10, No. 1, outer-voice reduction, bars 27–42.

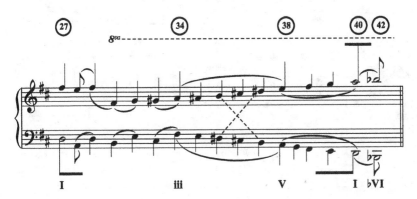

none other than the home tonic at bar 40—the mother's tonal region, but with a luminous transformation, from minor to major. What controls this impassioned progression is an ongoing stepwise ascent in the upper voice; beginning at bar 34, it moves in contrary motion with a stepwise descent in the bass, shown in reduction at Example 5.4. The goal of the exchange—the tonic major at bar 40—will then be exultantly celebrated, with repeated iterations.

But then! The arrival of the B♭ chord at bar 42 supersedes all else and becomes the *real* long-range goal—for me, a reference in reverse to the grace-note

B♭-to-A neighbor motion with which the mother's music began. The mother—"Mutter!"—is being called out by her "name," in the form of her signature opening gesture. The B♭ harmony ushers in a complete reprise of Edward's theme, now *fortissimo, pesante,* and texturally very full, with the melody an octave higher, appropriating the mother's own vast registral spacing (Example 5.5). If

Example 5.5 Brahms, Ballade, Op. 10, No. 1, bars 44–71.

Example 5.5 Continued

Edward is now "speaking" again, perhaps this is his much-delayed first poetic climax, where, in defiance, but also with the greatest anguish, he declares: "Oh I have struck my father dead" ("Ich hab' geschlagen meinen Vater tot"). We might even be tempted to hear the ballad's second climax—the curse—within the theme's sequential repetition: "A curse I will leave you and hell's fire" ("Fluch will ich euch lassen und höllisch Feuer"). In this hearing, the ballad's two climaxes have been compressed into one overwhelming outcry.

This time, Edward's theme does not swerve from emphatic cadential gestures in *either* G minor *or* C minor. But his passion cannot yet be stemmed: with the dynamics remaining *sempre fortissimo*, this pseudo-reprise spills over into dominant and then tonic fragments of his theme in the region of the Neapolitan, E♭—a surprising move, but maybe chosen as a means of releasing Edward's outpouring into a gentler major-mode context. Edward finally runs out of steam; the passage dissolves, and a written-out *ritardando* settles without conviction onto a half cadence in B♭, the very harmony with which the return of his theme began. Edward has come full circle, in despair.

As for the ballad's damning final line, we have no need to locate it in the music. By revisiting Mies's text underlay at Example 5.2, we'll see that he did not find a melodic fragment to accommodate the shorter, final verse in Edward's first declamation; here, in his last statement, that verse would be "Denn Ihr, Ihr rietet's mir!" ("because you, you counseled me to do it!"). There is no need for this final accusation: through allusions to her motives, the music of Brahms's B section has been insinuating the mother's collusion all along. Nor does the mother need to hear those words; she knows that they would only speak the truth. There is nothing left for her to do but lament her advice; together with her son, she will pay the heavy price of guilt. Brahms's varied reprise gives to the mother a greatly subdued final spotlight that she has so shamefully earned.

Hardly a "replay" of any aspect of the movement's opening dialogue, the A′ section simply transforms the mother's opening phrase, *sotto voce*, now elaborating upon it with a new staccato triplet figure in the lower register that "shadows" the mother's melody, lagging behind it by an eighth-rest. The effect is uncanny; the mother has lost her regal character—she seems to have become greatly diminished, even ghostly, and the sense of her remorse is palpable. A varied repetition of her phrase now turns not to the subdominant, as before, but to the very dark minor dominant (bar 64) and then to the whisperings (*pianissimo*) of diminished-seventh chords that initiate a long, slow, deeply melancholy chromatic descent over tonic pedal to the one and only authentic cadential gesture of the movement. The composer's characteristically unorthodox bass motion at the end—the descending arpeggiation A–F–D (bars 69–70)—embellishes one last instance of the mother's tell-tale falling fifths.

One can argue that, from a purely pragmatic viewpoint, there is good reason why Brahms did not sustain the ballad's dialogue structure to the bitter end: the stanzaic form of the ballad works well as a storytelling device, but the continuation of a musically strophic design throughout this solo piano work would have risked monotony in the absence of words. It must be acknowledged, however, that in 1878, twenty-four years later, Brahms returned to the "Edward" ballad and set its text as a vocal duet for alto and tenor. Perhaps he rose to this challenge in response to the enormous popularity of Carl Loewe's setting, published in 1824.[23] We must also note that Brahms's duet takes a varied strophic form and honors the "Edward" ballad's surprise ending, by placing the curse in the last moment of the duet.

But even without words, or without a musically strophic structure, a formal plan with a climax at the end might somehow have been possible for Brahms's Ballade. So, why did he resist? For James Parakilas, Brahms "is not abandoning that structure, but recasting it"; he is suggesting "a progression of utterances that at first respond to each other, but then lose themselves in self-absorption. Although this progression is very different from the narrative progression of 'Edward,' the music has a concentrated dramatic power that is clearly inspired by the narrative power of 'Edward.'"[24] Parakilas's idea of "self-absorption"—within Edward's monumental climax in the B section, and with the mother's inward-searching lament at the end—seems very good to me. But I think that this view can be greatly enhanced when we consider that Edward's appeals to his mother, through the composer's allusions to her music, bring her into focus as the implicated mastermind of the murder—the *other* unreliable character in the tale. In this light, Brahms's explicit focus upon the mother's music in the final section strikes me as a stroke of genius.

What does it mean to create an unreliable narrative *in fiction*? In my earlier article, I explored this question at length. Literary critic James Wood says: "We know that the narrator is being unreliable because the *author is alerting us... to that narrator's unreliability*. A process of authorial flagging is going on; the novel teaches us how to read its narrator."[25] In other words, the author and the reader are to a certain extent in collusion: the author encourages the reader to "read behind the back" of the narrator, or to "read between the lines."[26] From within the narrative discourse itself, we're encouraged to *participate*—to resolve textual contradictions or discrepancies.

Whether or not music, particularly music without a title, text, or program, can "narrate" in a comparable way remains a question in ongoing debate, expressly initiated by Jean-Jacques Nattiez in his famous 1990 essay, "Can One Speak of Narrativity in Music"?[27] An initial flurry of interest in musical narrativity began in the mid-1970s and led into the 1990s; since then, a new wave of activity has followed upon Byron Almén's 2008 *A Theory of Music Narrative*, in which Almén effectively summarizes earlier contributions, strives to rebut each of Nattiez's arguments, and develops a theory that draws upon the work of Northrop Frye, James Jacób Liszka, Eero Tarasti, Robert Hatten, and Vera Micznik.[28] Of the many essays on musical narrativity since Almén's, Seth Monahan's re-evaluation of the notions of musical "action" and "agency" has been influential,[29] and Michael L. Klein and Nicholas Reyland's edited collection of essays on musical narrative since 1900 represents an important breakthrough into the twentieth century and beyond.[30]

Within this wealth of early and recent writings, the notion of narrative "unreliability" *in music* has, to my knowledge, not been broached, though comparisons with different types of narrator in literature, both conventional and novel, have been explored. Returning to James Wood's "textural contradictions and discrepancies" in unreliable narratives, we can say, by analogy, that, in the case of his first Ballade, Op. 10, Brahms's displacement of the poem's final climax is a discrepancy; it contradicts the ballad's structure, perhaps even its implied meaning, and it conspires with both his tonal plan and his striking motivic interconnections to provoke our attention. Whether or not the composer alerts us to listen "between the lines" and beneath the surface, whether or not he wished above all to underscore the elements of unreliability, codependency, complicity, and criminality in the mother-son relationship, he invites us to ponder these issues as listeners and performers—to collude with him in attempting to understand this enigmatic work. The Ballade suggests an intellectual, literary, and psychological grasp of the "Edward" ballad that seems phenomenal for such a young composer at the threshold of his career.

Afterword

I offer this chapter, first and foremost, as an effort to place music analysis in the service of a new, admittedly speculative, view about the formal departure of Brahms's "Edward" Ballade from the poem's poetic structure. The question of why Brahms chose to engage with "Edward" lingers, if only "between the lines," among writers about the Ballade; and so it seems appropriate to conclude with thoughts about this question.

A mere perusal of the texts on the theme of love that Brahms chose to set as vocal solos in the early 1850s—for example, "Liebestreu" (Robert Reinick) and "Liebe und Frühling" I and II (Hoffmann von Fallersleben), from the Op. 3 collection; "Spanisches Lied," Op. 6; and "Parole" (Joseph von Eichendorff) from the Op. 7 collection—points by comparison to the extraordinary turn the composer made when he engaged with the patricide of the "Edward" ballad— a mythological tale of oedipal enormity and horror. What drew Brahms to address this subject, and to portray it with such gravity? We cannot know.

But we do know that, at some time between the end of June and the middle of October 1854, Brahms's new acquaintance in Düsseldorf, the art student Julius Allgeyer, introduced him to Herder's *Stimmen der Völker* and thus to the "Edward" ballad. The sleuth work of William Horne has established convincingly that the "Edward" Ballade was the last of Brahms's four ballades to have been composed, and that, unlike Ballades Nos. 3 and 4, it was entirely new; that is, unlike those two movements, it did *not* consist of a transformation of one of the earlier character pieces that Brahms had asked Joachim to review on 19 June of that year. We can also assume that the Ballades were finished by 21 October 1855, because Brahms reported to Frau Schumann that he had performed them for his Hamburg teacher, Eduard Marxsen. Clara was already familiar with them, so the Ballades as an opus must have been completed earlier—sometime after Allgeyer's gift of the Herder volume.[31] Whatever it was about the "Edward" ballad that fired the imagination of Brahms, it seems also to have inspired the title of the complete Op. 10 as a whole.[32]

The Scottish bard had not read Sophocles' Oedipus plays, of course; but surely both Percy and Herder had become acquainted with them. What about Brahms? Already at an early age, he was a voracious reader. Brahms scholars know that, from around the age of sixteen until 1854, he gathered favorite quotations from his readings, in little anthologies titled *Des jungen Kreislers Schatzkästlein* (*The Young Kreisler's Little Treasure Chest*)—clearly an effort to broaden his education; two of the hundreds of quotations are from Sophocles.[33]

The story of Brahms's friendship with Robert and Clara Schumann, beginning with his tap on their door at the end of September 1853, has gained the status of legend, and both Robert and Clara were involved in the early reception of Op. 10. After Robert's attempted suicide in February 1854, and then his request to be institutionalized at the private sanatorium in Endenich, the young Brahms spent two years "in complete if psychologically confused devotion to Clara and her family."[34] In this role he undertook a pleasant task in July of that year, spending happy hours arranging (and reading) the books and music in the Schumann library (see Chapter 1 of this volume). The part of Schumann's library now located at the Robert-Schumann-Haus in Zwickau does not list the Sophocles plays, but according to the index of Brahms's *own* library, catalogued by Kurt Hofmann in 1974, Clara Schumann sent Brahms a translation in German by F. W. G. Stäger (1841–1842) of Sophocles' tragedies (two volumes in one) in July 1855,[35] thus probably less than a year after he had completed the Ballades. It seems unlikely that Clara sent Brahms one of Sophocles' lesser-known extant plays; the gift was probably from the Theban Oedipus trilogy. Unlike the Stäger translation, where there are no markings, a second volume of Sophocles has been catalogued in Brahms's library, as translated by his friend Gustav Wendt (1884); here the only annotations to be found are in reference to Odysseus in *Ajax* (*Aias*) and to *Oedipus*.[36]

Brahms's veneration of Robert Schumann cannot be overstated; Schumann was his first renowned and unconditionally devoted advocate, the one who hailed him as "a young eagle," but who also repeatedly pressured him to begin writing orchestral music. As for Brahms's relationship with both Clara and Robert, we can let him speak for himself. In a letter of 16 August 1854 to friends in Winsen, he writes:

> Frau S[chumann] went with a friend on the 10th of this month to Ostend for the benefit of her health. I, after much persuasion, resolved to make a journey through Swabia during her absence. I did not know how greatly I was attached to the Schumanns, how I lived in them; everything seemed barren and empty to me, every day I wished to turn back, and was obliged to travel

by rail in order to get quickly to a distance and forget about turning back. It was of no use.... When one has found such divine people as Robert and Clara Schumann, one should stick to them and not leave them, but raise and inspire one's self by them.[37]

Biographer Florence May summarizes Brahms's role in the relationship: "The Schumanns' house had become a second home to him, and his place in the affections of its master and mistress that of a beloved elder son."[38]

In this light, it comes as no surprise that Brahms was eager to share his newly composed Ballades with both of the Schumanns. Clara's known response, on 8 November 1854, was to make a fabulous celebratory gift to Brahms, *One Thousand and One Nights* (*Tausend und eine Nacht*); she inscribes the volume "To the deeply esteemed Johannes Brahms in grateful remembrance of the wonderful magical sounds of his Ballades."[39] On 27 November Robert wrote to Clara from Endenich of his delight in studying the set of variations that would be published as Brahms's Op. 9, and he asks her to send him the Ballades. According to Horne, it appears from Brahms's correspondence with Julius Otto Grimm that, as one of the few friends allowed to visit Robert frequently in the sanatorium, he performed the Ballades and the Variations for him.[40] Schumann was thus one of the very first to hear the Ballades in person, and his shrewd comments about them stand as one of his last significant "reviews," marking the end of his distinguished career as a music critic. For context, I quote his remarks about the complete opus, from his letter to Clara of 6 January 1855:

> And the Ballades—the first one ["Edward"] wonderful, quite new; only the *doppio movimento*, the same as in the second one, I don't understand—doesn't it get too fast? [Brahms apparently revised this passage in the first Ballade, in response to Schumann's critique.] The finale beautiful/strange! The second one—how different, full of variety to give rich sustenance to the imagination; there are magical sounds in it. The final F♯ bass seems to lead into the third Ballade. What is the word for it? Demonic—magnificent, and the way it gets more and more secretive after the *pp* in the trio; the latter altogether transfigured and the return and finale! Did this Ballade perhaps make a similar impression on you, dear Clara? In the fourth Ballade, how lovely, that the strange first note of the melody alternates back and forth in the finale between minor and major and then stays ruefully in the major. Forward now to overtures and symphonies![41]

The overlapping of Robert's tragedy with the composing of the Ballades and, in response, with Brahms's ever closer devotion to the Schumann family leads back to that tantalizing, but probably unresolvable question: what compelled the composer to turn to the "Edward" ballad? In at least one case, a speculation has been intimated but then withdrawn, in the interests of propriety.[42] What we learn, from the facts and the actual circumstances of Brahms and the

Schumanns in 1854, is that Clara and Robert were among the first recipients of the Ballades, that they thus represent the first, though private, critical reception of Op. 10, that both were completely enchanted with this new work, and that neither of them seems to have been concerned with the topic, the content, or the criminality of the "Edward" tale and its relevance to the First Ballade. But even this is speculation. Perhaps it is Brahms's good fortune that there is nothing more we can know.

Chapter 6

The Transmission and Reception of Courtly Love Poetry in Late Folksong Settings by Johannes Brahms, Friedrich Wilhelm Arnold, and Wilhelm Tappert

Loretta Terrigno

Brahms's forty-nine folksong arrangements WoO 33, published in 1894, represent the culmination of his study of German folksong and its sources, a lifelong pursuit that occupied him from the 1850s to the 1890s.[1] During the preparation of WoO 33, Brahms's letters to Philipp Spitta imply that he had come to expect a treatment of folksong melodies that was not borne out by contemporary collections or arrangements. Franz Magnus Böhme's *Deutscher Liederhort: Auswahl der vorzüglicheren Deutschen Volkslieder, nach Wort und Weise aus der Vorzeit und Gegenwart* (1893–1894) (German treasury of song: a selection of exquisite German folksongs, according to texts and melodies from antiquity to the present) especially provoked Brahms's contempt, since this collection betrayed scholarly inaccuracies and an insensitivity to the provenance, national character, and artistic value of melodies.[2] Brahms's letters suggest that he responded to this neglectful state of folksong research and arrangement in his own collection of folksongs—a musical *Streitschrift*, or "manifesto in tones."[3] In a letter to Spitta on 6 April 1894, for instance, Brahms reveals that he planned a prose polemic alongside WoO 33, but ultimately destroyed the written component to let the music speak for itself:

> Dear fr[iend], I was serious about the polemic. But you'll get it tomorrow, transformed into something more beautiful, I hope. For while I was busy writing furiously, these old, beloved songs of mine came to mind.[4]

On its surface, Brahms's reference to "old, beloved songs" suggests that a simple love for certain melodies inspired him to revisit and draw from his own earlier settings and folksong study in WoO 33. But his nonchalant statement veils the intensity with which he carried out research into the songs' provenance. Later in the same letter from 6 April 1894, Brahms alludes to the depth of his scholarly pursuits and, further, admits his willingness to combine texts and melodies of different ages in No. 13 of his collection, "Wach auf, mein Hort":

> To you I don't need to say that I don't consider melodies of songs like "Wach auf, mein Hort" to be of the same age, also absolutely unworthy of the lovely

words; that I know the old melodies in Forster [Georg Forster, *Frische teutsche Liedlein* (New little German songbook) in 5 volumes, published 1539–1556], etc. very well—but am nevertheless glad to be able to sing songs such as that with so healthy, lively a melody. Not a folk tune? Fine, so then we have one more cherished composer and I need not be modest on his behalf as I am on mine.[5]

The circumstances that might have motivated Brahms to join specific texts and melodies in these folksongs, however, remain underexplored.[6] This chapter thus considers how Brahms's rigorous musicological investigation of sources exists meaningfully alongside his combination of courtly love texts with melodies that are not "authentic"—that is, archaic or transcribed directly from particular geographical regions or people. Further, by investigating Brahms's choice to unite certain poems and melodies, as well as his desire to recompose other folksong arrangements in WoO 33, we might rehear these seemingly familiar songs as Brahms's commentary on his music-historical past.

I will focus on three related topics. First, I will discuss how Brahms painstakingly disentangled the transmission of texts and melodies from sixteenth-century songbooks into nineteenth-century collections that adapted or modified them. Extensive annotations and cross-references throughout Brahms's personal library support his claim to "know the melodies in Forster well." Markings in Brahms's most cherished collection, the *Deutsche Lieder mit ihren Original-Weisen* (German songs with their original melodies) by Andreas Kretzschmer and Anton Wilhelm von Zuccalmaglio (1838–1840; hereafter KrZucc), as well as in Böhme's *Altdeutsches Liederbuch: Volkslieder der Deutschen nach Wort und Weise aus dem 12. bis zum 17. Jahrhundert* (1877) (Old German songbook: folksongs of the German people according to texts and melodies from the 12th to 17th centuries), and his *Deutscher Liederhort* (1893–1894) reveal that these books played a crucial role in Brahms's detailed comparison of collections of folksong texts, melodies, polyphonic lieder, and arrangements for voice and piano from the sixteenth to the nineteenth century.[7] In order to establish why Brahms might have joined archaic texts with modern melodies, we must therefore navigate Brahms's labyrinthine and meticulous comparison of a wide range of sources.

Second, I will demonstrate that Brahms's selection and treatment of modern melodies affects his portrayal of separation and fidelity in the courtly love poetry he includes in WoO 33.[8] Close readings of two songs, "Ach Gott, wie weh thut Scheiden" (No. 17) and "Mir ist ein schöns brauns Maidelein" (No. 24), which also exist as sixteenth-century polyphonic lieder and settings for voice and piano by Brahms's contemporaries Friedrich Wilhelm Arnold (1810–1864) and Wilhelm Tappert (1830–1907), respectively, will reveal Brahms's personal affinity for certain nineteenth-century melodies that he combines with poems derived from the sixteenth century. Brahms deftly sets each modern melody's chromaticism and characteristic tonal features in a manner that expresses archaic courtly love themes.[9]

Third, I will especially focus on the potential influence of the two nineteenth-century arrangements by Arnold and Tappert—both folksong researchers—on these settings (Nos. 17 and 24) from Brahms's collection. I will suggest that the songs by Arnold and Tappert provide Brahms with compositional inspiration as well as insight into the lineage of their texts and melodies.

Owing to Brahms's fusion of old and new materials, his folksong arrangements poignantly embody their transmission history and endorse the beauty and aesthetic value of their melodies and texts. Brahms's recomposition of "old, beloved songs" in this "more beautiful" polemic, as he described it to Spitta, argues against their neglectful treatment by preserving them in new, meaningful arrangements.

Brahms's Sources for "Ach Gott, wie weh tut Scheiden," WoO 33, No. 17: Melodic and Poetic Variants

Brahms's setting of "Ach Gott, wie weh tut Scheiden" in WoO 33 reflects his engagement with several sources that are listed below in abbreviated form and arranged chronologically in Figure 6.1. These include:

- Its original sixteenth-century courtly love poem, as printed in Georg Forster, *Frische teutsche Liedlein* (1549), Vol. 3; and a *Liedflugschrift* (Nürnberg: Gutknecht, ca. 1555);[10]
- Variants of this sixteenth-century poem in nineteenth-century collections—especially Ludwig Uhland, *Alte hoch- und niederdeutsche Volkslieder* (1844–1845) and Karl Simrock, *Die deutschen Volkslieder* (1851);

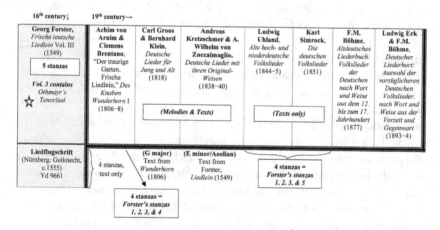

Figure 6.1 Chart of sixteenth- through nineteenth-century sources for "Ach Gott, wie Weh thut Scheiden" melodies and texts.

- Versions of its melody dating from the sixteenth and nineteenth centuries that appear in Forster (1549), Vol. 3; Carl Groos and Bernhard Klein (*Deutsche Lieder für Jung und Alt*, 1818); and KrZucc (1840); and
- Two nineteenth-century arrangements for voice and piano: (1) Brahms's own earlier arrangement ("Scheiden," WoO 32, posthum. No. 16, from 1858);[11] and (2) a setting (also titled "Scheiden") by the folksong collector F. W. Arnold.[12]

Markings in Brahms's personal library further indicate that he compared melodies for "Ach Gott" listed in KrZucc (1840) and in Böhme's *Altdeutsches Liederbuch* (1877) and *Deutscher Liederhort* (1893–1894), while ultimately choosing a similar melodic and textual pairing as that in Arnold's song. Both of Brahms's settings (WoO 32 and 33), moreover, share a tonal ambiguity with Arnold's "Scheiden." The manner in which both composers grapple with tonality in two similar nineteenth-century melodies provides insight into their portrayal of fated separation in a nineteenth-century adaptation of the courtly love poem.

Annotations in Brahms's copies of these three sources, shown in Figures 6.2, 6.3, and 6.4, respectively, show his efforts to trace the lineage of archaic and modern melodies for "Ach Gott." Figures 6.2 and 6.3 compare entry

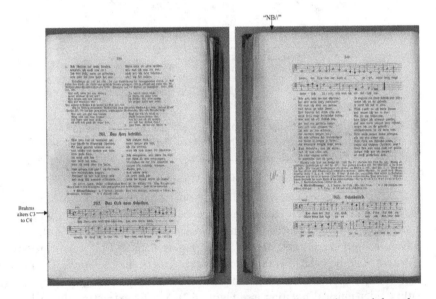

Figure 6.2 Entry No. 262 "Das Lied vom Scheiden," Franz M. Böhme, *Altdeutsches Liederbuch: Volkslieder der Deutschen nach Wort und Weise aus dem 12. bis zum 17. Jahrhundert* (Leipzig: Breitkopf und Härtel, 1877). A-Wgm3147/201B Archiv, Bibliothek und Sammlungen der Gesellschaft der Musikfreunde in Wien.

Figure 6.3 Entry No. 746 "Das Lied vom Scheiden," Ludwig Erk & Franz M. Böhme, *Deutscher Liederhort: Auswahl der vorzüglicheren Deutschen Volkslieder nach Wort und Weise aus der Vorzeit und Gegenwart* (Leipzig: Breitkopf & Härtel, 1893–1894).

No. 262 from Böhme's *Liederbuch* (Brahms's personal copy) with No. 746 from his later *Liederhort*. These entries contain two melodies: (1) the tenor part from a sixteenth-century *Tenorlied* by the Heidelberg composer Caspar Othmayr (given in both entries and dated 1549 in Figure 6.3); and (2) a new melody ("neuere Melodie") dated 1818, which appears only in the *Liederhort*. Böhme's earlier *Liederbuch* entry attempts to portray the melody's authenticity by imitating older musical notation (see Figure 6.2). Yet, by extracting the melody from its original context—Othmayr's four-voice *Tenorlied*—he obscures its compositional provenance. Brahms might well have disliked this type of faulty scholarship.[13]

Reception of Courtly Love Poetry   115

Figure 6.4 Entry No. 278, Andreas Kretzschmer & A. Wilhelm von Zuccalmaglio, *Deutsche Volkslieder mit ihren Original-Weisen*, Vol. 2 (Berlin: Vereins-Buchhandlung, 1840), 486–87. A.Wgm 1808/202B Archiv, Bibliothek und Sammlungen der Gesellschaft der Musikfreunde in Wien.

We know that Brahms sought out the original melodies cited in Böhme's critical notes in the 1877 *Liederbuch* (Figure 6.2) that he marked with "Note Bene."[14] We might also presume that Brahms would have matched Böhme's citation of "a modern, beautiful melody set by Carl Groos to the W[under]horn text" with the "neuere Melodie" in Böhme's *Liederhort* entry (Figure 6.3), which derives from the collection *Deutsche Lieder für Jung und Alt* by Carl Groos and Bernhard Klein (1818).[15] Yet Brahms's annotations beneath the melody printed in KrZucc (Figure 6.4) suggest that he was *also* aware of the discrepancy between its final pitch (E) and the pitch (G) that ends Böhme's "neuere Melodie" (compare Figure 6.3). Rather than consulting Groos-Klein directly to resolve this question, Brahms marks "die Obige?" ("the one above?") and "Deutsche Lieder für Jung und Alt, 1818" ("German Songs for the Young and Old, 1818") in KrZucc (Figure 6.4), as if expressing both his lingering interest in the noncorrespondence of these cadential variants and his doubt about their origin.

Brahms's concern for the provenance of these melodies also draws attention to the circumstances under which they were united with poetry. Othmayr and Groos-Klein attach their melodies to two different versions of the poem.[16] The first, Othmayr's five-stanza original, appears in Forster's *Liedlein* (1549). The second is an artful four-stanza adaptation of Othmayr's text by Achim von

Arnim and Clemens Brentano in *Des Knaben Wunderhorn* (1806). The chart in Figure 6.1 shows that subsequent nineteenth-century collections of texts, melodies, or both—including those by Groos-Klein (1818), KrZucc (1838–1840), Uhland (1844–1845), and Simrock (1851)—derived either five or four stanzas from the 1549 and 1806 versions, respectively.[17] Each poetic variant (see Nos. 1–3 in the appendix to this chapter) conveys contrastingly hopeful or despairing views of distant love.[18]

Although the earliest poem likely stems from Othmayr's lied, it is helpful to begin our discussion of its emotional content with a four-stanza variant circulated in a song pamphlet, or *Liedflugschrift* (1555), titled "ein schoen, new Lied" (see No. 1 in the appendix), which encapsulates the inevitable separation that characterizes courtly love.[19] In stanza 1, a suitor laments the painful parting ("Scheiden") from his beloved and describes his secret longing for his lady. Stanza 2 describes a garden in which flowers froze to death, implying that he lost his love too soon. Stanza 3 elevates the beloved to an empress ("Keyserin") in the speaker's thoughts, since only her image has the power to delight him, and stanza 4 mourns their fated separation. In keeping with the societal conventions of courtly love, which prevent their romantic union (stanza 4, line 5: "so kann es leider nicht gesein"), the speaker cannot renounce his maiden to pursue a joyful life (stanza 4, line 1: "meines Buhlens erwegen"), but must continue to pine for her.[20]

The five-stanza poetic variant likely originates with Othmayr's *Tenorlied* in Forster's *Liedlein* (1549) at a crucial juncture in the poem's transmission: whereas the *Liedflugschrift* only disseminated the text, Forster's songbook preserves its polyphonic setting.[21] Stanza 3 in this poetic version[22] (see No. 2 in the appendix) emphasizes concealed longing by dwelling in the speaker's desire for the maiden. Alluding to the beloved as the noblest type of flower ("von edler Art"), the speaker describes his glorified vision of her as the balm for his suffering *and* the cause of his secret grief. Although stanza 4 says that the maiden's image can dispel the speaker's pain ("Wann ich an sie gedenke, / verschwunden ist mir mein Leid"), stanza 5 expresses his mournful realization that parting is inevitable: "Es soll und muß geschieden sein!" ("It should and must be separation!").

Another formative juncture in poetic transmission occurs in 1806, as Arnim and Brentano print a four-stanza variant in *Des Knaben Wunderhorn*, titled "Der traurige Garten" (see No. 3 in the appendix) that omits stanza 5 from Othmayr's poem. Lacking this stanza,[23] "Der traurige Garten" ends optimistically with stanza 4, in which the envisioned beloved mitigates the speaker's suffering. The melody in Groos-Klein appears with this optimistic four-stanza variant. Finally, two related poetic variants shown in Figure 6.5, from Ludwig Uhland's *Alte hoch- und niederdeutsche Volkslieder* (1844–1845) and Karl Simrock's *Die deutschen Volkslieder* (1851)—the latter set by Brahms and Arnold—excise the hopeful ending from "Der traurige Garten." Brahms's

Uhland:	Simrock (set by Brahms and Arnold):	English Translation:
[1.] Ach gott, wie weh thut Scheiden! hat mir mein herz verwundt; so trab ich über die heiden und traur zu aller stund, der stunden der seind also vil, mein herz tregt heimlichs leiden wiewol ich oft frölich bin.	Ach, Gott, wie weh thut Scheiden! Hat mir mein Herz verwundt;[1] So trab ich über[2] die Haiden Und traur zu aller Stund. Der Stunden der sind allsoviel, Mein Herz trägt heimlich Leiden, Wiewohl ich oft fröhlich bin.	Oh, God, how painful parting is! It has wounded my heart. So I trot across the heath And lament every hour. The hours are so many, My heart bears secret suffering Although I often appear cheerful.
[2.] Het mir ein gertlein bawen von veil und grünem kle, ist mir zu frü erfroren, tut meinem herzen we; ist mir erfrorn bei sonnenschein ein kraut Je lenger je lieber, ein blümlein Vergiß nit mein.	Hatt mir ein Gärtlein bauet Von Veil und grünem Klee, Ist mir zu früh erfroren, Thut meinem Herzen weh; Ist mir erfroren[3] bei Sonnenschein Ein Kraut Jelängerjelieber, Ein Blümlein Vergißnitmein.[4]	I built myself a little garden Of violet and green clover, It froze to death too soon [And] wounded my heart. It froze in the sunshine A plant [of] honeysuckle, A little forget-me-not flower.
[3.] *(likely originates with Othmayr)* Das blümlein das ich meine das ist von edler art, ist aller tugend reine, ir mündlein das ist zart, ir euglein, die seind hübsch und fein, wann ich an sie gedenke wie gern ich bei ir wolt sein!	Das Blümlein das ich meine, Das ist von edler Art, Ist aller Tugend reine; Ihr Mündlein, das ist zart. Ihr Aeuglein, die sind hübsch und fein; Wenn ich an sie gedenke, Wie gern wollt ich bei ihr sein![5]	The flower that I mean Is of a noble kind, Is pure of virtue, Her little mouth is tender. Her little eyes are sweet and delicate, When I think of her How gladly I would be by her

[1] Brahms: verwund't
[2] Brahms: üb'r
[3] Brahms: erfrorn
[4] Brahms: vergiß nicht mein
[5] Brahms: wie gern ich bei ihr wollt sein

| [4.]
Solt mich meins buln erwegen
als oft ein ander tut,
sollt füren ein frölichs leben,
darzu ein leichten mut,
das kan und mag doch nit gesein;
gesegen dich gott im herzen!
es muß geschieden sein. | Sollt mich meines Buhlen erwegen[6]
Wie oft ein Andrer thut,[7]
Sollt führen ein frölich[8] Leben,
Dazu einen leichten Muth,
Das kann und mag doch nicht so sein;[9]
Gesegne dich Gott im Herzen,
Es muß geschieden sein. | Should I renounce my love
As others often do,
Should I lead happy life,
Should I be lighthearted,
But that cannot and may not be;
God bless your heart
We must remain separate. |

Final line emphasizes parting (as in 16th-century variants) & omits the hopeful last stanza of "Der traurige Garten" (1806):

| | Mich dünkt in all mein Sinnen,
Und wann ich bei ihr bin,
Sie sey ein Kaiserinne,
Kein lieber ich nimmer gewinn,
Hat mir mein junges Herz erfreut,
Wann ich an sie gedenke,
Verschwunden ist mir mein Leid. | I feel in all my senses,
And when I am with her,
She is like an empress,
I will never win one more dear,
She has gladdened my young heart,
When I think of her,
My pain disappears. |

[6] Brahms: meins Buhl'n erwehren
[7] Brahms: ein Ander tut
[8] Brahms: führ ein fröhlichs
[9] Brahms: gesein

Figure 6.5 Comparison of two poems: (1) "Ach Gott, wie weh thut Scheiden" in Ludwig Uhland, *Alte hoch- und niederdeutsche Volkslieder* (Stuttgart & Tübingen: Cotta, 1844–1845), 128–29; and Karl Simrock, *Die deutschen Volkslieder, gesammelt von Karl Simrock* (Frankfurt am Main: Brünner, 1851), 253.

annotation to the text that KrZucc prints (compare Figure 6.4)—"nicht bei Uhland"—confirms his awareness that Uhland's poem (Figure 6.5) omits stanza 4, allowing its final lines to correspond with sixteenth-century antecedents.[24] That is, Uhland and Simrock both retain Othmayr's stanzas 1, 2, 3, and 5, in which the final line ("es muß geschieden sein") foregrounds separation and the speaker's inevitable, secretly borne pain.

A comparison of the implied G-major ending of Groos's melody (Figure 6.3) with the definitive E-minor ending by KrZucc (Figure 6.4) further relates these keys to their poems. As if reflecting the positive fourth stanza in "Der traurige Garten," Groos's melody enables the possibility of cadencing in a hopeful G-major key.[25] (Brahms knew the Groos-Klein melody from Böhme's *Liederhort* [1893–1894] and from its appearance in Arnold's song, where it is paired with the textual variant by Simrock [1851].) But displaying a tendency to "romanticize" melodies, KrZucc alters this ending to $\hat{1}$ in E minor and prints a five-stanza text (labeled "Altdeutsch") that resembles Othmayr's poem,[26] as if imbuing the minor-mode melodic cadence with the poetic expression of inevitable longing. Brahms's settings of the melody from KrZucc and poem by Simrock in WoO 32, No. 16 and its successor WoO 33, No. 17 thus convey subtly different text-music relations than in Arnold's song. Brahms's arrangement even more fully captures the paradoxical union of hidden pain and bliss expressed in Simrock's adaptation of the courtly love poem.

Comparative Close Readings of Settings by Arnold and Brahms

Although Brahms's setting in E minor from 1858 ("Scheiden," WoO, 32 posthum. No. 16) sets the melody from KrZucc, it bears many similarities to Arnold's E-minor song ("Scheiden"), which uses the original melody from Groos-Klein.[27] Arnold sets the Groos-Klein melodic ending in strophes 1, 2, and 3, but concludes strophe 4 (and the song) with the E-minor cadence from KrZucc.[28] (See Figure 6.6.) As a result, his arrangement fluctuates between the implied keys of G major and E minor.[29] This same tonal ambiguity also occurs in Brahms's "Scheiden" (see Figure 6.7), and might be interpreted to portray the vacillation between longing and pleasure that characterizes separation in Simrock's poetic variant of the archaic text. By allowing the anachronistic union of an older text and two modern melodic variants, Brahms and Arnold privilege the melody's contrapuntal, harmonic, and expressive potential over its supposed authenticity.

Owing to its recurring Phrygian half cadences, Arnold's setting (Figure 6.6) separates G major and E minor more starkly than Brahms's song. But both settings seem to cast G major as a transitory key within a governing E-minor frame

Reception of Courtly Love Poetry

Figure 6.6 Friedrich Wilhelm Arnold, "Scheiden," Vol. 7, No. 1, from the *Deutsche Lieder aus alter und neuer Zeit* (ca. 1860–1870).

Figure 6.6 Continued

by exploiting multiple interpretations of pitches shared by the tonic triads in both keys. For example, phrases 1 and 2 in Arnold's setting contain two different harmonizations of the pitch B in the vocal melody. In phrase 1, the E-minor tonic yields to an imperfect authentic cadence (IAC) in G major (bar 4), but phrase 2 returns to E minor via a Phrygian half cadence (bar 8). This phrase seems to depict the poet's pining in every hour ("traur zu aller Stund") as an inescapable

Figure 6.7 Brahms, "Scheiden." WoO 32, No. 16 (text underlay for strophes 1–2 only).

lament by gravitating toward the characteristic half step ($\hat{6}$–$\hat{5}$ in the bass) in the relative minor key.[30] At the text "heimlich Leiden" ("secret pain") in bars 11–12, Arnold's harmonization of the $\hat{6}$–$\hat{5}$ motive (C–B) creates a sorrowful 7–6 suspension and derails the passage from an alternative harmonization: $\hat{4}$–$\hat{3}$ in G major. After a perfect authentic cadence (PAC) in G major ends strophes 1, 2, and 3 (bar 14), another $\hat{6}$–$\hat{5}$ motive in the piano's right hand (bar 16) reinforces this E-minor lamentation, overshadowing the preceding, ephemeral PAC in G major. A definitive PAC that supports the melodic descent $\hat{3}$–$\hat{2}$–$\hat{1}$ (bars 19–20) further enhances the sense of an inevitable turn toward E minor.

Since Brahms's "Scheiden" (WoO 32, No. 16) only sets the E-minor (or Aeolian) melody from KrZucc, it more subtly projects tonal ambiguity between an E-minor tonic and tonicizations of G major. (See Figure 6.7.)[31] Yet as in Arnold's setting, Brahms's tonicizations of G major sound transient, as if depicting the fleeting solace that the speaker experiences when picturing his beloved. Brahms's song begins in E minor, but enters G major in bar 2, leading to an IAC much like Arnold's phrase 1. (See Figure 6.7.) Rather than succumbing to E minor again, however, Brahms's song uses a descending sequence (with chord roots D–A followed by C–G in bars 5–8) to prolong G major before treating it as III (bar 8) en route to a PAC in E minor. Seizing upon the alternative harmonization of C–B at "heimlich Leiden" as $\hat{4}$–$\hat{3}$ in G major, Brahms's harmonization allows G major to linger where the text paradoxically associates concealed pain with the major mode. In conjunction with the tonal opposition between E minor and G major, a chromatic opposition in bars 8–9 between the longing of E♭ (♭$\hat{6}$ in G major) to descend and its enharmonic twin D♯ ($\hat{7}$ in E minor) to ascend reinforces the poetic dichotomy between longed-for union and inevitable separation.[32]

Brahms's recomposition of this song as WoO 33, No. 17, now in the paired keys of F minor and A♭ major (Figure 6.8), heightens its tonal ambiguity and demonstrates the melody's contrapuntal versatility. In this setting, phrases 1 and 2 (bars 1–8) reverse Arnold's harmonization: a Phrygian half cadence ending phrase 1 implies F minor (bar 4), while a plagal cadence in phrase 2 establishes A♭ major (bar 8). Like Brahms's 1858 setting, a sequence in bars 9–12 prolongs the major key until the text "heimlich Leiden" (bars 11–12) where the motive $\hat{4}$–$\hat{3}$ in A♭ major again merges the concepts of suffering ("Leiden") and bliss. After bar 12, however, Brahms combines melodic segments in counterpoint and thereby heightens tonal ambiguity at cadences. For instance, statements of the melody in the voice and in the bass (compare bars 1–3 and 14–16 in Figure 6.8) end with the motives F–E♭ and F–E♮, respectively, implying imminent cadences in A♭ major or F minor. Whereas the motive F–E♭ stems from the original folksong melody, sung by the voice, the piano's chromatically altered imitation (F–E♮) in bars 14–16 steers the song back into F minor. Just as the speaker either imagines the beloved or suffers from pining, the listener awaits a cadence in either the major or minor key.

Figure 6.8 Brahms, "Ach Gott, wie weh tut Scheiden." WoO 33, No. 17, bars 1–16 (strophes 1–2).

As Figure 6.9 shows, an artful contrapuntal display that ends the setting seems to reinforce its inevitable return to minor, as in WoO 32, No. 16, and Arnold's song. A sorrowful, stepwise descent from F_5 to F_4 in the vocal line (bracketed in bars 27–30 of Figure 6.9) is repeated in the piano postlude (bars

Figure 6.9 "Ach Gott, wie weh tut Scheiden." WoO 33, No. 17, bars 25–32 (strophes 3–4).

30–32) and placed in counterpoint with a melodic segment that originates in the vocal line (cf. bars 1–3). Brahms's harmonization of the voice's first octave descent (bars 27–30) moves between A♭ major and F minor, yet he harmonizes the piano's repetition of this melody firmly in F minor. The tonic and PAC supporting 1̂ (F) in bar 32 perhaps reflects the speaker's acceptance of fated parting.

In light of Brahms's curiosity about the differences between melodies by Othmayr, Groos-Klein, and KrZucc, it is significant that he selected a melodic variant (KrZucc) that would facilitate fleeting occurrences of the relative major key within a predominantly minor-mode harmonization, in conjunction with a poetic variant that foregrounds the unavoidable and paradoxically sweet pain of separation.

Brahms's Sources for "Mir ist ein schöns brauns Maidelein," WoO 33, No. 24: Melodic and Poetic Variants

The range of sixteenth- and nineteenth-century sources upon which Brahms drew in his research about "Mir ist ein schöns brauns Maidelein" again reveals a detailed comparison of archaic and modern melodies. These sources, summarized in Figure 6.10, include:

- Forster's *Liedlein* (1549 and 1556, respectively), Vols. 3 and 5;
- Carl Becker's *Lieder und Weisen vergangene Jahrhunderte* (1849);
- Böhme's *Liederbuch* (1877) and *Liederhort* (1893–1894); and
- Tappert's "Mir ist ein schön's braun's Meidelein," song no. 7 from the *12 alte deutsche Lieder für eine Singstimme mit Begleitung des Pianoforte frei bearbeitet von Wilhelm Tappert* (12 old German songs for solo voice with pianoforte accompaniment, freely arranged by Wilhelm Tappert) (ca. 1867), a setting for voice and piano.[33]

←16th century			19th century→					
Georg Rhau, *Bicinia gallica, latina, germanica Tomus I, II* (1545) Two-voice setting	Georg Forster, *Frische teutsche Liedlein* Vol. 3 (1549): Four-voice Tenorlied by C. Othmayr Vol. 5 (1556): Five-voice Lied by J.v. Brandt	*Liedflugschrift* (Nürnberg: Gutknecht, 1560) Yd 7831	Carl Becker, *Lieder und Weisen vergangener Jarhunderte* (1849)	F.W. Arnold, *Deutsche Lieder aus alter und neuer Zeit* (vol. 7, no. 12, c. 1860–70) "Die Liebste"	Wilhelm Tappert, *12 alte deutsche Lieder* (c. 1867) "Mir ist ein schön's braun's Meidelein"	F.M. Böhme, *Altdeutsches Liederbuch* (1877)	F.M. Böhme, *Deutsche Liederhort* (1893–4)	J. Brahms, *Deutsche Volkslieder* (1894) "Mir ist ein schöns brauns Maidelein"
G-Dorian melody	F-major melody	5 stanzas (text only)	5 stanzas G-major melody		4 stanzas (Becker)		5 extant stanzas	4 stanzas (Becker)

Figure 6.10 Chart of sixteenth- through nineteenth-century sources for "Mir ist ein schöns brauns Maidelein" (arrows match each nineteenth-century arrangement with its earlier melodic source).

Brahms seems to have been preoccupied with the settings by Tappert—a music critic and ardent Wagnerian—in which he likely perceived scholarly and compositional failings. Tappert sets a G-major melody from Carl Becker's *Lieder und Weisen vergangene Jahrhunderte* (1849), although his table of contents cites Forster's *Liedlein* (1549) as if to substantiate the adjective "alte" in the title of his collection.[34] Tappert's *12 alte deutsche Lieder*, therefore, seems to misrepresent the age or provenance of melodies to manufacture the impression of their archaism.[35] Moreover, a comparison of the settings by Tappert and Brahms will suggest that Brahms rectifies Tappert's ineffective harmonization of the chromaticism unique to Becker's modern melody, and in so doing seems to intensify the depiction of fidelity in its courtly love poem.

The G-major melody titled "Mir ist ein schöns brauns meidelein" in Becker's *Lieder und Weisen vergangener Jahrhunderte* (1849) shown in Figure 6.11—set by both Brahms and Tappert—evolved from two earlier melodies that appear in Böhme's *Liederbuch* (1877) and *Liederhort* (1893–1894): (1) a G-Dorian melody from a two-voice setting in Georg Rhau's *Bicinia gallica, latina, germanica Tomus I, II* [French, Latin, and German duets, Vols. I, II] (1545); and (2) an F-major melody excerpted from a polyphonic lied by Othmayr, no. 68 in Vol. 3 (1549) of Forster's *Liedlein*. Whereas Böhme's *Liederhort* (entries no. 450a and 450b) cites both the F-major melody from Forster's *Liedlein* and Rhau's modal melody fairly accurately, Brahms's annotations to Böhme's *Liederbuch*, which presents *only* the F-major melody and appears in Figure 6.12 (Brahms's personal copy), reveal its errors: namely, chromaticism in the

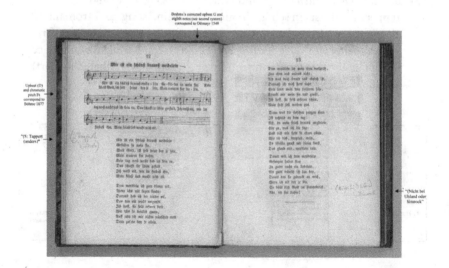

Figure 6.11 Carl Becker, *Lieder und Weisen vergangener Jahrhunderte. Worte und Töne den Originalen entlehnt* (Leipzig, 1849), 12–13. A-Wgm 2796/203B Archiv, Bibliothek und Sammlungen der Gesellschaft der Musikfreunde in Wien.

Reception of Courtly Love Poetry 127

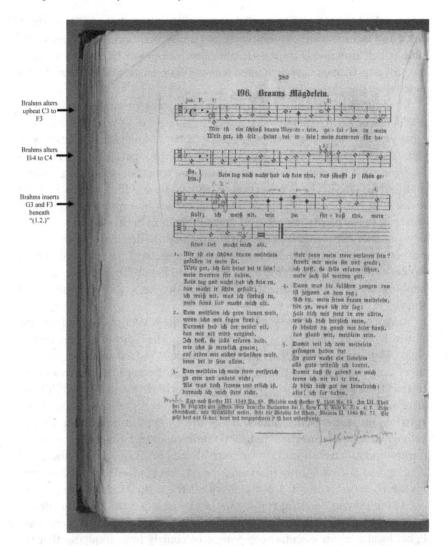

Figure 6.12 Entry No. 196 "Brauns Mägdelein," Franz M. Böhme, *Altdeutsches Liederbuch: Volkslieder der Deutschen nach Wort und Weise aus dem 12. bis zum 17. Jahrhundert* (Leipzig: Breitkopf und Härtel, 1877). A-Wgm 3147/201B Archiv, Bibliothek und Sammlungen der Gesellschaft der Musikfreunde in Wien.

F-major melody that Böhme attributes to Othmayr departs from the original lied (1549). Brahms's annotations clarify that the upbeat (C) and chromatic pitch E♭ (second system) in Böhme's printing instead correspond to the upbeat (D) and chromatic pitch F♮ in Becker's melody (compare Figures 6.11 and 6.12).[36] Brahms's pencil markings also include "(1. 2.)" above the third system and parentheses around the inserted pitches G_3 and F_3—corrected upbeats for each of the last two phrases in Othmayr's lied.[37] From Böhme's *Liederbuch* entry and Brahms's annotations we thus surmise that Becker—Böhme's possible (albeit unnamed) source—might have transposed Othmayr's F-major melody into G major, freely altered some of its pitches, and imbued it with new expressive chromaticism.[38]

In addition to studying Böhme's entries, Brahms annotated Tappert's *12 alte deutsche Lieder* in ways that suggest his irritation with the collection. For example, Tappert's table of contents—a list of complete melodies with source attributions—prints Othmayr's F-major tenor part and cites Forster's *Liedlein* with the date "1549," even though Tappert sets Becker's melody and fails to cite Becker's collection. Brahms's annotations to this F-major melody, in red pencil, highlight this discrepancy by supplying Becker's E♭ where Tappert prints the pitch C instead. Brahms writes "Becker" in the margin, as if clarifying that the chromatic pitch E♭ originates with Becker, not Othmayr.[39] Finally, Brahms cross-referenced Tappert's volume in Becker's collection (see Figure 6.11), writing "(S:[iehe] Tappert anders)," perhaps highlighting the inconsistency between Tappert's table of contents and the melody that he sets.[40]

Brahms's annotations to Becker's entry (Figure 6.11) also shed light on the transmission of its five-stanza courtly love poem. His indication to the bottom right of the text—"nicht bei Uhland und Simrock"—confirms that both authors' collections lack entries for Becker's poem. Becker's five stanzas derive instead from a *Liedflugschrift* (1560) by Gutknecht (listed in Figure 6.10) and were further altered by Brahms and Tappert.[41] Figure 6.13 shows the poetic adaptations by Tappert and Brahms, along with an English translation. Despite orthographic modernization and subtle differences in meaning between sixteenth- and nineteenth-century variants, all the poems foreground themes of longing and fidelity. Pining from afar, the speaker contrasts his pure longing for a maiden (in stanzas 1, 2, 3, and 5) with betrayal (in stanza 4), warning her not to fall prey to deceitful rumors spoken by jealous rivals who threaten to taint her purity in his absence. Throughout its transmission, the poem highlights loyalty as an essential component of courtly love, implying that the maiden will experience the speaker's full devotion only if she is faithful to him.

Brahms and Tappert use different stanzas from Becker's poem, as illustrated in Figure 6.13. Brahms adopts Becker's stanzas 1, 2, 3, and 5 and omits stanza 4, which describes the treachery of "false tongues," whereas Tappert retains Becker's stanzas 1, 4, and 5.[42] Lacking stanza 4, Brahms's poem emphasizes pure romantic longing and faithfulness. Yet in both adaptations, each stanza displays a dramatic progression toward its second half; the speaker's expository narration in lines 1–4 prepares his heightened desire for the maiden and her faithfulness in lines 5–8. For instance, lines 1–4 in stanza 1 of Brahms's adaptation describe the speaker's troubled separation from the "beautiful brownhaired maiden" that he wishes to be near ("Wollt Gott, ich sollt heut bei ihr

Reception of Courtly Love Poetry

Brahms, "Mir ist ein schöns brauns Maidelein"	Tappert, "Mir ist ein schön's braun's Meidelein"	English translation of Brahms's poem and Tappert's stanza 4:
Stanza 1 1 Mir ist ein schöns brauns Maidelein 2 Gefallen in den Sinn; 3 Wollt Gott, ich sollt heut bei ihr sein, 4 Mein Trauern führ dahin. 5 Kein Tag noch Nacht hab ich kein Ruh 6 Das schafft ihr schön Gestalt. 7 Ich weiß nicht, wie ihm fürbaß tu, 8 Mein Feinslieb macht mich alt.	Mir ist ein schön's braun's Meidelein Gefallen in mein Sinn; Wollt' Gott, ich könnt heut' bei ihr sein, Mein Trauern wär' dahin. Bei Tag und Nacht hab ich kein Ruh, Das schafft ihr schön Gestalt; Ich Weiss nit wie ich fürbass thu, Mein fein's Lieb macht mich alt.	A beautiful brown-haired maiden Has come into my mind If God wished I should be near her today, My suffering would depart. I rest neither day nor night, Her beautiful form causes this. I do not know how to move on, My darling makes me old.

Stanza 2
1 Dem Mägdlein ich gern dienen will,
2 Wenn ichs mit Fugen kunnt;
3 Darum hab ich der Neider viel,
4 Daß mir nit wird vergunnt.
5 Ich hoff, sie solls erfahren bald,
6 Wie ichs so treulich mein.
7 Auf Erd ich mir nichts wünschen wollt,
8 Denn zu sein bei ihr allein.
	Dem Meidlein ich gern dienen will,
	Wenn ich's mit Fug nur könnt,
	Darum hab ich der Neider viel,
	Weil mir's nit wird vergönnt.
	⌈ Sollt meine Treu verloren sein,
	  Kränkt sich mein Sinn und G'müth;
	  Ich hoff, sie solls erfahren schier,
	⌊ Mein Sach soll werden gut.
		Gladly I want to serve the maiden,
		If I could make an impact,
		Thus I have granted much to the enviers
		That I am not to have.
		I hope that she should soon experience,
		How faithfully I mean it:
		I would wish for nothing on Earth,
		Than only to be with her.

Stanza 3
1 Dem Maidlein ich mein Treu versprich,
2 Zu Ehrn und anders nicht.
3 Alls was doch fromm und ehrlich ist,
4 Danach ich stets mich richt.
⌈ 5 Sollt den mein Treu verloren sein,
  6 Kränkt mir mein Sinn und G'müt;
  7 Ich hoff sie solls erfahren schier,
⌊ 8 Mein Sach soll werden gut.
	Tappert omits lines 5–8 of stanza 2 and lines 1–4 of stanza 3.	I will pledge my loyalty to the maiden,
		To honor [her] and no other.
		All that is pious and honest,
		I shall always align myself with.
		Should my faithfulness be lost,
		My mind and feelings would fall ill,
		I hope she will experience it purely,
		My deed will be done well.

Stanza 4 *Brahms omits stanza 4.*	Denn was die falschen Zungen thun Ist jetzund an dem Tag, Ach du mein feines Mägdelein, Hör zu was ich dir sag': Halt dich mir stets in Ehr'n allein, Wie dich, Herzlieb mein; So b'hälst du Gunst mit dieser Kunst, Das glaub' mir Meidlein rein.	Because what the false tongues say Has now come to light. Oh you my dear maiden, Listen to what I say to you: Always hold in honor exclusively me As I do you, my lovely heart, So you will retain favor with this art, This believe me, pure maiden.
Stanza 5 1 Damit will ich dem Maidelein 2 Gesungen haben frei, 3 Zu guter Nacht ein Liedelein, 4 Alls Guts wünsch ich dabei, 5 Damit daß sie gedenkt an mich, 6 Wenn ich nit bei ihr bin. 7 So b'hüt dich Gott im Himmelreich, 8 Ade, ich fahr dahin!	Damit will ich dem Meidelein Gesungen haben frei, Zu guter Nacht mein Liedelein, All's Gut's wünsch ich dabei; Damit, dass die gedenkt an mich, Wenn ich nit bei ihr bin. So b'hüt dich Gott im Himmelreich, Ade! ich fahr dahin!	With this, to the maiden I have sung freely, A little song for good night, With this I wish [her] all good things, So that she will think of me When I am not with her. May got protect you in heaven, Farewell, I am departing!

Figure 6.13 Comparison of "Mir ist ein schöns brauns Maidelein" poems as adapted by Brahms and Wilhelm Tappert, with English translation.

sein, / Mein Trauern führ dahin"), whereas lines 5–8 reveal the restlessness and turbulent longing that her beautiful form causes ("Kein Tag noch Nacht hab ich kein Ruh / das schafft ihr schön Gestalt").

Drawing together these observations about Brahms's source study and poetic adaptation, the following comparative analyses will suggest that Brahms's contrapuntal treatment of motives and idiomatic harmonization of the distinctive chromaticism in Becker's melody reflects this dramatic arc toward lines 5–8 in each stanza, while Tappert's setting does an injustice to it. In an apparent effort to correct Tappert's inadequate response to expressive tonality implied by Becker's melody, Brahms recomposes elements from Tappert's song.

Comparative Close Readings of Settings by Tappert and Brahms

The form of Becker's melody, a sixteen-measure *Reprisenbar* containing two *Stollen* (sections A and A') and an *Abgesang*, consisting of a digression (section B) and reprise (section A²), is reflected in the cadential structure of Tappert's setting.[43] The closure-providing cadential paradigm I–vi–ii–V⁷–I in bars 3–4, 7–8, and 15–16 articulates perfect authentic cadences in G major to close sections A, A', and A² in strophes 1–3, whereas section B ends with a fleeting tonicized half cadence in G major (bar 12). (See Figure 6.14.)

Yet Brahms's markings—wavy lines and exclamation points near the melody and bass of bars 10–12 (transcribed in Figure 6.14 from his personal copy) imply that despite Tappert's suitable cadential structure, his harmonization of Becker's distinctive chromaticism in section B does a disservice to it. Tappert's harmonization also weakens the dramatic effect of section B, as this digression (i.e., contrasting melodic material in section B) sets lines 5–8 in the poem where the speaker's emotions are piqued.[44] Brahms's markings concern Tappert's harmonization of F♮ and C♯ in bars 10–11, coinciding with each stanza's emotional highpoint (e.g., in lines 5–6 of stanza 1, which describe the stirring effect of the maiden's beauty: "Kein Tag noch Nacht hab ich kein Ruh / das schafft ihr schön Gestalt"). Rather than harmonize F♮ and E across bars 10–11 with V⁷/IV followed by a root-position IV chord (C major), Tappert's pedal (G) creates a ⁶₄ chord on the downbeat of bar 11.[45] And instead of using the voice's C♯ (bar 11) to tonicize D major (V), Tappert harmonizes it with a neighboring common-tone diminished seventh chord. The resulting prolonged tonic across bars 10–12 seems to rob section B of the dramaturgically destabilizing effect of this alternative progression into the dominant region. Tappert's primarily chordal texture, further, lacks the contrapuntal and motivic integration that Brahms's setting embraces.

Brahms's setting, shown in Figure 6.15, recomposes the cadential design from Tappert's song as if to better realize the dramatic potential of Becker's *Reprisenbar* form. First, following perfect authentic cadences that end sections A (bars 1–4) and A' (bars 5–8), Brahms accommodates the dramatic and musical climax in section B (bars 9–12) with a tonicization of D major that better contextualizes F♮₅ and C♯₅ in Becker's melody. This imparts a more daring harmonic digression to the song before the tonic return in section A² (bars 13–16) and the piano postlude (bars 16–20). Brahms's development of motives derived from Tappert's setting (the neighboring ⁶₄ chord and cadential pattern I–vi–ii–V–I) might be heard to support this dramatic arc. Sections A and A', for instance, use the cadential pattern I–vi–ii–V–I above a tonic pedal (bar 3) and as the actual bass line (bar 7). A neighboring ⁶₄ chord to the G-major tonic in bar 1 (beat 3) also seems to correct Tappert's faulty rhythmic placement of the same progression by placing the ⁶₄ chord in a relatively weaker metrical

Reception of Courtly Love Poetry

Figure 6.14 "Mir ist ein schön's braun's Meidelein," No. 7 from *12 alte deutsche Lieder für eine Singstimme mit Begleitung des Pianoforte frei bearbeitet von Wilhelm Tappert* (Berlin, ca. 1867). Gesellschaft der Musikfreunde A-Wgm VI 36090.

Figure 6.14 Continued

Reception of Courtly Love Poetry

Figure 6.14 Continued

position (compare bars 1–2 in Figure 6.14, where Tappert's ⁶₄ chord appears on the downbeat).

Brahms's setting also incorporates Tappert's characteristic cadential paradigm (I–vi–ii–V–I), but more fully integrates it in the piano accompaniment with motives, such as a rising stepwise fourth, bracketed in bars 1–2 of Figure 6.15, that originate in Becker's melody. Section A, for instance, emphasizes a rising-fourth motive in the vocal line (bars 1–2), complemented by parallel sixths in the piano that resemble those found in Tappert's setting (compare the right hand in bars 3–4 of Figure 6.14). Brahms further develops these materials in A′ by (1) imitating the rising-fourth motive between the piano (bars 4–5) and voice (bars 5–6) to connect A and A′; and (2) expanding and varying the cadential pattern I–vi–ii–V as the harmonization that underlies bars 4–7.[46] Just as the narration of a dramatic premise in lines 1–2 of stanza 1 (the speaker's paradigmatic distance from the maiden in courtly love) presents themes for later elaboration, Brahms's accompaniment in sections A and A′ derives its rising-fourth motive from Becker's melody and realizes its simplest harmonic implications.

As the dramatic climax in stanza 1 (lines 5–6) reveals the effects of the maiden's provocative beauty, Brahms's section B develops these motives and progresses into the region of V (Figure 6.15, bars 10–12), fulfilling a more idiomatic harmonization of F♯ and C♯ than in Tappert's song. As if mimicking the speaker's increasing restlessness, Brahms's use of G♯ in the bass (bar 10) propels

Figure 6.15 Brahms, "Mir ist schöns brauns Meidelein," WoO 33, No. 24.

Reception of Courtly Love Poetry

Figure 6.15 Continued

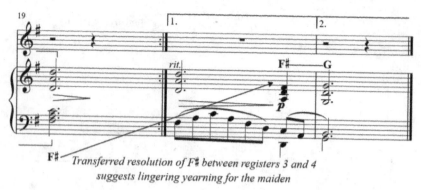

Transferred resolution of F♯ between registers 3 and 4 suggests lingering yearning for the maiden

Figure 6.15 Continued

the accompaniment through tonicizations of A major (V of V; bar 11) and D major (bar 12). That is, rather than interrupt the motion into D major by tonicizing C major, as Tappert's C-major $\frac{6}{4}$ chords implied, the pitch G♯ (supporting vii^7 of V) intensifies harmonic motion away from G major as the speaker's passion grows. A rising-fourth motive (C♯–D–E–F♯) in the piano's right hand (bars 11–12) also reinforces the sense of dramatic climax; it ascends above the voice's earlier F♯$_5$ (compare bar 10) to the leading tone F♯$_5$, which remains unresolved in that register. Pervasive rising-fourth motives, concealed within the piano's right hand (bracketed in bars 10–12), might also signify the maiden's ever-present image in the speaker's imagination, which transcends the constraints of physical separation.

Brahms's final, virtuosic treatment of these motives occurs during a tension-dissolving return to G major in A^2 (bars 13–16). In bars 13–14, Brahms weaves the recurring cadential bass line G–E–C–D within two dovetailed sequences: a descending-third sequence and a chromaticized ascending 5–6 sequence, then repeats an unelaborated form of its latter part leading to the cadence in bar 15. The piano postlude (bars 16–20) continues this sophisticated handling of counterpoint and harmony. The piano's right hand (bars 16–17) presents a rhythmic diminution of the arpeggiated left-hand figure (see brackets in Figure 6.15). In bars 18–19, a rising fourth in the bass (C♯–D–E–F♯) recalls the appearance of this motive at the melodic climax in the vocal line in bars 11–12. Finally, a transferred resolution of the pitch F♯ between registers 3 and 4 during the PAC in bar 20 recalls the earlier irresolution of F♯$_5$ in bar 12, a recollection that might signify the speaker's lingering yearning for the maiden.

In recomposing these basic elements from Tappert's arrangement, Brahms also makes manifest the nineteenth-century melody's distinctive harmonic and contrapuntal implications, which are based in the chromaticism that it accrued during its transmission from earlier sources. By examining Brahms's markings and reaction to Tappert's setting—an allusion of sorts, as discussed by Paul Berry and Janet Schmalfeldt in other songs by Brahms—we gain insight into how details of poetic and melodic evolution in "Mir ist ein schöns brauns Maidelein" might assume new meaning.[47]

Conclusion

Brahms's letters to Fritz Simrock about the publication of the *Deutsche Volkslieder*, WoO 33, reveal his deliberation over the collection's title. On 28 April 1894, Brahms entertains two options:

> I am still pondering over the title. Deutsche Volkslieder or Alte deutsche Lieder. With Klavier- or Pianoforte accompaniment?[48]

But on 7 May 1894, Brahms chooses the broader title:

> You have already printed "Alte deutsche L[ieder]" (Tappert). This [title] has already appeared with and without variation, and thus the simpler the better: Deutsche Volkslieder. (Fullstop.) With Klavier-accompaniment by J.B.[49]

Despite the outwardly practical focus of these letters, Brahms's reference to the clichéd adjective "alte" ("old" or "archaic") in Simrock's publication of Tappert's *12 alte deutsche Lieder* is suggestive, especially considering Brahms's apparent dislike of Tappert and his opaque reference to "old beloved songs" in the letter to Spitta one month earlier. Rather than claim an archaic provenance for the melodies in his own collection with the word "alte," perhaps Brahms's all-encompassing title "Deutsche Lieder" tacitly acknowledges the wide chronology of German songbooks that were integral to its creation, as demonstrated by Brahms's source study for "Ach Gott, wie weh tut Scheiden" and "Mir ist ein schöns brauns Maidelein."

Further research is necessary to advance the claim that Brahms's expressive recomposition throughout WoO 33 of existing poetry, melodies, and nineteenth-century settings reflects an "ideal," as he described it to Clara Schumann in 1860.[50] Indeed, an equally wide range of sources would likely affect an interpretation of the sacred poetry and narrative ballads that are arranged together with courtly love poems in WoO 33. Yet the two songs in this chapter offer preliminary evidence that Brahms's deep interest in the transmission, evolution, and enduring compositional value of their melodies and courtly love poems can influence the way we listen to these songs. We might conclude from these examples that just as Brahms's musical *Streitschrift* petitions eloquently—in tones rather than words—for a revitalized approach to *setting* German folksong, it also convincingly argues that our hearing of these songs should engage with their rich musical and poetic lineage.

Appendix

No. 1. "Ein schön new Lied: Ach Gott, wie weh thut scheiden," *Liedflugschrift* (Gutknecht: Nürnberg, 1555) held at the *Staatsbibliothek zu Berlin—Preußischer Kulturbesitz* (Yd 9661). [https://digital.staatsbibliothek-berlin.de/werkansicht/?PPN = PPN751839663]

[1] *(hidden pain)*

Ach Got[t] wie wee thut scheiden	Oh, God, how painful is parting,
hat mir mein hertz verwundt	[It] has wounded my heart
so zeuch ich uber die heide	So I go across the heath
un trawer zu aller stund	And lament in every hour.
Der Stund der sind im Jar so vil	The hours that are so many in the year
bringt mir ein heimlichs leiden	[That] bring me secret sorrow
wie wol ich offt frölich bin.	Although I often appear cheerful.

[2] *(garden metaphor)*

Ich thet mir ein gertlein pflantze	I planted myself a little garden
von feihel un grünem Klee	Of violets and green clover
Ist mir so fru erfroren	It froze to death so soon
thut meinem Herze wee	[It] wounded my heart
Ist mir erfroren bey Sun un Moneschein	It froze by sunshine and moonlight
Ein plümlein je lenger je lieber	A honeysuckle flower
ein kreutlein vergiß nicht mein.	A little forget-me-not.

[3] *(beloved as empress)*

Wenn ich an sie gedencke	When I think of her
vergangen ist mir mein leid	My sorrow has passed away
Deucht mich in meinen sinne	In my mind it seems to me
sie sey ein Keyserin werd	That she has become an empress
Sie hat mir offt mein herz erfreudt	She has often delighted my heart
Wenn ich an sie gedencke	When I think of her
verschwunden ist mir mein leidt.	My pain has disappeared.

[4] *(fated separation)*

Solt ich mich meines buhlen erwegen	Should I renounce my love
wie sich offt mancher thut	As many often do
Solt füren ein freies leben	Should I lead a free life
solt haben ein gute mut	Should I be cheerful
So kan es leider nicht gesein	Sadly, it cannot be so
Gesegen dich Gott im herzen	[May] God bless your heart
du bist mir die liebste mein.	You are my dearest.

No. 2. Five-stanza text in Georg Forster, *Frische teutsche Liedlein dritter Teil (1549)*, ed. Kurt Gudewill and Horst Brunner (Wolfenbüttel: Möseler Verlag. 1966 [1976]): 34–35.

[1] *(hidden pain)*
Ach Gott, wie weh tut Scheiden!
Hat mir mein Herz verwund't!
So drab ich uber d'Heiden
und traur zu aller Stund.
Der Stunden, der sein also viel,
mein Herz trägt Heimlich Leiden,
wiewohl ich oft fröhlich bin.

Oh, God how painful is parting,
[It] has wounded my heart!
So I trot across the heath
And lament in every hour.
Of hours there are so many in the year
[That] bring my heart secret suffering,
Although I often appear cheerful.

[2] *(garden metaphor)*
Hätt' mir ein Gärtlein bauet
von Veil und grünem Klee,
ist mir zu früh erfroren,
tut meinem Herzen weh.
Ist mir erfrorn bei Sonnenschein
ein Kraut Jelängerjelieber,
ein Blümlein Vergißnitmein.

I made myself a little garden
Of violet and green clover,
It froze to death so soon
[And] wounded my heart.
It froze in the sunshine
A plant [of] honeysuckle,
A little forget-me-not flower.

[3] *(Othmayr's stanza: glorified beloved)*
Das Blümlein, das ich meine,
das ist von edler Art,
ist aller Tugend reine,
ihr Mündlein das ist zart,
ihr Äuglein die seind hübsch und fein:
Wann ich an sie gedenke,
so wollt ich gern bei ihr sein.

The flower that I mean
Is of the noble kind,
Is pure of virtue,
Her little mouth is tender,
Her little eyes are sweet and delicate;
When I think of her
I would like to be with her.

[4] *(beloved as empress)*
Mich dunkt in all mein Sinnen
und wann ich bei ihr bin,
sie sei ein Kaiserinne,
kein lieber ich nimmer gwinn!
Hat mir mein junges Herz erfreut:
Wann ich an sie gedenke,
verschwunden ist mir mein Leid.

I feel [it] in all my senses
And when I am with her
She is like an empress
I will never win one more dear
[She] has gladdened my young heart:
When I think of her
My pain disappears.

[5] *(fated separation)*
Sollt mich meins Buhlen erwegen
als oft ein ander tut,
sollt führn ein fröhlichs Leben
dazu ein falschen Mut,
das kann und mag doch nicht gesein!
Gesegn dich Gott im Herzen:
Es soll und muß geschieden sein!

Should I renounce to my lover
As others often do,
Should I lead a happy life
And have a false demeanor;
This cannot and may not be!
[May] God bless your heart;
We are fated to part!

No. 3. "Der traurige Garten. *Frische Liedlein,*" *Des Knaben Wunderhorn* I (Heidelberg: Mohr u. Zimmer, 1806): 206.

[1]
Ach Gott, wie weh thut Scheiden, / Oh God, how painful is parting,
Hat mir mein Herz verwundt, / It has wounded my heart.
So trab ich über Heiden / So I trot across the heath
und traure zu aller Stund, / And lament every hour;
Der Stunden der sind alsoviel, / The hours are so many
Mein Herz trägt heimlich Leiden, / My heart bears secret pain,
Wiewohl ich oft fröhlich bin. / Although I often appear cheerful.

[2]
Hät mir ein Gärtlein bauet, / I built myself a little garden,
Von Veil und grünem Klee, / Of violet and green clover,
Ist mir zu früh erfroren, / It froze too soon,
Thut meinem Herzen weh; / And wounded my heart.
Ist mir erfrorn bei Sonnenschein / It froze in the sunshine
Ein Kraut Je länger je lieber, / A plant of honeysuckle,
Ein Blümlein Vergiß nicht mein. / A little forget-me-not-flower.

[3]
Das Blümlein, das ich meine, / The flower that I mean
Das ist von edler Art, / Is of a noble kind,
Ist aller Tugend reine, / Is pure of virtue,
Ihr Mündlein das ist zart, / Her little mouth is tender,
Ihr Aeuglein die sind hübsch und fein, / Her little eyes are sweet and delicate,
Wann ich an sie gedenke, / When I think of her,
So wollt ich gern bei ihr seyn. / I want gladly to be by her.

[4] *(positive ending)*
Mich dünkt in all mein Sinnen, / I feel in all my senses,
Und wann ich bei ihr bin, / And when I am with her,
Sie sey ein Kaiserinne, / She is like an empress,
Kein lieber ich nimmer gewinn, / I will never win one more dear,
Hat mir mein junges Herz erfreut, / She has gladdened my young heart,
Wann ich an sie gedenke, / When I think of her,
Verschwunden ist mir mein Leid. / My pain disappears.

No. 4. Comparison of two poems: (1) "Drei schone newe lieder, *Liedflugschrift* (Gutknecht: Nürnberg, 1560) held at the *Staatsbibliothek zu Berlin—Preußischer Kulturbesitz* (Yd 7831). [https://digital.staatsbibliothek-berlin.de/werkansicht/?PPN = PPN780034112]; and (2) Carl Becker, *Lieder und Weisen vergangene Jahrhunderte* (Leipzig: Kösling'sche Buchhandlung, 1849): 12–13.

Liedflugschrift by Gutknecht, Yd 7831 (Nürnberg: c. 1560)	English Translation of Liedflugschrift:	Carl Becker, *Lieder, Lieder und Weisen vergangener Jahrhunderte* (Leipzig: 1849): 12–13.	English Translation of Becker:
[1.] Mir ist ein feyns brauns megetlein gefallen in meinen syn, Wolt Gott ich solt heyud bay jr sein, mein trawren fur dahin, tag unde nacht hab ich kein rw das schafft ir schön gestalt, ich waiß nit wie im fürbaß thu, mein feins lieb macht mich alt.	A delicate brown-haired maiden Has come into my thoughts, Were God to want me near her today, My suffering would depart. Day and night I have no rest, Her beautiful form causes this, I do not know how to move on, My dear makes me old.	Mir ist ein schönß braunß meidelein Gefallen in mein sin, Wolt Gott, ich solt heint bey ir sein, Mein trauren fur dahin. Kein tag noch nacht hab ich kein ru, Das schafft ir schön gestalt, Ich weiß nit, wie im fürbaß thu, Mein feinß lieb macht mich alt.	A beautiful brown-haired maiden Has come into my thoughts, Would God to want me near her today, My suffering would depart. Neither day nor night, I have no rest, Her beautiful form causes this, I do not know how to move on, My dear makes me old.
[2.] Dem meydlein ich geren dienen wolt, wan ich das fugen kund, So hab ich doch der neyder vil, und die mirs hart vergund Ich hoff sie sols erfaren schier das ichs so trewlich mayn auff erdt ich mir nichts wunschen wolt wann sein bey jr allein.	I would gladly serve the maiden If I could make an impact But I have granted much to the enviers And they cruelly hurt me I hope she should feel it purely, That I mean it so faithfully, I would wish for nothing on Earth, If I were next to her alone.	Dem meydlein ich gern dienenwil, Wenn ich mit fugen kundt; Darumb hab ich der neyder vil, Des mir wit wirdt vergundt. Ich hoff, sie sols erfaren bald, Wie ichs so treulich gmein, Auff erdt ich mir nichts wünschen wolt Dem zusein bey ir allein.	I will gladly serve the maiden If I could make an impact. Thus I have granted the enviers That which I am not to have. I hope that she should soon experience How I mean it truly, I would wish for nothing on earth Than to be next to her alone.
[3.] Dem meydlein ich all mein trew versprich, zu eeren vnd anderst nit, Darzu was frumm vnd redlich ist, darnach ich mich stets richt, solt all mein trew verloren sein, krenckt mir hertz fin vnnd mut ich hoff sie sols erfaren schier mein sach sol werden gut.	I will pledge my faithfulness to the maiden, To honor [her] and not others, According to what is pious and honest, Always to align myself, Should all my loyalty be lost, My heart, mind, and courage would fall ill, I hope she should feel purely My deed will be well done.	Dem meydlein ich mein true versprich, Zu ehrn vnd anders nicht, Als was doch frumb vnd ehrlich ist, Darnach ich mich stets richt. Solt den mein true verloren sein, Krenckt mir mein sin vnd gmüt, Ich hoff, sie sols erfaren schier, Mein sach soll werden gut.	I will pledge my faithfulness to the maiden To honor [her] and no other, Since what is pious and honest, I always align myself. Should my faithfulness be lost, My thoughts and feelings would fall ill I hope she will experience it purely My deed should be done well.
[4.] Dann was die falschen zungen thun, das leit jetzt an dem tag hor zu du feins brauns megetlein, hor zu was ich dir sag. Ja halt dich stets an eeren allein Merck hertz lieb wie ich's main, so behelstu du gunst, nach disem wunsch, glaub mir brauns meidlein rein.	Since what the false tongues say Has come to light, Listen, you delicate maiden, Listen to what I say to you: Always uphold yourself to honor Realize, my lovely heart, how I mean it, So you will retain favor, according to this wish, Believe me, pure brunette maiden.	Dann was die falschen zungen thun Ist yetzund an dem tag: Ach, dir mein feinß braunß megdelein, Hör zu, was ich dir sag: Halt dich mir stets in ehren allein, Wie ich dich, hertzlieb, mein, So bhelstu gunst mit dieser kunst, Das glaub mir, meydlein rein.	Because what the false tongues say Has now come to light: Oh, you my delicate brown-haired maiden, Listen to what I say to you: Always hold in honor exclusively me, As I do you, my dear heart, So you will retain favor with this art This believe me, pure maiden.
[5.] Damit will ich dem megetlein, gesungen han so frey, zu guter nacht dem megetlein, Wuensch ich was jr gut sey, damit das sie gedenck an mich, wann ich vonn hynnen kumm, verschaffen gluck gaht nit hyndersich schafft als die schoen die frumm.	With this I will have to the maiden Sung so freely Good night, to the maiden I wish what is good for her So that with this she will think of me If I return from afar Obtaining happiness does not deceive, As the beautiful creates the pious.	Damit will ich dem meydelein Gesungen haben frey Zu guter nacht ein liedelein, Als guts witnsch ich dar bey; Damit das sie gedenckt an mich, Wenn ich nit bey ir bin. So bhüt dich Gott im himmelreich Ade, ich far dahin!	With this I will to the maiden Have sung freely A little song for good night, With this I wish [her] all good things, So that she will think of me When I am not with her. May God protect you in heaven Farewell, I am departing!

Chapter 7

Rehearing Brahms's Late Intermezzi
The Eternal Recurrence of Reflection

Tekla Babyak

The noted Bach scholar and friend of Johannes Brahms, Philipp Spitta (1841–1894), heard the composer's late intermezzi as fragments of a larger work that unfolds in the listener's mind, animated by memory, reflection, and rehearing. In a letter to Brahms from December 1893 Spitta observed that Opp. 118 and 119:

> are definitely meant to be absorbed slowly in silence and solitude, not only to think about afterwards, but also beforehand, and I believe that I have understood you correctly when I say that is what you meant by the term "intermezzo." "Pieces in between" ["Zwischenstücke"] have predecessors and followers, which in this case every player and listener has to make for himself.[1]

Spitta suggests that periods of silent reflection are demanded by the late intermezzi. Spitta's remarks bring these intermezzi into the orbit of other Brahms works that enclose the sung text within the framing device of a reflective prelude and postlude, such as *Schicksalslied*, as Nicole Grimes has demonstrated.[2] What Spitta is proposing here is a related phenomenon, except that the preludes and postludes are no longer overtly present in the works themselves.

Four of the six pieces in Op. 118 and three of the four pieces in Op. 119 are intermezzi. The salience of the intermezzo in both opera (following on the heels of Op. 117, which consists entirely of intermezzi) suggests that this genre holds a key to the aesthetics of Brahms's late piano music. Op. 118 begins and ends with intermezzi, while Op. 119 begins with one. Thus, even if each opus is performed as a cycle, these "bookend" intermezzi (and by extension the inner intermezzi as well) do not function as interludes in the traditional sense. Rather, as Spitta suggests, they carry connotations that imply a larger cycle of contemplation, which in turn requires a series of rehearings. That is, the reflection to which Spitta refers—anticipatory as well as retrospective in nature—is predicated on the memory of previous hearings.

Spitta suggests that Brahms's late intermezzi are designed for listeners with the emotional and intellectual ability to grasp the musical intricacies, as well as the time and space to experience this music in a setting conducive to introspection: "I can only hope that our virtuosi do not drag them [the intermezzi] into the concert hall. Ballades, Romances, Rhapsodies if you like; but the intermezzi? The public would sit there with such stupid facial expressions!"[3] Indeed, these works were generally not performed at public concerts.[4] On a few occasions, however, they were programmed as interludes that offered a reflective respite from virtuosity.[5]

Eduard Hanslick, similarly invoking the time-honored notion of private music for connoisseurs, referred to Opp. 118 and 119 as monologues that do not "win one over at first glance," going on to remark that "there is much ore buried in these pieces and this ore will long preserve them."[6] Here, Hanslick calls attention to the listener's active role in extracting the precious minerals from these works. His use of the term "monologue" suggests that the listener is perhaps also the performer, which, as Katrin Eich has observed, often was the case.[7] In fact, as we will see, the notational features of the intermezzi often engage the performer's eyes and hands in ways that inform an appreciation of the music.

In what follows, I examine how Brahms's late intermezzi draw the listener/performer into a cycle of rehearing and reflection generated by means of enigmatic passages that allow for multiple interpretations. The literature on Brahmsian ambiguity is substantial (including, for example, studies by Allen Cadwallader,[8] Edward T. Cone,[9] and Peter H. Smith[10]). However, scholars have yet to devote sufficient attention to the ways in which unresolved ambiguity can generate a cyclic temporality of listening. Pertinent here is Spitta's call, until now largely unheeded, for us to take the title "intermezzo" as a starting point for hermeneutic inquiry.

To this end, this chapter explores how Op. 118, Nos. 1 and 6, and Op. 119, No. 1, contain ambiguous passages that invite the listener to supply absent or implied musical material. This invitation allows for a different hearing each time these intermezzi are revisited, almost as though they could recur eternally with new insights to be gleaned on each encounter.[11] The listener's imaginative endeavors allow the Brahmsian intermezzi to fulfill the implications of their titles by being "works in between." They are framed by the work of reflection that takes place within the listener's mind.

The Emancipation of the Intermezzo

Before delving into a close reading of Brahms's late intermezzi it is helpful to sketch out a brief history of the intermezzo as a title and genre. The origin of the intermezzo dates back to early operatic conventions. John T. Hamilton notes that the genre of comic opera developed in the eighteenth century "from the comic intermezzi performed between acts of an opera seria."[12] This emancipatory process within the operatic domain predates the emancipation of the intermezzo in instrumental music. During the nineteenth century, the genre—insofar as we can call it that[13]—gradually extended its reach into the realm of instrumental music. In addition to a few brief linking movements labeled "Intermezzo" in Jan Ladislav Dussek's piano music, Felix Mendelssohn used the title for the scherzo-like third movements of his Piano Quartet No. 2 in F minor, Op. 2 (1823), and his String Quartet No. 2 in A minor, Op. 13 (1827). He also used it for the elegiac slow movement (composed in 1832) in the String Quintet No. 1 in A major, Op. 18, signaling a reflective turn that moved away from the genre's comic origins.[14] All of these intermezzi, however, retained the function of an interlude flanked by movements on either side. It was not until Robert Schumann's *Six Intermezzi*, Op. 4 (1832), that the intermezzo acquired an independent life. These are, to the best of my knowledge, the first stand-alone intermezzi. The move toward emancipation is in keeping with the nineteenth-century tendency for genres such as the prelude and the overture to break off from the larger contexts to which they had previously been attached.

Brahms's first published intermezzo appears as an "extra" movement in his Piano Sonata in F minor, Op. 5 (1853). Titled "Intermezzo (*Rückblick*)" (backward glance), this early work already signals his conception of the intermezzo as a space for reflective rehearing. According to his biographer Max Kalbeck, Brahms composed this intermezzo, along with what was to become the second movement, several months earlier than the remaining three movements.[15] This suggests that Brahms was potentially already moving toward an understanding of the intermezzo as a self-sufficient genre.

The retrospective mood of this "Intermezzo (*Rückblick*)," much of which looks back upon the second movement, resonates with German philosophical ideas that reach back to Hegel. In a formulation that exerted a powerful influence over nineteenth-century musical thought, Hegel contended that a historical era cannot be understood until it has drawn to a close, for "the owl of Minerva spreads its wings only with the falling of the dusk."[16] The owl's belatedly skyward gesture, performed at the cusp of twilight, indicates Hegel's notion of reflection as a retrospective act. Brahms, like Hegel, seems to have linked twilight to a retrospective mode of reflection. The poem that heads the second movement, "Junge Liebe," by C. O. Sternau, refers to the arrival of twilight and the shine of the moon.[17] The second movement and its reflective counterpart "Intermezzo (*Rückblick*)" thus can be heard in Hegelian terms as looking back upon the events of the day once the sun has set.

The third movement in Brahms's Ballades, Op. 10 (1854) offers another early example of his emerging conception of the intermezzo as a self-sufficient genre. William Kinderman observes its "special contrasting role" within "the overall design of these four interconnected pieces."[18] This early intermezzo, with its open fifths and nebulous tonality, can be heard as prefiguring the ambiguity that characterizes the later Brahmsian intermezzi. Joseph Joachim memorably remarked that the ambiguous phrases in the Op. 10 Intermezzo tend to "slip out of reach like a little eel."[19]

Ambiguity and Rehearing

Brahms's tendency to imbue his intermezzi with a reflective mood, already present in his earlier work, is intensified in the late intermezzi that serve as the focus of this chapter. As Spitta suggested, Brahms's late *Klavierstücke*, particularly the intermezzi, are designed for repeated listening interspersed with periods of reflection. I contend that Brahms conveys this invitation in part through employing ambiguity with regard to parameters such as form, harmony, and meter. Within the extensive literature on Brahms and ambiguity, scholars have rarely paid attention to the ways in which ambiguity can serve as a motivating force for rehearing.[20] Edward T. Cone comes the closest, perhaps, in his "Three Ways of Reading a Detective Story—Or a Brahms Intermezzo,"[21] in which he likens Op. 118, No. 1, to a narrative whose mysteries can only be decoded when hearing the work for the second time. He argues that a third hearing is necessary for full appreciation: only then can the listener synthesize the enjoyable surprises of the first hearing with insights gleaned from the second.

Cone stops at the third hearing. He implies that subsequent hearings will not be radically different. With pieces as rich as these late intermezzi, however, we need not limit ourselves to only three iterations of the listening process. Ambiguity has the potential to become more aesthetically productive with each hearing, enabling the listener to have a different experience each time (and perhaps also affording the performer the opportunity to play the piece differently each time). In the case of Op. 118, No. 1, the listener could choose to hear the initial C octave as an opening tonic, or as belonging to a dominant or mediant chord; this choice can be made anew for each hearing.

It is to Op. 118, No. 1, that I now turn as an example of the Brahmsian intermezzo as a genre framed by reflection. Spitta singled out this particular intermezzo in his aforementioned letter to Brahms, commenting ruefully on his inability to play it: "I can't succeed at all with the A-minor one, the archetype of the intermezzo as you mean the term."[22] Here, Spitta implies that these intermezzi might ideally be experienced through playing. This passage also suggests that Op. 118, No. 1, is almost the Platonic ideal of the Brahmsian intermezzo. This perception likely stems in part from its tonal ambiguity, which enables this intermezzo to serve as an exemplary vehicle for pre- and post-listening reflection.

The tonal enigmas in Op. 118, No. 1, saturate the piece, with the strongly implied tonic of F major of the opening measures, and the C major of the piece's first cadence (bars 9–10), and also prominent in the reprise, ultimately giving

Example 7.1 Brahms, Intermezzo, Op. 118, No. 1, bars 30–41.

way to A minor and then A major. As a result of this carefully engineered tonal ambiguity there is a cluster of dramatically significant moments toward the end of the intermezzo—a passage that provides the intermezzo's remarkable tonal denouement, as shown in Example 7.1. In bar 31, a sudden sustained E provides a moment of heightened expectancy, its temporary cessation of the busy texture also triggering a flood of reflections in the listener's mind. This E has a strong dominant quality, but it might also prompt thoughts about several important instances of the same pitch class earlier in the piece. Bars 17–20 employ a chromatically ascending bass line that culminated on E (note the deceptive progression in bars 19–20 that gives this culmination the quality of a surprise). This then leads to a high octave on E in bar 22, a registral extreme, that wrenches the music away from a straightforward reprise of the A section. This octave is followed by a prominent E in the bass on the downbeat of bar 23 supporting a first-inversion C-major chord.

In the second half of bar 31, the E in the bass is joined by a cadenza-like arpeggio on a D♯ diminished seventh chord. The E continues to resound as a pedal tone in bars 31–33, but its expected dominant function is somewhat blurred. This diminished-seventh arpeggio in bars 31–33 might echo the D♯ diminished-seventh chord in bar 12. This earlier chord marked an important juncture that helped redirect the harmony away from the F major that is implied by the opening measure and the tonicization of its dominant, C, at the first cadence.

Indeed, diminished-seventh chords play a central role in the sense of uncertainty that shapes this piece's close. Brahms's penultimate chord is a diminished-seventh instead of the more conventional dominant that we would expect at a cadence. In the context of what has come before, this chord also has the potential to activate a constellation of memories. Its diminished-seventh quality could be heard as referring back to the cadenza from bars 31–33. Its root, G♯, might even serve as a reminder of bar 11, in which this prominently articulated pitch helped to initiate the local shift toward A minor. More generally, bars 37–38 prompt reflection on the emotional journey enacted in this intermezzo. These bars suggest a *Sturm und Drang* topic evoked by the diminished triad, prominent tritones, low register, a drawn-out appoggiatura, and the *sf* marking. The music then settles, moving from agitation to calmness in just a few bars. Such an accelerated evocation of emotional lability calls for post-listening reflection in which the affective shifts can be re-experienced in slow motion.

As a final twist, the salience of the longed-for confirmatory tonic is heightened by Brahms's use of a Picardy third. As well as offering one further surprise on this already very unusual tonal journey, this major tonic chord also creates an open-ended conclusion that potentially sets up the A-major tonality of Op. 118, No. 2. This tonal link could be heard as creating a potential "multi-piece" composition, in keeping with Jonathan Dunsby's idea that the listener might find productive interconnections between the pieces within a single work.[23] In this case, the surprising final chord of Op. 118, No. 1, ushers in not only the tonality, but also the gentle, tender affect of the next piece.

Imagined (Re-)Harmonizations

One of the ways in which Brahms's intermezzi generate a cycle of rehearing and reflection is through the inclusion of sections that seem to be built as much by the musically knowledgeable listener as by the composer. Such opportunities for imaginative endeavors enable these pieces to be framed by the work of reflection that takes place within the listener's mind.[24] The concept of audience completion has a long pedigree that reaches back at least as far as the early stirrings of the Romantic movement. Thus Friedrich Schiller, writing at the cusp of the Romantic era (1794), noted that "the real and express content [wirkliche und ausdrückliche Gehalt] that the poet puts in his work remains always finite; the possible content that he allows us to contribute is an infinite quantity [unendliche Grösse]."[25]

Schiller's pedagogical aesthetic of teaching the audience member (listener) to contribute new material seems pertinent to the harmonic and formal processes that unfold in Op. 118, No. 6. The obsessive return of the main motive, as well as its resemblance to the "Dies irae" plainchant, has elicited much commentary. John Rink describes it as a "motivic shape whose pre-eminence virtually overwhelms all other structural aspects."[26] Less often noted, however, is the way in which this motivic saturation allows Brahms to model a creative mode of listening, with the harmonic implications of this recurring motive being reimagined at every turn.

This intermezzo opens sparsely, tentatively: the hushed monophony of the opening melody might be heard in Schillerian terms as creating an infinite space for the listener to contribute harmonic content.[27] Although its melodic outline suggests an E♭-minor triad, confirmation of this implied tonic harmony is delayed by the left-hand entry in bar 3 on vii°/V. The recurrences of this opening motive throughout the first section (bars 1–20) continue to eschew a clear statement of a root position tonic harmony in favor of vii°/V chords. The long-awaited tonic harmony in fact only materializes at the beginning of the restatement of the A section in bar 21. Yet, as Ryan McClelland observes, Brahms often employs strategies to "maintain destabilisation at preliminary thematic returns."[28]

In this case, the orientation of bars 1–20 toward B♭ minor undercuts the ostensible tonic return at bar 21, creating a paradoxical situation in which the music returns to a tonic that it had never comfortably inhabited. Adding to the ambiguity is the fact that the crucial major third is omitted from the dominant-seventh chord in bars 19–20; this absence of a leading tone, especially in light of the D♭s in the preceding bars, markedly weakens the perception of bar 21 as a tonic resolution. Patrick Miller suggests that the cadence in bars 19–21 could even be heard as i^7–iv in B♭ minor.[29] Rink similarly observes that "the ensuing E♭-minor return of the opening at bar 21" sounds "more like a subdominant than a tonic."[30]

In this sparse passage, Brahms thus offers the listener who hears the piece in real time two alternatives, each of which opens out onto different ways of hearing. The listener has the option of filling in the absent third with the pitch D♭ recently sounded in bars 17–18, or is free to make a more imaginative leap by mentally supplying a leading tone to E♭. In any case, the cadence soon dissolves into a destabilizing cascade of chromatic figuration. It is this figuration that leads to the reappearance of the "Dies irae" theme and diminished-seventh harmonization in bar 25.

The local harmonic versatility—and ambiguity—of the main motive is replicated on a larger level in the AABA form. The first two statements of the A section (bars 1–20 and 21–40) both end with similar cadential material consisting of the main motive transposed to the dominant. Yet this material leads in a different direction each time: its initial statement in bars 17–20 is immediately followed by a restatement of the A section. Its second occurrence,

Example 7.2a Brahms, Intermezzo, Op. 118, No. 6, bars 17–23.

Example 7.2b Brahms, Intermezzo, Op. 118, No. 6, bars 37–41.

however, ushers in the B section through a linear descent through a third in the bass from B♭ to G♭ (see Examples 7.2a and 7.2b).

The new direction is foreshadowed only slightly (and perhaps only heard as such in retrospect). This second iteration of the cadential figure does not move to the incomplete B♭ seventh chord that occurred in bar 20. Instead, on the second beat of bar 40 the B♭ present in both hands moves down by step to an A♭, forming a dyad with the sustained F. In light of the impending move to G♭ major, the new sonority could be heard as implying a D♭-major triad with a missing root. This implication, though by no means obvious on first listening, becomes stronger with each rehearing as the listener increasingly remembers (and potentially anticipates) the move to G♭ to come in the following bar. As in the first close of the A section, Brahms's sparse harmony invites our imaginative completion of a dyad into an applied dominant chord.

Within this overall AABA form, the threefold statement of the A section has some affinities with sonata form. Viewed schematically, the A section could be heard as an exposition that is recapitulated at bar 63. In fact, upon receiving the Op. 118 scores from Brahms, Clara Schumann expressed her appreciation in a letter (2 September 1893) in which she suggested that Nos. 2 and 6 could perhaps be considered sonata movements.[31] On the other hand, the tonal layout of Op. 118, No. 6, does not fully align with the tension-resolution principle of sonata form. The A section destabilizes our conventional certainty about tonic and dominant identity; we don't feel certain enough about our tonal home to know that we have moved away from it; the B section is never recapitulated in the tonic. In light of these anomalies, the structural layout of the piece might more profitably be heard as evoking a contemplative timelessness rather than a teleological drive toward closure.

Indeed, the boundaries between sections are blurred rather than polarized. The B section could be heard as composing out an important aspect of the "Dies irae" theme: the emphasis on G♭ in the opening motive turns out to be a foreshadowing of the relative major tonality of the B section. The unharmonized G♭ with which the piece began might thus be viewed retrospectively as a kind of promissory note in the sense of that term used by Edward T. Cone—a strikingly prominent note near the beginning of a piece that can generate expectations for its subsequent expansion.[32]

The "Dies irae" motive itself does not stay away for long; it returns emphatically in bars 53–54 and 60–62. This unusual eruption of the A section material within the B section has struck many listeners as a troubling event. Laurie McManus examines how the "breakthrough of the *dies irae* main theme in a B section with an otherwise heroic topos" might be connected to fin-de-siècle notions of psychological trauma and autobiographical narration.[33] Paul Berry similarly hears this return of the A-theme as a "collapse into familiar material" that becomes "a scene of weariness and loss" involving "shades of resignation."[34] The formerly melancholic motive is now "aggressively reharmonized,"[35] in part as a result of the dissonant combination of G♭ and F (see, e.g., bar 53). These pitches, so often heard in succession in the main motive, have now become simultaneous harmonic entities. This harmonic expression of a melodic feature attests to the power of the motive to generate different moods through the recombination of its constituent parts.

The motive takes on not only a new affect, but also a new role with respect to the piece's large-scale tonal journey. Rink observes that "it is the unexpected reappearance of the hitherto tonally destabilising main motive" that leads the music toward a long-awaited confirmation of E♭ as tonic.[36] This speaks to the versatility of this motive, which is capable of transforming itself from a destabilizing force into a stabilizing one. Such transformations provide the listener with a multiplicity of ways of experiencing Brahms's sparse melodic material.

This aspect of Brahms's musical design has implications for the process of rehearing and reflecting. When the listener rehears the main motive in its unharmonized form any (or all) of its various harmonizations might be cued as an imagined sonority. Peter H. Smith notes that "[t]he sum total of the process of hearing a motive that keeps switching meanings may indeed produce ambiguity."[37] As we have seen, this sum total also produces the desire to rehear the motive. Only through repeated listening can the motive be experienced in its rich multiplicity.

A Ritardando on Every Note

In a letter to Clara Schumann written on 4 May 1893, Brahms described the Intermezzo Op. 119, No. 1:

> The short piece is exceptionally melancholy, and it is not sufficient to say "play very slowly." Every bar and every note must sound like a ritardando, as if one wanted to extract the melancholy from every single one, with delight and contentment in the aforementioned dissonances![38]

Brahms's reference to a continual ritardando, as though trying to prolong the piece indefinitely, seems to suggest that the melancholic affect of this intermezzo stems in part from our perception of its transience—what we might refer to as its inevitable and necessary mortality. The bittersweet feeling that often occurs as a work of art draws to its close has been eloquently described by Alain Badiou as "the type of melancholy that overtakes the reader when reaching the last page of a magnificent novel."[39]

Brahms's letter suggests that this melancholy can become aesthetically pleasurable if the performer lingers on each note to mitigate the sense of loss. Prolongation is at the heart of this piece and its patterns of figuration. Ties, stems, and dots proliferate throughout the score, signaling pitches that continue to sound in overlapping resonance with other notes. Thus, when a new note arrives, it often becomes an addition to, rather than a replacement of, the preceding pitch. For the performer (and anyone else who reads the score), these visual signifiers of prolongation enact the "ritardando on every note."

Brahms's aesthetic of accumulation might be heard as expressing his desire to imbue the transitory with permanence. Supporting this point is the way in which the additive chains of thirds create a sense of the music extending into infinity.[40] At times the notation of these chains calls particular attention to this sense of quasi-infinite expansion across the keyboard. For instance, bars 43–44 of the retransition are notated in such a way as to encourage hand-crossing. The registral transfer of the chain of thirds thus finds itself enacted physically.[41]

The sense of lingering is enhanced by the canonical activity happening between the voices in sections such as bars 4–7 and 12–16 (see Example 7.3). It is as though the music, in its reluctance to relinquish each motive, seizes hold of the motive in a new voice to prolong its longevity. As with the ties discussed above, this polyphonic imitation is more apparent to the eyes than to the ears. Thus it likely addresses itself to the performer (who might also be the intended listener as well). Steven Rings hears these canons as an erudite technique that conveys "rational control and purposefulness."[42] Yet these canons could also be heard as gesturing toward something unattainable and therefore almost *irrational*: the desire to endow each motive with eternal life by perpetuating it through polyphonic imitation.

Example 7.3 Brahms, Intermezzo, Op. 119, No. 1, bars 1–16.

A sense of permanence, though, is elusive and perhaps cannot be achieved through a single hearing. Disappearance is inherent in the ephemeral nature of musical performance itself. As if to underscore the ephemerality of performance, the restatement of the A section (beginning at bar 47 and shown in Example 7.4b) creates the effect of moving at a faster pace. This effect is achieved through its use of sixteenth-note triplets in place of earlier sixteenth-note duplets. To be sure, diminution is a standard variation technique that, in this case, perhaps takes its inspiration from the triplet rhythms in the B section. However, in the context of this piece, the rhythmic diminutions might be heard as having a deeper meaning, expressing the acceleration of time as the end draws near, analogous to the way in which time appears to move faster with each passing decade of life.

Brahms was well aware of age-related temporal acceleration. This phenomenon figures prominently in his 1883 setting of Friedrich Rückert's poem "Mit vierzig Jahren" ("at forty years old"). The piano part, consisting mainly of quarter notes and eighth notes for most of the song, suddenly turns toward eighth-note triplets for the final line in bar 35 (see Example 7.4a). The text describes the gathering momentum that pulls us toward the "Port"—the final resting place. In this poetic context, the eighth-note triplets, functioning as a written-out accelerando, can be heard as symbolizing the inexorable hastening toward the end. Op. 119, No. 1, revisits and re-enacts this same phenomenon,

Rehearing Brahms's Late Intermezzi

Example 7.4a Brahms, "Mit vierzig Jahren," Op. 94, No. 1, bars 32–44.

Example 7.4b Brahms, Intermezzo, Op. 119, No. 1, bars 47–51.

in which the final stretch of a lifespan is marked by a melancholy-inducing quickening. It is as though these triplets in Op. 119, No. 1, enact the inevitability of the work's own mortality.

Brahms's reference to a "ritardando on every note" seems to fight against the acceleration that is built into the temporality of the music. Thus, to attain Brahms's desired goal of lingering on each note, the musical experience might further be prolonged through replaying and rehearing. Indeed, each note in Op. 119, No. 1, impels a reflective process that cannot fully be accomplished in real time. The ambiguous tonal orientation, wavering between B minor and D major, lends itself to multiple interpretations and thus multiple hearings.

Resolutions are sidestepped and displaced, causing the listener to engage in an ongoing process of rehearing and reinterpretation. For instance, the A♯s in bars 4 and 5 might suggest B minor. However, bar 6 transforms this pitch, respelling it as B♭, and the harmony now veers toward D major. In the first half of bar 11, the dominant of B minor briefly materializes before dissolving into a longer chain of thirds. The A♮ at the end of this same bar functions to cancel the previously heard leading tone, redirecting the music away from the recently implied tonic. When a B arrives in the bass on the second beat of bar 12, it no longer sounds as the root of a tonic chord, but is recontextualized as the seventh within a C♯ dominant-seventh chord that leads to F♯ minor. What emerges from this intricate succession of sonorities is a series of dissonances that often defy easy classification into harmonic and non-harmonic tones.

Complex interactions between D major and B minor occur not only at the local harmonic level, but also at the global level of form and in the way that this piece ends. The middle section is mostly in D major yet with a number of disruptive A♯s (sometimes spelled enharmonically as B♭s). The interplay between B and D has significant implications for the closing moments. Bars 58–61 seem poised to resolve to D major by means of a ii^7–V^7 cadential preparation. Yet, at the last possible moment, in bar 61, the harmony swerves away from D major with the introduction of A♯. In bar 62, the cadential preparation for D major begins again. This second pass brings to mind the "one-more-time" technique, a term used by Janet Schmalfeldt to describe a renewed attempt after an interrupted cadential progression.[43] This instance yields the same result as before: bar 65 essentially repeats the events in bar 61. But this time the music accepts this turn to B minor. The chain of thirds now continues all the way down to B to reach tonic closure.

Significantly, the notation (though not the sound) of Brahms's final chord encapsulates the ambiguity that has haunted the piece all along. The right hand suggests a D-major sonority (D–F♯), while the left hand has B–D. Thus, the tonic chord is split into the two competing keys that govern this piece, a separation that is especially palpable for the pianist when playing this chord, as notated, with overlapping hands. The F♯ in the top voice links back to the opening F♯. This tonal connection allows the end to lead back to the beginning in a cycle of rehearings, creating the archetypal nineteenth-century image of a spiral in which each cycle potentially offers a higher level of insight.[44] As Steven Rings has so eloquently observed, this piece "affords a sort of inexhaustible interaction."[45]

Conclusion

If a reflective frame informs Brahms's conception of the intermezzo, as this chapter has argued, then these works might not completely fulfill the promise of their titles until the listener has heard them at least once. These intermezzi cannot be preceded by reflection until there is material on which to reflect. Anticipatory reflection requires intimate familiarity with the piece and perhaps also with its companion pieces in the same set. Dunsby's notion of a "multi-piece" also suggests that the listener might find it fruitful to reflect on interconnections between works.[46] Thus, only with repeated hearings of the entire opus can a Brahmsian intermezzo actualize the potential contained in its title. This gradual fulfillment of potential resonates with what Schmalfeldt, with regard to the unfolding of structural functions, has theorized in terms of musical forms that enact a state of becoming.[47] The renewable process of reflection also creates a cyclic form, a cyclic intermezzo, extended over an indeterminate span of time. It is the listener who designs this form through structuring the interplay between silent reflection and hearing (or playing) the piece.[48] As I have sought to demonstrate, the emotional and compositional complexities of the late intermezzi invite recurrent cycles of reflecting and rehearing.

According to Brahms's student Gustav Jenner, "'enduring music' (*dauerhafte Musik*) was one of Brahms's favourite expressions"[49] to describe how his compositions were rooted in what he perceived as timeless principles. Enduring music, as Brahms understood the term, does not wither and fade with the passage of time and the whims of fashion. Similarly, Hanslick praised Opp. 118 and 119 for their durability, noting that "they do not speak immediately to the soul, nor flatteringly to the ear; for that reason, they do not need to fear such early withering."[50] Brahms's pursuit of a musical art that has this type of lasting quality is epitomized by the late piano pieces whose expressive intricacies are capable of sustaining our perpetual rehearings.

Chapter 8

Joachim and Brahms in the Spring and Summer of 1853

Formative Influences and Performative Identities Reconsidered

Katharina Uhde

The story of Johannes Brahms's and Joseph Joachim's first encounter, in April 1853, and ensuing decade-long friendship has been written many times. Their relationship extended from their enthusiastic early days together in Hanover and Göttingen to the well-documented counterpoint exchange (1856–1861)[1] and the famous collaboration on Brahms's Violin Concerto Op. 77—to which Joachim provided feedback and a cadenza—and beyond. If they hadn't left the world as two of the brightest luminaries in Austro-German musical life and custodians of Beethoven's legacy, biographers investigating their youth would have had an easier time separating "late" from "early." Florence May's, Max Kalbeck's, and Andreas Moser's accounts of their lives appeared around 1900, at a time when the sociocultural issues of their day resulted in glorifying "great man" narratives.[2] Kalbeck, for example, said "there has never been a more German artist than Joachim," and found "nothing gypsy-like in his being, such as the gypsy elements associated with Liszt and Reményi." Kalbeck construed Joachim's musico-cultural identity as "Germanic,"[3] which, in turn, distorted his view of the dynamics between the two friends.[4] Such "myths about Brahms," Natasha Loges and Katy Hamilton write, "have persisted despite longstanding evidence to challenge them."[5] Glorifying Brahms came at the cost of misrepresenting several side figures. Ede Reményi has served biographers mainly as a colorful foil: when cast against the morally inferior and artistically "corrupting" path of Reményi, the "noble" path of Brahms appeared in bold relief.[6] Only recent investigations have begun to disentangle facts from fiction for the spring of 1853.[7]

Brahms's exposure to *two* violinists—Reményi and Joachim—was formative in 1853, but the former's influence is more difficult to trace. There is evidence, however, in the form of sketches of aurally transcribed melodies Brahms heard Reményi perform. This prompts the broader question of how much value Brahms attributed to invented melodies at that time. Friedemann Kawohl argues, "From recollections, we know that Brahms rated pure inspiration relatively low but enormously valued the composer's craft" but adds that the "effort"[8] over "inspiration" principle was not yet as evident in the early 1850s.[9] "[T]he young Brahms," Kawohl argues, "was fascinated by Romantic literature, fully appreciated inspiration as the source of art, and his disparaging attitude only emerged as part of an aesthetic change of heart in 1860, expressed in works such as the *Variations on a Theme of Schumann* Op. 23 and *Variations and Fugue on a Theme of Handel* Op. 24."[10] In short, it is plausible that Brahms's views on melodies and invention in 1853 were still flexible. The melodies Brahms collected and transcribed, including those played by Reményi in 1853, helped to "ground and expand his compositional language" and strengthen the importance of oral transcribing practices. These are aspects of Brahms's musical persona that Moser and Kalbeck did not discuss in depth. Their "great man"[11] narratives are further problematic, therefore, when discussing young musicians still in their developing stages.

After providing a chronology and a critique of some of the classicizing issues in these early biographies, this chapter re-evaluates the early days of the Joachim-Brahms relationship from a compositional and performative angle by taking a fresh look at Brahms's still little-known *Hymne zur Verherrlichung des großen Joachim* ("Hymn in Adulation of the Great Joachim," hereafter *Hymne*) in the context of the practice of transcription.[12] Three collaborative sketches in Brahms's hand from January, April, and July each evince some *style hongrois*. A little-known Hungarian work by Joachim suggests that a *rethinking* of Kalbeck's Germanocentric view is also necessary. This rethinking, in turn, opens out onto a series of well-documented tensions in the music of the mid-nineteenth century between the performative and the intellectual, and between that which was considered to be truly German, and that which wore its ethnicity on its sleeve. Defying such polarizations, this reading of Joachim and Reményi highlights a shared ground between the two violinists, thus allowing for an alternative reading of a *style hongrois* passage in Brahms's *Hymne*. As I will argue, Brahms's musical "glorification" of Joachim may have elicited from his pen recent memories of Reményi. Finally, the chapter pulls together the two threads—the practice of transcription and the three occasion-based sketches—to problematize the binary oppositions relating to Joachim and Reményi and the clichés to which they have led, arguing instead that playing with Reményi may have influenced Brahms's "fiery" performing persona.

The Spring of 1853: Rethinking Early Biographies and Narratives

Investigating Brahms's and Joachim's early friendship is challenging. Kalbeck and Moser's biographies, based in part on verbal accounts, offer little verifiable evidence between March and July 1853. Florence May provides more of the timeline, while Styra Avins, Adam Gellen, Kurt and Renate Hofmann, and Joachim Thalmann offer some missing information, as Table 8.1 shows, rectifying some chronological issues.[13]

Table 8.1 Chronology and Sources

Date	Event/Source
1848	
11 March	Brahms hears Joachim in Hamburg (May, 96)
1853	
17 January	Brahms and Reményi rehearse (evidence: Brahms sketch A-Wgm, A 130, Blatt 28r, in Gellen, 315)
"Spring"	Brahms composes mvts. 1, 3, 4 of Sonata Op. 1 (McCorkle, 1)
9 and 14 April	Joachim plays *Hungarian Fantasy* in Hamburg (*Der Humorist* [16 April 1853]: 350) and Hanover (Moser II:90), respectively
19 April	Brahms leaves Hamburg with Reményi (Kalbeck 1904, I:70)
19 April	Brahms and Reményi embark on their tour (lost A-Minor sonata; Beethoven Sonata Op. 30, 2; Rondo ... by C. M. Weber; Elegy and Carnival by H. W. Ernst; Hungarian songs and dances; Concerto Op. 10 by Henri Vieuxtemps) (Hofmann and Hofmann, 12)
20 April	Brahms and Reményi play in Winsen/Luhe (Hofmann and Hofmann, 12)
21 April	"Concert in Winsen/Luhe, then trip to Celle, and from there a brief visit with Joachim in Hanover" (Hofmann and Hofmann, 12)
No date, [April]	Joachim hears Brahms's C-major Sonata (later Op. 1, ded. Joachim), Scherzo Op. 4; and "O versenk" (Moser I:126)
After April 21	Brahms and Reményi visit Joachim in Hanover (Hofmann and Hofmann, 12); a sketch of three *Magyar dalok* dedicated to Joachim marks this occasion
"Last week" April	Brahms and Reményi play in Winsen (May, 95)
2 May	Brahms and Reményi play in Celle, Dunckers Hotel (Moser, I:163; Hofmann and Hofmann, 14)
	Brahms and Reményi play in Celle (piano out of tune) (May, 97)
9, 11, 12 May	Brahms and Reményi play in Lüneburg (with special mention of Hungarian tunes), and Celle (May, 98–99)
15–17 May	Joachim performs at Niederrhein. Musikfest (May, 104)
18 May	Joachim leaves Düsseldorf for Weimar and spends "one week" there (May, 106)
22 May	Joachim in Weimar; rehearsal of *Hamlet* Overture (Kalbeck 1904, I:76)
ca. 26 May	Joachim spends "a day or two" in Hanover (May, 106)
"End of May"	Brahms and Reményi arrive in Hanover (Kalbeck 1904, I:74) Brahms "gets to know Joachim personally" (McCorkle, 2)

Table 8.1 Continued

Date	Event/Source
"End of May"	Joachim leaves Hanover for Göttingen (May, 108)
2 June	"I am leaving for Göttingen tomorrow" (Joachim, I:59)
4 June	"[Brahms and Reményi] met Joachim again in Göttingen" (Hofmann and Hofmann, 14); "[Brahms and Reményi] play Brahms's Sonata in A Minor [lost] at . . . Weenderstraße 82 [Wehner's residence]" (Michelmann, 95)
8 June	Brahms and Reményi's Hanover court concert (Geiringer, Bozarth [2006], 122; Hofmann and Hofmann, 14)
10 June	Reményi detained in Hanover concerning previous revolutionary activities (Vandermeulen, 71, 77); "deportation [Ausweisung] of . . . Reményi" (Hofmann and Hofmann, 14)
"Early in June"	Brahms and Reményi visit Liszt in Weimar (May, 108).
"Middle of June"	Brahms visits Joachim in Göttingen (May, 112)
14 June	Joachim matriculates at Göttingen university (Uhde, 145)
18 June	"First soirée" at Wehner's (without Brahms) (Michelmann, 97)
"End of June to middle of August"	"Stay with Joachim in Göttingen—encounter with Hoffmann von Fallersleben" (Hofmann and Hofmann, 14)
"First half of July"	Brahms has left Weimar for Göttingen (Reményi to Liszt, LaMara, 285)
17 July	Meeting at Wehner's with poet Hoffmann von Fallersleben; Joachim played "something by Bach and later a composition by himself" (Michelmann, 97)
22 July	Wehner's second soirée (Gasthaus Krone). Program: Concerto by Bach for two pianos; G major Trio by Beethoven; Romance by Joachim; Bach's Chaconne (Michelmann, 98)
[Summer]	"Second soirée," Göttingen. Program: ". . . concerto by Bach for two pianos, performed by Wehner and . . . Brahms; . . . trio in G Major for string instruments; Romance for piano and violin, composed by Joachim, subtly and deeply felt, and felicitously performed . . .; Chaconne of Bach." ("Göttingen im August," *Rheinische Musik-Zeitung für Kunstfreunde und Künstler* 4/178 [September 14, 1853]: 1338–39)
24 July	Joachim thought that his birthday was that day (Michelmann, 99)
"July 1853, Göttingen"	Songs Op. 3, Nos. 2–4; Op. 6, Nos. 5–6; lied *Die Müllerin*; *Hymne* for Joachim (McCorkle, 6–11; 16–20; 680; 671)
August	"Third soirée," Joachim plays Ernst, *Erlkönig* (*Der Humorist* [30 August 1853], 794) Concert of the "two students" (May, 114)
Middle of August	Brahms leaves Göttingen (May, 114)

(continued)

Table 8.1 Continued

Date	Event/Source
September	Brahms visits Wasiliewski, Brahms played "with great effect" the Rakóczy March (May, 115); Wüllner: "[in Cologne conservatory] he played us the just-finished C major sonata."
October	Brahms and Joachim rejoined in Hanover (May, 114)
28 October	*FAE* Sonata gathering in Düsseldorf (Brahms, Dietrich, Schumanns, Gisela and Bettina von Arnim, Joachim)

To recapitulate the main events: Reményi and Brahms knew each other by January, as a sketch of Hungarian national tunes in Brahms's hand dated 17 January 1853 suggests.[14] They began touring on 19 April 1853 (see Table 8.1 for their programming and concert venues). Reményi initiated contact with his old comrade Joachim, whom he had met in Vienna during their student days in the early 1840s under Joseph Böhm. This resulted in a visit to Hanover in April, as corroborated by the musical sketch presumably given to Joachim that day: "Hannover, April 1853."[15] According to May, the decisive meeting between Brahms, Reményi, and Joachim, which introduced Joachim to Brahms's compositions, occurred in late May, when Joachim visited Hanover before leaving for his Göttingen summer sojourn. The three definitely reunited in Göttingen on 4 June 1853; Brahms and Reményi remained just a few days before departing for a performance on 8 June in Hanover. Unforeseen circumstances led to Reményi's brief detention, after which Brahms and Reményi left Hanover for Weimar, bringing their tour to an end. Brahms's second trip to Göttingen occurred without Reményi ("Reményi is going to depart from Weimar without me, it is his will"); he arrived between the second half of June (according to May) and the first half of July (Reményi).[16] Feeling the weight of external pressure—such as the need to publish some of his compositions before "going back to Hamburg"— and having just been rejected by Reményi, Brahms was desperate.[17] Göttingen provided much-needed relief and inspiration to compose, and Joachim kept his promise to help and support Brahms, who departed in August for his Rhine tour. Joachim's assistance consisted of his offer to perform together with Brahms, including at the "second soirée" on 22 July (Table 8.1); writing letters of recommendation, which he gave Brahms and Reményi at their visit to Göttingen in early June;[18] arranging for a performance of Brahms's violin sonatas "to bring them to life," as documented in a note Joachim sent to Brahms;[19] playing with Brahms at informal performances that summer;[20] and writing a glowing letter about Brahms to the young composer's father, Jakob Brahms.[21]

This narrative of the early Brahms-Joachim friendship may not seem to offer anything new until it is considered in relation to the early biographies relating some of these events. Kalbeck wrote what is considered Brahms's "official" biography,[22] while Moser's Joachim biography was authorized by the violinist.[23] As Michael Musgrave notes, Kalbeck's account "at times . . . seems richer in poetry than in scholarship."[24] Moser lacks distance from his subject, with the biographer's voice often disappearing behind Joachim's presumed presence in several works.[25] Underpinning the Germanocentric "great man" portrayal of the Joachim-Brahms relationship are classicizing views on *Bildung*, ciphers, a polarized view of the activities of performance and composing, and an understanding of that which is perceived to be "true art," all of which results in a reductive understanding of Reményi.

The concept of *Bildung* that looms large in the nineteenth century also plays a large role in these biographical accounts. Since Goethe's *Italienische Reise* (1816–1817), travel was viewed as an important formative experience. Both Kalbeck and Moser followed established traditions regarding what exactly *Bildung* entailed. During these journeys of "education, of personal growth and maturing,"[26] musicians and composers were exposed to intellectual and cultural riches, promoting a "cultivation of an individual's intellectual, aesthetic and moral faculties through engagement with art and ideas."[27] According to Moser, Joachim's formation evolved via experiences in important musical and intellectual centers: Vienna, Leipzig, Weimar, Hanover, and, as a final stop, Berlin. Even Brahms's "Wanderschaft" in the spring of 1853 could qualify as a time of exposure to intellectual and cultural riches. It began on 19 April 1853 and, however romantic and lighthearted ("mit so leichtem Sinn sie unternommen wurde"), it nevertheless "followed a practical goal, namely to put to use the knowledge and skills gained up to this point," as Kalbeck suggests.[28]

The concept of *Bildung* in Moser's and Kalbeck's views does not include the types of knowledge Brahms gained through exposure to performance, such as the practice of listening and transcribing melodies. In keeping with recent performance-inclusive subareas within the field of musicology, this chapter frames Brahms's acts of transcription in relation to issues of listening and memory, also considering the act of commemoration in relation to performance.[29] Our knowledge of Brahms having written down familiar and unfamiliar tunes by ear, as Brahms seems to have done on several occasions that year, sheds light on Brahms's formative experience.[30] This practice of transcribing broadened Brahms's stylistic knowledge, laying a foundation for his future passion as a collector of folk melodies.[31]

We may add the practice of aural transcription to the list of compositional processes undermined by Kalbeck and Moser, in whose biographical accounts "composition" as a "true art" is afforded a privileged place, even if only implicitly. Acts of composing that emerge from performance, such as transcription sketches, are viewed as second-rate. (The same is true for album leaves, birthday gifts, and other occasional or simply less "worked-out" compositions.) This privileging, though in line with both Brahms's and Joachim's mid- and late-career historicist views, clashes with their early practice. Although "playing the piano—in private and public—was inseparable from his [Brahms's] artistic and compositional identity,"[32] we know little about how the art of transcribing featured in Brahms's practice: What did he listen for? What level of detail do early transcription sketches reveal? How was the original instrument—the violin—captured, in terms of idiom and texture? What elicited these sketches?

Questions of authorship add intriguing, albeit complicating, layers. If, as an *arranger*, Brahms wished "to enlarge the reach of music by making it more accessible to both amateur and professional musicians, including close friends," his goal as a *transcriber* of quasi-improvised melodies, such as those of Reményi, defies such easy description. Kalbeck and Moser—and Joachim and Brahms for that matter—did not reflect seriously on issues of authorship as it concerned Reményi's melodies, in part because of a general belief that these melodies were not a single composer's property but part of a country's cultural heritage. What motivated these transcriptions was Brahms's interest in how these melodies could be used to create something worthy of preservation for posterity. Valerie Geortzen writes that "[t]he layers of revisions found in Brahms's sources for his arrangements—autographs, manuscript copies and proofs—show his care in making these settings effective and pianistic."[33] Such markers of care and "effort" are much less visible in the transcriptions and sketches jotted down quickly in that spring and summer of 1853. Furthermore, whereas arrangements—as offshoots—can be compared to the original, there is no immediate way to compare Reményi's performance with Brahms's sketches, which resemble snapshots meant to fix a fleeting sounding impression on a tangible medium.

Thus, the concept of "true art" in the early accounts is problematic. Karen Leistra-Jones has shown that the need to protect this "true art" from "lesser music" resulted in almost warlike actions and rhetoric: "Cities needed to be won over, and boundaries against lesser music needed to be maintained ('draw the circle tighter') in order for Brahms's music to prevail." The "mission" of the mature violinist Joachim, indeed, was to dedicate himself in service of a wider and deeper "understanding for Beethoven's late quartets and 'advocacy for Brahms.'" In the words of Andreas Moser's 1901 biography of Joachim, which the violinist supervised, these were "good services which Joachim rendered his 'comrade-at-arms.'"[34] But the twenty-two-year-old Joachim was not yet concerned with these goals. Nor did the twenty-two-year-old have the disparaging attitude toward Reményi and his music, as he did later.

July 1853, Göttingen: *Hymne zur Verherrlichung des großen Joachim*

Daily life in Göttingen included composing, performing, and leisure. While Joachim took classes at the university and Brahms read and walked "through the streets and fields, always with a book and a pencil in his hand," the lively university town also afforded after-hours distraction at venues including the bar on "Weenderstraße next to the Jakobikirche."[35]

Joachim and Brahms lived at Nikolausberger Weg 21 (Figure 8.1). They occasionally attended meetings of "Corps Saxonia," a fraternity that exposed them to boisterous student songs.[36] Although lovesick,[37] Joachim was industrious; Brahms, meanwhile, focused mainly on composing songs (Table 8.2).

Brahms's *Hymne* is a small birthday composition in A major.[38] Sketched quickly and full of "Spott und Humor," it was preserved by mere coincidence.[39]

Figure 8.1 Joachim's and Brahms's Residence in Göttingen, July 1853. Emil Michelmann, *Agathe von Siebold: Johannes Brahms' Jugendliebe* (Göttingen: Ludwig Hätzschel & Co, 1930), 97.

Table 8.2 Brahms's and Joachim's Compositions/Sketches from January to July 1853

Date	Brahms	Joachim	Source
January 1853	Song Op. 3, No. 1		McCorkle
	[sketch] Brahms's transcription of Reményi's violin line		McCorkle
March 1853	Song Op. 7, No. 3		McCorkle
"Spring" 1853	Sonata Op. 1, movements 1, 3, and 4.	Overture to *Hamlet*	Uhde 2018, 108.
April 1853	[sketch] *Magyar dalok*, with Reményi		McCorkle
July 1853 (Göttingen)		*Three pieces*, Op. 5	D-LÜbi, MS 1991.2.53.7, Joachim to Heinrich Joachim, 25 July 1853.
	Songs Op. 3, Nos. 2–4		McCorkle
	Songs Op. 6, Nos. 5–6		McCorkle
	Die Müllerin (lied), fragment	[first sketches] Overture to *Heinrich IV*	D-LÜbi, MS 1991.2.53.7, Joachim to Heinrich Joachim, 25 July 1853.
	[sketch] *Hymne zur Verherrlichung*		McCorkle
		[revision] Concerto Op. 3	*Joachim* I:64, Joachim to Bargiel, 24 June 1853.

Like the *FAE* Sonata, which Brahms, Dietrich, and Schumann composed in October in anticipation of Joachim's arrival in Düsseldorf and presented to him on 28 October, the *Hymne* was also a collaborative effort, at least with regard to its performance. The dedication, which is intentionally kept in a humorous tone, concealing the fact that Brahms was the sole author, reads: "Hymn for the glorification of the great Joachim, offered [dargebracht] by some of his great admirers Gioseppo [Brahms?], Ottone [Brinkmann], and Arnoldino [Wehner], artists from Arcadia." Also present was the poet Hoffmann von Fallersleben (1798–1874), an old Göttingen aficionado.

Jacquelyn Sholes has discussed this composition in a probing essay that argues that musical commemoration for birthdays "is a subject ripe for exploration"[40] as they "provide a humanizing glimpse into Brahms's relationship with friends during a formative period of his career."[41] She provides an account of the "spirit of jest" in Brahms's *Hymne*, suggesting that the "piece gets off to a rocky start with the musicians not only playing instruments at which they lack proficiency but also playing up their ineptitude with slapstick-style, oafish mistakes and false starts written into the score." This prompts further questions, including whether one of the "oafish mistakes" has any additional meaning beyond the nature of "mistake"; whether the cadenza in the end is also *commemorative*—possibly pointing to Reményi and his "Hungarian heritage"; or whether it is simply "satirical," "a spoof of the virtuoso violinist Joachim himself" and *his* "Hungarian heritage"? This further causes us to ask how the act of listening—hearing Joachim perform his own music—might have elicited these references.[42]

There is certainly a good degree of humor in this *Hymne*, which impresses as an assemblage of quotations and paraphrases from Joachim's music, and even some stereotypical *style hongrois*. There is Haydnesque tuning and retuning resulting in two false starts, reminiscent of Haydn's Symphony No. 60 (Presto).[43] Adding to this potpourri is a reference to Brahms's lifelong indulgence in parallel fifths (bars 45–47). The hymn's main themes have verbatim references to Joachim's *Drei Stücke*, Opp. 2 and 5.

The waltz is in ABA compound ternary form (Table 8.3). The main theme of the A section (a') emerges in bar 17 after two false attempts at tuning. A charming twelve-bar sentence, a', consists of a presentation, continuation, and a cadential module.

Stepping closer, there are more oddities than the false starts. After the first misfired tuning, the music says: "Ach!,"[44] over three quarter rests

Table 8.3 Brahms, *Hymne zur Verherrlichung*, Form

Bar	1	17	29	49	69	77	1	17	29
	A			B			A		
	a	‖:a¹:‖	‖:b, a¹:‖	‖:c:‖	‖:d:‖	coda	a	‖:a¹:‖	‖:b, a¹:‖

(Example 8.1). It is worth considering that here Brahms offered the solution to a cipher perhaps intimated two measures earlier, on Joachim's name. This would play into a wider practice of imbuing musical compositions with musical ciphers practiced by the Schumann circle at this time.

The musical letters of "Joachim," A–C–H—"H" is "B" in English musical nomenclature—are rendered "A [rest] H" in the top voice of measure 5, thereby offering the partially deciphered version of the cipher. Because "Ach!" is a German word used as an exclamation of surprise, a parodying double meaning arises. In October, Schumann also pondered wordplay on Joachim's name:

> I recently brought out a salute, in charade form [Charadenform]. Three syllables: the first a God loved, the two others many readers love, and the whole we all love; the whole . . . shall live [Jo, Achim].[45]

Shortly thereafter, Schumann crafted the intermezzo for the *FAE* Violin Sonata ("frei aber einsam" was Joachim's personal motto), where he concentrated ten FAE-statements, and possibly also a musical cipher for Joachim, consisting of A–C–H (Example 8.2). Above the third piano statement of FAE, the bass of bars 12–13, Schumann worked into the piano treble the pitches A, C, and B (H).

Joachim's Piece for Violin and Piano, Op. 5, No. 3, provides another example of ciphers; here the cipher associated with Gisela (Gis-e-la, or G♯–E–A)

Example 8.1 Brahms, *Hymne zur Verherrlichung*, bars 1–7.

Example 8.2 Schumann, "Intermezzo" from *FAE* Sonata, bars 12–13.

von Arnim clearly emerges (Example 8.3). The perplexing melody, identical with Brahms's binary of the first A section (bars 17–28), most definitely would have triggered a smile from the performers.

There are more ciphers in the second binary part of Brahms's A section (bars 29–48), now in transposition and in a context that pulls the A-major key—in which G♯–E–A often appears due to its leading-tone G♯—to the relative F♯ minor, as outlined in the violin's and piano's E♯–C♯–F♯ in unison (G♯–E–A transposed down a minor third). While the meter of Brahms's version is ¾, emphasizing what Sholes paraphrased as a joyful "tongue-in-cheek waltz" (Example 8.4a),[46] the more somber original was in 4/4 meter (Example 8.4b).

Brahms had encountered Joachim's Romance Op. 2, No. 1, at Arnold Wehner's second soirée, which he quotes in bar 49, the opening of the *Hymne*'s

Example 8.3 Joachim, *Three Pieces*, Op. 5, No. 3, bars 1–3.

Example 8.4a Brahms, *Hymne zur Verherrlichung*, bars 29–37.

Example 8.4b Joachim, *Three Pieces*, Op. 5, No. 3, bars 26–29.

Example 8.5a Joachim, Romance Op. 2, No. 1, bars 29–37.

B section. Eight bars later, Brahms turns to the minor mode, thereby exploiting the stereotype of exaggerated emotionality inherent to the *style hongrois*. Large leaps of a descending augmented sixth and minor ninth also derive from Joachim's Op. 2, impelling the music higher toward a *style hongrois* cadenza on an implied dominant-minor-ninth-chord A–E–G–B♭ (the C♯ is delayed) (Examples 8.5a and 8.5b).

Joachim left an enthusiastic report of his birthday.[47] The amusing manner in which Brahms signed the hymn connects with a practice of using humorous pseudonyms that endured until June 1854.[48] For instance, Brahms considered

Example 8.5b Brahms, *Hymne zur Verherrlichung*, bars 64–75.

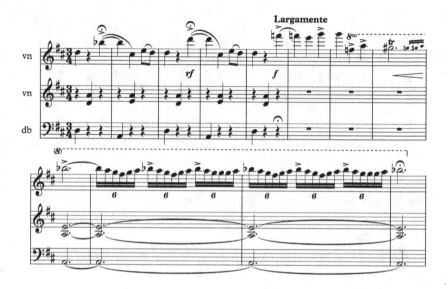

publishing his *51 Übungen für Klavier* as "Fantasiestücke in Callot's kühnster Manier," which revealed the composer's passion for E. T. A. Hoffmann's "Kreisler," a playful identification that was evident from the time of his Schumann Variations, Op. 9. Joachim was equally fascinated by alternative compositional identities, signing the manuscript for his *Hamlet* Overture "FAE," thereby disclosing "a piece of myself."[49] Such humorous, literary, or psychological references would disappear entirely from both composers' works in the course of the 1850s, confirming the changed "aesthetic" noted by Kawohl.

Most compelling about these references is a comparison of Brahms's *Hymne* and the original passages in Joachim's Op. 5, which reveal how *listening* to Joachim's performances that summer resulted in a transcription process akin to the ethnomusicological practice of transcribing from a live performance to paper.[50] Indeed, the medley-like nature of the references—recalling only the most memorable glimpses of Joachim's Göttingen pieces and forgetting some of the details—suggests that Brahms worked with such a process to transcribe the sound memories from his inner ear. For example, the opening theme of Joachim's Romance Op. 2 in B♭ major is recalled broadly without observing the correct dotted eighth note–sixteenth note rhythm; the fiery *sul G* passage from Joachim's Op. 5, No. 3, likewise, is sketched imprecisely with the rhythm altered to a loose dotted quarter note plus eighth note, instead of the sharp double-dotted quarter note plus thirty-second notes in the original (Op. 5, No. 3; see Example 8.4a). The expansive concluding gestures (descending leaps from Op. 2; see Example 8.5b) are harmonically distorted and transferred to D minor and crowned with fermatas. In all instances, the instrumentation is changed. The process of transcription here is not so different from the manner in which Brahms transcribed some of Reményi's melodies, as we shall explore below.

In the bouquet of stylistic references gathered in the *Hymne*, one is particularly characteristic: the *style hongrois* introduced via the minor-key version of the Op. 2, No. 1, opening, and the following wild violin cadenza (Example 8.5b). The *Hymne* may have been a birthday joke acknowledging the dedicatee's compositions, *and* his Hungarian identity. Jacquelyn Sholes's reading supports this hypothesis on the basis of stylistic and textural indications, including an instrumentation that resembles "Hungarian or 'gypsy' bands of the time, which often consisted of two violins, cimbalom, and double bass."[51] From Brahms's standpoint, whose collaboration with Reményi had just ended, breaking out into the *style hongrois* underscores a continuity with his musical activities earlier that year. That, in turn, leads us to another musical gift in the form of a manuscript in April 1853, when Brahms heard, performed, and notated *style hongrois* in another context—where the cimbalo and gypsy fiddle were explicitly evoked—and when Brahms met Joachim.

Performing *Style Hongrois* between January and July 1853

Like other nineteenth-century musicians, Brahms, Reményi, and Joachim constructed a *style hongrois* that employed distinctive musical patterns, dotted rhythms, and intensely contrasting musical characters alternating between melancholy and passionate abandon, a style close to Hungarian music that had circulated in print from 1780 on.[52] Because little literature about the *style hongrois* appeared before the 1850s, composers including Schubert and Weber drew from examples already circulating of the verbunkos, integrating them "into what is collectively called *style hongrois*."[53] The verbunkos circulated not only in print, but also in performance, especially in cities such as Vienna, "a hub of the *style hongrois*" that attracted traveling Romani bands performing in public places including coffeehouses. Both Joachim and Reményi had lived in Hungary before studying in Vienna during the 1840s; in contrast, Brahms's first *extensive* exposure to the *style hongrois* dated from the spring of 1853, through Reményi.[54]

According to Jonathan Bellman, "It was the performance significance of the Romani musicians (or their imitators, which everyone playing a Brahms Hungarian Dance in fact becomes) working their magic that gave the style not only the popularity but the power that it had."[55] Taking this claim that the *style hongrois* was to a considerable extent "performance-driven" as a point of departure, we will explore how performative memories created continuities between March and July 1853.

Brahms and Reményi in Hanover (April 1853)

That Brahms and Reményi visited Joachim already sometime between 21 and 31 April is evident from a manuscript signed in April 1853, which contains three Hungarian national melodies, *Magyar dalok*, notated in Brahms's youthful hand and annotated by Reményi.[56] Preserved today at the Joseph Joachim Partial Estate (housed at the Brahms-Institut in Lübeck), the manuscript includes a friendly dedication: "[undecipherable] Reményi and Brahms. Hanover April 1853. From a friend."[57] According to Bozarth, "The musicians gave this manuscript to Joseph Joachim while visiting him at the Hanoverian court in April 1853."[58]

Melody No. 1, "Andante con moto" (Example 8.6), features a similar version of a tune that Brahms had already notated on the "January 17, 1853" manuscript (Figure 8.2), in the second of two tunes.[59]

But the "Andante con moto" contains more elaborate dynamics, articulation, and character instructions. Specifically, markings like "doloroso" and "express." [sic] as well as "con fuoco" give evidence of a changeable and colorful *style hongrois*. The second melody of *Magyar dalok*, "Glorioso," has received the most scholarly attention of the three (and is therefore omitted here) because it features a version of the tune used later as a theme of Brahms's *Variations on a Hungarian Folksong*, Op. 21, No. 2.[60] The tune features a hand-written "not-so-lofty Hungarian text" next to the final bar line.[61]

Example 8.6 Brahms and Reményi, *Magyar dalok* No. 1, Andante con moto (D-Hs, BRA: Aa8).

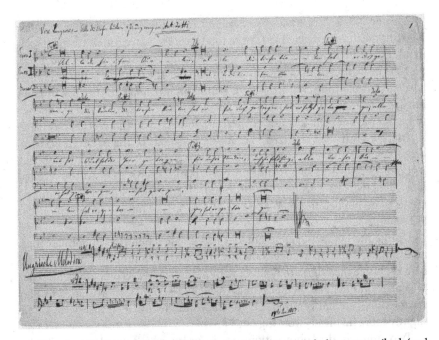

Figure 8.2 Johannes Brahms, sketch of two Hungarian melodies transcribed (and dated) 17 January, the day of the rehearsal with Reményi. A-Wgm, Signatur: A 130, leaf 28r. Archiv, Bibliothek und Sammlungen der Gesellschaft der Musikfreunde in Wien.

Example 8.7 Brahms and Reményi, *Magyar dalok* No. 3.

Melody No. 3, "col intense sentiment," is closely related to *Magyar dalok* No. 1 but features longer slurs in the top voice. Its instructions are again colorful, offering "Largamente" (bar 8), passionate ascending scalar flourishes, and the evocation of the cimbalo and the fiddle. The cimbalo is known for its special trait of "indiscipline," which Bellmann attributes to the instrument's idiosyncratic and clumsy sustaining pedal, a cluttering sound, and a tendency to be out of tune. On account of these attributes, its sound registers as being in friction with the "civilized" homogenous sound of the Western classical orchestra.[62] The repetitive alternating sixty-fourth notes under a legato slur in Liszt's *Hungarian Rhapsodies* provide "pianistic evocations of the cimbalom" evoking "background-strum[ming]."[63] The same kind of strumming seems to be implied in the *Magyar dalok* No. 3, "Col intense sentimento," bar 9 (Example 8.7).

Unlike the January sketch, notated in a single violin line in double-stops, revealing, as Bozarth argued, how Brahms heard the tunes from Reményi,[64] here the three melodies are notated with a simple bass accompaniment. After 21 April, Brahms and Reményi may have had several opportunities to play the melodies, so that Brahms had gone beyond the initial "transcription" to a slightly more involved "working out."

Two summarizing observations are in order, which depolarize Kalbeck's Joachim-Reményi portrayal. First, the *Magyar dalok* manuscript shows how the *style hongrois* and Reményi's skill inspired Brahms to sketch his own lines—first transcribing Reményi in January, then creating a collaborative sketch with presumably his own added accompaniments in April. The latter could be viewed as the result of a performative engagement over a period of time.

Second, the April sketch seems at first glance to document an event similar to the presentation of the *FAE* Sonata on 28 October 1853, and the birthday celebration of the hymn, sharing with the latter the *style hongrois* and the "Hungarian or 'gypsy' bands" texture, as Sholes avers. This is the first time that these three manuscript presentations—*Magyar dalok* (April 1853), *Hymne* (July 1853), and *FAE* Sonata (October 1853)—are mentioned together, even though Joachim was the recipient and dedicatee of all three manuscripts, and Brahms the musician who notated them (albeit only the Scherzo of the *FAE* Sonata).

Performed Style Hongrois and Joachim's Suppressed Hungarian Fantasy

Although Brahms, Joachim, and Reményi all performed *style hongrois* music that spring, Joachim's own *Hungarian Fantasy* remains unknown,[65] mainly because of his determined efforts to exchange his virtuoso reputation for a new performance persona. Deconstructing this binary opposition between virtuoso and "serious" musician allows for a more nuanced and historically informed account of the Hungarian elements of Joachim's persona and musical endeavors.

An essential ingredient of Kalbeck's/Moser's "great man" portrait of Brahms was that Joachim's Hungarian identity was undermined. While Reményi was discussed condescendingly, viewed as a "means" to that single achievement he accomplished in the biographers' eyes—introducing Brahms to Joachim—Joachim's portrait was crafted in a contrasting manner. Reményi, the "flamboyant and outgoing" musician, was viewed as "an ardent Hungarian," whose "national sentiment was reflected alike in his life and in his music,"[66] while Joachim was cherished for the established image of the violinist from the early 1900s, that of the reserved, most German, dignified *Geigerkönig*.

Table 8.4 shows that Joachim publicly performed a *Fantasy on Hungarian Themes* (1846–1850) with orchestra on 9 and 14 April 1853. This fantasy in *airs variés* form, likely based on an unidentified preexisting Hungarian theme, was rediscovered in 2016 (Example 8.8).[67] The tunes are loosely derived from each other, showing a unifying $\hat{1}$-$\hat{2}$-$\hat{3}$-$\hat{2}$-$\hat{1}$ contour.

Table 8.4 Performances of *Style Hongrois* Music by Brahms, Reményi, and Joachim (January to July 1853)

Reményi and Brahms	Joachim
17 January 1853 [informal performance resulting in sketch of only violin line]	
2 April 1853 [informal performance (?) from sketch]	9 April 1853, Hamburg [formal performance violin and orchestra from manuscript] Source: *Der Humorist* (16 April 1853), 350.
Concerts on the tour in Northern Germany between April 19 and June 4 [formal performance from sketch]	14 April 1853, Hanover [formal performance violin and orchestra from manuscript] Source: Moser, *Lebensbild*, II:90.
24 July 1853? [informal performance from sketch]	

Example 8.8 Joachim, *Hungarian Fantasy*, opening theme.

As Ian Pace has argued, "the *style hongrois* works of Liszt are quite different to those of Brahms, or of Schubert or anyone else," and evince "their own individuated approaches."[68] Thus, listing common, unifying *style hongrois* markers that Joachim's fantasy and Reményi and Brahms's sketches share does little to distinguish these composers' approaches.

What does help individuate these three composer-performers is their approach to their own Hungarian melodies. While Reményi continued most actively presenting them in public as his *chevaux de bataille* (he released his *Trois morceaux hongrois* only in 1881), Brahms eagerly continued collecting Hungarian and other folk tunes, as is evident in the many surviving sketches of the above-discussed sort, from many different national origins. He published his first *style hongrois* work—in variation form—as early as 1862. Joachim pursued the most unusual approach. Although formerly self-identified as a true "Magyarember" (Magyar),[69] and despite the "national sentiment" reflected in his music, no less than in Reményi's, he later changed his mind about the value of folk tunes "as such,"[70] favoring tunes *treated* in a classical form—that is, combining "folk and high art."[71]

Already in April 1853, when Joachim last performed the *Hungarian Fantasy*, he evidently had no desire to share its existence with Brahms and Reményi. This reflects Joachim's evolving views about what it meant to be an artist. It also reflects, as Robert Eshbach has suggested, a growing reluctance to be associated with Hungarians at a time when, as can be gleaned from Reményi's brief detention in Hanover, there was a certain hostility toward former Hungarian revolutionaries. In fact, Reményi's passionate, undisciplined, seemingly authentic Hungarian personality alienated the young Joachim, and may have triggered his psychological defense mechanism, as Beatrix Borchard puts it, prompting him to "split off" at least part of his "Magyarember" persona.[72]

Conclusion: *Style Hongrois* and Performativity

Could the formative influence of Reményi have left an impact on Brahms's performative identity? References to "fire" ("Feuer") and *con fuoco* in the works from the Göttingen weeks and an early documented assessment by Joachim of Brahms's playing seem to support this claim. Linking a "fiery" performance style to sharp rhythm and "fatalism," Joachim wrote about Brahms's performance style in 1853: "His playing shows the intense fire, and, I should like to say, 'fatalistic' energy and precision of rhythm which bodes well for the artist, and his compositions already betoken such power as I have seen in no other musician of his age."[73] Using his favorite philosophical term "fatalism,"[74] which appears periodically in his letters from 1847 onward, Joachim addressed a primarily performative quality, an "inevitable" forward momentum paired with rhythmic sharpness, that is, a tension between disparate movements through performance time: rhythmic accuracy and a fiery forward-pushing.

Joachim had particular ideas when it came to precise rhythm and rhythmic consequentiality (not making concessions for technical reasons) and found this quality especially important for the performance of Hungarian or gypsy music. He wrote in 1854: "The gypsies still play enthusiastically. . . . There is more rhythm . . . in their bows than in all north German orchestra players combined."[75]

Another instance of "Fire"—as a compositional directive—can be seen in Brahms's "Lied" Op. 3, No. 4, in E♭ Minor, which opens "Mit feurigem Schwung" (With fiery momentum). This directive connects to previous *"con fuoco"* pieces, including the "January 17th" sketch, and the third and fourth movements of his Piano Sonata Op. 1 (dedicated to Joachim). The consuming energy of this song accords with the "fire" topic, while the angular pianism of staccati and accents underscores the aggressive references in the text.

While Brahms's approach to *"con fuoco"* or "fire" did not originate in Göttingen, the persistence of "fire" in Brahms's performance practice and style indicates that this musical character helped define their Göttingen sound world. Perhaps, as Bellman avers, the *style hongrois* was indeed a performance-driven style, given that Reményi's Hungarian tunes left traces on Brahms's sketches from January and April, and that Brahms's "fiery" pianism—and Göttingen works—continued building on his experiences from the spring. The Aristotelian virtue theory—that *performing* a certain way means *acquiring* that quality—could be applied to Brahms. His music kept exploring Hungarian tunes, while both Brahms and Joachim began—perhaps that summer—to experiment more broadly with extroverted, passionate *"fuoco"* characters, showing the mobility of "fiery" styles across borders, within and outside the *style hongrois*.

This chapter has reviewed Brahms, Reményi, and Joachim's shared passion for melodies in the Hungarian style in the spring and summer of 1853, opening out onto their later dissimilar stance toward them. Reményi lived and breathed them, Joachim came to reject them (unless they were elevated within classical structures), and Brahms collected them as a means of stylistic expansion. Considering all three transcription (or transcription-like) sketches by Brahms from January, April, and July together allows an important continuity to emerge of a series of compositions for which Brahms held the pen as a Hungarian violinist performed. Drawing such a continuity allows us to problematize the established biographical patterns in Moser and Kalbeck whose "great man" portraits of Brahms and Joachim left little room for serious consideration of Reményi. Yet Reményi was a key player in this continuity: it is likely that he introduced Brahms to certain Hungarian melodies (in January); he inspired Brahms to revisit Hungarian melodies for the Joachim encounter in Hannover (April); he might even have left so strong an impression on Brahms that the latter remembered Reményi in the *style hongrois* passage composed for

Joachim's birthday *Hymne*. Indeed, Joachim had not shared his passion for the *style hongrois* with Brahms, but Reményi did. Reading the *style hongrois* passage in the *Hymn* as not only a *commemorative* but a com-*memorative* piece—his playing from memory styles heard and notated previously that year—allows us to challenge the familiar narrative of "works" originating through a process separate from performance. In other words, the hymn may have been composed with a distant memory of Reményi, whose silhouette in that memory was now overwritten by Joachim's presence. The impact that listening to, and performing with, Reményi and Joachim had on Brahms—which perhaps supported the development of Brahms's "fire"—suggests that part of Brahms's *Bildung* that spring and summer was performance-based and performative.

Chapter 9

Doesn't Play Well with Others
Performance and Embodiment in Brahms's Chamber Music with Piano

Anna Scott

Introduction

Doesn't play well with others: the report card comment every parent dreads. Children who play well with others listen, cooperate, and compromise—skills deemed predictive of success not only in adulthood, but in chamber music spheres as well, where playing well with others, in the sense of both properly and *ensemble* (together), requires the scrupulous coordination of individual competencies. The margins within which performers are said to play well together are fairly narrow in the chamber music of Johannes Brahms, where "good" playing is precise, clear, controlled, synchronous, and as close to the score as possible: norms that ensure a stable, neutral sonic template for the scholarly imagination. From his love of domestic music-making among friends, to his nostalgia for fin-de-siècle liberal Viennese values, Brahms's chamber music as currently performed is the soundtrack for existing and future ideas about who he was.[1] These ideas in turn provide the epistemic justification for performance norms dictating how his music should sound. This seemingly ideal symbiosis presents challenges for those negotiating between privileging the score as a text, or embracing procedures of sonic-embodiment with the music of Brahms. If an aspect of "rethinking Brahms" is playing his music differently, then playing differently must invite imprecision, licentiousness, and asynchrony into our performances. Yet performing this way in an industry obsessed with the existential threat of lowered standards, despite rising levels of virtuosity, could be career ending.

By applying nineteenth-century performance practices as embodied via the precise emulation of early recordings in Brahms's Sonata for Violin and Piano in A Major, Op. 100, and Piano Quintet in F Minor, Op. 34, this chapter seeks to challenge modern metrics for playing well together. This is done by using performance reviews to outline a broad set of rules to which both mainstream and period performances adhere, by demonstrating the inadequacy of documentary evidence of Brahms's musical contexts for those looking to break these rules, by arguing for an embodied "lo-fi" approach to applying sonic evidence of nineteenth-century performance practices, and by considering the implications of the resultant performances for the reflexivity of Brahmsian thought and practice. These performances explore what might lie beyond competence and unanimity, where players are encouraged to make sudden, bold, and risky moves in solo and accompanimental materials alike, where individual parts are allowed to organically diverge and reunite, and where missteps of tuning, technique, timing, and balance are tolerated and even amplified in order to create a more spontaneous, conversational, and improvisational atmosphere—one in which compromise can be just as perilous as intransigence. This chapter is methodologically rooted in research through performance where ambitious scholarly work is being carried out by skilled performers, and vice versa. Although no one can afford to ignore the lessons of early recordings, particularly concerning the phenomenon of style change over time, as explored by scholars including Daniel Leech-Wilkinson and Robert Philip, and the gaps between sonic and written evidence, as explored by performer-scholar Neal Peres Da Costa, there is a distinction to be made between approaches more heavily *weighted* toward either textual-procedural or sonic-embodiment concerns.[2]

Those in the first group often come from historical performance backgrounds in earlier repertoires. They tend to prefer period instruments, sparser tonal palettes, ornamental vibrato, and the selective application of sonic evidence when congruent with scores, treatises, and verbal accounts. Such work focuses on the systematization of musical procedures from a given period, the delineation of national and pedagogical schools, and the production of critical performing editions.[3] Those in the second group whose work leans toward sonic embodiment have a preference for modern instruments, denser tonal palettes, continuous vibrato, and the use of treatises and verbal accounts only when congruent with the sounds that convey their conception of the music. The precise emulation of early recordings is particularly important here, whether or not their constitutive procedural details make sense in relation to texts, and the extrapolation of embodied performance styles in ways that are as close to the sonic evidence, and as far from modern norms, as possible.[4]

Modern Chamber Performance Norms

There are practices so entrenched in how Brahms's chamber music is played that they often operate unnoticed, particularly where precision, clarity, control, synchronicity, and proximity to the score are concerned. Subtle nuances of tone, touch, and timing are permitted, but these must be "precisely timed and graded, allowing ensembles to behave as one player, to the extent that orchestras . . . can now operate highly effectively with no conductor." When all performances conform to the same set of scores and norms, the result is a situation where "such competence and unanimity (in ensemble and in belief) is taken as an absolute, as outside time, as permanently ideal." As Daniel Leech-Wilkinson observes: "The better it is, the more easily it's mistaken for that, and seen as the only option; and the more institutionalised it becomes . . . the harder it is to envisage alternatives."[5]

The narrowness of this ideal can lead to an overestimation of the differences between performances, which might explain why many performers and scholars refute its very existence. Fortunately for those seeking to outline these norms as a first step toward escaping them, the notion that Brahms's chamber music should sound a certain way is much less controversial in performance criticism spheres. Far from seeking to portray critics as narrow-minded for voicing the unsayable, and performers as unimaginative for obeying the invisible, in the following discussion of recent English-language reviews of performances of Brahms's Sonata for Violin and Piano in A Major, Op. 100, and Piano Quintet in F Minor, Op. 34, I simply seek to map out a set of norms underpinning what it conventionally means to play these works well.

In their 2018 recording of Brahms's violin sonatas, violinist Alina Ibragimova and pianist Cédric Tiberghien are said to execute "polished, respectable, and carefully-considered performances" in which "there is no outsized rubato, the score has been honoured in its many details, and there are few blemishes—musical or technical—of any kind."[6] While delivering note-perfect performances requires astonishingly advanced individual skills, as another critic writes in reference to a live 2017 performance of the Piano Quintet, Op. 34, exceptional ensembles are characterized by "remarkable unity . . . at the most critical moments, exquisitely nuanced dynamics, [and] all articulations synchronized to highly improbable tolerances."[7] Soloists must therefore listen, cooperate, and compromise in chamber settings—why play with others if not *together*?

Consensus must also be achieved where issues of textural blend and balance are concerned: qualities relentlessly honed in the realm of string quartet playing. As one reviewer notes in reference to the Takács Quartet's 2014 recording of Brahms's string quintets featuring violist Lawrence Power: "The blending of the instruments in this recording is something to behold. To all string players in training, here is a marvellous example of how to work closely with other[s]."[8] Inserting a pianist rather than a violist into this perfect state of tonal alchemy is trickier. In Brahms's piano quintet, Ursula Oppens "melt[s] easily into the ensemble texture" in a live 2011 performance with the Cassatt Quartet, while Jon Nakamastsu deftly avoids "overlording it like a concerto soloist" in a 2012 recording with the Tokyo Quartet.[9] Till Fellner's lightness of touch in a 2016 recording with the Belcea Quartet, however, is first praised because it "makes him less of a soloist, [and] more of an integrated texture," and then criticized because it "feels like he's responding rather than instigating," and "some listeners might reasonably like their Brahms with a burlier kind of pianism."[10] Brahmsian brawn, however, must also be carefully judged:

> If you love the Brahms Piano Quintet, you'll marvel at the fusion of power and clarity pianist Andreas Staier and the Leipzig Quartet achieve. The tricky tempo transitions in the outer movements are gauged to perfection, and no matter how intensely the musicians drive the climaxes, individual and combined timbres never turn raucous.[11]

The idea that there is a right (and wrong) way to handle notated detail, structure, and tempo—an approach paradoxically understood as neutral—suggests that competence and unanimity is best achieved when performers simply allow the inherent logic of the music "itself" to unfold naturally. In a live 2015 performance of the Sonata for Violin and Piano, Op. 100, by violinist Isabelle Faust and pianist Alexander Melnikov, temporal issues are "perfectly judged," with "both players allow[ing] the music to develop in an organic and unified way."[12] By surrendering to this logic, players allow themselves to be played by the music rather than the other way around: a state that the scholar Simon Høffding calls performative passivity, in which musicians can accurately predict what their colleagues are going to do without any advance planning. As Bin Kimura asserts, only when musicians submit to this state can music unfold "according to the necessity of a movement which is inherent to it": an impulse that transcends and subjugates the will of individual players, who "manipulate the little details, but abstain in awe of the beauty of the unfolding musical landscape."[13] While it is true that elite ensemble playing requires astoundingly little rehearsal, this is made possible, not by the music "itself," but rather by the narrowness of the available options. I know what my colleague will do because I know what they *cannot* do; the known far outweighs the unknown.

Chamber playing must sound conversational, improvised, and even risky. These qualities are at least partly believed to be embedded in the music itself, like the "conversational lilt" of the main theme in the fourth movement of the piano quintet, or "the genial dialogue that opens the [violin sonata's] first-movement Allegro amabile."[14] But players must also do their part. An intriguing pairing in this regard is violinist Leonidas Kavakos's sober meticulousness, and pianist Yuja Wang's more urgent flamboyance. Referring to their 2014 recording of the Brahms Violin Sonatas, one critic observes that while "the deeper logic of these works might be better served by a more neutral approach . . . the overall impression is of two distinct personalities in conversation about the music, and that's the chamber music ideal." The best of these conversations are tacit, however, as demonstrated by their live performance of the work later that year: "Over an hour of music had gone by and [Kavakos and Wang] had not looked at each other once while playing. They did not seem to need to."[15] Thanks to the narrowness of the norms within which even the most disparate of performers operate, cueing and eye contact are simply not needed: "for score-based music, it will in many cases be both necessary and sufficient to just play one's part correctly"; or, as a member of the Guarneri String Quartet puts it, "I haven't looked at these guys in years."[16] Any communication we do see onstage is thus either "theatrically employed" or a sign that "the normal mechanisms of co-performance are under pressure or have broken down."[17] Even the latter is usually fixable by listening alone.

Perhaps this conversational quality is entirely staged. Bruce Ellis Benson argues that genuine musical dialogues are both improvised and risky, with players being free "to play one thing instead of another, taking one path in place of all the others that beckon," while at the same time being forced to make the first move "without knowing that the other will reciprocate."[18] The moves players can make in Brahms's chamber music are indeed confined to subtle shadings of tone and timing, but this does not mean that this repertoire is inimical to improvisation and risk: it can be true *both* that no two performances are ever the same, *and* that the margins of this variation are extraordinarily narrow. What it does mean, however, as Høffding observes, is that what is "perceived as full of nuance and differentiation to the expert" is often "unnoticeable to the ordinary listener." It might be tempting to overestimate the impact of these shadings, but it behoves us to remember that "most listeners can clearly detect the improvised solo of the saxophonist in a jazz piece whereas few can find the traces of improvisation in [a] Beethoven quartet."[19] Perhaps this explains our discomfort when players deign to simply show up and do their jobs. Kavakos and Wang are criticized for a rare "jet-lagged readthrough" of the violin sonata in 2014, with the former playing "as if he would rather be anywhere else than at Carnegie Hall, his seeming disinterest perhaps hindering the usually charismatic Ms. Wang." As this critic argues, in the best chamber concerts "the performances *seem* spontaneous; the listener can sense musicians feeding off one another's energy, taking risks and enjoying a visceral experience together."[20] Kavakos and Wang can't make big moves in Brahms's music, but they can at least *look* like they might.

It is debatable whether more freedom is tolerated in historical performance spheres. Given Isabelle Faust and Alexander Melnikov's involvement in this arena, it is telling that an earlier review of their live 2015 performance of the Brahms Violin Sonatas makes no mention of period style. Though critiques of historical performance's transposition of modern norms onto old instruments have been around for some time, nineteenth-century performance practice scholar Robin Stowell is probably right to classify their approach to the sonata on a recording released that same year as "period instrument rather than historically informed." Faust plays a 1704 Stradivari and avoids any "portamento-edged, plum-coloured lyricism"; Melnikov plays an 1875 Bösendorfer with "striking clarity, mellowness, athleticism and lightness of touch."[21] The inclusion of period stylistic procedures, however, is no panacea where modern norms are concerned. For example, while one critic is "shocked" by violinist

Leila Schayegh and pianist Jan Schultz's 2020 recording of the violin sonata, which features period instruments *as well as* fluidity of ensemble, flexible tempi, rolled piano chords, and portamenti, the duo is praised for their "rhythmic spring and sense of pulse," their "technical adroitness," for "clearly aiming for the same objective," and for their light tone and sparse vibrato—holdovers, no doubt, from Schayegh's background in the historical performance of earlier repertoires.[22]

Comprising players from a similar background and led by pianist-scholar Neal Peres Da Costa, Australian ensemble Ironwood's 2017 recording of Brahms's Piano Quintet features gut strings, a replica 1868 Streicher fortepiano, and a whole host of period stylistic techniques. It too is praised for its tonal restraint, where "for once ensemble passages are not completely overpowering"; violinist-scholar David Milsom notes that "the technical standard of the playing is exemplary, and the recording itself made to a high standard"; and while another critic points out that Ironwood's quintet is more orthodox than their approach to the Piano Quartet No. 1 in G Minor on the same CD, this is deemed appropriate because the former "is by nature more orchestral, requiring less individuation and more integration."[23] The idea that cohesion must increase with ensemble size is an idea sometimes invoked in historical performance spheres and would appear to be grounded in a comment found in Louis Spohr's 1832 *Violinschule*. Spohr admonishes the "the Solo player in the Quartett to lay aside his peculiar manner of Solo playing." The bigger the musical group, the more vital it is that players "agree as much as possible."[24] However, Spohr's popularity is another holdover from performance practice research into earlier repertoires; it is not a given that larger ensembles require greater unity of approach, nor is this supported by the recorded evidence. While neither of these historical performances has been universally praised, to this listener they are beautiful—which is to say, highly skilled and coherent. Even their asynchronies sound coordinated and rehearsed: they offer a deliberative, consensus-seeking approach to period style. The performances that will be discussed later in this chapter may use the same stylistic procedures, but they belong to a different sound world, and operate according to an inherent necessity that is far less congruent with modern metrics of competence and unanimity.

The Verbal Evidence

To modern ears, ideas about who Brahms was and how his music should sound were far less imbricated when musicians within and adjacent to the composer's circle were making their own lo-fi recordings. How to treat verbal evidence of past performances is certainly far from clear. When a critic or friend from Brahms's circle comments that a performance was fast or that the ensemble was good or poor, what might this mean to us today when we are so far removed from the performance culture in which these writers were situated? The tendency is that even the most detailed descriptions of earlier styles seem to reinforce our modern norms, or they invite us to fill in missing data in ways that have the effect of leaving these norms intact.

Consider Brahms's sojourns with contralto Hermine Spies, who joined him in Switzerland for a series of private performances over a period of three summers beginning in 1886. As the Sonata for Piano and Violin in A Major, Op. 100, being composed at the same time potentially absorbed the quality of Spies's voice, along with the melodic material of songs like "Wie Melodien zieht es mir" and "Immer leiser wird mein Schlummer," Op. 105, Nos. 1 and 2, it is also intriguing to ponder *how* these works were performed.[25] Fortunately, we have Max Graf's vivid accounts of Brahms's 1890s performances with another contralto, Alice Barbi: "Accompanists of great singers perform in the same manner as lackeys laying a carpet at the feet of their mistresses. They are in the background, obsequious and bending to the whims of the artist and never step forth to attract attention. But not Brahms." As nothing here suggests that these soloistic tendencies included wild tempo fluctuations or sudden departures from the score, modern readers are free to assume that they were confined to issues of tone production. Graf confirms this by repeatedly remarking on the prominence of Brahms's basses—even in the tender "Wiegenlied," "the accompaniment of which is usually sublimated and pampering"—a feature that might also explain "the undertone of subterranean rumbling" in Brahms's 1891 performance of his Piano Trio in B major, Op. 8.[26] Brahms may not have easily melted into ensemble textures, but there's no reason to assume that he was overbearing either. Furthermore, any eccentricities of tone and technique at this time—like Clara Schumann's 1882 diary entry that "the pity is that Brahms plays more and more abominably—it's now nothing but thump, bang and scrabble"—are easily explained by his well-known later aversion to regular practice.[27]

Imagine, too, the music-making that went on at the private festivals Brahms frequented in Krefeld, just north of Düsseldorf: events whose massive programs often featured his Piano Quintet in F Minor, Op. 34. At one such festival in 1883, Brahms joined other visiting musicians at a local inn "for his morning pint." When the beer was served, he noticed that the opening measures of the quintet were engraved on the jug's lid. Thereafter he delighted in pushing the jug suddenly toward his companions and exclaiming, "'What is this from?, which was often followed by rollicking laughter."[28] To get a sense of whether this spirit of convivial togetherness permeated Brahms's Krefeld performances, consider pianist Fanny Davies's account of his 1887 performance of the Trio in C Minor, Op. 101, with violinist Joseph Joachim and cellist Robert Hausmann. His tempi were flexible, "but the balance was always there—one felt the fundamental rhythms underlying the surface rhythms." He shaped hairpins with dynamics *and* tempo, but primarily via slowing, "linger[ing] not on one note alone, but on a whole idea." His playing could be rough, but "there never failed to appear that routined and definite school of technique." And regarding the holy trinity of notated detail, structure, and time, Davies asserts that "all Brahms's passages ... are strings of gems, and that tempo which can best reveal these gems and help to characterize the detail at the same time as the outlines of a great work must be considered the right tempo." When she closes with Brahms's advice to "do it how you like, but make it beautiful," we are left with little doubt that we, too, would have found this performance beautiful.[29]

The Sonic Evidence

The solo recordings of the pianists who studied with Brahms and Clara Schumann are incompatible with modern metrics of musical quality. While Fanny Davies, Carl Friedberg, Adelina De Lara, Etelka Freund, and Ilona Eibenschütz all use devices like arpeggiation, dislocation, rhythmic alteration, and tempo modification, their *alteration* of notated detail, structure, and time is what lends their playing its palpable sense of imprecision.[30] They freely add, omit, and reduce materials; they disregard dynamic, articulation, and tempo indications; they rush everywhere possible and continuously blur pulse; they soften structural demarcations; and their performances are littered with wrong notes and memory slips. By precisely emulating their recordings, using Sonic Visualiser to work out nearly inaudible details, and apps like AnyTune to refine overall sweep, I embodied not only five idiosyncratic dialects of this stylistic language, but an extreme tolerance for discomfort and divergence as well. In Sound File 9.1a ▶ you can hear my imitation of Eibenschütz's 1952 recording of Brahms's Intermezzo in E Minor, Op. 119, No. 2, while in Sound File 9.1b ▶ you can hear my extrapolation of her style to the Intermezzo in B Minor, Op. 119, No. 1.

Once planted deep in the body, this waywardly soloistic impulse becomes an inherent necessity that transcends and subjugates, and that cannot easily be dampened, rationalized, or coordinated. As violist Emlyn Stam has demonstrated with his pivotal emulations of early solo, duo, and string quartet recordings, there was a time when players did precisely what Louis Spohr advised against, which was to preserve and even *amplify* this impulse when moving from solo to ensemble contexts. In his 1924 recordings of Bach's solo Chaconne from the Second Partita, BWV 1004, and Brahms's Clarinet Sonata, Op. 120, No. 1, violist Lionel Tertis engages in heavy portamenti, pitch alteration, extreme rushing and slowing, and some eccentric bowing, articulation, and ornamentation effects. In the sonata, however, these idiosyncrasies occur *in parallel with* those of pianist Ethel Hobday, an acquaintance of Brahms, with another layer being added by their combined use of daredevil tempo modifications and rhythmic alterations. This clash of the individual and collective is what results in frequent asynchrony, rhythmic ambiguity, handfuls of wrong notes, a general lack of attention to most details, and some "wild, rushed, and uncontrolled playing that would [today] be considered sloppy and inaccurate."[31]

In their 1921 recording of Tchaikovsky's "None but the Lonely Heart" with an unknown pianist, Lionel Tertis and soprano Zoia Rosovsky exhibit three different strategies for the unfolding of individual lines: complete independence, as if wholly unaware of one another; deliberate untogetherness, by playing around rather than with one another in order to ensure the audibility of both lines; and imitativeness, by echoing some aspect of the other's approach. All three strategies, however, lead to imprecision and asynchrony: even, and perhaps especially, when one feature of the performance is unified. Tertis falls nearly a beat behind the pianist, for example, while executing the technically awkward fingerings needed in order to match Rosovky's portamenti.[32] Just as much multilayering occurs in a 1935 recording of Beethoven's String Quartet, Op. 127, by the Klingler Quartet, a group with close ties to Brahms, Joachim, and Hausmann. Here, too, players deliver their lines in exaggeratedly individualistic ways while collectively executing wild tempo modifications and rhythmic alterations. Stam argues that the resulting asynchrony is so central to the Klingler's performance "that it must be a deliberate part of their practice."[33] The same could be said of Lionel Tertis and violinist Albert Sammons's 1933 recording of Mozart's Sinfonia Concertante, K. 364, with the London Philharmonic Orchestra. Despite piles of wrong notes, extensive alterations, heavy portamenti, abrupt rushing and slowing, and wide asynchronies, what Stam finds most compelling is how Tertis and Sammons, "who performed and recorded together over the course of many years, adopted and accepted independent approaches to the same motivic material within the same piece."[34]

There is no reason to assume that additional rehearsal would have made these performances any more competent and unanimous in a modern sense. Stam recalls how initially difficult it was for his quartet to maintain this level of inexactness without their performances falling apart. Over time, however, their playing did not become cleaner; rather, "counterintuitive or aesthetically displeasing" elements became so internalized that they began to feel natural—even if that meant "admitting a degree of chaos into [their] playing that none of [them] would have found comfortable in the context of a regular public concert."[35] Armed with this fearlessness, violinists Joan Berkhemer and Rada Ovcharova, violist Emlyn Stam, cellist Willem Stam, and sound engineer Geoff Miles joined me in exploring alternatives to playing well with others in Brahms's Sonata for Violin and Piano, Op. 100, and Piano Quintet, Op. 34.

It was still necessary to set certain constraints in order to thwart the pull of old habits. Rehearsal and recording sessions were strictly limited, and dedicated only to complete readings of each movement; in most cases, the recordings capture one of only two or three of these run-throughs. Our individual and collective approaches were left unplanned and uncoordinated: any impression of improvisation, dialogue, and danger on these recordings is a result of simply not knowing what our colleagues were going to do from one moment to the next. This was, of course, helped by our decision *not* to copy historical recordings of these works; we were confident that any differences between our performances and those of our early-recorded counterparts would be wholly in keeping with the epoch's wide margins of variability. Between run-throughs, Miles kept us focused on potentiality and divergence via verbal feedback and audio playback from the lo-fi microphone; in the editing phase, only two alterations per movement were permitted, provided these brought the performance closer to the spirit sought. Inserted passages were often messier, but more thrilling. The playing you will hear is undeniably risky.

Applying Embodied Performance Styles

It is no coincidence that critics often link standards of playing and recording. Modern hi-fi recording paradigms are typified by Morten Lindberg's comment that "as recording engineers and producers we need to do exactly the same as any good musician: interpret the music and the composer's intentions."[36] From the clinical set-up of studios, players' interactions with engineers, and our belief in the medium's transparency, to the ever-increasing capacity of microphones to capture a wide range of sonic spectrum (about 20–20,000 Hz), and the editing of recordings to otherwise unattainable standards of perfection, this paradigm encourages players to prioritize precision and synchrony over the spontaneous, improvisatory, and risky gestures that are associated with chamber playing in theory, but discouraged in practice. This irons out the hi-fi musical event, which sound engineer Miles likens to cartography. A map tells us where a river *is* rather than all the paths it could have taken by smoothing all its meandering twists and turns. Instead, Miles wants to re-attune players to a more fleeting sense of potentiality, where the musical event consists "of an infinite number of points, whereby in each fraction of a moment a different perspective on its possible paths might be experienced."[37]

As a means of challenging the norms of modern chamber music sound recording, the following renditions of Brahms's sonata and piano quintet were captured in an unusual way. Miles built an experimental limited bandwidth microphone that mimics historical acoustic recordings by exclusively capturing the middle frequency range of sound (about 200–5,000 Hz). The benefits of this lo-fi microphone are many: first, because the medium is not perceived as a transparent, it does not hyper-attune players to perfection, leaving them free to experiment with bolder, more individuated, spontaneous, and risky moves; second, these gestures are best captured by middle-range frequencies, to which human hearing is naturally more sensitive, as this is where finer sonic information resides; third, this detail includes information about the depth, velocity, inflection, tuning, and resonance of a given sound, elements associated with emotion, intention, and musicality; and fourth, this range is paradoxically captured in hi-fi by the lo-fi microphone, which, unlike its modern counterparts, does not suffer from mid-range distortion in order to be equally sensitive across a wide sonic spectrum.[38] This lo-fi paradigm then extends to the intimate recording spaces in which Miles works, where, via verbal and audio feedback, he keeps players focused on potentiality and divergence. The medium also engages listeners differently. By filling in the missing bandwidth data in an attempt to imagine how performances sounded live, audiences are transported into the recording space; by editing out the surplus bandwidth data in an attempt to imagine how their performance will sound in lo-fi, players are transported into audiences' homes.

Though at times jarringly reckless, surprisingly, these performances never fall apart; in fact, this wildness is often paradoxically cohesive. Consider the quintet's first movement, in Sound File 9.2a ▶ bars 122–54 (4:56–6:02). In an attempt to broaden tempo ahead of the extreme rushing to come, in bar 122 I play right-hand eighth notes early. This dislocates the piano from the viola, thereby adding to the wider asynchronous backdrop caused by the string players' variegated portamento strategies as they slide between intervals. Nothing here is played strictly together, but our death-defying rushing and raucous build-up of sound ensures a unified free-fall into bar 133. The cost of this cohesion, however, is being forced to begin the exposed material at bar 137 more quickly than I'd prefer. After the strings burst in like a speeding train at bar 145, I am desperately hanging on throughout the perilous leaps in bars 147–49, and yet we are still more or less together until bar 154. Note our disregard for modern notions of propriety in Brahmsian tone production: to cut through the clamor I play my right-hand sixteenth notes early at bar 150, but this only adds to the din. We also court disaster at the end of this movement. Rather than accelerating in bar 280 (11:00) toward a stable Tempo I as marked, we instead continue to rush, with the piano and quartet taking turns ramping tempo depending on who has the easiest material. I'm forced to drastically reduce bars 293–95 to keep up, but total breakdown never comes.

In the final push of the quintet's fourth movement, however, we allow our performance to alternate between moments of relative precision and extreme untidiness. Rather than establishing a stable tempo at Sound File 9.2d ▶ bar 342 (8:40), we again proceed to rush, only now via five very different triplet feels and acceleration strategies, resulting in patent asynchrony. The fleetingly cohesive effect of our snowballing tempo into bar 370, however, vanishes the moment we begin to rush anew, as does precision of intonation around bar 380, and proximity to the score in bars 387–91, where I'm forced to cut interstitial notes. But by bar 388 we are again back to playing relatively well together.

Contrast all this with our remarkably adroit playing during the equally terrifying accelerations in bars 394–423 and 423–66, despite the abrupt tempo change in bar 439, and despite more uncoordinated portamento strategies atop the piano's indistinct noodling from bar 445. Reduced playback speed reveals that even the section beginning in bar 467, with its built-in dislocations within the piano part, between the strings, and between piano and strings, is almost mathematically together—until the final two bars, that is, where players independently decide to either broaden or push tempo. It's not that we can't play well together; we simply allow our parts to organically dissociate and reunite, which is partly what gives this style its raw, emotional immediacy. This passivity, however, rests on each player's ability to suppress the instinct to detect and correct flaws the moment they occur.

Single players can also instigate divergence by making sudden, individualistic moves. As expected, this feels most intuitive in soloistic materials. Listen, for example, to how my extreme flexibility in the quintet's second movement, Sound File 9.2b ⏵ bars 21–23 and 26–27 (1:35–2:05), causes utter confusion and five-way asynchrony. In the first movement of the sonata, Sound File 9.3a ⏵ bars 50–66 (1:25–2:01), my heavy arpeggiation and dislocation, sudden lengthening and shortening of notes, and near-constant pushing and pulling of tempo, similarly force the violinist to second-guess the placement of his accompanimental asides. Sensing hesitation, I intensify rather than curtail these flexibilities, abruptly prolonging upper melodic notes in bars 58–59, before plunging into an even more wayward solo. That he knows when to come in at bar 66 is miraculous. In bars 137–44 (4:03–4:22), however, he is wholly unable to synchronize his accompanimental triplets with me, and at times we pull a full half-beat apart. But because he uses such a diffuse sound here, and because the soloist is the one imposing these flexibilities, the effect is loose and relaxed.

In the sonata's third movement, Sound File 9.3c ⏵ bars 49–77 (1:33–2:29), the piano now assumes a more dictatorial role in accompanimental materials. After taking the violinist by surprise in bars 54–58 with sudden slowing, arpeggiation, and elision, from bar 63 I reverse the typical soloist-accompanist dynamic by playing so loudly and restlessly, while reducing and rhythmically altering my materials, that I essentially drag the violinist along until I decide to slow dramatically in bar 74. This dynamic shifts at bar 90 (2:48), in a compelling example of how one player, now the violinist, can exert their conception of the music in a way that demands not surrender, but rather *amplified* freedom from their colleague. The cost of this, however, is another collective relinquishing of modern standards of competence and unanimity. Fleeting hive-mind moments, like our similar time feels in bars 96–98, seem accidental rather than engineered; moments of untogetherness convey the impression that we cannot even hear one another. This dynamic shifts once more in bar 112 (3:31), however, where my emphatic chord placement exerts the kind of leadership that demands subordination.

Subservience sometimes has undesirable consequences: listen, for example, to how my accompaniment at the outset of the quintet's fourth movement, in Sound File 9.2d ▶, bar 41 (1:41), is both too strict and not strict enough underneath the cello solo's subtle rhythmic nuances. When this material returns in bar 184 (4:57), a fluid tone creates a more forgiving cushion for these flexibilities. Returning to the quintet's first movement, in Sound File 9.2a ▶, bars 57–74 (2:16–2:57) we again get some awkward noodling in the piano underneath flexibly delivered string lines, but what's most offputting here is the nervous self-consciousness of both the violin ostinati in bars 59–60 and my triplets in bars 63–64. Tremolos or quicker ostinati would have been much better. This sense of uncertainty, followed by some hurriedly aggressive playing from the cello, first violin, and piano left-hand, is probably what causes the utter chaos throughout bars 69–74. Much the same happens when this material returns, beginning in bar 226 (8:32). The cellist in particular seems to struggle with accompanimental ostinati in this movement: compare, for example, the pleasing effect of his more diffuse delivery of these figures in bar 154 (5:59), with what happens when they move up an octave in bar 159. His frustration in the latter is palpable.

Interesting things happen, however, when the cellist adopts a more bullish approach. At the end of the quintet's second movement, in Sound File 9.2b ▶ bars 120–21 (7:48), listen to how he inexplicably rushes his accompanimental pizzicati while everyone else is slowing; asynchronous though the resultant effect might be, slower playback reveals that this is merely an illusion. There are also rushed cello pizzicati in the quintet's first movement, in Sound File 9.2a ▶ bar 51 (2:03), only now these convince me to abandon my more expansive approach, thereby mitigating any sense of untogetherness. Even more persuasive is the astonishing flexibility of his solo at bar 184 (7:00), which inspires me to rework my accompaniment into a countermelody. But despite the cellist's plasticity, my alterations, and the first violinist's understandable bewilderment, what sounds like extreme asynchrony is again revealed to be remarkably cohesive. That individual dominance can catalyze a collective impulse is further demonstrated shortly thereafter, in bar 193, where I begin to rush in order to regain control. This, however, seems to inspire the violist to further ramp tempo with his triplets, which in turn inspires the cellist to rush his pizzicati, all of which results in an unplanned, three-stage acceleration into my lightning-quick delivery of the material at bar 196.

The blurriness of distinctions between the intentional and unintentional, particularly where asynchrony is concerned, is revealed by comparing the first two Andantes of the sonata's second movement, in Sound File 9.3b ▶ bars 1–15 (0:00–1:15) and bars 72–93 (2:20–4:14). The first Andante largely hangs together thanks to a shared conception of how the music might unfold, some relatively straightforward violin playing, and a typical soloist-accompanist dynamic; I am continually arpeggiating and dislocating, adding a subterranean rumble of bass octave tremolos, and purposely playing around rather than with the violinist, but my role is supportive rather than antagonistic. In the second Andante, however, when the violinist unexpectedly draws out the sixteenth-note figure in bar 72, leading to our disjointed arrival on the downbeat of bar 73, we are faced with a decision: make the violin part more regular, or the piano part more passive. We do neither: the sense of calm I fight to maintain from bar 76 clashes with his restless melodic delivery; his playing becomes increasingly unpredictable while I refuse to reassure him that I am attempting to follow along; I even jettison my cushioning bass octave tremolos and magnify our discord by adding dislocated right-hand thumb lines. It is thus overly facile to call the more marked asynchrony of the second Andante unplanned: it may be less refined, but our unspoken decision to tolerate and amplify the discomfort of untogetherness is wholly deliberate.

This mindset can backfire, however. In the quintet's third movement, compare both iterations of Sound File 9.2c ▶ bars 150–57 (2:30–2:43 and 7:07–7:21). I play the first as written, but in the second I play right-hand materials as duplets, thereby dislocating myself from the strings' triplets, and leading to confusion and five-way asynchrony. Having found this effect pleasing rather than alarming, I then decide to similarly straighten out my materials in the second iteration of bars 186–89 (7:47–7:58) by playing them as eighth notes. But because the strings aren't playing triplets here, what this does is lend *more* cohesion to this passage as compared to how it sounds when played as written (3:09–3:20), and as compared to the chaotic two-against-three effect of the previous example. This style asks us to invite danger, but sometimes our best efforts go awry.

This mindset also has a built-in paradox: while it can often take a superhuman effort to create such divergence, the sense of potentiality and spontaneity we seek is undermined the moment this effort becomes audible. An example of this occurs at the end of the first movement of the sonata, from Sound File 9.3a ▶ bar 243 (7:23), where I begin dramatically under tempo before the violinist and I proceed to rush. Our varied acceleration strategies, however, lead to a two-way arrival at the climax in bar 250, after which our disjointed deceleration strategies, my dislocated inner right-hand notes, and the freeness of the violinist's delivery, all lead to a rather forced-sounding asynchrony until bar 258. Mysteriously, the same approach has a wholly different effect in the third movement, in Sound File 9.3c ▶ bars 123–41 (3:53–4:41). Despite breakneck speeding, total rhythmic ambiguity in the violin line, my drastic reduction and alteration of materials in bars 124–33, and some melodramatic slowing in bars 134–41, the effect is far more natural.

We thus have much to lose by *not* trying: like moments of remarkable unity, for example, where we seem to breathe as one. Listen to our inexplicably aligned time-feels in the first Vivace of the violin sonata's second movement, beginning in Sound File 9.3b ▶ bar 16 (1:12). There are also moments when the quartet persuades me to take bigger risks: in the quintet's fourth movement, for example, compare the pianistically treacherous passages in Sound File 9.2d ▶ bars 121–61 (3:39–4:21) and bars 279–320 (7:10–7:55). In the first, I try to curb the quartet's wild acceleration by holding back in bars 121–36, and by broadening both the upbeat-downbeat gestures in bars 141–45 and the accented chords in bars 152–58. The resultant asynchrony is not wholly convincing because my restraint has thwarted the passage's overall sweep. When this material returns, therefore, I allow myself to be carried along: my playing is less precise, but the effect is more exciting. If the cost of these moments is the occasional impression of derivativeness, so be it.

The muscularity of the string quartet comes startlingly to the fore in the quintet's second movement, where they consistently overpower the piano. This is another symptom of a soloistic mindset: when empowered to make bold moves, players begin fighting to be heard rather than to hear, resulting in massive accumulations of sound and an utter disregard for issues of balance. Pianists are usually the ones accused of dominating ensemble textures; in this style, and with this many string players, we don't stand a chance. In Sound File 9.2b ▶ bars 33–54 (2:21–3:26), listen to the somewhat aggressive tone of the second violin, viola, and cello lines, especially in bars 37–41, and the colossal build-up of sound they achieve until bar 55. Listen, too, to how the piano's vulnerable *pianissimo* tone around bar 61 (3:48) is drowned out by the quartet's rather literal interpretation of their *forte* indications, in what might be the only element of this performance that is closer to the score than what is typically heard today. And while our group sound in bars 103–18 (6:57–7:54) is riotous, bordering on shrill, this too is instigated by the strings.

This shift away from modern conceptions of playing well with others is facilitated at every turn by our chosen recording medium. At once immediate and distancing, stark and opaque, the lo-fi microphone inspires approaches ranging from pigheadedness to vulnerability, as so poignantly captured by the Sostenuto section of the quintet's fourth movement, in Sound File 9.2d ▶ bars 1–40 (0:00–1:44). Here, five individual stylistic dialects can be heard overlapping, deviating and merging in real time. No attempt is made to coordinate portamenti or rhythmic alterations, resulting in beat-to-beat dislocations; ambiguity of pulse and highly variegated tempo modification strategies lead to wide five-way asynchronies at key climactic moments. But what is most striking here is how this performance swims, searches, settles, and then floats away once more—that fleeting, divergent sense of potentiality I had hoped to achieve. The breathy, wavering quality of the string playing also conveys both a sense of trust and affection, as well as the domestic environs in which these recordings were made, with players and sound engineer alike crowded around a microphone that does not hear them the way they hear themselves.

Implications

In November 2020 this quartet performed in early-recorded style on a Dutch television program called *Podium Witteman*. The comments left by disgruntled viewers on the show's Facebook page demonstrate the extent to which the public has absorbed the rules of playing well together: "extremely ugly... as if it were the music from a horror film"; "very sloppily played... uneven in tempo and first violin very incorrect"; "bombastic, disappointing, too bad."[39] While it is heartening to have achieved a level of differentiation detectable by layperson and connoisseur alike, it doesn't take much imagination to guess how these viewers might receive the recordings discussed above. It is only hoped that such performances begin pointing to forms of musical beauty beyond competence and unanimity; skills that better capture the qualities we seek in chamber performances; and playing that reveals modern norms as a cautious sliver of what musicians are actually capable of, and of how these works can sound.

It is also hoped that this far less stable and neutral style of playing demonstrates the contingency of existing scholarship concerning questions of who Brahms was. Just as Brahms's Sonata for Violin and Piano in A Major, Op. 100, and the Piano Quintet in F Minor, Op. 34, can unfold in unpredictable, multifarious ways, so too can scholarly inquiries invite ambiguity, discord, and transformation. If rethinking Brahms involves playing his music differently, then playing differently means fostering more antagonistic ecosystems of thought and practice in this field—a dialogue whose genuineness might best be tested by the vulnerability and risk of not playing well with others. A move has been made, without knowing whether the other will reciprocate; a path has been chosen, without knowing where it might lead.

PART III
ANALYTICAL PERSPECTIVES

Chapter 10

First-Theme Syntax in Brahms's Sonata Forms

Julian Horton

Brahms and the New *Formenlehre*

James Webster's "The General and the Particular in Brahms's Sonata Forms" is notable not least for the rigorously empirical attitude toward the study of Brahms's mature sonata practices that it advocates. Webster adopts a comparative statistical approach, examining in detail the proportions of Brahms's sonata forms, beginning with the Op. 51 string quartets. For Webster, this methodology's value is that it offers "the possibility of a more or less objective description of the proportions and formal construction in any repertory of sonata-form movements, in a manner which permits convenient and meaningful comparison with any other repertory." Concluding that "the question of what Brahms accepted as "norms" or principles in writing sonata form movements seems . . . to have been taken too much for granted," Webster imagines "a comprehensive and highly differentiated morphological history of the sonata form," toward which his study constitutes "the first step."[1]

Although corpus-based approaches to the theory and analysis of form have flourished since Webster voiced this aspiration, important aspects of Brahms's sonata forms still await close empirical scrutiny.[2] Webster, for instance, applied his method to whole-movement forms and was more concerned with large-scale and inter-thematic relationships than with the details of Brahms's thematic construction. Research addressing Brahms's thematic syntax is of course plentiful; the work of Peter H. Smith on subject-answer designs and divisional overlap, Ryan McClelland on instability in Brahms's first themes, and Siegfried Kross on theme and formal process furnish prominent examples.[3] For the most part, however, these studies facilitate the analysis of formal strategies, rather than offering a strict empirical conspectus of intra-thematic habits. Furthermore, Webster's essay broaches the question of how the later sonata forms relate to the music up to 1868 only in passing. Empirical research spanning Brahms's oeuvre has the potential to shed systematic light on the ways in which his thematic designs change over a broader timespan.[4]

Responding to these lacunae, this essay reports on a corpus study of first themes in the first movements of Brahms's sonata-type works from Op. 1

Julian Horton, *First-Theme Syntax in Brahms's Sonata Forms* In: *Rethinking Brahms*. Edited by: Nicole Grimes and Reuben Phillips, Oxford University Press. © Oxford University Press 2022.
DOI: 10.1093/oso/9780197541739.003.0011

to Op. 120, No. 2. My aim is, in part, to provide a comprehensive picture of Brahms's first-theme syntax and thereby both to complement Webster's project, by reproducing its aims at the intra-thematic level, and to expand on it, by enfolding Brahms's entire oeuvre. At the same time, my aspirations range more widely because I use Brahms to instantiate a theoretical mentality, which might underpin the theory of Romantic form broadly conceived. In this respect, I offer a contribution to Romantic *Formenlehre*, which takes a particular stance in a live field of debate, central to which is the question of how best to position Romantic sonatas in relation to Viennese classicism. Theorists including James Hepokoski, Warren Darcy, Janet Schmalfeldt, Steven Vande Moortele, Seth Monahan, Peter H. Smith, Andrew Davis, Benedict Taylor, and myself have variously grappled with the looming fact that our orientating formal theories are derived overwhelmingly from the practices of Haydn, Mozart, and Beethoven.[5] The core issue, which Vande Moortele has styled as a tension between "negative" and "positive" approaches, is whether these theories should continue to be normative as we enter the nineteenth century.[6]

To answer this question affirmatively is to assume that nineteenth-century forms remain indentured to a set of eighteenth-century conventions, no matter how far composers stray from them in practice. This position approaches a definition of the concept of deformation advocated by Hepokoski, Darcy, Monahan, and others. As Hepokoski and Darcy explain it, deformation is "a technical term, referring to a striking way of stretching or overriding a norm."[7] In classical sonatas, deformations arise as counter-generic decisions: that is, as decisions that do not abide by the system of defaults that defines the "genre sonata form." Post-classical departures from classical orthodoxy instead reflect that orthodoxy by misreading ("deforming") it, thereby generating a dialogue between classical norms and Romantic deviations that may subsequently become normative, as composers increasingly select them as "lower-level defaults."[8] The classical "system," however, continues to orientate analysis, an anchorage Hepokoski and Darcy express in their insistence that "In addition to furnishing a new mode of analysis for the late-eighteenth-century instrumental repertory, [sonata theory] also provides a foundation for considering works from the decades to come—late Beethoven, Schubert, Weber, Mendelssohn, Liszt, Brahms, Bruckner, Strauss, Mahler, the 'nationalist composers,'" because classical sonata norms "remained in place as regulative ideas throughout the nineteenth century, even as the whole sonata-form genre . . . was continuously updated, altered and further personalized with unforeseen accretions, startling innovations, and more radical deformations."[9]

The alternative, which has been explored by theorists working in the traditions of William Caplin's form-functional theory, is to account for the particularity of nineteenth-century practice by stressing those features that render it distinctively post-classical. Vande Moortele, for example, seeks to enlarge upon Hepokoski and Darcy's concept of dialogic form, by situating classical precedents as "only one strand in a complex web of concurrent, partially overlapping, and at times contradictory dialogues" in which his chosen genre—the Romantic overture—is embedded. Vande Moortele summarily argues that "the monolithic model of a dialogue between a specific work (or group of works) and an abstract (composer- and work-transcendent) norm needs to be diversified in order to accommodate alternative modes of dialogue."[10] Grounding her work more thoroughly in the history of ideas, Schmalfeldt contrastingly explains the processual features of Romantic forms—and specifically the phenomenon of form-functional becoming, in which the formal function of material transforms retrospectively in light of dialectical reversals—as instantiations of a turn of mind in the orbit of Hegel's philosophy.[11] These approaches still reference eighteenth-century conventions, but they alleviate the burden of misprision that deformation imposes, by placing a weaker emphasis on departures from a system of classical norms.

My own work stresses *syntactic change* as a key to formal innovation: I maintain that any address on a composer's formal habits requires a detailed map of their syntactic predilections before large-scale strategies can be grasped or interpreted.[12] Brahms's departures from classical formal convention consequently need to be understood in relation to his material's syntactic protocols, because any formal event is necessarily implicated in a set of syntactically conditioned continuation decisions. A first-theme recapitulation, for example, demands explanation as a response to that theme's expositional properties before we seek to explain it in dialogue with a classical norm. Any sonata's strategic specificity is in large part a product of the syntactic interactions—what I call the work's *form-functional pathways*—which convey its design and resultant impression of "if . . . then" causal logic.[13] In the terms advocated by Hepokoski, the first-theme tonic return that initiates the development in the Fourth Symphony's first movement may very well be classified as a "Brahmsian deformation," which distinguishes it from the norms of the classical sonata.[14] But a failure to relate this event to the theme's expositional syntax cannot be compensated by pointing to a classical model from which it deviates, because the model is not a syntactic characteristic of the movement in hand.

I put this mentality into practice by reporting on a corpus study of thirty-six instrumental first movements by Brahms, which encompasses all sonata-type first movements in his instrumental oeuvre, with two omissions: the Academic Festival Overture Op. 80, which I regard as a *pot-pourri* overture that becomes a sonata in its latter stages, and which therefore doesn't have a clearly defined expositional first theme to classify; and the Horn Trio Op. 40, the first movement of which is not in sonata form. The study is empirical in the first instance and therefore only analytical in a limited sense. Its goals are first, to develop a thematic typology for Brahms; second, to enable empirically grounded assertions about Brahms's intra-thematic tactics; and third, to offer a case study of one set of formal pathways in Brahms's music, by tracing the relationships between initiating and cadential functions across the corpus.

I employ William Caplin's taxonomy of classical functions where pertinent, in partnership with modifications proposed by Schmalfeldt, Vande Moortele, and myself, and some sonata-theoretical terminology. There are of course also intersections with the analytical literature on Brahms, especially the work of Walter Frisch, Peter Smith, and Ryan McClelland, with which I engage on a case-by-case basis. Some of my terminology requires brief explanation:

1. I have loosened Caplin's prohibition on periods having similar medial and final cadences. I additionally designate as periods themes possessing strong periodic rhetoric but similar antecedent and consequent cadences; in those cases, the creation of a separate formal type seems unnecessary.
2. Hybrid themes are distinguished from compounds by the nesting of functions: hybrids employ the essential ingredients of Caplin's taxonomy in novel ways; compounds assemble larger themes from nested theme types, engaging in a kind of formal expansion I call "proliferation."[15]
3. I designate themes as periodic even if their antecedent is organized as a sentence, in order to distinguish recognizably periodic designs from larger compound formations.
4. I designate first themes as "A," and any materially contrasted subdivisions with qualifying integers (A1, A2, etc.). This means that a contrasting middle in a ternary theme is called A2. In cases where A2 functions as a contrasting middle, I append the label CM.
5. I define an evaded cadence, following Caplin, as any cadential progression leading on to a new phrase before the dominant has been allowed sufficiently to resolve to its tonic.[16]
6. I employ Schmalfeldt's open arrow "⇒" to represent "becoming," or the transformation of one function into another. As we'll see, there are only two thematic categories in which this appears with any regularity.
7. Finally, there is one sub-category of sentence, the presentation phrase of which has periodic properties, which Vande Moortele has called a "sentence with periodic presentation," designated as "spp" in the tables. I acknowledge that this could also be defined as a hybrid theme.[17]

Although my methodology owes much to the spirit of Webster's study, it is different in one key respect. Webster is concerned with *continuous* variables: his primary interest is in the relative proportions of the large-scale and inter-thematic functions of Brahms's sonata forms, measured in terms of bar length. This allows Webster to make statements about mean values and normative practices within standard deviation because his data can be expressed as a range of numerical values. My study, in contrast, is concerned with *discrete* variables: I am interested in syntactic categories—formal functions and theme types—which cannot be represented on a numerical continuum. For this reason, I make no claims about *normativity*, only about *prevalence*. Half cadences are a prevalent feature of Brahms's syntax; but the half cadence is a discrete category, and it would be empirically irresponsible to define it as a norm on the basis of prevalence.

Brahms and First-Theme Syntax

Table 10.1 attempts a typology of Brahms's first themes. One work—the Double Concerto Op. 102—appears twice, because the first theme has a distinct functional identity in Ritornello 1 (R1) and Solo 1 (S1). In the other concerti, this isn't really the case: in the Violin Concerto, Op. 77, the soloist's extended preface leads to a variant of R1 A's theme type, and this is essentially true of the Opp. 15 and 83 piano concertos as well, admittedly in different ways: Op. 15 comprises a leisurely new S1 preface, which is essentially periodic, but which in the end merges with R1's theme; in Op. 83, S1 supplies a vastly expanded variant of the theme that the soloist and orchestra collaboratively present at the work's opening.

The table provokes five general observations. First, in his entire oeuvre, Brahms employs only five stable types; category 5b, which I have titled "other," comprises four *sui generis* examples, to which I will return later. Second,

Table 10.1 Categorization by Type

Type	1. Period	2. Sentence	3. Grand antecedent +dissolving consequent	4. Hybrid	5. Compound 5a. Small ternary	5b. Other
Opus	1	77	11	2	5	8
	26	83	98	15	16	68
	34	90	100	18	25	81
	60	102 (R1)	120/2	51/2	36	114
		108		67	38	
		111		73	51/1	
				99	78	
				101	87	
				102 (S1)	88	
				115	120/1	
Total	4	6	4	10	10	4

Brahms does not favor straightforward classical conventions. Simple periods and sentences are not common; as we shall see, none of the four periods and few of the six sentences in the corpus relate unproblematically to classical precedents. Third, radical departures from classical convention—that is to say, themes having no obvious anchorage in some classical paradigm—are also a minority; and even then, their novelty resides in the unusual concatenation of functions rather than in the functions themselves. Fourth, Brahms's overwhelming preference is for hybrid or compound themes (twenty out of thirty-eight examples). Fifth, some types have fairly even chronological distribution (e.g., small-ternary themes, to which Brahms returned across his career from Op. 5 to Op. 120), while others do not (type 2, e.g., of which there are no examples before Op. 77; or type 3, which Brahms neglected between 1858 and 1884).

The relative dearth of simple sentences is especially notable. Given its absolute centrality to classical sonata syntax and the developmental concept of theme associated with Beethoven, the fact that Brahms writes not a single sentential first theme before 1878 is striking (although, as I'll show soon, sentential design doesn't disappear in Brahms, but migrates into other theme types). Moreover, although there are six type-2 entries in Table 10.2, very few of them simplistically resemble classical sentences. The closest we get is the Third Symphony, Op. 90, shown in Example 10.1. Discounting the two-bar anacrusis—which as Carl Dahlhaus showed is thematically critical, supplying as it does the theme's bassline and much else besides (see the brackets in the example)—bars 3–15 display a pretty clear sentential design, rounded with an elided perfect authentic cadence (PAC).[18] On the other hand, consider Example 10.2, which shows the first theme of Op. 77. The overall division into presentation, continuation, and cadence is clear, but both statement and response end cadentially, which lends bars 1–17 a periodic character. Following Vande Moortele, we could therefore call this a sentence with periodic presentation, except to say that both medial and final cadences are half-cadential, which feature, according to Caplin, precludes periodic classification (although, as I've indicated above, we can imagine a nineteenth-century period in which this is permissible).[19]

Table 10.2 Type 5a Themes: Sub-categories

	Complete	Incomplete (dissolving reprise)
Opus	5	16
	25	38
	36	51/1
	88	78
	120/1	87

Example 10.1 Brahms, Symphony No. 3, Op. 90, i, first theme.

Example 10.2 Brahms, Violin Concerto, Op. 77, i, R1 first theme.

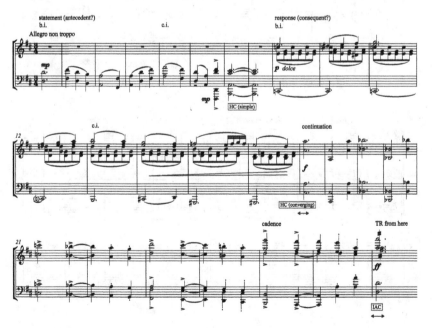

Brahms's periods are no less evasive. All four periodic themes are essentially sentential—both antecedent and consequent are sentences—meaning that Brahms never writes a periodic theme with a straightforward basic idea-contrasting idea antecedent design. The most problematic is the Op. 60 Piano Quartet, given in Example 10.3. Bars 1–31 self-evidently divide in two, given the recall of bar 1 in bar 11 after a half cadence, which posits bars 1–10 as an antecedent. After much phrase expansion, however, the consequent arrives, somewhat problematically, at bar 27 on a half cadence as well (recall again Caplin's injunction against periodic cadential similarity). This issue might be circumvented by stretching the consequent cadence to include the decisive V–i progression in bars 31–32, turning bars 27–32 into a covered PAC, although the attenuated dominant and implied E minor $^6_4$ chord in bars 28–30 strain the credibility of this reading. The consequent's expansion also generates decidedly

Example 10.3 Brahms, Piano Quartet No. 3, Op. 60, i, first theme.

First-Theme Syntax in Brahms's Sonata Forms 203

Example 10.3 Continued

unclassical proportions: a ten-bar antecedent yields to a seventeen-bar consequent with a four-bar extension.

These expansion techniques merit closer attention. As the overlay in Example 10.3 explains, we can with some license see both antecedent and consequent as a sentence prefaced by a thematic introduction, adapting Caplin's term.[20] The consequent, however, expands every aspect of the antecedent: the one-bar basic idea is doubled in size, so that the antecedent's two-bar basic idea + repetition mushrooms into a four-bar statement and response; and the antecedent continuation + cadence, which occupies six bars, inflates to eleven bars, thanks to the failure of bar 21's half cadence to establish closure. A third reading might fold bars 32–41[1] into the first theme as well, given that they comprise a variant of the antecedent, albeit one occurring entirely over a tonic pedal,

Example 10.4 Brahms, Piano Sonata No. 1, Op. 1, i, first theme.

producing a tripartite form. At this point, however, we leave the territory of current formal theory entirely, and Op. 60 transfers to category 5b.

Opus 60's theme is partly explicable as an intertextual gloss on the Piano Sonata Op. 1, shown in Example 10.4, a connection amplified by Op. 60's distended genesis, which stretches back to within two years of Op. 1's completion. Opus 60 depresses Op. 1's mode from C major to C minor, but both begin their consequent on ♭VII, perhaps reflecting the first movement of Beethoven's "Waldstein" Sonata as a common source of inspiration, which is also in C and supplies a I–V sentential statement with a ♭VII–IV response. Opp. 1 and 60, moreover, both begin with sentential periods, in which the antecedent continuation is enlarged in the consequent. Op. 1's antecedent ends with a compressed continuation + half cadence, the dominant of which is then prolonged over two bars. The consequent continuation adds two bars to this design, generating a dominant prolonged by elaborative upper and lower neighbor notes, before the PAC prevails in bars 16–17[1].

Hybridizations of classical functions (type 4) and expansive compound themes (type 5) are far more common and are regular features of the corpus. The Sonata Op. 2 affords an interesting early instance of hybridization (Example 10.5). This is almost a sentential period, except to say that there is no medial cadence; instead, the antecedent continuation phrase consists of a

Example 10.5 Brahms, Piano Sonata No. 2, Op. 2, i, first theme.

six-bar standing on V. The consequent does possess a cadence (a Phrygian half cadence), which follows a continuation that single-mindedly focuses on the liquidation of the *Hauptmotiv*'s second element. The syntax here plays two related games with convention. The antecedent's standing on V is a formula more commonly associated with framing functions (introductions) or what I would term linking functions (transitions; retransitions), which means that the antecedent's presentational status is immediately challenged by a form-functional cuckoo in the nest, which upsets our perception that bars 1–2 initiate a theme and transfers that burden onto bar 9, where the dominant resolves. In turn, the consequent's half cadence seems more at home in an antecedent phrase: we might imagine a counterfactual scenario, in which bars 9–15 are followed with a consequent closed with a PAC.

Example 10.6 contrasts this with a hybrid from the end of Brahms's career—the Clarinet Quintet Op. 115—which offers one of the most striking examples of Brahmsian proliferation. The theme is essentially a very large sentence, but Brahms incorporates smaller structures within it, which render the picture more complex. The relationship between the material of bars 1–2 and 6–9, for instance, implies a kind of statement-response design, albeit one in which differing conclusions are drawn from the same starting point at lower intrathematic levels. Bars 1–5 comprise an irregular compound basic idea, in which both the basic idea (b.i.) and contrasting idea (c.i.) are themselves miniature statement-response structures, as Example 10.6 clarifies, the latter given a one-bar extension, while the quartet pause over III to admit the clarinet's entry. Bars

Example 10.6 Brahms, Clarinet Quintet, Op. 115, i, first theme.

6–9 eliminate the contrasting idea, but by way of compensation double the size of the basic idea, creating a statement-response design that stretches the basic idea over two bars. Brahms moves from this through a continuation at bar 14 to a cadential phrase, in which the hoped-for PAC is once treated evasively and once deceptively before resolving categorically to demarcate the transition.

First-Theme Syntax in Brahms's Sonata Forms 207

More consistent evidence of proliferation is offered by Brahms's type-5 themes. The small ternary themes (type 5a) fall clearly into two sub-categories, classified in Table 10.2: complete ternary designs; and incomplete designs, in which the reprise dissolves into, or rather "becomes" the transition. Although one instance—the String Sextet Op. 36—is expansive on an almost Brucknerian scale, the ternary themes are mostly relatively compact. The most unequivocally tight-knit of the type-5a themes is that of the String Quintet Op. 88, shown in Example 10.7. A1 and A1[1] are periods, although the location of the reprise is blurred thanks to the technique of divisional overlap variously explored by Peter H. Smith and Carissa Reddick: the tonal reprise begins unequivocally in the middle of bar 15 with the beat-3 arrival on F; but this coincides with the beginning of the contrasting idea, not the basic idea, an elaboration of which has been in progress since bar 14.[21] And this variation is in turn emergent from the liquidatory process that characterizes the end of the contrasting middle,

Example 10.7 Brahms, String Quintet No. 1, Op. 88, i, first theme.

which, following a four-bar statement-response design, jettisons the first half of the basic idea from bar 13.

Type 5a themes with dissolving reprise are inevitably more loosely organized, as the first theme of the Piano Trio Op. 87, given as Example 10.8, makes

Example 10.8 Brahms, Piano Trio No. 2, Op. 87, i, first theme.

Example 10.8 Continued

apparent. The A1 section opens with a three-bar basic idea succeeded by two continuation phrases. In the first, a model is established (bars 4–5), sequenced (bars 6–7), and fragmented (bars 8–12). This process, however, produces no cadence; the liquidation of the descending octave motive in bars 8–12, labeled "x" in Example 10.8, instead culminates on I^6 at the start of bar 13. Brahms consequently tries again: bars 13–14 introduce a model, which is twice sequenced in bars 15–18, before A1 is closed with a reinterpreted half cadence in bars 19–21^1. Bars 21–32 furnish a contrasting middle (A2), which essentially follows a sentential scheme (statement and repetition in bars 21–24; model-sequence-fragmentation in bars 25–28; PAC in bars 29–33^1), although two factors complicate this interpretation. First, the counterpoint in bars 21–24 overlaps statement and repetition with an additional, imitative bass entry, creating two stretti between soprano and bass. Second, the functional identity of the cadential phrase is not straightforward. On the one hand, it exhibits obvious harmonic markers of a PAC, embedding an augmented sixth within a cadential $^6_4$, which we could interpret as ultimately resolved with the I chord with which A1^1 commences. On the other hand, A2 altogether suggests the dominant prolongation or emphasis that Caplin associates with classical contrasting-middle sections, which infrequently produces a PAC and more likely culminates in a dominant arrival or half cadence.[22] A1^1 then arrives unambiguously in bar 33, but from bar 37 A1's original continuation phrase is replaced by a new sequential ascent, from which point correspondence with A1 is broken and A1^1 becomes the transition (TR).

Symphony No. 4, Op. 98 (Example 10.9), supplies a subtle but representative example of type 3. Hepokoski and Darcy define the grand antecedent as "a lengthy, often multi-modular antecedent phrase," which is often sentential; they cite Mozart's last two symphonies, but it also has a symphonic pedigree in the first movements of Beethoven's Third and Seventh symphonies.[23] Opus 98's antecedent accordingly comprises an expansive sentence, which discloses an initial ambiguity in the relationship between presentation and continuation phrases, captured by the two readings overlaid in Example 10.9. Reading 1 understands bars 1–4 as a statement and response, meaning that bar 5 initiates the continuation by constructing a model-sequence progression out of the basic idea, which then fragments in the following bars. Reading 2 posits bars 1–8 as a compound statement-response phrase: the statement-response design in 1–4 comprises a statement at the next intra-thematic level; and the model-sequence progression in 5–8 is therefore reinterpreted as a second statement-response, which altogether supplies a response phrase to bars 1–4. The dissolving consequent begins in turn in elision with the antecedent's covered PAC at bar 19 and departs from its model into the transition at bar 27 in correspondence with bar 9.

Finally, four works—Opp. 8, 68, 81, and 114—depart entirely from classical typology. The First Symphony, Op. 68, and the "Tragic" Overture, Op. 81, share the tactic of building a compound theme by combining a sentence and a period. Op. 81 is shown in Example 10.10. The theme comprises a sentential period (A1) followed by a sentence (A2), both of which evidence proliferation. The antecedent, for example, reaches its cadence in bar 10, but Brahms

First-Theme Syntax in Brahms's Sonata Forms

Example 10.9 Brahms, Symphony No. 4, Op. 98, i, first theme.

appends a two-bar extension, which reinterprets the antecedent's V:PAC as a half cadence (HC). These bars are more than a dominant prolongation, however: rather, they occupy the phrase location of bars 1–2, which initially function as a thematic introduction. In effect, the extension folds the initial two bars into the theme's design, generating a brief region of becoming, which now annexes an extra two bars to the statement, returning in bar 12[1]. As Example

Example 10.10 Brahms, Tragic Overture, Op. 81, first theme.

10.10 shows, the introduction is more explicitly incorporated into the theme group at the end of the consequent, where it recurs as the gestural basis of the closing PAC. The sentence evidences cadential expansion: the cadential phrase in bars 29–33 closes with an imperfect authentic cadence (IAC); this is then repeated and expanded in bars 33–41 thanks to a two-bar deviation toward D♭, before the theme is closed with an emphatic PAC.

The first theme in the Allegro of Op. 68 is similarly conceived, except that it reverses the order of period and sentence; Opp. 8 and 114 are however *sui generis*. Op. 8 is in essence a small-ternary theme, but the contrasting middle and reprise are repeated, creating an A1–A2–A1^1–A2^1–A1^2 design, the final section of which has its ultimate cadence modified from authentic to plagal. The Clarinet Trio, Op. 114, is a variant of type 3: its grand antecedent is however bipartite: A1 comprises a c.b.i. plus an expanded response over a tonic pedal; A2 consists of a statement-response-fragmentation design; and neither unit has a proper cadence. Both A1 and A2 are reprised: the former is supplied with a reinterpreted HC; the latter dissolves into TR.

Form-Functional Pathways: Initiation and Cadence

In addition to this overarching typology, the corpus can be mined for more specific data, allowing us to build up a syntactic map of Brahms's thematic practice. To this end, Tables 10.3–10.6 focus on the various ways in which Brahms begins and ends his themes, in order both to gain a general understanding of his strategies of initiation and closure, and to sketch the form-functional pathways that they delimit, focusing particularly on emergent, common partnerships between types of initiating function and cadence.

Table 10.3 isolates initiating functions: that is, the ways in which Brahms begins his themes. Discounting the presence of introductions, there are four categories of initiating function in the corpus: basic ideas (b.i.); statement-response; compound basic ideas (c.b.i.), which is to say, a basic idea and a contrasting idea exhibiting no cadence; and antecedents, that is to say, compound basic ideas possessing a terminal cadence. These functions, it should be stressed, are independent of thematic type: an antecedent might form the first half of a simple period, the statement of a sentence with periodic presentation, the A1 section of a small-ternary theme, or the first half of a periodic A1 section of a small ternary theme, and so forth. In other words, Table 10.3 collates the lowest-level intra-thematic functions, which begin all of the themes classified.

The table also reveals the theme types that these functions initiate. It is immediately clear that Brahms overwhelmingly favors statement-response designs (eighteen out of thirty-eight themes), a preference that moreover spans all of the thematic types (specifically: three type 1, five type 2, two type 3, four type 4, two type 5a, and two type 5b). Self-evidently, Brahms's sentences begin

Table 10.3 Initiating Functions

Type:	Basic idea: Context:		Statement-response:	Context:	Compound basic idea:	Context:	Antecedent:	Context:
Opus:	34	type-1 sentential ant.	1	type 1 sentential ant.	36	type 5a A1	16	type 5a A1
	51/1	type 5a A1	2	type 4	67	type 4	18	type 4
	51/2	type 4	5	type 5a sentential A1	73	type 4	25	type 5a A1
	78	type 5a A1	8	type 5b hybrid A1	99	type 4	38	type 5a A1
	87	type 5a A1	11	type 3 antecedent (hybrid)	100	type 3 (c.b.i. as statement)	68	type 5b A1 (spp)
	120/2	type 3 gr. ant. (hybrid)	15	type 4	102 (S1)	type 4 (c.b.i. as statement)	77	type 2 (spp)
			26	type-1 sentential antecedent	114	type 5b A1	88	type 5a A1
			60	type-1 sentential antecedent				
			81	type 5b sentential A1				
			83	type 2 (incomplete)				
			90	type 2				
			98	type 3 gr. ant.				
			101	type 4				
			102 (R1)	type 2 (incomplete)				
			108	type 2				
			111	type 2				
			115	type 4 (b.i. of c.b.i. as statement)				
			120/1	type 5a A1				
Total:	6		18		7		7	

with statement-response forms; but what is striking is the extent to which this opening gambit infuses all the other theme types. A basic feature of his first-theme style is therefore the habit of migrating the initiating function that would commonly begin a sentence into other theme types. Brahms, we might argue, marginalizes the pure sentence because he is more interested in beginning other types with sentence-like functions.

The other initiating functions are minority interests distributed evenly across the corpus and more or less across the types. One obvious point is that Brahms composes seven straightforward antecedents, but none of them initiates a period. Rather, Brahms's antecedents always initiate compound, hybrid or sentential themes. Another point is that he is as likely to begin a theme with a basic idea and proceed straight to a continuation as he is to begin with a compound basic idea; and neither of these decisions is type-specific. In two cases, the Op. 100 Violin Sonata and the Op. 102 Double Concerto (S1), the c.b.i. forms the basic idea of a larger sentential design (this corresponding to Caplin's compound sentence), although in Op. 100 this initiates a grand antecedent, and in Op. 102 a hybrid-type theme.

Looking at the other end of Brahms's themes, Table 10.4 summarizes his cadential usage. It identifies seven cadence types across the corpus, specifying the work in which they occur, the thematic type and context, and introducing nuance where necessary (e.g., the kind of half cadence, or whether or not a PAC elides with its successor function). I have split the half cadences into two categories, depending on whether they close with an ultimate dominant, or else comprise an authentic cadence, which is reinterpreted as a half cadence.[24] In four special cases—Opp. 11, 15, 83, and 102 (R1)—no cadence occurs at all, for reasons that are context-specific and too complex to consider in any depth here. In situations where a theme type discloses only one cadential function (a sentence, for instance), I have described this as an end function, to avoid the cumbersome and tautological "cadential cadence."

Even at this stage, one point is clear, which is Brahms's overwhelming preference for half cadences. A large number, thirty-eight of the sixty-eight cadences identified, are half cadences, overshadowing the more modest community of twenty-two PACs and completely eclipsing IACs, deceptive, evaded, and plagal cadences, which are a minority property of Brahms's first-theme syntax. More substantive points emerge when we correlate this data with functional location, as Table 10.5 does. Reading from left to right gives a sense of how many of each cadence inhabits a given function; reading from top to bottom reveals the distribution of cadences across the functions. The antecedents are unproblematic, closing with HCs or IACs in both periodic and non-periodic contexts. The consequents contrastingly expose how problematic Brahms's periods are. Only one type-1 theme ends with a PAC (Op. 1), and of the other three, one (Op. 26) contrasts half cadences in different keys, and two (Opp. 34 and 60) have strong periodic rhetoric but employ contrasting half cadences in the same key. The

Table 10.4 Cadential Usage

Cadence	Opus	Type	Context	Total
PAC	1	1	consequent	
	8	5b	1. A1 end function; 2. A1¹ end function	
	18	4	end function	
	25	5a	1. A1 consequent; 2. A1¹ consequent (elided)	
	51/2	4	end function	
	67	4	end function (elided)	
	68	5b	1. A1 end function; 2. A2 consequent	
	73	4	end function (elided)	
	81	5b	1. A1 consequent; 2. A2 cadential (final cadence)	
	87	5b	A2 cadential (elided)	
	88	5a	1. A1 consequent (III:PAC); 2. A1¹ consequent (I:PAC)	
	90	2	end function (elided)	
	98	3	grand sentential antecedent end function (elided)	
	101	4	end function (elided)	
	102 (S1)	2	end function (elided)	
	111	2	end function (elided)	
	115	4	end function (final cadence; elided)	22
HC	1	1	antecedent (Phrygian)	
	2	2	end function (Phrygian)	
	5	5a	1. A1 end function (Phrygian); 2. A2 antecedent (v: simple); 3. A1¹ (Phrygian)	
	16	5a	1. A1 antecedent (Phrygian); 2. A1 consequent (simple)	
	18	4	antecedent (converging)	
	25	5a	1. A1 antecedent (simple); 2. A2 end function (converging III:HC)	
	26	1	consequent (vi:Phrygian)	
	34	1	1. antecedent (simple); 2. consequent?	
	36	5a	A2 end function (converging)	
	51/1	5a	1. A1 end function (simple); 2. A2 end function (♭vii:converging!)	
	60	1	1. antecedent (simple); 2. consequent (converging)	
	68	5b	A1 statement (converging)	
	77	2	1. statement (simple); 2. response (converging)	
	99	4	end function (19th-c.)	

First-Theme Syntax in Brahms's Sonata Forms

Table 10.4 Continued

Cadence	Opus	Type	Context	Total
	100	3	grand antecedent (sentential) end function (19th-c.)	
	120/1	5a	1. A1 end function (simple); 2. A1¹ end function (simple)	
	120/2	3	grand antecedent (hybrid) end function (simple)	26
HC (reinterpreted)	5	5a	A2 consequent (from V:PAC)	
	8	5b	A2 end function (from V:PAC)	
	26	1	antecedent (V:PAC⇒19th-c.)	
	38	5a	A1 end function (from V:PAC)	
	68	5b	A1 response (from V:PAC)	
	78	5a	A1 end function (V:PAC⇒19th-c.)	
	81	5b	A1 antecedent	
	87	5a	A1 end function (from V:PAC)	
	88		1. A1 antecedent (from V:IAC); 2. A1¹ antecedent (from V:IAC)	
	108	2	end function (from V:PAC)	
	114	5b	A1¹ (from V:PAC)	12
IAC	36	5a	A1 consequent	
	68	5b	A2 antecedent	
	77	2	end function (elided)	
	81	5b	A2 cadential (first time)	4
Deceptive	115	4	end function (second time)	1
Evaded	67	4	end function (first time)	
	115	4	end function (first time)	2
Plagal	8	5b	A1² end function	1
No cadence	11	3	—	
	15	2	—	
	83	2	—	
	102 (R1)	2	—	4

consequent cadence of the Piano Quintet, Op. 34, shown in Example 10.11, is especially troublesome. I have opted to class this as a species of half cadence, which assumes that V in bar 22 functions as an ultimate dominant and the tonic in bar 23 initiates a new progression. But as the example shows, a case might also be made for an elided IAC or perhaps evaded cadence (given the 6–5 motion in the soprano above î), if we think that the downbeat of bar 23 is integral to a definition of the cadential progression. The cadence's starting point is also unclear. The Parallel (P) and Leittonwechsel (L) transformations in bar 20 convert the Neapolitan sixth into its parallel enharmonic minor (G♭

Table 10.5 Cadential Usage by Function

	PAC	HC	HC reinterpreted	IAC	Deceptive	Evaded	Plagal	Total:
Antecedent (type 1)	—	Op. 1 Op. 34 Op. 60	Op. 26	—	—	—	—	4
Antecedent (other)	—	Op. 5 (A2) Op. 16 (A1) Op. 18	Op. 81 Op. 88 (A1 and A1¹)	Op. 68 (A2)	—	—	—	8
Consequent (type 1)	Op. 1	Op. 25 (A1) Op. 26 Op. 34 Op. 60	—	—	—	—	—	4
Consequent (other)	Op. 25 (A1 and A1¹) Op. 68 (A2) Op. 81 (A1) Op. 88 (A1 and A1¹) Op. 90 Op. 102 Op. 111	Op. 16 (A1)	Op. 5 (A2)	Op. 36 (A1)	—	—	Op. 8 (A1²)	10
Sentence (type 2)	—	—	Op. 108	Op. 77	—	—	—	5
Sentence (other)	Op. 68 (A1) Op. 81 (A2) Op. 98	Op. 5 (A1 and A1¹) Op. 100 Op. 120/1 (A1 and A1¹)	—	Op. 81 (A2 first time)	—	—	—	9

Hybrid end function (type 4)	Op. 18 Op. 51/2 Op. 67 (second time) Op. 73 Op. 101 Op. 115 (final cadence)	Op. 2 Op. 99	—	—	Op. 67 (first time)	9
Hybrid end function (other)	Op. 8 (A1 and A1¹)	Op. 51/1 (A1) Op. 120/2	Op. 38 (A1) Op. 78 (A1) Op. 87 (A1) Op. 114 (A1¹)	Op. 115 (second time)	Op. 115 (first time)	10
Statement (spp)	—	Op. 77	—	—	—	1
Statement (other)	—	Op. 68 (A1)	—	—	—	1
Response (spp)	—	Op. 77	—	—	—	1
Response (other)	—	—	Op. 68 (A1)	—	—	1
CM ending	Op. 87	Op. 25 Op. 36 Op. 51/1	Op. 8 (A2)	—	—	5
Total:	22	26	12	4	1	2	1	68

Example 10.11 Brahms, Piano Quintet, Op. 34, i, first-theme cadence.

major becomes F# minor), from which the music emerges in the following bar by treating a German sixth in F minor simultaneously as V of F# minor. The chord on the last beat of bar 23 should be a cadential $^6_4$, but the onward bass motion toward ii reframes it as the initiating tonic of a cadence, an impression reinforced by the fleeting motion through i^6 on bar 23's last triplet eighth note. If we think this progression is a type of expanded IAC, then the whole theme becomes a more straightforward, if oddly proportioned period.

The greater accumulation of consequent PACs in compound themes (six examples) reflects the simple fact that compounds are more numerous than periods. More significantly, Table 10.5 underscores the extent to which half cadences serve as end functions. Opp. 2, 5, 26, 34, 60, 99, 108, and 120/1 all do this unequivocally. In Opp. 100 and 120/2, the half cadence closes a grand antecedent, but because the consequent dissolves, no further first-theme cadence appears. And in the small ternary themes with dissolving reprise, all except Op. 87 have half cadences as their only cadential event. Op. 51/1 is perhaps the most extreme case, given that its A1 tonic half cadence is contrasted with an A2 closing half cadence in the leading-tone minor (B minor). In all, fourteen of the themes trade entirely in half-cadential closure, contributing to a loosening effect, which undermines the classical distinction, noted by Caplin, between the tight-knit syntax of first themes and the looser organization of second themes. Type-4 hybrid themes in contrast almost always close with a PAC, the two exceptions being Op. 2 and Op. 99.

Finally, Table 10.6 cross-references initiating and cadential functions, with the aim of mapping the relationships between the data compiled in Tables 10.3–10.5. The table collates all of the cadences that ensue from the four initiating functions. Reading from left to right, you can establish, for

Table 10.6 Initiating Functions and Resulting Cadences

	PAC	HC	HC reinterpreted	IAC	Deceptive	Evaded	Plagal	No cadence
Basic idea	Op. 51/2 (end function)	Op. 34 (ant.; cons.)	Op. 78 (A1 end function)	—	—	—	—	—
	Op. 87 (A2 end function)	Op. 51/1 (A1 end function; A2)	Op. 87 (A1 end function)					
		Op. 120/2 (gr. ant.)						
Total	2	5	2					
Statement-response	Op. 1 (cons.)	Op. 1 (ant.)	Op. 5 (A2 cons.)	Op. 81 (A2 end function first time)	Op. 115 (end-function second time)	Op. 115 (end-function first time)	Op. 8 (A1²)	Op. 11
	Op. 8 (A1 end function; A1¹ end function)	Op. 2 (cons.)	Op. 8 (A2)					Op. 15
		Op. 5 (A1; A2 ant.; A1¹)	Op. 26 (ant.)					Op. 83
	Op. 81 (A1 end function; A2 end function)	Op. 26 (cons.)	Op. 81 (A1 ant. end function)					Op. 102 (R1)
		Op. 60 (ant.; cons.)	Op. 108 (end function)					
	Op. 90 (end function)	Op. 120/1 (A1; A1¹)						

(continued)

Table 10.6 Continued

	PAC	HC	HC reinterpreted	IAC	Deceptive	Evaded	Plagal	No cadence
	Op. 98 (gr. ant.)	Op. 36 (A2 end function)	Op. 114 (A1¹ ant.)	Op. 36 (A1)		Op. 67 (first time)		
	Op. 101 (end function)	Op. 99 (end function)						
	Op. 102 (S1)	Op. 100 (gr. ant.)						
	Op. 111 (end function)							
	Op. 115 (end-function final cadence)							
Total	11	10	5	2	1	1	1	4
C.b.i.	Op. 67 (end function)				—	Op. 67 (first time)	—	—
	Op. 73 (end function)							
Total	2	3	1	1	—	1	—	—

Antecedent	Op. 18 (end function)	Op. 16 (A1 ant.; cons.)	Op. 38 (ant.)	Op. 68 (A2 ant.)	—	—	—
	Op. 25 (A1 cons.; A1¹ end function)	Op. 18 (ant.)	Op. 68 (A1 spp resp.)	Op. 77 (end function)			
	Op. 68 (A1 end function; A2 cons.)	Op. 25 (A1 ant.; A2 end function)	Op. 88 (A1 ant.; A1¹ ant.)				
	Op. 88 (A1 cons.; A1¹ cons.)	Op. 68 (A1 spp st.)					
		Op. 77 (spp st.; resp.)					
Total	7	8	4	2	—	—	—

example, how many PACs are produced by themes commencing with a basic idea, and also where these cadences sit within the theme. Table 10.6 further distills this evidence, by showing the number of internal and end PACs, HCs, and IACs that the four initiating functions produce (the distinction is not meaningful for deceptive and evaded cadences, both examples of which appear together in one theme's cadential function, or for plagal cadences, of which there is only one example, which serves as an end function). The table discloses information that is fundamental to the formal-strategic nature of Brahms's themes, because it reveals the modes of closure that a given model of thematic initiation is likely to produce: that is, it shows the ways in which Brahms's first-theme form-functional pathways are delimited, as a critical feature enervating Brahms's first-movement sonata forms in general.

Crucial here is the interaction of initiating functions with internal versus final cadences. Table 10.6, for example, shows that Brahms is almost as likely to end a theme commencing with a statement-response pair with an HC as he is with a PAC. The profile of initiating antecedents is instructive in a different way: they overwhelmingly begin themes in which internal half cadences proliferate (fourteen in all). Although only seven themes are initiated with an antecedent—Opp. 16, 18, 25, 38, 77, 68, and 88—between them they account for nearly half of Brahms's internal half-cadential usage. This statistic becomes explicable when we realize that five of the seven themes is a type-5 compound design, which means that cadential usage is a barometer of proliferation: the more expansive Brahms's themes, the more likely he is to deploy multiple interior half cadences. His least common strategy is to end a theme with an IAC; there is only one example, in the Violin Concerto, which is the culmination of a sentence with periodic presentation. The cadences in the grand antecedents are inevitably internal, because they lead on to dissolving consequents. Of the four instances, one has no cadences at all (the Serenade, Op. 11), and only one displays full closure at its antecedent's end (Op. 98). Grand antecedents, in other words, engender a relatively high degree of cadential provisionality.

These findings open up verdant analytical territory, which space permits me to sketch but not elaborate. The eventual goal of this project is to develop a composer-specific empirical method for mapping form-functional pathways, in a manner redolent of Robert Gjerdingen's work on eighteenth-century schema succession. If I know the full diversity of Brahms's first-theme syntax, and I have comparable data about his second-theme syntax and his medial-caesura and structural-cadential usage across each sonata form, then the totality of this information forms an inter-opus network of syntactic decisions, which is the sum of Brahms's first-movement sonata-formal syntactic strategies. I can then traverse this network in diverse ways, establishing, for instance, the relative prevalence of forms in which first-theme statement-response initiating functions yield dominant half-close medial caesuras, or dominant structural PACs, and so forth. Or I can pursue one complete pathway for one movement and relate this with precision to the total corpus.

Conclusions

If this survey puts a clear shape on the first-theme syntax of Brahms's first-movement sonata forms, it also generates numerous questions, if not controversies. Perhaps most obvious is the issue of how syntax interacts with developing variation, given its influence on accounts of Brahms's sonata-type thinking. Walter Frisch has argued that developing variation only really asserts itself with the Piano Quartet, Op. 26, the works before this instead exhibiting a kind of transformational technique, which is not developing variation proper.[25] More generally, both Adorno and Dahlhaus saw in Brahms's music a condition in which the logic of thematic development overrides classical form-functional priorities.[26]

Yet there is no predictable correlation between Brahms's syntactic and motivic-developmental decisions. Developing variation may well germinate with Op. 26, but this does not occasion a turn toward a more developmentally supportive thematic syntax in the early 1860s. By way of illustration, Table 10.7 tracks the use of theme types chronologically across the corpus. There is no clear correlation between a sustained engagement with developing variation after 1861 and any supporting change of syntactic priorities. If anything, between Opp. 26 and 51 at least there is an increased preoccupation with more recursive designs: that is to say, periods and especially small ternary themes. One thread here is a persistent interest in intra-thematic proliferation, culminating in Op. 36, the small-ternary theme of which spans an astonishing ninety-five bars. This leisurely design seems hardly compatible with a new aesthetic of cellular motivic process.

The more general question of the interaction of syntax and developing variation is no less evasive. Although the dissolution of functions is a common strategy, the idea that this responds to an overarching preoccupation with motivic process is difficult to substantiate. Brahms seldom engages in the kind of initial processual dialectic that commentators from Dahlhaus to Schmalfeldt have noted in Beethoven's "Tempest" Sonata, central to which is the argument that motivic action displaces syntactic identity.[27] Where becoming occurs, it generally serves the dissolution of a grand consequent or ternary reprise, but it never impinges on thematic function: we are not obliged to convert an introduction into a theme after the fact, for instance. There are some isolated cases of intra-thematic becoming, for example, the regression of the antecedent into an introductory function considered above in Op. 2, or the similar procedure in Op. 101, in which an initial statement-response is followed not by an orthodox continuation, but by a standing on V, which then yields to a

Table 10.7 Chronological Typology of Themes

Opus	Type	Year
1	Period	1852–1853
2	Hybrid	1852
5	Small ternary	1853
8	Other	1853–1854, rev. 1889
11	Gr. ant + diss. cons.	1857–1858
15	Hybrid	1854–1859
16	Small ternary	1858–1859
18	Hybrid	1859–1860
25	Small ternary	1861
26	Period	1861
34	Period	1862
36	Small ternary	1864–1865
38	Small ternary	1862–1865
51/1	Small ternary	ca. 1865–1873
51/2	Hybrid	ca. 1865–1873
60	Period	1855–1875
67	Hybrid	1875
68	Other	1862–1876
73	Hybrid	1877
77	Sentence (spp)	1878
78	Small ternary	1878–1879
81	Other	1880
83	Sentence	1881
87	Small ternary	1880–1882
88	Small ternary	1882
90	Sentence	1883
98	Gr. ant + diss. cons.	1884–1885
99	Hybrid	1886
100	Gr. ant + diss. cons.	1886
101	Hybrid	1886
102	Sentence (inc. R1; S1)	1887
108	Sentence	1886–1888
111	Sentence	1890
114	Other	1891
115	Hybrid	1891
120/1	Small ternary	1894
120/2	Gr. ant + diss. cons.	1894

First-Theme Syntax in Brahms's Sonata Forms

second sentence beginning in the relative major, thereby calling into question the initiatory function of bars 1–4. More often, Brahms is happy to allow the functional identity of his themes to remain untransformed, at least within the boundaries of first-theme function.

Neither is motivic-developmental saturation necessarily a common feature. The First Symphony constitutes an extreme case in this regard: the relentless contrapuntal variation of the "double" theme across the first-theme group, as Giselher Schubert called it, marks an outer limit of motivic density, which few other examples match, including the other symphonies.[28] In all, the study suggests that it is almost impossible to generalize a theory of developing variation that aligns with a theory of thematic syntax in any consistent way. If anything, syntax more often stands in an *antithetical* relationship with motivic action: motives initiate themes and processes of developing variation, but the two are neither necessarily synonymous nor coterminous.

A second, and possibly more tractable question concerns what Ryan McClelland has called Brahms's "principle of destabilised beginnings." Building on the tradition of thinking about Brahmsian ambiguity, McClelland sketches a taxonomy of instabilities in Brahms's first themes, understood as formal problems, through which the form has subsequently to work. McClelland's destabilizing features are harmonic or rhythmic-metric: they are either embedded chromatic or harmonically anomalous features, or else rhythmic-metric elements, which disturb the relationship between the material and its metrical context.

It is instructive to situate the phenomena McClelland identifies in relation to the present syntactic concerns; the Op. 36 String Sextet is a case in point. The destabilizing feature that McClelland identifies here is the intrusion of E♭ into A1's initiating function, shown in Example 10.12, which calls into question the stability of its G-major context.[29] E♭ is part of a hexatonic complex, which overlays the first theme: counterbalancing E♭ is a region of B major in the contrasting middle, which means that the symmetrical major thirds either side of G are misaligned with the form-functional divisions. E♭ reappears in A1^1, completing the symmetrical movement from the lower third to the upper third and back. None of this, however, undermines the theme's *form-functional*

Example 10.12 Brahms, String Sextet No. 2, Op. 36, i, opening.

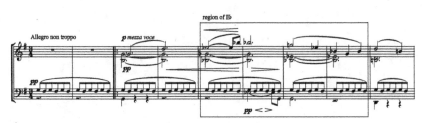

stability: the small-ternary design is schematic and tight-knit, thanks to the twenty-bar standing on V that secures the final tonic. In this case, the unstable features, which, as McClelland shows, Brahms later retrieves and stabilizes, appear in parallel with the first theme's form-functional design, but do not influence it. A theory of initial instability for Brahms could be augmented by an additional category, which is *syntactic* or *form-functional instability*: situations in which intra-thematic functions lose their integrity under the influence of contrapuntal-harmonic and/or rhythmic-metric characteristics.

Relating the taxonomy of syntax to the strategic question of instability in this way points to an analytical reconciliation of form-functional taxonomy and formal strategy, a connection that is informal at best in most analytical practice (taxonomy, as the domain of theory, is systematic; strategy, as the explanatory object of analysis, is not). By mapping the pathways that connect formal functions in relation to a data set, which is the sum of Brahms's form-functional decisions, we can at once explain the specific formal strategies of a given work and embed them in a taxonomy of syntactic practice. As a result, we move one small step closer to the objective of "a comprehensive and highly differentiated morphological history of the sonata form" that Webster advocates.

Chapter 11

Formal Elision in the Chamber Music of Mendelssohn and Brahms

A Case Study in Romantic *Formenlehre*

Benedict Taylor

The parallels between the life and work of Felix Mendelssohn and Johannes Brahms have often been noted. Born in Hamburg twenty-four years apart, both were perfectionists imbued with a pronounced work ethic and an enviable compositional technique, both had deep interest in and respect for the music of the past, and both were the foremost composers of their respective generations associated with "purely musical" values, in opposition to the mid-century polemics of the "New German" camp. Not least for this present chapter's concerns, both were strongly drawn to sonata form, and chamber music in the classical genres makes up a central part of their compositional output.

More seldom, though, have the musical links between the two composers been examined in any detail, and opinions have differed as to the extent, if any, of musical influence.[1] On the one hand, within Brahms's lifetime it was not uncommon for him to be cast as a follower of the Mendelssohn tradition, even (for detractors) something of a Mendelssohn epigone. "He writes fluently, articulately, cleanly, but without a trace of independent originality," wrote Tchaikovsky acerbically of Brahms's Op. 18 Sextet; "he is content with hackneyed musical ideas, which he borrows above all from Mendelssohn and mistreats a further time, and in imitating various superficial mannerisms of Schumann."[2] On the other hand, in the century following Brahms's death any links with his predecessor's music have often been understated, if not simply ignored. Perhaps the epitome of this tendency is provided by James Webster, who in a celebrated article on Brahms from the late 1970s was willing to declare that "Of Mendelssohn's influence on Brahms's large-scale instrumental music there is hardly a trace."[3]

Webster's assertion is representative of a strain of twentieth-century reception that paints a circumpolar picture of the development of nineteenth-century music, in which later nineteenth-century composers take their bearings almost entirely from classical predecessors, passing over the intervening Romantic generation.[4] Where Webster was unusual and pioneering at the time was in replacing a Beethoven-centric narrative with one that also included

Schubert. Still, whether we take 1827 or 1828 as our starting point, it would appear that there is little if any music from subsequent decades worthy of consideration—either by critics or, by inference, by composers. Webster's statement serves to support his thesis—inspired by a comment by Donald Tovey half a century before—that of post-Beethovenian composers only Schubert had any significant influence on Brahms, which he supports by the simple expedient of ignoring all the intervening music that might contradict this claim.[5] Although later scholars like John Daverio have sought to refine our understanding of Brahms's music by showing the probable influence of figures such as Robert Schumann, and Marie Sumner Lott has recently suggested links with the chamber music of George Onslow and Louis Spohr, the circumpolar narrative has proved tenacious.[6]

This perspective is paralleled in the recent North American development of *Formenlehre* or theories of musical form, in which the Viennese classical repertoire has provided the central focus for the formation of the two leading approaches. While William Caplin's theory of formal functions is confined in application to the music of Haydn, Mozart, and Beethoven, this same classical repertoire serves in the sonata theory of James Hepokoski and Warren Darcy as the normative model for later composers; later nineteenth-century works are "in dialogue" with the forms of Viennese classicism, and thus in his use of sonata form, Brahms is understood first and foremost as engaging with the practice of Haydn, Mozart, or Beethoven (at a stretch, also including Schubert).[7] While sonata theory is certainly open in principle to considering changing norms or "defaults" over time, in practice its application to later nineteenth- and early twentieth-century pieces often relates their forms directly back to classical norms, minimizing any influence that might have arisen from the intervening generations.[8] In this chapter, I seek to fill in some of the missing steps in this journey from classical norms to nineteenth-century formal practices with a focus, in the first instance, on resonances in thematic construction between the music of Mendelssohn and Brahms before further refining our view to consider formal commonalities in the music of the two composers in the context of a dynamic and changing sonata practice. In doing so, I aim to move away from the circumpolar narrative of nineteenth-century music around Beethoven or the classical style more generally, and, instead, to reveal a rich landscape of changing practices in formal functions in the first half of the nineteenth century that inform the music of Brahms.

Alte Bahnen: On Mendelssohn's Trail

There are, however, some fairly obvious traces of Mendelssohn in Brahms's large-scale instrumental music, indeed ones that Brahms famously acknowledged, albeit in his own, inimitably defensive manner. Probably the most well

Formal Elision in Mendelssohn and Brahms

known of these echoes is the influence of Mendelssohn's C Minor Piano Trio, Op. 66, on Brahms's C Minor Piano Quartet, Op. 60. Most clearly, Brahms's finale opens with running eighth-note figuration that openly alludes to that in Mendelssohn's first movement (see Examples 11.1a and 11.1b).

"Any ass can see that," one might imagine the composer retorting, and Brahms himself appears to have acknowledged the link.[9] In fact, more rewarding than merely noting the thematic borrowing in this case would be to explore the wider echoes of Mendelssohn's work and Mendelssohnian traits found throughout this movement. For instance, the opening theme of Brahms's secondary group (bar 55) is given over a first-inversion tonic, a procedure typical of Mendelssohn's practice, and found in his Trio's first movement, though rather less characteristic of Brahms; the chorale-like second theme (bar 75) is presented in distinct phrases interspersed with figuration, reminiscent of the chorale in the finale of Mendelssohn's Trio; while the recapitulation of the opening figuration is given over a $^6_4$ pedal, one of the most characteristic of all

Example 11.1a Brahms, Piano Quartet, Op. 60, iv, bar 1–3.

Example 11.1b Mendelssohn, Piano Trio, Op. 66, i, bars 1–3.

Mendelssohn's sonata traits.[10] Even the overall form of Mendelssohn's finale—whose recapitulation proceeds from the secondary theme as if continuing the thematic layout initiated with the return of primary material at the start of the development—is a prominent precedent for the type of rotational hybrid typical of Brahms's finales, sometimes termed a "Brahmsian deformation."[11] Indeed a persuasive interpretation of Brahms's movement as a deliberate "misreading" of Mendelssohn's work could be developed here.[12]

Less commonly noted, but no less transparent a borrowing, is Brahms's reworking of the main theme of this same Piano Trio's finale as the third movement of his F Minor Piano Sonata, Op. 5 (see Examples 11.2a and 11.2b); Op. 66 seems to have been a favorite of Brahms's. More frequently cited as an example of musical appropriation is the second theme of Brahms's Second Symphony, which from the composer's own admission onward has often been taken to allude to the second theme of Mendelssohn's Third Symphony. (Brahms claims

Example 11.2a Brahms, Piano Sonata, Op. 5, iii, bars 1–9.

Example 11.2b Mendelssohn, Piano Trio, Op. 66, iv, bars 1–5.

Formal Elision in Mendelssohn and Brahms

in a letter to Otto Dessoff to have "stolen" it, apparently from Mendelssohn; on the other hand, it actually sounds closer to an echo of his own well-known "Wiegenlied," Op. 49, No. 4.)[13]

Another thematic similarity—one that is unlikely to be entirely accidental—is the D-minor slow movement of Brahms's Second String Quintet (Op. 111, Example 11.3a), which reworks the basic idea of the D-minor slow movement of Mendelssohn's own Second String Quintet (Op. 87, Example 11.3b). In addition to the common underlying key (D minor), time signature ($\frac{2}{4}$), and tempo (adagio), the motivic and rhythmic constituents are the same (Brahms inverts Mendelssohn's opening figure), and both feature early motion to C-major harmony as V/F. (Compare bar 3 of the Brahms with bar 7 of Mendelssohn's movement; even the chain of dropping thirds in bars 7–9 of Mendelssohn's piece might seem proto-Brahmsian in this context.)

Example 11.3a Brahms, String Quintet, Op. 111, ii, bars 1–4.

Example 11.3b Mendelssohn, String Quintet, Op. 87, iii, bars 1–2, 7–9.

Perhaps the richest of all these reworkings is the intermezzo from Brahms's G Minor Piano Quartet, Op. 25 (Example 11.4a). On the surface this may not immediately suggest a Mendelssohnian model; however, this is in fact straight out of the Andante second movement of Mendelssohn's Octet (Example 11.4b). Unmistakable in both are the repeated pedal note (the dyad C–G in Mendelssohn, simply C in Brahms); the same motive (E♭–D–C–B♮–C), doubled identically in sixths; and the precipitous move to the Neapolitan D♭ (in Mendelssohn, via F minor, in Brahms more suddenly, though Mendelssohn's D♭ will prove more formally consequential). Even the unusual form of the

Example 11.4a Brahms, Piano Quartet, Op. 25, ii, bars 1–8.

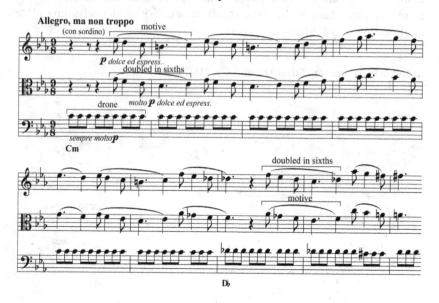

Example 11.4b Mendelssohn, Octet, Op. 20, ii, bars 1–5.

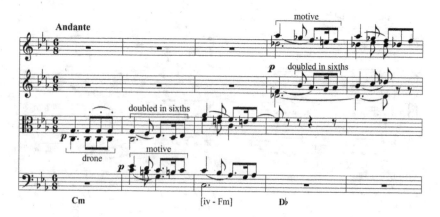

outer sections of Brahms's compound-ternary movement reflects something of the Mendelssohn piece. The second theme (bar 35) is given in the unusual subdominant, F minor,[14] which, following a brief retransition based on primary-theme material, is then reprised in the tonic before a coda based on the primary theme. In other words, there is a distinct element of the reverse reprise or "type 2" sonata procedure that is present at a more developed level in Mendelssohn's Andante.[15] Brahms's movement is in many respects a sped-up version of Mendelssohn's, and nonetheless characteristic despite this.

There are other possible examples of modeling that might be adduced—the duplicitous play between possible secondary tonalities in the first movement of Brahms's F Major Cello Sonata, Op. 99, for instance, which finds a clear antecedent in the opening movement of Mendelssohn's B♭ Major Cello Sonata, Op. 45—but the point is surely clear by now. Both in details of thematic construction and in formal design there are numerous, clear traces of Mendelssohn in Brahms's instrumental music.

I have dwelt at some length on demonstrating some of the more obvious similarities, curious coincidences, and overt borrowings, since this is a feature of Brahms's music that, for reasons of reception and long-entrenched prejudice, has long been overlooked and needs adequate acknowledgment.[16] Nevertheless, demonstrating influence can prove problematic, since the network of possible sources is almost invariably greater than will be accounted for now, and may be mediated through multiple sources, as well as being potentially unconscious in some cases (calling into question what criterion can be used to ascertain the validity of the claim). Rather than concerning ourselves with transmission as such, in this chapter I propose that it may be more productive to situate the question of musical resemblance more widely in the context of recent approaches to musical form, namely what has been dubbed the "Romantic turn" in the "New *Formenlehre*."[17] Where similarities exist between Mendelssohn's and Brahms's approaches to form—ones that appear idiosyncratic compared to a classical model derived from Haydn, Mozart, and Beethoven—these might alert us to a potentially distinct post-classical sonata practice, quite independently of the question of whether Brahms took these techniques from Schubert, Mendelssohn, Schumann, or whomever.[18] Obviously Brahms and Mendelssohn are only two of a vast number of composers writing in classical instrumental forms in the nineteenth century, but they are nonetheless the two who, more than any other in the century after Beethoven's death, seem to have found musical expression through sonata form most congenial.[19]

The following section will examine the commonalities between the two composers' formal procedures by spotlighting the technique of formal elision at one of the most significant structural junctures in sonata form, namely the onset of the recapitulation.[20] The corpus I will be using for this purpose is the chamber music of each composer: a body of some twenty-four works by Brahms, and the fourteen (or 14.5) works in this category written by

Mendelssohn after the age of sixteen, which are representative of his mature style (see Table 11.1). The reason for this choice of repertoire is twofold. Firstly, chamber music is closely associated in the nineteenth century with the classical tradition, and therefore offers an ideal repertoire for investigating the development of sonata form over the Romantic era. Secondly, both Mendelssohn and Brahms left a sizable body of works in this field (larger, for instance, than their respective symphonic outputs). Hence, if wishing to restrict our survey to a single genre or closely related set of genres, chamber music is the most promising category to take, offering as it does the largest sample size of sonata or sonata-related forms in the compositional output of these two figures.[21]

Although I will be suggesting in several places the likely influence of Mendelssohn on Brahms's practice, it is not always easy to claim exceptionality in this respect, and ultimately exploring the subtle differences between the two can be as rewarding as uncovering the broad commonalities. Paradoxically, analyzing Brahms's music from a perspective informed by Mendelssohn's practice helps to bring out what is distinctively Brahmsian about what the later composer does, despite—or probably because of—the often close similarities in formal procedure. This points in turn to wider changes in sonata composition over the nineteenth century, allowing us to deepen our understanding of Romantic form by focusing on its two most important practitioners in the decades after Beethoven.

Table 11.1 Chamber Works by Mendelssohn and Brahms Used in Corpus

Mendelssohn (1825–1847)	Brahms (1853–1894)
6 Quartets (Opp. 13, 12, 44, Nos. 1–3, 80) [½ Quartet (incomplete), Op. 81 i–ii]	3 Quartets (Opp. 51, Nos. 1–2, 67)
2 Quintets (Opp. 18, 87)	2 Quintets (Opp. 88, 111)
	2 Sextets (Opp. 18, 36)
1 Octet (Op. 20)	
2 Piano Trios (Opp. 49, 66)	3 Piano Trios (Opp. 8 [2 versions], 87, 101)
	3 Piano Quartets (Opp. 25, 26, 60)
	1 Piano Quintet (Op. 34)
	1 Horn Trio (Op. 40)
	1 Clarinet Trio (Op. 114)
	1 Clarinet Quintet (Op. 115)
1 Violin Sonata (Q26 [1838])	3 Violin Sonatas (Opp. 78, 100, 108)
2 Cello Sonatas (Opp. 45, 58)	2 Cello Sonatas (Opp. 38, 99)
	2 Clarinet Sonatas (Opp. 120, Nos. 1–2)

Formal Elision at the Point of Recapitulation

Brahms's "recapitulatory overlaps" have been the topic of renewed focus since a pioneering study by Peter Smith from 1994. Smith has discussed certain aspects of Brahms's practice—such as the technique of motivic liquidation and the harmonic implications for a Schenkerian conception of sonata form—in such works as the C Minor Quartet, Op. 51, No. 1; the F Major Cello Sonata, Op. 99; and the Fourth Symphony, Op. 98.[22] The principle of undercutting this formal juncture is, however, probably the most characteristic of all Mendelssohn's sonata procedures, and one where in many places one can trace close similarities in approach to Brahms. The recapitulation in the first movement of the Sextet in B♭ Major, Op. 18, provides a case in point, a piece that commentators have often considered Brahms's first mature chamber work.[23] This is the one moment in all of Brahms's chamber music that—to my mind—most clearly cries out a Mendelssohnian provenance.[24] There is the same sense of exhilaration, the dynamic surge of the returning theme emerging over a dominant pedal, the simultaneous contraction and yet expansion of the phrase from the form given at the start of the work in order to attain new registral heights. And despite this, the passage retains its Brahmsian identity.

As mentioned earlier, the recapitulation of the primary theme over a tonic $^6_4$ (or less frequently a $^6_3$) is one of the most distinctive traits of Mendelssohn's sonata forms, one seen as early as the finale of his first published work, the C Minor Piano Quartet, Op. 1, of 1822. This feature is certainly not unique to Mendelssohn, but there are relatively few examples before him, and one would be hard-pressed to find the same concentration in any other nineteenth-century composer. Of the fourteen chamber works by Mendelssohn considered, there are eleven movements featuring a reprise over a $^6_4$, and another five with a reprise given over a $^6_3$ (see Table 11.2).[25]

In other words, formal elision at the recapitulation is a distinctive practice in the most significant corpus of chamber music from the decades preceding Brahms. We might in fact wonder whether there could be a more specific model for Brahms. There are no string sextets by Mendelssohn, but there are two quintets, one of which is, like Brahms's work, an Op. 18, and the other, likewise, in B♭ major, and in this case the latter is the better match.[26] Mendelssohn's String Quintet No. 2 in B♭ Major, Op. 87, admittedly contains one of the less frequent $^6_3$ recapitulations, but the parallel is particularly prominent in the way the returning theme emerges in the inner voices and the climax spread out by keeping the registral expansion in the first violin in reserve until near the end of the phrase (in Mendelssohn soaring to b♭^{3}; in Brahms touching on this b♭ and then outdoing this by reaching a high c^4). In Brahms, the climb is more leisurely; the passage possesses a breadth, reflecting the underlying tranquility of his movement; Mendelssohn's has an urgency, a more frenetic quality, reflecting the darker, more emotionally troubled character of his piece.

Table 11.2 Instances of Large-Scale Formal Reprises Occurring over $^6_4$ or $^6_5$ Tonic Harmony in Mendelssohn's Chamber Music, 1825–47

$^6_4$ Reprise	$^6_5$ Reprise
Octet Op. 20/iii	Quartet Op. 44/1/iii
Quartet Op. 13/i	Quartet Op. 44/3/iv
Quartet Op. 13/ii (ternary form reprise)	Quartet Op. 87/i
Quartet Op. 44/2/i	Quintet Op. 87/iv ($^6_5$ already present in theme)
Quartet Op. 44/2/iii (+ intrathematic overlap)	
Quartet Op. 44/2/iv	Quartet Op. 80/i (multiple potential points of recapitulation)
Quartet Op. 44/3/ii (+ within sequence)	
Violin Sonata Q26/i	
Violin Sonata Q26/iii	
Cello Sonata Op. 45/i	
Piano Trio Op. 66/iii (a highly deformed sonata/rondo)	

A further example from Mendelssohn, again in B♭ major and in fact a harmonically closer match (though the mood is quite different), is the Cello Sonata, Op. 45, which approaches the $^6_4$ harmony from G♭ through an augmented-sixth style progression. Influence, though, is tricky to isolate, for although the general Mendelssohn resonance is unmistakable, there is in fact a specific passage from another composer that was also no doubt in Brahms's mind here.[27] That this composer is Schubert may not come as a surprise, even though the $^6_4$ recapitulation as such is not a particularly Schubertian feature. This is not from a recapitulation, however, and neither is it from a chamber work, but rather from the ("intrathematic") small ternary reprise of the primary theme within the opening movement of the B♭ Piano Sonata, D. 960 (bar 36). Brahms seems to be fusing (at least) two influences here: remembering the sound of the particular Schubert passage, the way it materializes as a sonorous moment, but using it in a Mendelssohnian location in a dynamic Mendelssohnian function. The G♭ approach recalls Schubert's passage, whereas the idea of recapitulating the primary theme over a $^6_4$, and the way the theme emerges within the texture—the upper dominant pedal with its suggestion of a new thematic idea, the ensuing registral expansion and dramatic pacing—all come from Mendelssohn.

Following the Sextet Op. 18, the $^6_4$ recapitulation is employed on several other occasions in Brahms's chamber music. A relatively straightforward example is given in the scherzo of the A Major Piano Quartet, Op. 26. Unlike Mendelssohn, Brahms rarely writes scherzi in sonata form. (When they are, this is almost invariably a case of expanding the rounded-binary outer section of a larger compound-ternary movement into a miniature sonata, and not of an entire movement, as so often with Mendelssohn.[28]) Thus, when Brahms *does* reference sonata organization in a scherzo, it is marked, and when this is combined with a $\substack{6\\4}$ recapitulation as here in Op. 26 it stands out more clearly as a potentially Mendelssohnian gesture. (See Table 11.3.)

What is particularly noteworthy from examining Brahms's wider output of chamber music, however, is how, having taken up this characteristic feature of another composer's style, he soon reworks and diversifies his procedures at this point in sonata form. The principle of smoothing or blurring the point of reprise remains, but the means used become more varied. Brahms develops an array of recapitulatory obfuscatory strategies, some of which relate to Mendelssohn's practice,[29] some of which have plausible precedent in other composers, and some of which are probably entirely his own. Table 11.4 shows some of the other main techniques used by Brahms for blurring his sonata recapitulations (these categories are not mutually exclusive).

In fact more characteristic of Brahms's practice than the $\substack{6\\4}$ recapitulation is surely the oblique arrival at the point of thematic reprise from ♭VI harmony. Again, this is not something Brahms invented: it is probably an outgrowth of the common eighteenth-century strategy of ending a development section on vi, a harmony that in some cases can be blurred by the composer with the opening of the reprise. (A good example is provided by the finale to Mozart's Piano Sonata No. 1, K. 279, while Mendelssohn's *A Midsummer Night's Dream* overture adeptly plays with the scheme.) Yet Brahms makes this technique peculiarly his own, above all in his use of ♭VI in the minor mode. For a brief case

Table 11.3 Instances of Large-Scale Formal Reprises Occurring over $\substack{6\\4}$ or $\substack{6\\5}$ Tonic Harmony in Brahms's Chamber Music

$\substack{6\\4}$ Reprise	$\substack{6\\5}$ Reprise
Sextet Op. 18/i	Piano Trio Op. 101/iv (in midst of harmonic progression)
Piano Quartet Op. 25/iii (non-sonata)	
Piano Quartet Op. 26/iii	
Piano Quintet Op. 34/i (ambiguous/diffused)	
Piano Quartet Op. 60/iv (diffused)	
Piano Trio Op. 8 (rev)/i (within sequence)	
Quintet Op. 111/i (owing to presentation of theme in bass)	
Clarinet Quintet Op. 115/i (already present in theme)	

Table 11.4 Other Categories of Elided or Blurred Reprise in Brahms's Chamber Music

---

On I^7
Violin Sonata Op. 78/i

Starts on ♭VI or other non-tonic harmony
String Quartet Op. 51/1/i

String Quartet Op. 51/2/i

Piano Quartet Op. 60/i (cf. 111/i)
Quintet Op. 111/iv (in original theme)

Oblique arrival on I (not prepared by V, or V/vi etc.)
Piano Trio Op. 87/i (within sequence)

Clarinet Sonata Op. 120/1/i (chromatic slipping)

Motivic overlap/blurring
Horn Trio Op. 40/iii (non-sonata)

String Quartet Op. 51/1/i

String Quartet Op. 51/2/i

Piano Trio Op. 87/i (within sequence)

Piano Trio Op. 8 (rev)/i

Preemptive tonic harmony (often in parallel mode)
Piano Quartet Op. 25/i

Piano Quartet Op. 26/i

Violin Sonata Op. 78/i

Clarinet Trio Op. 114/i

Clarinet Quintet Op. 115/i

Sectional division straddling original intrathematic boundary
Piano Quintet Op. 25/i

String Quartet Op. 51/2/ii (non-sonata)

String Quartet Op. 67/ii (non-sonata)

Redundant premature P reprise in non-tonic, followed by full P reprise
Piano Quartet Op. 25/iii (non-sonata)

Piano Quartet Op. 26/ii (non-sonata?)

Cello Sonata Op. 99/ii (non-sonata)

Premature P reprise in tonic, followed by full P reprise
Cello Sonata Op. 99/i

Suggestion of V/wrong tonic
Piano Trio Op. 87/iv

Formal Elision in Mendelssohn and Brahms

study, we might look at the first movement of the C Minor String Quartet, Op. 51, No. 1, perhaps the *locus classicus* for the Brahmsian "recapitulatory overlap," and compare it with the slightly different procedure in the opening movement of Mendelssohn's E Minor String Quartet, Op. 44, No. 2 (Examples 11.5a and 11.5b).

Example 11.5a Brahms, String Quartet, Op. 51, No. 1, i, bars 133–39.

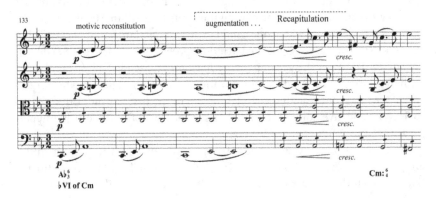

Example 11.5b Mendelssohn, String Quartet, Op. 44, No. 2, i, bars 160–72.

In Brahms's quartet, the start of the reprise is blurred by being approached out of ♭VI harmony, heard over a first-inversion A♭ chord (VI$^6_5$ substituting for the tonic minor in a typical Brahmsian ploy),[30] drawn out in augmentation, and given as part of a process of motivic reconstitution that has started a few bars previously. In Mendelssohn's work, a strong sense of ♭VI preceding the recall is also present, though the thematic return occurs in the midst of a cadential progression to the tonic, occurring over the penultimate ii^7–V stage. Motivically, the return is also prefigured, this time in diminution, submerged within a texture of "thematic" arpeggiations that grow out of the use of this primary-theme material in the closing theme just heard. In Mendelssohn, the melodic reprise comes where one would expect in the four-bar hypermeter, but the repetition of the G^7–C^7 in the harmonic progression (bars 165–67) desynchronizes this from the accompanying harmony.[31] Mendelssohn's subtle play with hypermeter and the desynchronization of harmonic and melodic phrases is replaced in Brahms with the stretching out of the first bar into three; nevertheless the effective point of return occurs at the start of a new four-bar hypermeasure (bar 137).

There are in other words, both strong similarities and important differences between the two composers. In both, the actual moment of return is blurred, such that we are not fully aware it has started until it is already well underway, and harmonic structure is dissociated from thematic design. But while Mendelssohn smooths the two together as part of a fluid onward sweep, Brahms diffuses the recapitulation function over an area of five or so bars.

The oblique harmonic arrival at the tonic and the principle of motivic linkage, witnessed in this last example, can be found in several further sonata recapitulations of both composers. For instance, Brahms approaches the tonic in the first movements of the Piano Trio, Op. 87, and Clarinet Sonata, Op. 120, No. 1, obliquely through a sequence that avoids suggestion of the dominant, a similar procedure as can be found in the sonata or sonata-rondo scherzos of Mendelssohn's String Quartet, Op. 44, No. 3, and Piano Trio, Op. 49. Likewise, Brahms is celebrated for his techniques of motivic linkage, although the permeation of sectional boundaries by ongoing motivic working is characteristic of nineteenth-century sonata forms in general, and as the example given from the String Quartet, Op. 44, No. 2, shows, instances can readily be found in Mendelssohn's music. (Another good example of motivic reconstitution is given by the sonata rondo finale of the Cello Sonata, Op. 45.)[32]

Of the numerous other comparisons between their respective recapitulatory strategies that can be made, one is the replacement of tonic harmony with the tonic seventh at the point of return, transforming I into V/IV, as found in the first movement of Brahms's G Major Violin Sonata, Op. 78, and the second movement of Mendelssohn's String Quartet, Op. 44, No. 2. Another common trait is the principle of intrathematic straddling, where a component of a thematic group is introduced surreptitiously prior to the harmonic return that occurs with the continuation into the latter part of the theme (normally rhetorically emphasized as the point of recapitulation). A nice example in Mendelssohn is the slow movement of his E Minor Quartet, an abridged ("type 1") sonata form where the primary theme returns at its original pitch level (bar 42) but in the midst of the retransitional progression prior to the attainment of root-position tonic harmony; the harmonic reprise (bar 47, once again given over a ⁶⁄₄) proceeds from the theme's consequent phrase. Effectively the preceding thematic statement becomes equivalent to the antecedent phrase of the primary theme, a single thematic unit straddling a much larger sectional boundary. Brahms offers his own variants of this type of procedure in the (non-sonata) slow movements of his own Quartets Op. 51, No. 2, and Op. 67, in which the first two segments (*a* and *b*) of the small-ternary primary theme return in the submediant, prior to the harmonic reprise that starts with the theme's ensuing (*a'*) phrase (bar 95 in Op. 51, No. 2/ii; bar 73 in Op. 67/ii).

A rather more ambiguous and individual application of this idea is found in the opening movement of Brahms's G Minor Piano Quartet, Op. 25. Here recapitulatory function is distended over two adjacent passages. The return of the primary theme's contrasting middle (*b* section) in the tonic major at bar 237 is followed by the continuation into its small ternary reprise (*a'*) in the tonic minor at bar 259. The earlier statement technically marks the return of primary theme material in the tonic, but is rhetorically understated, starting from the subsidiary central part of the theme, and thus on its arrival is unlikely to be heard as forming the recapitulation. Moreover, this material was originally stated in the relative major at the movement's outset (bar 11), so there is no literal return here either. Instead, the primary theme's small ternary reprise at bar 259 is set up as the evident moment of recapitulation. Brahms has thus preempted the return to the tonic before the ostensible recapitulation actually occurs—a feature characteristic of many of his later movements (including the first movements of Opp. 26, 78, 114, and 115) and quite distinct here from the practice of Mendelssohn. Again, the result is often to diffuse the sense of recapitulation over a larger span of music.

What makes the ploy even more ingenious in Op. 25 is that the theme's opening (*a*) segment has already been given in the tonic minor at the start of the development section quite some while before (bar 161); thus it is as if the return of the primary theme in the tonic is spread over two larger formal sections, dissociating sonata form's large-scale divisions from the thematic rotations.[33] This idea will be developed further in the finale of the following A Major Piano Quartet, Op. 26. When a tonic return of the primary theme at the head of the development is followed by a reprise that bypasses the already stated material, starting instead from the latter stage of the rotational cycle, the procedure results in the so-called Brahmsian deformation (already present, as we saw, in the finale of Mendelssohn's Op. 66 Trio).[34]

Just as characteristic as shortening, however, is duplication at this stage: idiosyncratic to Brahms is a repetition of the initial unit at the point of reprise, in which the first statement is somehow delegitimized. In the F Major Cello Sonata, for instance, the primary theme is recalled from bar 112 in the piano, softly and in augmentation but nevertheless over root-position tonic. Yet it is only at bar 128 as the theme is restated in the cello in normal note values that there is a real sense of recapitulation. Despite the preceding statement, Brahms subsequently provides a full restatement of both antecedent and consequent parts of the primary theme. The formal redundancy here is in marked contradistinction to Mendelssohn's tendency toward concision at the reprise. In several non-sonata slow movements, Brahms will also offer a (false) reprise in a non-tonic key followed by a full thematic statement in the correct key (found, for instance, in Op. 25/iii, Op. 26/ii, and again in Op. 99/ii).

Such comparisons could be extended at length. A larger question that would reward detailed examination would be these two composers' smoothing over of the sectional division at another crucial stage of sonata form, the juncture between exposition and development sections, through the avoidance or dissolution of the conventional cadential confirmation of the exposition's secondary key. For both composers, a perfect authentic cadence (PAC) in the secondary tonality (sonata theory's "essential expositional close" [EEC]—apparently an essential property of the eighteenth-century sonata) is often optional; weaker imperfect authentic cadences (IACs) are common, as is the tendency to have no cadence at all. The first movement of Brahms's Op. 18 presents a wonderful example, in which the long dominant pedal present from bar 107 becomes gradually drained of any functional potency and eventually resolves down to the tonic via $\hat{3}$ (bar 137). A multitude of approaches to the same end can be found throughout Mendelssohn's chamber music, from the repeated cadential remnants of Op. 44, No. 2, and avoidance of any cadence in the exposition of Op. 44, No. 1, to the penultimate dominant seventh that is violently broken off in Op. 80's first movement and the cadential dissolution of that quartet's finale. This would, however, be a topic demanding an even longer study. Instead, in order to round up the preceding discussion and bring this chapter to a close, I would like to offer some brief provisional conclusions and pointers to further study.

Conclusions

We can use such commonalities between these two composers' outputs in two ways: either to build up a fuller picture of nineteenth-century form and possible networks of intertextual relationship; or conversely, to analyze specifics: to highlight the uniqueness of each composer by asking what is the distinct *function* of this similar articulatory blurring in Brahms and Mendelssohn.

Unlike some other nineteenth-century composers who are uncomfortable with this feature and attempt to abandon it, Mendelssohn and Brahms both uphold the notion of recapitulation, but they find their own ways to manage the structural articulation of the reprise. To that end, the tendency to consider them "traditionalist" reveals that label to be a fairly empty term, which more sensibly collapses into a discussion of form, genre, and expectations. The differing approach in each composer's music points to the distinct stylistic qualities of each, as well as, potentially, their historical situation. In both, the de-synchronizing of the thematic from the harmonic recapitulation is common, but Mendelssohn generally elides the development with the recapitulation in the interests of continuity and dynamic sweep, whereas Brahms more often diffuses, spreads out, distends. In Mendelssohn, the use of the inverted tonic is much more widespread: it relates to a desire to keep formal boundaries open while still marking them to the listener, and implies a subtly different conception of sonata form. Mendelssohn's usage of the $^6_3$ or $^6_4$ reflects his highly nuanced command of cadential articulation (this is especially prominent in his secondary-theme groups—the continual returning to a $^6_3$ through evaded cadences, and not uncommonly the absence of any EEC); we still feel the force of the distinction between a PAC and an IAC in his music. In Brahms, on the other hand, there is a much greater use of chromatic and tertiary relations (most distinctively ♭VI) in place of the subtle cadential control of his predecessor; there are *some* instances of the $^6_3$ secondary theme but these are not as pronounced as in Mendelssohn, partly because Brahms's syntax and harmonic language is looser and more proliferative. (This in turn surely reflects the influence of composers like Schubert; the Sextet Op. 36 is a good exemplification of such traits.)

Unsurprisingly, though, there are significant underlying commonalities between the two composers' practice. We can see something of this if we compare what Mendelssohn and Brahms do with earlier, classical precedents for the $^6_4$ and $^6_3$ recapitulation. It will probably not have gone unobserved by many readers that there is one very celebrated example of each type in Beethoven: the F-minor $^6_4$ recapitulation in the first movement of the Piano Sonata No. 23 in F Minor, Op. 57, "Appassionata"; and the D-major $^6_3$ recapitulation in the first movement of the Ninth Symphony. What is curious—and distinct from Mendelssohn's practice, as from much of Brahms's too—is how these instances are confined to very specific formal problems. In both cases, Beethoven is reprising material which, superficially, seems prefatory, even though both, actually, are in tempo openings, and (above all in Op. 57) can be claimed to constitute a complete primary theme in form-functional terms. In other words, Beethoven is dealing with recapitulating something that originally seemed "before the beginning," though it intrinsically belongs to the thematic presentation. The result of his inverted tonic harmony at the point of recapitulation is a deferral of the harmonic "structural downbeat" to a later part of the recalled primary group, hence offering a solution to the problem of how to keep the initial thematic statement sounding provisional while still recapitulating it. In the later nineteenth-century cases, however, the elision of development and recapitulatory sections becomes much more frequent and points to a more fluid conception of sonata form in which sectional divisions are regularly overridden in the interests of a larger teleology. In Mendelssohn, indeed, it is common not to have a single PAC in the tonic from the end of the primary theme in the exposition until the coda.

As the foregoing discussion implies, one can often trace multiple lines of probable influence, which themselves can be furthermore interrelated. It would be mildly ridiculous to argue that all appearances of the $^6_4$ recapitulation in Brahms stem from one piece by Beethoven, given the small number of instances in Beethoven, and the enormous number in Mendelssohn; this simply reinscribes a familiar Beethoven-centric narrative. On the other hand, it would obviously be wrong to ignore these Beethoven pieces in cases when they do seem pertinent. Take, for example, the first movement of Brahms's Piano Quintet in F Minor, Op. 34, perhaps the most discussed example of the $^6_4$ reprise in his music. While it would be hard to deny that the "Appassionata" Sonata stands as one of the models for this passage given the common key and the movement's impregnation by $\flat$VI and $\flat$II harmonic coloring, to say that this example is simply referencing Beethoven's Op. 57 is too simplistic given the wider context for the procedure in Brahms's own earlier music as well as that of Mendelssohn and other composers, and not least the stark differences in how the return is handled. In Brahms's quintet, the reprise at the upbeat to bar 160 creeps up by stealth: thematically the outgrowth of the preceding motivic linkage technique that is continued through the motivic fragmentation of the following bars (cello, bar 162–63), it occurs hesitantly, *pianissimo*; it is only in the more emphatic continuation from the primary theme's contrasting middle (upbeat to bar 166) that the listener realizes the recapitulation is already underway. There is of course a play with the tonic major that might recall the dramatic arrival of this same key in the ensuing reprise of the theme's second phrase in Beethoven's movement, but almost everything else is different at this point, and in this respect the recapitulation of Op. 34 is manifestly following the strategies typical of Brahms's other reprises. Any Beethovenian influence is already integrated into Brahms's own compositional practice.

Even looking to an earlier piece that might seem a closer match, Brahms's own Piano Sonata in F Minor, Op. 5 (1853), we find the ostensible inverted tonic in the first movement (here a $^6_3$) handled quite differently from Beethoven's example. In Op. 5, the initial harmony at the point of recapitulation is a first-inversion tonic, but this is owing to the fact that the theme is reprised in the bass, and this lasts less than a quarter-note beat, resolving down by step to a root-position tonic. Brahms's procedure smooths over the juncture to create an effect of fluid continuity. There is little meaningful link with Beethoven's long recapitulatory $\substack{6\\4}$ in the "Appassionata": the use of the inverted tonic chord, itself of the utmost brevity, is hardly sufficient to warrant the comparison, since by 1853 the technique is widespread.[35] And of course between Op. 5 and Op. 34 Brahms has offered several instances of the $\substack{6\\4}$ reprise that more readily suggest the substantial Mendelssohnian precedent for this procedure—in the first movement of Op. 18 and the scherzos of Op. 25 and Op. 26. There is, in other words, a multilayered network of influence.

The ultimate thrust of this chapter is the by now evident point that we need to move away from the circumpolar narrative of nineteenth-century music around Beethoven or the classical style more generally—one that was advocated by Carl Dahlhaus and is still implicit in many applications of Hepokoski and Darcy's sonata theory to the Romantic repertoire. Almost half a century ago James Webster argued for replacing the Beethoven-to-Brahms narrative with a (Beethoven and) Schubert-to-Brahms one. This was a step in the right direction, but ignored the wealth of other pertinent models between these figures. John Daverio subsequently strove to add Schumann as the missing link between Schubert and Brahms—with some good grounds, though again passing over other obvious sources.[36] In this chapter I have argued for the necessity of adding Mendelssohn to this discussion, though there are no doubt other composers who would in turn demand consideration in an adequate account of Brahms's compositional practice.

Consider, for instance, Niels Gade, the finale of whose Violin Sonata No. 2 in D Minor (1849) recapitulates the first phrase of its primary theme over $\substack{6\\4}$ harmony, returning to root position for the phrase's continuation—a highly Mendelssohnian technique to be sure, but one that offers further precedent for Brahms's practice. Other instances of the $\substack{6\\4}$ recapitulation can be readily found in the following years, including the opening movements of Anton Rubinstein's Symphony No. 1 (1850), Robert Volkmann's C Minor Piano Sonata, Op. 12 (1854), and later in Max Bruch's Symphony No. 1 (1868). Perhaps the most famous example is given in the first movement of Schumann's "Rhenish" Symphony (1850), which both anticipates Brahms in its preemptive return to the tonic some bars before as well as foreshadowing the primary motive of the latter's Third Symphony a few bars later. The technique of commencing the primary theme recapitulation in vi, so closely associated with Brahms, is found earlier in the opening movement of Gade's Symphony No. 4 (1850) and the finale of Rubinstein's Symphony No. 1 from the same year. Or take Bruch's Symphony No. 2 (1868–1870), whose finale not only famously prefigures the "joy" theme in Brahms's First Symphony but whose first movement is permeated by the use of $\flat$VI$\substack{6\\4}$ so typical of Brahms, and whose recapitulation is similarly merged with the preceding development, the thematic reprise only gradually finding tonal focus by approaching the tonic F minor from its neighbors E minor and G minor.

In all these cases we see a range of nineteenth-century composers using procedures that would be exceptional in a classical sonata form, and yet appear to be commonplace in the following century. And hence, having advocated a picture of nineteenth-century sonata form based on the twin peaks of Mendelssohn and Brahms, I am now arguing that this is also clearly inadequate—though nevertheless this is a necessary stage toward building up a richer picture of sonata practice in the nineteenth century.[37]

Chapter 12

Compositional Range versus Compositional Ideal Type

Some Reflections on Brahms and Dvořák

Peter H. Smith

The musical and personal relationship between Brahms and Dvořák has long been a topic of fascination, with questions of influence at the forefront. Given Brahms's status as the older and more highly regarded artist, the tendency has been to trace Dvořák's reputed adaptation of Brahmsian compositional strategies. Still, as far back as 1983, Peter Petersen called for a more balanced view, transcending the biases of a chauvinistic German "mainstream" in relation to peripheral "nationalist" composers.[1] There have since been a handful of analytical studies of Dvořák's music, although the quantity has hardly kept pace with the attention lavished on Brahms.[2] These studies often still include comparisons with Brahms's approach, but with recognition that, although Brahms "made an important contribution to Dvořák's stylistic development . . . Dvořák's achievement was in large measure his own."[3] Some scholars have even speculated about Dvořák's possible influence on the older master rather than the reverse.[4]

Dvořák's music nevertheless remains understudied, and in this chapter serves as a route to rethinking Brahms. The intention is not to trace influence in one direction or the other. Rather, I analyze works of Dvořák that Brahms admired and compare them with compositions of Brahms. This analytical dialogue highlights less stereotypical aspects of Brahms's music and in the process achieves greater appreciation for Dvořák's artistry. The comparisons illustrate Brahms's embrace of compositional strategies not paradigmatically associated with him, both creatively in his own chamber music and critically in chamber works of Dvořák that received Brahms's approbation.

This reappraisal proceeds via two case studies. The first begins with the finale of Dvořák's String Quintet in E♭ Major, Op. 97, composed in 1893 during Dvořák's time in America. The movement is remarkable for its multileveled repetitiveness even by rondo standards. This repetitiveness, along with the finale's tunefulness, fits the cliché of Dvořák as a fount of charming ideas but lacking Brahms's powers of *Ausarbeitung* (working-out). Yet comparison with the finale of Brahms's Piano Quartet in G Minor, Op. 25, reveals a similarly repetitive, non-developmental form. The master of developing variation was willing to design a movement governed by very different principles from those conventionally associated with him. In both rondos, local and large-scale tonal continuities and recapitulatory-like restatements counterbalance the mosaic-like patterning. Ultimately, the repetitiveness allows both movements' codas to effect climax by breaking free of the regularity—a "breaking-out" as a special form of breakthrough.

The second case study focuses on the relationship between thematic and tonal content in sonata form, considering two movements by Brahms and one by Dvořák. The first movement of Brahms's Clarinet Sonata in F Minor, Op. 120, No. 1, epitomizes Brahmsian organicism—a multilayered saturation of motives that unifies the exposition's tonic and submediant key areas. Here we find quintessential exemplification of formal evolution on the opposite end of the Brahmsian spectrum from the additive processes of the Piano Quartet's finale. The first movement of Dvořák's String Quartet in E Major, Op. 80, takes a less exhaustive approach to integration of its own I–vi tonal pairing, exposing it to the criticism of being less unified in its treatment of motivic harmony.[5] Comparison with the first movement of Brahms's Violin Sonata in G Major, Op. 78, however, demonstrates the aesthetic value of juxtaposition, as opposed to seed-to-harvest processes, for the relationship between form and motivic harmony in the "ritornello script" that both movements enact.[6] Together, the case studies illustrate that it is a range of compositional resources, rather than one ideal type, that we may admire in Brahms and Dvořák—and that, we may speculate, they admired in each other.

Case Study I

Several preliminary points contextualize the analytical comparison of the finales in the first case study. Although Dvořák's finale ostensibly fits entrenched critical judgments, its idiosyncratic organization is no more representative of his approach than that of the Op. 25 finale is of Brahms's. In addition to composing a movement based on similar formal principles and thereby implicitly validating them, Brahms also took unqualified pleasure in Dvořák's American works. Although no assessment of the Op. 97 finale (or any other individual American movement) exists in the extant correspondence, Brahms commented generally about the compositions of 1893, writing to Simrock that, "I rejoice in [Dvořák's] cheerful creations."[7]

Although analysis reveals many similarities between the movements, crucial differences also exist. Even before delving into musical content, obvious contrasts caution against pushing the comparison too far. Brahms's Quartet was the work of an ambitious young composer yet to make his name, and Brahms programmed it on his all-important debut concerts in Vienna in 1862. Dvořák's Quintet was written long after he had become an internationally recognized figure and therefore an artist with little to prove. "[He] stated that he 'wanted to write something really melodious and simple'"[8] in the American works, surely a very different aim compared to Brahms's with the Quartet.

The movements are further contrasted in character as reflected by their modes—stormy minor for Brahms's Op. 25 and sunny major for Dvořák's Op. 97—and the vernacular style each evokes. Brahms created a fiery movement based on the *style hongrois*. Dvořák's jovial finale exhibits the "American tone" and "simplicity" that distinguishes the chamber works of 1893.[9] These differences are not a matter of a more profound artist outshining an inventive yet superficial understudy, but rather of contrasting compositional intentions.

Diverse intentions notwithstanding, a preponderance of thematic recurrence characterizes both movements. Tables 12.1 and 12.2 outline the forms. The opening refrains and the episodes trace small ternary forms, often including the standard repeat signs of two-reprise form. The tables depict these repetitive designs through a series of aba' labels across the center row of each table.[10] Burrowing down further (and not depicted in the tables) are the numerous patterns of repetition on lower levels. For instance, the [a] section of Brahms's refrain consists of a statement-digression-return pattern in bars 1–12, 13–18, and 19–30. On an even more local level, each of these sections houses a repetitive pattern. The statement and return passages themselves state and repeat a six-bar unit, and this unit itself consists of repetition of a three-bar idea. The middle section likewise states and repeats a three-bar phrase.

Dvořák's refrain is similarly repetitious. The modulating period of the [a] section adheres to the standard (i.e., repetitious) parallelism of antecedent and consequent (bars 1–4 and 5–8). These subunits, moreover, both follow the two-bar basic idea with a varied repetition rather than a more conventional contrasting idea. The [b] section of bars 9–16 presents three statements of its own, motivically derived, two-bar unit, before an internally repetitive variant based on fragmentation (bars 15–16) leads to the section's concluding fermata.

To avoid my own plunge into extreme repetition, I will not trace the similarly multilayered patterns of recurrence in the finales' episodes. The lower-level repetitions not depicted in the tables are clear enough for readers to discern directly from the scores. Less obvious are the ways the movements construct larger patterns of recurrence that the composers ingeniously counterbalance with characteristics of through-composition. What I have in mind are the large-scale ternary pattern of Brahms's movement and the overarching binary organization that Dvořák crafts.

Brahms's statement-contrast-return form highlighted at the top of Table 12.1 reflects patterns of recurrence on the immediately lower level, too. In the case of Part 1, an ABA' pattern governs the section, while statement and return of the C episode frames the CDB'C organization of Part 2. The bottom three rows of the table indicate that shifts of mode, relative keys, hypermeter, and tempo support recursive patterns on both levels. Part 1 encloses B♭ major

Table 12.1 Brahms, Piano Quartet, Op. 25, iv, Formal Outline

	1 Statement					2 Contrast				3 Return			
Bars	1–79				80–115	116–54	155–72	173–205	206–37	238–55	256–93	294–362			363–405
	A				B	A'	C	D	B'	C	A"	Dev. and RT			A''' = Coda
Bars	1	31	61	67	80	92	104	116	155	161	167	173	189	198	206	218	238	244	250	256	294	303	313	363
	a	b	overlap	a'	a	b	a'	a	a	b	a'	a	b	a'	a	RT	a	b	a'	b	on D	on B	on C+B	a'
Recap. "scattering"								[a] section of refrain						recap. of B in major tonic					[b] section of refrain				[a'] section of refrain
Tonality	g minor: i				III				i	G major: I		vi ⎯⎯ V/vi	"I" V/vi–vi–V		g: i V		V i	
Hypermeter	3-bar groups				4-bar groups				3-bar groups	3-bar groups		4-bar groups	4-bar groups		3-bar groups		3-bar groups	4-bar groups		3-bar groups
Tempo	Presto								Meno presto			Poco sost. + dim.	In tempo		Meno presto		Tempo I	Meno presto, accel. to			Molto presto

Table 12.2 Dvořák, String Quintet, Op. 97, iv, Formal Outline

	Part 1						Part 2				Coda
Bars	1–32		33–56		57–67	68–113	114–45	146–71	172–82	183–228	229–86
	A		B		A'	C	A	B'	A"	C	A-based Coda
Bars	1	9	17 (⇒TR in 26–32)	33	41	49 (⇒TR in 52–56)	57	68	83	99	114	122	130 (⇒TR in 139–45)	146	154	162 (⇒TR in 165–71)	172 (⇒TR in 180–82)	183	198	214	
	a	b	a'	a	b	a'	a'	a	b	a'	a	b	a'	a	b	a'	a'	a	b	a'	
Comments							only [a'] section of refrain							recap. of B in minor tonic			only [a'] section of refrain				
Tonality	I		iii		I	♭VII	♭III	i			I	WI ——— I	I
Dynamics			[b] begins pp, crescendos to mp, then mf at [a'], and culminates on ⟶ ff at A'			p and pp (f only briefly at 107)					[b] begins pp, rises to p, then reaches mf and f in [a'], and culminates on ⟶ ff at A"			pp and p (mf and piu f only at [a'])	f, ff, and fff
Character	dance rhythms (dotted)		dance rhythms (triplets)		dance rhythms (dotted)	lyrical	dance rhythms (dotted)	dance rhythms (triplets)	dance rhythms (dotted)	lyrical	dance rhythms (dotted and triplets)

within a G-minor frame, while Part 2 does the same for E minor within G major, now at a slower tempo (*meno Presto*). Part 3 then returns to the G-minor thematic material and tempo of Part 1, sandwiching the G major and *meno Presto* of Part 2 on the larger level. The balancing of keys a minor third above and below the tonic—G–B♭–G and G–E–G—will emerge as yet another similarity with Dvořák's finale. Alternation of three- and four-bar hypermeter further contrasts the framing sections (A and C) from the middle sections (B and D), as summarized in the second row up from the bottom of the table.

The binary subdivision that Table 12.2 asserts for Dvořák's movement receives its own manner of multidimensional support. Its main basis is a global repetition of refrain/episode alternations: the ABA′C of Part 1 is answered by Part 2's AB′A″C, with an A-based coda following. The A sections launching these two parts (bars 1 and 114) are both complete statements of the refrain's aba′ form, which delineates their large-scale initiating function. The internal A′ and A″, by contrast, present only the [a′] phrase (bars 57–67 and 172–82). These abbreviated returns complete the textural-dynamic expansions that occur across the preceding B episodes and in that sense group with those sections. More decisive breaks at the C entrances support this grouping, with the C statements culminating the two parts of the binary form. The table traces, toward its bottom, the dynamic expansion from B to abbreviated A, and the change in character from dance-like B and A to soft, lyrical C.

A fascinating component of both movements is the manner in which Brahms and Dvořák compose across the forms' large-scale subdivisions to create end-accented trajectories, even while sustaining the aesthetic of repetition. Brahms achieves this continuity by crafting a non-contiguous process of recapitulation—paradoxically another technique of recurrence—scattered across the largest ternary pattern.[11] The end of Part 1 initiates the process by restating only the refrain's [a] section (bars 116–54). The [b] section returns considerably later to launch Part 3 (bar 256), which eventually concludes with the refrain's final component of return: the restatement of [a′] as coda (bar 363).

There are two additional touchpoints of reprise: the sonata-form-like tonic grounding of B material at bar 206 and the climactic double return of the C episode at bar 238. All of these restatements sustain momentum through equivocation regarding a full sense of return. Despite its recapitulatory tonal characteristic, the return of the B theme lacks dominant preparation. It also maintains instability by immediately modulating back to the E-minor key of the D episode. The B′ episode's G tonic is prolongational rather than structural. The main tonal motion is from the V/E that concludes the D episode at bar 205 to the E-minor expansion in bars 210^2–17, as Roman numerals in the "Tonality" row of Table 12.1 indicate. The B′ section also quickly merges into a forward-driving retransition (bars 218–37) to the "true" return of G at the arrival of the C episode. Yet although the C episode's G-major tonic is structural, this double return remains a step removed from the ultimate goal in terms of mode (major not minor), thematic material (C not A), and tempo (*Meno presto* not Tempo I). Those characteristics coalesce only at the A-based coda of bar 363, which forms the climactic goal of the scattering process's various forms of delay.[12]

Dvořák also softens sectionalization through partial restatements and tonal continuities. The above-described incomplete returns of the refrain allow the momentum of the B sections to flow onward to the more substantial breaks that occur at the C episodes. Yet both C episodes are distant from the tonic—♭III and ♭VI—and sustain momentum through that status. Indeed, the second, presumably recapitulatory instance at bar 183 defers an expected E♭ tonic via deceptive resolution of the home dominant.

The first C episode (bar 68) achieves additional continuity through the bridge of ♭III it initiates across the form's binary subdivision. This G♭ tonicization remains in place across what otherwise would be a recapitulatory return of the refrain at bar 114. The prolonged G♭ forms the center of a quasi-palindrome straddling the binary form, similar to the tonal "balancing" in Brahms's movement. In Part 1, the B material tonicizes G minor, the key a major third above the tonic. In Part 2, the return of the C episode tonicizes C♭, the key a major third below. In the center and across the bifurcation of the two-part form sits the mutual tonicization of the chromatic third relation, G♭, of the C episode and A refrain.

Mode also plays a decisive role, contributing to goal directedness in the face of repetition as in Brahms's rondo. The return of the B section at bar 146 grounds the G-minor theme in the tonic, but it is the minor tonic. E♭ major returns only later, and initially this occurs with the refrain at bar 172—one of the above-described partial returns absorbed into a broader trajectory from B episode to non-tonic C entrance. The next stage of equivocal recapitulation arises when this ♭VI return of C finally makes its way to the tonic for its [a'] section at bar 214. This strategy creates continuity across the end of C and the refrain-based coda of bar 229. As in Brahms's finale, it is only in this final section that a fully satisfactory home tonic arrives in its original mode and affiliation with A material—the breakthrough moment in both movements mentioned at the outset.

Aspects of rhythmic organization and refrain-episode motivic links offer final opportunities to compare these unusual movements. Dvořák's finale again superficially appears to confirm hackneyed critiques of the composer. The movement's repetitiousness results in nearly unvaried four- and often eight-bar hypermeter. As the cliché would have it, Dvořák's melodic invention is enviable, but there is an absence of "working-out" and the resulting elasticity of Brahmsian musical prose. The only exceptions to rhythmic regularity are the compound period of the C theme (8 + 7 in bars 68–82), the brief transitional passages connecting the refrains and episodes, and several segments of the coda. Example 12.1 provides one instance, with an interpretation of the hypermetric irregularity. The example also illustrates the motivic linkage based on the circled G–D fourth that smooths the otherwise sharp boundary. More broadly, the three rondo themes share intervallic relationships, as Example 12.2 suggests.

Example 12.1 Dvořák, String Quintet, Op. 97, iv, phrase expansion in transition to B episode.

Compositional Range vs Compositional Ideal Type

Example 12.1 Continued

Example 12.2 Dvořák, String Quintet, Op. 97, iv, motivic connections among themes.

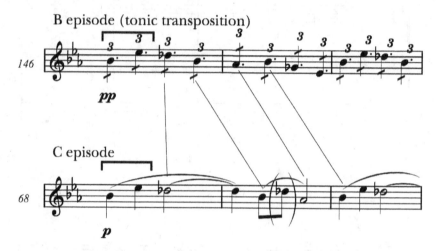

Before we hastily judge this modest amount of development as a compositional deficiency, we should recognize the similar absence of prose-like construction in Brahms's finale. Brahms actually presents more abrupt shifts from section to section and consistently symmetrical hypermeter. Each section simply ends with a hard break before the next launches, although an F♯–G motive provides linkage across many of the formal boundaries.[13] Example 12.3 suggests that hypermetric reinterpretations of this motive and a sixteenth-note idea join the linking process to invest dynamism into an additive process. Still, these reinterpretations result from temporal repositioning of unaltered motives. Absent are the extensive intervallic reshapings of these or the movement's other ideas characteristic of developing variation. The listener must wait until the retransition in Part 2 (bars 218–37) and the developmental passage in Part 3 (bars 294–362) for the fluid motivic development that more characteristically animates Brahms's forms from the outset.

Brahms does trace a diverse pattern of hypermeters compared to Dvořák's consistently duple hierarchy. This is unsurprising, however, given Dvořák's intention "to write something really melodious and simple." Brahms's three- and four-bar periodicities indicated in Table 12.1 build, on higher levels, to

Compositional Range vs Compositional Ideal Type

Example 12.3 Brahms, Piano Quartet, Op. 25, iv, hypermetric reinterpretation of linking dyad.

Example 12.3 Continued

Compositional Range vs Compositional Ideal Type 261

Example 12.3 Continued

an array of hypermeters—large-scale equivalents of 12/8, 3/8, and 4/8 for the A, B, and C sections, respectively, and multileveled duple organization for the D episode.¹⁴ These hypermeters enter through abrupt fiat, as one section follows another. The patterns, moreover, remain largely unvaried within their sections. As compelling as it all is—and this is unquestionably a thrilling movement—the metric changes are not byproducts of a process of motivic evolution, as Schoenberg attributed to Brahmsian musical prose.

Case Study II

If one were searching for a prototypical example of developing variation to contrast with the Op. 25 finale's additive processes, the first movement of Brahms's Clarinet Sonata in F Minor, Op. 120, No. 1, would be a strong candidate.[15] The merger of form and content across the exposition's tonic and submediant key areas embraces pitch motives, chordal sonorities, tonal pillars, and the key scheme itself. The relationships permeate both horizontal and vertical pitch space on multiple hierarchical levels. Further integration arises through the chronological growth of the relationships from melodic details, to local harmonies, and onward to enlargements across the formal sections. The metaphor of organic growth seems apropos, especially compared to the paratactic procedures of the Op. 25 finale.

I begin this second case study by focusing on the Clarinet Sonata to facilitate engagement with its complexities. Once this ideal type of developing variation is on the table, we will be in a position to compare, first, the less painstaking but no less effective integrative strategies in Dvořák's E-major Quartet. Lest we take the comparison to confirm the traditional view of Brahms as the superior composer, the case study concludes with a survey of similar processes of juxtaposition, as opposed to seed-to-harvest organization, for motivic harmony in Brahms's G-major Violin Sonata. I hasten to stress that I am not claiming that Dvořák's Quartet and Brahms's Violin Sonata are devoid of developing variation (or that the Op. 97 and Op. 25 finales are without motivic processes either). These compositions nevertheless reap the aesthetic rewards of contrast and alternation in developing their motivic harmonies, in contrast to the near-obsessive integration in the Clarinet Sonata. Both composers possessed expansive toolkits that allowed them to range from paratactic formal processes like those of the finales, to intensely developmental organization like that of the Clarinet Sonata, but also to equally compelling strategies in between as represented by the Quartet and Violin Sonata.[16]

The Clarinet Sonata's motivic process begins immediately and evolves across the exposition's formal demarcations. The P zone alternates two themes: a quasi-introductory opening phrase ($P^{1.0}$ of bars 1–4) and the main

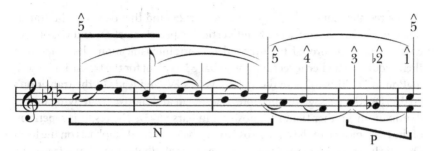

Example 12.4 Brahms, Clarinet Sonata, Op. 120, No. 1, i, graph of $P^{1.0}$ (bars 1–5¹).

theme proper of bars 5–12 ($P^{1.1}$); the themes then return in bars 13–24 and 25–32. Example 12.4 highlights two motives in $P^{1.0}$: a D♭ neighbor and a G♭ passing tone. The addition of G♭ to the passage's F natural-minor pitch collection anticipates the pitch collection of the D♭ key of the first of the two subordinate themes. (This is a three-key exposition, with a D♭-major S^1 at bar 38 and a C-minor S^2 at bar 53.) A hint of the seed-to-harvest integration of tonic and submediant key areas is intimated from the outset.

The sentential $P^{1.1}$ extends the influence of the motivic D♭ and G♭ into the vertical dimension. The i and iv harmonies of $P^{1.1}$'s basic idea and its repetition receive embellishment via 5–6 motions over bass F and B♭ (bars 5–6 and 7–8). Although the resulting D♭ and G♭ ⁶₄ sonorities are not independent harmonies (they are byproducts of the i$^{5-6}$– iv$^{5-6}$ progression), they manifest the first step in the evolution from melodic to harmonic expression of the motivic content. The ⁶₄ position will emerge as a characteristic feature of the nascent motivic verticalities, analogous to the specifically neighboring and passing identities of the D♭ and G♭ motives in the horizontal dimension.

The process of development continues with the return of the $P^{1.0}$ idea in bars 13–16, as expansion of $P^{1.1}$'s half-cadential dominant. The passage harmonizes the D♭ neighbor with ii^{ø7} rather than VI in bar 15. It nevertheless brings, to the clarinet's thematic surface, the statement of the motive submerged in the piano's accompaniment at $P^{1.1}$'s half cadence of bars 11–12 (also with ii^{ø7}). The dominant expansion continues with a varied repetition of $P^{1.0}$ in bars 17–24, but one that indeed harmonizes D♭ with the submediant and G♭ with ♭II (bars 19–20 and 24). What had been the neighbor and passing origins of the motivic process in the original, purely linear $P^{1.0}$, now include in $P^{1.0}$ the harmonies they had generated in $P^{1.1}$. What is more, VI and ♭II once again appear in the characteristic ⁶₄ position. VI even receives its first hint of tonicization in bars 19–20, adding a glimmer of the key-scheme component to the thematic process. That the tonicization includes the A♭–G♭–F motive in the bass will have ramifications for the modulation to D♭ for the S^1 theme.

The restatement of $P^{1.1}$ that follows at bar 25 (and that becomes the transition) maintains the horizontal and vertical expressions of D♭ and G♭, but re-emphasizes them through textural and dynamic intensification. The Neapolitan then acquires a higher-level function at bar 33 as pivot for the transition's modulation to D♭. This ♭II⁶ is reinterpreted as D♭'s IV⁶ and leads to the transition's goal V/D♭. The passage further integrates form and motive by arriving on the dominant in $^6_4$ rather than root position in bars 36–37. The result is repetition of the G♭–F motive in the bass across the arrival of S¹, and emphasis on the local D♭ tonic in the emblematic $^6_4$ position—the very attributes that characterize the just-described seed for this tonicization across bars 19–20.

Example 12.5a labels surface transformations of $P^{1.0}$'s neighbor and passing segments as they now comprise S¹. The recurrence of these motives at their original pitch develops the aforementioned embedding of D♭'s pitch collection in $P^{1.0}$. Brackets in Example 12.5b highlight further pitch-specific repetitions buried deeper in S¹. Going a step further—and most astonishingly—Example 12.5c indicates that even as D♭ has risen to the status of tonal pillar, the harmony remains an offshoot of the opening F tonic. Brahms renders motivic even the contrapuntal origin of S¹'s expanded D♭ $^6_4$ chord in the i^{5-6} voice leading, as part of the enlargement. This D♭ also reflects the motivic status of the Neapolitan function. VI⁶ becomes a ♭II⁶ pivot for the modulation to C minor for S² at bar 53, and it does so specifically with the pre-dominant function and $^6_4$ position characteristic for a Neapolitan, as Roman numerals beneath the graph highlight.

Although this motivic integration is extensive even by Brahmsian standards, other passages rival it. Example 12.6 summarizes the prominence of D♭ as climax of the development, the return of $P^{1.0}$ in the Neapolitan to initiate the thematic reprise at bar 130, and the folding back of the prolonged submediant into the tonic for $P^{1.1}$'s recapitulation via a reversal of the motivic 5–6 voice leading.[17] Here Brahms emphatically practiced what he preached to his student Gustav Jenner about the necessity of making the form a consequence of the musical ideas.[18]

The persistence of D♭ as a tonic shadow marks the i/VI relationship as a tonal pairing. The tendency to intertwine i and VI aligns the movement with broader nineteenth-century trends of tonal dialectics. Although tonal pairing has diverse manifestations, it generally refers, as here, to a persistent interaction between two tonics within and across formal sections, in contrast to the unambiguously "uni-centered" approach of the eighteenth century. It may not be surprising that Dvořák also embraced tonal pairing, given Wagner's influence on him and extensive use of the technique. But like Brahms, Dvořák adopted tonal dialectics in the apparently conservative, and ultimately monotonal, context of sonata form.[19]

Compositional Range vs Compositional Ideal Type   265

Example 12.5 Brahms, Clarinet Sonata, Op. 120, No. 1, i.
(a) P^1 motives in S^1 antecedent phrase (bars 38–46^1)
(b) motivic enlargements in S^1
(c) motivic basis of large-scale tonal pillars

An emblematic example arises in the first movement of Dvořák's String Quartet in E Major, Op. 80. Comparison with the Clarinet Sonata reveals a less thoroughgoing saturation of tonic-submediant relations, exposing the movement to the old criticism of Dvořák as overflowing with thematic inspiration but falling short of Brahmsian standards of development. On the other hand, a persistence of large-scale I–vi juxtapositions and a novel recapitulatory strategy endow the movement with its own compelling formal narrative,

Example 12.5 Continued

(b)
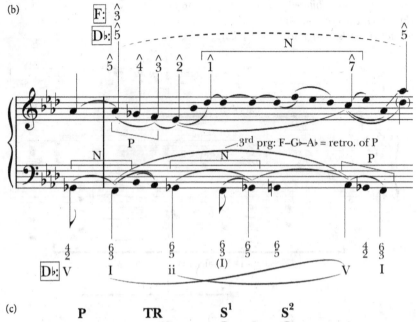

(c)
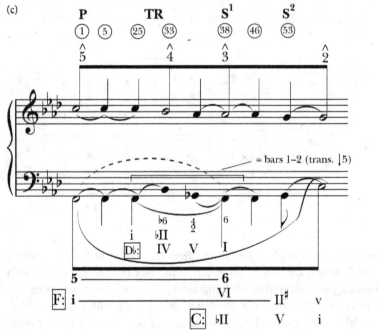

Example 12.6 Brahms, Clarinet Sonata, Op. 120, No. 1, i, motivic tonal pillars in dev. and beginning of recap.

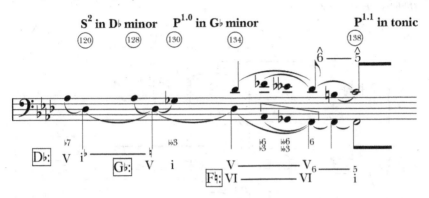

and one whose recapitulation outstrips the Clarinet Sonata's in making the form a consequence of the ideas.[20] I follow examination of these characteristics with comparison to the first movement of Brahms's Violin Sonata in G Major, Op. 78. The Sonata demonstrates that Brahms also employed collocation to motivate tonal-thematic relationships in the "ritornello script" the movement shares with Dvořák's Quartet.[21]

Dvořák's movement houses a two-key exposition, with a subordinate theme in the submediant at bar 50 like Brahms's S¹. In contrast to the Clarinet Sonata's gradual process of motivic evolution, Dvořák more baldly anticipates the I–vi middleground progression with an extensive tonicization of C♯ within the P zone (bars 17–31), as seen in Example 12.7a. The connection is also thematic: P's C♯ passage states the three main melodic ideas of S, as outlined in Example 12.7b. This thematic-harmonic anticipation is complemented by tonal recollection in the S zone: S recalls P's tonic through tonicization of E in bars 54–55 and 70–71. The tonal reversal—E: I and VI♯ become C♯: III and i—produces the harmonic vacillation characteristic of pairing. The result is a prototypical nineteenth-century continuity across the key areas, similar to the unity of P and S¹ in the Clarinet Sonata and in contrast to classical-style tonal polarity.

The integration is nevertheless less exhaustive than the Clarinet Sonata's motivic saturation. Dvořák's P zone touches on C♯ in bars 7, 13–14, and 15–16 and even approaches 6̂ from B♯.[22] In each case, C♯ is part of expansion of E's dominant.[23] There are no vertical anticipations of the two C♯ tonicizations to come, either as sonorities generated contrapuntally from the E tonic or as more independently functioning harmonies. Nor do we encounter a persistent ⁶₄ position, foreground tonicizations, interactions with a motivic Neapolitan,

Example 12.7 Dvořák, String Quartet, Op. 80, i, thematic connections across P and S.
(a) bars 17–19 and 26–29 of P
(b) bars 50–51 and 75–78 of S

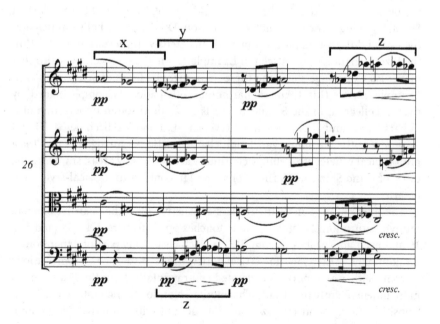

Compositional Range vs Compositional Ideal Type

Example 12.7 Continued

emblematic 5–6 voice leading on multiple levels, or the emergence of these characteristics in a gradual process of growth.[24]

Before we precipitously judge Dvořák's strategy inferior, it is worth recalling Brahms's enthusiasm for the E-major Quartet. In the process of accepting

Dvořák's dedication of his D-minor Quartet in a letter of March 1878, Brahms requested that Dvořák also send him the E-major Quartet, so that Brahms could recommend both works to Simrock for publication.[25] In a letter to Simrock of April 1878, Brahms stressed that "the best that a musician must have, Dvořák has, and is also in these [quartets]."[26] Elsewhere in the correspondence, Brahms emphasized to Simrock that he did not make supportive comments like this lightly.[27] That Brahms put his weight behind string quartets in particular speaks volumes, given his reverence for the genre and his own delay in publishing any until the Op. 51 pair of 1873.

We can only speculate about which characteristics of Op. 80 Brahms found most compelling. The E/C♯ pairing is nevertheless so prevalent that we can be fairly confident that Brahms found it persuasive.[28] So how does the pairing influence the form, even if in a somewhat different manner than the dense integration of the Clarinet Sonata? The crucial, post-exposition passages include: the initiation and climax of the development; the expansion into a "second development" of the C♯ tonicization within P's recapitulation; the swerve, in the tonic return of S, into C♯ and S's eventual close in that tonally-paired key; and the resolution of the tonal pairing in the coda.

The development sustains the E/C♯ duality by departing from P in the tonic at bar 93. Although the specifically tonic return of P in this location is notable in a first movement (as opposed to a rondo finale)—and likely is motivated by the pairing—the strategy is hardly unique. Brahms followed the practice in, for instance, the first movements of his G-major Violin Sonata (as already mentioned), G-minor Piano Quartet, C-minor Piano Trio, E♭-major Clarinet Sonata, and Fourth Symphony, and Dvořák did likewise in the first movements of his Eighth Symphony, E♭-major Piano Quartet, and A♭-major String Quartet.[29] Although a retransitional V prepares the return in the E-major Quartet (bars 87–92), the tonic persists for only six bars and includes a destabilizing seventh (D♮), suggesting that it is a prolongational rather than a structural harmony.[30] The result is that this tonic P is made less structurally significant than S's middleground C♯, with the exposition's pillars thus weighted as $I-V^{/vi}-vi^{♭-♯}-(V-I)$. The reversal of tonal perspective instantiated by S's subsidiary emphasis on E, continues on a larger formal level—E as subsidiary *within* S is followed by E as subsidiary *following* S, all following the opening P in which C♯ is subsidiary within E.

The development keeps C♯ active through tonicization at bar 126 (with C♯ spelled as D♭), followed by a *fortissimo* climax still above bass C♯ at bar 130. The pairing with E remains palpable through progression from this tonicized vi to the home dominant that ushers in the recapitulation at bar 138.[31] E remerges in the primary position, in a reversal of the state of affairs as S progressed to the development: $vi^{♭-♯}-(V-I)$ at the end of the exposition reverts to $^{VI}-V-I$ at the end of the development. Again, the strategy is more akin to juxtaposition compared to the Clarinet Sonata's evolutionary return of VI to i via a reversal of the motivic 5–6 voice leading, rather than motion to a conventional retransitional V.

A "second development" within the recapitulation (bars 154–98) magnifies the original stress on C♯ and S-theme motives within the P zone, even as this C♯ remains subordinate to E. The tonic-submediant vacillation continues as this second development becomes the transition and culminates on a medial caesura (MC) on V/E in bar 194. Just as the development's C♯ had yielded to the retransitional V, so, too, does the second development progress from submediant to dominant. The caesura prepares the tonic return of the first part of S at bar 199. This first part then leads to a freshly composed second caesura, also on V at bar 211. The second MC, however, resolves deceptively to the motivic vi at bar 214, and this tonicized submediant governs the remainder of S's recapitulation (214–30^1).

The situation is remarkable because, on the one hand, it includes the traditional characteristics of a harmonically closed expository S, and the recapitulation of a substantial portion of that S in the tonic. Yet rather than follow with the expected course—continuation of the restatement to closure in the home key—the shift to C♯ produces the extraordinary circumstance of the *un*-transposed return of S material and closure for the recapitulation in the same C♯ key as in the exposition. This late elevation of C♯ is underscored by S's maintenance of its original subsidiary tonicization of E (bars 218–19). But the alternation also migrates to a higher level since S now manifests E→C♯ directional tonality. The marked character of the recapitulation's C♯ close apotheosizes the E/C♯ duality. C♯ usurps E at the very moment that the home tonic would conventionally resolve the tonal drama of sonata form, a convention the movement invokes through S's initial tonic return.

Brahms's recapitulation in the Clarinet Sonata seems tame by comparison: an abbreviated P zone in the minor tonic (bars 138–45) leads via a brief transition (bars 145–52) to restatement of S^1 in the major tonic (bars 153–67), with F minor returning for S^2 (bars 168–205). Formal convention gains the upper hand with tonic restatement pervasive, in contrast to Dvořák's intensification of his tonal dialectic through freshly composed passages. It is Dvořák who more extensively crafts the recapitulation as a consequence of the musical idea.

The coda finally unravels the E/C♯ braid with a P-based phrase at bar 234 leading to a closing E cadence at bar 244. The subsequent expansion of the closing E tonic includes a final recollection of the tonal duality—the beautiful, shimmering C♯ sonority of Example 12.8. That this sonority "reduces" C♯ to a byproduct of a 5–6 motion over an E pedal does nothing to diminish its poignancy. Dvořák chooses a compelling alternative to Brahms's strategy. Rather than beginning with an embryonic I$^{5-6}$ motion and allowing the submediant gradually to emerge and grow, he exposes the distilled essence of the I/vi relationship as culmination for the previous mid- and large-scale juxtapositions.

272   Analytical Perspectives

Example 12.8 Dvořák, String Quartet, Op. 80, i, distilled essence of I/vi pairing in coda.

Like Dvořák's quartet movement, the first movement of Brahms's Violin Sonata in G Major, Op. 78, develops a motivic harmony in a manner distinct from the all-encompassing integration of the Clarinet Sonata. The approach is distinct, too, from the Quartet's tonal pairing. Comparison of these movements serves to illustrate neither a pecking order of artistic integrity nor the absence of developing variation and organic unity, but the mastery of both composers in marshalling a range of strategies relevant to varied musical contexts. Indeed, Brahms's Op. 78 first movement is as compelling a sonata form as any in the composer's oeuvre. The work's great personal significance, as an expression of consolation to Clara Schumann on the death of her son Felix (Brahms's godson), all but guarantees that this would be the case.

The Sonata's first movement, like those of the other two compositions, stresses a third-related harmony in its P zone. III♯ enters at bar 11 without the multidimensional foreshadowing of the Clarinet Sonata or even the modulatory preparation of the String Quartet. The A section of the P zone's small ternary form (bars 1–10) presents a beautifully uncomplicated harmonic progression as it moves from opening tonic to a tonicized, half-cadential dominant. The result is an arresting, fresh shift to III♯ at the entrance of the B section (bars 11–20), a spontaneity underscored by the sudden change from metric consonance to dissonance (unperturbed 👫 in the A section to 👫 against 👫 in the B section). Voice leading integrates the III♯ within a I–III♯–V progression, as Example 12.9 suggests. The A and B sections also connect via B's development of A's seminal dotted rhythm.[32] The formal context nevertheless seems calculated to allow III♯ to enter as a novel harmonic color rather than as the gradual germination of a previously planted tonal seed.

The form likewise abruptly exits the III♯ expansion, although voice leading again assimilates the mediant into its tonal context—here the III♯–IV–ii–V motion that culminates the B section. The A′ section (bar 21), which merges into the transition, and the subordinate theme (bars 36–60¹) set aside III♯, even as Brahms unifies the exposition via his emblematic melodic-motivic evolution.[33] This is a very different world from that of either the Clarinet Sonata or Quartet, where the motivic submediant remains omnipresent. The mediant relation returns only later and in a manner that sustains, as its own type of characteristic feature, the potential to manifest a striking change of harmonic color.

The context for this return-at-a-distance is curious. The subordinate theme recedes to its point of closure at bar 60¹. Rather than highlighting the closing D tonic in the closing zone, Brahms shifts suddenly to III♯ of D. Like the B major of P, this III♯ has not been prepared by S. Rather, it recalls the original I–III♯ relationship now transferred to the dominant key, including the extemporaneity of its entry. Although the passage expands the F♯ sonority, F♯ functions locally as V/B, in a further recollection of the original tonicized B mediant. The passage also maintains the function of III♯ as a chord that participates in motion to V, as Example 12.10 indicates at bar 70. Once the D tonic returns at bar 74, it begins to tilt toward its subdominant, and this gravitation to G prepares the tonic return of P that initiates the development at bar 82. The strategy affiliates the form with the Type III ritornello script that also underlies Dvořák's quartet

Example 12.9 Brahms, Violin Sonata, Op. 78, i, voice leading context for III# in P².

movement, and here, too, the rescoring of P signals the launch of the development rather than an exposition-repeat feint.

Like S, the development forgoes III# or any idiosyncrasies overtly traceable to it. Most obviously, there is no climactic mediant analogous to the dramatic submediants in the developments of the Clarinet Sonata and String Quartet.

Compositional Range vs Compositional Ideal Type

Example 12.10 Brahms, Violin Sonata, Op. 78, i, voice leading context for III# in C.

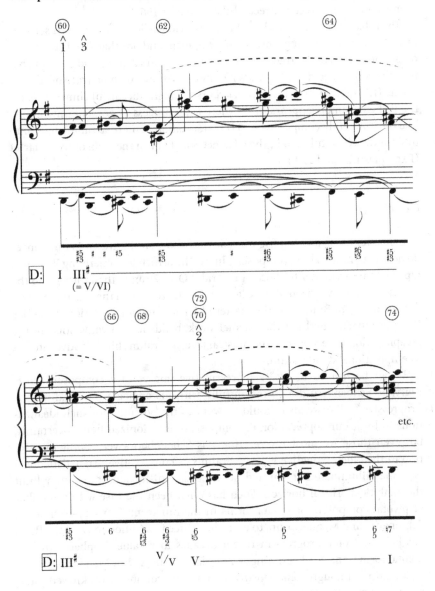

This strategy allows the recapitulation of P's A and B sections at bars 156 and 165 to retain spontaneity as a marker of III#'s motivic identity. The G-major return of S at bar 174 prepares the closing zone's III# so that it, too, maintains its novel character and, in addition, achieves a heightened connection with the P zone's B major. The closing theme (bar 198) returns down a fifth (as S does), so the I–III♯ progression—now G–B—forms a pitch-specific match with P's harmonic motion, just recently recapitulated in bars 156–73.

The P-based coda at bar 223—the fourth "ritornello" of the Type III script—provides a final long-range motivic development and one that affects tonal reconciliation. The coda retraces P's A and B ideas (bars 223–34 and 235–43), but now the B theme joyfully expands A's closing G tonic, with no trace of the coloristic III♯. Tellingly, the resolution occurs through a beautiful climactic fiat—the B theme simply appears in G. There is no process of gradual unwinding, like the differently compelling 6–5 transformation of motivic submediant into tonic at the recapitulation of the Clarinet Sonata or in the coda of the Quartet (Examples 12.6 and 12.8).

Conclusion

This chapter has examined five movements, whose similarities and differences do not break neatly along composerly lines. The principles underlying Brahms's Op. 25 finale are closer to those of Dvořák's Op. 97 rondo than they are to the intense motivic evolution of the Clarinet Sonata. Although the Clarinet Sonata fits our image of Brahms as the master of form-content integration, Dvořák's E-major Quartet, and not the clarinet work, bends formal convention in the recapitulation in response to the musical idea, as Brahms himself advocated as a compositional desideratum.

It can be helpful to create representative images of a composer's creativity, as Schoenberg did so insightfully with his apologia for "Brahms the Progressive."[34] But we also should be wary of the potential for such idealizations to limit our appreciation of composers—less lionized figures certainly, but even those we most revere. This was Schoenberg's very point in reaction to the older, reductive view of Brahms as conservative. An artistic ideal type may illuminate but, through its necessary distortion, it also may limit the analytical-critical horizon. Such has often been the case with a number of pivotal composers of sonata forms in the nineteenth century—Schubert, Schumann, and Mendelssohn, to name just three in addition to Dvořák. There has been welcome progress in recent decades to revalue Schubert's instrumental forms, and the beginnings of similar advances with Mendelssohn and Schumann. Although some worthy efforts have countered hackneyed judgments of Dvořák, much work still remains, as comparison with the considerably larger volume of analytical-theoretical scholarship on Brahms readily demonstrates.

My strategy has been to rethink Brahms in tandem with a comparative reappraisal of Dvořák. What I have presented is only an initial contribution to what I hope will be fresh perspectives on both composers. That Brahms's music continues to inspire such reflection, even in the face of the extensive scrutiny it has attracted, is among its greatest tributes. If Dvořák's compositions still interested Brahms "naturally" as late as 1893, to the extent that he studied the American works closely enough to proofread every note, then surely this repertoire must be worthy of our analytical scrutiny too.

Chapter 13

Intentional Transgressions

Transformation and Prolongation in Selected Works by Brahms

Frank Samarotto

Brahms's rambunctious Waltz in G♯ Minor, No. 14 from his Op. 39, seems unsteady from the outset, and it is not long before it goes off the rails. Bar 8 takes a vertiginous turn to G minor—G *natural*, a half-step lower than expected. Now, amid the tumult, this is a perplex: how can the tonic, the touchstone of stability, be lowered a half-step and still maintain rapport with the jumping-off point? (To be sure, this might be understood as an enharmonically written seventh degree; I will argue that this is not the case here.) The tonic, and the dominant as well, serve as structural pillars undergirding tonal coherence; a chromatic alteration of the roots of either would seem to threaten to undermine that coherence, a circumstance I do not typically associate with the music of Brahms.

And, to be sure, a particular series of events would have to eventuate in order to bring about a genuine deformation of coherence, and these would usually be rather more elaborate than our waltz's transgressive turn (about which more later). These events, I think, are not common. To support that assertion, it will be useful to propose a boundary between harmonic pathways that bend coherence but remain guided by it, and those that, over time, sever ties with tonality's tonal pillars, if only temporarily.

But others might contend that the second leg of my dichotomy is better explained by disregarding diatony's guiding framework altogether. As Richard Cohn has put it: "Neo-Riemannian theory arose in response to analytical problems posed by chromatic music that is triadic but not altogether tonally unified. Such characteristics are primarily identified with the music of Wagner, Liszt, and subsequent generations, but are also represented by some passages from Mozart, Schubert, and other pre-1850 composers.... [S]ome nineteenth-century triadic music [is] to some extent tonally disunified, and, to that extent, 'post-tonal.'"[1] This makes clear that the concern for overall tonal coherence so central to the Schenkerian approach is not at all required by Neo-Riemannian theory. Indeed, Cohn might seem to imply that the logic of Neo-Riemannian organization is essentially anti-tonal.[2] So it is hardly surprising that finding such transformational passages within the bounds of works commonly called tonal would lead some to find these works "tonally disunified," even when they fall well within the common-practice tradition. But is such a finding justified or, more important, could it be analytically persuasive, and under what circumstances?

It seems to me that such situations are really rather rare in the common-practice repertoire. My game plan here will be to argue the norm by pointing to the exception, to show what I consider typical by carefully identifying the special case. I will begin by setting out some abstract issues, and will then turn to the music of Brahms, first to a piece that I regard as unproblematically tonal, then to more complex situations in which transformational steps might engender a tangible conflict with prolongational coherence. Furthermore, I hope to show that these conflicts can be central to a work's expressive meaning.

First, some basic principles, specifically, why is there an issue of conflict at all? I would propose that this arises because transformational and prolongational theories exemplify two fundamentally different sorts of generative structures. Transformational theories can be conceptualized as a series of operations applied to *Klänge* (sonorities) that occur successively without *necessarily* being governed by an overall referential *Klang* or a tonal center. This can be visualized as a series of horizontal steps, as shown in Figure 13.1a.[3] To be sure, it can be argued that an underlying symmetry, or at least a uniformity of recursive operation, can provide a coherent organization to these steps, but still, in the absence of an overriding context, this symmetry renders all *Klänge* hierarchically equal. Whatever sort of coherence this is, it is not generated by any principle of tonal centricity.

A prolongational approach to tonal coherence could be visualized as in Figure 13.1b, in which a single basic triad is understood to generate a hierarchy of middleground elaborations; the consequence of this is that every foreground event is implicitly derivable from a single background tonality.[4] This is quite similar to Figure 13.1c, the original Figure 1 of *Der freie Satz*; this figure was Schenker's graphic representation of his concept of tonal coherence.[5] Rather significantly, it includes a reference to *Diatonie* (the diatonic framework) as a background element; the implication is that diatonic *Stufen* (prolonged harmonies, and, pointedly, not just a single tone or triad) play a controlling role in assuring coherence, providing reference points of contact with tonality at all levels.

Even if we stipulate to the validity of the dichotomy set out in Figures 13.1a and 13.1b, we need not accept that any series of Neo-Riemannian transformations automatically entails a departure from tonal coherence; some of these might be applied to fairly common chord successions.[6] Nor is it enough just to locate an unusual or chromatic chord progression or sequence; the tradition of tonal music is surely robust enough to accommodate a rich array of chromaticism. To speak convincingly of tonal conflict or disunity, I propose that two conditions must be satisfied: first, one needs to show that a transformational

a)

b)

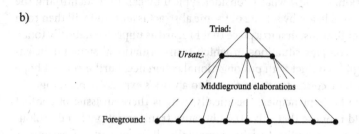

c)

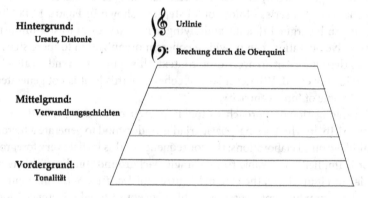

Figure 13.1 Transformation vs. prolongation.

step is *actualized* in the music, and then one must show whether this step is compatible with the overall prolongation or whether it is inexorably in conflict with it.

What do I mean when I say "actualized in the music"? In part, that a tonal event is a feature foregrounded for its own sake, not merely a latent aspect.[7] Such a possibility is beautifully illustrated by David Lewin, in his description of a transpositional network of motives in the last movement of Brahms's Horn Trio, Op. 40. Lewin explicitly distinguishes between places where "a traditional Schenkerian approach . . . reveals more than does [an] intervallic/transpositional approach," and passages where "[the] networks take on a life of their own, [and become] autonomous structures [that] interact with [local] events or

Intentional Transgressions 281

perhaps even determine them."[8] The passage he cites is the end of the development, with the dominant arriving in bar 143; from this point of departure, the horn melody rings once, and then again, but bent by a force that deflects its harmonic path. It is the harmonic deflection that is foregrounded, actualized by our hearing the horn melody dip deeper than before. We quickly recover from this dizzy spell, regain our moorings on the dominant, and find solid footing with the tonic return. Something was dragging us away from that return, but the design certainly makes clear that we were still standing on the dominant, as we often do at the close of a development. The downward cycle of major thirds briefly occludes our awareness of tonal orientation. The effect might be compared to an airplane in free fall; we momentarily feel that we are floating in zero gravity. In reality, however, gravity is very much in effect; it is only that a force is temporarily suspending our sensation of it. In some ways, this metaphor mirrors Lewin's contrast between the passive attitude of observers looking out on distances in Cartesian space and a more active transformational attitude in which one actually executes the traversal of that distance—except that in tonal contexts I might reverse subject and object; when a traversal is unexpected it can sweep along the passive listener like a wave. Whether as agent or patient, the actualized harmonic motion is foremost in our experience.

How might one chart this interplay of forces? I suggest some more specific ways in the general models shown in Figure 13.2. Figure 13.2a, Type 1, shows diatonic coherence in the manner depicted in Figure 13.1b, but at a more foreground level; to concretize this I have juxtaposed a simple example illustrating a common harmonic progression interpreted in a voice-leading sketch. This embodies diatonic coherence; the beginning, the ending, and the straightforward progression that links them all reinforce the composing-out of the tonic harmony. A listener easily identifies each bass tone with the underlying diatonic framework; even the raised $\hat{4}$ serves only to secure the clarity of key.

Figure 13.2b, Type 2, shows a less common situation, one that puts a bit of strain on diatonic coherence. We encountered this situation in the finale of the Horn Trio in the example glossed by Lewin.[9] It can be described as a major-third cycle but that can be misleading. I propose a more dynamic interpretation, aimed at charting the fluctuating rapport with the underlying diatony. As the initial tonic descends by a major third, diatony sags slightly but holds: ♭VI audibly sounds the sixth scale degree, albeit flattened. So far, so good. The next step is not so easy, and the identity of the next root not so transparent. A prospective hearing seeks to maintain major thirds and assumes a descent through A♭ to F♭, but the ear rebels against the notion of ♭IV (or at very least regards it as unlikely). At some point—hard to specify exactly—a retrospective hearing becomes more plausible, and the ear reinstates the diatonic framework, preferring E♮, the familiar third scale degree, as more likely than ♭$\hat{4}$. The area of diatonic reinterpretation is marked by crossed lines; diatony is still present, but there is an area of uncertainty and reorientation, brought

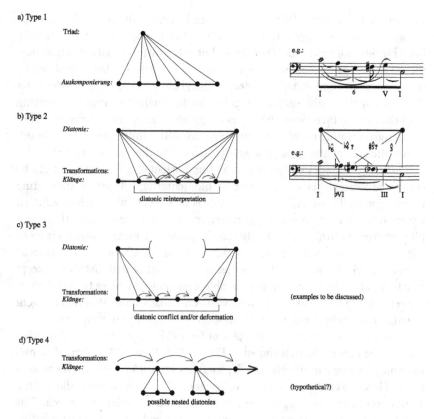

Figure 13.2 Models of coherence.

about by the motions through equal steps, a transformational operation nested within the diatony and contending with it. These relentless steps put stress on its tonal coherence but do not, I believe, ever supplant it.

Setting aside these abstract models for the moment, it will be valuable to consider an actual example of how Brahms can embed a major-third cycle in an unambiguous tonic prolongation and, more important, how the diatonic uncertainty this cycle entails can be rendered an organic part of work's tonal structure, turning a liability into an asset. Example 13.1 shows the opening of the slow movement of the Brahms's Clarinet Sonata, Op. 120, No. 1. Complex harmonic displacements conceal a simple diatonic progression, within which the first chromatic tone, E♮ (bar 3), is unexpected, and its evaded resolution to E♭ even more so. This is a *sub rosa* hint that the E♮ might be behaving as an F♭, and it is more explicit at the corresponding place in bar 15 (see Example 13.1b and compare the coda, shown in Example 13.1c). This E♮/F♭ ambivalence is implicated in the work's luminescent middle section, which executes a gentle fall to ♭VI and then major III, each apparent key dissolving as we find ourselves

Intentional Transgressions 283

Example 13.1 Brahms, Clarinet Sonata, Op. 120, No. 1, ii, a chromatic detail.

back on I and the reprise of the opening. Example 13.2a sketches this middle section in some detail.[10]

Refer now to the deeper middleground in Example 13.2b. The prominent F over IV (see bar 23, the beginning of the B section) is inflected to F♭, then transformed into E♮, which then resolves to E♭, just as in the opening. Now this is indeed a subtle integration of the major-third cycle into the work's motivic life, but it also demonstrates my point: if the diatonic reinterpretation necessitated by the major-third cycle were truly disruptive of tonal coherence, one would have to say the same about the fluctuation between E♮ and F♭ in Brahms's opening phrases cited in Example 13.1, where I should think that tonal coherence is not in question. With this subtle embedded play of enharmonics,

Example 13.2 Brahms, Clarinet Sonata, Op. 120, No. 1, ii, bars 31–49, voice-leading sketch.

a) voice-leading sketch showing middle section in more detail

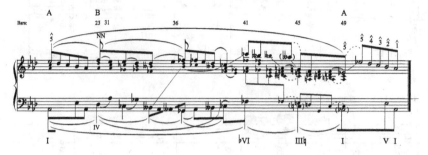

b) the same at a deeper level of middleground

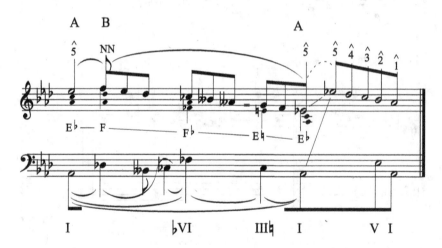

Brahms invites us to embrace the reinterpretation of scale degrees as a part of tonality's richness, rather than a challenge to its stability.

Returning to my abstract examples, Figure 13.2c, Type 3 depicts a situation in which a series of transformational steps lead to a harmony that is difficult to reconcile with the overall tonality, either because that harmony cannot be identified with any scale step of the prevailing tonality, even through mixture, or because it suggests a scale step so altered that it distorts the sense of prolongational coherence.[11] Type 3 is quite rare; it requires a rather particular set of circumstances to lead to an irreconcilable conflict with diatony and deformation of a prolonged tonal background. This might be a momentarily lapse, soon to be corrected, or a large-scale pathway leading to collapse, like a house of cards. It is this rare Type 3 situation that will be considered in the three analyses that follow. I submit the exceptional circumstances of these three works by Brahms as argument for assuming the Type 2 model in the vast majority of cases, and for tonality's robustness in the face of scale-degree uncertainty.

Before proceeding to analysis let us take one more step into abstraction, for completeness' sake. In Figure 13.2d, I extrapolate a hypothetical Type 4 in which areas of diatony occur only in local isolation and in which some other, perhaps transformationally derived, coherence might be in effect. This is not a possibility one encounters in the music of Brahms and it is not one I will consider here.[12]

Waltz, Op. 39, No. 14

For a first possible Type 3, let us return to the G♯-minor Waltz already cited, now analyzed in greater detail in Examples 13.3–13.5. This boisterous dance is always on the edge of a hemiola, thwarted by an odd turn, both melodically and harmonically, in the fourth and eighth bars. The first turn takes the harmony a step down to F♯, suggesting that a descending tetrachord is underway. However, the second bump, four bars later, careens off course to G major, a lowered tonic chord (as we have already noted). That it is meant to be heard as an altered tonic is confirmed by the reprise of this phrase at bar 25, where the harmonic deflection is corrected to the expected and conformant V–I. This is highlighted in the partial rhythmic analysis in the aligned Examples 13.3a and 13.3b; compare the voice-leading sketch in Example 13.5.[13] The passage that follows the anomalous G♮ pointedly fluctuates between E minor and E major, a part of the uncertain state of G at this point. Following the double bar, it is just this chromatic detail that shows variation among the other versions that Brahms made, as noted in Example 13.4.[14] The issue comes to a head in bar 21, when a persistent G⁷ chord finally gives way to the real dominant, with G♮ being reinterpreted as F𝄪.

My précis of the middleground in Example 13.5b shows that I reject a more typical reading of a descending fourth in the bass in favor of elevating the lowered tonic chord to greater status. It surely conflicts with our sense of tonic as a solid foundation, but it seems to me to be truer to the piece: the path to this chord is abrupt but deliberate, so clearly foregrounded by the design. I take this piece to be an example of Brahms actualizing a series of harmonic steps (most of them, taken on their own, quite standard progressions!) to create a momentary tonal diversion, for clearly mock-serious effect.

Rhapsody, Op. 79, No. 1

By contrast, a stern seriousness dominates the Rhapsody in B Minor, No. 1 from Op. 79, which is ruled by tumultuous impulse.[15] It is a virtual essay in

Example 13.3 Brahms, Waltz, Op. 39, No. 14, the opening and its reprise.

Example 13.4 Brahms, Waltz, Op. 39, No. 14, a variable chromatic detail.

as in 4-hand and easier 2-hand versions
(transposed from A minor)

motion through equal-interval cycles, and so contains built-in challenges to the diatonic framework. I will discuss most of the opening B-minor section, beginning with Example 13.6a. The work's opening octave is at least ambiguous: I hear it prolonging an implied dominant, a V which is eventually stabilized as its own key at the end of the first sixteen bars.[16] Within this prolonged dominant we are propelled through an interval cycle of upward minor thirds, from F♯ to A to C until an augmented sixth curtails this force and brings us to the expected V of F♯. This overview comprises the main content of the middleground sketch at Example 13.6b.

Truly disruptive action begins with the second interval cycle, which is charted in Example 13.7. The hard-won F♯ arrival suddenly gives way to D major and a gently nostalgic reworking of the opening melody; note the prior A♯s are recalled as neighboring B♭s. So begins an odyssey: A brief meditation in D minor is interrupted by B♭ major (at bar 39), and very quickly by G♭ major (in bar 43). This is where things go awry: normally we would hear this G♭ as a notational enharmonic, visually different but aurally equivalent to the diatonic V of B minor, namely, F♯. And it could turn out to be exactly that, except that an added augmented sixth takes us to F major, forcing us to hear that F-major chord as a goal dominant—the *wrong* dominant! We find ourselves a half-step off track, in a harmonic cul-de-sac, one that is elaborately prolonged to solidify its presence.

Could we perhaps reinterpret this F♮ as a leading tone to F♯? The scales that mark the end of our journey do nothing to help us; they rather do the opposite. There is no way out but to wrench the lowered V out of its tonal aporia, to restore diatony by sheer force of will, one scale supplanting another. I think this represents a true Type 3 situation, where a transformational path, in this case a cycle of major thirds, leads us past the point where tonal coherence is fully in effect, creating a hiatus in the overall prolongation. This anomalous bass plan is indeed corrected in the return of the A section, as the overview in Example 13.8 shows. But everything in this work's ethos seems to warrant an extraordinary reading of its structure, one prefigured yet unforeseen in its first chromatic note E♯.

Example 13.5 Brahms, Waltz, Op. 39, No. 14, voice-leading sketches.

Example 13.5 Continued

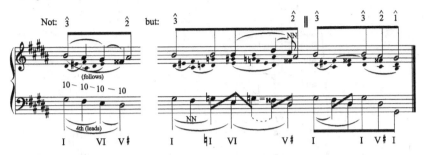

Ein deutsches Requiem, Op. 45, "Denn wir haben hie keine bleibende Statt"

My final example will draw on the German Requiem, on the first section of the sixth movement, the whole of which is a kind of gigantic prelude and fugue. Reduced sections of the score appear in the examples, but access to the full score may be helpful. Indeed, the orchestration is telling: a mystical aura surrounds the opening pair of chords (see Example 13.9). It is not just the registrally distant woodwinds: the harmonic succession of G major–D minor–G major is a sphinx-like enigma. I hear the D-minor chord as a divider within the V, as I show in Examples 13.10a and 13.10b, but this hearing does not mitigate our sense that this is a piece where even the simplest relation of a fifth is rendered problematic. As with the Rhapsody, the opening prolongs the dominant; here it is a harmonic expression of having "no continuing place" (*keine bleibende Statt*), but seeking one to come (*die zukünftige suchen wir*). The melodic arch hints a prophecy not yet realized: the melodic rise in bar 10 hints at a future, but the D♮ is immediately deflected to D♭ (with motivic significance!).

In Example 13.11a, the baritone enters in a passage of great moment: Behold, I will show you a mystery (*Siehe, ich sage euch ein Geheimnis*). His words lead us from the dominant of C minor to an elaborate cadence on D♭—truly a mystery, in that it bends the perfect-fifth-divider prolonging V into a diminished-fifth divider (see Example 13.10c). The harmonic connection between G and D♭ is strained but made viable by the upper voice enlargement of the D–F motion. (This connection is helped by the appearance of the woodwinds in the same register as bar 2.) This harmonic distortion is bit of a stretch already, but even as we take it in, the arrival at D♭ is swiftly usurped by a Baroque cadence formula that drops a fifth to G♭ minor (written by Brahms as F♯ for notational simplicity). "We shall not all sleep, but we shall be transformed" (*Wir werden nicht alle entschlafen, wir werden aber alle verwandelt werden*), and indeed we

Example 13.6 Brahms, Rhapsody, Op. 79, No. 1, bars 1–16, the first interval cycle.

a) foreground sketch

b) middleground sketch

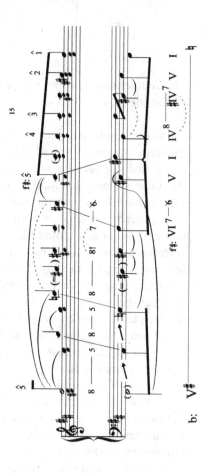

Example 13.7 Brahms, Rhapsody, Op. 79, No. 1, bars 1–66, the second interval cycle.

Example 13.8 Brahms, Rhapsody, Op. 79, No. 1, the bass plan of the B-minor part.

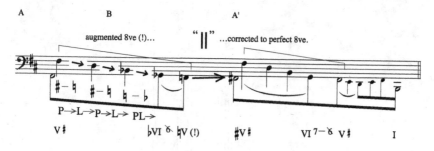

have been: this apparent ♭V has lost contact with the C minor diatony. I do not believe we should hear it as an F♯ neighbor to V of C minor—as charted in Example 13.11c, the transformational path prohibits this direct connection. Appropriately, we depart this patch of ♭V by retracing our steps through D♭ (written as C♯), albeit in the role of V of F♯ minor.

The subsequent course of the piece confirms that this submergence into G♭ minor is a step too far, venturing outside of the tonal framework. This is made evident by repeated attempts to bring D♭ into closer relation with the diatonic dominant G. This begins with Example 13.12, the sounding of the last trumpet, where a jarring succession of nearly unrelated harmonies wrenches us from D♭ back to V, which finally ushers in the first C-minor outburst ("the trumpet shall sound"; *Denn es wird die Posaune schallen*).

The denouement is briefly traced in Example 13.13. The exclamation, "Death, where is thy sting?" (*Tod, wo ist dein Stachel?*; see the inset), with a falling bass that recalls the F♯ minor section, sets in motion a dramatic ascent from D♭ again to G; this final enactment of passage culminates in a breathtaking cadence, shown at the end of Example 13.13b, one that restores D to its natural state as II progressing to V. The conflict is expunged; the tonal allegory is complete.

To recapitulate: the opening chords prepare us to hear the divider flattened as shown in Example 13.10, and to hear that opening chord succession as vastly expanded as it is tonally deformed. The move beyond even this, to a tonally challenging G♭, is a step too far and represents a genuine conflict with diatony; it thus represents my third category, a temporary suspension of tonal coherence, briefly treading beyond its limits.

The three foregoing analyses illustrate situations where events, precipitous in the case of the Waltz, painstaking in the case of the Rhapsody, and miraculous in the case of the Requiem, take us along a path that steps beyond the boundaries of tonality. I would argue that these transgressions are not an artifact of a theory too narrowly circumscribed, but are rather inscribed in the pieces themselves. They are, I believe, the expressive core of these works, to be

Example 13.9 Brahms, *Ein deutsches Requiem*, vi, bars 1–18.

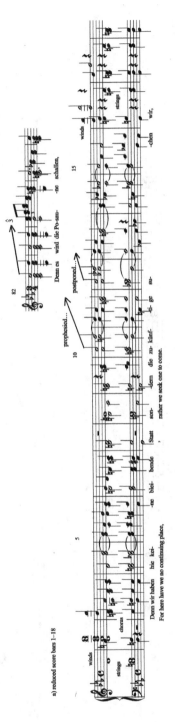

Example 13.10 The divider within V.

The divider within V

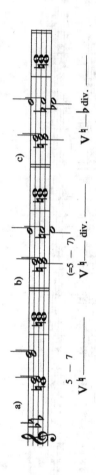

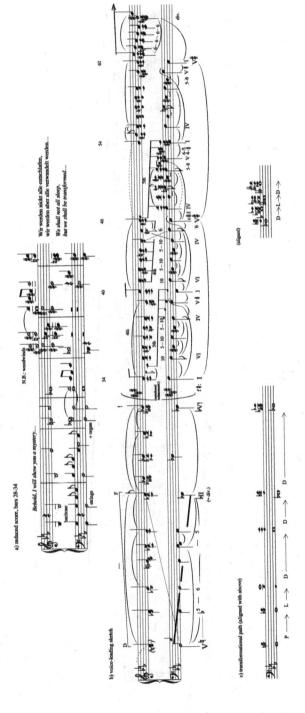

Example 13.11 Brahms, *Ein deutsches Requiem*, vi, bars 28–66.

Example 13.12 Brahms, *Ein deutsches Requiem*, vi, bars 67–86.

Example 13.13 Brahms, *Ein deutsches Requiem*, vi, bars 107–22.

valued for the particularity of their anomaly. This particularity would be lost if we ignored the tonal framework within which it operates; neither should we minimize the extravagant power of these unusual passages. Adherence to tonality is not to be taken as a mark of value but neither is it irrelevant. Some transgressions are intentional, and may even be transformative.

PART IV

MONUMENTS AND MEMORIALIZATION

Chapter 14

Images, Monuments, Constructs
Johannes Brahms in the Culture of Remembrance

Wolfgang Sandberger

Translated by Reuben Phillips

We encounter Johannes Brahms not only through his music. Whoever sits in the Tonhalle in Zürich can spot the likeness of Brahms in the "Composers' Heaven" on the ceiling of the concert hall that was opened in 1895. In this decorative illusion Brahms, already within his own lifetime, entered the heaven through a triumphal arch in the company of seven other composers. The plaques or Brahms busts that are to be seen today in concert halls worldwide are indicators of his canonization. In the nineteenth century, concert halls were quasi-imaginary museums of music history. Like temples of art, temples of music also required "masterworks" and their respective star composers—in short, heroes. The plaques, busts, and images in concert halls represent for the immaterial art of music the field of tension between aesthetic and historical observation. On the one hand they point by their very nature to the historicity of music, on the other they are geared toward venerating the creators of "masterworks" and thereby equally assuring their identity-forming past and future. At the same time, with respect to Brahms, canon-forming categories such as "classicism," "metaphysical aura," "sublimity," "exclusivity," "hierarchization," "memory," and "monumentality" also play a central role.[1] We are aware of these categories even in the tongue-in-cheek play of a caricature. Shortly after the death of the composer on 3 April 1897, Otto Böhler, an illustrator active in Vienna, represented *Brahms's Arrival in Heaven* (*Die Ankunft Brahms' im Himmel*) in an amusing papercut-Parnassus.[2] In this heaven aesthetic partisanship is long since forgotten. Brahms is received with open arms by Bruckner of all people. The humorous silhouette and the concert hall ceiling in Zürich are related: both depictions evoke notions of a Parnassus, in each case Brahms joins an already established group of composers; both are thus iconographic documents of Brahms's canonization. These markers of memorial culture multiplied after the death of Brahms; monuments were erected, memorial plaques affixed, life memoirs written, and editions were conceived. We find the most significant Brahms monuments in the town of Meiningen, in his birthplace Hamburg, and in Vienna, the city that was at the center of his creative activity. The locations where the composer took summer retreats also developed posthumously to focal points of Brahms veneration.

The canonization process began within Brahms's own lifetime; his era was, after all, virtually inscribed with the signature of remembrance. Brahms belonged to that century that had, already in 1839—in contrast to the "philosophical" eighteenth century—been dubbed the "historical century."[3] It was during this century that the bourgeois religion of art sought its Pantheon with the corresponding saints of art, a century with an inclination toward the large and the monumental that is as fascinating as it is disconcerting, and that is reflected in numerous gigantic projects of completely different types: in Leopold von Ranke's giant edifice of world history; in Honoré de Balzac's *Comédie humaine*, which was to comprise over 200 volumes; in Wagner's Gesamtkunstwerk; and in Leo von Klenze's Walhalla. Brahms was, however, not admitted to the Walhalla above the Danube near Regensburg until 14 September 2000—as the thirteenth musician after Handel, Gluck, Haydn, Mozart, Beethoven, Wagner, Bach, Schubert, Bruckner, Reger, Richard Strauss, and Weber.[4]

Brahms himself was thoroughly suspicious of this inclination toward monumentality. For in excess frequently lies the seed of failure. The aesthetic values of Brahms were more modest, even though he was also concerned with a lasting existence in the canon. *Dauerhafte Musik* (enduring music) was, as is well known, a favorite expression of Brahms. "What he meant by this," as his composition student Gustav Jenner recorded, "was that music that was deeply rooted in the very basis of the spirit of music and nowhere came into conflict with it, in contrast to that which clung floundering to the surface and, as original and charming as it might appear, is only all too quickly swept away by the stream of time, because it is not capable of satisfying a deeper artistic need of humankind."[5] The compositional and historical aspiration that lay behind this ideal of an enduring music is enormous, though still rather modest compared to the artistic and ideological concepts of the late nineteenth century. Nonetheless Brahms himself also pursued very deft strategies to fulfill the prerequisites for his canonization. Works such as *Ein deutsches Requiem*, with which he achieved international recognition in 1868, reflect not least the self-reflexive quest for a promising position in the coordinate system of musical history, simply on new terrain.[6]

Our notions of Brahms—beyond the actual music—are to this day directly shaped by aspects of his iconographic canonization and its attendant discourses; the actual images, busts, and monuments have helped to define the images of Brahms in the collective consciousness. In keeping with the "rethinking" that is central to this book, this chapter singles out certain iconographic examples of memorial culture in order to gain new perspectives on Brahms through the patterns of his reception.

Poses and Positioning

Our exploration begins—on first appearance straightforwardly—with the physiognomy of the composer. Our notions of Brahms are shaped by photos of him as an elderly man: there stands or sits a comfortable, serious gentleman with a big white bushy beard; one can almost smell his cigar as he pensively looks into the camera (see Figure 14.1). In the late snapshots by Maria Fellinger[7] we see the apparently melancholic individual who, according to Richard Heuberger's recollection, when in a good mood would let his choir sing "Das Grab ist meine Freude" (The grave is my joy).

Figure 14.1 Johannes Brahms, 15 June 1896. Photograph by Maria Fellinger, Brahms-Institut an der Musikhochschule Lübeck, Nr. 10440.

However, the "old melancholic Brahms," who in the private photograph[8] from 15 June 1896 is only just sixty-three, is not only a biographical, but also an aesthetic-historical construct.[9] The dominance of images of the elderly Brahms corresponds in a peculiar manner with the notion that Brahms has always been a "late," "end-of-an-era" composer, whereby the "late works" overlay *pars pro toto* the early compositions. The nostalgic-elegiac tone of many works from the late period—such as many of the piano pieces and the chamber music with clarinet—is identified as the authentic "tone" of Brahms. Characteristically even a key work like *Ein deutsches Requiem* is described in the literature as really being a work of the mature, late Brahms. A requiem does not appear suitably compatible with a thirty-five-year-old.

Brahms himself certainly highlighted aspects of the melancholic in his music. But when he designated compositions such as the B-minor Intermezzo from Op. 119 as "exceptionally melancholy" (*ausnehmend melancholisch*)[10] and himself—in the context of the Second Symphony and the "Warum" Motet, Op. 74—as a "deeply melancholic person" (*schwer melancholischen Menschen*),[11] specifically what he meant by melancholy requires nuanced differentiation. The one-dimensional view of the "ponderous north German" in any case hides the fact that particularly for the late Brahms the "ideal of lightness, effortlessness, gracefulness"[12] became important. By the same token, Brahms the "profound-German" venerated Johann Strauss and hardly anyone would suspect that the rather Francophobic composer[13] also enthused over Georges Bizet's *Carmen*, which, in a letter to Elisabeth von Herzogenberg he cited as a "a very particular beloved of mine."[14] This *Carmen* infatuation casts a significant light on the issue of how open Brahms also was toward other aesthetic positions. Some years later, Friedrich Nietzsche would write about *Carmen* in his text *Der Fall Wagner*: "This music appears perfect. It comes forth as light, nimble, and courtly. It is lovable, it doesn't sweat"[15]—words that could also have come from Brahms. What surprising common ground in a text that not only contains the sharpest polemic against Wagner, but also directs at Brahms the vicious expression "melancholy of impotence" (*Melancholie des Unvermögens*).[16]

The dominance of late photos and also the etched portraits and the busts from the final decades reinforce a perception of Brahms that is conceived "from the end." From this perspective the development of the composer seems compelling and his place in music history clearly defined: Brahms the symphonist and chamber musician is the great antipode of Wagner and Bruckner, the bourgeois figurehead of a conservative faction with the aesthetic idea of "absolute music" emblazoned on its banner. Much honored and decorated, Brahms was held already by his contemporaries as *the* heir to the classicists, whose works, at the same time, were thought to reflect the spirit of the fin de siècle. Already in 1892 Brahms was described by his friend, the Bach biographer Philipp Spitta, as the quasi-universal heir of music history: "There is no musician who could be more literate in his art."[17] From this perspective Brahms is likewise the composer who had to struggle with an oppressive tradition, especially that of Beethoven. Dependent on music-aesthetic alignment, this image of the "Beethoven-heir" is connected to the notion of Brahms either as the "consummator" or as the "imitator" who was born too late. Both perceptions are, however, perceptions from the rear-view mirror, as it were. Retrospectively, Brahms was taken by many as the terminal point of an aesthetic-historical development, as the composer who (with national-chauvinistic undertones) had secured the "world renown of German music for the last time."[18]

But seen from the beginning, from the various starting points, we perceive a different Brahms. The young Brahms from the area of Hamburg known as the *Gängeviertel* ("Quarter of Narrow Alleyways") was a romantic firebrand full of ambivalences, tensions, and discontinuities. He assimilated Romantic worldviews and identified himself with Capellmeister Johannes Kreisler who stemmed from the pen of E. T. A. Hoffmann. To Clara Schumann the twenty-one-year-old wrote: "I often quarrel with myself, that is Kreisler and Brahms quarrel. But each usually has his decided opinion and wrestles it out."[19] This " 'Kreisler junior' attitude" served less as a means of Romantic-narcissistic self-fashioning, but rather as a "playfully reflective vehicle of his artistic energy."[20] The best-known illustrations of this young Brahms are the consciously androgynously tinged silverpoint drawings of the French writer and painter Jean-Joseph Bonaventure Laurens.[21] Considering these three drawings, which Laurens produced in Düsseldorf in October 1853, Schumann described the young man with dreamily sunken gaze and long blond hair as one of "the most beautiful and ingenious of youths."[22] The double portrait with the Hungarian violinist Eduard Reményi was made before these drawings—a daguerreotype[23] that shows Brahms standing and the violinist sitting. This young Brahms is less tangible today and many details in his musical socialization are still unclear, his sensational advancement outside of all academic institutions in any event proceeding very differently from what is immediately suggested by a middle-class career model. As a little experiment let us set next to the photo of the elderly Brahms the earliest original photographic portrait that shows Brahms alone (see Figure 14.2).

The contrast with his elderly image could hardly be greater; Ludwig Finscher previously assessed it as greater than with any other composer of the nineteenth century.[24] The photograph was taken by Berta Wehnert-Beckmann in November/December 1853 in the musical metropolis of Leipzig, where the young pianist and composer had to pass his first crucial test. Following Robert Schumann's enthusiastic article "Neue Bahnen," the young man, supported by further accompanying letters, was to be launched in Leipzig into the musical world and to negotiate the printing of his first compositions by the prestigious publisher Breitkopf & Härtel. Whether the

Figure 14.2 Johannes Brahms, Leipzig 1853. Brahms-Institut an der Musikhochschule Lübeck, Nr. 10020.

photograph came about immediately at the time of the first stay (from 17 November) or during the second stay (from 1 December) is unclear. The image shows a young man sitting at a table, shy and highly sensitive, who at that time had also captured the imagination of the banker's daughter Hedwig von Salomon: "He [Brahms] now sat opposite me, this young hero of the day, this Messiah promised by Schumann; blond, ostensibly delicate, but already in the twentieth year with developed features, albeit innocent of all passion."[25] In this photographic portrait we see the young artist that also impressed Hector Berlioz and Franz Liszt who were then present in Leipzig.

But let us look more closely at the portrait. It is striking how Brahms stages himself in this Leipzig studio: with the traditional gesture of the Romantic melancholic, supporting his head with his left hand. From here there is a point of reference to the late Brahms. But it is difficult to decide whether, in this self-staging, Brahms is specifically alluding to the prominent depiction of Robert Schumann from 1850 (daguerreotype by Johann Anton Völlner; see Figure 14.3) or is just intuitively following the topos of the Romantic artist-genius.

It is fairly certain that Brahms would have seen the Schumann portrait in Düsseldorf shortly before this photograph was taken. Clara Schumann at any rate found this Schumann depiction and the drawing by Eduard Bendemann that followed it to be "completely marvellous";[26] she made sure that it was this portrait that became lodged in collective memory up until the present as the popular image of Schumann. Already for Robert Schumann the primary function of such a portrait was the commercial interest in his own marketing. The photograph of Brahms is not a snapshot either, but rather a staging in a studio: the young musician quite deliberately presented himself in this pose to public view.

Figure 14.3 Robert Schumann. Daguerreotype by Johann Anton Völlner, Robert-Schumann-Haus Zwickau.

Images of Jupiter

Beyond specific portraits and drawings, descriptions of his outward appearance are also of interest with respect to images of Brahms in the collective memory. Dominant here in particular are the idealized and heroic depictions of the aging composer. By contrast, the young composer and musicologist Adolf Sandberger provided a rather unbiased and unvarnished portrayal of Brahms, who by 1888 had long since become famous. On 10 January of that year the twenty-three-year-old Sandberger noted in his travel diary:

> The most interesting acquaintance [in Vienna] was probably Brahms, to whom I was introduced by the singing teacher [Josef] Gänsbacher. Brahms is short and bowlegged, has a big wobbly belly and is rather sloppily dressed. The head is very interesting, a real, high forehead, which shows the intellectual work. He looked like a Bacchus and, being somewhat sleepy, drank a great deal of beer and felt himself at ease. Only when he donned his pince-nez was he somewhat imposing and the eyes then glanced sharply and urgently.[27]

The "short, squat" (*kurze, gedrungene*) figure of the composer was not lost on Brahms's friend Joseph Viktor Widmann either, but how differently the Swiss author depicts it with his striking choice of words:

> [. . .] the complete appearance, as it were, exuded energy. The lionlike wide chest, the herculean shoulders, the mighty head that the [piano] player sometimes threw back with an energetic jolt, the thoughtful, beautiful forehead, as though glowing from inner illumination, and the Germanic eyes, radiating a wonderful fire between the blond eyelashes, an artistic personality that appeared to be saturated with brilliance right up to its very fingertips. There also lay something confidently victorious in this countenance.[28]

The image of Hercules or Jupiter was not just consistently invoked by Widmann. The beard that Brahms sported since the end of the 1870s played an essential role in this process.[29] The bearded Brahms effectively overgrew the earlier images. It was precisely in the beard-framed face that friends saw a "Jupiter head," which to them seemed "like a symbol of the now completely steadfast figure of the composer, absolutely clear and sure of his goals."[30] This Jupiter figure turns out to be a bourgeois idealization, one that represented artists as icons of Olympic proportions with pseudo-religious bearing. The official Brahms portraits of the 1880s, in particular, appear to show the bearded composer as a figure of identification for the self-confident bourgeoisie, complete with waistcoat, watch chain, and necktie (see Figure 14.4).

The photograph of the fifty-six-year-old stands as an exemplary Brahms-image of "calculated moderation"[31] that at the same time counters the idea of the bohemian or superficial artist, as was definitely Brahms's intention. Max Graf already perceived the bourgeois stance to be a deceptive gesture,

Figure 14.4 Johannes Brahms, Berlin 1889. Brahms-Institut an der Musikhochschule Lübeck, Nr. 10300.

when he described the "bourgeois exterior appearance" as a "classical façade" (*klassische Front*) that "hid so much romantic passion and romantic longing." According to Graf, it is too easily overlooked that this was "a defence mechanism against the tempests of manly emotion, a form of protection against the vulnerability of the soul, and that Brahms regarded the bourgeois lifestyle merely as a safeguard against the emotional and spiritual fantasy that had so strongly affected his youth."[32] Only seldom has posterity kept such ruptures in view.[33] And yet the composer himself could ironically satirize this "classical façade." The singer Felix Kraus, who had presented the *Vier ernste Gesänge*, Op. 121, reports in his memoirs:

> On the next day he sent me his almost life-sized image (photograph by C. Brasch in Berlin from the year 1896) in a beautiful frame signed with his name in the lower right corner, while on the left there was the melody of "Dies Bildnis ist bezaubernd schön" ("This image is enchantingly lovely") from the *Zauberflöte* in music notation, not in major but in *minor*, which he accompanied with the words: when one is such an old fellow and has so many lines and wrinkles then one really *has* to write that in *minor*![34]

Brahms in the "Composers' Heaven"

By at least the last two decades of his life spent in his adopted city of Vienna, Brahms was a leading personality in the international musical scene as a pianist, conductor, and composer, and was greatly admired and revered. Numerous distinctions and honorary memberships were bestowed upon him. Already in 1881 Clara Schumann noted in her diary that it was "a great satisfaction" to see Brahms "so well recognized."[35] This recognition was likewise reflected in etchings and busts that originated already within the lifetime of the composer. Representative here are the Brahms busts by Viktor Tilgner (1844–1896) and Rudolf Küchler (1867–1954). Tilgner completed his bronze bust in 1891, notably not from a model, but rather from life: Brahms had been induced to sit for the Viennese sculptor. Tilgner's picturesque, neo-Baroque style corresponds with the artistic aims of the Viennese Hans Makart, with whom he was friendly. Below the flowing coils of hair, the bust with its affectedly curved large mustache mirrors the "expression of inspired genius, of creative power and alertness."[36] By contrast, the young Küchler, who had studied at the Wiener Akademie, in 1893 modeled facial features, adorning beard, necktie, and the folds of clothing from a photograph.[37] In light of these busts it is perhaps less surprising that Brahms was elevated into the "Composers' Heaven" already during his own lifetime. When on 20 October 1895 he conducted his *Triumphlied*, Op. 55, for the opening of the large hall of the Tonhalle in Zürich, he would have been able to spot his likeness in the central ceiling painting of the hall looking suggestively over Beethoven's shoulder. Together with Bach, Handel, Gluck, Haydn, Mozart, Beethoven, and Wagner, he had entered the muses' heaven through the triumphal arch (*Ehrenpforte*)[38]—as the only composer of this ensemble who was still alive! This process of canonization within his lifetime is quite spectacular and, in view of the "readability" of such a visual canon in the public space of a concert hall, notable in the context of memorial culture.

The inauguration of the new Tonhalle in Zürich in October 1895 was a memorable event.[39] On the day of the concert, as the sixty-two-year-old Brahms was led into the new hall amid the "roaring jubilation"[40] of the auditorium, his perception of his own person in the "Composers' Heaven" quite disturbed him.[41] According to one account he was deeply moved, according to another he rather detachedly indicated that his portrait was wrongly displayed next to Beethoven and Wagner in the "Composers' Heaven" since he was still among the living.[42]

In its visual rhetoric, the ceiling painting by the Viennese painters Karl Johann Peyfuss (1865–1932) and Peregrin von Gastgeb[43] is a magnificent example of a nineteenth-century decorative scheme (see Figure 14.5). The visual program spontaneously evokes associations of traditional motifs such as the "apotheosis" and the "Parnassus," whereby music itself is triumphantly lifted

Images, Monuments, Constructs

Figure 14.5 Ceiling painting, Tonhalle in Zürich.

into the heaven. Instead of individual works, their creators are presented. In relation to Brahms, the particular arrangement of the composers who have entered the heaven through the triumphal arch is of interest. From left to right we see the composers symmetrically grouped by the balustrade of a balcony. Brahms, Beethoven, and Wagner form a trio; Gluck and Haydn a duo in the middle; with Bach, Mozart, and Handel constituting another group of three. The depiction is thus subtly structured both historically and hierarchically; the individual composers are by no means equal in the way that is suggested by a uniform series of portrait plaster busts, as in the heavily war-damaged Odeon in Munich, or as is implied by the nameplates of equal size in other nineteenth-century concert halls. Through the separation of the figures in Zürich the three groups are combined with each other in an artful manner; the trio that is directly by the balustrade ostentatiously and emphatically completes the inner circle of Viennese Classicism: Beethoven, Haydn, Mozart.

Beethoven dominates the group of three on the left, while with Brahms and Wagner the two current representatives of the great partisan battle are depicted—that aesthetic controversy that, at the end of the nineteenth century, could still pointedly be reduced to the formulaic question: who is the legitimate heir of Beethoven?[44] If Brahms looks over Beethoven's shoulder, as it were, then a relationship is established that is exactly the reverse of the reality of Brahms's life. In the music room of his Viennese apartment in the Karlsgasse Brahms had set the bust of Beethoven on the wall high above the piano—almost literally breathing down his neck. On closer inspection it could be speculated whether the likeness of Brahms might have been retrospectively inserted into the Zürich visual program, whether the idea of integrating a living composer into the muses' temple may thus not have been fixed from the start. The fact that Brahms slightly protrudes on the left-hand side beyond the lower architectural circular arch that surrounds the collective group of figures assigns him a special role. In 1895 Brahms was the only composer in this group still alive and, in the aesthetic illusion, it seems as if he has newly joined the other composers, therefore not yet completely or only just belonging. Brahms comes, as it were, from the aesthetic present. Admittedly, the fact that the left-hand trio corresponds, in terms of numbers at any rate, with the group on the right contradicts the idea of a later addition. It is probable that the final visual program coincided with the invitation to Brahms to conduct the opening concert.

At the opening of the Tonhalle in Zürich in 1895, Brahms was thus present in three ways. Firstly, very tangibly, as the conductor of his *Triumphlied*. Secondly, as a composer with a work that, on the one hand, invoked history in the sense of style adaptation, and on the other, casts an eye toward the future in its visionary, eschatological orientation. (The ceiling painting with its fanfares of an imaginary heavenly music corresponds in a curious manner to the *Triumphlied*'s "picture in sound.") And finally, Brahms's likeness was resplendent in the "Composers' Heaven" of the new Tonhalle, a building that, more than any other, represented the cultural self-confidence of the flourishing city and its leading middle classes. Beyond the ephemeral music Brahms was canonized in this ceiling program, integrated as a living composer into an already historical ensemble, thus stylized as both a historical and future guiding model. The Zürich middle classes, for whom the new Tonhalle had an identity-forming role, could have found no composer more suitable than Brahms for this act of self-legitimization, for at the same time, as a living exponent of the art of music, Brahms provided a justification of the new institution. At any rate, no other composer could have taken over this function. His friend Widmann encapsulated this in a poetic tribute that—according to the

Neue Zürcher Zeitung—was offered to Brahms after further laurel wreaths on 24 October in a private gathering at night:[45]

> Oh! Great Master! Wreaths and words
> do not reach your heights. Merely as a token of thanks
> in return for your coming among us,
> accept them both. You know this house shall serve
> the divine art of music. Now into the distance,
> always under the bright star of your genius![46]

Monuments

If Brahms's elevation into the Zürich "Composers' Heaven" during his own lifetime was a rather singular event, after the death of the composer there arose the need for further public and lasting tributes. In this process the memorial markers took very different forms: firstly there are the actual monuments, the figures and busts that were erected to the composer after his death. The most artistically significant are in the Thuringian *Residenzstadt* Meiningen (1899, Adolf von Hildebrand), in Brahms's birthplace Hamburg (1909, Max Klinger), and at the site of his most intensive creative activity, in Vienna (1903, Ilse Conrat and 1908, Rudolf Weyr). As different as these monuments might be in their aesthetic conception, they correspond more or less with the photographs of the elderly composer that dominate the collective, popular consciousness; the Czech sculptor Milan Knobloch responded to this tradition with a marble bust created in 2000 for the Walhalla. Very deliberately, it features a youthful artist without a beard.

Adolf von Hildebrand (1847–1921) characteristically fashioned his Meiningen monument after a photograph that shows the elderly Brahms with a beard (see Figure 14.6).[47] The bronze bust on a high stone pedestal forms the central point of the almost semi-circular exedra construction that Hildebrand designed together with the architect Carlo Sattler in the English Garden.[48] Joseph Joachim delivered the official speech at the unveiling of the monument on 7 October 1899.[49] In the handwritten dictation of his speech Joachim described one of Brahms's major compositions as a memorial, a monument in tones, whereby through sheer exaggeration of a biographical detail he ignored the complex genesis of the work:

> We are still under the profound impression of the harrowing sounds [of the Requiem] that have only just faded away in the church. They flew from the pious soul of one mourning a much-loved mother who struggled to find comfort for his pain. For how many thousands of people the transfigured tones have already been a balm, how many generations will yet be uplifted by them! There is no nobler monument of childlike piety to record in all of art

Figure 14.6 Brahms Monument by Adolf von Hildebrand, Meiningen, 1899.

history. A monument less perishable than bronze! Brahms was a good person as much as he was great; a benefactor of humanity![50]

The design of Brahms's Honorary Grave at Vienna's Central Cemetery lay in the hands of the young sculptor Ilse Conrat, who at the time of the solemn unveiling on 7 May 1903, Brahms's seventieth birthday, was just twenty-three years old.[51] Already prior to the designing of the grave she had modeled impressive Brahms busts, which unquestionably secured her the commission and, at the same time, show a type of artistic development in the sense of concentration and reduction.[52] In the busts of 1903 created directly before the designing of the grave monument, the head of the composer, as it were, grows out of the untreated block of material with the sunken head turned inwards—the allusion to Auguste Rodin, whom Conrat had visited in Paris, is unmistakable (see Figure 14.7).

The marble grave monument, which was executed relatively independently from the earlier busts, merges gravestone with a portrait bust, whereby Brahms is shown in the pose of the thinker, head propped on his hand, in front of an open score. To be made out in delicate reliefs on the gravestone towering behind Brahms are a female nude shown from behind and a male figure. A piece of cloth appears to connect both, the ends of which are pressed to the lips of the male figure as though in a kiss. A newspaper critic of the *Wiener Mode* at that time interpreted this allegorical representation in the following way:

> The muse bears the silent lyre toward heaven like a sacred object, as though she wanted to return the precious jewel of the deity. A veil blows down from the lyre; it is the immortal music of the master that lives on among us! The

Figure 14.7 Brahms Bust by Ilse Conrat, 1903. Brahms-Institut an der Musikhochschule Lübeck.

youth presses the veil to his lips and brings the sounding legacy down to comfort humankind.[53]

The unveiling of the grave monument in Vienna was a distinguished social event that found a wide response in the media. In the presence of leading politicians and many honorary guests, the Singverein of the Gesellschaft der Musikfreunde opened proceedings with the chorus "Nachtwache" (from Brahms's Op. 104) under the direction of Ferdinand Löwe: "When the tones had died away, the actor Reimer stepped forward and delivered Max Kalbeck's 'Iambs' in memory of Brahms."[54]

A few years later in 1908 (again on Brahms's birthday), the monument by Rudolf Weyr (1847–1914) was unveiled in Vienna. Wehr was—like Victor Tilgner—a prominent sculptor of the Makart era and was involved in many decorative interiors of the Vienna Ringstraße. Weyr positioned Brahms with a reflective bearing on a throne-like chair above a stepped pedestal. After the submission of the model the jury had requested that the artist revise the monument, as is reflected in various drawings by Weyr that are preserved in the print room of the Akademie der bildenden Künste in Vienna. The most notable change in the execution is the appended female figure with lyre, a personification of mourning music, on the steps at the feet of the composer. Whether this is really an aesthetic improvement in comparison to the original conception of the monument is questionable.

In actual fact the traditional Brahms monuments have begun to falter. The monument by Max Klinger that was unveiled on 7 May 1909 in Hamburg and can be seen today in the Musikhalle is also affected by this process (see Figure 14.8). It shows a towering Brahms enveloped by muses and genii, a person who—albeit carved in Carrara marble—appears to ascend into celestial realms. Today we struggle to see the composer through the eyes of this sculptor, to whom Brahms had dedicated the *Vier ernste Gesänge*, Op. 121, in thanks for the 41 drawings and etchings of the *Brahms-Phantasie*.[55]

To conclude, let us consider the page titled "Accorde" from Klinger's *Brahms-Phantasie* from 1894, as it provides a point of departure for a further strand of reception that cannot be elaborated further: the engagement with

Figure 14.8 Brahms Monument by Max Klinger.

Images, Monuments, Constructs

Brahms's music in images (see Figure 14.9). This page from Klinger might jar with us at first, for it exhibits, in a surreal scene with different visual planes, the summoning up of the sublime, which Klinger appears primarily to have associated with Brahms's music. The terrace-like structure on the right with the pianist and the female figure functioning as a muse symbolize the sphere of the artist. The left-hand side of the image provides a view of a grandiose, jagged snowy mountainscape; a sailing boat threatened with wreckage in the agitated sea heads toward a cypress grove, reminiscent of Arnold Böcklin's famous *Toteninsel* (*Isle of the Dead*). The spheres of nature and art are represented by the gestures of the woman and the oversized harp supported by Triton that is crowned with a tragic mask. Klinger, who must have picked out the gloomy and tragic in Brahms's music above all else, hints in this image at feelings and phantasies that could be awakened in the artist through music: his psychological attunement "resounds" in the conception of nature that becomes the seascape. This page is also cited here because it shows—at least as a singular example—the degree to which perceptions of Brahms around 1894 could already be distinct from the dichotomy that is still popular today of "absolute music"/"program music."

Artistic engagement with Johannes Brahms and his music is also ongoing. An example of this is the Brahms Gallery of the Musikhochschule in Lübeck, which was established in the context of the foundation of the Lübeck

Figure 14.9 Max Klinger, "Accorde" from the *Brahms-Phantasie*, Opus XII, Berlin 1894, Brahms-Institut an der Musikhochschule Lübeck.

Brahms-Institut in 1991 and the annual Brahms Festivals that take place there. In this Lübeck gallery there are depictions of Brahms by Johannes Grützke (1997), Arnim Mueller-Stahl (2006), Dietrich Fischer-Dieskau (2006), and Gunther Fritz (2008), among others, and engagements with his music through painting such as the "Optical Score for Johannes Brahms" by Günther Uecker (2001).[56]

Chapter 15

Templates of Grief

Brahms's Requiem and the Dresdner Kreuzchor, 1939–1949

Martha Sprigge

Dresden, 1945

In a letter to his brother and sister-in-law at the end of October 1945, music journalist Karl Laux (1896–1978) gave a sobering account of his life in Dresden after the Allied aerial attack on the city on 13 February that same year.[1] This was the night that British and American air forces targeted Dresden, killing between 18,000 and 25,000 people and leaving the city's Baroque historical center in ruins.[2] Like many residents of the Saxon capital, Laux and his wife Maria suffered considerable damage to their health in the firebombing, leaving them in hospital for months.[3] After they had recovered physically, they tested the patience of friends, who took them in because their home had been entirely destroyed in the Allied attack. Laux described how they were trying to buy furniture so that they could relocate to two rooms that were quite derelict, but would suffice while they pieced their lives back together. He had even acquired an old Bechstein piano for their new space.[4]

Amid the immense physical destruction, non-Jewish German residents of the city were facing questions of moral culpability in the wake of the Nazi era and their nation's total defeat in the Second World War. The collapse of the Third Reich prompted an existential crisis. German citizens did not openly respond to the Holocaust or take responsibility for their actions in the Third Reich, leading German Jewish philosopher Hannah Arendt to accuse her fellow citizens of an "inability to feel" for those persecuted under Nazi rule.[5] But guilt and trauma often manifested themselves in indirect ways.[6] Laux's response to denazification was practical and individualistic: he reported that he had had some success resuming work in the Soviet Occupation Zone (or SBZ), because he had not joined the Nazi party and had professional difficulties as a result during the Third Reich.[7] This was a rare asset in the early postwar months, when occupying forces were frantically attempting to establish denazification procedures for German citizens, most of whom had supported the

Third Reich to some degree.[8] While Laux's self-assessment might seem shallow, even opportunistic, in light of subsequent debates about collective guilt (known in German discourse as the *Schuldfrage*, or the question of German guilt), it was in keeping with responses to denazification in the immediate postwar years.[9] Victor Klemperer summarized the situation with biting clarity in a diary entry from 11 May 1945, three days after Victory in Europe Day (VE Day). Klemperer—fellow Dresdner, famed diarist, linguist, and German Jew—reflected bitterly that "the Third Reich is already almost as good as forgotten, everyone was opposed to it, 'always' opposed to it; and people have the most absurd ideas about the future."[10]

Perhaps confirming Klemperer's assessment about the concerns of the city's residents was the fact that Laux noted how "Dresden's artistic life, despite the rubble . . . is back up and running."[11] In other documents from the same era, Laux recounted intimate concerts in destroyed homes, where musicians would perform from scores they had on hand. These were invariably pieces from the Austro-Germanic canon, including chamber works by Brahms.[12] The city's large-scale musical institutions restarted performances shortly after the war's end, too, making do in the city's open spaces, or performing amid the ruins to bring music to grief-stricken audiences. The Dresdner Philharmonie gave their first performance on 8 June, and the Dresdner Kreuzchor sang in their first postwar Vespers service on 1 July 1945.[13] By the end of 1945, three of Dresden's prominent musical institutions—the Kreuzchor, the Philharmonie, and the Bachverein—had joined forces to stage three performances of Johannes Brahms's *Ein deutsches Requiem*: on 26 September, 3 November, and on Totensonntag (Sunday of the Dead, 24 November).[14]

Brahms's Requiem and the Music of German Suffering

Prior to 13 February 1945, Dresden had been renowned as a city of culture (a *Kulturstadt*). Overnight, the Allied attack on the city had transformed it into a "city of civilian victims" (an *Opferstadt*, victim city).[15] Images of the city's famous Baroque skyline in ruins circulated on both sides of the Iron Curtain, and continue to shape the city's post-catastrophic identity.[16] The widespread efforts to restore musical life in the Saxon capital as quickly as possible after the war's end represent some of the earliest attempts to reconcile these two identities—to use the known parameters of cultural life to comprehend the distress brought on by war, guilt, defeat, and occupation. Reports of the Dresdner Kreuzchor going about their everyday activities point to an effort to restore normalcy, even as they were grieving the loss of eleven choristers who died in the firebombing. In this moment of profound crisis, musicians and audiences alike turned to repertoires that brought them comfort and familiarity. They had done the same in the darkest months of the war, as the Kreuzchor gave performances of Brahms's Requiem on Totensonntag throughout the war.

For the Dresdner Kreuzchor, the three performances of Brahms's Requiem in the final months of the Second World War were Janus-faced: they mark the start of a postwar tradition of commemorating the firebombing with what became annual performances of a large-scale Requiem, and they reinforce this institution's role as arbiters of the mourning customs of the Lutheran church. In his work on Brahms's Requiem, Robin Leaver argued that the composition belongs to a genre of music performed specifically for Totensonntag (which marks the close of the liturgical year in the German Protestant church).[17] The Kreuzchor started performing Brahms's Requiem on Totensonntag in 1939. Throughout the postwar period, the Kreuzchor have publicized their annual performance of the Brahms Requiem as a long-standing custom.[18] The origins of this tradition are intricately connected to the choir and congregation's experiences of the Third Reich and the Second World War. In addition to providing an outlet for grief throughout the war, these annual performances of the Requiem reinforced, through performance, the musical customs of Totensonntag that had informed Brahms's mourning work. The choir were—and remain—renowned for their performances of choral works by Heinrich Schütz, Johann Sebastian Bach, and other composers from a canon of German Protestant mourning music that influenced Brahms's own Requiem.[19] These works were the musical means by which the Dresdner Kreuzchor responded to the wartime years and their aftermath in both performance and composition.[20]

The Kreuzchor's sustained engagement with Brahms's choral mourning music during and in the early aftermath of the Second World War prompt us to rethink these repertoires in light of their circulation in twentieth-century Germany. This chapter thus joins a number of recent reconsiderations of Brahms's Requiem in light of its performance history in German-speaking regions, from its date of composition to the present day.[21] By focusing on the musical mourning customs of a single institution, I explore the ways that Brahms's choral mourning music—as well as the Lutheran death culture that inspired it—took on local significance within a specific community at a time of immense political and personal upheaval. Yet Dresden's precarious musical life in the late wartime and early postwar years was not unique in Germany, nor in Europe.[22] Musical life in German cities continued amid the ruins of the air war, capturing war-weary audiences by staging scenes of German suffering. Brahms's Requiem was heard across Germany at this precarious time. On 14 April 1945, for example, the Berlin Singakademie staged a performance of the work. Celia Applegate notes how "director Georg Schumann assembled his chorus of lamentation literally on the edge of the ruined shell of the Berlin Philharmonic Hall, the boom of advancing Soviet artillery audible in the not-so-far distance."[23]

These performances can be considered part of a larger practice of *Trümmerkünste* (the rubble arts): artistic responses to Germany's aerial destruction that aestheticize the debris.[24] Large-scale memorial works from the Austro-Germanic canon were a staple of ruin concerts, even though these works would have presented significant logistical challenges in terms of performers and space.[25] Critiques of early postwar music-making rightly draw attention to how these ruin concerts foregrounded German suffering. By centering on wartime damage and the catastrophic effects of the air war, ruin concerts became an avoidance mechanism for confronting the nation's past.[26] Music from the Austro-Germanic canon gave voice to German suffering at a time when occupation forces were focused on making German citizens aware of their guilt or even enacting revenge.[27] For the most part, denazification efforts in the late 1940s were focused on personnel rather than culture (which comes through in Laux's reflections on the early postwar months). Concert repertoires did not change significantly and were thus an ideal means for expressions of grief that could not be expressed verbally either for political reasons or psychological blockages—often both. As Anke Pinkert has noted, scholars of postwar Germany should be careful not to confuse a lack of public discourse about German guilt from its absence in early postwar society. German guilt and suffering coexisted, and need to be analyzed in more multifaceted ways.[28]

I endeavour to address these emotional surpluses in late wartime and early postwar Dresden by examining the Kreuzchor's musical mourning customs in the decade between the start of the Second World War in 1939 to the founding of the German Democratic Republic (East Germany, or the GDR) in 1949. My chronological purview is guided by the choir's own memorial practices: 1939 was the year that their tradition of performing Brahms's Requiem on Totensonntag commenced. A focus on this decade also allows me to chart how the cantor of the Kreuzkirche—Rudolf Mauersberger (1889–1971)—led the choir through everyday crises presented by the war and its eventual end. I follow an approach to German history that undercuts the idea that the end of the Second World War in 1945 marked a breaking point, or "zero hour" (*Stunde Null*) for German culture.[29] The Dresdner Kreuzchor mourned different types of losses, including civilians who died in aerial attacks and soldiers who died fighting for the Reich, using the same set of Lutheran repertoires. There was a continuity of mourning customs throughout the war and into the early postwar period. In his responses to the Second World War, Mauersberger turns not only to Brahms's German Requiem, but to the liturgical mourning lineage that shaped Brahms's own works as templates for grief.

The Dresdner Kreuzchor in the Third Reich

Founded in 1236, the Dresdner Kreuzchor is the second oldest boys' choir in the world.[30] From 1930 to 1971, Mauersberger held the position of Kreuzkantor, directing this world-renowned choir throughout the final years of the Weimar Republic (1930–1933), the Third Reich (1933–1945), the Soviet Occupation Zone (1945–1949), and in the first two decades of the GDR (1949–1971). His career stability during such a politically tumultuous time is a revealing marker of the cultural significance of the Kreuzchor in Dresden and Germany, the status of the Protestant church under different political regimes,[31] and Mauersberger's political complicity in the Third Reich. Mauersberger joined the Nazi Party in 1933 and the Kreuzchor became members of the Hitler Jugend (the Nazi youth group, the Hitler Youth).[32] Pamela Potter describes the pitfalls of studying musical culture in the Third Reich and its aftermath, noting that too many scholars have condemned complicit artists and valorized those who were Nazi victims, as they seek to evaluate past political activities using present-day rubrics.[33] For instance, in some literature about the Kreuzchor, Mauersberger is described as so intensely focused on musical excellence at the Kreuzchor that he made political decisions to protect the cultural heritage it represents.[34] Yet Mauersberger's political decisions are representative of a wider trend, reflecting what Neil Gregor calls the "deeper associations" between the cultural values promoted by the Nazis and those of the surrounding time periods.[35] In the GDR, Mauersberger and the choir faced a new and different set of compromises. Mauersberger received a number of accolades for his contributions to cultural life. During this period, the choristers' education—which had been the purview of the Lutheran church for centuries—was the subject of scrutiny by the Ministry of Culture in the secular socialist state.[36]

This brief overview makes it clear that the Dresdner Kreuzchor was considered ideologically useful under different political regimes because it represented and embodied German cultural heritage. In this regard, the choir is emblematic of a larger pattern across Germany's oldest and most illustrious musical institutions. Nazi ideologies were bolstered by these institutions, and cultural alliances in the Third Reich were the norm rather than the exception.[37] But perhaps more tellingly, as Potter has persistently argued, though the Nazi Party may have brought changes in cultural policy, its bureaucratic organizations did not shape cultural realities.[38] The majority of Germany's musical ensembles—especially outside the capital—continued to perform the same repertoires for attentive audiences throughout the Third Reich and well into the Second World War.[39] The Kreuzchor, for example, did sometimes perform in the uniform of the Hitler Jugend and at political events.[40] For much of the school year, though, the Kreuzchor's musical life during the Nazi era was one of continuity. Surviving Vespers service booklets indicate a regular performance schedule of a cappella choral works from the Renaissance era and other *stile antico* repertoires from later centuries, including an increased performance of new works in a historicist modernist vein by composers such as Hugo Distler (1908–1942).[41]

Their frequent performances of the music of Heinrich Schütz (1585–1672) indicates the ways in which Mauersberger's musical decisions were concordant with the cultural politics of the time while also representing a commitment to the institutional history of the Kreuzchor. Schütz is one of Dresden's most celebrated musicians. Most of his Lutheran church music dates from his long career in the Saxon capital from 1615 to 1672. Over half of his time in Dresden was marked by the extended conflict of the Thirty Years' War (1618–1648).[42] Schütz scholars have noted the extensive ways in which the war shaped Schütz's music, particularly the collection of a cappella motets published in 1648 under the title *Geistliche Chormusik*.[43] Schütz's a cappella choral works were a staple of Vespers services, where the choir perform without accompaniment. During the Second World War, associations in Schütz's wartime music became an expressive anchor for Mauersberger and the Kreuzchor. For both practical and expressive reasons, selections from Schütz's *Geistliche Chormusik* were regularly programmed during Vespers services throughout the war.[44]

More broadly, Mauersberger's career at the Kreuzkirche coincided with a nationwide Schütz revival—one which the choir contributed to significantly throughout Mauersberger's time as cantor, establishing *Schütz-Tage* (a Schütz festival) and embarking on a substantial recording project in the 1960s.[45] Bettina Varwig describes how Schütz reception history in the 1930s was molded to suit political ideals: a "vocabulary of obdurate strength in defence of the fatherland ... became more dominant in the lively discourse about Schütz between the two world wars, which increasingly assimilated the composer into an ever more narrowly formulated ideal of German art as manly and combative."[46] The Kreuzchor did perform a number of new works that bolstered this nationalistic agenda of the Third Reich, but their performance repertoires changed much less than the wider rhetoric surrounding German musical works.[47] Far more than the cultural policies of the Third Reich, it was the Dresden firebombing in February 1945 that affected the performing patterns of choir and cantor for years to come, and caused immense ruptures for choristers and the local community. Thus, as Neil Gregor has demonstrated in a series of micro-historical essays about other aspects of German musical life, it is helpful to take a local approach to understanding the choir's customs during periods of political upheaval.[48]

Totensonntag Rituals during the Second World War

In keeping with a local approach, consider how the Kreuzchor's position as a hallmark of the German choral tradition shaped the everyday lives of choristers, particularly during the wartime and early postwar years. Now an institution that is over 800 years old, choristers' day-to-day practices still bear the imprints of liturgical choral practices from early modern Europe, where the main church in the city had a resident choir.[49] Members of the Dresdner Kreuzchor (known as Kruzianer) are school-aged boys between the ages of nine and eighteen, who primarily come from the region of Saxony. They are educated together at the Dresdner Kreuzschule (now the Evangelisches Kreuzgymnasium), where they receive training in choral music from the Kreuzkantor, as well as lessons on an instrument.[50] Those who are not local to Dresden attend the boarding school. The Kreuzchor's connections to centuries-old Lutheran musical traditions are forged through daily experience.

The choir's prominent position as both a cultural and religious institution shaped their activities during the Second World War. Prior to the firebombing in February 1945, they held services throughout the school year, from late August or early September until June of the following year. This included performances for Vespers on Saturday evenings, their typical Sunday worship, and occasional concerts in Dresden and surrounding towns.[51] Their concert schedule had been curtailed significantly over the course of the war: the Nazi propaganda minister, Joseph Goebbels, had initiated a concert ban in August 1944. Even after this edict, though, performances that were part of church services were deemed exempt and continued into the final months of the war.[52] The Kreuzchor's last Vespers service before the firebombing was on Saturday, 10 February 1945. At the end of the printed program is the date of the next planned Vespers service, which was supposed to take place on 17 February 1945.[53]

As they continued performing, the impact of the war manifested in two main ways: older choristers were called up to the Wehrmacht (the German Army), and as the conflict reached its final stages, material resources became scarcer. Programs from 1944, 1945, and 1946 are typed or sometimes even handwritten on reused paper, rather than printed in the church' typical gothic font. The services printed in Figure 15.1 show the comparison: the first (15.1a) is from the Totensonntag service on 26 November 1933, and the second (15.1b) is the order of service for Vespers the evening before Totensonntag in 1944. In both services the choir and congregation sing Luther's hymn "Mitten wir im Leben sind" (In the midst of life we are in death) in call-and-response.[54] In 1944, this hymn was more than a familiar custom. Its lines had particular resonance as Germans faced the increasing certainty of defeat and the war came to a drawn-out close.[55]

The comparison of these two services points to the ways that Protestant mourning music became a framework for comfort and consolation that was both tied to the Kreuzchor's long-standing musical traditions and that took on specific resonances and emotional meaning in the final years of the Second World War. Take, for instance, Schütz's motet "Selig sind die Toten" ("Blessed Are the Dead"), from *Geistliche Chormusik*. The madrigalisms that permeate Schütz's setting of Revelation 14:13 strike a delicate balance between expressing the sorrow felt by those in mourning with the emphasis on rest and peace for the deceased in the biblical text. On Totensonntag in 1944, everyone in the

Figure 15.1a Order of Service for Totensonntag Service, 26 November 1933, 6 P.M. © SLUB Dresden / Sachsen.Digital (CC BY-SA 4.0)

Geistlicher: Herr, lehre uns bedenken, daß wir sterben müssen!
Gemeinde: Auf daß wir klug werden.

1. Vorlesung: Psalm 90 1—12

Chor: „Geistliches Lied" . . . . Wolfgang Fortner (geb. 1906)

Der Mensch lebt und bestehet nur eine kurze Zeit. Und alle Welt vergehet mit ihrer Herrlichkeit. Es ist nur einer ewig und an allen Enden,	und wir in seinen Händen. Und der ist allwissend. Und der ist heilig. Und der ist allmächtig, ist barmherzig, Halleluja ewig, ewig seinen Namen.

2. Vorlesung: Joh. 14 1—6, 10 27—30

Chor:
Mit Fried und Freud ich fahr dahin,
in Gottes Wille;
getrost ist mir mein Herz und Sinn,
sanft und stille.
Wie Gott mir verheißen hat,
der Tod ist mein Schlaf worden.

Gemeinde:
Das macht Christus, wahr Gottes Sohn,
der treue Heiland,
den du mich, Herr hast lassen sehn,
und machst bekannt,
daß er sei das Leben
und Heil in Not und Sterben.

Den du hast allen vorgestellt mit großen Gnaden, zu seinem Reich die ganze Welt heißen laden durch dein teuer heilsam Wort, an allem Ort erschollen.	Er ist das Heil und selig Licht für die Heiden, zu erleuchten, die dich kennen nicht, und zu weiden. Er ist deins Volk Israel Preis, Ehre, Freud und Wonne.

3. Vorlesung: Offenbarung 12, 11, 14, 13, 21 1—4

Chor:
Ich hab von ferne,
Herr, deinen Thron erblickt
und hätte gerne
mein Herz vorausgeschickt,
und hatte gern mein müdes Leben,
Schöpfer der Geister, dir hingegeben. (:/:)

Gemeinde:
Jerusalem, du hochgebaute Stadt,
wollt Gott, ich wär in dir!
Mein sehnend Herz so groß Verlangen hat
und ist nicht mehr bei mir,
Weit über Berg und Tale,
weit über blaches Feld
schwingt es sich über alle
und eilt aus dieser Welt.

Figure 15.1a Continued

Chor: Das war so prächtig,
was ich im Geist gesehn!
Du bist allmächtig,
drum ist dein Licht so schön.
Könnt ich an diesen hellen Thronen
doch schon von heute an ewig wohnen!

Gemeinde: O Ehrenburg, sei nun gegrüßet mir,
tu auf der Gnaden Pfort!
Wie große Zeit hat mich verlangt nach dir,
eh ich bin kommen fort
aus jenem bösen Leben,
aus jener Nichtigkeit,
und mir Gott hat gegeben
das Erb der Seligkeit.

Chor: Ich bin zufrieden,
daß ich die Stadt gesehn;
und ohn Ermüden
will ich ihr näher gehn,
und ihre hellen, goldnen Gassen
lebenslang nicht aus den Augen lassen.

Gemeinde: Wenn dann zuletzt ich angelanget bin
im schönen Paradeis,
von höchster Freud erfüllet wird der Sinn,
der Mund von Lob und Preis.
Das Halleluja reine
man singet in Heiligkeit,
das Hosianna feine
ohn End in Ewigkeit.

~ Ansprache ~

Einzelstimmen: Ach Herr, laß dein lieb Engelein
am letzten End die Seele mein
in Abrahams Schoß tragen;
Den Leib in seinem Kämmerlein
gar sanft ohn einge Qual und Pein
ruhn bis zum jüngsten Tage.
Alsdann vom Tod erwecke mich,
daß meine Augen sehen dich
an aller Freud, o Gottessohn,
mein Heiland und mein Gnadenthron.
Herr Jesu Christ erhöre mich,
erhöre mich, ich will dich preisen ewiglich.

Gemeinde:

Christus, der ist mein Leben Sterben ist mein Gewinn; dem hab ich mich ergeben, mit Fried fahr ich dahin.	Mit Freud fahr ich von dannen zu Christ, dem Bruder mein, auf daß ich zu ihm komme und ewig bei ihm sei.

Ich hab nun überwunden
Kreuz, Leiden, Angst und Not;
durch seine heilgen Wunden
bin ich versöhnt mit Gott.

Figure 15.1a Continued

Geistlicher: Selig sind die Toten, die in dem Herrn sterben von nun an, Halleluja!
Gemeinde: Ja, der Geist spricht, daß sie ruhen von ihrer Arbeit, und ihre Werke folgen ihnen nach. Halleluja.

Gemeinde:
Gloria sei dir gesungen
mit Menschen- und mit Engelzungen,
mit Harfen und mit Zimbeln schön.
Von zwölf Perlen sind die Tore
an deiner Stadt, wir stehn im Chore
der Engel hoch um deinen Thron.
Kein Aug hat je gesehn,
kein Ohr hat je gehört
solche Freude.
Des jauchzen wir
und singen dir
das Halleluja für und für!

Feier des Heiligen Abendmahls

Geistlicher: Sei getreu bis in den Tod,
Gemeinde: So will ich dir die Krone des Lebens geben.

Gemeinde:
O wie selig seid ihr doch, ihr Frommen,
die ihr durch den Tod zu Gott gekommen!
Ihr seid entgangen aller Not,
die uns noch hält gefangen.

Schreib meinen Nam aufs beste
ins Buch des Lebens ein,
bind meine Seele feste
ins Lebensbündelein
der, die im Himmel grünen
und vor dir leben frei;
so will ich ewig rühmen,
daß treu dein Herze sei.   (Spendelied)

Nach dem Gottesdienst findet die Feier des Heiligen Abendmahls statt, zu der besonders alle Trauernden der Gemeinde herzlich eingeladen sind.

Die Sammlung beim Ausgang aus dem Gottesdienste
ist bestimmt für Kriegshinterbliebene und Kriegsgräberfürsorge.

Kommt, wir wollen wieder zum Herrn, denn er hat uns zerrissen, er wird uns auch heilen. Er hat uns geschlagen; er wird uns auch verbinden.   Hosea 6, 1.

Figure 15.1a Continued

Vesper in der Kreuzkirche
z. Z. in der Sophienkirche
am Sonnabend, den 25. November 1944, 17 Uhr.

Orgel: Joh. Seb. B a c h (1685 - 1750) Triosonate Nr. 2 in c moll
für Orgel. I. Vivace, II. Largo, III. Allegro.

Heinrich Schütz (1585 bis 1672) Zwei Motetten aus der "Geistlichen
Chormusik:
So fahr hin mit Freuden"
Ich

Ich fahr ich hin, zu Jesu Christ, mein Arm tu ich ausstrecken, so
schlaf ich ein und ruhe fein, kein Mensch kann mich aufwecken,
denn Jesus Christus, Gottes Sohn, der wird die Himmelstür auftun,
mich führen zum ewigen Leben.

"Selig sind die Toten."

Selig sind die Toten, die in dem Herrn sterben von nun an.
Ja, der Geist spricht: Sie ruhen von ihrer Arbeit und ihre Werke
folgen ihnen nach.

V o r l e s u n g .

Chor: Mitten wir im Leben sind mit dem Tod umfangen. Wen suchen wir,
der Hilfe tu, dass wir Gnad erlangen? Das bist du; Herr, alleine.
Uns reuet unsre Missetat, die dich, Herr, erzürnet hat.
Heiliger Herre Gott! heiliger starker Gott! heiliger barmherziger Heiland, du ewiger Gott! lass uns nicht versinken in des
bittern Todesnot. Kyrie eleison.
Gemeinde:
Mitten in der Höllen Angst unsre Sünd uns treiben. Wo soll'n wir
denn fliehen hin, da wir mögen bleiben? Zu dir, Herr Christ, allei
vergossen ist dein teures Blut, das genug für die Sünde tut.
Heiliger Herre Gott! heiliger starker Gott! heiliger, barmherziger
Heiland, du ewiger Gott, lass uns nicht entfallen von des rech-
ten Glaubens Trost. Kyrie eleison.

G e b e t und S e g e n .

Heinrich Schütz: Teile aus den "Musikalischen Exequien".
(Konzert in Form einer teutschen Begräbnismissa).

Intonatio:
Chor: Nacket bin ich von Mutterleibe kommend.
Nacket werde ich wiederum dahin fahren, der Herr hat's gegeben,
der Herr hats genommen, der Name des Herrn sei gelobet. Herr Gott
Vater im Himmel erbarm dich über uns. Christus ist mein Leben, Sterben ist mein Gewinn. Siehe, das ist Gottes Lamm, das der Welt Sünde
trägt. Jesu Christe, Gottes Sohn, erbarm dich über uns. Leben wir
so leben wir dem Herren, sterben wir, so sterben wir dem Herren,
darum wir leben oder sterben, so sind wir des Herren. Herr Gott
heiliger Geist, erbarm dich über uns.

Figure 15.1b Order of Service for Vespers, Saturday Evening, 25 November 1944, 5 P.M. © SLUB Dresden / Sachsen.Digital (CC BY-SA 4.0)

Chor: Es ist allhier ein Jammertak, Angst, Not und Trübsal überall, des Bleibens ist ein kleine Zeit, voller Mühseligkeit, und wer's bedenkt, ist immer in Streit.

Knabenstimmen am Altar und Bässe:

Der Gerechten Seelen sind in Gottes Hand und keine Qual rühret sie an, für den Unverständigen werden sie angesehen, als stürben sie und ihr Abschied wird für eine Pein gerechnet und ihr Hinfahren für Verderben, aber sie sind in Frieden.

Chor:
Weil du vom Tod erstanden bist, werd ich im Grab nicht bleiben, mein höchster Trost dein Auffahrt ist, Todsfurcht kannst du vertreiben, denn wo du bist, da komm ich hin, dass ich stets bei dir leb und bin, drum fahr ich hin mit Freuden.

Intonatio:
Herr nun lässest deinen Diener......
              du
Chor:
in Frieden fahren, wie du gesagt hast allen Völkern. Denn meine Augen haben deinen Heiland gesehen, welchen du bereitest hast für allen Völkern, ein Licht zu erleuchten die Heiden und zum Preise deines Volks Preis und Ehr.
Selig sind die Toten, die in dem Herren sterben, sie ruhen von ihrer Arbeit und ihre Werke folgen ihnen nach. Sie sind in der Hand des Herren und keine Qual rühret sie.

Mitwirkende:

Der Kreuzchor; Orgel: Kreuzorganist Herbert Collum;

Leitung: Kreuzkantor Prof. Rudolf Mauersberger.

Nächste Kreuzchorvesper am Sonnabend, den 2. **November** 17 Uhr in der Sophienkirche.

Eingelegte Beckengelder sind für den Kreuzchor bestimmt.

Figure 15.1b Continued

choir or congregation would have been mourning friends, family members, and acquaintances who had died—or were presumed dead—in the war.

In addition to using long-standing Totensonntag rituals to reflect on the wartime years, the Kreuzchor played a role in forging mourning rituals for the city and its Lutheran congregants. Their annual performances of Brahms's *Ein deutsches Requiem* illustrate this point. The Kreuzchor's tradition of performing Brahms's Requiem began in the first year of the Second World War.[56] They continued this custom throughout the war, though they faced logistical difficulties that prevented performances in some years. These performances provided Dresden's Christian communities with a public space of mourning and consolation during a period of trauma and uncertainty. In the opening of his memoirs, Heinrich Magirius (a Kruzianer from 1945 to 1952) vividly recalls hearing Brahms's Requiem for the first time before Totensonntag in 1944.[57] The "hammering" text of the Requiem's second movement ("Denn alles Fleisch, es ist wie Gras") triggered "eschatological" memories from the final year of war.[58] Magirius compiled his memoirs around the time of his eightieth birthday in 2014, which might have inflected his memory of total defeat feeling inevitable. Nevertheless, the close association he maintains between the Requiem and the final months of war indicates that Brahms's music offered a vast interpretive canvas for listeners to process their experiences, both during the conflict and long after.

In his analysis of Brahms's Requiem, Leaver notes affinities with Lutheran burial chorales, and traces the lineage of these traditions through Heinrich Schütz and J. S. Bach to Brahms and on to Max Reger. The early performance history of the Requiem does not indicate that audiences and performers made connections between Brahms's musical language and Totensonntag. As R. Allen Lott has shown in his reconsideration of the Requiem's liturgical origins and influence, the most prevalent date on which Brahms's work was performed during the first fifteen years of its circulation was during Holy Week.[59] There were performances held on Totensonntag (also referred to as *Todtenfest* or *Bußtag*, depending on the region), but this date was less common.[60] Moreover, at the time Brahms wrote this work, musical connections to a longer lineage of Lutheran funerary music—including those of Schütz—would have been known to church musicians, but not necessarily to a wider Christian community.[61]

When the Kreuzchor started performing the Requiem to mark Totensonntag in 1939, they reinforced connections between Brahms's Requiem and Lutheran mortuary customs of the Renaissance and Baroque periods for the Kreuzkirche congregation. These lineages remain central to the choir's performance repertoires to this day. Each year, their memorial services in November—which now take place to mark Totensonntag and *Volkstrauertag* (the national day of mourning)—include the same works and settings of biblical texts that influenced Brahms's mourning oeuvre. We can see this in the Vespers programs shown in Figure 15.1b, from 1944, when the choir performed three mourning works by Heinrich Schütz. The motet "Selig sind die Toten" shares a text with the closing movement of Brahms's Requiem, and Schütz's *Musikalische Exequien* is considered one of the main precursors to Brahms's work. On Totensonntag in 1945, they performed J. S. Bach's "Wenn ich einmal soll scheiden," from the St. Matthew Passion, followed by two settings of biblical texts by Rudolf Mauersberger himself, including a setting of "O Tod wie bitter bist du," from Ecclesiastes, which Brahms had set in his *Vier ernste Gesänge*, Op. 121 (1896).[62] Even as the Requiem became increasingly connected to secular constructions of national identity, the Kreuzchor's performance customs emphasized the work's origins in the customs of the Lutheran church.

The Kreuzchor's Totensonntag performances are indicative of a larger trend across wartime Germany. With news of the German army's losses deliberately withheld to focus on victory, churches provided informal reports about the war dead.[63] As cities across the Reich became targets in Allied bombing campaigns, ministers offered allegorical interpretations of wartime events in their sermons, to provide solace to their congregation and explain these catastrophes within a Christian worldview.[64] It is difficult to underestimate the significance of the church for providing a semblance of familiarity and means of sense-making during a time of immense loss. With so many institutions destroyed or disbanded by the end of the war, Christian churches were among the few institutions to survive the war with their organizational infrastructure intact.[65] We see this with the Kreuzkirche: even with their building in ruins, the choir remained in regular contact after the firebombing, and they resumed their activities in a temporary location during their first postwar season.[66]

Mourning Choristers through the Lutheran *Ars Moriendi*

During the war, the Kreuzchor held services to commemorate members of their closest musical community—deceased choristers. Surviving evidence in the choir's archive indicates that they made use of the tradition of the Lutheran *ars moriendi* (the "art of dying") to provide consolation for their community members.[67] For example, on 13 October 1944, choristers sung in a graveside service for Herbert Blumstock, a Kruzianer who died in a bombing attack the week earlier.[68] They sang five works—a combination of burial chorales and texts with recognizable musical settings associated with Lutheran mourning, including one text that Brahms set in the third movement of his Requiem.[69] Singing burial chorales at the grave of the deceased began during the Reformation, when it was carried out by local boys' choirs.[70] Around Blumstock's grave, the Kreuzchor performed these final rites for a member of their own community, ensuring a "good death" by singing in accordance with Lutheran custom.

Their memorial activities continued at their Vespers service the following evening (Saturday, 14 October 1944). The service was performed in memory of two former choristers: Blumstock and Lothar Weichhold, who had died after injuries he sustained on the Eastern front at the age of nineteen.[71] The brief biographical information provided in the notes for these services is a stark reminder of the different nature of wartime losses, and a glimpse into the impact of "total war" (an acceleration of the conflict that Goebbels announced in a frenzied speech on 18 February 1943) on German citizens. It is unclear how they learned of Weichhold's death, but the Kreuzkirche's leaders took responsibility for funeral rites. Weichhold and Blumstock were mourned at a joint service, and with the same music: the motet *Unser Leben ist ein Schatten* by Johann Bach (1604–1672), Johannes Brahms's motet *Warum ist das Licht gegeben*, and J. S. Bach's setting of the chorale *Gib dich zufrieden und sei stille*.[72]

The details of this service in the archive are partial, with information about the repertoire sung and not the topic of the late wartime sermon. Nevertheless, this fragmented glimpse into the Kreuzchor's wartime mourning activities gives us a sense of the multitude of emotional and cultural connections that might have been present for choristers and congregation as they used music to mourn during wartime and early postwar services. Some might have found resonances of the Nazi "cult of the dead hero" in the Vespers service.[73] The brief notice about Weichhold's death makes it clear that he was part of the Reich's army and died for its cause. Nazi burial culture celebrated fallen soldiers as heroes of the Third Reich, honoring them with jingoistic memorial ceremonies and a national "heroes' day of mourning" (*Heldengedenktag*).[74] Musically, commemorative repertoires for new Nazi rituals were drawn from works that evoked Brahms's Requiem: several composers had taken this piece as a model for new memorial works.[75] Moreover, at a point in the war when the German army was losing more battles, the Kreuzchor used music to name Weichhold and mourn him specifically. Anonymous death and burial were associated with being outside the Nazi state: anonymity was deliberately dehumanizing and was enforced within the spaces of Nazi genocide.[76]

Musicologists who have examined Brahms reception in the Third Reich draw attention to how the nascent jingoism in some of his music and cultural outlooks resonated with the Nazi's cultural ideologies.[77] For some audiences, this made Brahms's music an ideal canvas for ideological projection. The German Requiem became one such site for forging cultural continuities between the German nationalism of the later nineteenth century and the genocidal distortion of nationalism fostered in the Third Reich.[78] Reinhold Brinkmann has argued that Nazi musical aesthetics borrowed from preexisting repertoires but did so in a way that distorted the concept of the sublime. The "National Socialist sublime," he writes, "resembles the political ideology of the Nazis in general, exemplified by the loss of the subjective factor on the one hand, and the overwhelming power of a collective will—the *Gemeinschaft*, the *Volk*—on the other, with the Führer as its symbolic representation."[79]

Nazi burial culture tells a partial story of musical griefwork in Germany during the Second World War. For as publicly celebrated as the Wehrmacht was, new burial customs did not replace other long-standing German mourning rituals, even as they borrowed from them liberally. Across the country, German churches continued to provide comfort in the wake of loss and to enact mourning rites for their community members. In the case of the Dresdner Kreuzkirche, these rites positioned Brahms's mourning music back within the Lutheran customs from which he had found inspiration almost a century earlier. Though the Kreuzchor were remembering a member of the Wehrmacht at their Vespers service in October 1944, the rituals the choir performed had regional significance, as did the custom of Vespers itself. In fact, the notes about Blumstock and Weichhold's memorials are the only thing that differs from their conventional Vespers services. Most Saturday evenings during the school year, the Kreuzchor perform a cappella vocal works drawn from a vast repertoire of Christian (primarily, but not exclusively, Lutheran) *stile antico* sacred music. The services Mauersberger and the Kreuzchor performed for Blumstock and Weichhold reaffirm the customs of the choir and their community.

Brahmsian Grief after the Dresden Firebombing

As with most of the city's cultural institutions, the Dresden firebombing played a significant role in the choir's postwar identity.[80] Eleven choristers died in the Allied attack on the city on 13 February 1945. Their home church, the Kreuzkirche, and school, the Kreuzschule, were both heavily damaged. The choir's library was completely destroyed.[81] Many of those who survived left the city. Mauersberger walked to his hometown over fifty miles away, while choristers at the boarding school sheltered in the neighboring town of Meissen, under the care of pastoral staff.[82] With his musical community scattered across Saxony, Mauersberger's first responses to the firebombing manifested in composition rather than performance. During Holy Week in 1945, he penned the a cappella, *stile antico* mourning motet *Wie liegt die Stadt so wüst*, setting texts drawn from the Lamentations of Jeremiah.[83] His chosen lines from the Lamentations are a response to the firebombing forged through allegory rather than testimony.[84] The zenith of this work is an allusion to Brahms's mourning motet *Warum ist das Licht gegeben*—a piece that the choir had performed six months earlier at Blumstock and Weichhold's memorial Vespers.[85]

Mauersberger's motet was the starting point in the Kreuzchor's personal and collective responses to the firebombing.[86] Despite the immense practical challenges of the city's rubblescape, the choir returned to Dresden and resumed rehearsals in June 1945.[87] With most of the old city center in ruins, they moved around the city in the first postwar decade, attending a temporary location for 1945–1946, while also performing in destroyed buildings and churches in undamaged neighbourhoods.[88] Vespers services scheduled between Christmas and the first anniversary of the firebombing were canceled due to a lack of heat.[89] But other performances went ahead despite these immense logistical difficulties. For some of the pieces the choir sang during these early postwar months, Mauersberger recalled the music from memory, and choristers then transcribed his scores so that the choir had enough parts.[90]

Their performances filled an emotional need for the city's shell-shocked residents: a memorial Vespers (*Gedenkvesper*) service on 4 August 1945, held in the ruins of the Kreuzkirche, drew a crowd of thousands.[91] At this service the choir sang mourning motets from the Lutheran funerary tradition. The service opened and closed with two newly composed a cappella works by Rudolf Mauersberger that fit within these customs, including the premiere of *Wie liegt die Stadt so wüst*.[92] The 4 August 1945 Vespers was one of many services performed for those who lost their lives in the firebombing, including annual performances on the anniversary of the attacks. The most important of these pieces in the early postwar years was Brahms's Requiem. In addition to the three performances they gave in the final months of 1945 (mentioned at the outset of this essay), the Kreuzchor also performed this work on the anniversary of the attacks in 1946, 1947, and 1948.[93] Thus for a three-year period in the years after the Second World War, the Kreuzchor's customs for Totensonntag and for the firebombing were linked by both repertoire and ritual practice. The choir still perform an annual service around the time of the firebombing to this day. In some years, they use the Brahms Requiem to commemorate this local trauma.[94]

In the late 1940s, Mauersberger adapted Brahms's memorial templates further, by writing his own Requiem. Mauersberger consistently said that he was drawn to composition as a necessity in the aftermath of the firebombing, as the choir's library was destroyed the night of 13 February 1945.[95] First premiered in 1948, his *Dresdner Requiem* has many parallels with Brahms's earlier work.[96] Like Brahms, Mauersberger described how this work arose from the liturgical need for a Lutheran Mass for the Dead.[97] He forged the polychoral piece by setting biblical passages from both the New and Old Testaments, movements of the Roman Catholic Mass in German translation, and the music and text of Lutheran chorales. He revised the work several times in the 1950s and in its final version (1960), the work is thirty-seven movements long, divided across five sections that align with the Roman Catholic Requiem Mass: Introitus, Kyrie, "Vergänglichkeit, Tod, Dies Irae" (Transitory, Death, Dies Irae), Sanctus, and Agnus Dei.[98]

Musically and textually, Mauersberger's Requiem bears the markers of Lutheran funerary customs, such as a prominence of movements set a cappella and *stile antico*, quotations of burial chorales, biblical passages referring to death and resurrection, and instances of structural symmetry within and across movements.[99] Regional and national customs are prevalent, too, including the use of funerary trombones, and a setting of the chorale "Es ist gewißlich an der Zeit" in movement 19, which is known as the *Deutsches Dies Irae*.[100] Mauersberger evokes his predecessor through the title: his Requiem was originally titled the *Liturgisches Requiem*, but the revised title more closely resembles Brahms's *Ein deutsches Requiem*. Such individual evocations no doubt resonated with members of the Kreuzchor through their Totensonntag performances. For all of the specific connections to Brahms, though, it is important to note that Mauersberger composed in a style of historicist modernism that enhances these associations to Lutheran funerary music because he held a commitment to choral music by virtue of his lifelong position as a church musician.[101]

In Mauersberger's Dresden memorial works, the composer was both positioning himself within the historiography of Lutheran mourning music and responding to the aftermath of the Dresden firebombing and the Second World War. The heart of his Requiem is a multi-movement section titled "Transitory, Death, Dies Irae" (movements eight through twenty-two). It is within this section that Mauersberger engaged in the most biblical exegesis, crafting texts for each movement by taking short passages—sometimes single verses—from across the New and Old Testaments to respond to the Dresden firebombing through musical and textual allusions.[102] His textual choices reveal a deep familiarity with the Lutheran Bible, as Brahms had shown in several of his vocal mourning works as well.[103] Mauersberger's selected texts in this section of the work are reflections on fire, death, material remains, and judgment at the end of life. We have seen how the choir was involved—directly and indirectly—in the cultural machinations of the Third Reich. Though guilt remained a difficult topic to discuss openly and directly in the postwar period, there are ways that the aftermath of the Third Reich and the firebombing manifest in Mauersberger's Requiem through his choice of biblical texts on the topics of guilt and sin.[104]

Brahms aligned his Requiem with a Lutheran outlook on mourning, which focuses on providing comfort for the living rather than memorializing the deceased.[105] The circumstances facing Mauersberger in the late 1940s may have led him to include this extended pontification on death and fear of judgment at the end of life. At the same time, the imperative to provide comfort is interspersed throughout the central section of the Requiem. Mauersberger sets texts from the Gospel of John and Revelation that provide reminders of faith, and the final movements of each subsection close with a chorale performed by a "distant choir" (*Fernchor*).[106] This choir, which in the Kreuzkirche are positioned in the balcony of the church, are meant to represent the deceased.[107] This compositional choice echoes that made by Heinrich Schütz in the *Musikalische Exequien* (1636). In this work, Schütz used a second, distant, choir to conjure ideas of heaven and the afterlife. This was in keeping with contemporary reflections on the music of heaven, yet allowed Schütz to create a subtle musical presentation of heaven that did not directly evoke the sounds typically associated with celestial representation in music.[108] Musical comfort looks and sounds different in Brahms and Mauersberger's Requiems, but both composers drew inspiration from previous generations of Lutheran composers to formulate musical expressions of mourning and consolation in their works.

Around the time Mauersberger was composing his Requiem, official narratives of the firebombing were starting to shift. In 1946 and 1947, Soviet Occupation Authorities had prevented public services on the firebombing anniversary, fearing a massive outpouring of grief.[109] But in 1949, city officials began organizing events to mark the firebombing. Their anxieties about collective mourning were overpowered by the propagandistic potential the Allied attack on Dresden presented for promoting East Germany's founding narratives.[110] The Kreuzchor became a formal part of these rituals in the 1950s. Their performance repertoire for these annual commemorations enhances the idea that Mauersberger's Requiem was considered a successor to Brahms's renowned work in the genre. To commemorate the firebombing in 1948, the choir had performed Brahms's Requiem; in 1949, they performed Mauersberger's Liturgical Requiem.[111]

The confluence of Germanic style seen in Mauersberger's Requiem arguably made it easier for the ruling authorities to uphold a religious work as a symbol of Dresden's destruction in an officially atheist country. As Elaine Kelly has shown in her study of nineteenth-century music in East Germany, musicologists reframed Brahms's compositional process as fitting within the historical narratives of "Erbe"/heritage and "tradition" in the 1950s.[112] This stripped Brahms's choral music of its sacred associations. With Mauersberger, avoiding the sacredness of his music was more difficult: he was alive, conducting one of the oldest church choirs in the world. But the ruling communists presented themselves as the "protectors" of a long-standing cultural heritage, and the Kreuzchor was an integral part of local and national musical traditions. Moreover, both choir and cantor embodied Dresden's "phoenix rising from the ashes" mentality, which was an integral part of the city's postwar narrative.[113]

Conclusion: Lutheran Lineages of Loss

In this chapter I have explored the significance of Brahms's Requiem and other choral mourning works to the Dresdner Kreuzchor, showing how these works took on local meanings and associations during the Second World War and after the Dresden firebombing. In the immediate postwar context, Lutheran mourning music bridged a chasm between the Kreuzchor's common cultural memory—the conventions that they have practiced in some form since the institution was founded in 1236—and the traumatic cultural memory of 13 February 1945. Brahms's Requiem accrued new associations because of its uses for mourning the firebombing.

Though *Ein deutsches Requiem* took on specific meanings for Dresden's local communities between 1939 and 1949, the Kreuzchor's engagements with Brahms can be situated within a rich posthumous reception history of his Requiem, particularly in German-speaking countries. For instance, Sven Hiemke has surveyed homages to Brahms's Requiem, which range from memorial works for Brahms himself, to works that allude to the original work in the context of mourning a range of individual and communal losses throughout the twentieth century.[114] In the *Dresdner Requiem*, Mauersberger's musical engagements with Brahms's Requiem are at the level of genre rather than direct quotation. Nevertheless, through his compositions, Mauersberger and the Kreuzchor participated in a trend of alluding to Brahms's Requiem to express loss in a way that had personal and collective resonances. In German-speaking regions, Brahms's Requiem became a musical language through which to formulate responses to grief in the twentieth century in both composition and performance.

Brahms positioned himself within a lineage of Lutheran mourning music, though his Requiem was subsequently taken up in primarily secular contexts beginning in the 1860s and continuing into the twentieth century.[115] Composers working in Protestant institutions across Germany have adapted these customs too, positioning themselves within the musical lineage that Brahms evoked so clearly in his own mourning works. When Brahms wrote *Ein deutsches Requiem*, he called on long-standing conventions of Lutheran mourning music to create a genre that he felt was absent from the Lutheran liturgy: a Mass for the Dead. Mauersberger's responses to the Dresden firebombing extended many of Brahms's customs forward into the twentieth century. As a corollary, Mauersberger repositions Brahms within the sacred customs that inspired his work but that quickly became detached from it.[116]

Mauersberger's musical responses to the Dresden Firebombing adapt Protestant burial customs that date back to the Renaissance, and had previously informed Brahms's memorial repertoires. As the annual commemoration of Dresden became increasingly propagandistic, Mauersberger's music ensured the use and adaptation of Lutheran mourning rituals as part of this day of remembrance. By focusing on the works performed at these annual commemorations, we see how Dresden's postwar memorial politics remained grounded in sacred practices. Moreover, the city's musical expressions of loss are saturated with continuities to the Third Reich, and extend back well before the supposed ruptures of the Nazi era. The circulation of Brahms's Requiem is part of this entangled history of Germany's commemorative politics. Examining the Kreuzchor's mourning customs in postwar Dresden further contributes to our understanding of Brahms's complicated legacy in twentieth-century Germany.

Chapter 16

"Aimez-vous Brahms?"

The History of a Question

Daniel Beller-McKenna

Françoise Sagan's 1959 novel *Aimez-vous Brahms* . . . provided a catchphrase that helped frame numerous studies of the composer's work over the ensuing decades. Much as Arnold Schoenberg's formulation "Brahms the Progressive" had led to numerous take-offs ("Brahms the Ambivalent"; "Brahms the Programmatic"; "Brahms the Romantic";[1] etc.), Sagan's title was quickly echoed in a 1962 ballet (*Aimez-vous Bach?*) and a 1963 novel (*Aimez-vous Wagner?*). Later it was borrowed, more famously, by Peter Gay for his 1977 landmark essay on Brahms and modernism, and later for a major review-essay by Charles Rosen in 1998.[2] Inevitably, a 1989 *Musik-Konzepte* volume took the step of combining tropes: *Aimez-vous Brahms the Progressive?*[3] Schoenberg and Sagan's pithy titles are so often emulated because they serve a clear purpose. Schoenberg's statement stakes out a provocative perspective and dares the reader to disagree. In place of the prevailing sense of Brahms as the last representative of the forms, conventions, and contrapuntal undergirding of the common-practice period, Schoenberg claims the mantel of progress for him, a status normally associated with Brahms's rivals, Wagner and Liszt. Sagan's question situates Brahms's legacy in simpler terms, as it forces us to consider one of the basic elements in a composer's value: do we like their music?

In an essay originally presented at a 2018 symposium devoted to Brahms reception in France between the Franco-Prussian War and the First World War, Nicolas Dufetel rightly calls into question the relevance of Sagan's book for the study of Brahms reception. He notes that in various interviews around the time of the book's publication, Sagan suggests that Brahms serves an abstract function in the title of her book. In one case, she explains that Brahms was chosen because he wasn't too famous and, elsewhere, she offers that the question is more symbolic than substantive. Dufetel reports: "In a television interview with Pierre Dumayet, Sagan said that the title was a simple and inquisitive question to ask a girl, much like 'Aimez-vous Chopin? Aimez-vous Brahms? Que pensez-vous de Dieu?'" It is only "the intention of the question" that is important, not the answer."[4] Here Sagan is channeling her heroine, Paule, who states, "it was one of those questions young men had asked

Daniel Beller-McKenna, *"Aimez-vous Brahms?"* In: *Rethinking Brahms*. Edited by: Nicole Grimes and Reuben Phillips, Oxford University Press. © Oxford University Press 2022. DOI: 10.1093/oso/9780197541739.003.0017 her when she was seventeen."[5] But as I will argue later in this essay, even the lack of Brahmsian substance in Sagan's book in fact does tell us something of where his music stood around 1960. More important, whereas her book is not a great gauge of French taste for Brahms (after all, as Dufetel emphasizes, it is not even stated as a question in her title, which lacks a question mark), that core question was near the surface of Brahms reception in France from his own lifetime through the mid-twentieth century (and notably it often hinged on his reputation as a stuffy old-fashioned romantic, which occasioned Schoenberg's gambit). Sagan's title is, then, not so much a starting point as an echo of a long-standing problem in the reception of Brahms's music in France. This essay charts three moments in French-language Brahms-reception, each marked by the question, "aimez-vous Brahms?" exactly or almost exactly in that formulation. The three examples range from a concert series announcement in 1908, to a recalled conversation by a Parisian cultural historian in 1945, to Sagan's book title from 1959 and the reverberations in its 1961 film setting. In each instance the context for the question (musical, social, or historical) and the identity of the person posing it help situate the French take on Brahms's music and his legacy, attached as it was to a variety of historical crosscurrents.

Timing is everything. Establishing his career in the last third of the nineteenth century, Brahms found it harder to crack French concert programs than had his Austro-German predecessors. Haydn's and Mozart's music was performed in Paris during their lifetimes (Haydn's to great acclaim), and Beethoven came to represent that most public of instrumental genres, the symphony, at the time that regular symphonic concert-series became a staple in France during the late 1820s. The success of those three Germanic composers normalized the appearance of German instrumental music on French concert programs, benefiting Weber, Mendelssohn, Schumann, and many other German composers who followed them through the middle of the nineteenth century. Brahms's career, however, did not take off until 1868 with the premiere of his German Requiem, followed by a string of larger works in the 1870s. It was precisely those years, however, that saw the first harsh critiques of Brahms's works from leading figures in French music: Lalo, Saint-Saëns, Fauré, and Alfred Bruneau, among others. Those years coincided with a strongly anti-Teutonic, nationalist movement in response to France's humiliating defeat in the Franco-Prussian War of 1870. Whereas earlier German classic-romantic composers were grandfathered in, French taste for Brahms (and for newer German symphonists generally) developed slowly and grudgingly against the "Ars Gallica" mentality of the newly formed Société Nationale de Musique. Jim Samson has also pointed to the relative de-emphasis in Paris of public choral singing and amateur music-making as edifying in comparison with large German cities. Music in Paris, Samson argues, was "a craft to be cultivated excellently, and above all to be left to the professionals."[6] This sealed off another potential avenue to Brahms's acceptance in Paris during the last third of the nineteenth century, given the importance of choral music to his reputation.

Brahms's music was certainly heard in France in the later nineteenth and early twentieth centuries. In a short overview from the Brahms anniversary year of 1997, Marc Vignal surveyed Brahms's reception in France, enumerating many performances of Brahms's music there from the 1860s onward. Citing concerts featuring Brahms by staunch Wagnerians Charles Lamoureux and Jules Pasdeloup, Vignal lists performances of every type of piece in Brahms's oeuvre (piano, chamber, orchestral, choral, and lied), noting the rising resistance to Brahms by some musical opinion shapers along the way.[7] Like his admirers Lamoureux and Pasdeloup, some of Brahms's early French detractors were strong followers of Wagner, as were most of Brahms's prominent detractors in the next generations, including Poulenc, Dukas, and d'Indy. Whereas the weightiest discussions of Wagner took place in the literary realm, following Baudelaire's lead and the symbolists' admiration for Wagner's modernity, the relevant effect of Wagnerism on Brahms's reception came from an embrace by the composers I have listed (and others) of various progressive features associated with the *Musikdrama*. In much the same vein as the New Germans, French Wagnerians' criticism of Brahms coalesced around his use of older forms into which, they complained, he could breathe life but could not produce anything forward-looking.

Raymond Bouyer, 1908: Armand Parent's Brahms Project

Thus, unlike the continuing reverence for Johann Sebastian Bach, the enduring status of Beethoven, and the pervasive influence of Wagner, there was no love expressed for Brahms among the French musical elite at the turn of the twentieth century. Although the issue of whether one likes any given composer no doubt comes up in common conversation all the time in any country, I have not uncovered the formulation "aimez-vous x" widely in French-language musical journals during the time in question. It is notable then that, without searching too far, one finds it uttered at least twice in the first half of the twentieth century in the French press, and then, of course famously in Sagan's book title. The first instance occurs in the Belgian music newspaper *Le Guide musical* from 15 March 1908, in an announcement of an upcoming series of performances. "Do you like the music of Brahms?" asks the author, art and music critic Raymond Bouyer (1862–1935). He himself continues: "I'll tell you more when I have heard everything, or at least his twenty-four works of chamber music, as the tireless Armand Parent is letting us be the first to hear them this year at the Schola."[8] Parent, a Belgian violinist, was perhaps Brahms's greatest champion in Paris at the turn of the century. Since 1892, he had frequently dedicated entire concert programs to Brahms's chamber works, and he has been credited with sparking new interest in performances of Brahms's music in Paris. In a 1993 article, Michel Stockhem chronicles the slow and limited success of Parent's Brahms concerts. Surveying Brahms's presence on Parisian concert programs prior to Parent, Stockhem observes that Brahms's music was "sparingly disseminated, almost exclusively near to Germanophile circles of the initiated. In a country where the awakening to chamber and symphonic music was still quite fresh, where progressive musicians tried intensely to forget that Wagner had been German, Brahms was considered emblematic of a Germanic type of pedant, very *Herr Doktor Professor*, artistically dead from the desiccating influence of Teutonic military ambition."[9]

Stockhem also traces the engagement of *Le Guide musical* as a champion of Parent's Brahms project, crediting critic Hugues Imbert (whom he describes as "a critic among the most prolific, if not the most profound, of the turn of the century") with converting the *Guide* from a leading Wagner organ of the time to a "Brahmin" venue through a series of reviews beginning in 1894.[10] Imbert died in 1905, leaving the *Guide*'s Parent/Brahms coverage to others like Bouyer. From his 1908 notice, we could be misled to think that Brahms's music was gaining acceptance in France a decade after his death. But misgivings about his music and his historical position that had slowed its introduction to Parisian audiences from the start were still firmly in place in the first decade of the twentieth century. Parent had been at this for sixteen years, so the sheer volume of works presented in his 1908 concert series, a high point in Brahms's presence in Paris, indicates how slow the process was to win over French audiences. As further evidence, the reviewer, Raymond Bouyer, a venerable critic of art and music in Paris, claims he will have to hear these twenty-four works before answering his own rhetorical question. More important, the question implies that not every reader *will* like the music of Brahms, and it almost takes the form of a challenge (as in, "You had *better* like Brahms if you are going to subject yourself to four full evenings of his music.") Bouyer's ensuing commentary raises some of the old complaints—"the four symphonies, more interesting than transporting"; "the violin concerto . . . which always seemed icy to us"—before he renders this judgment, so typical of his time and place: "Let's say that the austere musician, celebrated by the enthusiastic pen of Hugues Imbert and Fantin-Latour's Schumannian pencil, never counted, dead or alive, among the controversial geniuses, because his work, eminently orthodox, does not appear combative or confused; it is so fundamentally Germanic that it does not attract the French taste at first glance. . . . Let us content ourselves with listening to the music of Brahms. . . . Analysis before synthesis! And let us beware of ready-made judgments!"[11] Thus, Bouyer's question, "Aimez-vous la musique de Brahms?," nevertheless acknowledges the prejudice with which French audiences approached his music and argues for keeping an open mind (ear?) as his music becomes better known in France.

Whereas some of the Parisian music audience may have heeded that advice, Brahms's stock failed to rise among the musical establishment in France. Vincent d'Indy, an ardent Wagnerian, sums up the established French assessment of Brahms just four years later (1912) in his *Cours de composition*, a collection of his foundational lectures at the Schola Cantorum:

> Perhaps alone among the Germans, Brahms inherited something of Beethoven's gift for the development of ideas, but more from a thematic than from a tonal point of view. His ideas and harmonies are not banal, but they are rarely distinctive. Such as they are, Brahms manages them with talent, and to use a vulgar expression, "he works his dough" but this "dough" often sticks to his pen, and when it does his style becomes heavy and indigestible. Moreover as tonal relationships don't seem to interest him much, many of his works sound awkward and tedious.[12]

D'Indy's take on Brahms is significant in general, given his prominence as a teacher and a leader of the post-1870 French school that had its own classicizing tendencies. Arguing that Brahms, in his attempt to emulate Beethoven, works himself into a muddle (as the dough sticks to his pen), d'Indy concludes: "Anyone endowed with artistic sense should have respect for Brahms; but he is not easy to love. For his works, honestly composed as they are, seldom radiate that true charm that touches and stirs the heart."[13] (Or, in the words of an anonymous 1908 reviewer of d'Indy's Second Symphony, Brahms's symphonies are "so opaque, so heavy, so desperately classic in the wrong sense!"[14]) The problem to d'Indy and his followers was not merely that Brahms looked to the past rather than moving music forward, but also that he failed to achieve the emotional effect that his forebears had, never "stirring the heart." Instead, to their ears, his ideas became "awkward and tedious."

To make his point, d'Indy briefly assays Brahms's three piano sonatas as incomplete and failed attempts to work out cyclical sonata form. "The Sonatas," he writes, "are interesting because of the tendency they manifest toward cyclical construction: but this conception, still vague, is far from its complete realization."[15] After tracing themes in the Sonata in F Minor (Op. 5, the most overtly cyclical of the group), offering compliments and mild rebukes as he proceeds, d'Indy concludes: "We see from these examples that there is, in Brahms, a rather clear tendency toward the redevelopment of the sonata form, by means of certain thematic modifications or variations, none of which can be traced in the works of his German contemporaries. It is always the latent cyclical design that dictates these incomplete attempts, whose full realization was left, almost exclusively, to César Franck and the French school."[16] Here, critically, Brahms's alleged shortcomings are measured pointedly against his French contemporaries. For d'Indy, then, one can surmise that part of his aversion to Brahms's music stems from the latter's German identity.

German music was generally met with resistance in France during the First World War. Brahms received a relative pass, if only because he had never been widely accepted by the French in the first place. By contrast, an open nationalist campaign against Wagner's music was carried out in the press during the war, led on the musical front by his admirer Saint-Saëns, who valued Wagner's music but was repelled by its close identity with the German Reich under Wilhelm II.[17] Brahms had hardly gained enough of a foothold to be a similar subject of patriotic scorn. So little, in fact, that when Jean Cocteau came to Wagner's defense, not wishing to exclude all German music, his omission of Brahms speaks loudly: "Wagner is indigestible, *but* a genius. Munich art is dreadful, but we should not mistake it for a French return to sublime simplicity. I will not brush my teeth with Odol [a turn-of-the-century German toothpaste] anymore, *but* I will not deprive myself either of Schubert, or Bach, or Beethoven."[18] Cocteau is making a distinction between Wagner's national associations and his musical style. He was, of course, a leading voice in the call for a distinctly French form of modernism, one that eschewed the emotional excesses of romanticism and undergirded the French neo-classicism of the 1920s and 1930s.

All nationalist sentiments aside, both Brahms and Wagner were due to lose program space as the new music of Stravinsky and Les Six (and the newly appreciated music of Satie) came to the fore in Paris during those decades. That said, both composers' profiles improved in France in the mid to late 1930s. Wagner's operas started to be performed again by 1921 and gained considerable attention through Furtwängler's productions throughout the 1930s. Vignal cites a turn toward more favorable critiques and a rise in the number of performances of Brahms's music from 1935 onward, singling out Alfred Cortot's *Cours d'interprétation* as an example: "The French are wrong to regard Brahms as a man of average talent. It is, in truth, a very powerful constructor that is the author of this Sonata in F minor (Op. 5).... The work is imbued with a greatness which must be reflected in the interpretation one gives it. Brahms has been criticized for his ambition, his desire for the sublime: he not only had a desire for it, he achieved it."[19]

Henri Davenson, 1945: Brahms as a Composer of the Past

Of course, the Nazi occupation of France in the summer of 1940 turned French reception of iconic German composers on its head. The frequency of performances of Brahms and (especially) Wagner, took on an inverse relationship to their acceptance by French audiences.

This leads to the next appearance (to my knowledge) of our question in the French cultural press, one that occurs at the tail end of the Second World War. This time, it is turned around and posed to a French writer. In his April

1945 essay "French Music or Music in France," cultural historian Henri-Irénée Marrou (1904–1977), writing under his pen name, Henri Davenson, recounts a recent meeting with a young musician: "The other day, during a political event, I met a young Austrian musician. This one, happy to discover after a moment that we could talk about something other than the status of immigrants, immediately started a conversation. His first question: 'Aimez-vous Brahms?' I answered immediately, of course, 'the first of the bores,' to the dismay of my Austrian friend." Davenson's complaint against Brahms is all too familiar, but he quickly moves to dismiss it, indicating an important change in Brahms's status in France: "Have you noticed? Brahms is the litmus test that separates French musicians and musicians from Central Europe: for us academism, for them the last of the Big Three Bs, a classic equal to Johann Sebastian or Ludwig.... We must move beyond this; to succeed in the field of musical taste, as in the field of politics, in getting past the sterile cult of incommunicable difference: that, let us be clear, would be less an eclipsing of nationalism than a profound examination of it."[20]

Unlike the critics I cited previously, Davenson treats Brahms strictly as a musician of the past; the experience of the Second World War creates a breach from which he will emerge, not just as a composer accused of aping music of the past, but truly a figure of the past himself. In calling for a truce ("to succeed in the field of musical taste ... in getting past the sterile cult of incommunicable difference"), Davenson de-emphasizes the significance of Brahms's Germanness, and is willing to move beyond it, focusing instead on the different perspectives of the French listener and the Central European listener. This becomes the central theme of his essay: that French music is a manner of listening to music, that music in France is more important than music from France (criticizing Fauré and elevating Mussorgsky along the way). He closes:

> We will therefore defend French music here. A position that arms our critique with a perfect freedom of judgment with regard to the music currently produced in France. We intend to make this critique severe, demanding,—strong. It seems to me that music in France is at this moment on the brink of a great period of renewal. History shows that the great rebirths emerge more often from a foreign influence assimilated with ardor than from a culture of pure national routine: the *Pléiade* [a group of sixteenth-century French poets] broke with tradition. They established themselves slavishly in the school of Italian Humanism, and yet they bore the true grandeur of France.[21]

To be sure, Brahms has little place in this moment of renewal in French music. It is not that Davenson has no use for music of the past; indeed most of his writing on music (including three books) focuses on antiquity and the Middle Ages.[22] Rather, he wants to elevate composers whose music inspires a classical humanistic outlook ("light, order, beauty, *visio pacis*," he states), specifically one that looks past nineteenth-century Romanticism.[23] Romanticism was not the charge levied against Brahms by Davenson (although it was certainly a common critique). Rather, Brahms was judged too academic to be suitable for inspiring a way forward.

Fifteen years after this essay, Davenson was invited to write a reflection piece for the same journal, *Esprit*. There, in 1960, he averred, lamentably, that the breaking down of national barriers had not occurred, that a modern Europe had not taken shape. He specifically recalls the question "Aimez-vous Brahms?"—presumably in light of Sagan's book of the previous year— and offers that Brahms remains a sticking point between France and Central Europe, and that his music has not made significant inroads in Parisian concert programs during the intervening years:

> There would be a lot to say about the evolution of taste in France within a single generation. In retrospect, I am struck by the extent to which the unity of Europe, which is being completed before our eyes, has taken a long time to be achieved. For a long time, the word "music" did not have the same meaning in Paris, Milan or London, to say nothing of Germany. It seems ridiculous to say it again, but the question "Do you like Brahms?" (With question mark, o Julliard) has been, during all this time, the shibboleth, the infallible detector at the crossing of the Rhine; I have often explained that the historic role of the old, bearded man had been filled in France by César Franck, of d'Indy, the Schola cantorum; have things really changed?[24]

Davenson's assessment of the intervening years notwithstanding, Brahms ranked sixth (admittedly, a distant sixth) among composers who appeared on orchestral programs in Paris in 1951 according to a report in the *Musical Times* that year.[25] Likewise a *New York Times* article of 1956 reports an enthusiastic reception of the Second Symphony performed by the Boston Symphony Orchestra under Charles Munch to open the concert season that year: "Brahms has only very recently been accepted in France, but tonight's highly charged performance . . . was enthusiastically acclaimed."[26] And, as Davenson himself points out, recordings of Brahms's music were ever more plentiful in France by the end of that decade.

More important, however, Brahms's reputation had shifted after the war (if not necessarily for the better). His reputation as a cold, academic composer had been replaced by the notion that he was a dated romantic. In his 1977 essay "Aimez-vous Brahms? Reflections on Modernism," Peter Gay lays out the then-prevalent take on the composer:

> Brahms is not difficult but easy. He strikes the modern ear, in fact, as all too easy, with those long yearning melodies announced by the cello, and the thick resounding tutti produced by his sizable orchestra. Even his chamber

music—that demanding, spare genre that reveals all—often sounds oddly symphonic. Much of it lacks the acerbity, the dry wit, the intimacy of classical chamber music; with its all-too-pleasing themes and sonorous scoring, it approaches at times the kind of music played by a discreet ensemble in resort hotels to the clatter of spoons and the hum of conversation.

He adds, "The literature of condescension that has collected around Brahms the "romantic classicist," is too familiar to require recital."[27]

Françoise Sagan, 1959: Forgetting Brahms

Rest assured, Gay is setting up what he sees as the common perception only to argue that Brahms was a true modernist, the "progressive" Schoenberg had claimed. But Gay rightly introduces the prevailing romantic idea of Brahms through the work from which he borrowed his title, Françoise Sagan's 1959 book, *Aimez-vous Brahms . . .*, which was the twenty-four-year-old Sagan's fourth book, having already made her mark with her first novel, *Bonjour Tristesse*, in 1954 at the age of eighteen. Like her previous novels, *Aimez-vous Brahms . . .* involves problematic personal relationships among restless characters to form a biting critique of modern French society and its mores.

She was not the first *enfant terrible* on the French scene to draw on Brahms's romantic aura to critique postwar French society. Louis Malle's film *Les Amants* from the previous year employs the Folia-based theme and variations second movement of Brahms String Sextet, Op. 18, as its soundtrack. Brahms's melody, which is heard as the film opens (and, along with its variations, repeatedly throughout the film) is only one among a number of icons that Malle uses to outline a conflict, as the film's heroine, Jeanne Tournier (played by Jeanne Moreau) rebels against a stifling set of centuries-old social conventions that repress her. As we hear the entire thirty-two-bar theme, the opening credits unfold against an old and odd map. This is the famous *Carte de Tendre*, an allegorical map devised in the mid-seventeenth-century salon of novelist and philosopher Madeleine de Scudéry, who replaces the names of places with emotional states, virtues, and vices. As Joan DeJean states in her book *Tender Geographies*, "Scudery maps out the land of Tenderness in order to suggest that individual contracts could be recognized as equally binding alternatives that would return to women control over their own destinies," and that it offered "multiple amorous trajectories."[28] Whereas Scudéry spearheaded a social movement outside of, and in some ways antagonistic to, the Regime, the folia model to which Brahms makes reference is its political antipode, associated as it was with the Royal court: in distinction to the earlier Spanish and Italian versions of folia, this one originated with Jean-Baptiste Lully in the 1670s when he was the musical face of the court of Louis XIV, and thus carries an aura of absolutism.[29] At the same time, Brahms's theme provides a metaphor for control and the limits of expression with predetermined boundaries through its very genre (theme and variations). Although of a different era, the historical tinge of the folia theme reinforces Brahms's association with the past, adding a level of social, even political meaning to Brahms's musical identity. Malle is thus able to capture Jeanne Tournier's predicament through the combination of the *Carte de Tendre* and the Sextet, as she seeks to free herself from culturally determined expectations of her role as a wife, and by an upper-class life that she increasingly considers shallow and artificial, all of which rests on centuries-old paradigms. In Malle's words, "What I had in mind was a denunciation of the hypocrisy of the ruling class and what women were supposed to be[:] good wives and mothers and stick to that."[30]

Unlike Malle, who saturates his film with Brahms's music without once referencing the composer, Sagan takes nearly the opposite tack; Brahms features in her title, but his music is barely (and only vaguely) mentioned in the book. But just as Malle engages Brahms in a question of identity (i.e., Jeanne Tournier's social identity as a woman in postwar France), Sagan's book similarly uses Brahms to provoke the heroine Paule's identity crisis. Sagan's first three books featured morally rebellious young women in conflict with the older generation, a dynamic that is reversed in her fourth book, *Aimez-vous Brahms. . . .* Now the heroine, Paule, is a thirty-nine-year-old Parisian dressmaker who is becoming increasingly uneasy with her lack of stability and security as mid-life descends, a predicament that is only exacerbated by her long-term affair with Roger, an unfaithful lover her own age. Enter Simon, a twenty-five-year-old American in search of a purpose in life who falls in love with Paule and pursues her ceaselessly, initially to her amusement and annoyance, until she finally gives in after yet another of Roger's flings with a younger woman. In the end, Paule returns to Roger, realizing that she can never really take her relationship with Simon seriously.

Prior to the development of her relationship with Simon, *Aimez-vous Brahms . . .* is rife with references to Paule's growing awareness that she has lost touch with her younger self, and the first page of the short book clearly maps out the distinction:

> Paule gazed at her face in the mirror and studied the accumulated defeats of thirty-nine years, one by one, not with the panic, the acrimony usual at such times, but with a detached calm. As though the tepid skin, which her two fingers plucked now and then to accentuate a wrinkle or bring out a shadow, belonged to someone else, to another Paule passionately concerned with her beauty and battling with the transition from young to youngish woman: a woman she scarcely recognized. She had stationed herself at this mirror to kill time only to discover—she smiled at the thought—that time was gradually killing her, aiming its blows at an appearance she knew had been loved.[31]

Not only does Paule see the woman in the mirror as somehow removed from herself ("someone else," "a woman she scarcely recognized"); within the first few pages of the book Sagan repeatedly presents Paule's despair over the current state of her life: "this uneasy listlessness"; "her deserted flat stuck out to her as odious and useless"; "she felt thoroughly dejected"; "sitting down on the bed with tears in her eyes"; "she brooded gently, bitterly, on her loneliness." Paule's unhappiness with her life is a critical component of her identity dilemma, which is eventually spurred by Brahms.

Sagan does not mention Brahms until roughly a third of the way through the book. While still wooing Paule, Simon leaves a note under her door: "'There is a wonderful concert in the Salle Pleyel at six,' Simon wrote, '*Aimez-vous Brahms?*' . . . She smiled on account of the second sentence: *Aimez-vous Brahms?* It was one of those questions young men had asked her when she was seventeen." This evokes a fit of forgetfulness in Paule. "'Come to think of it,'" she asks herself, "'did she care for Brahms?'" Having located a recording of a Brahms concerto in her collection (on the back of, what else, a Wagner overture), listening to Brahms only seems to exacerbate Paule's condition:

> She put the concerto on, found the beginning romantic and forgot to listen to all of it. She awoke to the fact when the music stopped and was angry with herself. Nowadays she took six days to read a book, lost her place, and forgot music. She could not keep her mind on a thing, except fabric samples and a man who was never there. She was losing herself, losing track of herself; she would never be herself again. *Aimez-vous Brahms?* For a moment she stood by the window; the sunlight hit her full in the eyes and dazzled her. And this little phrase, *Aimez-vous Brahms?* seemed suddenly to reveal an enormous forgetfulness; all that she had forgotten, all the questions that she had deliberately refrained from asking herself. *Aimez-vous Brahms?* Did she care for anything, now, except for herself and her own existence?[32]

Paule's inability to remember whether she liked Brahms reveals a mid-life crisis, in which she doesn't know who she is anymore. Paule forgets whether she likes Brahms just as she has trouble making up her mind whether she really loves Roger. This marks a decided change of Brahms's status in French culture from when Raymond Bouyer asked his readers, "Aimez-vous la musique de Brahms?" in his announcement of Armand Parant's planned series of concerts in 1908. Whereas Bouyer's query suggested a lack of full familiarity among Parisian concertgoers, and even a little resistance to Brahms, Paule's inability to answer the question comes not from a lack of exposure, but rather a lack of focus. When she listens to the record, Brahms is too familiar; the music passes her by without her realizing it. In the course of a half-century, Brahms has gone from being underrepresented in the Parisian music scene at the turn of the century, to the shibboleth that divides French and German through the end of the Second World War, to becoming all too familiar. Now he can be found along with Wagner on a disc (although Paule thinks to herself that she knows the Wagner overture on the flip side "by heart") in the record collection of a middle-aged, middle-class Parisian woman. His music is part of a tradition that is firmly entrenched; he is the past.

That reading is borne out to a degree by Sagan's own comments. In a 1960 interview she says of the question in her title: "It is a question you are asked when you're twenty [echoing Paule's comment above], a young man's question. . . . At twenty they ask, 'Do you believe in God?' 'Do you like Nietzsche, or Brahms?'—questions that have nothing to do with private and daily life. These are questions that you pass aside later, that you discuss less and less, that you forget. Afterwards you're asked, 'Do you like flounder?' 'Have you seen such and such a film?' 'Whom are you sleeping with?' "[33] Lumping Brahms in with Nietzsche and God places him beyond musical taste, even beyond music history per se. Perhaps this is merely an extension of Davenson's "shibboleth," Brahms as a dividing line, recalling (and reaffirming) Dufetel's comments near the beginning of this essay, that the title *Aimez-vous Brahms . . .* should probably be seen as more literary-musical than historical. At the same time, Sagan's treatment of Brahms marks a culmination in his reception in France from something vitally divisive to something of the past: "nothing to do with private and daily life."

Goodbye Again, 1961: Brahms as All Too Familiar

We never get much of an idea from Sagan which work Brahms Paule put on the record player, nor what was played at the concert (which she did agree to attend with Simon): only that it was "a concerto."[34] When the book was adapted to film in 1961, however, director Anatole Litvak entrusted the soundtrack to French composer Georges Auric, who radically transformed Brahms's role.[35] Although the dialogue in the film stays very close to that of the book (and Sagan worked closely with Litvak), Auric adapts the first theme from the Poco allegretto third movement of Brahms's Third Symphony as an *idée fixe* to represent Paule throughout the film, thus elevating his music from invisible to paramount. (This despite the disappearance of Brahms's name from the original American title for the film when it was rebranded *Goodbye Again*.) If, per Dufetel, Sagan's book is not a good barometer of French Brahms reception, Litvak's film might be even further off the mark; it is directed by a Ukrainian-born Lithuanian American; its dialog is in English; the screenplay was written by an American (Samuel A. Taylor); and only one of its three stars (Yves Montand) is French. Nevertheless, its soundtrack offers a unique view on the French taste for Brahms, given George Auric's career trajectory and his lived history. Auric is probably best known as a composer for his involvement in the French modernist group Les Six during the 1920s, although film scores make up his steadiest output from the mid-1930s until the 1960s when he turned his attention away from composing. He was already working on film and ballet scores with the likes of Cocteau and Diaghilev before embarking on a series of scores for socialist-themed films in the 1930s, which engendered a shift toward a populist style anchored by a more accessible musical language.[36] In *Goodbye Again*, Auric uses the Brahms theme to frame the plot and mark the flow of the story. His craftsmanship shines most brightly in the variety of lighter guises in which he sets the theme: a languid solo guitar arrangement; a polka-like piano miniature; a cabaret dance-band number; and a torch song. But Auric came of age during the early twentieth-century resistance to Brahms among the French musical elite; he studied with d'Indy at the Schola Cantorum, and he lived through the shifts in those tastes outlined in this essay. Thus, it is not surprising that, in addition to the various popular settings, Auric's soundtrack also projects the long-standing French notion of Brahms as a stuffy, dated romantic.

To begin with, the Poco allegretto theme is one of Brahms's most pathos-laden symphonic melodies; the constant rise of the melody only to fall repeatedly to incomplete cadences, epitomizes romantic yearning. Auric presents the melody in a full-throated orchestral rendition at the beginning (the opening credits), the middle (the Brahms concert), and at the close of the film. In the first instance, Auric arranges the theme with a heavy hand as part of the score to accompany the opening credits. Brahms's melody emerges forcefully (at first in *forte* unison) as Paule walks past a poster for the Brahms concert she later will attend. That same unison scoring returns at the very close of the film, developing out of the guitar solo mentioned above as Paule dejectedly prepares for bed after Roger cancels their date. As in Sagan's book, this scene reprises an identical moment from earlier in the story, although in the film the original scene's underscoring failed to transition from guitar to orchestra. Between the two scenes, of course, Paule had freed herself from her frustrating relationship with Roger, finding some vicarious connection with her lost youth through her relationship with Simon (renamed "Philip" in the film). Auric's overbearing scoring of the Poco allegretto theme at opposite ends of the film implies Paule's entrapment in her middle-aged present. And if it is too simplistic to equate Brahms with that which is "old" and "stuffy" here, one can at least hear Brahms in his more familiar orchestral setting as counter to all that is new, young, and free—which in Paule's case equates with Philip.

Unlike these two non-diegetic instances of the orchestral theme, its other iterations come near the middle of the film, first as Paule plays a recording at home, and shortly thereafter as Paule and Philip argue in the stairwell of the concert hall as the orchestra's performance of the third movement, already in progress, plays in the background. They have arrived (unrealistically) late for the symphony as they return from intermission. During the first half of the concert, where Auric could perhaps have inserted any Brahms concerto to maintain some fidelity to Sagan's text, he instead chose the C-major fourth movement of Brahms's Symphony No. 1 in C Minor—the only other music by Brahms heard in the film. Litvak's unusual construction of this scene captures the old image of Brahms as a romantic (already presented by the dramatic scoring of the Poco allegretto theme in the opening credits) while simultaneously deconstructing Davenson's Brahms-as-German ("the infallible detector at the crossing of the Rhine"). After Paule and Philip meet in the lobby, the scene fades into the concert hall, picking up with the first restatement of the fourth movement's hymn-like main theme. As the movement progresses (skipping over the *animato* second theme in G major), Paule drifts into a reverie, triggered perhaps by the epaulettes of the two soldiers in uniform seated directly in front of them. At this point Brahms's meaning becomes muddied. Paule recalls sitting at a sidewalk café, watching a military parade, where she met Roger for the first time. Brahms's C-major theme has distinct march-like characteristics in its prominent dactyl-spondee rhythms and in the martial scoring of some passages, exemplified by the wind heavy statement with which the scene begins. In other contexts, showing a military parade in conjunction with this music might reinforce Brahms's German identity in contradistinction to France. Yet the marchers here are clearly a French military band in postwar Paris, which conjures inherently anti-German notions. Litvak and Auric have hardly turned Brahms into a French hero. Rather, this scene indicates the degree to which Brahms's music has been loosened from its earlier moorings by 1961. Although just a year earlier Davenson questioned whether Brahms's meaning had changed when he wrote the second of his essays to raise the question "aimez-vous Brahms?," this scene, along with Auric's reframing of the Poco allegretto theme in popular styles, indicates that by 1961, Brahms's music had become familiar enough in France that it could be divorced from its earliest connotations.

PART V
AFTERLIVES OF BRAHMS

Chapter 17

Brahms's *Serious Songs* in the Orchestral Imagination

Two Episodes in the Arrangement History of Op. 121

Frankie Perry

During the coronavirus lockdown of Spring 2020, the pianist Igor Levit livestreamed a series of fifty-two "house concerts" over social networking sites, freely available to all with a stable internet connection.[1] Untethered from the programming restraints of his usual concert schedule, Levit chose the repertoire for his near-daily performances freely and spontaneously: while the series featured many stalwarts of the piano repertoire, Levit also chose pieces from its peripheries, allowing lesser-known music to reach audiences much larger than usual, as thousands tuned in to each recital. Levit found himself drawn to music that "seemed relevant at the time," and to music which "promised to provide inner strength and emotional support," both for himself and for his audience.[2] In October 2020, it was announced that this "Hauskonzert" project had won for Levit the annual Prize for Understanding and Tolerance from the Jewish Museum Berlin, in recognition of his "deeply humanitarian" work.[3]

A selection of the music from the project formed the basis of a new double album by Levit, *Encounter*, which was recorded in May—two months into the lockdown—and released by Sony Classical in September 2020. At the center of this album are transcriptions for solo piano of the final two works completed by Johannes Brahms, both written in 1896, the year before his death. The *Four Serious Songs* (*Vier ernste Gesänge*, Op. 121) are presented in Max Reger's 1912 version, and six of the *Eleven Chorale Preludes* (*Elf Choralvorspiele*, Op. 122), written originally for organ, are given in a 1902 transcription by Ferruccio Busoni.[4] Both are unlikely choices: the chorale preludes are little-known, marginal within Busoni's catalog of transcriptions let alone within Brahms's keyboard oeuvre; the *Serious Songs*, on the other hand, are so celebrated in their original version that the inclusion of a voiceless rendition on a solo piano album invites us to consider why these works were chosen, in these versions, at this time.

Most obvious, perhaps, is the subject matter of the two works. The passages from the Old Testament used in the first three of the *Serious Songs* ruminate, with "varying shades of pessimism,"[5] on death—they are, as Brahms wrote, "momentous words, heavy with meaning."[6] The *Chorale Preludes* have a similar gravitas: for the most part, Brahms chose Lutheran hymn tunes concerned with matters of death and the afterlife, and Busoni's whittling down of Brahms's eleven to six further heightens this topical priority, as the retained final sequence of the two settings of "Herzlich tut mich verlangen" and "O Welt ich muß dich lassen" now constitutes half the set.[7] Yet, both Op. 121 and Op. 122 balance their pessimistic overtones with espousals of hope and, importantly, love—they encourage reflection upon the most serious of topics, but they also bring comfort and consolation. While both "contemplate the human condition without relying on religious dogma,"[8] the performance of Op. 121 without its biblical words arguably makes the work more accessible—linguistically and spiritually—to a diverse twenty-first-century audience. It is little wonder, then, that these works spoke to Levit as he sought out music for his lockdown project that makes us consider the "basic questions of love and death, of loneliness and the possibility of truly loving one's neighbour."[9]

Levit's project was at once a solitary enterprise—an "extraordinary inner journey"—and a means for him to forge meaningful connections, musical and human, with as wide an audience as possible.[10] The status of the works as transcriptions is telling here. In Nicole Grimes's words, Brahms distills in Op. 121 a "monumental scale of conception" into "the most intimate of forms," and the act of transcription brings a further process of distillation.[11] The transcription turns the songs inward, into pieces more akin to chorale preludes: hearing Op. 121 and Op. 122 side by side allows the former to lean into the introspection inherent to this latter genre. While the rich intertextuality of Op. 122 means their textual (and musical) origins are known only to those versed in Lutheran musical heritage, the literal manner of transcription in the case of Op. 121 means that the subsumed words lie much closer to the surface. This is demonstrated in Reger's score, where the texts are printed above the staves, encouraging the pianist to play with them in mind (Example 17.1). A video broadcast of Levit performing Reger's transcription, from London's Wigmore Hall in October 2020, showed how deeply certain passages of the text were felt by Levit, who visibly mouthed or breathed occasional words—sometimes single syllables—as he played.[12] Yet the human voice is palpably absent, fittingly for a time when musicians were stripped of their livelihoods, a time of quarantine, isolation, and mourning.

* * *

Reger's transcription sits toward the beginning of the long and varied afterlife of Brahms's *Serious Songs* in arrangement. There have been versions for organ, which perhaps draw the non-religious Brahms's "godless" songs into more explicitly Christian performance settings, and there have been performing editions that switch out the low male voice for various solo instruments—most often cello, trombone, bass trombone, or tuba for their registral and (some say)

The Four Serious Songs in Orchestration

Example 17.1 Max Reger, *Johannes Brahms, Op. 121: Vier ernste Gesänge für Klavier allein (mit hinzugefügtem Text) von Max Reger* (Berlin: Simrock, 1912), bars 1–7.

timbral accord with the human voice.[13] There have also been several orchestrations and orchestral reimaginings of the songs, which will be the focus of this chapter. It is perhaps unsurprising that these songs, with their deeply personal yet "universal" texts, have been taken into the orchestral arena through arrangement considerably more than any of Brahms's other lieder, their message seemingly outgrowing their small-scale accompanimental medium. Among several suggestions that the songs sit uneasily within the genre of the lied, Lucien Stark wrote that they "expand the concept of art song" in order to facilitate an introspective, individual exploration of the same "ethical and spiritual matters" that the Requiem addresses on a "universal scale."[14]

The apparent predisposition of the songs for orchestral treatment also owes much to long-running speculation that Brahms had intended either to orchestrate the songs, or to incorporate some of their themes into a new orchestral work. The single-page manuscript document upon which this speculation is based—catalogued as "A 122" in the archive of the Gesellschaft der Musikfreunde—displays on one side a sketch of Op. 121/iv, and on the other a sketch for an unrealized E♭-major work, with annotations indicating orchestral scoring.[15] Included in these orchestral jottings is a clear transcription, transposed into E♭ major, of four bars from the second song of Op. 121, along with possible further references to the first and third of the *Serious Songs*. This, along with the shared key (and manuscript page) of the sketch with Op. 121/iv, led Max Kalbeck to conclude that Brahms had envisaged a "symphonic cantata" or a "fantasy on previously existing songs."[16] While this claim has been called into question by scholars including George Bozarth, David Brodbeck, and, most thoroughly, Daniel Beller-McKenna on the grounds that most of the orchestral sketch "bears only a passing relationship to Op. 121,"[17] what is important here is not what might (or might not) have been if Brahms had developed the sketch further, but rather how Kalbeck's early conclusions laid the ground for the widespread reception of the songs as "symphonic."[18]

When examining the "composed reception" of specific musical works, it is obvious that the layers of interpretive history that grow up around them will provide points of entry for later arrangers and composers—a good example of this being the thematization of mental illness in many late twentieth-century reimaginings of Robert Schumann's late music.[19] In the case of the *Serious Songs*, there are numerous, interweaving interpretive "hooks" that are amplified through later arrangements: one is the idea of the songs' unfulfilled orchestral potential; another is the revered status of the songs as Brahms's last "great" work; and another is the sense that the composer was "staring death in the face"[20] as he wrote the songs. In the two case studies that follow, each constituting an "episode" in the arrangement history of Op. 121, I chart the songs' significance for individual interpreters—and their audiences—at distinct points in their reception history. The first is a straightforward orchestration by the British conductor Malcolm Sargent (1895–1967), who worked on his version at a time of personal, albeit highly public, crisis in 1944; the circumstances of its creation heavily informed its public reception, and it received considerable acclaim and frequent performance for two decades before the score—and its emotional significance for mid-century British audiences—faded into obscurity. The second version I examine is from 2005, by composer Detlev Glanert (b. 1960), who adds four preludes and a postlude to his stylistic orchestration of Brahms's score, creating a single, through-composed work lasting twenty-five minutes. For different reasons, both Sargent's and Glanert's versions have been considered highly personal endeavors that demonstrate, respectively, a biographical or musical "affinity" with Brahms on the part of the arranger. An indication of where these versions sit chronologically within the orchestration history of Op. 121 is given in Table 17.1.[21]

Episode 1: 1944

The orchestrations by conductors Erich Leinsdorf and Malcolm Sargent were both completed in 1944, in the United States and the United Kingdom respectively. For Leinsdorf, the dramatic stature of Brahms's *Serious Songs* superseded the scale of the voice-piano setting—he was "always cognizant that the piano is a bit frugal for music of that kind of tremendous power."[22] In his writings, Leinsdorf described transcription as a tool that should be wielded judiciously by conductors in order to better "advocate" for a musical work—in this case, he deemed the orchestra a more suitable "medium" for the powerful

Table 17.1 Select Orchestrations of the *Serious Songs*, Noting the Primary Occupation of Each Arranger

1934	Günther Raphael: composer	Orchestration (Breitkopf & Härtel, 1934)
1944	Malcolm Sargent: conductor	Orchestration (Oxford University Press, 1959)
1944	Erich Leinsdorf: conductor	Orchestration (Boosey & Hawkes, 1978)
ca. 1952	Ludwig Misch: musicologist/conductor	Orchestration (Schott, 1952)
1981	Karl Michael Komma: composer	Orchestration (Carus, 1983)
2004	Detlev Glanert: composer	Orchestration (Boosey & Hawkes, 2004)
2004/2005		Orchestration with added preludes: *Vier Präludien und ernste Gesänge* (Boosey & Hawkes, 2005)
2007	Henk de Vlieger: composer/arranger	Orchestration (Schott, 2007)
2013	Eberhard Kloke: conductor/arranger	Orchestration of the first three songs, with interpolations/additions: *Drei ernste Gesänge für tiefe Stimme, einem Rezitator ad lib., Transkription für Orchester*, Op. 28/1 (Boosey, 2013)
		Chamber ensemble version of the above: *Drei ernste Gesänge für tiefe Stimme, einem Rezitator ad lib., Transkription für Kammerensemble*, Op. 28/2
2013	David Matthews: composer/arranger	Orchestration: strings only (Faber, 2013)

"message" of the songs.[23] Leinsdorf's positive and pragmatic views on practices of transcription and arrangement were shared by Sargent, who often stated his belief that "music itself matters more than the colour of it."[24] Put bluntly, it is clear that neither conductor intended, creatively, for their orchestration to be anything other than a means to a communicative end; neither used the orchestral medium to advance a particular interpretation or analysis, and neither claimed "authenticity" to Brahms's own orchestral style. While we do not know for sure why Leinsdorf turned to these "little requiems," as he called them, at this time, we do know that he orchestrated the songs in the midst of his brief conscription into the US Army—he had received US citizenship in 1942, after emigrating from Austria shortly before the Anschluss.[25] A much fuller picture remains of the provenance of Sargent's version, and also of its reception—which, while mostly forgotten today, tells a moving tale about the orchestral circulation of the *Serious Songs* in mid-century Britain.

Sargent's orchestration is, for the most part, thickly scored. "Heavy double basses" underpin low, rich string textures at the start of the first song, while an oboe cuts through to accentuate the vocal line; forceful pizzicati and frenetic violin lines track the turbulence that develops as the song progresses.[26] Greater textual variegation is found in the subsequent songs, where evocative sonorities coalesce around important textual and musical moments: horns are used to gently herald the shift to the major in the third song, and shimmering harp and violin textures envelop the consolatory heart of the fourth. The orchestration was premiered in the summer of 1944, as part of the Liverpool Philharmonic's series of concerts "For the Man in the Street"—a morale-boosting enterprise that aimed to attract local workers and families with low prices and a relaxed atmosphere.[27] While perhaps not "morale-boosting" in the typical rousing sense, this context allowed for music that had long offered comfort and contemplation to connoisseurs to be heard by a broader cross-section of society, and immediate comprehension of the texts would have been aided by the fact that Sargent's version was performed (at the premiere and thereafter) in English translation.[28]

The inescapability of war to the circumstances of the arrangement is inscribed quite literally in an early version of the score, which was lacerated by a splinter from a shattered window when a V1 bomb fell close by. The composer Elisabeth Lutyens, who had been copying the score for Sargent, claims that in this moment, the score saved her life: she had moved it away from the window, to dry the ink over the fire, moments before the blast hit, thus escaping the "huge slices of glass" that fell onto her empty desk.[29] This circumstantial quirk was especially evocative for Lutyens given the subject matter of the songs, and serves as a reminder of the sheer proximity of death and destruction to everyday life at the time the songs were orchestrated. However, Sargent's orchestration was borne of more immediately personal upheaval: he set to work on his version at the bedside of his daughter Pamela, in the months leading up to her death from complications of polio on 23 August 1944 at age twenty.[30] Pamela had contracted the disease in 1937, and lived for the final years of her life in a convalescence home where she was visited frequently by her father. While Brahms insisted that a low male voice should perform his songs (writing to Fritz Simrock that "it would be ridiculous to expect a girl or a tenor to sing them"), Sargent had a female voice in mind for the version dedicated to his daughter.[31] The orchestration received its early performances in the weeks before and after Pamela's death, with Nancy Evans and Kathleen Ferrier as soloists. While he continued to conduct performances in subsequent years,

Sargent kept the score and parts unpublished and in his private property for fifteen years, and during this time he was very particular about allowing other conductors and orchestras to perform it.[32]

The context of the orchestration impacted upon its reception before, during, and long after its heyday on the concert stage in the mid-to-late 1940s and 1950s. Sargent's fame meant public awareness of his personal circumstances, which inevitably swayed responses to the orchestration by performers and audiences alike. Recollections by Evans and Ferrier demonstrate how completely the knowledge of Pamela's illness and death hung over their performances: Evans, who sang the premiere, recalled that "Sargent was moved and so was I. Tears were streaming down his face while we were doing it. It was heartbreaking to see such emotion in a man who was usually so controlled."[33] And on 26 August, Ferrier's diary noted the distressing absence of Sargent from the podium at her performance that evening, three days after Pamela's death.[34] In the shift from laborious closeness—musical, tactile, and emotional—in the process of the orchestration, to the public expression of grief in its performances, the dual personal and universal significance of the *Serious Songs* in Brahms's life find close parallels in Sargent's roles as father, arranger, and director. That Op. 121 was written so late in Brahms's life, in the midst of a chain of bereavements, and was first played by the composer for fellow mourners after Clara Schumann's funeral, has meant that the songs have always been imbued with a sense of biographical profundity. In his early study of Brahms's life and work, Kalbeck lists possible friends whose deaths and illnesses may have been on the composer's mind as he wrote the songs; and his influential discussion of the songs is followed directly by a detailed, moving description of the death and burial of his esteemed friend.[35] In the history of the songs in performance and arrangement, Evans's account of tears "streaming down [Sargent's] face" sits together with Gustav Ophüls's recollection that "large tears rolled down [Brahms's] cheeks," as both remembered loved ones as they performed.[36] Brahms's songs are thus inscribed through their orchestration with another layer of personal authorial anguish—grief upon grief.

The orchestration would later accrue a further layer of emotional significance for its British listeners. Sargent is said to have arranged the songs with Ferrier's voice in mind, and during her lifetime Ferrier made the arrangement famous. It became a staple of her repertoire: she sang it in orchestral concerts across the United Kingdom, including in each of her final five Proms appearances (all under Sargent's baton) between 1949 and 1952, and her recordings of both the orchestrated version and the original score joined her beloved interpretations of Mahler, Gluck, and folksongs as popular choices on the BBC radio program "Desert Island Discs."[37] The 1949 live recording of the orchestration (conducted by Sargent) bears witness to the heart-on-sleeve expressive vocal style for which Ferrier was known—she apparently found the third song "almost impossible to sing without choking with emotion" in knowledge of Sargent's grief—and her vocal commitment is matched by a palpable orchestral intensity, with string portamenti and frequent rallentandi on Sargent's part.[38] Ferrier would typically sing the orchestrated songs in English translation, which is given in parallel with the German in Sargent's score; her preference for singing in her native language is implied in a letter where she refers to performing the *Serious Songs* in German as "an awfie sweat!"[39] It is curious that Ferrier would continue to perform (and record) the voice-piano score in German while using English in the orchestral version: setting aside the potential political dimension of choosing English over German in wartime, perhaps the amplification of the "universal" message of Brahms's songs in their orchestral mediation fostered an urge to communicate them more directly to British audiences by removing a potential linguistic barrier; or perhaps the close association of Sargent's and Ferrier's names with the orchestration, and their popularity with British audiences, meant that the version itself came to be perceived as "British."[40]

The shock of Ferrier's death at the height of her career, at age forty-one in 1953, was felt widely by British musicians and audiences alike: the incomprehensibility of life cut short compounded the acute sense of musical loss, prompting eulogies from far and wide.[41] On learning of Ferrier's death, Sargent spoke of both "intense personal sorrow" and of "one of the most distressing things that has happened to music, not only for Britain, but the whole world."[42] The difficulties Ferrier experienced singing the *Serious Songs* in the knowledge of Sargent's situation were now exchanged for similar feelings on the part of audiences and critics as they listened to Ferrier's recordings with awareness of her own fate.[43] This poignancy was not lost on Sargent, who affirmed that "Brahms's Four Serious Songs will always remain in the memory of anyone who heard her sing them."[44] Later descriptions of Sargent's orchestration in biographies and in program notes hear in the music the twin losses of Pamela's death and Ferrier's: Richard Aldous writes that Sargent "made this arrangement for Kathleen Ferrier, who would also die at an early age"; Sam Dobson speaks of Ferrier's death as a "twist of fate"; and Michael Kennedy, recalling a performance of the songs with Ferrier and the Hallé Orchestra in 1952, lamented in Shakespearean terms, and with a nod to the third song: " 'O Death, how bitter art thou' . . . within a year [Ferrier was] dead, the lass unparallel'd."[45] The drawing together of Ferrier's death, Pamela's, and Brahms's in the discourse surrounding Sargent's orchestration demonstrates well how particular arrangements can have very specific meanings for particular audiences, constructed by time, place, and circumstance.

Episode 2: 2004–2005

The sixty years that separate the orchestrations by Sargent and Leinsdorf with the versions by Detlev Glanert (b. 1960), as well as their respective priorities

The Four Serious Songs in Orchestration

as conductor and composer, make it impossible to compare them like-for-like. While for conductors like Sargent and Leinsdorf, arrangement served the practical purpose of broadening the reach of musical works and amplifying the "message" of the original, for Glanert and many other composers of his generation, practices of arrangement and reimagining are carefully cultivated as parts of their creative identities. Works based on preexisting music—be that through "straightforward" arrangement, creative reimagining, or looser compositional response—form a substantial subset of Glanert's output, and Brahms is the source composer to whom he has turned most frequently. Indeed, many commentators have spoken of Glanert's "affinity" with Brahms, which stems in part from their shared home city: "of all the composers who have fed into his DNA, none looms so large as Brahms, a fellow native of Hamburg."[46] While Glanert has embraced this geographical connection, he has also found it difficult to escape, stating that it is impossible for a Hamburg-born composer living today not to establish a relationship with the "phenomenon of Brahms."[47] Between 1996 and 2020, there have been nine explicitly Brahms-based works, many of which reference either the composer or the source work in their title (these are detailed in Table 17.2). This literalism is important, as it demonstrates how practices of arrangement and reimagining—as distinct from broader uses of tonal, textural, and formal allusion in "neo-Romantic" composition more generally—are central to Glanert's work.[48] His first published works based on Brahms were small-scale, minimally interventionist chamber arrangements in the 1990s, but over time, his Brahms engagements have become more ambitious, both in type and in scale. The culmination of Glanert's Brahms project thus far is the ongoing series of four orchestral works, each of which responds to one of Brahms's four symphonies—a concept somewhat akin to that of Wolfgang Rihm's *Symphonie: Nähe Fern*.[49] In Glanert's case, as with the constituent movements of Rihm's symphony, the *Brahms-Fantasie* (2011–2012), *Weites Land* (2013), and *Idyllium* (2018) have all entered the contemporary orchestral repertoire both as companion pieces for their respective symphonies and as standalone works. For one critic, the *Brahms-Fantasie* "movingly evoked Brahms's central place in the great Germanic tradition"; another described the same piece as "smart, striking music gracefully putting an edgy contemporary sensibility on the music of the past."[50]

If the modest chamber arrangements and the elaborate orchestral fantasies sit at opposite ends of Glanert's spectrum of reimagining, then his two engagements with the *Serious Songs* can be located somewhere in the middle. Glanert first turned to Op. 121 in 2004, when he made a straightforward orchestration of the songs. This version is performed occasionally, as an alternative to the older arrangements by the likes of Sargent and Leinsdorf; it is published by Boosey & Hawkes and has been recorded once to date. Glanert's version has a greater kinship than the mid-century orchestrations with Brahms's own orchestral style, which doubtless owes something to the shift away from

Table 17.2 Detlev Glanert's Arrangements of and Compositional Engagements with Brahms (1996–2018)

Glanert title and year		Source work	Type of engagement
1996	*Variationen über ein Thema von Schumann*, Op. 9 For octet: cl-bn-hn-2 vln-vla-vc-cb	*Variationen über ein Thema von Schumann*, Op. 9 For piano	Chamber arrangement
1997	*Vier Klavierstücke*, Op. 119 For octet: cl-bn-hn-2 vln-vla-vc-cb.	*Vier Klavierstücke*, Op. 119 For piano	Chamber arrangement
2004	*Vier ernste Gesänge*, Op. 121 For bass baritone and orchestra	*Vier ernste Gesänge*, Op. 121 For voice and piano	Orchestration
2004-5	*Vier Präludien und ernste Gesänge* For bass baritone and orchestra	*Vier ernste Gesänge*, Op. 121 For voice and piano	Framed orchestration: orchestrated songs with freely composed preludes
2008	*Walzer*, Op. 39 For violin and piano	*Walzer*, Op. 39 For piano	Chamber arrangement
2011-2012	*Brahms-Fantasie (Heliogravure für Orchester)* For full orchestra	Symphony No. 1	Compositional response
2013	*Weites Land (Musik mit Brahms für Orchester)* For full orchestra	Symphony No. 4	Compositional response
2017	*Vier Choralvorspiele* For full orchestra	*11 Choralvorspielen für Orgel*, Op. 122 For organ	Orchestration
2018	*Idyllium (Metamorphosen nach Brahms für Orchester)* For full orchestra	Symphony No. 2	Compositional response

"maximalization" in performances of nineteenth-century music in the wake of "historically informed performance" movements.[51] The orchestration style is also more consistent throughout the four songs and, to my ears, does not enhance particular passages, as Sargent's does. The thousand-word program note for the work in the liner booklet of this recording mentions Glanert and his "sensitive" orchestration in only one sentence, billing him as a facilitator for new orchestral pairings of Op. 121 (in this case, Dvořák's Requiem) rather than as a creative voice worthy of note.[52] In this scenario, the arranger is relegated to the status of an "invisible translator," to borrow Lawrence Venuti's influential term, of songs which remain firmly "by" Brahms.[53] That Glanert returned to the *Serious Songs* so soon, less than a year after his initial orchestration, might suggest that he wished to put more of himself into the orchestrated songs, to be recognized alongside Brahms as a co-creator, rather than as a "mere" arranger. The return to the *Serious Songs* paid off: Glanert's *Four Preludes and Serious Songs* (*Vier Präludien und ernste Gesänge*, 2004–2005) found immediate critical acclaim: it remains one of his most frequently performed works, and has been recorded twice thus far.[54] For Erica Jeal, the version marks the point at which Glanert's "affinity with Brahms crystallised to extraordinary effect," and for Guy Rickards, its "sublime fusion of both composers" makes it the most successful of the composer's Brahms-based music.[55] Rainer Nonnenmann, who has written widely on the composed reception of nineteenth-century music, wrote in a rare unfavorable review that Glanert's reimagining was "too dependent on the original" and lacked the critical edge of "composed interpretations" in the Zender tradition.[56] But closeness to, and kinship with, the original is precisely the point of Glanert's framed orchestration: "the music starts in his world, slid[es] slowly into our world, and then fall[s] back again."[57] For Glanert, practices of arranging and reimagining nineteenth-century music are born of a desire "to build up, not to destroy" a sense of musical heritage, but it seems that the fullness of his embrace of the musical past is still not fully accepted in certain quarters where the legacy of mid-century modernism looms large.[58]

The *Preludes and Serious Songs* add four preludes and a postlude to the orchestrated songs, creating a continuous, twenty-five-minute new work. The preludes build passageways that navigate musical and subjective shifts between successive songs, but each of Glanert's interjections also forges its own path, developing ambitious trajectories based on small motivic kernels. These interpolations serve to expand the contextual universe of Brahms's songs, drawing attention to musical links between Op. 121 and its Brahmsian precedents (especially the Requiem), and pushing the sound-world forward chronologically, with passages that clearly evoke Mahler and the Second Viennese School. This takes place exclusively in the gaps between the songs: beyond the unobtrusive orchestration, there is no authorial interference with the songs once their first bar lines are reached. By using this clearly delineated authorial mode, Glanert alludes to historical precedents that stretch from Brahms's own time to much later. A prominent example from performance history might be the "mosaic" sequences formed by Clara Schumann in her weaving together of short keyboard works with transitions and preludes.[59] Into the twentieth century, a similar improvisatory technique was used by Hans Pfitzner, who, as Nicholas Attfield has detailed, inserted connective interludes between the songs of cycles such as Schumann's *Dichterliebe* and the Op. 39 *Liederkreis*.[60] Pfitzner also offers a compositional precedent with his orchestration of eight *Frauenchöre von Robert Schumann*, to which he added "short modulatory passages" between the originally separate songs. For Attfield, Pfitzner's modus operandi here bespeaks not "recompositional license," but rather an "unbending commitment to Schumann's settings," as the creative intervention is made entirely *around* the songs.[61] Yet even amid many precedents, the closest precursor for Glanert's *Preludes and Serious Songs* is surely Wolfgang Rihm's *Das Lesen der Schrift*, which was premiered in 2002 and comprises four orchestral interludes to be played between movements of a full-orchestral performance of Brahms's Requiem. Indeed, the two works are linked by the personnel of their premieres—conductor Kent Nagano and the Deutsches Symphonie-Orchester Berlin—which took place just three years apart; and Habakuk Traber has suggested that the existence of Glanert's work may well owe something to the success of Rihm's, which defied critical skepticism in advance of its premiere.[62]

Still, these interstitial expansions of Brahms remain highly unusual among recent composed reimaginings of the musical past, in that the movements of their respective source pieces are used in full and are left as "untouched" as possible. Other works that use a similar process of dual authorship through linear structural interjection—such as Berio's *Rendering*—do not mark out their boundaries for creative reimagining so clearly.[63] The reason for this, I suggest, has to do with the tenor of seriousness—both textual and musical—that comes with both the songs and the Requiem, leading some to feel that such music should be handled with the utmost care and "respect." Indeed, with the exception of Eberhard Kloke's orchestration,[64] the catalog of arrangements of Op. 121 to date is notably less interventionist than that of any major song cycle or set by Schubert, Schumann, or Mahler, while several straightforward arrangements and editions of the Requiem have appeared in the twenty-first century.[65] In the critical reception of Glanert's *Preludes and Serious Songs*, the persistence of *Werktreue* values is inescapable: Jeal writes that "in the hands of a more egotistical composer this would be disastrous, but Glanert shows both affection and respect"; Colin Anderson heard "respect and imagination" in Glanert's framed orchestration; Nonnenmann prefaced his critical review of the version with a favorable note that "Glanert approaches the original with respect."[66]

Glanert's engagement with the *Serious Songs* has further bypassed some of the charges of "infidelity" (to the source work and to the source composer) that often beleaguer arrangements on account of its association with

The Four Serious Songs in Orchestration

Brahms's unrealized orchestral sketch.[67] It is well documented that Glanert's framed orchestration was motivated, in part, by his knowledge of the "A 122" manuscript—information that has been reiterated multiply in paratexts surrounding the published score, in program and broadcast listings, and in critical commentary.[68] The only extended scholarly commentary on the version to date—an essay by Habakuk Traber—notes that "Brahms did not rule out an orchestral version of his Op. 121. From the distance of one hundred and ten years, Glanert carried out what Brahms may have planned himself."[69] While Traber's designation of an "orchestral version" is vague, others are more misleading about the contents of Brahms's sketch, with one program note claiming that "sketches exist for the orchestration of three songs."[70] Whatever information Glanert himself was working with, the prominence made of this historical impetus has endowed the *Preludes and Serious Songs* with a sense of fidelity to Brahms, along with a tacit authorization to take up the gauntlet thrown down by the "A 122" sketch.

Glanert does not attempt an historically informed counterfactual rendering of what Brahms might have done with the sketch material, but instead allows his freely composed preludes and postlude to cast into relief the musical material and the music-historical surroundings of Op. 121.[71] Traber has already commented upon Glanert's heightening of latent links, mainly melodic in nature, to the German Requiem and the fourth symphony already present in the *Serious Songs*.[72] In the third and fourth preludes, Glanert extends the referential reach of his added passages beyond Brahms's oeuvre. An unexpected climactic moment in the third prelude, which bears no clear resemblance to any motivic material within Op. 121, gives a "flash of Mahler's sound-world" and a simultaneous invocation of the North German Baroque through a fleeting *Totentanz* (Example 17.2).[73] A web is spun here linking Brahms's musical heritage, Mahler's, and Glanert's, and the Hamburg connections of all three were not lost on those present at its performance during the opening festival of the Elbphilharmonie in 2017, a celebration of the city's musical past and present.[74] In the fourth prelude, the semitonal descent between the end of the third song (E major) and the beginning of the fourth (E♭) is broached through meandering, taut string lines of ambiguous harmonic character, which have also widely invoked Mahler for listeners, in this case his "haunted" late Adagios (Example 17.3).[75]

Glanert's postlude recalls motifs from all four songs (Example 17.4). In mind of long scholarly debates about the coherence of the fourth song at the end of the set—both musically and philosophically—the postlude's prominent recapitulation of motifs from across the songs adds structural weight and, perhaps, credence, to the consolatory concluding message of "Wenn ich mit Menschen- und mit Engelzungen redete." But Glanert's final orchestral comment on Brahms's songs also points beyond them. When heard in its orchestral guise, the rise from D minor to E♭ major in the overarching tonal trajectory

Example 17.2 Glanert, *Vier Präludien und ernste Gesänge*, "Totentanz"-like passage in Prelude 3, bars 273–77.

Example 17.3 Glanert, *Vier Präludien und ernste Gesänge*, "Mahlerian" line in the first violins. Prelude 4, bars 345–50.

Example 17.4 Glanert, *Vier Präludien und ernste Gesänge*. Appearance of motifs from all four songs in the Postlude (bars 489–96). L–R: bars 489–91, clarinet (Op. 121, iv); bars 490–91, oboe (iii); bars 492–3, flute (i); bars 494–5, horn (ii).

of the work evokes the "progressive tonality" usually associated with late-Romantic symphonism; Traber points specifically to Mahler's fifth and seventh symphonies, both of which present a semitonal rise and a modal switch between their first and last movements (the fifth travels from C♯ minor to D major; the seventh from B minor to C major).[76] This additional invocation of Mahler, in the large-scale structure of the composite work, is especially pertinent in light of existing hypotheses surrounding Brahms's orchestral sketch. The conjectural "symphonic cantata" of Kalbeck's musings would be, he suggested, "illuminated and seized by a similar 'primal light' (*Urlicht*)" to that of Mahler's second symphony.[77] Nicole Grimes has recently reinvigorated scholarly debate surrounding the sketch material, giving time and traction to this particular point of Kalbeck's that had hitherto not been afforded by musicologists. Grimes draws out further parallels between Op. 121 and Mahler's second symphony: both engage with literary, religious, and philosophical thought beyond what can be immediately perceived in their scores, and through these allusions Grimes traces parallel moves in both from a Schopenhauerian pessimism to a Nietzschean "transformation of tragedy into joy" (in Mahler's case, from the chaotic, pessimistic message of the *Wunderhorn* song filtered through the Scherzo, to the setting of Klopstock's "Resurrection Ode" in the finale).[78] On a musical level, the funereal openings of both give way to an unforeseeable and (perhaps self-consciously) "naive" sense of religious optimism in their respective E♭-major finales.[79]

Glanert's between-the-gaps orchestral explorations gently reimagine the musical past, while their containment as preludes and postlude carefully shields accusations of disruptive irreverence. The success of his version—and the contingency of this success upon his careful, "respectful" treatment of Brahms—might be understood as a composed confirmation of the position Brahms's last songs continue to hold at the peak of the Austro-German canon. That the amplifying effect Glanert's orchestral frame brings to the music, message, and reception of Brahms's songs is achieved through discursive compositional intervention sets it apart from the similar sense of amplification achieved in Sargent's orchestration: there, public appreciation of the version owed much to the biographical parallels between Brahms's situation, Sargent's own, and, later, Ferrier's. But in both cases—as indeed with Levit's recording of Reger's transcription during the coronavirus pandemic—the reception of the later versions is always inflected by the canonicity, and widespread familiarity, of Brahms's original songs.

* * *

In 2017, Glanert turned his arranging hand to Brahms's "last musical sign of life," the *Chorale Preludes* Op. 122, orchestrating four of them for Yannick Nézet-Séguin and the Philadelphia Orchestra.[80] In fact, for such relatively little known pieces, they have been orchestrated surprisingly frequently: in addition to a lavishly scored version by Virgil Thomson, complete with tubular bells, from 1957–1958, two arrangers of the *Serious Songs* listed in Table 17.1, Erich Leinsdorf and Henk de Vlieger, have also orchestrated either selections or all of the *Chorale Preludes*.[81] Both Op. 121 and Op. 122 have clearly appealed to arrangers on account of their lateness, their textual preoccupation with death, and specifically their association with Clara Schumann: in the preface to his version, Glanert comments that the *Chorale Preludes* were written "as a direct response to the death of Clara Schumann,"[82] and he suggests that Brahms's use of Baroque stylistic devices indicates a desire to elevate his personal grief to a "higher spiritual, human and universal level."[83] De Vlieger, in a lengthy note on his version, mentions Brahms's response to Schumann's death, and the composer's own failing health; he then recounts having begun the orchestration shortly after the death of his father.[84] These comments mirror the pervasive reception tropes of the *Serious Songs*, which, as I have shown in this chapter, are amplified through the work's arrangement history, and this suggests a shared rationale for later adaptations of Op. 121 and Op. 122. Unlike in the case of the *Serious Songs*, however, here arrangement is almost an act of advocacy for orchestrators of the marginalized *Chorale Preludes*.[85] De Vlieger hopes that his orchestrations will "contribute to the accessibility" of Op. 122, and Glanert claims to have avoided making "compositional additions" for the same reason—his straightforward orchestrations aim to bring the *Chorale Preludes* to a larger audience through concert hall performance (this hands-off stance contrasts with the embellishments of Busoni's early transcription).[86] Hearing Op. 121 and Op. 122 in the same medium—be that in orchestration or in solo piano transcription, as they are heard on Levit's disk—both amplifies and further constructs the shared musical and spiritual preoccupations of the two works, offering a more holistic impression of Brahms's final music where the perceived "greatness" of the *Serious Songs* is tempered by the understated, Baroque-oriented musings of the *Chorale Preludes*. These interweaving arrangement histories move late Brahms in and out of the concert hall, the organ loft, the recital stage, and the home, accumulating meaning all the while that enriches the source works and their significance in our lives and in our listening.

Chapter 18

Hearing Rihm Hearing Brahms
Symphonie *"Nähe fern"* and the Future of Nostalgia

Nicole Grimes

In 2011 the director of the Luzerner Sinfonieorchester, Numa Bischof Ullmann, commissioned Wolfgang Rihm to write four orchestral pieces as pendants to the Brahms symphonies. It was fitting that he should do so, for this commission not only followed a close collaboration between Rihm and the Lucerne Festival for many years, but it also continued Rihm's tradition of writing new works in response to the music of Johannes Brahms. The 1977–1978 composition *Klavierstück Nr 6* features Brahms's Intermezzo in E♭ Minor, Op. 118, No. 6, by way of what I have referred to elsewhere as a "vanishing point."[1] The title of the 1985 composition *Brahmsliebewalzer* conjures up Brahms's *Liebesliederwalzer*. Written for solo piano, however, Rihm's dance movement is more akin to one of Brahms's sixteen waltzes in the Op. 39 set than it is to a work for two pianos with vocalists intoning witty poetry.[2] *Brahmsliebewalzer* was inspired by Rihm's engagement with Brahms's biography—specifically with his reading of the music critic Richard Heuberger's *Brahms-Erinnerungen*.[3] *Das Lesen der Schrift* (2001–2002) comprises four pieces for orchestra intended to be incorporated between individual movements of *Ein deutsches Requiem*. *Ernster Gesang* (1996) was written for Wolfgang Sawallisch and the Philadelphia Orchestra at the conductor's request. Responding to his prolonged immersion in Brahms's last published opus, the *Vier ernste Gesänge*, Op. 121, Rihm confessed that the mysteries of those lieder revealed themselves gradually. This prompted him to prioritize the "primary tone color of clarinets, horns, and low strings" in *Ernster Gesang* and to explore Brahms's "harmonic constellations,"[4] whose "sharp and perhaps cloudy sweetness" would not let him go.[5] Rihm reflects on the ephemeral nature of this Brahmsian enterprise:

> As I composed it during the last days of the year 1996 in Badenweiler, I was both filled with and empty of Brahms. The repercussions, the constellations that existed in my memory, disappeared when I wanted to grasp them or force them into a concrete form. Their appearance is thus always their immediate disappearance as well. What remains is an intonation, a turning of events that wavers between arrival and departure.[6]

Table 18.1 Rihm, *Symphonie "Nähe Fern,"* Formal Outline

Movement	Nähe fern 1	Song	Nähe fern 2	Nähe fern 3	Nähe fern 4
Tempo marking	Adagio	Ruhig fließend	Quasi Andante, scorrevole	Allegro sostenuto, ma energico	Energico (Allegro sostenuto)
Time Sig	3/4	4/4	3/8	3/8	3/4
Tonality	All movements are notated without key signature				
Date of completion	2 April 2011	Originally 2004 Orchestration, 5 April 2012	11 May 2011	12 October 2011	15 May 2012

Rihm's five-movement work, as outlined in Table 18.1, comprises four orchestral pieces written as pendants to Brahms's Four Symphonies, its interpolated second movement being an orchestration of "Dämmrung senkte sich von oben" from Rihm's *Goethe Lieder* composed in 2004. The piece is scored for an early nineteenth-century orchestra, with the exception of the tuba.[7] In its entirety, the duration of the composition is about 47 minutes, each of the "Nähe fern" movements lasting between 10 and 12 minutes, and the song being almost 4 minutes long. As we will see, whereas the five movements may be played together as a multi-movement work, any one of them may be extracted and played along with other repertoire.

This chapter explores Rihm's engagement with Brahms in relation to *Symphonie "Nähe fern"* of 2012. It explores the historicist approach to composition shared by these two composers who were working more than a century apart from one another, and considers their mutual preoccupation with art and literature, and the degree to which their music is intricately linked with this shared intellectual heritage. Goethe's poem "Dämmrung senkte sich von oben" forms a central point in this chapter, which opens out in several directions: onto the question of how the music of Brahms and Rihm is coded by German literary history; onto the treatment of tonality which becomes a metaphor for the imagery of distance and closeness that is intrinsic to *Symphonie "Nähe fern"*; and onto a discussion of modes of listening, of hearing, and of perception in relation to the enduring influence of aesthetic humanism over two centuries of German music and letters.

Artistic Affinities

By 2011, when he began work on *Symphonie "Nähe fern,"* Rihm's relationship with Brahms had intensified:

The older I get, the more I love Brahms. A few years ago I heard all four Brahms symphonies with Daniel Barenboim and the Staatskapelle Berlin over two evenings in Munich. These pieces with which I had been familiar since my earliest youth sparked off a sort of "symphonic aspiration" in me: the desire to be able to give form to the flow of development as the intrinsic element of musical invention. Line has long been my musical obsession. In Brahms we experience the lines, the melodic flow, as something immensely organic and at the same time constructed. One generates the other, everything is development.... In fact, I just had to go further along a path that had already been explored, to take the concepts further, in order to get away from Brahms while moving forward with Brahms. Because it could only be about that: shaping something of my own that took up the thread of a conversation and moved it on a stage further. So, no philology, but distant proximity—proximate distance [*ferne Nähe—nahe Ferne*].[8]

This imagery of being at once close to Brahms while also being distant, of being at once saturated with Brahms while also being empty of his music, pervades Rihm's discussion of his Brahmsian compositions. Thomas Meyer has occasioned Rihm to elaborate on this use of imagery. After the dress rehearsal of "Nähe fern 3" in Lucerne in February 2012, Meyer asked Rihm if he was still saturated with Brahms as he had been for *Ernster Gesang* sixteen years earlier. Rihm responded:

> I did not even get soaked, maybe I'm already fully saturated. I just approached things from my memory. I only had the scores of the respective symphonies there and kept looking back.[9]

Following the successive premieres of each of the four orchestral movements between June 2011 and June 2012, Rihm's *Symphonie "Nähe fern"* was premiered as a whole in August 2012 as part of the Lucerne Festival.

Rihm explicitly states that with this composition he did not want to write a historical symphony in the style of Brahms.[10] Instead, he positions himself among the composers who enter into a dialog with a composer of the past, primary among whom is Brahms himself, as for instance with pieces such as Two Gavottes, WoO. 3, in A Minor and A Major (after Gluck); his arrangement of a Gavotte from Gluck's *Iphigénie en Aulide*, WoO. Anh. 1, No. 2; Bach-Brahms Chaconne in D Minor for the left hand; *Variations on a Theme of Robert Schumann*, Op. 9; *Variations and Fugue on a Theme by Handel*, Op. 24; and the *Variations on a Theme of Paganini*, Op. 35, to name just a few.

In this respect and others, Brahms and Rihm share a strong historicist approach to music. Whereas the sphere of Rihm's allusions stretches back to Gesualdo and Bach, it also reaches to his near contemporaries such as Stockhausen. A significant part of Rihm's output responds to a number of prominent German composers from the long nineteenth century. Among them are Schubert, Schumann, and Mahler. Rihm's *Erscheinung: Skizze über Schubert*

(1978) for nine string players, *Ländler* (1979) arranged for 13 string players, and *Goethe Lieder* (2004–2007) are strongly evocative of Schubert. "Eine Art Traumbild" from the seventh scene of the chamber opera *Jakob Lenz* (1977–1978) responds to Schumann's *Kinderszenen*,[11] while the third movement of his Piano Trio *Fremde-Szenen* I–III (1982–1984) called "Charakterstück" also conjures up thoughts of Schumann. Rihm's *Abgesang* of *Morphonie, Sektor IV* for string quartet and orchestra (1972–1973), the large orchestral adagios *Dis-Kontur* (1974) and *Sub-Kontur* (1974–1975), and Symphony No. 2 (1975) and No. 3 (1976–1977) are strongly suggestive of Mahler.[12]

While Rihm asserts that "music answers music,"[13] in the case of *Symphonie "Nähe fern,"* music must also answer literature. In its final form the complete work incorporates an orchestral version of the third of Rihm's 13 *Goethe Lieder*, "Dämmrung senkte sich von oben" (Dusk has fallen from on high) for voice and piano.[14] The inclusion of the poetry of one of Germany's New Humanist poets from the early nineteenth century signals an artistic kinship between Rihm and Brahms that goes beyond the musical, drawing on a shared intellectual and literary heritage.

This mutual preoccupation with art and literature is evident in the diaries and notebooks of both Brahms and Rihm containing excerpts of favorite passages, or recording their thoughts on artists and writers.[15] Both composers, moreover, have a propensity toward philosophical reflection in their music, and both were largely preoccupied with the poetry of the New Humanists at the turn of the nineteenth century, that is, Goethe, Schiller, and Hölderlin. Brahms was one of very few musical figures to have set Hölderlin in the nineteenth century, intuiting the complex poetic and philosophical meaning of Hölderlin's *Hyperion* in his 1871 composition *Schicksalslied*, Op. 54.[16] Brahms's artistic sensitivity to Hölderlin's poetry was not to be equaled until the late twentieth-century compositions of Benjamin Britten, Hans Werner Henze, Luigi Nono, and Rihm himself.[17] Among Brahms's major pieces for choir and orchestra are his setting of Schiller's poem "Auch das Schöne muß sterben" as *Nänie*, Op. 82, and Goethe's *Harzreise im Winter* as the *Alto Rhapsody*, Op. 53. Rihm also composed a *Harzreise im Winter* in 2012 for baritone and piano as the most extended of his *Goethe Lieder*, along with an array of lieder after Schiller and Hölderlin, the most extensive of these being the *Hölderlin-Fragmente*.[18] Perhaps the strongest affinity between Brahms and Rihm is the degree to which their instrumental music is coded by German literary history. In this respect, they join Mahler as composers who have a capacity to entirely reimagine their lieder in instrumental music (and vice versa).

More generally, a quintessentially German mindset underpins this continuum of German music and letters. *Symphonie "Nähe fern"* is characterized by a rich network of allusion and reference. These cultural references accrue over time in an incremental manner. Constantin Behler's notion of nostalgic teleology is apposite to describe the layering process at play in this music.

Table 18.2 Levels of Nostalgic Teleology in Rihm, Symphonie "Nähe Fern"

Goethe's poem* (1828) (Imaginary China)	Brahms's setting of poem* (1873)	Brahms's 4 Symphonies (1871–1885)	Rihm's setting of poem* (2004)	Rihm, Symphonie: Nähe Fern (2012)

* Poem: Goethe, "Dämmrung senkte sich von oben," *Chinesisch-deutsche Jahres- und Tageszeiten* (1827–1830)

Behler's evocative term, which, simply put, concerns artworks that simultaneously look to the past and to the future, captures the intrinsically temporal nature of Schiller's output, which postulates a metaphor for renewal, and a theme of reawakening that has been deeply influential since the late eighteenth century.[19] Much like Schiller's neo-Hellenic poetry, *Symphonie "Nähe fern"* looks both to the past and the future by including allusions not only to the artistic output of Brahms, but also enfolding layers of cultural reference to Goethe (1749–1832) and, through that poet, glimpses further back to an imaginary world, in this instance the ancient world of China, for which Goethe was inspired by the English translation of Chinese novels.[20] (See Table 18.2.)

"Dämmrung senkte sich von oben"

"Dämmrung senkte sich von oben" is No. VIII of the fourteen poems in Goethe's late collection *Chinesisch-deutsche Jahre- und Tageszeiten* (*Chinese-German collection of seasons and hours*) begun in 1827 when the poet was seventy-eight, shortly after the *West-östlicher Divan*. Goethe's seasonal pattern in the cycle moves from spring (poems 1 to 6), to summer (poems 7 and 8), and then to autumn (poems 9 to 14), although autumn is never mentioned by name and there are no poems about winter. (See Table 18.3.) The collection is bookended by the meditations of a Chinese court official. Within these bookends lies a lengthy reflection on the passing of time and the nature of love, which is interrupted only once by the evocative description of nocturnal moonlight contained in this poem. "Dämmrung senkte sich von oben" occupies a pivotal position within this collection, therefore, for in this poem the sun has already given way to twilight and in the second stanza the scene is suffused with images of moonlight.[21] This double imagery witnesses a turn, both within the poem and within the cycle: the poem ushers in autumn and it is during this poem that twilight begins. What follows, No. VIII in Goethe's *Chinesisch-deutsche Jahre- und Tageszeiten*, is a series of contemplations on "the eternal law according to which the rose the lily bloom" (Poem XI), and following which "only now, the blossom time of roses having passed, one realizes what a rosebud means" (Poem IX).[22]

Table 18.3 Goethe, *Chinesisch-deutsche Jahre- und Tageszeiten*

1. Sag, was könnt uns Mandarin (Tell us Mandarins enquiring)	**Spring**
2. Weiß wie Lilien, reine Kerzen (Pure as candles, lilies' whiteness)	
3. Ziehn die Schafe von der Wiese (From the meadow sheep are leaving)	
4. Der Pfau schreit häßlich (The peacock's cry is horrid)	
5. Entwickle deiner Lüste Glanz (When evening sun's gold rays)	
6. Der Guguck wie die Nachtigall (The cuckoo and the nightingale)	
7. War schooner als der schönste Tag (Than fairest day she was more fair)	**Summer**
8. Dämmrung senkte sich von oben (Twilight down from high has drifted)	
9. Nun weiß man erst, was Roseknospe sei (Only now do we know the rosebud at last)	**Autumn**
10. Als Allenschönste bist du anerkannt (Most beautiful of all you are acclaimed)	
11. Mich ängstigt das Verfängliche (Theorizing's reprehensible)	
12. Hingesunken alten Träumen (Man's old dreaming here disposes)	
13. Die stille Freude wollt ihr stören? (Why now disturb my quiet elation?)	
14. Nun den! Eh' wir von hinnen eilen (Well now! Before we dash away)	

"Dämmrung senkte sich von oben," Johann Wolfgang von Goethe (1828)

Dämmrung senkte sich von oben,
Schon ist alle Nähe fern;
Doch zuerst emporgehoben
Holden Lichts der Abendstern!
Alles schwankt ins Ungewisse
Nebel schleichen in die Höh;
Schwarzvertiefte Finsternisse
Wiederspiegelnd ruht der See.

Nun im östlichen Bereiche
Ahn ich Mondenglanz und -Glut,
Schlanker Weiden Haargezweige
Scherzen auf der nächsten Flut.
Durch bewegter Schatten Spiele
Zittert Lunas Zauberschein,
Und durchs Auge schleicht die Kühle
Sänftigend ins Herz hinein.

Dusk has fallen from on high;
all that was near now is distant.
But there the evening star appears
Shining with its lovely light!
All becomes an uncertain blur,
The mists creep up the sky.
Ever blacker depths of darkness
are mirrored in the silent lake.

Now in the eastern reaches
I sense the moon's light and glow;
The branching hair of slender willows
Frolics on the nearby water.
Through the play of moving shadows,
The moon's magic light quivers down;
And coolness steals through the eye
Soothingly into the heart.[23]

The dialectic of distance and closeness that is played out in many of Goethe's late works is encapsulated in the second line of this poem from which Rihm has borrowed for the title of his symphony: "Dusk has fallen from on high; / all that was near now is distant" ("Dämmrung senkte sich von oben / Schon ist alle nähe fern"). In this poem, which describes a moonlight landscape with mist, Paul Bishop notes "the ability of the seeing eye to traverse space and render what is—spatially, as well as temporally—distant but nevertheless present."[24] That which is both distant and close for Goethe might be understood to be the two different cultures that find a meeting place in this poem: an imaginary ancient Chinese culture and the German literary world that Goethe inhabits. Similarly, in *Symphonie "Nähe fern,"* the nineteenth-century realm of Brahms's symphonies meets the twenty-first-century output of Rihm. The "coolness" that "steals through the eye soothingly into the heart" in Goethe's poem ("Und durchs Auge schleicht die Kühle / Sänftigend ins Herz hinein") does so by way of sensuous perception, arguably bypassing reason.[25] This is consistent with Rihm's approach to the Brahmsian source as he worked from memory in composing *Symphonie "Nähe fern"* during the period 2011–2012.

Goethe's poem sets in motion a series of artistic responses that we might chart along a continuum from Goethe to Brahms's 1873 setting of "Dämmrung senkte sich von oben" as the first of his *Acht Lieder und Gesänge*, Op. 59, through Rihm's rendering for voice and piano in his *Goethe Lieder* (2004), and on to the orchestration of that song as part of the symphonic work that was premiered at the Lucerne Festival in 2012.[26] Rihm speaks of *Symphonie "Nähe fern"* as "shaping something of my own that took up the thread of a conversation and moved it on a stage further."[27]

The poem itself might also be helpfully understood as a metaphor for the compositional process that underpins *Symphonie "Nähe fern,"* with Brahms serving as "the evening star" ("der Abendstern") that appears to Rihm. The expressive reach of Goethe's poem extends beyond the second movement in which it is set. All five movements of the *Lucerne Symphony*, as it has come to be called, are soaked with Brahmsian references.[28] Rihm's description of his earlier piece *Ernster Gesang* as being "at once filled with and empty of Brahms" ("*Brahmsreich und Brahmsarm zugleich*") applies equally well here.

"Alles schwankt ins Ungewisse": Brahms and Rihm

Brahmsian colors are evident in "Nähe fern 1" in manifold ways, not least in the orchestration. With the exception of Rihm's use of a tuba, the scoring is redolent of Brahms. As was the case in *Ernster Gesang*, clarinets, horns, and the lower strings feature heavily in this movement and this instrumentation is found in concentrated form at its very opening. Both Brahms's Symphony No. 1 and "Nähe fern 1" also emerge out of a small chromatic cell, the latter gradually expanding its range through movement by semitone, and incrementally spreading out from cellos and basses to include clarinets, bassoon, horn, and trumpet. Rihm engages with the distinctive angularity of Brahms's first movement, and repeatedly conjures up the solemnity of its instrumentation through the use of timpani and by alluding to timpani textures in other instruments, for instance the figuration in the flute at bar 22 as the full orchestra is heard for the first time.[29] Just as Brahms pays tribute to Beethoven with the allusions in his First Symphony, Rihm here pays tribute to Brahms. The famous alphorn theme from Brahms's fourth movement (see Example 18.1a) is just discernible at bar 80 in the horns. Similarly, the motif heard initially at bar 21 of the introduction to Brahms's first movement (which later governs the Allegro) is conspicuous in the passage leading to the climactic sostenuto chords at bar 83 of "Nähe fern 1" (Examples 18.1b and 18.2). This gives rise to an outburst of Rihm's volcanic force. A telescoping of the instrumentation ensues at bar 97 in a "misterioso" passage that eschews the horns, trumpets, and trombone. Combined with a more reminiscent Brahmsian harmony, the proximity to Brahms is more evident here than anywhere else in the movement.

The orchestration of Rihm's earlier song "Dämmrung senkte sich von oben" as the interpolated second movement of *Symphonie "Nähe fern"* also evokes a distinctly Brahmsian soundscape. The clarinet once again plays a prominent role here, its weaving together with the voice making it a particularly poetic choice. Although the harmonic realm of Rihm's song is distant from Brahms, the richness of the baritone voice seems redolent of Brahms's Op. 59 setting of this poem written in 1873.[30] Rihm's orchestration of the Goethe poem seems to bring together the timbral character of both these Brahms compositions for voice and clarinet.

"Nähe fern 2" opens with a thunderclap of timpani and double basses that gives way to a smeared reminiscence of one of two motivic excerpts that veer in and out of focus throughout this movement, their mercurial presence changing on each occasion. The first is the theme that appears in bar 44 of the first movement of Brahms's Second Symphony. (See Example 18.3a, motif x.) This passes like an illusion through bars 10–16 of Rihm's score so that, as Goethe would have it, "all becomes an uncertain blur" ("Alles schwankt in Ungewisse"). If "Nähe fern 1" "was more of a harmonic space that was gradually paced out," Meyer observes of "Nähe fern 2" that everything is developed from the flowing energy that . . . dominates Brahms's Second Symphony."[31]

Example 18.1 Brahms, Symphony No. 1, Op. 68, fourth movement: a) Alphorn theme; b) second movement, theme at bar 21ff.

Example 18.2 Rihm, "Nähe fern 1," *Symphonie "Nähe fern,"* bars 80–86 (pp. 13–14). © Universal Edition A. G. Wien.

Example 18.2 Continued

Example 18.3 Brahms, Symphony No. 2, Op. 73, first movement: a) bar 44ff.; b) bars 2–5.

The second fragment that pervades this movement is the theme heard in the horns in bars 2–5 of the first movement of Brahms's Op. 73 (see Example 18.3b, motif y), an apparition of which is evident in bars 32–35 of Rihm. Motif x again comes into focus at bars 64–67. Michael Sattler describes the effect well: "in each movement one hears the harmonies, motifs, and characters of the associated Brahms symphonic template as it were subtly shimmering through from behind a curtain, sometimes more sometimes less clearly recognizable."[32] The flickering appearance of motif y in the cellos and basses at bar 137 gives way to a melody in the violins marked "quasi lontano," an evocation of distance, the full significance of which will not become fully apparent until "Nähe fern 4." Just as "Nähe fern 2" opened with motif x, it closes with one further obscured reminiscence of motif y at bar 255, now heard in the clarinets and shrouded by long, sustained chords in the horns. (See Example 18.4.)

Of the four orchestral movements in *Symphonie "Nähe fern"* associated with Brahms's four symphonies, the density of the motivic particles is greatest in the final two—"Nähe fern 3" and "Nähe fern 4"—which correspond to Brahms's Third and Fourth Symphonies. Fabrice Fitch hears "Nähe fern 3" as being "prone to bombastic outbursts, which, reminiscent though they may be of their model (and typical of their composer), don't necessarily endear themselves on that account."[33] In the final movement of *Symphonie "Nähe fern,"* the increasing density of Brahms's motivic particles brings with it an intensifying sense of distance that relies on a dreamlike vision of the stacked thirds that we have come to think of as one of Brahms's compositional fingerprints.[34] Rihm acknowledges a different compositional process in this final movement:

> Unlike pieces 1–3, the issue here is not approaching (an imagined) Brahmsian composition, but distance, *distancing oneself* from it. . . . For the sounds become "distant" and are heard "from a distance."[35]

The dialectic between distance and closeness is further evoked by discreet staging as "Nähe fern 4" draws to a close. Immediately before the large-scale "Adagio" that ends the movement, the trumpeters are instructed to perform synchronous gestures as if playing in a trance. They then leave the stage, walking in opposite directions, with the score stipulating that they give the impression that they are actors in a quasi-religious production. Once off stage, they position themselves "In der Ferne" ("in the distance"). The next trumpet entry, as shown in Example 18.5, is marked *fff*, yet Rihm clarifies that this dynamic is relative: "In the hall, it should sound as if played loudly in the distance."

As the piece draws to a close, we hear the *fff* of the distant trumpets against the *ppp* of the strings and timpani, before all of the particles of intertextuality disappear: "quasi 'ofz in niente'" ("as though fading away into oblivion").

Example 18.4 Rihm, "Nähe fern 2," *Symphonie "Nähe fern,"* bars 249–64 (pp. 32–33). With the kind permission of Universal Edition A. G. Wien.

Distance and Closeness in *Symphonie "Nähe fern"*

The performance direction at this critical juncture at the end of Rihm's work—*lontanissimo*—is redolent of the layers of meaning in this composition, and can be understood as a microcosm of the larger process at play within this

Example 18.4 Continued

piece—that is, a large-scale utterance of nostalgic teleology. A direct translation of *lontano* is "far," so that *lontanissimo* can be translated as "distant."[36] With such a distinctive performance direction we may understand Rihm to convey more than a direction for the off-stage position of the trumpets, for *lontanissimo* also conjures up historical distance. It is immediately suggestive

Example 18.5 Rihm, "Nähe fern 4," *Symphonie "Nähe fern,"* bars 168–95 (pp. 28–30). © Universal Edition A. G. Wien.

of Ligeti's *Lontano*, a work that, as Amy Bauer posits, "folds elements from separate corners of music history into its embrace."[37] In a nineteenth-century context it is suggestive of the penultimate dance in Robert Schumann's *Davidsbündlertänzer*, "Wie aus der Ferne (come da lontano)." *Symphonie "Nähe Fern"* therefore shares a kinship with a form of composition that Ligeti describes: "behind the music there is other music, and behind that more

Example 18.5 Continued

still—a kind of infinite perspective, as if one saw oneself in two mirrors, with the never-ending reflection that this produces."[38]

The relationship between tonality as a form of *Heimat* and the writings of the New Humanist poets in Germany at the end of the eighteenth century occupies a pivotal position in this imaginary hall of mirrors. Novalis, as Andrew Bowie observes, "had characterized philosophy as 'homesickness' and claimed

Example 18.5 Continued

that music allowed us temporarily to feel at home, thus suggesting that music can do what philosophy cannot, namely reconcile us for a time at an affective level with our transience and finitude."[39] Tonality itself plays out such a quest toward homewardness with its implicit "drama of leaving home, of spatial derangement and complexity, and the search for return."[40] Julian Johnson draws an explicit connection between the impact of historical events in Europe in the early twentieth century and music's loss of this capacity to return home, to be reconciled. He cites Viktor Ullmann's "Abendphantasie," one of his three settings of Hölderlin written while imprisoned in Terezin, as an example of how "this wandering, winding, searching song seems to reach out for the promise of homecoming that tonality promises but which, by 1944, was either impossible or meaningless."[41]

Rihm has argued that there is no such thing as tonality, only harmony, a theoretical position that is reinforced in practice by the absence of a key signature in *Symphonie "Nähe fern."*[42] This richly intertextual symphonic work once again addresses the issue of music's capacity to allow one to feel at home. It does so without direct recourse to tonality, even if it conjures up the tonal tradition:

> Stacked thirds that force their way out of the key (or into it?), mediants, the foundation of the harmonic sphere, colours—all of this carries within it a close relationship to "Brahms 4," but at the same time wants to escape it. Now I must follow that movement; perhaps it leads—to paraphrase Novalis—"ever homewards" ("immer nachhause").[43]

The manner in which Rihm inscribes such concepts of *Heimweh* and homecoming onto this symphony, with its rich network of associations with Brahms, and Goethe raises significant historical and philosophical questions pertinent not only to Rihm but, more broadly, to a number of composers from the late twentieth century.

The nostalgic element at play in the work of the generation of composers who came to maturity in the 1970s has been met with critical and scholarly dissent over the past four decades. Hermann Danuser, for instance, has repeatedly cast what he calls "neo-Romanticism" pejoratively as anachronistic. He acknowledges the nostalgia that is central to this repertoire but does not recognize its nostalgic teleology. In other words, Danuser positions neo-Romanticism as looking only to the past and, at that, only to the immediate past.[44] Such a perspective is not confined to musical commentators.

Ligeti, for instance, was representing a wider point of view within the composer's community when he wrote in 1978 that: "I quite agree with the complete rejection of the last twenty years on the part of the young composers.... But they should do something genuinely new, instead of returning to late-Romantic, pathos-filled music."[45] Bauer has underlined Ligeti's ambiguity in his attitude toward the nostalgic in music: he was at once highly critical of it, yet contrary to this critical stance, in many of his own pieces, he "sought to evoke a vanished place or time." This is evident, for example, in the Horn Trio (also a homage to Brahms) and the 1982 composition *Drei Phantasien nach Friedrich Hölderlin*. Ligeti's commentary on his own historically conscious output seems to betray an unconscious affinity with the historicism he criticizes. His 1974 articles on Mahler's forms exemplify the point, for here as Bauer observes, he celebrates "not only their sense of physical space, but [also] their sense for historical reflection."[46] Drawing a connection with his own compositional process in *Lontano* Ligeti remarks of Mahler:

> ... we can grasp the work only within *our tradition*, within a certain musical education [by which he refers to Germanic music]. If one were not quite acquainted with the whole of late-Romanticism, the quality of being at a distance ... would not be manifest in this work. For this reason, the piece is double-edged: it is in a sense traditional but not literally as with Stravinsky, it does not treat exact quotations from late romantic music, but certain types of later romantic music are just touched upon. ... The forms can be heard from a distance and from long ago: almost, as it were, like the post horn from Mahler's Third Symphony.[47]

Ligeti's reflections on the historically conscious nature of the tradition to which he refers speaks to the manner in which "music answers music," to recall Rihm's evocative phrase, and this historically conscious mindset has a bearing on our understanding of *Symphonie "Nähe fern."*[48] Rihm describes his procedure in that composition:

> Obviously no quotations; echoes, to be sure, but as if they were early forms. As if they had not yet taken on the shape they will have in Brahms. An original configuration reconfigured.[49]

Perhaps it is as straightforward as Meyer suggests: that to immerse oneself in the possibilities of composing means "ascertaining what Brahms did with the material by composing it, but at the same time also tracing what he could have composed from it. That does not mean a correction, but an alternative." Meyer further suggests that "Brahms would certainly not have composed music à la Rihm—he did not (yet) have this possibility. But Rihm can rethink these possibilities."[50] In this sense, Rihm's composition can be understood as a form of analysis, although he is eager to point out that just as Hitchcock's *The Birds* is no ornithological film, his own *Symphonie "Nähe fern"* is not "musicological literature. This is not a seminar paper about Brahms. It is something that has taken place in the living object."[51]

Rihm Hearing Brahms

Nonetheless, a temporal paradox is at play in Rihm's *Symphonie "Nähe Fern."* If we consider this composition through a teleological Schoenbergian lens whereby a seed imbues a musical work with motivic unity, then the impression we find in Rihm's symphony is not that of the composer beginning with the same motivic kernels as Brahms did and imagining them anew. For it is impossible to reverse the process of growth and developing variation that is integral to Brahms's oeuvre.[52] Rather, the impression is of Rihm casting Brahms's fully formed compositions through a prism and, from the filtered shards of light that are projected, initiating the Brahmsian process anew. Rihm seems fully aware of the implications of this temporal paradox:

> I wanted to create something like preparations (*Vorfelder*) where the things still unordered twirl in their own dynamic and drift, as if an inspirational environment that would later be populated by Brahms is already populated by motivic particles which then become Brahms'.[53]

The word *Vorfeld* is challenging to translate in a musical context. A literal translation tells us it is that which stands in the run-up to something, or that which stands ahead of something. In the context of Rihm's discussion of *Symphonie "Nähe fern"* perhaps the most apposite translation is "preparation." Meyer elaborates on the term *Vorfeld*: "The prefix 'vor' ('pre-') is essential: pre-lude, pre-history, it is about the state ('Zustand') before the composition, thus also before the decomposition, it is about the state ('Zustand') of the 'unrealized' ('noch'), the preparation (*Vorfeld*) where things 'unrealized' whirl around in a disordered manner."[54] He further clarifies that "the 'Vorfeld' proves to be conceptually inadequate if it is understood too much as a state and not as a field of movement."[55] The spatial and temporal implications of Rihm's treatment of these Brahmsian particles—and his description of his own compositional process—indicate that his dynamic engagement with Brahms is at a much "deeper level than that of quotation."[56]

Listening, Perceiving, Hearing

The order in which a listener encounters Rihm's *Nähe Fern* in relation to the Brahms symphonies has a profound impact on how they will experience Rihm's composition. Rihm stipulates that no knowledge of Brahms is required in order to appreciate these pieces in their own right.[57] "One can perceive and hear and come to completely different conclusions."[58] Of course, there is a particular—if limited—audience who are deeply familiar with Brahms's music, those whom Meyer refers to as the "auditory sponges that are saturated with Brahms" ("Brahmsvolle Hörschwämme"). For those people, listening to *Symphonie "Nähe fern"* "always means listening to Brahms, but it also means hearing the Brahms in us (near or far)."[59]

In live performances, the movements of *Symphonie "Nähe fern"* have been positioned in various ways in relation to Brahms's symphonies. At the premier performance at the Lucerne Festival, Rihm's orchestral movements were performed before the Brahms symphonies, thereby emphasizing the idea of the *Vorfelder*; during the radio broadcast of "Nähe Fern 3," Rihm was played after Brahms's Symphony No. 3 so that the listener would first be saturated with Brahms; at the premiere of the entire cycle, Brahms's symphonies were left out entirely.[60] The experience of listening at home that has become so prevalent during the age of the coronavirus pandemic presents further possibilities for how one might curate their own listening experiences of *Symphonie "Nähe fern"* in relation to Brahms, beyond the options available in the concert hall. The English language seems inadequate to describe the modes of listening that can arise from such curated adventures. Meyer writes of "Brahms mithören auf Brahms hinhören" ("listening with (*mithören*) Brahms hearing (*hinhören*) Brahms").

Such listening experiences heighten our awareness of where meaning is considered to reside in these various musical works: whether it is in Brahms's compositions, in Rihm's compositions, or latent somewhere between the two. In this respect, Rihm's symphonic work speaks to a type of German Romanticism that aspires to translate, central to which is Goethe who read, productively misunderstood, and mistranslated swathes of literature from distant cultures, not least that of ancient China.[61] Peter Szendy draws a distinction between an arrangement and a translation of a piece of music that is helpful to our consideration of *Symphonie "Nähe fern,"* even if we admit that that composition does not fit neatly into either of these two categories. Szendy provocatively proposes that "translation is possible only because the original needs to be transformed in order to survive."[62] He clarifies that "translation does not aim for meaning, then, since meaning is waiting *in suspense* [*en souffrance*], endlessly deferred".[63]

> Now it seems to me that what arrangers are signing is above all a listening. Their hearing of a work. They may even be the only listeners in the history of music to write down their listenings, rather than describe them (as critics do). And that is why I love them, I who so love to listen to someone listening. I love hearing them hear.[64]

Conclusion

The layering effect that comes from listening to Rihm hearing Brahms, and that pervades Rihm's *Sinfonie "Nähe Fern,"* is inextricably bound up with nostalgic teleology that, in turn, concerns the enduring influence of aesthetic humanism over two centuries of German music and letters. The three-stage schema of aesthetic humanism—which looks back to an earlier ideal unity of human nature and espouses its recovery as the goal of cultivation, morality, and history—is manifest on both a micro- and a macro-level. At a micro-level, each individual artwork embedded in this composition—that is, Goethe's poem and the imaginary oriental landscape from which it is drawn, Brahms's setting of Goethe's poem, Brahms's four symphonies, and Rihm's setting of Goethe's poem—incorporates elements of the past (whether a technique, an allusion, a quotation, a form, or a distant culture) by way of looking forward to some sort of a return, a reawakening. At a macro-level, each artwork reaches beyond its individual ontological boundary and therefore transcends the individual work. As a result, *Symphonie "Nähe Fern"* intuits and records a process from a world-embedded consciousness to a philosophically reflective consciousness. The process of *Bildung* that underpins this entire enterprise is beset by an essential homesickness or nostalgia that is equally as concerned with the individual as it is with the collective. While it is a psychic process that relates back to the inner emotional life of the individual, it is also a quintessentially German phenomenon. It is rooted in the thought of German-language writers and composers. Each work, moreover, helps us to define the paradigm through which memories are told.

As a result of the nostalgic teleology with which it is imbued, *Symphonie "Nähe fern"* blurs the boundaries between the notion of memory as a province of history (which is bound up with specific tangible events or artworks), and the notion of memory as a province of the imagination (which is bound up with the recovery of a perceived former state—whether real or imagined, temporal or atemporal, chronological or anachronistic). Inherent to this composition are elements that both look to the past and may be taken up again in the future. Regardless of the direction of our enquiry, whether it is retrospective, projected forward, or suspended in time, this change of perspective allows us to grapple with fundamental questions regarding the nature of German music, and creates a space for the emergence of new patterns within one coherent extended period of recent German history.

Chapter 19

Specters and "Derangements"
Michael Finnissy's Summonings of Brahms the Progressive

Edward Venn

Over the course of his long composition career, which at the time of writing has resulted in over 500 works,[1] the British composer Michael Finnissy (b. 1946) has regularly incorporated references to a large number of other composers.[2] Amid the sheer diversity of the source material, spanning the gamut of Western art music as well as folk musics from around the world, one might single out the three hours' worth of material in the *Verdi Transcriptions* (1972–2005), and the twenty-one pieces on Gershwin in *Gershwin Arrangements* (1975–1988) and *Gershwin* (1989–1990).[3] However, the borrowed material is rarely identifiable (as is the case, say, in the music of composers such as Berio and Zimmermann). Rather, Finnissy "fragments, transforms, [and] juxtaposes elements of a large number of different pieces of music to construct a rich motivic stew within which each component is significant *not so much for what it represents in itself* but rather more for what it represents as part of this new form."[4] In this context, Finnissy's engagement with the music of Brahms is noteworthy less for its prominence (when compared to Verdi and Gershwin) and more for the fact that Finnissy *does*, atypically, draw on the ways in which the music can be thought of as standing for a particular tradition.

Finnissy has described Brahms as "an early crush ... at one stage ... a bit temporary in [his] impact."[5] Such admiration received expression in *Romance (with Intermezzo)* for piano (1960), in which Finnissy employed "micro-motives in a state of continuous flux" in a post-Schoenbergian take on developing variation.[6] The filtering of Brahms through a Schoenbergian lens is not coincidental: Brahms, in his guise of "the Progressive," has played a key role in his reception in British music of the twentieth and twenty-first centuries.[7] But what is at stake here for Finnissy's later music is not simply the importance given to specific technical characteristics of Brahms's music within the Schoenbergian tradition, but the larger claims that this tradition makes on musical teleology and value.

The central text here is of course Schoenberg's "Brahms the Progressive," which positions Brahms at a crucial juncture in music history, looking back to the innovations and practices of Bach, Haydn, Mozart, Beethoven, and Schubert, and, by implication, forward to the music of Schoenberg.[8] The

Specters and "Derangements"

narrative that emerges is marked by a collapse of temporalities—Brahms's past, present, and future—that is, perhaps, an inevitable consequence of any composer's creative response to earlier music (including Finnissy). Nevertheless, the intensity with which Schoenberg pursues his task, the temporal dislocations he effects, and the teleological questions he raises are unusually pronounced, and this is true, too, for much subsequent musical and musicological literature about Brahms.[9] By proposing that Brahms is central to a particular musical tradition—a tradition that is unquestioned in terms of artistic value and its own cultural centrality—but at the same time rendering him insubstantial by virtue of belonging neither fully to his own time nor Schoenberg's (nor, by extension, our own), Schoenberg unwittingly sows the seeds for a critique of that tradition.[10]

In contrast to Schoenberg's relatively uncritical (or possibly even cynical) appropriation of the figure of Brahms for his own aesthetic purposes, Finnissy's musical response to Brahms is alert to the constructed, contestable nature of identity and in particular the (unwitting) instabilities of the Schoenbergian Brahms the Progressive. To demonstrate this, I shall in this chapter focus on two of Finnissy's most telling responses to Brahms that belong to a rich seam of pieces that engage with folk music and "reveal a very personal reflection upon the relationship between history/tradition, society and the individual."[11] Nevertheless, both Schoenberg and Finnissy's representations of Brahms can, in their differing ways, be read productively through the lens of Derridean hauntology, and in particular his notion of *spectrality*.[12] Hauntology, as construed here, is a critical practice that examines how particular representations of figures or concepts (here, the spirit of Brahms) are bound—in the form of *specters*—to a particular ontology (not least to offer a way of modeling the rethinking of Brahms more widely, and not solely in the context of late modernist composition).[13] In Schoenberg's case, the ontology of Brahms "the Progressive" is that of the logic of rigorous motivic working and flexible rhythms; there is no question of Schoenberg's self-identification with Brahms and his Austro-German musical heritage.[14] In Finnissy's case, what is at stake is the *resistance* to such a unitary binding: he offers instead multiple specters, multiple ontologies, each as self-consciously mediated as the other. In doing so, Finnissy inverts Schoenberg's claims for centrality, unmooring both Brahms within tradition, and tradition within culture. But this isn't a sense of throwing the baby out with the bathwater (or exorcizing the specter with the holy water): Finnissy rejects neither Brahms nor his legacy but offers instead an intense probing of the Brahmsian spirit, laying bare the dynamics of summoning. It is a way of critically rehearing the Brahms-Schoenberg tradition through a rethinking of Brahms in order to prompt a reappraisal of what it might yet mean in the twenty-first century.

Finnissy and Brahms

Finnissy's increasingly ambiguous relationship to Brahms over the course of his musical life has been described by Ian Pace as one of "recurrent fascination but something of a love-hate relationship."[15] Thus in *Folklore 3* for piano (1993–1994),

> Finnissy works in references to composers who, either as a result of integration or rejection, had a substantial effect on him. This material as a whole provides a chronological account of Finnissy's developing musical mind, and as he says in the note to the piece, the "infinity of traces that historical processes leave on the self." Allusions abound to compositional styles, in particular those of Brahms (the "progressive" as described by Schoenberg, a view that was once shared (but later violently rejected) by Finnissy), Scriabin, Ives and Bussotti.[16]

Sehnsucht (1997) for string quartet, embeds references to both versions of Brahms's solo songs of the same title within its opening bars.[17] The titles of the two 2009 chamber works *Piano Quartet in A Major (1861–62)* and *Piano Quartet in C Minor (1861)* both evoke specific works by Brahms. *Mit Arnold Schoenberg* (2000–2008), for piano, reverses the direction of travel observed in earlier works, by beginning with Schoenberg, and only from there bringing in Brahms (a citation of the passage from Brahms's String Quartet in C Minor, Op. 51, No. 1, discussed in Schoenberg's "Brahms the Progressive"). Lest the critical dimension of this citation be underestimated, note that *Mit Arnold Schoenberg* is the second of three pieces in Finnissy's larger *Second Political Agenda*. Likewise, Finnissy's preface to *Folklore* makes clear the political dimensions of the work, citing Gramsci, and making no bones about the perceived "insular and conservative" nature of England (not to mention its "Hypocrisy. Bigotry").[18]

The most direct confrontation with Brahms (and the tradition that he represents for Finnissy) can be found in the piano trio *In stiller Nacht* (1990, revised 1997) and *Brahms-Lieder* for piano (2015). *In stiller Nacht* offers three "different views of Brahms's manner or style" (two of which were with reference to Schoenbergian traditions), exposing the mediated nature of any representation or presentation of Brahms's music. Such mediations are, of course, the result of particular discursive practices; they are always ideologically driven. So too, was Finnissy's decision to use Brahms's setting of the folksong "In stiller Nacht" (WoO 33, No. 42) as the source material. For Finnissy, Brahms's manner is best observed in "those works where the raw material is not his," including "his cycle of German folksong arrangements."[19] This in itself is a gently radical way for Finnissy to orient himself toward Brahms's legacy, eschewing those works that might sit more squarely in the Schoenbergian image of Brahms the Progressive in favor of (possibly) less ideologically loaded, but no less composerly, material.[20]

Similarly, Finnissy turned to four of Brahms's folksong arrangements WoO 33 for the four movements of his *Brahms-Lieder*, filtering them through what are at times more-or-less recognizable Brahmsian textures and figurations, and employing developing variation (taken paradoxically, at times, to such extremes to render the music amotivic). For Arnold Whittall, this flux serves yet another critical function, bringing "Schoenbergian notions of 'liquidation' . . . into the foreground as an index of modernism's need to discount the old classical truths."[21] These truths, in part, include the values and certainties of the Brahmsian tradition. Through the intense application of the technical apparatus available to composers of this tradition (developing variation) to the same tradition's materials (including folksongs), Finnissy effectively dissolves both form and content in a vivid demonstration of the fragility of identity.

As a critical practice, Finnissy's methods evoke the process by which, as Karl Marx put it, "[a]ll that is solid melts into air, all that is holy is profaned, and man is at last compelled to face with sober senses his real conditions of life, and his relations with his kind."[22] More specifically, by following the compositional logic of the Brahms-Schoenberg tradition "to its final consequences, one finds an excess which cannot be construed within the rules of logic, for the excess can only be conceived as *neither* this *nor* that, or both at the same time—a departure from all rules of logic."[23] This is the logic too of the Derridean specter; it is the means by which meaning is evacuated from a sign and identity eroded. But excess inheres too in the material substance of Finnissy's music—composed into the score in its profusion of textures, topical and intertextual allusions, and motivic material—and its virtuosic demands on the performer.[24]

In stiller Nacht

In stiller Nacht was commissioned by the Bekova Sisters; one of the stipulations of the commission was that the piece was to be in "the manner, or style" of Brahms.[25] The concert series was to include all of Brahms's Piano Trios (hence the request). Yet this posed certain problems: Ian Pace reported in 1996 that "Finnissy was annoyed by the patronizing request for stylistic composition and the associated nostalgia for a composer he detests."[26] Nevertheless, Finnissy offered up in *In stiller Nacht* an attempt at a kind of pastiche, "at least so far as it 'sounds' to [Finnissy], and so far as he can 'analytically' extrapolate [Brahms's] compositional methodology and apply it to different material."[27]

As Jonathan Cross has observed, style is thus treated predominantly by Finnissy as a question of process rather than content.[28] In hauntological terms, *In stiller Nacht* becomes a question of engaging with the spirit, rather than the flesh, of Brahms's music; it is a summoning of Brahms's specter on Finnissy's own terms. Specifically, *In stiller Nacht* is a meditation on the multiple Brahms that are passed down through tradition, presenting (to use Finnissy's own description of much of his music) "an uncomfortable... synthesis."[29]

Brahms's setting of the folksong "In stiller Nacht, zur ersten Wacht" WoO 33, No. 42 (1894) provides the source material for Finnissy's "arrangement (or quite possibly 'derangement') of an arrangement," *In stiller Nacht*.[30] The opening of the song is given in Example 19.1a. The melodic line set by Brahms begins with a one-bar motif (labeled *x*) followed by its immediate, exact repetition, all over a tonic prolongation; it is followed by a two-bar contrasting idea (motif *y*) that ends with a half cadence. This forms the antecedent to an eight-bar period in which the consequent, beginning with a transposed variant of the opening idea (motif *x*1), moves from dominant to tonic (although Brahms undercuts the final cadence to avoid too strong a closure). George Bozarth has observed that "[t]he distinctive feature of [Brahms's] setting for solo voice... is the metrical displacement of the accompaniment... creating a mood of hushed disquiet."[31] This serves gently to blur the boundaries of the otherwise normative and rigid periodic structure of the vocal line.

The non-alignment might also be the source of one of the most characteristic qualities of Finnissy's derangement, in which the three instruments of the piano trio "start together but continue independently, as exactly as possible in their different tempi. It is not essential that the parts finish together" (the opening of each part is given in Examples 19.1b–d;[32] the layout in the example is to bring out motivic relationships between each line, but no necessary alignment between layers is implied).[33] Finnissy goes much further than Brahms: not only are these instruments independent, but "[t]he structure and psychological dynamics of each part differ, presenting a range of responses to Brahmsian 'style' or 'manner.'"[34] Each instrument thus offers, in the language of hauntology, a different "specter" of Brahms, constructing his image according to the different traditions that Finnissy makes him represent.

The first of these specters can be heard in the violin part, which Finnissy describes as "the closest to a parody of Brahms (at least so far as it 'sounds' to me, and so far as I can 'analytically' extrapolate his compositional methodology and apply it to different material...)."[35] What emerges cannot be mistaken for Brahms: rather, we might think of it as an encounter between two composers, in which Finnissy approaches the folksong melody via his own, individual, response to Brahms's music. As Finnissy acknowledges, to compose a work "in the manner of Brahms" can only be "in inverted commas. Eventually, no more nor less than you, I can only be (creatively) what I am."[36] Comparison between the upper line of Example 19.1a and the violin part of Example 19.1b demonstrates how this works in practice. First, as the annotations above the line demonstrate, Finnissy replicates the motivic content of the first line of "In stiller Nacht" and, to a greater extent, the pitches (allowing for octave transpositions at the opening). Gentle elisions between motifs (such as the overlap between the E completing the second utterance of motif *x* with the G♮ beginning motif

Example 19.1 (a) Brahms, "*In stiller Nacht*," WoO 33, No. 42 (1894), bars 1–5; Finnissy, In stiller Nacht, opening of individual parts for (b) violin, (c) cello, and (d) piano. "In Stiller Nacht" by Michael Finnissy © Oxford University Press 1990, revised 1997. Extracts reproduced by permission. All rights reserved.

y, and the F♯ at the boundary between *y* and *x*1) recall the use of similar techniques elsewhere in Brahms's output.[37] Second, the minim tread of Brahms's setting can still be taken as a point of departure for the violin line, but the absence of a time signature and irregular bar lengths, coupled with surface irregularities (not least the use of complex tuplets) suggests a more spontaneous, folk-like character. The anacrustic character of the opening G♯ in the piano in Brahms's setting is, for instance, conveyed in Finnissy's notation: the precise rhythms of a dotted-sixteenth-note rest followed by a thirty-second note tied over to a dotted half note might indicate to the performer a particular sense of "pushing" the beat on the first entry, throwing the weight of the phrase toward the notated downbow on the double stopped B/G♯. Third, from the outset the material is subject to development: the repetition of the opening motif is exact neither rhythmically nor in pitch content; in the latter case it is subject to an inexact transposition. Finnissy's extrapolation of Brahms's technique already begins to anticipate Brahms in his Schoenbergian "Progressive" manner. The source material might be folk-like, but the compositional procedures are knowingly sophisticated.

The flickers of developing variation heard in the violin part are explicitly reworked in the cello line in the guise of Schoenberg's "Brahms the Progressive," understood here by Finnissy as a "proto-modernist."[38] Accordingly, the opening melodic material of "In stiller Nacht" is elaborated into "a twelve-note 'grundgestalt,'" and from there passes through "derivatives of this 'objectified' material in a Second Viennese School manner."[39] The derivation of this grundgestalt, and its relationship to developing variation, might be modeled analytically as follows. First, the cello line contains three embellished references to the opening motivic neighbor note, inverted (in the case of the first and third repetitions—see Example 19.1c). Second, Finnissy takes the rise and fall of the half cadence of motif *y* in Brahms's setting and integrates it with motif *x′*; cadential thrust is thus lost within Finnissy's free-flowing reworking, not least as the line rises to the high F♯ of *x*1 to create a new climax at the end of the phrase. The result in this instance is to foreground Brahmsian developmental procedures by unshackling them from traditional phrase structures. Omitting repetitions, eleven distinct pitch classes are employed in the opening phrase, which, taken in abstract along with the absent twelfth pitch (a D♯), becomes a source of further development.

The opening of the piano part is characterized by metrical complexity, as well as textural contrasts (a hint of which can be observed in the shift of register and relative simplification of the material in the opening of the second bar of Example 19.1d). To a greater extent, this is no more or less than a reworking of the metrical ambiguities and textural juxtapositions to be found in the accompaniment to Brahms's setting of "In stiller Nacht"—most notably the contrasting tessitura of the accompaniment to motifs *x* and *y*. The low E and A in the left hand of Finnissy's setting offers a ghostly echo of Brahms's opening harmonies. But Finnissy also exploits different tonal languages within this setting, rapidly shifting between them or even combining them: the very opening, for instance, superimposes the first four pitches of the grundgestalt of the cello line over a white-note set in the bass, before the material dissolves into something altogether more complex.

Any such correspondences between Finnissy's piano part and Brahms's "In stiller Nacht" soon give way to a more fractured surface, in which predominantly monodic textures alternate with dense polyphony. Finnissy argues that, "taking Brahms-Schoenberg-Cage as its axis[,] the piano fragments the material even further, in some ways removing it to the remotest point from Brahms, in others . . . certainly the closest to Brahmsian 'actuality.'"[40] Although Finnissy does not expand upon his reasons for admitting Cage into this tradition, plausible reasons (beyond the simple fact that Cage studied with Schoenberg) might be suggested. First, for all of its apparent superficial differences in approach, Cage's treatment of repetitions and variations of material owes much to Schoenbergian (and hence Brahmsian) models.[41] Second, with its abrupt juxtapositions, one is reminded in Finnissy's piano part for *In stiller Nacht* of Cage's apparent enthusiasm for the "stop-and-go" form of Schoenberg's Double Variation/Fugue in his 1934 *Suite* (which itself owed something to the precedent of the second movement of Brahms's String Quintet Op. 88). But Finnissy's approach (and not just in the piano part) resonates with Cage's exhortation to treat works from the past (including, but not limited to music) "as material rather than as art," which is to say that it becomes something that can be used freely, without deference to its former function and identity, and "put together with other things."[42] In this way, Cage's inclusion as part of a Brahms-Schoenberg-Cage axis serves at once to destabilize, and with it, acknowledge the de-centering of, the Brahms-Schoenberg axis from *the* musical mainstream to become one of a number of coexisting traditions.[43] The specter of Brahms that is summoned here is thus one that could only arise from the vantage point of late modernism, in which his music can be treated as an artifact to be repurposed, its symbolic value attenuated to the point of insubstantiality.

This much can be gleaned from an overview of *In stiller Nacht* as a whole. Brahms's setting falls into four four-bar subsections that together present a simple aa'bc form (in which the melodic apex is reached in the b phrase, and the cadence, recalling the shape of motif *y*, in the c phrase); the whole is then repeated for the second verse. Finnissy's similarly offers a repeat. However, the opening material and a short concluding passage of each part are not repeated, and there is no necessary reason (or even likelihood) why the parts would return to the start of the repeat at the same time, less still end at the same time. Musical closure therefore becomes a site of contestation between the two settings. In a recent interview, Finnissy has spoken of how he is "careful to avoid cadences and conventional punctuation";[44] recomposing Brahms's closural devices lays bare the constructed nature of tonal rhetoric.

Comparison between Brahms and Finnissy's violin surrogate for Brahms (Examples 19.2a and 19.2b) reveals at first a close similarity in contour (and to a greater extent, rhythm). The lines part ways at the $\hat{2}$–$\hat{1}$ cadence in the voice at bar 16, whereupon the violin embarks on a short reminiscence of the climactic melodic gesture ("ist mir das Herz zerflossen") before ending enigmatically. The considerable distance, however, in pitch content between the two lines indicates the extent to which the cumulative application of Brahmsian compositional techniques over the course of *In stiller Nacht* has sundered the musical surface from its source. The conclusion of the cello part (Example 19.2c) initially strays far closer to Brahms's original than the violin line, though it omits

Example 19.2 (a) Brahms, "In stiller Nacht," WoO 33, No. 42 (1894), bars 10–17 (melody only); (b) Finnissy, *In stiller Nacht*, violin (lines 16–18); (c) Finnissy, *In stiller Nacht*, cello (lines 13–18). "In Stiller Nacht" by Michael Finnissy © Oxford University Press 1990, revised 1997. Extracts reproduced by permission. All rights reserved.

the cadential $\hat{1}$. Instead, the material essays in retrograde (with some permutation) much of the original grundgestalt, in a closural gesture far more akin to serial procedures than Brahmsian tonal practice. In doing so, it substitutes one cadential convention for another, neither of which proves to be conclusive. The emphasis, therefore, is on open-ended, continuous development rather than the closed, four-square phrasing of the original, a specter of process rather than of form.

The text of the folksong "In stiller Nacht" describes the way in which the protagonist hears a distant lament, carried to them by the wind. Not only is the protagonist moved to tears by what they hear, but also nature itself provides physical responses to the otherwise acousmatic, disembodied sorrow (the moon sets, the stars stop shining, and birds and beasts grieve).[45] The distance between the poetic description here and that which happens in Finnissy's arrangement-derangement is not so great. In Finnissy's hand, a voice comes to us not on the wind, and not singularly, but multiply, and whispered by spectres. And these whispers are given substance not by nature, but rather culture, mediated by musical traditions.

Arnold Whittall has observed that, in Finnissy's musical thinking, "a simple opposition between diatonicism and atonality fails to do justice to the richness of late-modernist musical realities."[46] In the same vein, the multiple musical perspectives of *In stiller Nacht* intertwine and interact in such a way as to offer an equally rich portrait of Brahms as perceived from the late twentieth century, eschewing blunt oppositions in favor of a more complex, "uncomfortable synthesis" of contrasting viewpoints. In performance, the unpredictable and sometimes dense alignment of parts creates an uncertain, unstable musical environment in which the different lines—and hence different spectres of Brahms—emerge unpredictably.[47] As such, no effort is made to smooth over the numerous contradictions and tensions within our cultural image of Brahms. Rather they are teased out, if not foregrounded, and presented to the listener as a spur for critical engagement.

Brahms-Lieder

In a pre-concert talk before the pianist Augustus Arnone performed Finnissy's monumental *The History of Photography in Sound* (1995–2001) in New York on 23 March 2015,[48] the composer described how his "pieces just start, and they just stop," as if in a dreamlike state.[49] This sense of open-endedness has been a consistent feature of Finnissy's compositions, reflecting an interest in challenging the aesthetic of formal coherence and self-contained work.[50] Elsewhere, Finnissy has linked such ideas to the work of Marcel Duchamp, who "forced his audience to think, setting them the task of mentally completing the artwork," as well as that of Satie, in which "the surface (frequently borrowed from elsewhere: plainsong or ragtime) is contradicted by the structure and actual substance (repetition, fragmentation, surreal verbal commentary, bizarre spelling). You're listening to disruption rather than 'organic' development." And, in the same context, Finnissy suggested that "[c]omposing is also dealing with Memory. Individual memory, collective memory. The decaying and eventual disappearance of what anyone can remember."[51] Drawing together these lines of thought provides a way into Finnissy's *Brahms-Lieder*, written for Arnone (and indeed, begun in the United States in the month that Arnone performed *The History of Photography in Sound*). Each of the four movements, as in *In stiller Nacht*, draws on settings from Brahms's *Deutsche Volkslieder* WoO 33. Nevertheless, the diffusion of these songs into the texture of each movement (decaying and disappearance) as well as the ambiguous, dreamlike forms Finnissy constructs, situates *Brahms-Lieder* at a considerable critical distance from their source.

This distance manifests itself less in the musical surface (although the songs form a radical departure from Brahms's original) and more, as in *In stiller Nacht*, in the way that musical procedures are employed. Pace has suggested that "in all of the songs . . . the material (in all parts) is in a continual state of flux, as Brahms's type of 'developing variation' is reconfigured in a much late[r] post-tonal context."[52] Whittall, building on this observation, suggests that "it is by no means clear that Finnissy uses basic shapes with as explicit a connection to the motivic processes of pre-modernist music as Brahms or Schoenberg do. . . . this opens up the radically different ideas about continuity and musical character that are apparent when 'pure' Brahms, or Schoenberg, are compared with 'pure' Finnissy."[53] *Brahms-Lieder*, therefore, can be said to form a positive critique of developing variation to balance that presented in *In stiller Nacht*. Specifically, Finnissy appears to be asking what happens when the technique is decoupled from an aesthetic ideology grounded in formal coherence and instead pressed into service in the context of an open-ended, and at times athematic, discourse. In short, Brahms's specter is being made to haunt a very different musical environment.

Nevertheless, the audible presence of Brahms within *Brahms-Lieder* is elusive at most. The allusions are at their most cryptic in the third movement, marked Allegro martellato—Sempre Allegro. The movement begins with white-note clusters in the bass over which a declamatory upper line, *fff* and mostly thickened with added notes thirds, fifths, or sixths below, rings forth. This, Pace suggests, is a reference to typical Brahmsian pianistic figurations,[54] but the musical language and rhetoric serves to obscure both stylistic origins and, often, the audibility of the material. After four such outbursts, the dynamic drops slightly (to *f*) and an active figuration in the left hand added, mostly above middle C, for three further declamations. The mood suddenly changes: although still largely in the treble register, the line fragments further in increasingly hushed, enigmatic statements before ending on an isolated, unaccompanied high C♯. This abrupt shift of musical perspective, in lieu of more conventional closural devices, speaks to Finnissy's somewhat cinematic approach to musical structure, quite at odds with Brahmsian rhetoric.[55]

A similar cinematic edit marks the end of the second movement, Scherzoso delicato, in which the Romantic piano textures of the majority of the movement (which alternates between spacious, lighter material [as in Example 19.3b] and somewhat more intricate writing [Example 19.3c]) suddenly thin to two voices (Example 19.3d). Pace suggests that the closing passage contains "a series of inverted fragments from Brahms's [WoO 33] No. 35, 'Soll sich der Mond nicht heller scheinen'" (see Example 19.3a). Primed with this information, it is possible to imagine traces of Brahms's original haunting Finnissy's movement. It is not too fanciful, for instance, to identify the bass motion F♯–D in bars 1–2 of the Brahms recurring in Finnissy's opening (Example 19.3b). But deeper intertextual connections can be conceived. The text of the folksong begins as if *in media res*. Similarly, one can also understand Finnissy's opening, like the song text, as if part of an ongoing discourse that we are only just privy to (his "pieces just start"). As such, the listener is presented with fragments of the melody of "Soll sich der Mond" that are already in the midst of continuous developing variation, as part of a transformational process that has neither beginning nor end. The lack of a clear statement of what *is* being developed is significant, however. This is the logic of the Derridean specter, for it renders the Brahmsian source insubstantial, neither present nor absent, undermining teleological notions of origin and destination.

As an illustration of this developmental attitude, consider the opening motif of "Soll sich der Mond." Finnissy's reworking—which I shall come to shortly—focuses more on motivic shape rather than specific intervallic content, and my analysis of WoO 33, No. 35, reflects this concern. In this light, the opening rising contour of a leap followed by a step (Example 19.3a, bracket *a*)— a shape that is immediately followed by its transposed repetition—becomes significant. The close of the first clause—a descending leap followed by a step— inverts the contour (labeled I(*a*)). Admittedly, there is a risk, when looking for motivic correspondences between *Brahms-Lieder* and their sources, that an analyst might latch onto any similar contour and imbue it with a significance it might not have (especially when the contour, in dense textures, may not be perceptually salient). Nevertheless, the consistency with which the motivic fragments are deployed within particular sections suggests that they have a compositional function. Specifically: there appears to be a relationship between the distribution of pianistic textures and motivic shapes. In Example 19.3b, the outer voices employ a variant of the contour based on retrograde motion—a descending step and then leap (R(*a*))—while the inner voice presents recollections of the original contour *a*. Example 19.3c, which marks the onset of the first texturally contrasting section at bar 11, makes most use of a the retrograde of the inversion of *a* (i.e., RI(*a*)), suggesting that the change

Example 19.3 (a) Brahms, "Soll sich der Mond nicht heller scheinen," WoO 33, No. 35 (1894), bars 1–4; Finnissy, *Brahms-Lieder*, ii, (b) bars 1–5; (c) bars 11–12; (d) opening of final unbarred section. Extracts from *Brahms-Lieder* © Verlag Neue Musik, Berlin.

of texture is intensified by a change of motivic focus. The opening of the final section, Example 19.3d, employs nearly all of the variants of the contour, but in addition closely follows the melodic contour of Brahms's entire first clause (*b*, reworked by Finnissy as *b′*). The process speaks to (Schoenbergian) developing variation, but the degree to which Finnissy's dense compositional workings obscure the audibility of this technique serves to weaken it as a guarantor of aesthetic coherence.

The specter of Brahms in the first movement, Lento pianissimo espressivo—Più mosso subito molto agitato e misterioso, is far less shadowy. As Pace has shown, the presence of the melody of WoO 33, No. 30, "All mein Gedanken," can be detected at multiple points within the alto voice, modeled, as August Arnone suggests, on textures from Brahms's Op. 10, No. 4.[56] Whittall has noted how Finnissy significantly alters both the tempo (slower) and texture (more complex) of the borrowed material from "All mein Gedanken" so that the melody is "absorbed into something else ... rather than simply quoted with a different accompaniment."[57] It is conceivable that, in performance, a pianist might choose to emphasize this inner voice (and with it, decide whether to respect Brahms's metrical emphasis or Finnissy's shifting of notated upbeats to downbeats). However, Finnissy's expression markings (*pianissimo espressivo*), liberal use of dampening and sustain pedals, and intricate interplay of rhythms and contrapuntal lines all suggest a hazy, veiled atmosphere in which no line is afforded particular emphasis (compare this with *In stiller Nacht*). At most, Brahms might be spotted as if through a heavy, almost opaque gauze, "as if from the other side."

At over three minutes long, the final movement is the longest of the set (none of the others lasts much beyond two minutes), though this is perhaps its only concession to conventional notions of finales. The source here is WoO 33, No. 29, "Es war ein Markgraf überm Rhein," and something of the extended narrational quality of the song—for instance, the flowing accompaniment of Brahms's setting of verses 3 and 4, paralleled in bars 15–20 of Finnissy's reworking—is retained. So too, to a greater extent, is Brahms's melodic line, which in Finnissy's hands is rendered somewhere between the more explicit quotations of the first movement and the developmental allusiveness of the second. The opening of the original is given in Example 19.4a. It can be divided into five fragments, which I have labeled *c–g* (the reason for separating

Example 19.4 (a) Brahms, "Es war ein Markgraf überm Rhein," WoO 33, No. 29 (1894), bars 1–4; (b) Finnissy, *Brahms-Lieder*, iv, bars 1–4. Extracts from *Brahms-Lieder* © Verlag Neue Musik, Berlin.

out *d* from *e* will become clear). There is a musical rhyme to match the poetic one: the first half of the phrase (*c–e*) outlines a tonal progression ending with a half cadence; the second phrase (*f–g*) surveys similar harmonic material but is reworked to end with a perfect authentic cadence. The opening is thus a charming model of tonal and harmonic conventionality.

The material derived from "Es war ein Markgraf" remains close to Finnissy's musical surface; as a result, of all the *Brahms-Lieder*, the final movement is the one that has the strongest potential to project tonal hierarchies.[58] Here, developing variation seems to be employed not to diffuse and disperse musical identity (as in Example 19.3) but rather to prise apart and examine as if under a microscope the constituent elements of tonal function. For this exploration to work, the resemblance between source and reworking has to remain audible; annotations to Example 19.4b show how this is achieved. Thus, the ordering of the motivic fragments of Brahms's first phrase are reversed, and while Finnissy's setting of motifs *e–c* in the tenor voice may begin and end with what are more-or-less dominant chords (as did Brahms), tonal cause and effect is suspended. The treble voice (beginning bar 2) appears to allude to the start and end of Brahms's motifs *d* + *e* and *g*—Finnissy's chromatic alteration at the beginning of the former intensifies the implied chromatic voice leading between contrapuntal voices, but the emphasis is shifted away from the final A back to the D in the upper voice. This destabilizing of the tonic occurs in the lower voices too: the descending cadential melodic motion $\hat{5}–\hat{1}$ of Brahms's second phrase (of which *g* consists of the last four notes) is displaced to the bass in the middle of Finnissy's opening phrase, to be answered in the tenor voice by a corresponding rise from $\hat{2}–\hat{5}$ that derives from *f*. Finnissy ends the phrase with an unambiguous statement of an E-major chord at the start of bar 4, thereby upending the tonic-dominant relationship of Brahms's original setting. By drawing on developing variation to separate out and fragment tonal functions, as well as dislocating thematic motif from formal syntax, Finnissy reconceives Brahmsian thinking for a post-tonal musical environment.

* * *

For Derrida, the "being-with specters" is, in part, "a *politics* of memory, of inheritance, and of generations."[59] Observing the Brahmsian specters in Finnissy's music through a Derridean lens thus provides a model for ways of thinking about how other composers, performers, and listeners grapple with the politics of tradition in their own rethinking of Brahms. In Finnissy's case, his summoning of multiple specters of Brahms filtered through the Brahms-Schoenberg tradition (and encapsulated in the idea of "Brahms the Progressive") offers a model of critical musical practice that interrogates the musical values, aesthetic ideologies, and compositional techniques of this tradition and its centrality in Western musical culture. Although the only deliberate relationship between *In stiller Nacht* and *Brahms-Lieder* is their shared

Specters and "Derangements"

response to Brahms, their summoning and derangement of Brahmsian specters might be taken as a two-part argument. In the first instance, the successive transformation of inherited images of Brahms in *In stiller Nacht* has something of a parodic function (the humor threaded through Finnissy's output must not be overlooked). Nevertheless, the underlying question of the nature of (musical) identity and the values that we attach to it is of the utmost seriousness. By taking the compositional techniques of the Brahms-Schoenberg tradition—developing variation—to their logical conclusion, Finnissy demonstrates how both identity and value are social constructs, thereby rendering immediately suspect any uncritical claims for the centrality of this tradition.

In *Brahms-Lieder*, Finnissy returns to the same territory of *In stiller Nacht*, that of Brahms the Progressive as folksong arranger. Here, developing variation is decontextualized, denuded of its former role as a means of providing unity and formal coherence and instead offering a means of negotiating the dreamlike logic of Finnissy's musical syntax, within which fragments of recognizable motifs and harmonic functions drift occasionally to the surface, before plunging back down into the depths of the unconscious. Here, Finnissy perhaps comes closest to "being with" the ghost of Brahms.

Notes

Introduction

1. For discussions of how Brahms's death was discussed in the Viennese press, see Sandra McColl, *Music Criticism in Vienna 1896–1897: Critically Moving Forms* (Oxford: Oxford University Press, 1996); Ingrid Fuchs, "Der Versuch musikhistorischer Einordnung Brahms' und Bruckners in den Wiener Nachrufen," in *Bruckner-Symposion: Bruckner, Vorbilder und Traditionen: im Rahmen des Internationales Brucknerfest Linz 1997*, ed. Uwe Harten (Vienna: Musikwissenschaftlicher Verlag, 1999), 221–9. Two of the first-published Brahms memoirs were by the composer's friends Dietrich and Widmann. See Albert Dietrich, *Erinnerungen an Johannes Brahms in Briefen besonders aus seiner Jugendzeit* (Leipzig: Otto Wigand, 1898); and Joseph Viktor Widmann, *Johannes Brahms in Erinnerungen* (Berlin: Gebrüder Paetel, 1898). The earliest detailed Brahms biographies were by Hermann Deiters (published 1898), Max Kalbeck (published 1904–1914), and Florence May (published 1905).

2. Wilibald Nagel, *Johannes Brahms als Nachfolger Beethoven's* (Leipzig & Zürich: Gebrüder Hug., 1892); Philipp Spitta, "Johannes Brahms," in *Zur Musik. Sechzehn Aufsätze* (Berlin: Gebrüder Paetel, 1892), 387–427.

3. See Norbert Meurs, *Neue Bahnen? Aspekte der Brahms-Rezeption 1853–1868* (Köln: Studio, 1996).

4. Paul Berry, *Brahms among Friends: Listening, Performance, and the Rhetoric of Allusion* (New York: Oxford University Press, 2014); Katy Hamilton and Natasha Loges, eds., *Brahms in the Home and the Concert Hall: Between Private and Public Performance* (Cambridge: Cambridge University Press, 2014); Marie Sumner Lott, *The Social Worlds of Nineteenth-Century Chamber Music: Composers, Consumers, Communities* (Urbana: University of Illinois Press, 2015); Natasha Loges and Katy Hamilton, *Brahms in Context* (Cambridge: Cambridge University Press, 2019).

5. Otto Biba et al., eds., *Brahms' Schubert-Rezeption im Wiener Kontext. Bericht über das internationale Symposium Wien 2013* (Stuttgart: Franz Steiner Verlag, 2017); Jacquelyn Sholes, *Allusion as Narrative Premise in Brahms's Instrumental Music* (Bloomington: Indiana University Press, 2018).

6. Natasha Loges, *Brahms and His Poets: A Handbook* (Woodbridge: The Boydell Press, 2017); Julian Horton, *Brahms's Second Piano Concerto, Op. 83: Analytical and Contextual Studies* (Leuven: Peeters, 2017); Katharina Loose-Einfalt, *Melancholie, Natur, Musik: zum Horntrio von Johannes Brahms* (Mainz: Schott, 2017); Sven Hiemke, *Johannes Brahms, ein deutsches Requiem* (Kassel: Bärenreiter, 2018); Nicole Grimes, *Brahms's Elegies: The Poetics of Loss in Nineteenth-Century German Culture* (Cambridge: Cambridge University Press, 2019); R. Allen Lott,

Brahms's *A German Requiem: Reconsidering Its Biblical, Historical, and Musical Contexts* (Rochester, NY: University of Rochester Press, 2020).

7. Heather Platt and Peter Smith, eds., *Expressive Intersections in Brahms* (Bloomington: Indiana University Press, 2012); Scott Murphy, ed., *Brahms and the Shaping of Time* (Rochester, NY: University of Rochester Press, 2018).

8. Laurie McManus, *Brahms in the Priesthood of Art: Gender and Art Religion in the Nineteenth-Century German Musical Imagination* (New York: Oxford University Press, 2021).

9. Clive Brown, Neal Peres da Costa, and Kate Bennett Wadsworth, *Performing Practices in Johannes Brahms' Chamber Music* (Kassel: Bärenreiter, 2015); Christopher Dyment, *Conducting the Brahms Symphonies: From Brahms to Boult* (Woodbridge: The Boydell Press, 2016).

10. Anonymous, "A Work for This Moment: 'A German Requiem' by Brahms," *Deutsche Welle*, https://www.dw.com/en/a-work-for-this-moment-a-german-requiem-by-brahms/a-53079994 (accessed 1 December 2020).

11. See Lori Holcomb-Holland, "Protestors Delay St. Louis Symphony," *New York Times* (5 October 2014), and Robert Siegel, "A Ferguson Protest Brings New Meaning to Brahms' Requiem in St. Louis," NPR website, 6 October 2014, https://www.npr.org/sections/deceptivecadence/2014/10/06/354101823/a-ferguson-protest-brings-new-meaning-to-brahms-requiem-in-st-louis (accessed 1 December 2020).

12. Accounts of this performance are provided in Michael C. Duff, *The Cowboy Code Meets the Smash Mouth Truth: Meditations on Worker Incivility*, Law Archive of Wyoming Scholarship, Faculty Articles 69 (2015): 100–25 (124–25); and Robert Samuels, 'Protestors Interrupt St. Louis Symphony with 'Requiem for Mike Brown,'" *Washington Post* (5 October 2014).

13. See Alexandra Kedves, "Der Regisseur koppelt Brahms mit Black Lives Matter," *Basler Zeitung* (29 June 2020), 12. For an account of Stemann's initiative in English, see https://www.schauspielhaus.ch/en/journal/18090/corona-passion-play-what-is-that; Daniele Muscionico, "Die neuen Leiden des jungen Virus: Jetzt hat auch das Theater sein Corona-Evangelium," *Neue Zürcher Zeitung* (28 June 2020); Sarah Stutte, "Dem Virus ins Gesicht lachen," Kirche Schweiz website, 29 July 2020, https://www.kath.ch/newsd/dem-virus-ins-gesicht-lachen/ (accessed 1 December 2020). Kimberly Jones is coauthor, with Gilly Segal, of *I'm Not Dying With You Tonight* (Naperville IL: Sourcebooks Fire, 2019). For the full video of the protest speech Jones gave on 9 June 2020 from which the excerpts at the end of the *Corona Passion Play* are taken, see https://www.youtube.com/watch?v=llci8MVh8J4 (accessed 1 December 2020).

14. Langston Hughes, "Home," in *The Ways of White Folks* (New York: Vintage, 1933). For a discussion of Hughes's short story "Home" in relation to the Black Lives Matter movement and classical music, see Kira Thurman, "Singing Against the Grain: Playing Beethoven in the #BlackLivesMatter Era," *The Point* 17 (28 September 2018): https://thepointmag.com/examined-life/singing-against-grain-playing-beethoven-blacklivesmatter-era/ (accessed 9 March 2022).

15. M. H. Abrams, *Natural Supernaturalism: Tradition and Revolution in Romantic Literature* (New York: W. W. Norton, 1971).

16. Jonathan Miller, *The Afterlife of Plays*, Fifth Distinguished Graduate Research Lecture (San Diego: San Diego State University Press, 1992), 27, 28, 29, and 34.

17. For a collection of Zehnder's other drawings see *C. Zehnder, Maler-Architekt, 1859–1938: Ideal-Architekturen* (Zürich: ETH, 1981). We are grateful to Styra Avins for alerting us to the existence of Zehnder's Brahms drawings.

Chapter 1

1. I am grateful to Robert Anderson, Walter Frisch, and Nicole Grimes for their thoughtful reading of this chapter.
   The primary source materials relating to Schumann's time at Endenich have been transcribed and collated. See Bernhard R. Appel, ed., *Robert Schumann in Endenich (1854–1856): Krankenakten, Briefzeugnisse und zeitgenössische Berichte*, Schumann Forschungen 11 (Mainz: Schott, 2006), 117–22.

2. "Von mir nur noch, daß ich mich wohl befinde, bei Schumann zu meiner großen Wonne die Bücher und Notenbibliothek geordnet habe und jetzt den ganzen Tag dort sitze und studire. Ich habe mich selten so wohl befunden, als jetzt in dieser Bibliothek wühlend." Albert Dietrich, *Erinnerungen an Johannes Brahms in Briefen besonders aus seiner Jugendzeit* (Leipzig: Otto Wigand, 1898), 17–18. All translations are my own unless otherwise noted.

3. No complete listing survives for the items that would have been in the Schumann library. I am grateful to Thomas Synofzik for supplying me with details of the large number of volumes that are now preserved in the collection of the Robert-Schumann-Haus in Zwickau.

4. For an influential study exploring Brahms's Kreisler identification see Siegfried Kross, "Brahms and E. T. A. Hoffmann," *19th-Century Music* 5/3 (1982): 193–200.

5. Robert Schumann, *Tagebücher*, ed. Gerd Nauhaus, vol. 3, part 2 (Leipzig: VEB Deutscher Verlag für Musik, 1982), 635–38. The writings on Robert Schumann's literary enthusiasms and their significance for his musical activities are voluminous. See, for example, Uwe Schweikert, "Das literarische Werk—Lektüre, Poesie, Kritik und poetische Musik," in *Schumann-Handbuch*, ed. Ulrich Tadday (Kassel: Bärenreiter, 2006), 107–26; Bernhard R. Appel and Inge Hermstrüwer, eds., *Robert Schumann und die Dichter: Ein Musiker als Leser* (Düsseldorf: Droste, 1991); John Daverio, *Robert Schumann: Herald of a "New Poetic Age"* (New York: Oxford University Press, 1997); John MacAuslan, *Schumann's Music and E. T. A. Hoffmann's Fiction* (Cambridge: Cambridge University Press, 2016).

6. Johannes Brahms, *Des jungen Kreislers Schatzkästlein: Aussprüche von Dichtern, Philosophen und Künstlern*, ed. Carl Krebs (Berlin: Deutsche Brahms-Gesellschaft, 1909). For further information about the 1909 publication and the

Schatzkästlein notebooks more generally, see Reuben Phillips, "Between Hoffmann and Goethe: The Young Brahms as Reader," *Journal of the Royal Musical Association* 146/2 (2021): 455–89.

7. Josef W. von Wasielewski, *Robert Schumann. Eine Biographie* (Dresden: Kunze, 1858), 286.

8. "'Haben Sie sich auch schon in der Composition versucht?' frug ihn Schumann, und, auf Brahms' bejahende Frage, 'haben Sie Ihre Manuscripte bei sich?['] 'Ich kann sie ohne Noten auf dem Clavier spielen,' 'dann spielen Sie etwas, dort steht der Flügel.' Brahms setzt sich an den Flügel, Schumann lässt ihn kaum ein Stück beendigen, unterbricht ihn dann mit den Worten: 'das muss Clara hören,' holt seine Frau herbei, 'hier, liebe Clara, sollst Du Musik hören, wie Du sie noch nicht gehört hast; jetzt fangen Sie das Stück noch einmal an, junger Mann.'" Adolf Schubring, "Schumanniana Nr. 11: Schumann und Brahms. Brahms' vierhändige Schumann-Variationen," *Allgemeine musikalische Zeitung* 3/6 (5 February 1868): 41–42 (42).

9. Max Kalbeck, *Johannes Brahms*, vol. 1 (Berlin: Deutsche Brahms-Gesellschaft, 1908), 114.

10. The source for this is the daughter of Theodor Avé-Lallemant, who suggests that her father introduced Brahms to Schumann at a soirée. See Thomas Synofzik, "Brahms und Schumann," in *Brahms-Handbuch*, ed. Wolfgang Sandberger (Kassel: Bärenreiter, 2009), 63–76 (63–64).

11. "Brahms zum Besuch (ein Genius)." Robert Schumann, *Tagebücher*, 3/2: 637.

12. Robert Schumann, "Neue Bahnen," *Neue Zeitschrift für Musik* 39/18 (28 October 1853): 185–86.

13. Previously, on 9 September 1853, Schumann had finished the novel *Siebenkäs*. Robert Schumann, *Tagebücher*, 3/2: 635 and 638.

14. The source for this claim is Max Kalbeck. See his *Johannes Brahms*, 1:119. No trace of the quartet, however, survives. For an exploration of possible connections between *Prinzessin Brambilla* and Robert Schumann's *Carnaval*, Op. 9, see MacAuslan, *Schumann's Music*, 37–69.

15. "Schumanns Brahms-Artikel ist ein Bekenntnis zur Tradition der Romantik und er ist ein Bekenntnis zu Brahms, den Schumann einzig für berufen hielt, die Tradition der Romantik fortzuführen." Ulrich Tadday, "Tendenzen der Brahms-Kritik im 19. Jahrhundert," in *Brahms-Handbuch*, ed. Wolfgang Sandberger (Kassel: Bärenreiter, 2009), 112–27 (116).

16. "Am Clavier sitzend, fing er an wunderbare Regionen zu enthüllen. Wir wurden in immer zauberischere Kreise hineingezogen." Schumann, "Neue Bahnen," 185.

17. "jedes so abweichend vom andern, daß sie jedes verschiedenen Quellen zu entströmen schienen. Und dann schien es, als vereinigte er, als Strom dahinbrausend, alle wie zu einem Wasserfall, über die hinunterstürzenden Wogen den friedlichen Regenbogen tragenden und am Ufer von Schmetterlingen umspielt und von Nachtigallenstimmen begleitet." Schumann, "Neue Bahnen," 185–86.

18. Constantin Floros, *Brahms und Bruckner: Studien zur musikalischen Exegetik* (Wiesbaden: Breitkopf & Härtel, 1980), 99–102.

19. Clara: "Er hat bei Marxsen in Hamburg studiert, doch das, was er uns gespielt, ist so meisterhaft, daß man meinen müßte, den hätte der liebe Gott gleich so fertig auf die Welt gesetzt. Eine schöne Zukunft steht Dem bevor, den wenn er erst für Orchester schreiben wird, dann wird er erst das rechte Feld für seine Phantasie gefunden haben!" Robert: "Ich dachte, . . . es würde und müsse nach solchem Vorgang einmal plötzlich Einer erscheinen, der den höchsten Ausdruck der Zeit in idealer Weise berufen wäre, einer, der uns die Meisterschaft nicht in stufenweiser Entfaltung brächt, sondern, wie Minerva, gleich vollkommen gepanzert aus dem Haupte des Kronion spränge." "Wenn er seinen Zauberstab dahin senken wird, wo ihm die Mächte der Massen, im Chor und Orchester, ihre Kräfte leihen, so stehen uns noch wunderbarere Blick in die Geheimnisse der Geisterwelt bevor." Floros, *Brahms und Bruckner*, 101. It remains difficult to untangle the exact nature of Clara Schumann's contribution to this famous essay. Some of her diary entries might well reflect Robert's spoken comments, though it seems very likely that his ideas about Brahms as a pianist and composer would have been developed in conversation with his wife. See also Synofzik, "Brahms und Schumann," 67.

20. The letter was addressed to Amtsvogt [Baliff] Blume, who lived Winsen-an-der-Luhe, outside of Hamburg. Styra Avins, ed., *Johannes Brahms: His Life and Letters*, trans. Josef Eisinger and Styra Avins (Oxford: Oxford University Press, 1997), 53–54.

21. "Lieber Joachim, Acht Tage sind wir fort, und noch haben wir Ihnen und Ihren Gesellen kein Wort zukommen lassen! Aber mit sympathetischer Tinte habe ich Euch oft geschrieben, und auch zwischen diesen Zeilen steht eine Geheimschrift, die später hervorbrechen wird.

"Und geträumt habe ich von Ihnen, Lieber Joachim; wir waren drei Tage zusammen—Sie hatten Reiherfedern in den Händen, aus denen Champagner floß—wie prosaisch!—aber wie wahr!" Johannes Joachim and Andreas Moser, eds., *Briefe von und an Joseph Joachim*, vol. 1 (Berlin: Julius Bard, 1911), 153–54.

22. Robert Schumann, *Tagebücher*, 3/2: 646 (entry from 14 January 1854). Brahms's copy of the Hoffmann volume is preserved in Archive of the Gesellschaft der Musikfreunde in Vienna, shelf mark: Brahms-Bibliothek 256 (see Figure 1.5).

23. The entries believed to be by Brahms run from late February until December 1854. Brahms's handwriting was identified by a slip of paper pasted into the household book by Ferdinand Schumann, son of Robert and Clara, and former owner of this source. Robert Schumann, *Tagebücher*, 3/2:649.

24. Berthold Litzmann, *Clara Schumann. Ein Künstlerleben nach Tagebüchern und Briefen*, vol. 2 (Leipzig: Breitkopf & Härtel, 1906), 323.

25. Avins, ed., *Life and Letters*, 68.

26. Valerie Woodring Goertzen, "At the Piano with Joseph and Johannes: Joachim's Overtures in Brahms's Circle," in *Brahms in the Home and the Concert Hall: Between Private and Public Performance*, ed. Katy Hamilton and Natasha Loges (Cambridge: Cambridge University Press, 2014), 168.

27. "An Ihnen lerne ich immerfort, daß man Lebenskraft (= lebenskräftiges Schaffen) nich aus Büchern holen kann, sondern nur aus der eigenen Seele." Beatrix Borchard, *Clara Schumann: Musik als Lebenform* (Hildesheim: Olms, 2019), 38.

28. Robert-Schumann-Haus Zwickau; Archiv-Nr.: 10315–iA4/C1.

29. "Der theuren Clara vom jungen Kreisler. 16 Jan. 56." *Autographen und Handzeichnungen. Auktion am 28. Oktober 1937*, J. A. Stargardt Antiquariat, 17. The current whereabouts of this volume is unknown.

30. Siegmund Helms, "Johannes Brahms und Johann Sebastian Bach," in *Bach-Jahrbuch 57* (Berlin: Evangelische Verlagsanstalt, 1971), 13–81 (15).

31. This list was assembled by drawing on three earlier investigations of the Brahms library. Eusebius Mandyczewski, "Die Bibliothek Brahms," *Musikbuch aus Österreich* 1 (1904): 7–17; Kurt Hofmann, *Die Bibliothek von Johannes Brahms. Bücher- und Musikalienverzeichnis* (Hamburg: Verlag der Musikalienhandlung Wagner, 1974); Eva Krill, "Die Bibliothek von Johannes Brahms: Zur literarischen Geistigkeit des Komponisten" (PhD diss., University of Vienna, 2001).

32. Berthold Litzmann, ed., *Clara Schumann, Johannes Brahms: Briefe aus den Jahren 1853–1896*, vol. 1 (Leipzig: Breitkopf & Härtel, 1927), 8.

33. Variations 10 and 11 in Brahms's work were added later and are dated August 1854. For a helpful summary of the scholarship on this composition see Katrin Eich, "Die Klavierwerke," in *Brahms-Handbuch*, ed. Wolfgang Sandberger (Kassel: Bärenreiter, 2009), 347–48.

34. "Kleine Variationen über ein Thema von Ihm. Ihr zugeeignet."

35. "1. Siehe zu, daß dich die Schule zum Leben führe, daß du immer festen Boden fühlst, daß sich dein Wissen nicht als trübes Mittel zwischen deine Kunst u. Natur stelle u. du nicht etwa nur lernst, täglich ein größerer Manierist zu werden. / Kunstblatt. 2. Es muß sich ein Zunftwesen edlerer Art bilden, das alles der Kunst Unwürdige ausstößt. / J. Feski." The seven entries shown in Figure 1.3 correspond to entries 503–9 of the 1909 Deutsche Brahms-Gesellschaft publication edited by Carl Krebs (hereafter, Krebs 503–9).

36. As Martin Geck notes, Schumann's model in the use of poetic mottos was the *Morgenblatt für gebildete Stände* published by the firm of Cotta. See his *Robert Schumann: The Life and Work of a Romantic Composer*, trans. Stewart Spencer (Chicago: University of Chicago Press, 2013), 48.

37. Geck, *Life and Work of a Romantic Composer*, 49.

38. For an account of the publication circumstances surround Schumann's writings, see Gerd Nauhaus, "Nachwort," in Robert Schumann, *Gesammelte Schriften über Musik und Musiker*, ed. Gerd Nauhaus and Ingeborg Singer, vol. 2 (Wiesbaden: Breitkopf & Härtel, 1985), 307–22.

39. "'Es hat gefallen' oder: 'es hat nicht gefallen' sagen die Leute. Als ob es nichts Höheres gäbe, als den Leuten zu gefallen!" "Licht senden in die Tiefe des menschlichen Herzens—des Künstlers Beruf!" Robert Schumann, *Gesammelte Schriften* (Leipzig: Georg Wigand, 1854), 4:278. Krebs 584–85.

40. "welch Gemüt, welcher Geist, welche reiche Phantasie! Je mehr man ihn kennt, [um] so mehr muß man ihn ins Herz schließen." Nauhaus, "Nachwort," 307.

41. The *Dichtergarten* manuscript is preserved in the Robert-Schumann-Haus in Zwickau. Archiv-Nr.: 4871/VIII,1–A3.

42. Robert Schumann, *Dichtergarten für Musik: eine Anthologie für Freunde der Literatur und Musik*, ed. Gerd Nauhaus and Ingrid Bodsch (Bonn: Stadt Museum, 2007), 11.

43. "In der Zeit hab' ich immer wieder an meinem Garten gearbeitet. Er wird immer stattlicher; auch Wegweiser habe ich hier und da hingesetzt, daß man sich nicht verirrt, d.h. aufklärenden Text. Jetzt bin ich in die uralte Vergangenheit gekommen, in Homer und das Griechenthum. Namentlich im Plato habe ich herrliche Stellen entdeckt." Schumann, *Dichtergarten*, 14.

44. The visit is documented both by Schumann's diary and by a surviving borrowing slip from the public library. From the borrowing slip it can be seen that Schumann was examining works by three writers: Claudius Aelianus, Aristotle, and Horace. Appel, ed., *Robert Schumann in Endenich*, 44 and 482.

45. "Dienstag, den 21. Februar, schliefen wir wieder die ganze Nacht nicht; er sprach immer davon, er sei ein Verbrecher und solle eigentlich in der Bibel lesen usw. Ich merkte überhaupt, daß sein Zustand immer aufgeregter wurde, wenn er in der Bibel las, und kam dadurch auf die Idee, daß er sich beim Lesen derselben, als er für seinen Dichtergarten sammelte, vielleicht zu sehr in Dinge hineinvertieft, die seinen Geist verwirrten, wie denn seine Leiden fast durchgängig religiöser Art, förmliche Überspannung war." Appel, ed., *Robert Schumann in Endenich*, 48–49.

46. Frederick Niecks, trans., "Robert Schumann and Bettina von Arnim," *Monthly Musical Record* 53/632 (1 August 1923): 230–32. For the original German see Appel, ed., *Robert Schumann in Endenich*, 265.

47. "Nicht unwahrscheinlich ist es, daß er im Sinne hatte, Schumann mit seiner Sammlung ein willkommenes Geschenk zu machen, gewissermaßen als Untergärtner seines 'Dichtergartens.'" Kalbeck, *Johannes Brahms*, 1:184.

48. Entries from Zedlitz and Menzel's Kunstblatt also appear in another Schumann source: Robert's notebooks of poetic mottos assembled between 1825 and 1852, known as his *Mottosammlung*. Brahms's copying of other entries from the *Dichtergarten* manuscript, however, makes this the more likely source. Leander Hotaki, ed., *Robert Schumanns Mottosammlung: Übertragung, Kommentar, Einführung* (Freiburg: Rombach, 1998).

49. Sotheby & Co., *Catalogue of Valuable Printed Books, Illuminated and Other Manuscripts, Autograph Letters and Historical Documents, Oriental Miniatures, Etc.* (London, 1935), 65.

50. Daverio, *Robert Schumann*, vii.

51. Kalbeck reports that Brahms claimed to have set the complete works of Eichendorff and Heine: "Den ganzen Eichendorff und Heine hab' ich in Musik gesetzt." Kalbeck, *Johannes Brahms*, 1:133.

52. It is hard to establish which of Brahms's surviving early piano works would have been included in this planned publication. See Robert Pascall, *Brahms beyond Mastery: His Sarabande and Gavotte, and Its Recompositions* (Farnham: Ashgate, 2013), 7–8.

53. Also of note here is the humorous list of rules that Brahms drew up for the female choir he conducted in Hamburg in the late 1850s. This document, written in a deliberately antiquated German, is signed "Johannes Kreisler/alias: Brahms." Wienbibliothek im Rathaus, H.I.N.32885.

54. There was an obvious similarity between Brahms's title and the subtitle of Hoffmann's *Fantasiestücke*: "Leaves from the Diary of a Traveling Enthusiast" (*reisenden Enthusiasten*). Hoffmann's device of presenting an editor (*Herausgeber*) as an author has been helpfully theorized through the concept of *Herausgeberfiktion*. See Uwe Wirth, *Die Geburt des Autors aus dem Geist der Herausgeberfiktion: Editoriale Rahmung im Roman um 1800* (Munich: Wilhelm Fink, 2008).

55. For a discussion of this issue see Mark Evan Bonds, "Idealism and the Aesthetics of Instrumental Music at the Turn of the Nineteenth Century," *Journal of the American Musicological Society* 50/2 (1997): 387–420.

56. "Sie ist die romantischste aller Künste, beinahe möchte man sagen, allein echt romantisch, denn nur das Unendliche ist ihr Vorwurf. . . . Die Musik schließt dem Menschen ein unbekanntes Reich auf, eine Welt, die nichts gemein hat mit der äußern Sinnenwelt, die ihn umgibt, und in der er alle *bestimmten* Gefühle zurückläßt, um sich einer unausprechlichen Sehnsucht hinzugeben." E. T. A. Hoffmann, *Werke*, vol. 1 (Frankfurt am Main: Insel Verlag, 1967), 37.

57. "O Musik! Nachklang aus einer entlegnen harmonischen Welt! Seufzer des Engels in uns!" Krebs 6.

58. Krebs 370.

59. "Mir ist bei der Musik, als hörte ich eine laute Vergangenheit oder eine laute Zukunft. Die Musik hat etwas Heiliges, sie kann nichts als das Gute malen, verschieden von andern Künsten." Krebs 362.

60. "Mir aber ist das ein Jammerpoet, / Dem nicht immer sein Volk vor Augen steht." Krebs 137.

61. "Die Genügsamkeit des Publikums ist nur ermunternd für die Mittelmäßigkeit, aber beschimpfend und abschreckend für das Genie." Krebs 149.

62. "Ein großer Teil des Publikums hat überhaupt nur Sinn und Kraft für das Mittelmäßige. Das aber kann mann verlangen, daß die, welche bloß das Gemeine oder Mittelmäßige verstehen und lieben, sich des Urteils über eigentliche geniale Kunstwerke enthalten." Krebs 521.

63. On the history of this important concept see E. V. K. Brill, "The Philistine Concept in German Literature," *European Studies Review* 7 (1977): 77–93.

64. Quoted in Daverio, *Robert Schumann*, 123.

65. "Hebt noch etwas den Spießbürger empor am Ohr, so ist's zwei-, höchstens dreierlei: 1. wenn aus einem halbtoten Pianissimo plötzlich ein Fortissimo wie en Rebhuhn aufknattert; 2. wenn einer, besonders mit dem Geigenbogen, auf dem höchsten Seile der höchsten Töne lange tanzt und rutscht, und nun kopfunten in die tiefsten herunterklatscht; 3. wenn gar beides vorfällt. In solchen Punkten ist der Bürger seiner nicht mehr mächtig, sondern schwitzt vor Lob." Krebs 457; Schumann, *Dichtergarten* 250.

66. "Vor jedem steht ein Bild des, was er werden soll; / Solang' er das nicht ist, ist nicht sein Friede voll." Krebs 386.

67. "Das wahre Genie richtet sich zwar zuweilen an fremden Urteile auf, aber das entwickelte Gefühl seiner Kräfte macht ihm bald dies Krücke entbehrlich." Krebs 147.

68. "Aus dem Leben heraus sind der Wege zwei dir geöffnet, / Zum Ideale führt einer, der andre zum Tod. / Siehe, daß du beizeiten noch frei auf dem ersten entspringest, / Ehe die Parze mit Zwang dich auf dem andern entführt." Krebs 553.

69. Crucial here are Brahms's sympathies for Viennese liberalism and his engagement with classical German literature (notably Goethe, Hölderlin, and Schiller). Margaret Notley, *Lateness and Brahms: Music and Culture in the Twilight of Viennese Liberalism* (New York: Oxford University Press, 2007); Nicole Grimes, *Brahms's Elegies: The Poetics of Loss in Nineteenth-Century German Culture* (Cambridge: Cambridge University Press, 2019).

70. "Sie ist Erziehung zur Persönlichkeit, Erziehung eines frey handelnden Wesens, das sich selbst erhalten, und in der Gesellschaft ein Glied ausmachen, für sich selbst aber einen inner Werth haben kann." Immanuel Kant, *Über Pädagogik* (Königsberg: Friedrich Nicolovius, 1803), 35. (These words do not appear in Brahms's collection.)

71. "Er hat gewiß seine geheime innere Welt—er nimmt alles Schöne in sich auf und zehrt nun innerlich davon." Berthold Litzmann, *Clara Schumann. Ein Künstlerleben*, 2:291.

Chapter 2

1. A number of acknowledgments are due: to the librarians of the Thomas J. Watson Library at the Metropolitan Museum, New York, and the librarians of the Print Collection and the Arts and Architecture Collection of the New York Public Library my grateful thanks for guiding me through their enormous repositories. I am indebted to Peter Bloom, whose extensive knowledge of the music scene of nineteenth-century France was most helpful in the early stages of my research, and to John MacAuslan, former administration director of the National Portrait Gallery (London) and musicologist, who kindly shared his observations on a wide range of European art from the Renaissance to the twentieth century. Josef Eisinger untangled several knotty passages in German, and Simon Eisinger prepared most of the illustrations. Last but not least, I wish to thank my editors, Nicole Grimes and Reuben Phillips, who kindly but persistently helped to give the chapter its present shape.

Recently several studies have appeared that address Brahms's interest in art, most notably Reinhold Brinkmann, "Zeitgenossen: Johannes Brahms und die Maler Feuerbach, Böcklin, Klinger, und Menzel," in *Johannes Brahms: Quellen-Text-Rezeption-Interpretation: Internationaler Brahms-Kongress, Hamburg 1997*, ed. Friedhelm Krummacher and Michael Struck, with Constantin Floros and

Peter Petersen (Munich: Henle Verlag 1999), 71–89; Leon Botstein, "Brahms and 19th Century Painting," *19th Century Music* 14/2 (1990): 154–68; Jan Brachmann, "Johannes Brahms und Max Klinger—eine Kunstfreundschaft," *Brahms-Studien* 15 (2008): 69–87; and Brachmann's "Form und Sinn des Buches—Betrachtungen zur *Brahms-Phantasie* von Max Klinger," an essay for the facsimile edition of *Brahms-Phantasie Op. XII*, published by the Johannes-Brahms-Gesellschaft (Hamburg: Verlag Ellert & Richter, 2017). Adolph Menzel is discussed in Reinhold Brinkman's *Late Idyll: The Second Symphony of Johannes Brahms* (Cambridge, MA: Harvard University Press, 1997), and in Nicole Grimes, *Brahms Elegies: The Poetics of Loss in Nineteenth-Century German Culture* (Cambridge: Cambridge University Press, 2019). Feuerbach is considered in some detail in Grimes's Chapter 2, "*Nänie* and the Death of Beauty." Natasha Loges also focuses on Feuerbach and Brahms in "Exoticism, Artifice and the Supernatural in the Brahmsian Lied," *Nineteenth-Century Music Review* 3/2 (2006): 137–68. For an excellent survey of Brahms's general interests in the arts, see Loges's chapter "Visual Arts," in *Brahms in Context*, ed. Natasha Loges and Katy Hamilton (Cambridge: Cambridge University Press, 2019), 286–95.

2. "Er steckt voller Tollheiten—als Düsseldorfer Malergenie hat er sich sein Appartement voll der schönsten Fresken in Callots Manier ausgemalt, d.h. lauter Fratzen und Madonnengesichter—." Letter from Julius Otto Grimm to Joseph Joachim, [April] 1854. *Johannes Brahms Briefwechsel*, vols. V and VI: *Johannes Brahms im Briefwechsel mit Joseph Joachim*, ed. Andreas Moser, 2 vols. (Berlin: Deutsche Brahms-Gesellschaft, 1908; repr. Tutzing: Hans Schneider, 1974), V:28. Moser's date has been corrected. See Styra Avins, *Johannes Brahms Life and Letters* (Oxford and New York: Oxford University Press, 1997), 41, footnote 19.

3. E. T. A. Hoffmann, "Jacques Callot," in *Fantasiestücke in Callot's Manier, Blätter aus dem Tagebuche eines reisenden Enthusiasten* (Bamberg: bei E. F. Kunz, 1819), 3–4; in English, see E. T. A. Hoffman, "Jacques Callot," in *E. T. A. Hoffmann's Musical Writings: Kreisleriana, The Poet and the Composer, Music Criticism*, ed. David Charlton, trans. Martyn Clarke (Cambridge: Cambridge University Press, 1989), 76–78.

4. "Hogarth kaufe ja nicht. Schöne Kupferstiche sind ja die Hauptsache ... es ist zu spät, Hogarth jetzt noch erklären zu wollen, wir werden wohl immer mit Lichtenbergs Anfang zufrieden sein müssen. Die Stiche finde ich vielleicht einmal billig und schön, dann will ich sie kaufen." Berthold Litzmann, *Clara Schumann-Johannes Brahms: Briefe aus den Jahren 1853–1896* (Leipzig: Breitkopf & Härtel, 1920), 1:208; in English, see Avins, *Life and Letters*, 159.

5. Some beginning! Georg Christoph Lichtenberg's *Commentaries* are still considered the most important of the various attempts to explain all the details of Hogarth's scenes, and a work of literature in its own right. Brahms would have known the *Ausführliche Erklärung der Hogarthischen Kupferstiche* (Göttingen: Dieterich, 1795). In English, see Georg Christoph Lichtenberg, *Hogarth on High Life: The Marriage à la Mode series from Georg Christoph Lichtenberg's Commentaries* (London: Pallas Athene, 2010).

6. Florence May, *The Life of Johannes Brahms*, 2 Vols., 2nd ed. (London: William Reeves, 1946), 2:478.

7. For details of the excursion see Avins, *Life and Letters*, 103.

8. Brahms's life in Karlsruhe's artist circle is vividly described in Ekkehard Schulz, "Brahms' Karlsruher Freundes-und Bekanntenkreis," in *Johannes Brahms in Baden-Baden und Karlsruhe; Ausstellung der Badische Landesbibliothek Karlsruhe*, ed. Joachim Draheim, Ludwig Finscher, Frithjof Haas, Klaus Häfner, Jeannot Heinen, Brigitte Höft, and Ekkehard Schulz (Karlsruhe: Badische Landesbibliothek, 1983), 35–57.

9. See S. Avins and J. Eisinger, "Sechs unveröffentlichte Briefe von Brahms," *Brahms-Studien* 13 (2002): 33–35. In English, see "Six Unpublished Letters," in *For the Love of Music*, ed. Darwin Scott (Lucca: Lim antiqua, 2002), 105–36.

10. Ulrich Christoffel, *Anselm Feuerbach* (Munich: Bruckmann Verlag, 1944), 60.

11. See Natasha Loges, "Exoticism, Artifice and the Supernatural in the Brahmsian Lied," *Nineteenth Century Music Review* 3/2 (2006): 137–68. The essay is an important exploration of the artistic goals they shared.

12. See May, *Life of Brahms*, 2:478. Brahms's two historical etchings memorialized important historical moments: Daniel Chodowiecki's engraving "Ziethen Seated before His King," the military hero of the Seven Years' War seated before his grateful sovereign, Frederick the Great; and "Der Friedensschluß zu Münster" (The Peace Treaty at Münster), an engraving of the painting by Bartholomeus van der Helst. These etchings are discussed later in this chapter on pp. 54–55.

13. "Anselm weiss sehr oft nicht, was er schreibt, und was er spricht, nicht einmal was er denkt. Er tobt sich aus, wie eine Naturgewalt, die eben trift, wo sie trift… sein Geist und sein Gemüt geht auf in der künstlerischen Empfindung… muß man ihn, wenn man richtig handeln will, nehmen als ein gutes, aber schrecklich ungezogenes Kind, das ungebärdig ist." Henriette Feuerbach to Julius Allgeyer, Heidelberg, 18 March 1866, in Hermann Uhde-Bernays, *Henriette Feuerbach, Ihr Leben in Briefen* (Berlin: Meyer & Jessen, 1912), 253–55.

14. Peter Russel, *Johannes Brahms and Klaus Groth: The Biography of a Friendship* (Aldershot: Ashgate 2006), 69–72.

15. "Ich bitte Sie, ihm ein geneigter wohlmeinender Freund zu bleiben und sich sein Wohl angelegen sein zu lassen, wie Sie es bei Ihrem innerlichen Gleichgewicht und ihrer Sicherheit so wohl vermögen." Henriette Feuerbach to Johannes Brahms, 23 February 1875, Heidelberg, in Uhde-Bernays, *H. Feuerbach Briefen*, 297–98.

16. For more on *Nänie* and its connection to Feuerbach see Nicole Grimes, "The Ennoblement of Mourning: *Nänie* and the Death of Beauty," in *Brahms's Elegies*, Chapter 2.

17. See J. V. Widmann, *Erinnerungen an Johannes Brahms* (Repr. Zurich and Stuttgart: Rotapfel-Verlag, 1980), 94, and *Sizilien und andere Gegenden Italiens* (Frauenfeld: Verlag J. Huger, 1898), 167, 179.

18. Brahms to Joseph Viktor Widmann, 17 December 1894, in *Johannes Brahms Briefwechsel*, vol. VIII: *Johannes Brahms: Briefe an Joseph Viktor Widmann, Ellen*

und Ferdinand Vetter, Adolf Schubring, ed. Max Kalbeck (Berlin: Deutsche Brahms Gesellschaft, 1915; repr. Tutzing: Hans Schneider, 1974), 138.

19. Louis Viardot, "Ut pictora musica," *Gazette des Beaux-Arts* 1 (1859): 19–33.

20. "Symphonies," in John Neubauer, *The Emancipation of Music from Language* (New Haven, CT: Yale University Press, 1986), 199–200.

21. Quoted in Edward Lockspeiser, *Music and Painting: A Study in Comparative Ideas from Turner to Schoenberg* (New York: Harper & Row, 1973), 47.

22. In 1869: "De tout ce que j'ai entendu de moderne, c'est l'oeuvre de ce jeune 'élève de Schumann,' si talentueux, qui me fit la meilleure impression." Jean-Jacques Lévêque, *Henri Fantin-Latour* (Paris: ACR Editions Internationale, 1996), 36. Fantin-Latour's interest in Brahms grew; by 1874 his wife and sister added the Op. 39 waltzes to their repertory. First "Hommage" was painted in 1877.

23. Botstein, "Brahms and Nineteenth-Century Painting," 163. In 1885, Böcklin, residing in Florence until April, moved to Zurich. Brahms was in neither place that year. Botstein is quoting Rolf Andree, *Arnold Böcklin: Die Gemälde* (Basel: Friedrich Reinhardt und Prestel, 1977), who in turn is quoting Adolf Frey, *Arnold Böcklin nach den Erinnerungen seiner Zürcher Freunde* (Stuttgart and Berlin: Cotta, 1912). A likely date is sometime between 22–25 November 1887, when Brahms was in Zurich for a few days and may have visited through the good offices of their mutual friend, the writer Gottfried Keller.

24. Arnold Böcklin and Heinrich Alfred Schmid, *Arnold Böcklin: eine Auswahl der hervorragendsten Werke des Künstlers in Photogravüre* (Munich: Photographische Union, 1899–1901). Brahms received the first edition of the work. See Brahms's letter to Widmann in Johannes Brahms, *Johannes Brahms Briefwechsel*, VIII:138.

25. Wilhelm Engelmann, *Daniel Chodowieckis sämmtliche Kupferstiche* (Leipzig: Verlag von Wilh. Engelmann, 1857). It was this catalogue that was used, in the New York Public Library Print Room, to find the illustrations included in the present essay.

26. "Ich sollte mich schämen einen solchen Schatz zu besitzen—aber ich wünsche doch auch für meine Kunst keinen bessern Liebhaber als ich es hier bin." *Johannes Brahms Briefwechsel*, vol XIII: *Johannes Brahms im Briefwechsel mit Th. Wilhelm Engelmann*, ed. Julius Roentgen (Berlin: Deutsche Brahms Gesellschaft, 1918; repr. Tutzing: Hans Schneider, 1974), 58–60, especially 60.

27. ". . . die innern, philosophischen und dichterischen Kunstgehalt und in Absicht auf die Kentniss des menschlichen Herzens und der Welt, die darin überall so hervorleuchtet." Engelmann, *Chodowieckis Kupferstiche*, 8–9.

28. In addition, Brahms's library contained Chodowiecki's own *Von Berlin nach Danzig. Eine Künstlerfahrt im Jahre 1773* (Berlin: Amsler & Ruthardt, 1883), and a German-language edition of Laurence Sterne, *Tristram Schandy's Leben und Meinungen*, vol. 1 (Hannover: Gebrüdern Hahn, 1810), and vols. 2 and 3 (Leipzig: Salomo Lincke, 1801), with illustrations by Chodowiecki.

29. "Ich wollte versuchen, Dir einiges zu plaudern von Menzel, dem großen Künstler (wohl dem größten unsrer Zeit) und dem prächtigen Menschen. . . . Mir ist ein besonderes Pläsier, daß er der einzige unsrer berühmten Männer ist, der in

den bescheidensten bürgerlichen Verhältnissen lebt. Seine Zimmer sind nicht halb so hoch und groß wie die Deinen, und ein so übereinfaches Atelier hast Du noch nicht gesehen." Brahms to Clara Schumann, *Clara Schumann-Johannes Brahms Briefe*, 2:614.

30. See, for instance, Michael Fried, *Menzel's Realism: Art and Embodiment in Nineteenth-Century Berlin* (New Haven, CT, and London: Yale University Press, 2002), 5; and Karl Scheffler, *Adolph Menzel: Der Mensch, das Werk* (Berlin: Cassirer, 1915), who discusses how Menzel's short stature affected his self-esteem throughout his life.

31. The others being the American Thomas Eakins (1844–1916) and Caspar David Friedrich (1774–1840). For more on this aspect of Menzel's art see Fried, *Menzel's Realism*, in particular Chapter 10, "Time and the Everyday."

32. Quoted in Claude Keisch and Marie Ursula Rieman-Reyer, eds., *Adolph Menzel, 1815–1905: Between Romanticism and Impressionism* (New Haven, CT, and London: Yale University Press in association with the National Gallery of Art, Washington. 1996), 125.

33. "Vor allem war es mir bei diesen Sachen nicht um 'Illustration' zu tun, sondern darum, von den Empfindungen aus, in die uns Dichtung und vor allem Musik zieht, uns blind ziehen, Blicke über den Gefühlskreis zu werfen, und von da aus mitzusehen, weiterzuführen, zu verbinden oder zu ergänzen. Das letze Wort scheint frech. Es ist es aber kaum, da mir für das Gesamte eine Idee zugrunde lag, die wohl im Stimmungsgehalte Ihrer Werke vorhanden war, aber für diesen Fall unausgesprochen blieb." Letter from Klinger to Brahms, December 1893, sent along with the proof sheets and some sketches. Quoted in Karin Mayer-Pasinski, *Max Klingers Brahmsphantasie* (Frankfurt am Main: Rita G. Fisher Verlag, 1981), 20. Translated by Avins and Josef Eisinger.

34. The opening etching of the Brahms-Phantasie, "Accorde," is discussed elsewhere in this volume as Figure 4.3. See Chapters 4 and 14.

35. "Ich sehe die Musik, die schönen Worte dazu—und nun tragen mich ganz unvermerkt Ihre herrlichen Zeichnungen weiter, sie ansehend, ist es, als ob die Musik ins Unendliche weiter töne und Alles aussprüche, was ich gern hätte sagen mögen, deutlicher als die Musik es vermag und dennoch ebenso geheimnißreich und ahnungsvoll. . . . Schließlich aber muss ich denken, alle Kunst ist dieselbe und spricht die gleiche Sprache." Letter written from Vienna, 29 December 1893. *Johannes Brahms an Max Klinger*, ed. Ernst Eggebrecht and Hans Schulz (Leipzig: Private publication, 1924), 5–6. The complete letter is translated in Avins, *Life and Letters*, 710.

36. "Es sind ganz herrliche Blätter, und wie gemacht, alles mögliche Erbärmliche zu vergessen und sich in lichteste Höhen tragen zu lassen . . . mit welcher Lust man immer weiter und tiefer hinein sieht und denkt." Letter written from Vienna, 6 January 1894. *Johannes Brahms Briefwechsel*, VIII:133.

37. The list is compiled from Viktor Miller zu Aichholz and Max Kalbeck, *Ein Brahms-Bilderbuch* (Vienna: R. Lechner, 1905), with details supplied by the present author.

38. Kurt Hofmann, *Die Bibliothek von Johannes Brahms* (Hamburg: Karl Dieter Wagner, 1974), 40.

39. See Brahms's letter to Clara Schumann, 14 August 1855, in Avins, *Life and Letters*, 105.

40. On Brahms and the uncanny or "unheimlich," see Risa Okina, "Brahms and the Uncanny," PhD diss., Temple University (2020); and Edward Venn, "Thomas Adès and the Spectres of Brahms," *Journal of the Royal Musical Association* 140/1 (2015): 163–212.

41. [Editors] For an alternative view of Brahms and the working classes, see Elaine Kelly, *Composing the Canon in the German Democratic Republic: Narratives of Nineteenth Century Music* (Oxford: Oxford University Press, 2014), in particular 56 and 138.

42. An exception here is the *Sistine Madonna*, but it would be difficult to make the case that Brahms's interest in the work was religious, rather than being due to his great appreciation of Renaissance art and the beauty of Raphael's painting. For a selection of writings on the topic of Brahms and religious belief see Heather Platt, *Johannes Brahms: A Research and Information Guide* (New York and London: Taylor and Francis, 2011), 134–35; and Thomas Quigley, *Johannes Brahms: An Annotated Bibliography of the Literature through 1982* (Metuchen, NJ: Scarecrow Press, 1990), 450, and (by the same author) *Johannes Brahms: An Annotated Bibliography of the Literature from 1982 to 1996* (Lanham, MD: Scarecrow Press, 1998), 444. See in particular Daniel Beller-McKenna, *Brahms and the German Spirit* (Cambridge, MA: Harvard University Press, 2004); Jan Brachmann, *Kunst, Religion, Krise: Der Fall Brahms* (Kassel et al: Bärenreiter, 2003); Nicole Grimes, *Brahms's Elegies: The Poetics of Loss in Nineteenth-Century German Culture* (Cambridge: Cambridge University Press, 2019), particularly Chapter 4; R. Allen Lott, *Brahms's A German Requiem: Reconsidering Its Biblical, Historical, and Musical Contexts* (Rochester, NY: University of Rochester Press, 2020); and Hanns Christian Stekel, *Sehnsucht und Distanz: Theologische Aspekte in den wortgebundenen religiösen Kompositionen von Johannes Brahms* (Frankfurt am Main and New York: Peter Lang, 1997).

Chapter 3

1. Adolf Glaßbrenner, *Berlin wie est ist und—trinkt*, 2 vols. (Berlin: Arani, 1987). The present whereabouts of Hecht's gift is unknown. Because the editor of the Brahms-Hecht correspondence consulted closely with Hecht in the making of his edition, we have reason to place credence in his identification of Glassbrenner as the author of the pamphlets and in his report that Hecht had acquired them from an antiquarian. See *Johannes Brahms Briefwechsel* (hereafter *Briefwechsel*), 19 vols. to date (consisting of 16 orig. vols., rev. eds., Berlin, 1912–1922; repr. Tutzing: Hans Schneider, 1974; and a *Neue Folge* consisting of 3 vols. to date, Tutzing: Hans Schneider, 1991-), Vol. 7: *Johannes Brahms im Briefwechsel mit Hermann Levi, Friedrich Gernsheim sowie den Familien Hecht und Fellinger*, ed. Leopold Schmidt (1910), 233n.

2. Mary Lee Townsend, "The Politics of Humor: Adolf Glassbrenner and the Rediscovery of the Prussian *Vormärz* (1815-1848)," *Central European History* 20 (1987): 29-57 (30); Heinz Bulmahn, *Adolf Glassbrenner: His Development from Jungdeutscher to* Vormärzler (Amsterdam: John Benjamins, 1978).

3. "Da kommen Ihre Berliner Hefte als Buch und ehe ich mich der 'heiteren' Lektüre hingebe, muß ich Ihnen dafür allerschönsten Dank sagen. Ob es wohl eine heitere sein wird? Ich bin auch darin verwöhnt, grade jetzt stecke ich zum X^t male mitten im *Tristram Schandy*. Aber an jene jämmerliche Zeit muß man sich zuweilen erinnern, an seine früheste Jugendzeit aber mag man es gern, und wie haben wir s. Z. jene Blätter verschlungen!" Letter of 9 January 1897, in *Briefwechsel* 7:233-34. Brahms owned all three volumes of Sterne's novel in German translation. Unless otherwise noted, the cited volumes in Brahms's library are listed in Kurt Hofmann, *Die Bibliothek von Johannes Brahms: Bücher- und Musikalienverzeichnis* (Hamburg: Karl Dieter Wagner, 1974).

4. Dieter Langewiesche, "Revolution in Germany: Constitutional State–Nation State–Social Reform," in *Europe in 1848: Revolution and Reform*, ed. Dieter Dowe, Heinz-Gerhard Haupt, Dieter Langewiesche, and Jonathan Sperber, trans. David Higgins (New York and Oxford: Berghahn Books, 2001), 120-43 (121).

5. On the deliberations in Frankfurt, see Brian E. Vick, *Defining Germany: The 1848 Frankfurt Parliamentarians and National Identity* (Cambridge, MA, and London: Harvard University Press, 2002). For more succinct accounts, see Mary Fulbrook, *A Concise History of Germany*, 3rd ed. (Cambridge: Cambridge University Press, 2019), 116-22; and James J. Sheehan, *German History 1770-1866* (Oxford: Clarendon Press, 1989), 656-729.

6. Christopher Clark, *Iron Kingdom: The Rise and Fall of Prussia, 1600-1947* (Cambridge, MA: Belknap Press of Harvard University Press, 2006), 468-509.

7. David Blackbourn, *History of Germany 1780-1918: The Long Nineteenth Century*, 2nd ed. (Malden, MA: Blackwell, 2003), 130-31.

8. John Breuilly and Iorwerth Prothero, "The Revolution as Urban Event: Hamburg and Lyon during the Revolutions of 1848-49," in *Europe in 1848*, ed. Dowe et al., 371-98.

9. Katherine Aaslestad, *Place and Politics: Local Identity, Civic Culture, and German Nationalism in North Germany during the Revolutionary Era* (Leiden and Boston: Brill, 2005), 327-28.

10. Richard J. Evans, *Death in Hamburg: Society and Politics in the Cholera Years, 1830-1910* (New York: Penguin, 2005), 4-5.

11. Johannes Brahms, *Des jungen Kreislers Schatzkästlein: Aussprüche von Dichtern, Philosophen und Künstlern*, ed. Carl Krebs (Berlin: Deutsche Brahms-Gesellschaft, 1909); Eng. trans. as *The Brahms Notebooks: The Little Treasure Chest of the Young Kreisler*, trans. Agnes Eisenberger, annotations by Siegmund Levarie (Hillsdale, NY: Pendragon Press, 2003). On this important source, see Reuben Phillips, "Brahms as Reader" (PhD diss., Princeton University, 2019). "Brahms as Reader," 1-128.

12. Ferdinand Freiligrath, *Neuere politische und soziale Gedichte*, vol. 1 (Cologne: Selbstverlag der Verfassers; Düsseldorf: W. H. Scheller, 1849), and Freilingrath, *Neuere politische und soziale Gedichte*, vol. 2 (Düsseldorf: Selbstverlag der Verfassers, 1851).

13. Max Kalbeck, *Johannes Brahms*, rev. ed., 4 vols. in 8 (Berlin: Deutsche Brahms-Gesellschaft, 1915–1921; repr., Tutzing: Hans Schneider, 1976), 1:183.

14. Georg Herwegh, *Gedichte eines Lebendigen*, 9th printing (Stuttgart: G. J. Göschen, 1871).

15. Jost Hermand, "On the History of the 'Deutschlandlied,'" in *Music and German National Identity*, ed. Celia Applegate and Pamela Potter (Chicago and London: University of Chicago Press, 2002), 251–68.

16. [August Heinrich] Hoffmann von Fallersleben, *Mein Leben*, 6 vols. (Hannover: Carl Rümpler, 1868), 5:215, 224. Both visits are discussed briefly in Peter Clive, *Brahms and His World: A Biographical Dictionary* (Latham, MD: Scarecrow Press, 2006), 227.

17. Styra Avins and Josef Eisinger, "Six Unpublished Letters from Johannes Brahms," in *For the Love of Music: Festschrift in Honor of Theodore Front on his 90th Birthday*, ed. Darwin F. Scott (Lucca: Antigua, 2002), 105–36 (115–19).

18. Abigail Green, "Political and Diplomatic Movements, 1850–1870: National Movement, Liberal Movement, Great-Power Struggles, and the Creation of the German Empire," in *Germany 1800–1870*, ed. Jonathan Sperber (Oxford and New York: Oxford University Press, 2004), 69–90 (76–84).

19. Jürgen Habermas, *The Structural Transformation of the Public Sphere: An Inquiry into a Category of Bourgeois Society*, trans. Thomas Burger (Cambridge, MA: MIT Press, 1989).

20. Madeleine Hurd, "Oligarchs, Liberals, and *Mittelstand*: Defining Civil Society in Hamburg, 1858–1862," in *Paradoxes of Civil Society: New Perspectives on Modern Germany and British History*, ed. Frank Trentmann (New York: Berghahn Books, 1999), 283–305 (284). See also Hurd, *Public Spheres, Public Mores, and Democracy: Hamburg and Stockholm, 1870–1914* (Ann Arbor: University of Michigan Press, 2000), 1–92.

21. Hurd, "Oligarchs, Liberals, and *Mittelstand*," 284–85.

22. Ludwig Aegidi, "Erinnerung an und von Emanuel Geibel," *Deutsche Revue über das gesamte nationale Leben der Gegenwart* 23/1 (January–March 1898): 6–24 (13n). These studies do not seem to have been noted previously in modern scholarship on Brahms.

23. Walter Hübbe, *Brahms in Hamburg* (Hamburg: Lütcke & Wulff, 1902), 35; Florence May, *The Life of Brahms*, 2 vols. (London: Edward Arnold, 1905), 1:259.

24. Clark, *Iron Kingdom*, 510–17.

25. Otto von Bismarck, speech to the Prussian Landtag, 30 September 1862 ("Blood and Iron"), quoted in English translation in https://germanhistorydocs.ghi-dc.org/sub_document.cfm?document_id=250 (accessed 20 March 2021).

26. For an excellent concise account, see Blackbourn, *History of Germany*, 184–95.

27. Entry from May 1883 in the diary of Laura von Beckerath, in Kurt Stephenson, *Johannes Brahms und die Familie von Beckerath* (Hamburg: Christians Verlag, 1979), 28: "Erzählung der Möglichkeit, mit Bismarck bei Graf Fleming in Baden zusammengetroffen zu sein, aber aus demokratischen Gründen zu seinem jetzigen Ärger gemieden."

28. Siegfried Kross, *Die Chorwerke von Johannes Brahms* (Berlin and Wunsiedel: Max Hesses, 1958), 153, 160–61; Hans Michael Beuerle, *Untersuchungen zu den A-cappella-Kompositionen: Ein Beitrag zur Geschichte der Chormusik* (Hamburg: K. D. Wagner, 1987).

29. Burkhard Meischein, "Weltliche Chorwerke A Cappella," in *Brahms Handbuch*, ed. Wolfgang Sandberger (Stuttgart and Weimer: J. B. Metzler, 2009), 314–29 (319); Daniel Beller-McKenna, *Brahms and the German Spirit* (Cambridge, MA, and London: Harvard University Press, 2004), 149–51 (150).

30. In addition to the source cited in the previous footnote, see Daniel Beller-McKenna, "The Scope and Significance of the Choral Music," in *The Cambridge Companion to Brahms*, ed. Musgrave, 171–94 (178), and Beller-McKenna, "5 Lieder, for Four-Part Men's Chorus, Opus 41," in *The Compleat Brahms*, ed. Leon Botstein (New York: Norton, 1997), 342–44.

31. Carl Lemcke, *Lieder und Gedichte* (Hamburg: Hoffmann und Campe, 1861). Brahms's copy is dated "Joh. Brahms 1862," as noted in Hofmann, *Die Bibliothek von Johannes Brahms*, 69. On Brahms and Lemcke, see Natasha Lodges, *Brahms and His Poets: A Handbook* (Woodbridge, UK: Boydell Press, 2017), 265–75.

32. Misreading the documentary evidence, Kalbeck assigned "Geleit" to 1862 and asserts that the other three Lemcke settings were probably written "around the same time (1861–2) in Hamburg." See Kalbeck, *Johannes Brahms*, 2:13. No primary source for this piece is preserved. On my revised dating of all four Lemcke settings, see David Brodbeck, *Brahms and German National Sentiment* (tentative title, in progress).

33. "Ich schwing' mein Horn in's Jammerthal," Op. 41, No. 1, by contrast, not only differs from these songs in subject matter, as we shall see; its key, B♭ major, stands at a point of some remove from that which prevails in the Lemcke group.

34. This might be translated as "in the damned bi-, bo-, ba-, in the barracks." I have adapted my translations of the texts used in Op. 41 from those available at the LiederNet Archive (https://www.lieder.net/lieder/get_text.html?TextId=29861), where they are credited to Linda Godry (accessed 20 March 2021).

35. Margit L. McCorkle, *Johannes Brahms: Thematisch-bibliographisches Werkverzeichnis*, published following joint preliminary work with Donald McCorkle (Munich: Henle, 1984), 148.

36. On "Welsche" as a pejorative for the French, see Ute Schneider, "Die Erfindung des Bösen: Der Welsche," in *"Gott mit uns": Nation, Religion und Gewalt im 19. und frühen 20. Jahrhundert*, ed. Gerd Krumeich and Hartmut Lehmann (Göttingen: Vandenhoeck & Ruprecht, 2000), 35–51.

37. A few of these are also noted in Kerstin Schüssler-Bach, "'Einigermaßen zeitgemäß': Brahms' Männerchöre im politischen Kontext der 1860-er Jahre,"

Brahms Studien, vol. 16, ed. Beatrix Borchard and Kerstin Schüssler-Bach (Tutzing: Hans Schneider, 2011), 113-26 (119). "Gebt Acht" expresses generalized liberal-nationalist sentiments but lacks this allusive web.

38. Anna Wierzbicka, *Understanding Culture through Their Key Words: English, Russian, Polish, German, and Japanese* (New York and Oxford: Oxford University Press, 1997), 156-70 (163).

39. James M. Brophy, "The Rhine Crisis of 1840 and German Nationalism: Chauvinism, Skepticism, and Regional Reception," *Journal of Modern History* 85 (March 2013): 1-35. See also Cecilia Hopkins Porter, "The *Rheinlieder* Critics: A Case of Musical Nationalism," *Musical Quarterly* 63 (1977): 74-98.

40. David Brodbeck, *Defining Deutschtum: Political Ideology, German Identity, and Music-Critical Discourse in Liberal Vienna* (New York: Oxford University Pres, 2014), 123-24.

41. For a concise but lucid discussion, Randall Lesaffer, "1864," in *Oxford Public Law International* (https://opil.ouplaw.com/page/545/1864, accessed 6 July 2020). For a more extended treatment, see Mark Hewitson, *Nationalism in Germany, 1848-1866: Revolutionary Nation* (New York: Palgrave Macmillan, 2010), 291-344.

42. Sheehan, *German History 1770-1866*, 682. On the Schleswig-Holstein question from the German liberal point of view in 1848, see Vick, *Defining Germany*, 142-49. Also useful is Steen Bo Frandsen, "Denmark 1848: The Victory of Democracy and the Shattering of the Conglomerate State," in *Europe in 1848*, ed. Dowe et al., 289-311.

43. Peter Russell, *Johannes Brahms and Klaus Groth: The Biography of a Friendship* (Aldershot, Hampshire, and Burlington, VT: Ashgate, 2006), 17-21.

44. Here I rely on Hewitson, *Nationalism in Germany*, 291-344; Green, "Political and Diplomatic Movements," 82-85; Sheehan, *German History 1770-1866*, 890-92; and John Breuilly, "Revolution to Unification," in *Nineteenth-Century Germany: Politics, Culture and Society, 1780-1918*, 2nd ed., ed. John Breuilly (London: Bloomsbury Academic, 2020), 123-42 (129-31).

45. Green, "Political and Diplomatic Movements," 82.

46. On the boom in "patriotic war songs and heroic celebratory rhetoric" occasioned by this historical moment, see Friedhelm Brusniak and Dietmar Klenke, "Sängerfeste und die Musikpolitik der deutschen Nationalbewegung," *Die Musikforschung* 52 (1999): 29-54 (40). The authors do not make mention of Brahms's Op. 41. By contrast, Schüssler-Bach and Kross both seem to sense that Op. 41 is related in some way to events in the Elbe duchies, but because, like McCorkle, they follow Kalbeck in dating the songs to 1861-1862, they are unable to make the case for it. Schüssler-Bach, "'Einigermaßen zeitgemäß,'" 122; and Kross, *Die Chorwerke von Johannes Brahms*, 150-51.

47. Undated letter from Brahms to Josef Gänsbacher from early 1866, quoted in Kalbeck, *Johannes Brahms*, 2:219-20. Letter from Hermann Levi to Brahms of 5 May 1866, in *Briefwechsel*, 7:26-27. Undated letter from Brahms to Julius Allgeyer of May 1866, in Alfred Orel, *Johannes Brahms und Julius Allgeyer: Eine Künstlerfreundschaft in Briefen* (Tutzing: Hans Schneider, 1964), 39, trans. in

Johannes Brahms: Life and Letters, ed. Styra Avins, translations by Josef Eisinger and Styra Avins (Oxford and New York: Oxford University Press, 1997), 34.

48. See Brahms's letters to P. J. Simrock of 6 September 1865 and Breitkopf & Härtel of 16 September, respectively, in *Briefwechsel*, Vol. 9: *Johannes Brahms: Briefe an P. J. Simrock and Fritz Simrock*, ed. Max Kalbeck (1917): 45–46; and *Briefwechsel*, Vol. 14: *Johannes Brahms im Briefwechsel mit Breitkopf & Härtel, Bartolf Senff, J. Rieter-Biedermann, C. F. Peters, E. W. Fritzsch und Robert Lienau*, ed. Wilhelm Altmann (1920): 116–18.

49. "Ein Heft mit 5 Männerchor-Liedern. Durchaus unschwer zu singen, natürlich einigermaßen zeitgemäß." Letter of 18 June 1866, in *Briefwechsel* 9:51–52 (emphasis added).

50. Ludwig Uhland, *Alte hoch- und niederdeutsche Volkslieder mit Abhandlung und Anmerkungen herausgegeben*, 2 vols. (Stuttgart & Tübingen: J. G. Cotta'schen Buchhandlung, 1844–1845), 1:481. Sophie Drinker, *Brahms and His Women's Choruses* (Merion, PA: Sophie Drinker, under the auspices of Musurgia Publishers, A. G. Hess, 1952), 95. May, *Life of Brahms*, 1: 70–82.

51. "Bei Euch ist es den doch wirklich so schlimm, daß man fast hoffen könnte, bald das Erfreulichste erleben zu müssen. Aber die Welt geht langsam vorwärts, einstweilen können wir wohl den Preußen immerhin für den Krakehl danken, ohne das geht's gar nicht vorwärts." Undated letter of August 1866 from Brahms to Gänsbacher, in Alfred Orel, *Johannes Brahms und Julius Allgeyer: Eine Künstlerfreundschaft in Briefen* (Tutzing: Hans Schneider, 1964), 40; translation by Josef Eisinger.

Chapter 4

1. "Für dein *Te Deum* schönsten Dank. Ich bin einstweilen nur darin spaziert, aber mit größtem Interesse und vieler Freude.—Einstweilen stolperte ich noch jedesmal, wenn die Harfe oder die Geigendämpfer kamen! Zeigt sich vielleicht in solchem Fall, daß wir in Gefahr sind, in zwei Sprachen zu reden?" Letter from Brahms to Wüllner, in *Johannes Brahms Briefwechsel*, Vol. XV: *Johannes Brahms im Briefwechsel mit Franz Wüllner*, ed. Ernst Wolff (Berlin: Verlag der deutschen Brahms-Gesellschaft, 1922), 172. See also p. 166, where Wüllner solicits Brahms's feedback on the score of his *Te Deum*, which he planned to send in the coming days. Translations are my own unless otherwise indicated.

2. "Aber warum soll man sie nicht anwenden, wo es—wie in einem *Te Deum*—darauf ankommt, der Klangwirkung nicht bloß möglichsten Glanz, sondern hier und da—in den zarteren Stellen—auch möglichst die Farbe der Verklärung (ich finde keinen anderen Ausdruck) zu geben; z.B. bei dem *Sanctus* der Engel, bei der Erwähnung des heiligen Geistes, des Himmelreiches, der Ewigkeit, usw. Schumann hat im Faust (Ariel, Doktor Marianus) und Du selbst im Deutschen Requiem, (wo die Harfe so wunderschön wirkt) die Anwendung derselben für verwandte Stimmungen nicht verschmäht." Wüllner to Brahms, February 1890, in

Johannes Brahms im Briefwechsel mit Franz Wüllner, 174. Wüllner prefaced this with a confession; the material with harp came from an earlier piece, commissioned by Ludwig II for his wedding in 1867, which was called off. Ludwig had specifically requested harp, and Wüllner saw no reason to leave it out.

3. With thanks to Sophie Hoffmann in the rare books department at Universitäts- und Landesbibliothek Münster for access to this score.

4. For a comprehensive summary of the harp's symbolism, see Hans Joachim Zingel, "Die Harfe als Symbol und allegorisches Attribut," *Die Musikforschung* 19/1 (1957): 39–48.

5. Hans Joachim Zingel, "Die Einführung der Harfe in das romantische Orchester," *Die Musikforschung* 2/2 (1949): 192–204 (194).

6. Jean-Georges Kastner, *Traité général d'instrumentation* (Paris: Prilipp, 1837), 24; and Hans-Werner Küthen, "Ein verlorener Registerklang: Beethovens Imitation der Aeolsharfe," *Musik & Ästhetik* 34 (2005): 83–92 (83).

7. Hugh MacDonald, *Berlioz's Orchestration Treatise: A Translation and Commentary* (New York: Cambridge University Press, 2004), 331.

8. This chapter focuses on Brahms's vocal-orchestral works; however, the imagery of the Aeolian harp on a grave is also taken up in Eduard Mörike's poem "An eine Äolsharfe," set by Brahms in Op. 19, No. 5.

9. Another early symphonic work in the Austro-German tradition with harp is Antonín Dvořák's Symphony No. 3 in E♭ Major, which premiered in 1874. The symphony was known only to a limited circle, which included Brahms, and underwent revisions by Dvořák in the 1880s before its posthumous publication in 1911. César Franck's Symphony in D minor calls for harp and is contemporary with Bruckner's Eighth Symphony and Mahler's First Symphony. The Russian symphonists Balakirev and Rimsky-Korsakov (devotees of Berlioz) used harp, but Tchaikovsky used harp only in his ballets and the *Manfred* Symphony, not in Symphonies Nos. 1–6.

10. Victor Ravizza, "Sinfonische Chorwerke," in *Brahms Handbuch*, ed. Wolfgang Sandberger (Stuttgart: Metzler, 2009), 279–302 (300–1). Schumann wrote that "Ich kann mir keine Idee von dem Zusammenklang dieser beiden Instrument machen." Grimm wrote of the first three that "Mit den drei Harfen und Hornliedern kann ich nicht zur Vernunft kommen, sie wollen mir durchaus nicht eingehn ... aber das Fingalstück ist herrlich." (Quoted in Ravizza). Julius Otto Grimm to Johannes Brahms, August 1860. See *Johannes Brahms Briefwechsel*, vol. IV: *Johannes Brahms im Briefwechsel mit J. O. Grimm*, ed. Richard Barth (Berlin: Deutsche Brahms-Gesellschaft, 1912; repr. Tutzing: Schneider, 1974), 103–4.

11. MacDonald, *Berlioz's Orchestration Treatise*, 73.

12. See chamber works for horn and harp by Frédéric Duvernoy (1765–1838), Martin Pierre Dalvimare (1772–1839), François-Joseph Naderman (1781–1835), Louis François Dauprat (1781–1868), and Nicholas Charles Bochsa (1789–1856).

13. For more on Ossian in music, see: R. Larry Todd, "Mendelssohn's Ossianic Manner, with a New Source—*On Lena's Gloomy Heath*," in *Mendelssohn and*

Schumann: Essays on Their Music and Its Context, ed. Jon W. Finson and R. Larry Todd (Durham, NC: Duke University Press, 1984), especially 145–46 and 153; John Daverio, "Schumann's Ossianic Manner," *19th-Century Music* 21/3 (1998): 247–73, especially 259.

14. For examples of the harp and horn in Ossianic contexts, see Niels Gade's cantata *Comala* (1846), No. 5 *Ballade*; Jean-François Le Sueur's opera *Ossian, ou Les Bardes* (premiered 1804), which calls for 12 harps; and Étienne Méhul's opera *Uthal* (1806), which pairs harp and horn in the overture. According to Richard Heuberger, Brahms was both familiar with and admiring of this opera. Richard Heuberger, *Erinnerungen an Johannes Brahms; Tagebuchnotizen aus den Jahren 1875–1897*, ed. Kurt Hofmann (Tutzing: H. Schneider, 1971), 49.

15. Translations of the Requiem text are from the Authorized King James Version of the Bible.

16. Nicole Grimes, *Brahms's Elegies: The Poetics of Loss in Nineteenth-Century German Culture* (New York: Cambridge University Press, 2019), 95–8.

17. Daniel Beller-McKenna, "Distance and Disembodiment: Harps, Horns, and the Requiem Idea in Schumann and Brahms," *Journal of Musicology* 22/1 (2005): 47–89 (48–49). Beller-McKenna takes John Daverio's "Requiem Idea," based on elegiac works by Brahms and Schumann, as his starting point. See John Daverio, *Crossing Paths: Schubert, Schumann, and Brahms* (New York: Oxford University Press, 2002), 186–90.

18. See the *Schicksalslied*, bars 52–61, and the *Alto Rhapsody*, bars 116ff.

19. "And when he had taken the book, the four beasts and four and twenty elders fell down before the Lamb, having every one of them harps, and golden vials full of odours, which are the prayers of the saints," Revelation 5:8.

20. "... höchst originelle Pizzicati in der Begleitung—ob Brahms dabei an die Harfen der 24 Aeltesten gedacht, die er in der Apokalypse auch gefunden? Sehr gut, daß er die wirkliche Harfe verschmäht hat—sie ist zwar auf Malereien das specifische Engelsinstrument, aber für Kirchenmusik nicht 'hoffähig,' man denkt (wie in Rossini's Messe) bei ihr gleich an den Salon—die Großpriesterin unter den Instrumenten ist und bleibt die Orgel." The review appeared in the *Wiener Zeitung* on December 11, 1872, following a performance at the *Gesellschaft* conducted by Brahms. Markéta Štědronská, ed., *August Wilhelm Ambros Musikaufsätze und - Rezensionen 1872–1876, Historisch-kritische Ausgabe*, Band I (Vienna: Hollitzer Verlag, 2017), 344.

21. Curiously, Berlioz called for harps in his own *Messe solennelle* (1824) and twelve harps in the *Te Deum* (1849), but he reserves them for the final, instrumental movement, "Marche pour la présentation aux drapeaux." Would Berlioz have agreed or disagreed with Ambros on the "acceptability" of harps in church music?

22. This topic is taken up in much of the secondary literature on Brahms. For scholarship that relates to his religion (or lack thereof) and the Requiem, see especially Michael Musgrave, *Brahms: A German Requiem* (Cambridge: Cambridge University Press, 1996); and Daniel Beller-McKenna, *Brahms and the German Spirit* (Cambridge, MA: Harvard University Press, 2004).

23. Nominalization of the verb *verklären*, which means "to heighten (*erhöhen*) something into the unearthly (*Überirdische*) and lend to its appearance an inner glow or radiance." *Duden Online*, https://www.duden.de/rechtschreibung/verklae ren (accessed 17 March 2021).

24. "Und ebenso ist es mit dem geheimnisvollen Strome in den Tiefen des menschlichen Gemütes beschaffen. Die Sprache zählt und nennt und beschreibt seine Verwandlungen in fremden Stoff;—die Tonkunst strömt ihn uns selber vor. Sie greift beherzt in die geheimnisvolle Harfe, schlägt in der dunkeln Welt bestimmte, dunkle Wunderzeichen in bestimmter Folge an,—und die Saiten unsres Herzens erklingen, und wir verstehen ihren Klang." Wilhelm Heinrich Wackenroder and Ludwig Tieck, "Das eigentümliche innere Wesen der Tonkunst und die Seelenlehre der heutigen Instrumental-musik," in *Phantasien über die Kunst*, ed. Wolfgang Nehring (Stuttgart: Reclam, 1973), 77–87 (82–83).

25. Peter Tenhaef links this to the harp's symbolic association with the absolute (and consequently the concept of absolute music) in "Die Harfe und die absolute Musik," *Die Musikforschung* 46/4 (1993): 391–410 (391–94).

26. On intellectual and aesthetic intuition, see Dalia Nassar, *The Romantic Absolute: Being and Knowing in Early German Romantic Philosophy, 1795–1804* (Chicago: University of Chicago Press, 2014), especially 5–7; 223–24.

27. Daverio, *Crossing Paths*, 190.

28. Grimes, *Brahms's Elegies*, 2.

29. Hermann Kretzschmar, for example, describes Beethoven's Symphony No. 5 in terms of the *per aspera ad astra* archetype in *Führer durch den Concertsaal. I. Abtheilung: Sinfonie und Suite* (Leipzig: A. G. Liebeskind, 1887), 88.

30. See James Webster, "The *Alto Rhapsody*: Psychology, Intertextuality, and Brahms's Artistic Development," in *Brahms Studies*, Vol. 3, ed. David Brodbeck (Lincoln: University of Nebraska Press, 2001), 19–45 (24, 25, and 43–44). Table 2.1 on p. 24 contains a list of "Meaningful C minor to C Major Progressions" ranging from Mozart to Brahms, organized by broadly defined thematic categories.

31. Other examples cited by Webster include Brahms's Piano Trio in C minor, Op. 101, and "Auf dem Kirchhofe," Op. 105, No. 4—both of which foreground harp-like arpeggiations in the piano. He finds resonances between the *Alto Rhapsody* and the coda of the Op. 101 finale. See Webster, "The *Alto Rhapsody*," 40–41.

32. Christopher Reynolds, "Brahms Rhapsodizing: The *Alto Rhapsody* and Its Expressive Double," *Journal of Musicology* 29/2 (2012): 191–238 (226).

33. For the critical reception of the ending to *Schicksalslied*, see Grimes, *Brahms's Elegies*, 27–31. For different attempts to reconcile the conflict between *Schicksalslied*'s E♭–C-minor–C-major tonality and form, see John Daverio, "The 'Wechsel der Töne' in Brahms's 'Schicksalslied,'" *Journal of the American Musicological Society* 46/1 (1993): 84–113; Reynolds, "Brahms Rhapsodizing," 191–238.

34. See Grimes, "Brahms's Ascending Circle: Hölderlin and *Schicksalslied*," Chap. 1 in *Brahms's Elegies*, 18–63, especially 52–55.

35. Reynolds, "Brahms Rhapsodizing," 221–22.

Notes

36. Quoted and translated in Grimes, *Brahms's Elegies*, 28. As Grimes observes, though, Hanslick and many others understood the ending as Brahms's reinterpretation of the poem, rather than interpreting the poem within the context of its original novel.

37. For a study of musical monumentality in relation to cultural memory and historiography, see Alexander Rehding, *Music and Monumentality: Commemoration and Wonderment in Nineteenth-Century Germany* (New York: Oxford University Press, 2009).

38. This image is almost identical to one of the pedestal reliefs on the Beethoven-Denkmal in Bonn, in this case identified as a representation of "Phantasie." Ernst Linderoth, ed., *Bonn im Spiegel der Jahrhunderte: eine Sammlung heimatkundlicher Zeitungsartikel* (Bonn: Bonner Heimat- und Geschichtsverein, 1992), 118.

39. See "nēnia" in P. G. W. Glare, ed., *Oxford Latin Dictionary*, 2nd ed. (Oxford: Oxford University Press, 2012), 1287. In eighteenth-century Latin-Greek-German dictionaries, *nenia* is defined as a *Klaglied* (song of lament). For example, Andreas Reyher and Christian Juncker, *Theatrum Latino-Germanico-Graecum sive lexicon linguae latinae* (Leipzig: Klosius, 1712), 1485.

40. For this reading of the poem, see K. F. Hilliard, "'Nänie': Critical Reflections on the Sentimental in Poetry," *Publications of the English Goethe Society* 75/1 (2006): 3–13 (4); Joachim Wohlleben, "Ein Gedicht, ein Satz, ein Gedanke—Schillers 'Nänie,'" in *Wahrnehmungen in Poetischen All. Festchrift für Alfred Behrmann*, ed. Klaus Deterding (Heidelberg: Winter, 1993), 60. Both cited by Grimes, who relates this reading of the poem to Brahms's composition in *Brahms's Elegies*, especially 67–68 and 81–88. See also Eftychia Papanikolaou, "Brahms, Böcklin, and the *Gesang der Parzen*," *Music in Art* 30/1–2 (2005): 154–65 (158–59).

41. For Klinger's association of the figures of Homer and Hölderlin, see Marsha Morton, *Max Klinger and Wilhelmine Culture: On the Threshold of German Modernism* (London: Routledge, 2014), 33.

42. For in-depth studies of the musical and visual symbolism in the *Brahmsphantasie* and its reception, see Karin Mayer-Pasinski, *Max Klingers Brahmsphantasie* (Frankfurt am Main: Rita G. Fischer Verlag, 1982); Ursula Kersten, *Max Klinger und die Musik*, 2 vols. (Frankfurt am Main: Peter Lang, 1993); Thomas K. Nelson, "Klinger's *Brahmsphantasie* and the Cultural Politics of Absolute Music," *Art History* 19/1 (1996): 26–43; Jan Brachmann, "*Ins Ungewisse hinauf*": *Johannes Brahms und Max Klinger im Zwiespalt von Kunst und Kommunikation* (Kassel: Bärenreiter, 1999); Walter Frisch, *German Modernism: Music and the Arts* (Berkeley: University of California Press, 2005), 93–106; and Kevin C. Karnes, "Max Klinger, Gesamtkunstwerk, and the Dream of the Third Kingdom," in *A Kingdom Not of This World: Wagner, the Arts, and Utopian Visions in Fin-de-Siècle Vienna* (New York: Oxford University Press, 2013), 37–65.

43. Letter from Klinger to Brahms, quoted in Karin Mayer-Pasinski, *Max Klingers Brahmsphantasie*, 20.

44. "Aber es sind nicht Illustrationen im gewöhnlichen Sinne, sondern ganz herrliche, wundervolle Fantasien über meine Texte. Ohne weiteres (ohne einige Erklärung) würdest Du aber gewiß öfter den Sinn und den Zusammenhang mit dem Text vermissen." Quoted in Mayer-Pasinski, *Max Klingers Brahmsphantasie*, 22–23. I have taken the liberty of translating "Du" as "one" instead of "you," which gives Brahms a condescending tone, but Schumann had not yet seen the *Brahmsphantasie*.

45. Max Klinger, *Malerei und Zeichnung* (Leipzig: [s.n.], 1891), 22–23.

46. Brachmann's argument is similarly based on Klinger's work as a sociological dialogue with Brahms. See *"Ins Ungewisse hinauf,"* 51ff (also cited in Frisch, *German Modernism*, 97fn30). Brachmann further points to the "elitism" and "exclusive" nature of Klinger's *Brahmsphantasie*, observing that the artist had only 150 exemplars printed, and that each one cost 300 Deutschmarks in 1894, the value of which would have been approximately €3,000 in 2017 at the time Brachmann was writing. See Jan Brachmann, "Form und Sinn des Buches—Betrachtungen zur *Brahms-Phantasie* von Max Klinger," essay for the facsimile edition of *Brahms-Phantasie Op. XII*, published by the Johannes-Brahms-Gesellschaft (Hamburg: Verlag Ellert & Richter, 2017), ix–xxv.

47. Paul Kühn, *Max Klinger* (Leipzig: Breitkopf & Härtel, 1907), 69. With thanks to the editors for bringing this source to my attention.

48. On the complementary nature of these two images, see Mayer-Pasinski, *Max Klingers Brahmsphantasie*, 39–42; Nelson, "Klinger's *Brahmsphantasie*," 35.

49. Paul Kühn believed this to be Brahms's likeness, although Mayer-Pasinski finds the connection tenuous (see p. 36 of *Max Klingers Brahmsphantasie*). Indeed, most ancient portrayals of Dionysus are bewhiskered. Kühn, *Max Klinger*, 207. For Mayer-Pasinski's exegesis of this image, see *Max Klingers Brahmsphantasie*, 29.

50. Mayer-Pasinski, *Max Klingers Brahmsphantasie*, 37–9.

51. Letter from Brahms to Klinger, cited and translated in Frisch, *German Modernism*, 96. For the German, see Mayer-Pasinski, *Max Klingers Brahmsphantasie*, 20.

Chapter 5

1. About Huckleberry, Wayne C. Booth has written: "It is most often a matter of what [Henry] James calls *inconscience*; the narrator is mistaken, or he believes he has qualities which the author denies him . . . the narrator claims to be naturally wicked while the author silently praises his virtue behind his back." Booth, *The Rhetoric of Fiction*, 2nd ed. (Chicago and London: University of California Press, 1983 [1961]), 159. For Greta Olson, Huck provides a clear case of narrator fallibility, as opposed to untrustworthiness; his misperceptions are *"situationally motivated . . . by his age, his superstitions . . . as well as his as yet literal understanding of the shallow moral norms he has been exposed to"* (Olson, "Reconsidering Unreliability: Fallible and Untrustworthy Narrators," *Narrative* 11/1 (2003): 102.

2. Brian Boyd, "Shade and Shape in *Pale Fire*: Debates about *Pale Fire*," *Nabokov Studies* 4 (1997): 173. Nabokovians in the late 1990s generally pitted "Shadeans" against "Kinboteans." Shadeans argued that the (fictional) John Shade composed both his poem and the complete Commentary; Kinboteans believed that Kinbote is the author of both. For the wildest view I've encountered, Boyd holds that Shade inspires Kinbote's Commentary from the grave, that is, in the role of a "shade." libraries.psu.edu/nabokov/boydpf2.htm (accessed 31 March 2021). Though hardly a Nabokov scholar, I venture that what the flesh-and-blood author accomplished in *Pale Fire* is just too brilliant to be accepted in the world of fiction as the work of two completely contradictory characters, with such divergent writing styles. Boyd puts this well: "Poem and commentary interact in a complex interplay of simultaneous and successive ironies. We respond first to the outrageous comedy of the disjuncture between poem and ostensible annotation, which manages to be at once a barbed satire, a harmonious and multifaceted revelation of character, and a resonant moral critique" (Boyd, "Shade and Shape," 180). For more on this and on the literary cottage industry that *Pale Fire* has spawned, see the electronic discussion and information-sharing group *Zembla*. https://libraries.psu.edu/nabokov/contr.htm (accessed 31 March 2021).

3. *Atonement*, the film, was directed by Joe Wright, with screenplay by Christopher Hampton; Working Title Films, 2007.

4. Briony says: "[H]ow can a novelist achieve atonement when, with her absolute power of deciding outcomes, she is also God? . . . No atonement for God or novelists, even if they are atheists. It was always an impossible task, and that was precisely the point. The attempt was all" (Ian McEwan, *Atonement* [New York: Nan A. Talese, Doubleday, 2001], 350–51). James Phelan questions the ethical integrity of both Briony and McEwan; the author's delayed disclosure is analogous to Briony's, and similarly transgressive, in that he has "implicitly misidentified the nature of this narrative up to this point." James Phelan, "Narrative Judgments and the Rhetorical Theory of Narrative: Ian McEwan's *Atonement*," in *A Companion to Narrative Theory*, ed. James Phelan and Peter J. Rabinowitz (Oxford: Blackwell, 2005), 333.

5. Booth's canonized definition of reliability is as follows: "For lack of better terms, I have called a narrator *reliable* when he speaks for or acts in accordance with the norms of the work (which is to say, the implied author's norms), *unreliable* when he does not" (Booth, *The Rhetoric of Fiction*, 158–59). Booth gauged the (un)reliability of a narrative by the degree of ironic "distance" between the "norms" of the implied author and those of the narrator, on such matters as facts, events, and values (154, passim).

6. Janet Schmalfeldt, "From Literary Fiction to Music: Schumann and the Unreliable Narrative," *19th-Century Music* 43/3 (2020): 170–93.

7. Phelan develops the metaphor of an "axis of communication," to propose that both authors and narrators typically make three distinct kinds of communication, with authors communicating to their "authorial audience" (the readers), and narrators addressing their narratees. Each of the three corresponds to one of

the narrator's *three roles*: narrators *report*, they *interpret*, and they *evaluate*. The six types of unreliable narration arise from these roles: narrators might *mis*report or *under*report; *mis*interpret or *under*interpret; and *mis*evaluate or *under*evaluate. (Any one of these six activities usually involves another.) These groups require different activities on the part of the reader. With the "mis-" group, the audience must reject the narrator's words and reconstruct alternatives; with the "under-" group, the reader must supplement the narrator's view. See James Phelan, *Living to Tell about It: A Rhetoric and Ethics of Character Narration* (Ithaca, NY, and London: Cornell University Press, 2005), 18–20, passim.

8. Dorrit Cohn's term "discordant narration" covers several of the narrator-types I mention. See Cohn, "Discordant Narration," *Style* 34/1 (2000): 307–16.

9. I am indebted to Eric Elder, candidate at the time of this writing for the degree of PhD in musicology (music theory and analysis) at Brandeis University, for the engraving of this and all other music examples in my article.

10. Dillon Parmer, "Brahms and the Poetic Motto: A Hermeneutic Aid?," *Journal of Musicology* 15/3 (1997): 380–81.

11. Parmer, "Brahms and the Poetic Motto," 384.

12. For later fiction with two unreliable narrators or characters, two examples come to mind: Emily Brontë's *Wuthering Heights* (Mr. Lockwood and Nelly Dean) and Henry James's "The Liar" (Colonel Capadose and Oliver Lyon, the third-person teller of the story—note that his name gives the clue).

13. Paul Mies, "Herders Edward-Ballade bei Joh. Brahms," *Zeitschrift für Musikwissenschaft* 2 (1919–1920): 225–32.

14. From Michael Musgrave: "The pattern of question and answer can be traced throughout, culminating in Edward's final statement: 'The curse of heaven shall ye for me bear.' However, Brahms contrives to produce a rounded A B A form from the successive stanzas by evolving a central, development section from the figure of the second reply, its growing intensity reflecting the *mother's anguished questioning*, the tragic revelation of the *true victim, the father*, reflected in the quiet closing reprise of the opening." Musgrave, *The Music of Brahms* (Oxford: Clarendon Press, 1985), 24, my emphasis.

15. From Walter Frisch, speaking about Brahms's titles for his piano works in general, including the Ballades, Op. 10: "in the nineteenth century titles like those employed by Brahms had lost the more specific or generic associations they had carried in earlier periods. As such, it is probably a mistake for a listener or critic to attach too much meaning to Brahms's titles beyond a general indication of *Stimmung* or mood." Walter Frisch, "Brahms: From Classical to Modern," in *Nineteenth-Century Piano Music*, ed. R. Larry Todd (New York: Schirmer Books, 1990), 336.

16. From James Parakilas: "Instead of making up a new program for Brahms, it would be reasonable to conclude that since the sensational revelation at the end of the poem is an inescapable part of the poem's narrative structure, Brahms, in ending his Ballade as he did, was not taking the poem primarily as a narrative, or programmatic model." Parakilas, *Ballads without Words: Chopin and the*

Tradition of the Instrumental Ballade (Portland, OR: Amadeus Press, 1992), 142. Parakilas later offers a finely nuanced interpretation of Brahms's Ballade, which I discuss below.

17. Charise Hastings, "From Poem to Performance: Brahms's 'Edward' Ballade, Op. 10, No. 1," *College Music Symposium* 48 (2008): 83–97.

18. Max Kalbeck, *Johannes Brahms, 1833–1862* (Vienna and Leipzig: Wiener Verlag, 1904), 197; Mies, "Herders Edward-Ballade," 226.

19. Günther Wagner, *Die Klavierballade um die Mitte des 19. Jahrhunderts* (München: Katzbichler), 78; Parmer, "Brahms and the Poetic Motto," 386; Hastings, "From Poem to Performance," 86.

20. Hastings, "From Poem to Performance," 89, 88.

21. For example, see Roger Fiske, "Brahms and Scotland," *Musical Times* 109 (1968): 1106–7 and 1109–11.

22. From Hastings: "Although the positive direction of the Allegro is illusory, I try to communicate as much conviction as possible by picturing Edward, seething with passion, creeping toward his unsuspecting father with blade bared" ("From Poem to Performance," 91).

23. Loewe scores his Ballade for only one voice; this presumably calls upon the singer to alternate vocal characters for the mother and the son. The first of Schubert's three lesser known 1827 strophic duets, for male and female, was not published until 1862; the other two versions did not appear until 1895.

24. Parakilas, *Ballads without Words*, 142–43.

25. James Wood, *How Fiction Works* (New York: Picador; Farrar, Straus and Giroux, 2008), 5; my emphasis.

26. As a reader's technique for detecting literary unreliability, the colloquial "reading between the lines" is Seymour Chatman's expression, in Chatman, *Story and Discourse: Narrative Structure in Fiction and Film* (Ithaca, NY: Cornell University Press, 1978).

27. Jean-Jacques Nattiez, "Can One Speak of Narrativity in Music?" *Journal of the Royal Musicological Association* 115/2 (1990): 240–57.

28. Byron Almén, *A Theory of Musical Narrative* (Bloomington: Indiana University Press, 2008). Northrop Frye, *Anatomy of Criticism: Four Essays* (Princeton, NJ: Princeton University Press, 1957); James Jacób Liszka, *The Semiotic of Myth: A Critical Study of the Symbol* (Bloomington: Indiana University Press, 1989); Eero Tarasti, *A Theory of Musical Semiotics* (Bloomington: Indiana University Press, 1994); Robert Hatten, *Musical Meaning in Beethoven: Markedness, Correlation, and Interpretation* (Bloomington: Indiana University Press, 1994); and Vera Micznik, "Music and Narrative Revisited: Degrees of Narrativity in Beethoven and Mahler," *Journal of the Royal Musical Association* 126/2 (2001): 193–249. For reviews of Almén's study, see Arnold Whittall, *Music and Letters* 91/2 (2010): 299–303; and David Bretherton, *Music Analysis* 31/3 (2012): 414–21.

29. Seth Monahan, "Action and Agency Revisited," *Journal of Music Theory* 57/2 (2013): 321–71.

30. Michael L. Klein and Nicholas Reyland, eds., *Music and Narrative since 1900* (Bloomington: Indiana University Press, 2013).

31. William Horne, "Brahms's Op. 10 Ballades and His *Blätter aus dem Tagebuch eines Musikers*," *Journal of Musicology* 15/1 (1997): 98–115; see especially 99 (on Marxsen) and 103–9.

32. Horne speculates that Brahms's title may also have been influenced by Robert Schumann's unpublished Ballade cycle, Vom Pagen und der Königstochter, which Clara may have played privately from a manuscript for him and other friends in the spring of 1854; Horne draws attention to several similarities between the two collections.

33. See Johannes Brahms, *The Brahms Notebooks: The Little Treasure Chest of the Young Kreisler*, ed. Carl Krebs, trans. Agnes Eisenberger (Hillsdale, NY: Pendragon Press, 2003). Brahms's title pays tribute to E. T. A. Hoffmann's wild and crazy Capellmeister Johannes Kreisler, the eponymous character of his *Kreisleriana* collection of 1813. The quotations in translation from Sophocles are as follows: No. 28, "A state has ceased to exist when it becomes the property of one individual" (15); and No. 219, "Even if you reach far and wide, you will not recognize divinity if it does not reveal itself directly to you" (109).

34. Michael Musgrave, *A Brahms Reader* (New Haven, CT, and London: Yale University Press, 2000), 24.

35. Here is the entry in the inventory of Brahms's library: "Sophokles. Tragödien von Friedrich Wilhelm Georg Stäger. Urschrift und Uebersetzung. (Zwei Bände in einem.). Halle, 1841, 1842. Verlag von Richard Mühlmann. 379, 417, S. Hldr. Auf dem Vorsatzblatt: 'Dem theuren Johannes als freudigen Gruss beim Wiedersehen Clara Sch.(umann) July 55.'" Kurt Hofmann, *Die Bibliothek von Johannes Brahms* (Hamburg: Verlag der Musikalienhandlung Wagner, 1974), 108. I am grateful to Reuben Phillips for supplying me with details of the Hofmann publication.

36. I thank Nicole Grimes for this information. In the Wendt translation, *Ödipus*, Zweites Epeisodias, p. 295, line 822, she observes the question mark at the end of this line and notes that Brahms crossed it out, as follows: "Der Mann, der ihn erschlagen! War ich Frevlor den?" The following translation has been suggested: "The man who killed him; was I the sinner/provocateur [Frevlor], or villain [Frevler], then?" Whatever Brahms's small revision means, it suggests that he sustained a long-standing interest in the actions and the character of Oedipus.

37. Florence May, *The Life of Johannes Brahms*, Vol. 1 (London: Edward Arnold, 1905), 164.

38. May, *The Life of Johannes Brahms*, 1:165.

39. "Dem innig verehrten Johannes Brahms in dankbarer Erinnerung der herrlichen Zauberklänge seiner Balladen von Clara Schumann. Hamburg, d. 8. Nov. 1854." Hofmann, *Die Bibliothek von Johannes Brahms*, 115.

40. Horne, "Brahms's Op. 10 Ballades," 114.

41. From Eduard Hanslick, the first publisher of Schumann's letters from Endenich, "Robert Schumann in Endenich (1899)," trans. Susan Gillespie, in *Schumann and His World*, ed. R. Larry Todd (Princeton, NJ: Princeton University

Press, 1994), 277. Schumann's last observation is particularly insightful. The head motive of the Fourth Ballade, in B major, introduces the incomplete neighbor motion D♮-to-D♯, thus anticipating the tension between B minor and B major throughout the movement. For the German original see Kalbeck, *Johannes Brahms, 1833–1862*, 195.

42. From Malcolm MacDonald: "Perhaps we would transgress the bounds of propriety to speculate why Brahms should have chosen, in the aftermath of Schumann's tragedy, to evoke this tale of the son who has slain his father at the mother's behest: but one suspects that the symbolism must have held a strong significance for him." Malcolm MacDonald, *Brahms* (Oxford: Oxford University Press, 1990), 86.

Chapter 6

1. The collection is published as *Deutsche Volkslieder Mit Clavier-Begleitung von Johannes Brahms* (Berlin: N. Simrock, 1894) in seven books of seven songs each. Songs 42–49 consist of arrangements for soloist and chorus with piano accompaniment.

2. Franz Magnus Böhme, *Deutscher Liederhort, Auswahl der vorzüglicheren Deutschen Volkslieder, nach Wort und Weise aus der Vorzeit und Gegenwart. Gesammelt und erläutert von Ludwig Erk. Im Auftrage und mit Unterstützung der Königlich Preußischen Regierung nach Erk's handschriftlichem Nachlasse und auf Grund eigener Sammlung neubearbeitet und fortgesetzt von Franz M. Böhme* (Leipzig: Breitkopf und Härtel, 1893–1894), 1–3.

3. See Imogen Fellinger, "Brahms' beabsichtigte Streitschrift gegen Erk-Böhmes 'Deutscher Liederhort,'" in *Brahms-Kongress Wien 1983*, ed. Susanne Antonicek and Otto Biba (Tutzing: Hans Schneider, 1988); and Styra Avins, ed. *Johannes Brahms: Life and Letters*, trans. Josef Eisinger and Styra Avins (New York: Oxford University Press, 1997).

4. Avins, *Johannes Brahms: Life and Letters*, 714–15.

5. Avins, *Johannes Brahms*, 715. As Virginia Hancock shows, Brahms received a hand-copied transcription of Forster's *Frische teutsche Liedlein* as a gift following the German Requiem premiere in 1869. Before then, he may have accessed these pieces from Gustav Nottebohm or copies in the Vienna City Library. See Virginia Hancock, "Brahms's Links with German Renaissance Music: A Discussion of Selected Choral Works," in *Brahms 2: Biographical, Documentary, and Analytical Studies*, ed. Michael Musgrave (Cambridge: Cambridge University Press, 1987), 101ff.

6. Two studies indicate the breadth of this topic. George Bozarth investigates the original sources for the text and melody in Brahms's song "In stiller Nacht," WoO 33, No. 42. Hancock describes Brahms's combination of archaic texts with modern melodic treatment in Op. 22. See George Bozarth, "The Origin of Brahms's

In Stiller Nacht," Notes 53/2 (1996): 363–80; and Hancock, "Brahms's Links with German Renaissance Music."

7. Fellinger, "Brahms's beabsichtigte *Streitschrift*" describes many of Brahms's markings in Böhme's 1877 *Liederbuch*.

8. I use the term "courtly love" to describe themes such as chivalry and loyalty that are found in Medieval German lyrics, and which might be understood to derive from twelfth-century Provençal poetry. See Roger Boase, *The Origin and Meaning of Courtly Love: A Critical Study of European Scholarship* (Manchester: Manchester University Press, 1977). Albrecht Classen further describes the significance of sixteenth-century German songbooks in preserving popular poetry on a range of concepts, including courtly love themes. See Albrecht Classen, "Tradition and Innovation in 15th and 16th Century Popular Song Poetry: From Oswald von Wolkenstein to Georg Forster," in *Fifteenth-Century Studies* 37, ed. Barbara I. Gusick and Matthew Z. Heintzelman (Rochester, NY: Camden House, 2012), 1–16.

9. This new pairing of texts and melodies resembles contrafacta. Brahms's underlined passages in *Die historischen Volkslieder der Deutschen vom 13. bis 16. Jahrhundert: gesammelt und erläutert von R.v. Liliencron* (Leipzig: Vogel, 1869), held by the Gesellschaft der Musikfreunde (A-Wgm 2952/203B), suggest his interest in sixteenth-century compositions that recombine texts and melodies from existing sources. Brahms's "Zwei Gesänge" Op. 91 offer another instance of his expressive recomposition of the hymn tune "Josef, lieber Josef mein." See Daniel Beller-McKenna, *Brahms and the German Spirit* (Cambridge, MA: Harvard University Press, 2004), 18–30.

10. Staatsbibliothek zu Berlin—Preußischer Kulturbesitz Digital: https://digital.staatsbibliothek-berlin.de/werkansicht/?PPN=PPN751839663 (accessed 28 December 2020).

11. Eusebius Mandyczewski, ed., *28 Deutsche Volkslieder* (Leipzig: Breitkopf und Härtel, 1926). Brahms's *16 Deutsche Volkslieder* (WoO posthum. 37) and *12 Deutsche Volkslieder* (WoO posthum. 35) also contain a setting of "Ach Gott" for three female voices and an SATB a cappella setting, respectively. These arrangements adapt the melody and harmonization in WoO 32, No. 16. See Heather Platt, "Brahms's Laboratory: Probing the Limits of Competing Tonal Centers." Paper presented at the Nineteenth Century Music International Conference, Toronto, 2014. For more on Brahms's earlier versions of songs in WoO 33, see Michael Musgrave, "Die '49 Deutschen Volkslieder' für eine Singstimme (Chor) und Klavierbegleitung WoO33 und ihre früheren Fassungen," in *Spätphase(n)?: Johannes Brahms' Werke der 1880er und 1890er Jahre Internationales musikwissenschaftliches Symposium Meiningen 2008*, ed. Maren Goltz and Wolfgang Sandberger and Christiane Wiesenfeldt (Munich: Henle, 2010).

12. The song is published in the *Deutsche Lieder aus alter und neuer Zeit: gesammelt und mit Clavierbegleitung versehen von F .W. Arnold* (Elberfeld: F. W. Arnold, ca. 1860–1870), Vol. 7, no. 1. Brahms's markings throughout his personal copy of this collection (A-Wgm, VI 36734) indicate that he studied all nine volumes closely. George Bozarth surmises that "[j]udging from the publisher's numbers and

from references in nineteenth-century bibliographies, volumes in Arnold's collection began to appear in the early 1860s and continued to be issued until about 1870." Werner Morik claims 1864 as the publication date. See Bozarth, "The Origin of Brahms's *In Stiller Nacht*," 372, and Werner Morik, *Johannes Brahms und sein Verhältnis zum Deutschen Volkslied* (Tutzing: Hans Schneider, 1965).

13. Böhme's unscholarly tendencies are discussed in Nils Grosch, "The Old German Folksongs: Tracing a Philological Fake," *Muzikološki zbornik* 49/2 (2013): 23–32.

14. Brahms's characteristic "NB" marking appears throughout the books in his library as evidence that he cross-checked sources. Annotations in Brahms's copy of Forster's *Frische Liedlein* (titled *Ein ausbund schöner Teutscher Liedlein* in his copy held by the *Gesellschaft der Musikfreunde*) indicate that he cross-checked Othmayr's lied and corrected the first pitch of Othmayr's melody in Böhme's *Liederbuch* (1877) from C_3 to C_4 (see Figure 6.2). Brahms also corrected the first pitch in Othmayr's melody (changing E_4 to C_5) in his copy of Böhme's *Liederhort* (1893–1894).

15. Carl Groos and Bernhard Klein, *Deutsche Lieder für Jung und Alt* (Berlin: Realschulbuchhandlung, 1818). *Bayerische Staatsbibliothek* digital: mdz-nbn-resolving.de/urn:nbn:de:bvb:12-bsb10113951-8 (accessed 28 September 2020).

16. The composer of the melody in Groos-Klein remains unnamed. See Lisa Feurzeig, ed. *Deutsche Lieder für Jung und Alt* (Middleton, WI: A-R Editions, 2012).

17. Böhme's entries from 1877 and 1893–1894 merely summarize all existing stanzas.

18. I'm grateful to Harald and Sharon Krebs and Katharina Uhde for their guidance with poetic translations.

19. Contrary to the title "new Lied" in song printings of the late Middle Ages, these songs were often modifications of previously established texts and melodies. The four-stanza *Liedflugschrift* text might therefore reflect an adaptation of Othmayr's five-stanza poem. See Walter Salmen, "Das gemachte 'Neue Lied' im Spätmittelalter," in *Handbuch des Volksliedes: Historisches und systematisches. Interethnische Beziehungen, Musikethnologie*, ed. Rolf Wilhelm Brednich, Lutz Röhrich, and Wolfgang Suppan, 2 vols. (Munich: W. Fink, 1973–1975), 407–20.

20. Brahms chose the verb "erwehren" ("to renounce") in stanza 5, line 1.

21. The important role of sixteenth-century songbooks and pamphlets in preserving and disseminating melodies and texts is discussed in Grosch, *Lied und Medienwechsel im 16. Jahrhundert*.

22. Othmayr may have added this stanza to a pre-existing text. According to a study of the Heidelberg Liedmeister, "it seems . . . that one may well regard the composers of Forster's generation in general as arranger-editors of the text. Indeed, *they mainly use extant texts that they change or parody for their purposes* [emphasis added]." See Carl Phillipp Reinhardt, *Die Heidelberger Liedmeister des 16. Jahrhunderts* (Kassel: Bärenreiter, 1939), 58.

23. Böhme encloses stanza 4 in brackets to show its omission from these sources.

24. In his copy of Uhland's *Alte hoch- und niederdeutsche Volkslieder* held at the Gesellschaft der Musikfreunde, Brahms underlines "erwegen" (stanza 4) and writes "begeben" in the margin, as if he was deciphering these verbs.

25. This interpretation of F♯–G as $\hat{7}$–$\hat{8}$ in G major permits a harmonization that begins and ends in different keys. This phenomenon, called "directional tonality," occurs in works by Schubert and Schumann. See Harald Krebs, "Third Relation and Dominant in Late 18th- and Early 19th-Century Music," PhD diss., Yale University, 1980; and Benjamin K. Wadsworth, "Directional Tonality in Schumann's Early Works," *Music Theory Online* 18/4 (2012).

26. Zuccalmaglio often altered melodies in a manner described as "romantic coloration." See Walter Wiora, *Die rheinischbergischen Melodien bei Zuccalmalgio und Brahms: Alte Liedweisen in romantischer Färbung* (Bad Godesberg: Voggenreiter, 1953), 109.

27. Max Friedländer's song "Wie Weh thut Scheiden," No. 90 from the *Hundert Deutsche Volkslieder für eine Singstimme mit Begleitung des Klaviers* (Leipzig: Peters, 1886), also musically resembles Brahms's 1858 setting. Friedländer's song pairs the E-minor melody from KrZucc with the *Wunderhorn* text.

28. As with Platt's reading of "Gunhilde," WoO 32, No. 10, in E Aeolian (without raised leading tone), the melody in KrZucc also expresses this mode. See Platt, "Brahms's Laboratory."

29. Platt compares types of "tonal pairing" between E minor and G major that are evident in Brahms's earlier and later settings of "Gunhilde," "Du, mein einzig Licht," "Es ritt ein Ritter," and "Ach Gott, wie Weh thut Scheiden" from WoO posthum. 32, 35, and 37, as well as in WoO 33. See Platt, "Brahms's Laboratory."

30. Historically this semitone is associated with lamentation. See Carl Schachter, "The Prelude in E Minor, Op. 28, No. 4: Autograph Sources and Interpretation," in *Chopin Studies 2*, ed. John Rink and Jim Samson (Cambridge: Cambridge University Press, 1994).

31. This is because D♯ remains absent until the authentic cadence ending the song (bar 9). Platt cites a similar situation in Brahms's "Gunhilde," WoO 32, No. 10.

32. Similar, meaningful oppositions between ♯$\hat{5}$ and ♭$\hat{6}$ occur in Schubert's songs. See Steven G. Laitz, "The Submediant Complex: Its Musical and Poetic Roles in Schubert's Songs," *Theory and Practice* 21 (1996): 123–65.

33. Tappert's *12 alte deutsche Lieder* appears under "Ubersicht neu erschienener Musikwerke" in vol. 32 of the *Leipziger Allgemeine musikalischer Zeitung* (7 August 1867).

34. Yet for some melodies, Tappert cites Becker along with relevant archaic sources.

35. A review of Tappert's *12 alte deutsche Lieder* in the *Neue Zeitschrift für Musik* further claimed that Tappert altered the rhythm of melodies too severely in his settings: "Die altdeutschen Lieder erscheinen etwas zu frei bearbeitet, was die oft wesentlichen rhythmischen Aenderungen betrifft, welche sich Tappert mit den in ursprünglicher Gestalt beigefügten, überwiegend recht charakteristischen Originalweisen gestattet hat. Aus wenigstens erschienen

dieselben fast durchgängig nicht als Verbesserung, sondern als abschwächende Modernisierung." "Kammer und Hausmusik: Lieder für eine Singstimme mit Begleitung des Pianoforte," H . . . . n [pseudonym], *Neue Zeitschrift für Musik* 64/ 18 (24 April 1868): 153–54.

36. In contrast with this chromaticism, which necessitates a change in melodic direction, Rhau's Dorian melody (Böhme's entry no. 450b) contains a stepwise ascent to F_5 at the corresponding location. Incidentally, Tappert set Rhau's melody (transposed to F minor and supplied with chromatic alterations) as song no. 10 in the *12 alte deutsche Lieder* with a new poem and title: "Wer unter eines Mädchens Hand."

37. Figure 6.12 shows Brahms's correction of the upbeat C_3 to F_3, of C_4 to $B\flat_4$ (bar 3) and of E_4 to G_4 (bar 12) as in Othmayr's tenor part. Brahms also underlines Böhme's incorrect source attribution for the melody: a five-voice lied by Jobst vom Brandt from Vol. 5 of Forster's *Liedlein* (1556).

38. Becker cites Forster's *Liedlein* as the source for the G-major melody, supporting this hypothesis that he transposed Othmayr's melody. But another relevant source must be mentioned: the *Christliche Reuter Lieder* by Philippen zu Winnenberg (Strasburg: Jobin, 1586). A G-Mixolydian melody in this collection (No. VI, p. 32) resembles Becker's tune almost exactly. Although this source is cited atop entry no. 450a in Böhme's *Liederhort*, it is not explained further.

39. *12 alte deutsche Lieder für eine Singstimme mit Begleitung des Pianoforte frei bearbeitet von Wilhelm Tappert* (Berlin: Simrock, ca. 1867), Gesellschaft der Musikfreunde A-Wgm VI 36090. Brahms also notates "CB" (Becker's initials) near this alteration.

40. Brahms's penciled eighth notes (Figure 6.11, second system) correspond to Othmayr's melody.

41. *Staatsbibliothek zu Berlin—Preußischer Kulturbesitz Digital*: https://digital.staatsbibliothek-berlin.de/werkansicht/?PPN=PPN780034112 (accessed 28 December 2020). A comparison of the *Liedflugschrift* and Becker's poem (see No. 4 in the appendix to this chapter) shows this evolution. The text in Rhau's *Bicinia Germanica* resembles the *Liedflugschrift* but omits stanza 4.

42. Tappert joins lines 1–4 of stanza 2 with lines 5–8 of stanza 3, excising eight lines from the poem.

43. The term *Reprisenbar* originates with Alfred Lorenz in *Das Geheimnis der Form bei Richard Wagner* (Berlin: Hesse, 1924–1933). William Rothstein further analyzes Wagner's use of extended *Reprisenbar* forms in *Phrase Rhythm in Tonal Music* (New York: Schirmer, 1989). Becker's *Reprisenbar* form melody offers a rare modulation to the subdominant. See Morik, *Johannes Brahms und sein Verhältnis zum Deutschen Volkslied*, 70–71.

44. Megan Kaes Long examines dramatic, phrase-structural, and tonal implications of Italian, German, and English texts on other sixteenth-century forms, such as the canzonetta and balletto. See Megan Kaes Long, *Hearing Homophony: Tonal Expectation at the Turn of the Seventeenth Century* (New York: Oxford University Press, 2020).

45. Bar 11 (downbeat) recalls two previous neighboring ⁴₂ chords (see bars 2 and 6, asterisked in Figure 6.14).

46. This variation consists of "composing out" IV and ii chords (bars 5–6) to replace a tonic prolongation (compare bars 1–2).

47. Berry and Schmalfeldt discuss Brahms's recompositions and allusions to songs by other composers. Examples include "Es liebt sich so lieblich im Lenze," Op. 71, No. 1, and "Dämmrung senkte sich von oben," Op. 59, No. 1 (see Paul Berry, *Brahms among Friends: Listening, Performance, and the Rhetoric of Allusion* [New York: Oxford University Press, 2014], Chapter 2 and page 9 respectively); and "Meine liebe ist grün," Op. 63, No. 5 (see Janet Schmalfeldt, "Brahms, again the 'Master of Allusion,' with his Godson in Mind," *Ars Lyrica* 21 [2012]: 115–54).

48. "Ich selbst denke noch über den Titel nach. Deutsche Volkslieder oder Alte deutsche Lieder. Mit Klavier- oder Pianoforte-begleitung?" *Johannes Brahms Briefwechsel*, Vols. XI and XII: *Johannes Brahms Briefe an Fritz Simrock*, ed. Max Kalbeck, 2 vols. (Berlin: Deutsche Brahms-Gesellschaft, 1919; repr. Tutzing: Hans Schneider, 1974), 2:127.

49. "'Alte deutsche L.' haben Sie selbst schon herausgegeben (Tappert). Mit und ohne Variation ist das schon oft gesagt, und so bleibt wohl nur das einfache: Deutsche Volkslieder. (Punkt.) Mit Klavierbegleitung von J.B." Kalbeck, ed., *Johannes Brahms Briefe an Fritz Simrock*, 2:128.

50. "Songs are sailing such an erroneous course nowadays that one cannot impress the ideal too sharply on oneself. And that's what folk-song is for me." Avins, *Johannes Brahms*, 212.

Chapter 7

1. "Sie sind recht zum langsamen Aufsaugen in der Stille und Einsamkeit, nicht nur zum Nach-, sondern auch zum Vordenken und ich glaube Sie recht zu verstehen, wenn ich meine, dass Sie derartiges mit dem 'Intermezzo' haben andeuten wollen. 'Zwischenstücke' haben Voraussetzungen und Folgen, die in diesem Falle ein jeder Spieler und Hörer sich selbst zu machen hat." *Johannes Brahms Briefwechsel*, vol. XVI: *Johannes Brahms im Briefwechsel mit Philipp Spitta*, ed. Carl Krebs (Berlin: Deutsche Brahms-Gesellschaft, 1920; repr., Tutzing: Hans Schneider, 1971), 95–96. All translations are my own unless otherwise noted.

2. Nicole Grimes, *Brahms's Elegies: The Poetics of Loss in Nineteenth-Century German Culture* (Cambridge: Cambridge University Press, 2019), 18–63.

3. "Nun wünsche ich nur, dass unsere Virtuosen sie nicht in den Conzertsaal zerren. Ballade, Romanze, Rhapsodie meinetwegen; aber die Intermezzi? Mit welch dummem Gesicht wird das Publicum dasitzen." *Briefwechsel Brahms-Spitta*, 96.

4. Steven Rings points out that "Brahms only once performed any of the late piano pieces in a semiformal concert: at the Tonkünstlerverein on 31 October 1893. All other known performances were in the homes of friends (at the Fellingers' in Vienna and the Villa of Miller zu Aichholz in Gmunden)." Steven Rings, "The

Learned Self: Artifice in Brahms's Late Intermezzi," in *Expressive Intersections in Brahms: Essays in Analysis and Meaning*, ed. Heather Platt and Peter H. Smith (Bloomington: Indiana University Press, 2012), 48.

5. Op. 118, No. 6, was performed on 8 February 1894 in a public concert in which "[a]s a change of pace between overtly virtuosic works for both instruments, Brüll had presented the Vienna premiere of the E♭-minor Intermezzo and just three more of Brahms's latest piano pieces (the Romanze and Ballade from Op. 118 and the Rhapsody from Op. 119)." Paul Berry, *Brahms among Friends: Listening, Performance, and the Rhetoric of Allusion* (New York: Oxford University Press, 2014), 333.

6. Quoted in Rings, "The Learned Self," 25 and 30.

7. Katrin Eich, "Where Was the Home of Brahms's Piano Works?," in *Brahms in the Home and the Concert Hall: Between Private and Public Performance*, ed. Katy Hamilton and Natasha Loges (Cambridge: Cambridge University Press, 2014), 102.

8. Allen Cadwallader, "Foreground Motivic Ambiguity: Its Clarification at Middleground Levels in Selected Late Piano Pieces of Johannes Brahms," *Music Analysis* 7/1 (1988): 59–91.

9. Edward T. Cone, "Three Ways of Reading a Detective Story—Or a Brahms Intermezzo," *Georgia Review* 31/3 (1977): 554–74.

10. Peter H. Smith, "You Reap What You Sow: Some Instances of Rhythmic and Harmonic Ambiguity in Brahms," *Music Theory Spectrum* 28/1 (2006): 57–97 (59).

11. I borrow this term from Walter Kaufmann's translation of "ewige Wiederkunft" as "eternal recurrence." In *The Gay Science* (as well as in several other works), Nietzsche asks the reader to imagine that each life cycle might recur eternally. Friedrich Nietzsche, *The Gay Science*, trans. Walter Kaufmann (New York; Toronto: Random House, 1974), 273.

12. John T. Hamilton, *Music, Madness, and the Unworking of Language* (New York: Columbia University Press, 2008), 59.

13. Frank Samarotto refers to the intermezzo as "an elastic genre" in the context of pointing out that the third movement of Brahms's First Symphony has often been heard as an intermezzo. Frank Samarotto, "Fluidities of Phrase and Form in the 'Intermezzo' of Brahms's First Symphony," *Intégral* 22 (2008): 117–143 (117).

14. During the 1820s, the intermezzo was gaining currency as a serious genre in literary circles as well: in 1823, Heinrich Heine published a series of poems under the title *Lyrisches Intermezzo* (the work which served as the source for the sixteen poems that Robert Schumann later set in *Dichterliebe*).

15. "Allegro, Scherzo und Finale (Satz 1, 3 und 5) wurden im Oktober 1853 komponiert; das Andante und das mit ihm korrespondierende 'Rückblick' überschriebene Intermezzo (Satz 2 und 4) waren früher enstanden, vielleicht unterwegs auf seiner Rheinreise oder noch in Hamburg." "The Allegro, Scherzo and Finale (movements 1, 3, and 5) were composed in October 1853; the Andante and the corresponding movement headed 'Intermezzo: Rückblick' (movements 2 and

4) originated earlier, maybe on the way to his Rhineland journey or when he was still in Hamburg." Max Kalbeck, *Johannes Brahms* (Berlin: Deutsche Brahms-Gesellschaft, 1908), 1:120.

16. G. W. F. Hegel, *Philosophy of Right*, trans. T. M. Knox (Oxford: Oxford University Press, 1952), 20. For discussion of Hegel's influence on nineteenth-century musical culture, see Thomas Christensen, "Fétis and Emerging Tonal Consciousness," in *Music Theory in the Age of Romanticism*, ed. Ian Bent (Cambridge: Cambridge University Press, 1996), 55–56.

17. The verse used by Brahms as a heading is "Der Abend dämmert, das Mondlicht scheint, Da sind zwei Herzen in Liebe vereint, Und halten sich selig umfangen." "Twilight is falling, the moonlight is shining, there two hearts are united in love and keep themselves wrapped in bliss." This translation is taken from Dillon Parmer, "Brahms and the Poetic Motto: A Hermeneutic Aid?," *Journal of Musicology* 15/3 (1997): 353–89 (354).

18. William Kinderman, "'Capricious Play': Veiled Cyclic Relations in Brahms's Ballades Op. 10 and Fantasies Op. 116," in *Bach to Brahms: Essays on Musical Design and Structure*, ed. David Beach and Yosef Goldenberg (Rochester, NY: University of Rochester Press, 2015), 122.

19. Quoted in Kinderman, "Capricious Play," 119.

20. A philosophical approach to repetition in the late intermezzi has been put forward by Tim Howell, "Brahms, Kierkegaard, and Repetition: Three Intermezzi," *Nineteenth-Century Music Review* 10 (2013): 101–17. He focuses on repetition within pieces. What I propose to examine here is the somewhat different process of revisiting a piece across an indeterminate span of time.

21. Cone, "Three Ways of Reading a Detective Story."

22. "Nicht einmal das a-moll will mir gelingen, der Typus des 'Intermezzo' wie Sie es meinen." *Briefwechsel Brahms-Spitta*, 96.

23. Jonathan Dunsby, "The Multi-Piece in Brahms: Fantasien Op. 116," in *Brahms: Biographical, Documentary, and Analytical Studies*, ed. Robert Pascall (Cambridge: Cambridge University Press, 1983), 167–89 (176).

24. Pre-Brahmsian precedents for the evocation of unheard sounds include Schumann's *Auf einer Burg*, Op. 39, No. 7 (1840), in which the final dominant-type sonority implies a tonic resolution to A minor. See R. Larry Todd, "Late Brahms, Ancient Modes," *Nineteenth-Century Music Review* 15 (2018): 421–42 (432). In the Schumann song, however, the identity of the unheard chord is obvious (it is clearly a tonic chord), whereas in Brahms the listener is free to imagine a wide variety of possible chords/sounds.

25. Quoted in Charles Rosen, *The Romantic Generation* (Cambridge, MA: Harvard University Press, 1995), 93. Rosen interprets this passage by Schiller as a commentary on how "the artist cannot completely control public understanding."

26. John Rink, "Opposition and Integration in the Piano Music," in *The Cambridge Companion to Brahms*, ed. Michael Musgrave (Cambridge: Cambridge University Press, 1999), 79–97 (94).

27. Unharmonized openings such as this one are part of a larger tendency for Brahms to use what Ryan McClelland calls "destabilised beginnings." Ryan McClelland, "Brahms and the Principle of Destabilised Beginnings," *Music Analysis* 28/1 (2009): 3–61.

28. McClelland, "Destabilised Beginnings," 3.

29. Patrick Miller, "Tonal Structure and Formal Design in Johannes Brahms's Op. 118, No. 6," in *Music from the Middle Ages through the Twentieth Century: Essays in Honor of Gwynn S. McPeek*, ed. Carmelo P. Comberiati and Matthew C. Steel (New York: Gordon and Breach, 1988), 213–34 (224).

30. Rink, "Opposition and Integration," 95.

31. Letter from Clara Schumann to Brahms on 2 September 1893: "nicht zu sprechen von den grösseren Stücken 'Andante Teneramente' und 'Andante largo et mesto,' die so wunderbar interessant sind! (was heisst: mesto?) Sind die beiden letzteren nicht Sonatensätze?" Berthold Litzmann, ed., *Clara Schumann, Johannes Brahms: Briefe aus den Jahren 1853–1896* (Leipzig: Breitkopf & Härtel, 1927), 2:527.

32. Edward T. Cone, "Schubert's Promissory Note: An Exercise in Musical Hermeneutics," *19th-Century Music* 5/3 (1982): 233–41.

33. Laurie McManus, "Prostitutes, Trauma, and (Auto)-Biographical Narratives: Revisiting Brahms at the *Fin de Siècle*," *19th-Century Music* 42/3 (2019): 225–48 (247).

34. Berry, *Brahms among Friends*, 343.

35. Berry, *Brahms among Friends*, 341.

36. Rink, "Opposition and Integration," 95.

37. Smith, "You Reap What You Sow," 59.

38. "Das kleine Stück [Op. 119, No. 1] ist ausnehmend melancholisch, und 'sehr langsam spielen' ist nicht genug gesagt. Jeder Takt und jede Note muss wie ritard. klingen, als ob man Melancholie aus jeder einzelnen saugen wollte, mit Wollust und Behagen aus besagten Dissonanzen!" Litzmann, ed., *Clara Schumann, Johannes Brahms*, 2:513.

39. "L'espèce de mélancolie qui gagne le lecteur quand vient la dernière page d'un magnifique roman." Alain Badiou, *L'immanence des vérités: L'être et l'événement* (Paris: Fayard, 2018), 544.

40. These chains of thirds are a compelling stimulus for analytical reflection, prompting many studies of their tonal and motivic implications. See, for example, Allen Cadwallader, "Motivic Unity and Integration of Structural Levels in Brahms's B Minor Intermezzo, Op. 119, No. 1," *Theory and Practice* 8/2 (1983): 5–24; Roland Jordan and Emma Kafalenos, "The Double Trajectory: Ambiguity in Brahms and Henry James," *19th-Century Music* 13/2 (1989): 129–44; Felix Diergarten, "Melancholie des Unvermögens: Der Brahmssche Ton und das Intermezzo Op. 119, 1," *Musik & Ästhetik* 7/26 (2003): 42–53. A brief consideration of Op. 119, No. 1, also appears in David Lewin, "A Formal Theory of Generalized Tonal Functions," *Journal of Music Theory* 26/1 (1982): 43–45.

41. Rings observes that this is a "vivid instance of a common procedure in the intermezzi, in which the composer asks the performer to execute a motion that in

some sense physically manifests the technical idea at work in the music." Rings, "The Learned Self," 40.

42. Rings, "The Learned Self," 36.

43. Janet Schmalfeldt, *In the Process of Becoming: Analytical and Philosophical Perspectives on Form in Early Nineteenth-Century Music* (New York: Oxford University Press, 2011), 48.

44. Nicole Grimes has written perceptively about the "Romantic notion of the ascending circle" in which "the protagonist must earn his return to wholeness by striving incessantly along a circuitous path." Grimes, *Brahms's Elegies*, 38.

45. Rings, "The Learned Self," 28.

46. Dunsby, "The Multi-Piece in Brahms."

47. Schmalfeldt, *In the Process of Becoming*.

48. Such attentive listening habits are still being practiced today. See Mark Mulligan, Keith Jopling, and Zach Fuller, "The Classical Music Market: Streaming's Next Genre?," a MIDiA Research White Paper commissioned by IDAGIO (May 2019). This report, an "online consumer survey of 8,000 adult music consumers across eight markets: the USA, UK, Germany, Austria, Denmark, Sweden, Mexico and South Korea," indicates that 45 percent of classical listeners "prefer focused listening at home" (7). This persistence of focused listening practices is the case despite the rise of new technologies such as streaming (used by 31 percent of classical music listeners). Also noteworthy is that over half of the listeners in this survey use headphones (18). This perhaps increases the sense of privacy when listening. The use of headphones resonates in an interesting way with Brahms's own time when piano works such as the late intermezzi might have been heard in private, maybe by a listener/performer playing alone at the piano.

49. "'Dauerhafte Musik' war ein Lieblingsausdruck von Brahms. Er meinte damit jene Musik, die in dem tiefen Untergrund des Geistes der Musik wurzelt." Gustav Jenner, *Johannes Brahms als Mensch, Lehrer und Künstler* (Marburg: N. G. Elwert'sche Verlagsbuchhandlung, 1905), 74.

50. Quoted in Rings, "The Learned Self," 31.

Chapter 8

1. David Brodbeck, "The Brahms-Joachim Counterpoint Exchange: or, Robert, Clara, and 'the Best Harmony between Jos. and Joh.,'" in *Brahms Studies*, ed. David Brodbeck (Lincoln: University of Nebraska Press, 1994), 1:30–88.

2. Natasha Loges and Katy Hamilton, "Mythmaking," in *Brahms in Context*, ed. Natasha Loges and Katy Hamilton (Cambridge: Cambridge University Press, 2019), 383–93 (385).

3. Joachim as "Germanic," see John Knowles Paine, Theodore Thomas, and Karl Klauser, eds, *Famous Composers and Their Works* (Boston: J. B. Millet, 1891), 4:864; Andreas Moser, *Joseph Joachim, Ein Lebensbild*, 2 vols. (Berlin: B. Behr, 1898), II:276, stresses Joachim's ability to bring to his interpretations the "Tiefsinn

germanischer Kunst"; newspapers frequently noted that Joachim was a "durch und durch Deutscher Künstler" (*Mährisches Tagblatt* 22 [27 June 1901]: 5).

4. "In der Tat hat es nie einen deutscheren Künstler gegeben als ihn." "Nichts Zigeunerisches in seinem Wesen, wie Liszt und Reményi." "[Er neigt im Charakter] so ganz zur germanischen Art." Max Kalbeck, *Johannes Brahms, 1833–1862* (Vienna and Leipzig: Wiener Verlag, 1904), I:94.

5. Loges and Hamilton, "Mythmaking," 385.

6. Robert Eshbach, "Joachim, Reményi . . . and Brahms," paper presented at the 2012 meeting of the American Brahms Society. See https://josephjoachim.com/2014/09/29/remenyi-before-brahms/ (accessed August 2020).

7. Joachim Thalmann, *Untersuchungen zum Frühwerk von Johannes Brahms* (Kassel: Bärenreiter, 1989), 95.

8. "[A]rt is a 'possession only gained with effort.'" Friedemann Kawohl, "Copyright," *Brahms in Context*, 246–256 (248), cites Wolfgang Sandberger, "Brahms im Dialog mit der Musikforschung seiner Zeit," in *Brahms Handbuch*, ed. Wolfgang Sandberger (Stuttgart: J. B. Metzler, 2009), 142–52 (146).

9. Kawohl, "Copyright," 247.

10. Kawohl, "Copyright," 249, cites Jan Brachmann, *Kunst—Religion—Krise. Der Fall Brahms* (Kassel: Bärenreiter, 2003).

11. Loges and Hamilton, "Mythmaking," 385.

12. "Transcriptions are usually made from manuscript sources of early (pre-1800) music and therefore involve some degree of editorial work. It may also mean an Arrangement, especially one involving a change of medium (e.g. from orchestra to piano). In ethnomusicological transcription, music is written down from a live or recorded performance." Ter Ellingson, "Transcription (i)," *Grove Music Online*, 2001, https://www.oxfordmusiconline.com/grovemusic/view/10.1093/gmo/9781561592630.001.0001/omo-9781561592630-e-0000028268 (accessed 22 December 2020); William Horne also used the term "transcription" in discussing how Brahms utilized the sketch transcribed from Reményi's playing in January as an "artifact" that was later turned into an "art-music product." William Horne, "Brahms's Variations on a Hungarian Song," in *Brahms Studies*, ed. David Brodbeck (Lincoln: University of Nebraska Press, 2001), 3:47–128 (58).

13. The following sources appear in abbreviated form in Table 8.1: Renate Hofmann and Kurt Hofmann, *Johannes Brahms: Zeittafel zu Leben und Werk* (Tutzing: Hans Schneider, 1983); Joseph Joachim and Andreas Moser, eds, *Briefe von und an Joseph Joachim*, 2 vols. (Berlin: Julius Bard, 1911); Max Kalbeck, *Johannes Brahms, 1833–1862*, 4 vols. (Vienna and Leipzig: Wiener Verlag, 1904); La Mara (Ida Maria Lipsius), *Briefe hervorragender Zeitgenossen an Franz Liszt: 1824–1854* (Leipzig: Breitkopf & Härtel, 1895); Florence May, *The Life of Johannes Brahms* (London: Edward Arnold, 1905); Margit L. McCorkle, *Johannes Brahms Thematisch-Bibliographisches Werkverzeichnis* (Munich: G. Henle Verlag, 1984); Moser, *Joseph Joachim*; Katharina Uhde, *The Music of Joseph Joachim* (Rochester, NY: Boydell & Prewer, 2018); and A. Vandermeulen, ed., *Enthüllungen aus der*

höheren Region der politischen Spionage, in Berichten eines ungarischen Judas Ischarioth (Berlin: Hoffschläger, 1862).

14. Eshbach, "Joachim, Reményi . . . and Brahms."

15. Adam Gellen, "Eduard Reményis Jugendjahre und seine Beziehung zu Johannes Brahms—Eine biographische Skizze," *Studia Musicologica* 49/3-4 (September 2008): 295-319 (318).

16. "Reményi wird von Weimar ohne mich fortgehen, es ist sein Wille," letter from Brahms to Joachim, Weimar, 29 June 1853, in *Johannes Brahms Briefwechsel*, Vol. V *mit Joseph Joachim*, ed. Andreas Moser, 2 vols., 3rd ed. (1908; 1921; repr., Tutzing: Schneider, 1974): *Briefe von und an Joseph Joachim*, I:3. (Hereafter, *Johannes Brahms Briefwechsel*, V.)

17. "Trüge ich nicht den Namen Kreisler, ich hätte jetzt vollwichtige Gründe, etwas Weniges zu verzagen, meine Kunstliebe und meinen Enthusiasmus zu verwünschen und mich als Eremit (Schreiber?) in die Einsamkeit (eines Bureaus) zurückzuziehen und in stille Betrachtung (der die kopierenen Akten) zu versinken. Ja, Liebster, so vollwichtige Gründe, daß mir mein erzwungener Humor jetzt schon ausgeht und ich Ihnen bittre Wahrheit so ernst erzählen muß, wie ich sie empfand. Reményi wird von Weimar ohne mich fortgehen, es ist sein Wille, mein Betragen gegen ihn konnte ihm nicht den geringsten Anlaß geben. . . . Es war mir wirklich nicht nötig, noch eine so bittere Erfahrung zu machen. . . . [I]ch muss mindestens zwei oder drei meiner Werke verlegt sehen, damit ich meinen Eltern frisch und freudig ins Gesicht sehen kann. . . . Sie aber, liebster Herr Joachim, möchte ich dringend bitten, die Hoffnung, die Sie mir in Göttingen machten, womöglich zu erfüllen und mich dadurch ins Künstlerleben einzuführen." Letter from Brahms to Joachim, Weimar, 29 June 1853, in *Johannes Brahms Briefwechsel*, V:3

18. Hans Küntzel and Agathe Schütte, *Brahms in Göttingen: Mit Erinnerungen von Agathe Schütte, geb. von Siebold* (Göttingen: Edition Herodot, 1985), 16.

19. During their short stay in Göttingen in early June, Brahms and Reményi stayed at the "Gasthaus Krone (Weender Straße)." Küntzel and Schütte, *Brahms in Göttingen*, 15.

20. Küntzel and Schütte, *Brahms in Göttingen*, 24, reports of an artist and Göttingen resident, William Unger, who recalled later in life: "[E]r [Joachim] wohnte in dem Vogelschen Hause. . . . Wir hatten nun *oft* Gelegenheit, die beiden spielen zu hören." (Emphasis added.)

21. Küntzel and Schütte, *Brahms in Göttingen*, 15.

22. Michael Musgrave, "Frei aber Froh: A Reconsideration," 19th-Century Music 3/3 (1980): 251-258 (252).

23. Heather Platt, "Other Instrumentalists," in *Brahms in Context*, eds. Loges and Hamilton, 215-226 (226).

24. Musgrave, "Frei aber Froh: A Reconsideration," 252.

25. A violin student of Joachim, Moser also coauthored a three-volume *Violinschule* (1905) in which it is difficult to discern his contribution due to a lack of distinction between his and his master's views.

Notes

26. Robert Eshbach, "Digression: The Road to Jewish Emancipation" (2013), https://josephjoachim.com/2013/08/05/digression-the-road-to-jewish-emancipation/ (accessed 20 March 2020).

27. Karen Leistra-Jones, "Leipzig and Berlin," in *Brahms in Context*, eds. Loges and Hamilton, 33–43 (39).

28. Kalbeck, *Johannes Brahms, 1833–1862*, I:70.

29. For two recent samples of scholarship, see Darla Crispin and Bob Gilmore, eds., *Artistic Experimentation in Music* (Leuven: Leuven University Press, 2014) and Aaron Williamon, Jane Ginsborg, Rosie Perkins, George Waddell, *Performing Music Research* (Oxford and New York: Oxford University Press, 2021).

30. Christian Thorau and Hansjakob Ziemer, "Introduction: The Art of Listening," in *The Oxford Handbook of Musical Listening in the 19th and 20th Centuries*, ed. Christian Thorau and Hansjakob Ziemer (New York: Oxford University Press, 2019), 1–36 (20).

31. "But of these master composers [Bozarth lists Haydn, Mozart, Beethoven, Mendelssohn, and Schumann], only Brahms (to my knowledge) set about collecting folk-songs, German and otherwise, to study their very nature in order to ground and expand his compositional language." George S. Bozarth, "Folk Music," in *Brahms in Context*, ed. Loges and Hamilton, 164–75 (164).

32. Katrin Eich, "As Pianist," in *Brahms in Context*, ed. Loges and Hamilton, 80–87 (80).

33. Goertzen, "As Arranger," in *Brahms in Context*, ed. Loges and Hamilton, 98–113 (101).

34. Leistra-Jones, "Leipzig and Berlin," 42, quotes Moser, *Joseph Joachim*, II:240–41.

35. Hugh Macdonald, *Music in 1853: The Biography of a Year* (Woodbridge: Boydell & Brewer, 2012), 71; Küntzel and Schütte, *Brahms in Göttingen*, 22.

36. Küntzel and Schütte, *Brahms in Göttingen*, 23.

37. Joachim to von Arnim, 3–4 December 1853, in *Briefe von und an Joseph Joachim*, ed. Moser and Joachim, I:113.

38. Joachim knew then that 24 July was not his birthday; later he found out that it was 28 June.

39. Johannes Brahms, *Hymne zur Verherrlichung des großen Joachim. Walzer für zwei Violinen und Kontrabaß oder Violoncello*, ed. Klaus Stahmer (Hamburg: J. Schuberth & Co, 1976), 9.

40. Jacquelyn Sholes, "Music for Birthdays: Commemorative Birthday Pieces in Johannes Brahms's Circle (1853–1854) and Elsewhere," in *Cultures of Memory in the Nineteenth Century: Consuming Commemoration*, ed. Katherine Grenier and Amanda Mushal (New York: Palgrave Macmillan, 2020), 61–80 (61).

41. Sholes, "Music for Birthdays," 61.

42. Sholes, "Music for Birthdays," 62.

43. We must nonetheless reject Stahmer's hypothesis relating the piece to the "Kaffernbund" on the basis that the "Kaffernbund" is a concept first mentioned on

10 November 1854, thereby postdating this piece by more than a year. Letters in the primary sources referencing the "Kaffernbund" include: 10 Nov. [1854] (*Johannes Brahms Briefwechsel*, V:73); 16 Nov. 1854 (*Johannes Brahms Briefwechsel*, V:75); 31 Dec. 1854 (*Johannes Brahms Briefwechsel*, IV: *Johannes Brahms im Briefwechsel mit J. O. Grimm*, ed. Richard Barth [Berlin: Deutsche Brahms-Gesellschaft, 1912; repr. Tutzing: Schneider, 1974], 14 (hereafter *Johannes Brahms Briefwechsel*, IV); Jan 1855 (*Johannes Brahms Briefwechsel*, IV:18); mid-Nov. 1854 (*Johannes Brahms Briefwechsel*, V:223); January 1864 (*Johannes Brahms Briefwechsel*, V:331).

44. In a recording of the *Hymne zur Verherrlichung des grossen Joachim* there is further text, going beyond the "Urtext," which reads: "Ach! Das ist nicht so. Ach! Noch einmal. Eins, zwei, drei . . .," which gives the proposed reading of a possible Jo-ACH-im cipher, more authority.

45. "Neulich brachte ich beim Glas Wein eine Gesundheit aus in Charadenform. Drei Silben: die erste liebte ein Gott, die zwei andern lieben viele Leser, das Ganze lieben wir alle; das Ganze und der Ganze soll leben [Jo, Achim]," Schumann to Joachim, 13 October 1853, in Moser, *Joseph Joachim*, I:85–86.

46. Sholes, "Music for Birthdays," 62–63.

47. "Eine interessante Bekanntschaft war mir Hoffmann von Fallersleben . . . den ich mir . . . kecker und trotziger gedacht hatte. . . . Gestern feierte man hier . . . meinen Geburtstag; die Beweise von freundlicher u. liebenswürdiger Gesinnung thaten mir wohl." D-LÜbi, MS 1991.2.53.7.

48. By June 1854, Joachim recommended to Brahms that "alles äußerlich Auffallende gerade von genialen Naturen jetzt vermieden werden müsse," and followed this guideline himself. Joachim to Brahms, 27 June 1854, in *Johannes Brahms Briefwechsel*, V:51.

49. "[E]in Stück von mir selbst," D-LÜbi, MS 1991.2.53.4, Joachim to Heinrich Joachim, 25 April 1853.

50. Ellingson, "Transcription," *Grove Music Online*.

51. Jacquelyn Sholes, "Music for Birthdays," 62–64.

52. Katharina Uhde, "Rediscovering Joseph Joachim's 'Hungarian' and 'Irish' [Scottish] Fantasias," *Musical Times* (Winter 2017): 75–99 (86).

53. Csilla Pethő: "'Style hongrois': Hungarian Elements in the Works of Haydn, Beethoven, Weber and Schubert," Studia Musicologica Academiae Scientiarum Hungaricae 41/1–3 (2000): 199–284.

54. Thalmann, *Untersuchungen zum Frühwerk von Johannes Brahms*, 33–34.

55. Jonathan Bellman, "Performing Brahms in the *Style Hongrois*," in *Performing Brahms: Early Evidence of Performance Style*, ed. Michael Musgrave and Bernhard D. Sherman (Cambridge: Cambridge University Press, 2003), 327–48 (340).

56. Bozarth, "Folk Music," 165.

57. "[undecipherable] Reményi és Brahms. Hannover April 1853. barátjától." D-Hs, BRSA: Aa8.

58. Bozarth, "Folk Music," 170.

59. Bozarth, "Folk Music," 170.

Notes

60. Bozarth, "Folk Music," 169–70.

61. Bozarth, "Folk Music," 169–70: "Akkor csinos a bakkancsos, ha gatyája végig rongyos, térgye kilóg a gatyából, mint a rózsa bimbójából." (Then the man who wears soldier's boots is pretty, if his breeches are torn down, his knees sticking out of his pants, as the rose from its bud.)

62. Jonathan Bellman, "The Hungarian Gypsies," in *The Exotic in Western Music*, ed. Jonathan Bellman (Boston: Northeastern University Press, 1998), 89.

63. Bellman, "Performing Brahms in the *Style Hongrois*," 325.

64. Bozarth, "Folk Music," 170.

65. Joachim's later contributions to the *style hongrois* include the *Hungarian Concerto*, Op. 11, and *Variationen über ein eigenes Thema*, Op. 10 for viola.

66. Gwendolyn Dunlevy Kelley and George P. Upton, *Edouard Remenyi Musician, Litterateur and Man* (Chicago: A. C. Mclurg, 1906), 9.

67. Uhde, "Rediscovering Joachim's Fantasias."

68. Ian Pace, "Performing Liszt in the Style Hongroise," *Liszt Society Journal* 32 (2007): 55–90 (68).

69. Joachim to Heinrich, October 1848, in Moser, *Joseph Joachim*, I:17.

70. "Die Melodie an sich hat keinen großen Wert, und verdankt ihre Wirkung lediglich dem Takte. Mir ist überhaupt widerstrebend Wirkungen durch etwas anderes als durch künstlerische Mittel zu erzielen; und auf Zufälle zu spekulieren war mir immer gegen die Würde des Künstlers. Das mag Reményi thun und ich werde ihn um seine Erfolge nicht beneiden." Joachim to his parents [undated], GB-Lbl, Additional MS 42718.

71. George S. Bozarth and Walter Frisch, "Brahms, Johannes," in *The New Grove Dictionary of Music and Musicians*, 2nd ed. (London, 2001), 4:120–227.

72. Beatrix Borchard uses the concept "finding identity through splitting-off" ("Identitätsfindung durch Abspaltung") in *Stimme und Geige. Amalie und Joseph Joachim* (Vienna: Böhlau, 2005), 129.

73. "In seinem Spiele ist ganz das intensive Feuer, jene, ich möchte sagen, fatalistische Energie und Präzision des Rhythmus, welche den Künstler prophezeien, und seine Kompositionen zeigen jetzt schon so viel Bedeutendes, wie ich es bis jetzt noch bei keinem Kunstjünger seines Alters getroffen." Kalbeck, *Johannes Brahms, 1833–1862*, I:74.

74. Uhde, *The Music of Joseph Joachim*, 149.

75. "Die Zigeuner spielen noch enthusiastisch . . . es ist mehr Rhythmus . . . in ihren Bogen, als in allen norddeutschen Kapellisten zusammengenommen." Joachim to Liszt, 16 November 1854 in Moser, *Joseph Joachim*, I:227.

Chapter 9

1. See Katy Hamilton and Natasha Loges, eds., *Brahms in the Home and the Concert Hall: Between Private and Public Performance* (Cambridge: Cambridge University Press, 2014); Paul Berry, *Brahms among Friends: Listening, Performance,*

and the Rhetoric of Allusion (Oxford and New York: Oxford University Press, 2014); and Margaret Notley, *Lateness and Brahms: Music and Culture in the Twilight of Viennese Liberalism* (Oxford and New York: Oxford University Press, 2006).

2. See Daniel Leech-Wilkinson, *The Changing Sound of Music: Approaches to Studying Recorded Musical Performances* (CHARM, 2009), www.charm.rhul.ac.uk/studies/chapters/intro.html (accessed 10 March 2021); Robert Philip, *Early Recordings and Musical Style: Changing Tastes in Instrumental Performance, 1900–1950* (Cambridge: Cambridge University Press, 1992), and *Performing Music in the Age of Recording* (New Haven, CT: Yale University Press, 2004); and Neal Peres Da Costa, *Off the Record: Performing Practices in Romantic Piano Playing* (Oxford and New York: Oxford University Press, 2012).

3. See Clive Brown, *Classical and Romantic Performing Practice 1750–1900* (Oxford and New York: Oxford University Press, 1999); David Milsom, *Theory and Practice in Late Nineteenth Century Violin Performance* (Aldershot: Ashgate, 2003); David Hyun-Su Kim, "The Brahmsian Hairpin," *19th-Century Music* 36/1 (2012): 46–57; Kai Köpp, "Hohe Schule des Portamentos: Violintechnik als Schlüssel für die Gesangspraxis im 19. Jahrhundert," *Dissonance* 132 (2015): 16–25; and Clive Brown, Neal Peres Da Costa, and Kate Bennett Wadsworth, *Performing Practices in Johannes Brahms's Chamber Music* (Kassel: Bärenreiter, 2015).

4. See George Barth, "Effacing Modernism, or How to Perform Less Accurately through Listening," *Historical Performance* 1 (2018): 148–89; Sigurd Slåttebrekk, *Chasing the Butterfly: Recreating Grieg's 1903 Recordings and Beyond* (2010), www.chasingthebutterfly.no (accessed 10 March 2021); Anna Scott, "Romanticizing Brahms: Early Recordings and the Reconstruction of Brahmsian Identity," PhD diss., Leiden University (2014); and Emlyn Stam, "In Search of a Lost Language: Performing in Early-Recorded Style in Viola and String Quartet Repertoires," PhD diss., Leiden University (2018).

5. Daniel Leech-Wilkinson, "The Fabulous Status Quo," *Challenging Performance*, Chapter 2, https://challengingperformance.com/the-book-2/ (accessed 19 March 2021).

6. Richard Masters, "Review of *Brahms Violin Sonatas, Alina Ibragimova & Cédric Tiberghien*," 2019, http://www.musicweb-international.com/classrev/2019/Oct/Brahms_violin_CDA68200_RM.htm (accessed 12 January 2021).

7. David Noel Edwards, "Schumann, Brahms Piano Quintets: Truly Titanic Performances at Close Encounters with Music," *Berkshire Edge*, 4 November 2017,https://theberkshireedge.com/review-schumann-brahms-piano-quintets-truly-titanic-performances-at-close-encounters-with-music (accessed 12 January 2021).

8. Paul Ballam-Cross, "Brahms: String Quintets (Takács Quartet, Lawrence Power)," *Limelight Magazine*, 6 January 2015, www.limelightmagazine.com.au/reviews/brahms-string-quintets-takacs-quartet-lawrence-power (accessed 12 January 2021).

9. Allan Kozinn, "Sharp Interplay and Melting Lyricism," *New York Times*, 4 July 2011,www.nytimes.com/2011/07/05/arts/music/cassatt-quartet-and-ursula-oppens-at-bargemusic-review.html (accessed 12 January 2021); Michelle Dulak

Notes

Thomson, "Astounding Control: Tokyo Quartet on Brahms," *San Francisco Classical Voice*, 14 December 2012, www.sfcv.org/reviews/tone-control-tokyo-takes-on-brahms (accessed 12 January 2021).

10. Kate Molleson, "Brahms: String Quartets, Piano Quintet CD Review—Angst, Ardency and Brilliance," *The Guardian*, 6 October 2016,www.theguardian.com/music/2016/oct/06/brahms-string-quartets-piano-quintet-cd-review-belcea-quartet-till-felner-alpha (accessed 12 January 2021).

11. Jed Distler, "Brahms: Piano Quintet/Staier," *Classics Today* www.classicstoday.com/review/review-11464 (accessed 12 January 2021).

12. Robert Beattie, "The Brahms Violin Sonatas Impressively Done by Faust and Melnikov," *Seen and Heard International*, 15 June 2015, https://seenandheard-international.com/2015/06/the-brahms-violin-sonatas-impressively-done-by-faust-and-melnikov (accessed 12 January 2021).

13. Bin Kimura, *L'entre: une approche phénoménologique de la schizophrénie* (Grenoble: Editions Jérôme Millon, 2000), 43, in Simon Høffding, *A Phenomenology of Musical Absorption* (London: Palgrave Macmillan, 2018), 245.

14. Jed Distler, "Fresh Insights from an Old Master in Brahms Quintet," *Classics Today*,www.classicstoday.com/review/fresh-insights-old-master-brahms-quintet (accessed 12 January 2021); Vivien Schweitzer, "Violin and Piano, in an Evening's Conversation," *New York Times*, 6 May 2011, www.nytimes.com/2011/05/07/arts/music/christian-tetzlaff-at-weill-recital-hall-review.html (accessed 12 January 2021).

15. James Manheim, "Review of *Brahms: The Violin Sonatas, Leonidas Kavakos & Yuja Wang*," *AllMusic*, www.allmusic.com/album/brahms-the-violin-sonatas-mw0002625014 (accessed 12 January 2021); Laura Furones, "So Full of Melodies: Kavakos and Wang Play Brahms's Sonatas," *Bachtrack*, 21 October 2014, https://bachtrack.com/review-brahms-kavakos-wang-madrid-october-2014 (accessed 12 January 2021).

16. Høffding, *Musical Absorption*, 222; David Blum, *The Art of Quartet Playing: The Guarneri String Quartet in Conversation with David Blum* (New York: Alfred Knopf, 1986), 236.

17. Høffding, *Musical Absorption*, 232, 223.

18. Bruce Ellis Benson, *The Improvisation of Musical Dialogue: A Phenomenology of Music* (Cambridge: Cambridge University Press, 2003), 141, 168.

19. Høffding, *Musical Absorption*, 226.

20. Vivien Schweitzer, "Seeking an Intimate Sound across a Cavernous Expanse," *New York Times*, 23 November 2014, www.nytimes.com/2014/11/24/arts/music/leonidas-kavakos-and-yuja-wang-play-brahms-and-respighi.html (accessed 12 January 2021). Emphasis added.

21. Robin Stowell, "Faust and Melnikov Finish Their Brahms Survey, Eight Years On," *The Strad* (November 2015), www.thestrad.com/brahms-violin-sonatas-no2-in-a-major-op100-no3-in-d-minor-op108-dietrich/schumann/brahms-fae-sonata-schumann-three-romances-op94/1139.article (accessed 13 March 2021).

22. Martin Cotton, "*Brahms: Violin Sonatas, Leila Schayegh & Jan Schultz*," *Classical Music*, 1 March 2020, www.classical-music.com/reviews/chamber/brahms-violin-sonatas-2 (accessed 12 January 2021).

23. Paul Ballam-Cross, "Brahms: Piano Quartet No. 1, Piano Quintet," *Limelight Magazine*, 10 March 2017, www.limelightmagazine.com.au/reviews/brahms-piano-quartet-no-1-piano-quintet-ironwood (accessed 12 January 2021); David Milsom, "Ironwood: Brahms, Piano Quartet No. 1; Piano Quintet," *The Strad*, 30 October 2017,www.thestrad.com/reviews/ironwood-brahms-piano-quartet-no1-piano-quintet/7240.article (accessed 12 January 2021); Gordon Kerry, "Brahms: Tones of Romantic Extravagance," *Music Trust*, 2 February 2017, https://musictrust.com.au/loudmouth/brahms-tones-of-romantic-extravagance-piano-quartet-no-1piano-quintet (accessed 12 January 2021).

24. Louis Spohr, *Violinschule*, trans. C. Rudolphus (London: Wessel & Co. [no date; original edition, 1832]), 230.

25. Berry, *Brahms among Friends*, 9, 322.

26. Max Graf, *Legend of a Musical City: The Story of Vienna3* (New York: Philosophical Library, 1945; repr. 1969), 191–96. EPUB version (2013) courtesy of the New York Philosophical Library.

27. Berthold Litzmann, *Clara Schumann: An Artist's Life, Based on Material Found in Diaries and letters*, trans. Grace E. Hadow, 2 vols. (London: Macmillan, 1913; repr. Cambridge: Cambridge University Press, 2013), II:368.

28. Heinz von Beckerath, "Erinnerungen an Johannes Brahms: Brahms und seine Krefelder Freunde," *Die Heimat (Krefeld)* 29/1–4 (1958): 81–93; in English, "Heinz von Beckerath Remembering Johannes Brahms: Brahms and His Krefeld Friends," trans. Josef Eisinger, introduced and annotated by Styra Avins, in *Brahms and His World*, ed. Walter Frisch and Kevin C. Karnes (Princeton, NJ: Princeton University Press, 2009), 349–80 (355).

29. Fanny Davies, "Some Personal Recollections of Brahms as Pianist and Interpreter," in *Cobbett's Cyclopedic Survey of Chamber Music*, ed. W. W. Cobbett (London: Oxford University Press, 1929[repr. 1963]), 182–84, reproduced in George Bozarth, "Fanny Davies and Brahms's Late Chamber Music," in *Performing Brahms: Early Evidence of Performing Style*, ed. Bernard D. Sherman and Michael Musgrave (Cambridge: Cambridge University Press, 2003), 170–219 (172–76).

30. For details of my copies and extrapolations of recordings by De Lara and Eibenschütz, see Scott, "Romanticizing Brahms"; for Davies, Friedberg, and Freund, see Anna Scott, "To Change One's Skin According to the Music at Hand," in *Practice in Context: Perspectives on Historically Informed Practices in Post-Classical Music*, ed. Claire Holden, Eric Clarke, and Cayenna Ponchione-Bailey (Oxford: Oxford University Press, forthcoming).

31. Stam, "Lost Language," 128.
32. Stam, "Lost Language," 114.
33. Stam, "Lost Language," 157.
34. Stam, "Lost Language," 141.
35. Stam, "Lost Language," 178, 206.

36. Morten Lindberg, "The Nordic Sound," *2L*, www.2l.no (accessed 13 January 2021).

37. Geoff Miles, as paraphrased in Stam, "Lost Language," 56.

38. For an overview of the phenomenon of mid-range distortion in modern microphones and its musical implications, see Stam, "Lost Language," 57–59; for further reading, see Keith Howard, "Euphonic Distortion: Naughty but Nice?," *Stereophile* (30 April 2006), https://www.stereophile.com/reference/406howard/index.html (accessed 18 July 2021); Andrew Simpson, "Implications of Nonlinear Distortion in the Ultrasonic Capacitive Microphone: Why Is the Wide-Bandwidth Condenser Microphone a Bad Idea?" (Poland: Simpson Microphones, 2009); and John Willet, "The Symmetrical Microphone Capsule and the Quest for the Perfect 'Acoustic Window,'" AES UK 13th Conference (March 1998): "Microphones & Loudspeakers," http://sound-link.co.uk/docs/Acoustic%20Window.pdf (accessed 19 July 2021).

39. *Podium Witteman*, Facebook, 29 November 2020, "Buitengewoon lelijk. Sorry. Alsof het de muziek uit een horrorfilm was"; "Bijzonder slordig gespeeld. Ongelijk in tempo en eerste viool zeer onjuist"; "Bombastisch, viel tegen, jammer," translated by author, www.facebook.com/podiumwitteman/posts/2906246876265844 and www.facebook.com/podiumwitteman/posts/2906342542922944 (accessed 3 March 2021).

Chapter 10

1. James Webster, "The General and the Particular in Brahms's Sonata Forms," in *Brahms Studies: Analytical and Historical Perspectives*, ed. George Bozarth (Oxford: Clarendon Press, 1990), 49–78 (76).

2. For an important recent example concerned with Romantic sonata form, see Steven Vande Moortele, *The Romantic Overture and Musical Form from Rossini to Wagner* (Cambridge: Cambridge University Press, 2017).

3. Peter H. Smith, "Brahms and Subject/Answer Rhetoric," *Music Analysis* 20/2 (2001): 193–236; Ryan McClelland, "Brahms and the Principle of Destabilised Beginnings," *Music Analysis* 28/1 (2010): 3–59; Siegfried Kross, "Thematic Structure and Formal Process in Brahms's Sonata Movements," in *Brahms Studies: Analytical and Historical Perspectives*, ed. George Bozarth (Oxford: Clarendon Press, 1990), 423–43.

4. This is of course not to suggest that no large-scale studies of Brahms's sonata forms predate Webster's essay. Well-known examples include Robert Pascall, "Formal Principles in the Music of Brahms" (PhD diss., Oxford University, 1973) and Arno Mitschka, "Der Sonatensatz in den Werken von Johannes Brahms" (PhD diss., Johannes Gutenberg-University of Mainz, 1961). Elaine Sisman has adopted a similar, corpus-based approach toward Brahms's slow-movement forms; see "Brahms's Slow Movements: Reinventing the 'Closed' Forms," in *Brahms Studies: Analytical and Historical Perspectives*, ed. George Bozarth

(Oxford: Clarendon Press, 1990), 79–103. My point is rather to stress Webster's empirical-statistical method and its potential, when conjoined with aspects of the new *Formenlehre*, for illuminating the details of Brahms's thematic construction.

    5. See, for example, James Hepokoski, "Monumentality and Formal Process in the First Movement of Brahms's Piano Concerto in D minor, Op. 15," in *Expressive Intersections in Brahms: Essays in Analysis and Meaning*, ed. Peter H. Smith and Heather Platt (Bloomington: Indiana University Press, 2012), 217–51; Warren Darcy, "Bruckner's Sonata Deformations," in *Bruckner Studies*, ed. Timothy L. Jackson and Paul Hawkshaw (Cambridge: Cambridge University Press, 1997), 256–77; Janet Schmalfeldt, *In the Process of Becoming: Analytic and Philosophical Perspectives on Form in Romantic Music* (New York: Oxford University Press, 2011); Steven Vande Moortele, "In Search of Romantic Form," *Music Analysis* 32/3 (2013): 404–31, and *The Concert Overture and Musical Form from Rossini to Wagner*; Seth Monahan, "Success and Failure in Mahler's Symphonic Sonatas," *Music Theory Spectrum* 33/1 (2011): 37–58; Peter H. Smith, "Dvořák and Subordinate Theme Closure: 'Positive' Analytic Results from a 'Negative' Approach to Romantic Form," *Journal of Music Theory* 64/2 (2020): 203–40; Andrew Davis, *Sonata Fragments: Romantic Narratives in Chopin, Schumann and Brahms* (Bloomington: Indiana University Press, 2017); Benedict Taylor, *Mendelssohn, Time and Memory: The Romantic Conception of Cyclic Form* (Cambridge: Cambridge University Press, 2011); and Julian Horton, "Criteria for a Theory of Nineteenth-Century Sonata Form," *Music Theory and Analysis* 4/2 (2017): 147–91.

    6. Vande Moortele, *The Concert Overture and Musical Form from Rossini to Wagner*, 10.

    7. James Hepokoski and Warren Darcy, *Elements of Sonata Theory: Norms, Types, and Deformations in the Late-Eighteenth-Century Sonata* (New York and Oxford: Oxford University Press, 2006), 615.

    8. See, for example, Hepokoski and Darcy, *Elements of Sonata Theory*, 39–40 on the system of medial-caesura defaults.

    9. Hepokoski and Darcy, *Elements of Sonata Theory*, vii.

    10. Vande Moortele, *The Romantic Overture and Musical Form from Rossini to Wagner*, 12.

    11. Schmalfeldt, *In the Process of Becoming*, 10–11 and 25–37.

    12. See, for example, Julian Horton, "Formal Type and Formal Function in the Post-Classical Piano Concerto," in *Formal Functions in Perspective*, ed. Nathan Martin, Steven Vande Moortele, and Julie Pednault-Deslaurier (Rochester, NY: University of Rochester Press, 2017), 77–122, and "Rethinking Sonata Failure: Mendelssohn's Overture *zum Märchen von der schönen Melusine*," *Music Theory Spectrum* 43/2 (2021): 299–319.

    13. I have developed a partner concept to the form-functional pathway—the *processual network*—in "Rethinking Sonata Failure," especially at 306. Form-functional pathways describe the music's intra-thematic syntax in terms of the total range of discrete syntactic variables in a given corpus and their temporal relationships; processual networks capture the conceptual basis of the pathway's

stage-by-stage material logic. The specific concatenation of functions in a theme, for instance those that produce a sentence-period hybrid, define its form-functional pathway; the concept or concepts, for example proliferation, which account for the ways in which the theme is generated from its material, define its processual network. The interaction of pathway and network I regard as central to any sonata's formal strategy.

14. Hepokoski defines this rather gnomically as a "non-repeating exposition"; see *Sibelius: Symphony No. 5* (Cambridge: Cambridge University Press, 1993), 7, n. 17; and also Robert Pascall, "Some Special Uses of Sonata Form by Brahms," *Soundings* 4 (1974): 58–63.

15. On the concept of proliferation, see, for example, Julian Horton, *Brahms's Piano Concerto No. 2, Op. 83: Analytical and Contextual Studies* (Leuven: Peeters, 2017), 46–48.

16. For a definition, see William Caplin, *Analyzing Classical Form: An Approach for the Classroom* (New York and Oxford: Oxford University Press, 2013), 131–2.

17. Vande Moortele, "In Search of Romantic Form," 412–15.

18. Carl Dahlhaus, *Nineteenth-Century Music*, trans. J. Bradford Robinson (Berkeley and Los Angeles: California University Press, 1989), 269–71.

19. On cadential closure in the classical period, see Caplin, *Analyzing Classical Form*, 79–87.

20. Caplin, *Analyzing Classical Form*, 133–34.

21. Smith, "Liquidation, Augmentation, and Brahms's Recapitulatory Overlaps," *19th-Century Music* 17/3 (1994): 237–61; and Carissa Reddick, "Becoming at a Deeper Level: Divisional Overlap in Sonata Forms from the Late Nineteenth Century," *Music Theory Online* 16/2 (2010): 1–5.

22. See Caplin, *Analyzing Classical Form*, 210–14 and 221–22.

23. See Hepokoski and Darcy, *Elements of Sonata Theory*, 77.

24. On the reinterpreted half cadence, see Caplin, *Analyzing Classical Form*, 90–92.

25. See Walter Frisch, *Brahms and the Principle of Developing Variation* (Berkeley and Los Angeles: University of California Press, 1984), 77: "[In Op. 26] We encounter for the first time in Brahms the flexible kind of developing variation that Schoenberg so admired in the Andante of Op. 51 No. 1."

26. I have in mind Theodor W. Adorno, *Philosophy of New Music*, trans. Robert Hullot-Kentor (Minneapolis: University of Minnesota Press, 2006), 47; and Carl Dahlhaus, *Between Romanticism and Modernism: Four Studies in the Music of the Later Nineteenth Century*, trans. Mary Whittall (Berkeley: University of California Press, 1980), 42 and 50. Adorno's views on the relationship between theme and form are extensively analysed from a Brahmsian perspective in Margaret Anne Notley, *Lateness and Brahms: Music and Culture in the Twilight of Viennese Liberalism* (Oxford: Oxford University Press, 2007), 72–106.

27. For example, in Dahlhaus, *Nineteenth-Century Music*, 13–15; and Schmalfeldt, *In the Process of Becoming*, 23–57.

28. Giselher Schubert, "Themes and Double Themes: The Problem of the Symphonic in Brahms," *19th-Century Music* 18/1 (1984): 10–23.

29. For McClelland's analysis of Op. 36, see "Brahms and the Principle of Destabilised Beginnings," 10–13.

Chapter 11

1. Notable exceptions are Hans Kohlhase, "Brahms und Mendelssohn: Strukturelle Parallelen in der Kammermusik für Streicher," in *Brahms und seine Zeit*, ed. Constantin Floros, Hans Joachim Marx, and Peter Petersen, *Hamburger Jahrbuch für Musikwissenschaft* 7 (Laaber: Laaber Verlag, 1984): 59–85; David Brodbeck, "Brahms's Mendelssohn," in *Brahms Studies*, ed. David Brodbeck (Lincoln: University of Nebraska Press, 1998), 2:209–31. Also see Wulf Konold, "Mendelssohn und Brahms: Beispiele schöpferische Rezeption im Lichte der Klaviermusik," in *Brahms-Analysen: Referate der Kieler Tagung 1983*, ed. Friedhelm Krummacher and Wolfram Steinbeck (Kassel: Bärenreiter, 1984), 81–90; and the volume *Konstellationen: Felix Mendelssohn und die deutsche Musikkultur, Felix Mendelssohn und Johannes Brahms*, ed. Wolfgang Sandberger (Lübeck: Brahms-Institut an der Musikhochschule Lübeck, 2015), esp. Peter Gülke, "Brahms und Mendelssohn: Festvortrag zur Ausstellungseröffnung," 74–77.

2. Tchaikovsky, review of a performance of Brahms's Sextet, Op. 18, from November 1872, quoted by Kohlhase, "Brahms und Mendelssohn," 59, emphasis and translation mine. Ludwig Wittgenstein later famously linked the two figures as well, noting that "there is definitely a certain kinship" that extends beyond "the individual passages in Brahms's works that are reminiscent of those in Mendelssohn." In his case, though, Wittgenstein read Brahms as the "improved" version of Mendelssohn, who did "with complete rigour what Mendelssohn did half rigorously." See Wittgenstein, *Culture and Value*, ed. G. H. von Wright, trans. Peter Winch (Oxford: Wiley and Blackwell, 1998), 19.

3. James Webster, "Schubert's Sonata Form and Brahms's First Maturity (II)," *19th-Century Music* 3/1 (1979): 52–63 (56).

4. On nineteenth-century compositional history as circumpolar, speaking specifically of the symphony after Beethoven, see Carl Dahlhaus, *Nineteenth-Century Music*, trans. J. B. Robinson (Berkeley and Los Angeles: University of California Press, 1989), 152.

5. Tovey's observation is from his 1928 "Franz Schubert," reprinted in Donald Francis Tovey, *Essays and Lectures on Music* (London: Oxford University Press, 1949), 123.

6. John Daverio, *Crossing Paths: Schubert, Schumann, and Brahms* (New York: Oxford University Press, 2002); Marie Sumner Lott, "Domesticity in Brahms's String Sextets, Opp. 18 and 36," in *Brahms in the Home and the Concert Hall: Between Private and Public Performance*, ed. Katy Hamilton and Natasha Loges (Cambridge: Cambridge University Press, 2014), 43–94.

7. William Caplin, *Classical Form: A Theory of Formal Functions for the Instrumental Music of Haydn, Mozart, and Beethoven* (Oxford and New York: Oxford University Press, 1998); James Hepokoski and Warren Darcy, *Elements of Sonata Theory: Norms, Types, and Deformations in the Late-Eighteenth-Century Sonata* (New York: Oxford University Press, 2006). Hepokoski has turned attention specifically to Brahms in a subsequent essay, "Monumentality and Formal Processes in the First Movement of Brahms's Piano Concerto No. 1 in D Minor, op. 15," in *Expressive Intersections in Brahms*, ed. Heather Platt and Peter H. Smith (Bloomington: Indiana University Press, 2012), 217–51, and in the recent *A Sonata Theory Handbook* (New York: Oxford University Press, 2020), ch. 12, "Brahms, Symphony No. 1 in C Minor, Op. 68/iv (Adagio—Più andante—Allegro non troppo, ma con brio—Più allegro)."

8. See particularly the criticism made by Steven Vande Moortele in a review of Seth Monahan's monograph on Mahler's symphonies (one of the most important and valuable applications of sonata theory to the post-classical repertory), "Seth Monahan: *Mahler's Symphonic Sonatas*," *Music Theory Spectrum* 40/1 (2018): 166–71.

9. As reported by George Henschel, *Personal Recollections of Johannes Brahms* (Boston: R. G. Badger, 1907), 30.

10. This recapitulation of the primary theme's accompanimental figuration (bar 173) is separated here from the reprise of the actual theme, which occurs some bars later, now over ⅔ of B minor (bar 188)—a feature typical of Brahms's diffusion of recapitulatory functions across a wider span of music. Brahms's procedure is in some ways the inverse of Mendelssohn's in his movement. Mendelssohn begins with what is apparently nothing more than figuration, used to construct an opening sentential phrase, but gradually introduces more characteristic melodic material; Brahms starts off with a less ambiguous complex of accompaniment and theme, but then separates the two in the recapitulation.

11. There are of course precedents for this design in other composers as well as in Brahms's earlier works; the comparison with Mendelssohn's example is salient in this case given the numerous other correspondences with his movement. On the "Brahmsian deformation" (an "expanded type 1 sonata" in sonata-theory terminology) see Hepokoski and Darcy, *Elements of Sonata Theory*, 349–50 (the term "Brahmsian deformation" is not in fact used here, but is by Hepokoski in earlier writings, such as his pioneering *Sibelius: Symphony No. 5* [Cambridge: Cambridge University Press, 1993], 94). Brahms's use of this form has received substantial scholarly discussion: see especially Robert Pascall, "Some Special Uses of Sonata Form by Brahms," *Soundings* 4 (1974): 58–63; John Daverio, "From 'Concertante Rondo' to 'Lyric Sonata': A Commentary on Brahms's Reception of Mozart," in *Brahms Studies*, ed. David Brodbeck (Lincoln: University of Nebraska Press, 1994), 1:115–19 (who terms the design "amplified binary"); and Joel Galand, "Some Eighteenth-Century Ritornello Scripts and Their Nineteenth-Century Revivals," *Music Theory Spectrum* 30/2 (2008), 239–82.

12. Referring to Harold Bloom's well-known theory of the artistic "anxiety of influence," an approach that was very popular in musicology during the 1990s. A good example is given by Mark Evan Bonds, *After Beethoven: Imperatives of Originality in the Symphony* (Cambridge, MA: Harvard University Press, 1996), which takes as a postulate a Beethoven-centric historiography of nineteenth-century music.

13. Brahms, letter of June 1878 to Otto Dessoff, in *Johannes Brahms Briefwechsel*, Vol. XVI: *Johannes Brahms im Briefwechsel mit Philipp Spitta. Briefwechsel mit Otto Dessoff*, ed. Carl Krebs (Berlin: Deutsche Brahms-Gesellschaft, 1922), 192. Brahms doesn't name Mendelssohn at this point, but Dessoff's reply (letter of 7 July 1878, XVI:198) makes it clear Brahms was meaning this work. Like me, Dessoff finds this "Mendelssohn=Brahms thievery" not that pronounced: "between the 2nd theme of the [Mendelssohn] A minor Symphony and yours is exactly as much similarity as between the spires of St Stephen's and Strasbourg: they are two spires."

14. This unexpected use of the subdominant minor might even be linked to the early motion to F minor in Mendelssohn's movement, the feature initially missing at a local level in Brahms's reworking.

15. Brahms's design is quite unschematic, and while I am not convinced by a rounded binary reading (see, e.g., Ryan McClelland, *Brahms and the Scherzo: Studies in Musical Narrative* [Abingdon: Ashgate, 2010], 155–67), I would hesitate to call it a type-2 sonata either. On the slow movement of Mendelssohn's Octet as a "type 2 sonata" see Hepokoski and Darcy, *Elements of Sonata Theory*, 364; further, Peter H. Smith, "The Type 2 Sonata in the Nineteenth Century: Two Case Studies from Mendelssohn and Dvořák," *Journal of Music Theory* 63/1 (2019): 103–38.

16. On the idea of allusions in Brahms's music more generally see Christopher Reynolds, *Motives for Allusion: Context and Content in Nineteenth-Century Music* (Cambridge, MA: Harvard University Press, 2003).

17. See, e.g., Steven Vande Moortele, *The Romantic Overture and Musical Form from Rossini to Wagner* (Cambridge: Cambridge University Press, 2017), 1; as well as my review, "Julian Horton, *Brahms's Piano Concerto No. 2, Op. 83*, and Steven Vande Moortele, *The Romantic Overture and Musical Form from Rossini to Wagner*," *Music Analysis* 37/3 (2018): 415–27.

18. In this sense, the present chapter is part of a broader collaborative project I am undertaking that seeks to further the incursion of recent *Formenlehre* into the nineteenth century, challenging the earlier, sometimes uncritical application of a formal model derived from late eighteenth-century music to a mid-nineteenth-century repertory.

19. Indeed, if anything the sonata idea is even more central for Mendelssohn's formal thinking than for Brahms, in that not just outer movements, but also his slow movements and scherzos, are often structured as some variant of sonata form; in Mendelssohn, it is not uncommon for an entire four-movement work to consist of sonata-based forms, something that never occurs in Brahms.

20. Mendelssohn's smoothing over of this point has also been addressed from a Schenkerian perspective by Erez Rapoport in *Mendelssohn's Instrumental*

Music: Structure and Style (Hillsdale, NY: Pendragon Press, 2012), 73–104; on Mendelssohn's possible influence on Brahms, see 176–80. Reinhold Brinkmann offers brief analyses of seven of Brahms's reprises in "Anhand von Reprisen," in *Brahms-Analysen: Referate der Kieler Tagung 1983*, ed. Friedhelm Krummacher and Wolfram Steinbach (Kassel: Bärenreiter, 1984), 107–20, though he is more concerned with demonstrating how each example responds to the individual treatment of material in the foregoing movement than with the question of formal blurring.

21. Whether "chamber music" should be considered a genre is debatable; restricting the term to subcategories like "string quartet" or "instrumental sonata" would seem preferable (although even here one might be caught in disputes over whether quartets belong to the same genre as quintets or sextets). "Chamber music" functions more in the classificatory sense of "genus" here, of which quartets, duo sonatas, etc., can be considered individual "species." On the advisability and virtues of generic restriction when considering sonata practice, see especially Vande Moortele, *The Romantic Overture*, 1–6; on questions of genre in Brahms's chamber music (with particular reference to the two sextets), see especially Michael Kube, "Brahms' Streichsextette und ihr gattungsgeschichtlicher Kontext,' in *Die Kammermusik von Johannes Brahms: Tradition und Innovation*, ed. Gernot Gruber (Laaber: Laaber Verlag, 2001), 149–74; and Sumner Lott, "Domesticity in Brahms's String Sextets."

22. Peter H. Smith, "Liquidation, Augmentation, and Brahms's Recapitulatory Overlaps," *19th-Century Music* 17/3 (1994): 237–61, "Brahms and Schenker: A Mutual Response to Sonata Form," *Music Theory Spectrum* 16/1 (1994): 77–103, and "New Perspectives on Brahms's Linkage Technique," *Intégral* 21 (2007): 109–54. Also see Carissa Reddick, "*Becoming* at a Deeper Level: Divisional Overlap in Sonata Forms from the Late Nineteenth Century," *Music Theory Online* 16/2 (May 2010).

23. Both Tovey and Harold Truscott, for instance, consider Op. 18 to be Brahms's first completely successful chamber work (judging the Op. 8 Trio in its first, 1854 version). See Donald Francis Tovey, "Brahms's Chamber Music," in *Essays and Lectures on Music* (London: Oxford University Press, 1949), 220–70; and Harold Truscott, "Brahms and Sonata Style," *Music Review* 25/3 (1964): 186–201.

24. Additionally, Wolfgang Ruf considers the popular "Canzonetta" from Mendelssohn's E♭ String Quartet, Op. 12, to be the only precedent for the pizzicato close to Brahms's movement; see "Die zwei Sextette von Brahms: Eine analytische Studie," in *Brahms-Analysen: Referate der Kieler Tagung 1983*, ed. Friedhelm Krummacher and Wolfram Steinbach (Kassel: Bärenreiter, 1984), 121–33 (132).

25. Two of Mendelssohn's early chamber works prior to 1825 also manifest this ⁶⁄₄ recapitulation—the finale of the Piano Quartet, Op. 1, and second movement of the Piano Quartet, Op. 2.

26. As Sumner Lott notes, string sextets are in fact a rarity before Brahms's Op. 18, with only two published examples traceable (Louis Spohr, Op. 140, and Ferdinand David, Op. 38, the latter for a different combination of instruments;

see Sumner Lott, "Domesticity in Brahms's String Sextets," 45–46). That Brahms's first sextet was published as Op. 18 is surely no coincidence. Christopher Reynolds observes how giving works identical opus numbers to previous canonical works in the genre was a way of affirming one's place in a tradition: the opus number 18 is associated with Mozart's three "Prussian" Quartets, Beethoven's first set of quartets, Mendelssohn's first quintet, and Brahms's first sextet (see *Motives for Allusion*, 144). One may furthermore notice a gradated increase in forces from four instruments (Mozart, Beethoven) to five (Mendelssohn) to six (Brahms).

27. Yet another milder B♭ major precedent would be the recapitulation in the first movement of Beethoven's Fourth Symphony. Beethoven's retransition settles *pianissimo* on a distant B major, whose F♯^{7} dominant then resolves as an Italian Sixth to a B♭ $^6_4$; this harmony gradually builds up through a crescendo to the primary theme reprise (given with a root-position tonic).

28. Brahms's scherzi possessing sonata qualities include the present example of the A Major Piano Quartet, Op. 26/iii; the Horn Trio, Op. 40/ii; Symphony No. 4, Op. 98/iii; Cello Sonata, Op. 99/iii; and Clarinet Quintet, Op. 115/iii. Of these, only the Symphony and Clarinet Quintet movements do not follow the traditional rounded-binary structure within a larger compound ternary design. Op. 98/iii is a sonata rondo with elements of expanded type-1 design (not dissimilar to several of Mendelssohn's mature sonata-form scherzi), while Op. 115/iii offers an intriguing and formally inventive amalgamation of a framing D-major Andantino and an internal B-minor sonata-like design (Presto non assai) that starts off as if a variation of the opening Andantino.

29. Nearly all the other movements by Mendelssohn in my survey feature some type of harmonic blurring, elision, or at the very least the use of an IAC in place of a PAC at the point of reprise; of the fourteen works examined, only two movements have a clear PAC at the start of the recapitulation (Quintet Op. 18/ii and Quartet Op. 80/iv).

30. This is one of Brahms's favorite devices; it can be found prominently in the finale to the Op. 8 Piano Trio (both versions), the third movement of the Op. 34 Quintet, and the First Piano Concerto.

31. This example is discussed in more detail in my chapter "Mendelssohn and Sonata Form: The Case of Op. 44 No. 2," in *Rethinking Mendelssohn*, ed. Benedict Taylor (New York: Oxford University Press, 2020), 192–95. An example of a recapitulation actually starting on vi harmony is given in the slow movement of Mendelssohn's F Major Violin Sonata, Q26 (bar 57).

32. More idiosyncratic of the earlier composer, however, is the use of a lyrical countermelody, normally starting a few bars prior to the reprise, to smooth over the sectional join, or the rotational blurring of closing theme and primary theme when based on similar material (e.g., in the opening movement of the E Minor Quartet, Op. 44, No. 2, above, or that of the C Minor Piano Trio, Op. 66).

33. In the case of Op. 25/i, the contrasting middle *b* theme is also partially stated at the start of the development (bar 171), so it is not literally a case of splitting up a single statement of the primary theme over two sections.

34. As witnessed by Op. 26, this practice is typical above all of Brahms's finales: later instances of its use in a chamber music context include the F Minor Piano Quintet, Op. 34; C Minor String Quartet, Op. 51, No. 1; B Major Piano Trio, Op. 8/iv (revised version); D Minor Violin Sonata, Op. 108/iv; Clarinet Trio, Op. 114/iv; and F Minor Clarinet Sonata, Op. 120, No. 1/iv.

35. This is not to deny that the "Appassionata" is likely to have been one of the works Brahms had in mind when writing Op. 5: merely that the fleeting use of the first-inversion tonic at the actual point of reprise has a negligible relation to Beethoven's much longer recapitulation of his first theme over a second-inversion tonic.

36. For instance, Daverio overlooks the obvious Mendelssohnian precedents for the ¾ recapitulation in Brahms—a point picked up on in Christopher Reynolds's review of Daverio's *Crossing Paths* in *Journal of the American Musicological Society* 57 (2004): 664–73.

37. In this, my chapter finds common ground with the enterprise set out by Julian Horton in "Criteria for a Theory of Nineteenth-Century Sonata Form," *Music Theory and Analysis* 4/11 (2017): 147–91, which has served as a stimulus for my approach here.

Chapter 12

1. Peter Petersen, "Brahms und Dvořák," in *Brahms und seine Zeit*, ed. Constantin Floros et al. (Laaber: Laaber-Verlag, 1984), 125–46.

2. Analytical studies of Dvořák's instrumental music include David Beveridge, "Romantic Ideas in a Classical Frame: the Sonata Forms of Dvořák" (PhD diss., University of California, Berkeley, 1980); Hartmut Schick, *Studien zu Dvořáks Streichquartetten* (Laaber: Laaber-Verlag, 1989); Leslie Kinton, "A Documentary Study and Schenkerian Analysis of Dvořák's Symphony in D Minor, Op. 70" (PhD diss., University of Toronto, 2008); Markéta Štědronská, *Die Klavierkammermusik von Antonín Dvořák: Studien und Vergleiche mit Werken von Brahms* (Tutzing: Hans Schneider, 2008); Carissa Reddick, "Formal Fusion and Rotational Overlap in Sonata Forms from the Chamber Music of Brahms, Dvořák, Franck, and Grieg" (PhD diss., University of Connecticut, 2009); Daniel Partridge, "Harmony, Form, and Voice Leading in the Mature Works of Antonín Dvořák" (PhD diss., City University of New York, 2012); and Xieyi Zhang, "Tonicizations, Periods, and Period-Like Structures in the Music of Dvořák" (PhD diss., City University of New York, 2019). There has also been valuable scholarship of a more historical bent, for instance, Michael Beckerman, *New Worlds of Dvořák: Searching in America for the Composer's Inner Life* (New York: W. W. Norton, 2003).

3. David Beveridge, "Dvořák and Brahms: A Chronicle, an Interpretation," in *Dvořák and His World*, ed. Michael Beckerman (Princeton, NJ: Princeton University Press, 1993), 79.

4. Michael Beckerman, "Dvořák and Brahms: A Question of Influence," *The American Brahms Society Newsletter* 4/2 (1986): 6–8; and David Beveridge, "Echoes of Dvořák in the Third Symphony of Brahms," *Musik des Ostens* 11 (1989): 221–30.

5. Here I apply, to Brahms and Dvořák, Dahlhaus's concept of "individualization of harmony" in which "harmonic progressions and even some individual chords in Wagner have the same significance as a leitmotiv." "Issues in Composition," in *Between Romanticism and Modernism: Four Studies in the Music of the Later Nineteenth Century*, trans. Mary Whittall (Berkeley: University of California Press, 1980), 73.

6. Joel Galand, "Some Eighteenth-Century Ritornello Scripts and Their Nineteenth-Century Revivals," *Music Theory Spectrum* 30/2 (2008): 239–82.

7. Beveridge assembles, in English translation, all ten extant letters of the Brahms-Dvořák correspondence and surveys relevant passages from the composers' correspondence with Simrock, including this letter of January 1894 ("Dvořák and Brahms," 81). My quotations throughout are from Beveridge's translations. Brahms's familiarity with the American works of 1893 cannot be in doubt. He immersed himself in them after accepting Simrock's request to correct the prepublication proofs, commenting that they would "interest me naturally" (Letter from Brahms to Simrock on 22 December 1893).

8. Klaus Döge, "Dvořák, Antonín," *Grove Music Online*, 2001, https://www.oxfordmusiconline.com/grovemusic/view/10.1093/gmo/9781561592630.001.0001/omo-9781561592630-e-0000051222 (accessed 31 March 2021).

9. Döge, "Dvořák, Antonín."

10. The [a′] section of the Quartet's refrain emerges via a Brahmsian formal overlap. Brahms forgoes restatement of bars 1–12 and fuses retransitional and reprise functions in bars 61–66.

11. John Daverio discusses Brahms's recapitulatory "scattering," in which expository passages eventually return but are redistributed non-contiguously rather than recurring in immediate succession. "From 'Concertante Rondo' to 'Lyric Sonata': A Commentary on Brahms's Reception of Mozart," in *Brahms Studies*, ed. David Brodbeck (Lincoln: University of Nebraska Press, 1994), 1:111–38.

12. Like the return of the C episode, a retransition prepares the coda. These are the only instances of such continuity in the movement. The minor mode, A-section material, and *tempo primo* do return prior to the coda, at bar 256. This entrance nevertheless serves as a stepping stone to the later formal moment. The theme at bar 256 is the refrain's [b] section and thus fails to achieve the fullest form of return—the articulation of G minor by the opening material. The earlier moment also lacks the climax provided by the coda's resolution of an extensive retransitional dominant. The coda's *molto presto* intensifies the climax.

13. As I explore in "New Perspectives on Brahms's Linkage Technique," *Intégral* 21 (2007): 139–49.

14. As analyzed by Scott Murphy, "On Metre in the Rondo of Brahms's Op. 25," *Music Analysis* 26/3 (2007): 323–53.

15. My analysis summarizes my interpretation in "Brahms and the Neapolitan Complex: ♭II, ♭VI, and Their Multiple Functions in the First Movement of the F-minor Clarinet Sonata," in *Brahms Studies*, ed. David Brodbeck (Lincoln: University of Nebraska Press, 1998), 2:169–208. Other, insightful analyses include Roger Graybill, "Brahms' Integration of Traditional and Progressive Tendencies: A Look at Three Sonata Expositions," *Journal of Musicological Research* 8/1–2 (1988): 143–47; James Webster, "The General and the Particular in Brahms's Later Sonata Forms," in *Brahms Studies: Analytical and Historical Perspectives*, ed. George Bozarth (Oxford: Oxford University Press, 1990), 69–72; and David Beach and Ryan McClelland, *Analysis of 18th- and 19th-Century Works in the Classical Tradition* (New York: Routledge, 2012), 258–76.

16. For discussion of intense motivic integration in Dvořák, see my analysis of the first movement of the E♭-major Piano Quartet in "Form and the Large-Scale Connection: Motivic Harmony and the Expanded Type-1 Sonata in Dvořák's Later Chamber Music," *Music Theory Spectrum* 40/2 (2018): 269–75.

17. The graph spells all instances as D♭ and G♭ despite Brahms's use of C♯ and F♯ prior to bar 136.

18. Jenner, "Johannes Brahms as Man, Teacher, and Artist," in *Brahms and His World*, rev. ed., ed. Walter Frisch and Kevin Karnes (Princeton, NJ: Princeton University Press, 2009), 385, 413.

19. On Brahms's tonal pairing in sonata form, see my "Tonal Pairing and Monotonality in Instrumental Forms of Beethoven, Schubert, Schumann, and Brahms," *Music Theory Spectrum* 35/1 (2013): 77–102.

20. Schick (*Studien zu Dvořáks Streichquartetten*, 166–89) also explores these tonic-submediant interactions.

21. The term *ritornello scripts* is Galand's. He uses it to categorize sonata forms based on various patterns of P return, often in the tonic but also possibly in other keys ("Some Eighteenth-Century Ritornello Scripts"). Dvořák's Op. 80 and Brahms's Op. 78 include three tonic statements of P: at the outset, following the exposition, and at the recapitulation. This pattern affiliates the movements with Galand's Type III script. The movements' P-based codas also function as "ritornellos," a feature Galand additionally associates with Type III.

22. The B–B♯–C♯ motions in bars 13–15 prepare the tonicization of C♯ at bar 17. As Dvořák expands the home dominant for the return to E at bar 38, he reverses the chromatic motion in both the cello and first violin: C♯–C♮–B (bars 32–34 and 36–38). In yet another reversal, the S theme includes a B–B♯–C♯ motion in the cello, as its local E tonicizations return to C♯ (bars 55–57 and 71–73). Thus, motion to C♯ triggers chromatic ascent with B♯; motion to E, chromatic descent with C♮.

23. See, for instance, the B–A–F♯–D♯–B bass arpeggiation across bars 5–9, with each pitch governing one bar of the V^7 expansion. The C♯'s effect momentary shifts to vii^{ø7} at bars 6 and 7.

24. The one exception arises with the $^6_4$ chord above E in bar 43, a sonority that does indeed grow from the E $^5_3$ in bars 38–41 via a 5–6 motion. The passage also includes B♯–C♯ in the violins and a hint of tonicization via the vii$^{o4}_3$/vi on beat 4 of

bar 42. P and S otherwise stress C♯ in root position; no parallelisms among C♯ $\S$ chords materialize.

25. Brahms already knew the E-major Quartet from his service on the jury for the Austrian State Stipendium. It was one of the compositions that Dvořák submitted in his winning application of 1876, Brahms's second year on the jury. Brahms's letter requesting the E-major Quartet appears in Beveridge, "Dvořák and Brahms," 66.

26. Beveridge, "Dvořák and Brahms," 67.

27. Brahms, in a letter of December of 1877 recommending Dvořák's Moravian Duets to Simrock, stressed his stinginess with recommendations (Beveridge, "Dvořák and Brahms," 63).

28. Brahms's correspondence about the Quartet was based on his familiarity with an earlier, 1876 version. In 1888, Dvořák revised the Quartet and published it as Op. 80. Although no record survives of Brahms's judgment of the revisions, the changes do not have a substantial impact on the first movement's form, as Beveridge notes ("Romantic Ideas in a Classical Frame," 337).

29. I cite first movements to distinguish the post-exposition tonic return of P from standard sonata-rondo convention in finales. Some of these movements follow Galand's Type III script, in which yet another tonic P also launches the recapitulation. This is the practice we will see in the E-major Quartet and Brahms's G-major Violin Sonata. Others are instances of a binary sonata form with an exposition and an "expanded recapitulation."

30. The addition of D♮, new accompanying voices, and a new imitative continuation ensure that the tonic return of P will not be confused, even momentarily, with an exposition repeat.

31. The harmonic progression and C♯-C♮-B bass leading to the retransitional dominant follow the pattern established by the return to E from C♯ within the original P zone (bars 32-34).

32. The dotted rhythm joins other aspects of developing variation to unify the themes in the first movement and, indeed, across the three-movement cycle.

33. See Walter Frisch, *Brahms and the Principle of Developing Variation* (Berkeley: University of California Press, 1984), 116-20, for an interpretation of the Sonata's motivic process.

34. Arnold Schoenberg, *Style and Idea*, ed. Leonard Stein (Berkeley: University of California Press, 1984), 398-441.

Chapter 13

1. Richard Cohn, "Introduction to Neo-Riemannian Theory: A Survey and Historical Perspective," *Journal of Music Theory* 42/2 (1998): 167-80 (168).

2. For a contrary view that transformational theory is not at all antithetical to tonality, see Steven Rings, *Tonality and Transformation* (New York: Oxford University Press, 2011).

3. To be clear, this graphic depiction is my own, based on my understanding of transformational processes.

4. Even in the exceptional situation of works clearly not in a single key, it is arguable that parts of the piece can still cohere to an individual triad in the manner pictured here.

5. This reproduces the original Figure 1 of *Der freie Satz* in the 1935 edition, which was redacted in the Jonas edition. *Der freie Satz*, Vol. III of *Neue musikalische Theorien und Phantasien* (Vienna: Universal Edition, 1935; 2nd ed., ed. and rev. Oswald Jonas, Vienna: Universal Edition, 1956); *Free Composition*, trans. and ed. Ernst Oster (New York: Longman, 1979). The differences between my Figure 13.1b and Schenker's are not critical to the issue at hand.

6. For instance, Neo-Riemannian transformations easily describe root motions by third, an ubiquitous feature of common-practice music.

7. Of course, standard features of a tonal work are often more latent than apparent, but unusual features need special pleading, on the grounds that extraordinary claims require extraordinary evidence.

8. David Lewin, *Generalized Musical Intervals and Transformations* (New Haven, CT: Yale University Press, 1987), 165 and 168.

9. It is worth noting that major-cycles can prolong both tonic and dominant harmonies equally effectively and commonly.

10. Consult the score for the subtle details of the dissolution of the apparent keys F♭ and C major.

11. Mixture conventionally includes interchanges between major and minor, applied to the third and/or the root, as well as the special inclusion of the Phrygian (lowered) II. Raising the roots of tonic, dominant, and subdominant can be construed as a type of leading-tone chromaticism; lowering those roots is normally considered disruptive of their function and therefore not viable.

12. See Cohn's later stand, which describes how: "the splitting of a tone's scale-degree constituency can have a ripple effect, destabilizing the diatonic collection and the tonic that is claimed to anchor it"—which I would place in Type 3. He also notes that "while the local spans are classically tonal, the middleground tonics adhere to a different logic"—which could be a description of my Type 4. (Cohn's discussion begins with music of Schubert, not Brahms.) See *Audacious Euphony: Chromatic Harmony and the Triad's Second Nature* (New York; Oxford: Oxford University Press, 2012), 9 and 11 respectively.

13. In Example 13.5a full and partial bar lines are used to indicate metric grouping of four and two bars respectively; larger grouping is indicated by numbering in italics between the staves.

14. Note that the simplified version, made by Brahms, is in A minor and shows a similar variation at this point.

15. For more on the rhapsodic character of this piece, see my treatment in "Against Nature: Interval Cycles and Prolongational Conflict in Brahms's Rhapsody, Op. 79, #1," in *A Composition as a Problem III: Proceedings of the 3rd*

International Conference on Music Theory, Tallinn, March 9–10, 2001, edited by Mart Humal (Tallinn, Estonia: Scripta Musicalia, 2003), 93–108

16. For a different view, see Peter H. Smith, "You Reap What You Sow: Some Instances of Rhythmic and Harmonic Ambiguity in Brahms," *Music Theory Spectrum* 28/1 (2006): 57–97.

Chapter 14

1. "Einführung," in *Der Kanon in der Musik. Theorie und Geschichte. Ein Handbuch*, ed. Klaus Pietschmann and Melanie Wald-Fuhrmann (Munich: Edition Text + Kritik, 2013), 9–24 (10).

2. See the illustration in Wolfgang Sandberger and Stefan Weymar, eds., *Johannes Brahms—Ikone der bürgerlichen Lebenswelt? Ausstellungskatalog des Brahms-Instituts an der Musikhochschule Lübeck* (Lübeck: Brahms-Institut an der Musikhochschule Lübeck, 2008), 33.

3. Eduard Schmidt, *Umrisse zur Geschichte der Philosophie* (Berlin: Ferdinand Dümmler, 1839), 26.

4. See Wolfgang Sandberger, "Johannes Brahms in der Walhalla, Rede zum Festakt," *Literatur in Bayern* 61/62 (2000): 2–11.

5. "Er meinte damit jene Musik, die in dem tiefen Urgrund des Geistes der Musik wurzelt und nirgends mit ihm in Widerspruch gerät, im Gegensatz zu derjenigen, welche haltlos an der Oberfläche des Nebensächlichen klebt und, mag sie noch so originell und reizvoll wirken, vom Strom der Zeit nur zu schnell fortgerissen wird, da sie einem tieferen Kunstbedürfnisse der Menschheit nicht zu genügen vermochte." Gustav Jenner, *Johannes Brahms als Mensch, Lehrer und Künstler* (Marburg: N. G. Elwert'sche Verlagsbuchhandlung, 1905), 74.

6. Wolfgang Sandberger, "Kompositorische Selbstpositionierung. 'Ein deutsches Requiem' von Johannes Brahms und die musikhistorische Konstellation von 1868," in *Das Jahr 1868. Musik zwischen Realismus und Gründerzeit. Zürcher Festspiel-Symposium 2018*, ed. Laurenz Lütteken (Kassel: Bärenreiter, 2019), 89–108.

7. Maria Fellinger (1849–1925), daughter of the composer Josephine Lang-Köstlin, was not only a gifted painter and photographer but also a sculptor. She produced small busts and statues of Brahms modeled on her snapshots. Fellinger published her photos in 1900 as the portfolio *Johannes Brahms—Bilder*. The heavily augmented second edition (Leipzig: Breitkopf & Härtel, 1911) additionally contained photographs of the Viennese apartment of the composer and the grave at the Vienna Central Cemetery. The *Brahms-Bilderbuch* by Viktor von Miller zu Aichholz (Vienna: R. Lechner, 1905) with commentary from Max Kalbeck also contributed to the popularization of the composer.

8. Not until the 1890s did Brahms consent to being photographed in a private setting.

9. On this topic see Maren Goltz, Wolfgang Sandberger, and Christiane Wiesenfeldt, eds., *Spätphase(n)? Johannes Brahms' Werke der 1880er und 1890er*

Jahre. Internationales musikwissenschaftliches Symposium Meiningen 2008 (Munich: Henle, 2010).

10. Johannes Brahms, letter to Clara Schumann, May 1893, in Berthold Litzmann, ed., *Clara Schumann, Johannes Brahms: Briefe aus den Jahren 1853–1896*, vol. 2 (Leipzig: Breitkopf & Härtel, 1927), 513.

11. Johannes Brahms, letter to Vincenz Lachner, August 1879, cited in Reinhold Brinkmann, *Johannes Brahms. Die zweite Symphonie* (Munich: Edition Text + Kritik, 1990), 75.

12. ". . . das Ideal des Leichten, Unangestrengten, Graziösen . . ." Ludwig Finscher, "Kunst und Leben. Bemerkungen zur Kunstanschauung von Johannes Brahms," in *Johannes Brahms. Quellen—Text—Rezeption—Interpretation. Internationaler Brahms-Kongreß Hamburg 1997*, ed. Friedhelm Krummacher and Michael Struck (Munich: Henle, 1999), 31–41 (37).

13. See here Wolfgang Sandberger, ed., *Konfrontationen. Musik im Spannungsfeld des deutsch-französischen Verhältnisses 1871–1918. Symposium und Ausstellungskatalog* (Munich: Edition Text + Kritik, 2018).

14. ". . . eine ganz besondre Geliebte von mir . . ." Johannes Brahms, letter to Elisabet von Herzogenberg, 21 December 1883, in *Johannes Brahms im Briefwechsel mit Heinrich und Elisabet von Herzogenberg*, ed. Max Kalbeck (Tutzing: Schneider, 1974), 15.

15. "Diese Musik scheint mir vollkommen. Sie kommt leicht, biegsam, mit Höflichkeit daher. Sie ist liebenswürdig, sie schwitzt nicht." Friedrich Nietzsche, "Der Fall Wagner. Ein Musikantenproblem," in *Der Fall Wagner, Götzendämmerung. Nachgelassene Schriften (August 1888–Anfang Januar 1889), Nietzsche Werke. Kritische Gesamtausgabe*, section 6, vol. 3 (Berlin: Walter de Gruyter, 1969), 1–48 (7).

16. Walter Kaufmann offers an alternative translation of "Melancholie des Unvermögens" as "melancholy of incapacity." See Walter Kaufmann, trans. and ed., *The Basic Writings of Nietzsche* (New York: Random House, 2000), 643.

17. "Es giebt keinen Musiker, der in seiner Kunst belesener wäre." Philipp Spitta, "Johannes Brahms," in *Zur Musik. Sechzehn Aufsätze* (Berlin: Gebrüder Paetel, 1892), 385–427 (390).

18. ". . . die Weltgeltung der deutschen Musik zum letzten Mal . . ." Wilhelm Furtwängler, "Johannes Brahms. Vortrag, gehalten anläßlich des Brahms-Festes in Wien 1931 [sic]," in *Brahms. Bruckner. Mit einem Nachwort über Wilhelm Furtwängler von Dr. W. Riezler* (Leipzig: Reclam, 1942), 3–18 (4).

19. "Ich habe oft Streit mit mir, das heißt, Kreisler und Brahms streiten sich. Aber sonst hat jeder seine entschiedene Meinung und ficht die durch." Johannes Brahms, letter to Clara Schumann, 15 August 1854, in *Clara Schumann, Johannes Brahms: Briefe*, ed. Litzmann, 1:9.

20. ". . . spielerisch reflektierte Vehikel seiner künstlerischen Energie..." Matthias Schmidt, *Johannes Brahms: Ein Versuch über die musikalische Selbstreflexion* (Wilhelmshaven: F. Noetzel, 2000), 85.

21. See Brahms-Institut an der Musikhochschule Lübeck, digitales Archiv, Inv. Nr. ABH 1.7.1.32.

22. "... [einen der] schönsten und genialsten Jünglinge..." Robert Schumann, letter to Clara Schumann, 27 November 1854, in *Robert Schumann Briefe: Neue Folge*, ed. F. Gustav Jansen (Leipzig: Breitkopf & Härtel, 1904), 402.

23. Brahms-Institut an der Musikhochschule Lübeck, digitales Archiv, Inv. Nr. ABH 1.7.1.69. This daguerreotype is frequently shown back to front. Brahms's parting must sit on the right hand side in the reproduction—with his right hand he clasps his heart.

24. Finscher, "Kunst und Leben. Bemerkungen zur Kunstanschauung von Johannes Brahms," 31.

25. "Er [Brahms] saß mir nun gegenüber, dieser junge Held des Tages, dieser von Schumann verheißene Messias; blond, anscheinend zart, und hat doch im zwanzigsten Jahr schon durchgearbeitete Züge, obgleich rein von aller Leidenschaft." Max Kalbeck, *Johannes Brahms* (Tutzing: Schneider, 1976), 1:145–46.

26. "... ganz herrlich..." Diary entry by Clara Schumann, 20 March 1850, in Berthold Litzmann, *Clara Schumann. Ein Künstlerleben. Nach Tagebüchern und Briefen* (Leipzig: Breitkopf & Härtel, 1906), 2:208.

27. "Die interessanteste Bekanntschaft [in Wien] war wohl Brahms, dem ich durch den Gesanglehrer Gänsbacher vorgestellt wurde. Brahms ist klein und krummbeinig, hat einen dicken wackeligen Bauch und ist ziemlich schmierig gekleidet. Der Kopf ist sehr interessant, eine echte hohe Stirn, der man die geistige Arbeit ansieht. Er sah aus wie ein Bachus [sic] und etwas müde, trank viel Bier und fühlte sich behaglich. Nur wenn er seinen Zwicker aufsetzt, hat er etwas Imponierendes und die Augen blicken dann scharf und dringend." Adolf Sandberger, *Tagebuch meiner Reise nach Wien und Italien. Dezember [18]87–Juni 88*. Original in possession of the family; a copy is present in the Handschriftenabteilung of the Bayerische Staatsbibliothek, Ana 431, Schachtel 12a.

28. "... die ganze Erscheinung war gleichsam in Kraft getaucht. Die löwenhaft breite Brust, die herkulischen Schultern, das mächtige Haupt, das der Spielende manchmal mit energischem Ruck zurückwarf, die gedankenvolle, schöne, wie von innerer Erleuchtung glänzende Stirn und die zwischen den blonden Wimpern ein wunderbares Feuer versprühenden germanischen Augen[,] eine künstlerische Persönlichkeit, die bis in die Fingerspitzen hinein mit genialem Fluidum geladen zu sein schien. Auch lag etwas zuversichtlich Sieghaftes in diesem Antlitz." Joseph Viktor Widmann, *Johannes Brahms in Erinnerungen* (Berlin: Gebrüder Paetel, 1898), 17–18.

29. Joachim Reiber, "Wallender Wall—Der Bart des Johannes Brahms," in *Festschrift Otto Biba zum 60. Geburtstag*, ed. Ingrid Fuchs (Tutzing: Schneider, 2006), 425–30.

30. "... wie ein Symbol des nun vollkommen gefestigten, in ihren Zielen absolut klaren und sicheren Gestalt des Tondichters...." Reiber, "Wallende Wall."

Notes

31. Stefan Weymar, "Johannes Brahms—Ikonographie und Erinnerungsstücke," in *Johannes Brahms. Ikone der bürgerlichen Lebenswelt?*, 32–35 (32).

32. ". . . Verteidigungsmechanismus gegen den Sturm männlichen Gefühls . . ., ein Schutz gegen die Verletzlichkeit der Seele und daß Brahms die bürgerliche Lebenshaltung nur als Sicherung gegen die seelische Phantastik ansah, die seine Jugendzeit so stark bewegt hatte." Max Graf, *Legende einer Musikstadt* (Vienna: Österreichische Buchgemeinschaft, 1949), 157.

33. See here Laurenz Lütteken, "Brahms—eine bürgerliche Biographie?," in *Johannes Brahms. Ikone der bürgerlichen Lebenswelt?*, 10–15.

34. "Am nächsten Tage sandte er mir sein beinahe lebensgroßes Bild (Photographie von C. Brasch in Berlin aus dem Jahre 1896) in einem schönen Rahmen, das er in der rechten Ecke unten mit seinem Namen signiert hatte, während links die Melodie von 'Dies Bildnis ist bezaubernd schön' aus der 'Zauberflöte' in Noten steht, aber nicht in Dur, sondern in *Moll*, was er mit den Worten begleitete: 'Wenn man so ein alter Kerl ist und so viele Runzeln und Falten hat, dann *muß* man das schon in *Moll* schreiben!'" Felix von Kraus, *Begegnungen mit Anton Bruckner, Johannes Brahms, Cosima Wagner. Aus den Lebenserinnerungen von Dr. Felix Kraus (1870–1937)* (Vienna: F. Hain, [1961]), 43.

35. ". . . eine große Genugthuung" . . . Brahms "so anerkannt zu sehen . . ." Litzmann, *Clara Schumann: ein Künstlerleben* (Leipzig: Breitkopf & Härtel, 1910–1912), 3:421.

36. ". . . Ausdruck von inspirierter Genialität, von Schöpferkraft und Wachheit . . ." Johanna Lessmann, in "*. . . in meinen Tönen spreche ich.*" *Für Johannes Brahms 1833–1897. Ausstellungskatalog Museum für Kunst und Gewerbe Hamburg 1997*, ed. Otto Biba and Jürgen Neubacher (Hamburg: Museum für Kunst und Gewerbe, 1997), 59.

37. See Sandberger and Weymar, eds., *Johannes Brahms. Ikone der bürgerlichen Lebenswelt?*, 35.

38. For comparison see also the title page of Johann Mattheson, *Grundlage einer Ehrenpforte* (Hamburg: author's edition, 1740).

39. For further details see Wolfgang Sandberger, *Imagination und Kanon. Der "Komponistenhimmel" in der Zürcher Tonhalle von 1895* (Winterthur: Amadeus Verlag, 2015).

40. ". . . brausendem Jubel . . ." Kalbeck, *Johannes Brahms*, 4:420.

41. Reactions to the event in the form of letters have unfortunately not survived. Apart from a telegram to Viktor von Miller zu Aichholz (21 October) Brahms wrote no letters during his stay in Zürich in October 1895. See Wolfgang Sandberger and Christiane Wiesenfeldt, *Brahms-Briefwechsel-Verzeichnis (BBV): chronologisch-systematisches Verzeichnis sämtlicher Briefe von und an Johannes Brahms, gefördert von der Deutschen Forschungsgemeinschaft*, with the assistance of Fabian Bergener, Peter Schmitz and Andreas Hund, www.brahms-institut.de, 2010 (accessed 31 March 2021).

42. When faced with a Brahms bust standing on Max Kalbeck's bookcase, Brahms commented to his future biographer: "You see that other people also hit upon the senseless idea of relocating me onto the ceiling." Kalbeck, *Johannes Brahms*, 4:421.

43. For both Viennese painters only limited information is recorded, and for Gastgeb the birth and death dates are also missing in the *Allgemeines Künstler-Lexikon*, vol. 50 (Munich and Leipzig: Sauer Verlag, 2006), 86.

44. The particular biographical connections of both composers to Zürich may have played a background role in the conception, because at first glance it might be doubted whether Wagner as a music-dramatist properly belongs in the concert hall, even if his overtures, *Vorspiele* and individual musical-dramatic scenes (the *Liebestod*, etc.) were of course heard there. After his demission as theater capellmeister in 1850, Wagner took on the direction of the elite concerts of the Allgemeine Musikgesellschaft Zürich as a conductor. See Laurenz Lütteken, ed., *Kunstwerk der Zukunft—Richard Wagner und Zürich (1849–1858)* (Zürich: Verlag Neue Zürcher Zeitung, 2008).

45. *Neue Zürcher Zeitung*, 21 October 1895. Cited in Werner G. Zimmermann, *Brahms in der Schweiz. Eine Dokumentation* (Zürich: Atlantis Musikbuch-Verlag, 1983), 110.

46. "O! grosser Meister! Kranz und Wort erreichen / nicht Deine Höhe. Nur als Dankeszeichen / Dafür, dass unter uns Du bist erschienen, / Nimm beides an. Du weißt, dies Haus soll dienen / Der heil'gen Tonkunst. Nun in alle Ferne / Stets unter Deines Genius hellem Sterne!"

47. See here Maren Goltz, "Feine Unterschiede: Komponisten, Dichter und Interpreten in der Memorialikonographie Meiningens," *Imago Musicae* 25 (2012): 145–86 (152–53).

48. A few years before Adolf von Hildebrand reflected on the interplay between architecture and sculpture. See his *Das Problem der Form in der bildenden Kunst* (Strasbourg: Heitz, 1893).

49. Joseph Joachim, *Festrede zur Enthüllung des Brahms-Denkmals in Meiningen, 7. Oktober 1899. Diktierte Niederschrift mit autografen Korrekturen und Ergänzungen*, Staats- und Universitätsbibliothek Carl von Ossietzky, Hamburg, Signatur: Brahms-Archiv, NL Joseph Joachim.

50. "Wir sind noch unter dem tiefen Eindruck der erschütternden Klänge [des Requiems], die kaum in der Kirche verrauscht. Sie sind doch dem frommen Gemüth eines um die heißgeliebte Mutter Trauernden entquollen, der für seinen Schmerz nach Trost rang. Wie viel Tausenden waren die verklärten Klänge schon Balsam, wie viel Generationen werden sich noch daran erheben! In der ganzen Kunstgeschichte giebt es kein edleres Denkmal kindlicher Pietät zu verzeichnen. Ein Monument unvergänglicher als Erz! Brahms war ein guter, wie er ein großer Mensch war; ein Wohltäter der Menschen!" Cited by Jürgen Neubacher in "*. . . in meinen Tönen spreche ich,*" 4.

51. Her name is also occasionally written as Conrad; after her marriage in 1910 she was known as Ilse von Twardowski-Conrat. Today the Jewish sculptor is sadly

still much too little appreciated. She shared the fate of many persecuted artists, committing suicide on 9 August 1942 on receiving notification of her transportation by the Munich Gestapo.

52. On the sculptor's development see Sylvia Mraz, "Die Bildhauerin Ilse Twardowski-Conrat. Studien zu Leben und Werk" (MA diss., University of Vienna, 2003).

53. "Die Muse trägt die ausgeklungene Leier wie ein Heiligtum gegen den Himmel, gleichsam als wolle sie das köstliche Kleinod der Gottheit zurückstellen. Ein Schleier weht von der Leier herab; es ist die unsterbliche Musik des Meisters, die unter uns fortlebt! Der Jüngling drückt den Schleier an seine Lippen und bringt das tönende Vermächtnis der Menschheit hinunter zum Trost." Unknown critic, *Wiener Mode* 18 (1903), cited in Mraz, "Die Bildhauerin Ilse Twardowski-Conrat," 39.

54. "Als die Töne verklungen waren, trat Hofschauspieler Reimers vor und sprach Max Kalbecks, dem Andenken Brahms gewidmete 'Jamben.'" Unknown critic, *Wiener Bilder. Illustrirtes Familienblatt*, 13 May 1903. The paper also contained several photographs of the occasion.

55. On the *Brahms-Phantasie* by Max Klinger see Jan Brachmann, *"Ins Ungewisse hinauf..." Johannes Brahms und Max Klinger im Zwiespalt von Kunst und Kommunikation* (Kassel: Bärenreiter, 1999), and Wolfgang Sandberger, "'... ganz herrliche, wundervolle Fantasien über meine Texte'—Johannes Brahms und Max Klinger," in *Johannes Brahms. Zeichen, Bilder, Phantasien. Katalog zur Ausstellung des Brahms-Instituts an der Musikhochschule Lübeck* (Lübeck: Brahms-Institut an der Musikhochschule Lübeck, 2004), 7–88.

56. See the booklet *Brahms-Galerie* compiled by Friedhelm Döhl and published by the Musikhochschule Lübeck, 2014.

Chapter 15

1. Mscr. Dresd. X 1, 13. Karl Laux to Franz and Frau Hildegard Laux. Dated 27 October 1945. Housed in Karl Laux's Nachlass at the Sächsische Landesbibliothek—Staats- und Universitätsbibliothek (SLUB), Dresden.

2. There have been wide discrepancies about the death toll of the Dresden firebombing, ranging from 10,000 to 200,000. Dietmar Süss discusses the general difficulty of recording accurate death counts for the air war across German cities in *Death from the Skies: How the British and Germans Survived Bombing in World War II*, trans. Lesley Sharpe and Jeremy Noakes (Oxford and New York: Oxford University Press, 2011), 452–54. These difficulties were compounded in Dresden, where the death toll was subject to ideological distortions in both East Germany and the United Kingdom.

3. Mscr. Dresd. X 1, 13. "In Kürze also unser Schicksal: wir wurden in der Nacht vom 13. auf 14. Februar total ausgebombt. Am Aschermittwoch-Morgen standen wir vor der Trümmern unseres Hauses, vor den Trümmern unserer

Habe. Wir waren über Nacht Bettler geworden. Nicht nur das: einfolgende unverantwortlichen Verhaltens der Leute unter uns blieben wir, unsere Wohnung beobachtend und kleine Brände löschend, zu lange oben, sodass wir schließlich durch die den Treppenaufgang schon anfressenden Flammen mussten. Die Folge davon schwere Verbrennungen an den Händen, im Gesicht. Wir wurden ins Krankenhaus eingeliefert, ein Bild des Jammers, unsere Wunden eiterten wochenlange, bei Maria ging aus Leben und Tod. Dazu Luftangriffe, die Erwartung der Dinge, die da kommen sollten, es war eine schreckliche Zeit."

4. Mscr. Dresd. X 1, 13. "Nun hausen wir bei Bekannten. Als Untermieter. Als Ausgebombte, d.h. Als eben Geduldete (trotz aller Freundschaft). Und wir versuchen uns wieder ein Leben, ein Heim, eine Existenz aufzubauen. Wir haben jetzt zwei leere Zimmer in Aussicht. Allerdings ohne Glas, ohne Gas, ohne Wasser. Soll alles nachkommen. Ohne Möbel. Wir sind dabei uns welche zu kaufen. Auch Bücher, Noten kaufe ich mir mühsam zusammen, soweit es möglich ist, solche zu bekommen. Ein Glück: ich konnte mir wieder einen Flügel kaufen, einen (sehr alten) Beckstein."

5. Hannah Arendt, "The Aftermath of Nazi Rule: Report from Germany," in *Essays in Understanding, 1930–1954: Formation, Exile, and Totalitarianism*, ed. and trans. Jerome Kohn (New York: Harcourt, Brace, & Co. 1994), 249.

6. Monica Black, *Death in Berlin: From Weimar to Divided Germany* (Cambridge and New York: Cambridge University Press, 2010), 145–86; Robert Moeller, *War Stories: The Search for a Usable Past in the Federal Republic of Germany* (Berkeley: University of California Press, 2001), 1–20; Anke Pinkert, *Film and Memory in East Germany* (Bloomington: Indiana University Press, 2008), 19–83.

7. Mscr. Dresd. X 1, 13. Karl Laux to Franz and Frau Hildegard Laux. Dated 27 October 1945. "Als Nicht als von den Nazis Gezeichneter (Buch: "Musik in Gefahr" usw.) habe ich Aussichten, mitmachen zu können." Laux's denazification questionnaire and other biographical sketches from after 1945 are available in his archive: SLUB Mscr. Dresd. X 1, Box 1, Items 1–7.

8. Elizabeth Janik, *Recomposing German Music: Politics and Musical Tradition in Cold War Berlin* (Leiden and Boston: Brill, 2005), 129–55; David Monod, *Settling Scores: German Music, Denazification, and the Americans, 1945–1953* (Chapel Hill and London: University of North Carolina Press, 2005), 44–95.

9. Karl Jaspers, *The Question of German Guilt*, trans. E. B. Ashton, with an introduction by Joseph W. Koterski (New York: Fordham University Press, 2001).

10. Victor Klemperer, *I Will Bear Witness: A Diary of the Nazi Years, 1942–1945*, trans. Martin Chalmers (New York: The Modern Library, 2001), 478. Klemperer, who was a language professor at the Technical University of Dresden until he was removed from his position in 1935, was married to an Aryan woman, Eva. He resolutely decided to remain in Germany during the Third Reich. The Dresden firebombing paradoxically saved his life: the Nazi authorities had scheduled to send Dresden's remaining Jewish population to death camps before the firebombing. After the firebombing he discarded his Jewish identity papers and went under a

different name for the remaining months of the war. See Henry Ashby Turner Jr., "Victor Klemperer's Holocaust," *German Studies Review* 22/3 (1999): 385–95.

11. Mscr. Dresd. X 1, 13. Karl Laux to Franz and Frau Hildegard Laux. Dated 27 October 1945. "Wir Ihr auf der Rückseite ersehen könnt, ist das Kunstleben Dresdens trotz aller Trümmer (es ist schrecklich, die schöne Stadt!) wieder heftig in Gang."

12. Mscr. Dresd. X 24, 3–51.

13. Many of the Dresdner Philharmonie and the Dresdner Kreuzchor's programs have been digitized and made available online through Sachsen.digital: https://sachsen.digital/sammlungen/ (accessed 13 December 2020).

14. Stadtarchiv Dresden/Kreuzschul-Archiv, Collection: Kreuzchor nach 1945, Signature: 20.1.3, No. 1368. "Wiederbeginn der Tätigkeit des Dresdner Kreuzchores 1945 und seine Mitwirkung während des Jahres 1945."

15. Tony Joel, *The Dresden Firebombing: Memory and the Politics of Commemorating Destruction* (London: I. B. Tauris, 2013), 45–81. The idea that Dresden was a city of civilian victims was originally put forward in Nazi propaganda, by Joseph Goebbels. It became persistent in postwar Britain, too, through the work of Holocaust denier David Irving. His book *The Destruction of Dresden* (London: W. Kimber, 1963) was internationally popular at the time of its publication, though it has since been discredited. See D. D. Guttenplan, *The Holocaust on Trial* (New York: W. W. Norton, 2002).

16. Steven Hoelscher, "'Dresden, a Camera Accuses': Rubble Photography and the Politics of Memory in a Divided Germany," *History of Photography* 36 (2012): 288–305. One of the most enduring accounts of postwar Dresden for English-speaking audiences comes from Kurt Vonnegut's *Slaughterhouse Five, or The Children's Crusade: A Duty-Dance with Death* (New York: Random House, 1969), 229–30. For a discussion of this novel and its connection to Dresden's memory politics see Anne Fuchs, *After the Dresden Bombing: Pathways of Memory, 1945 to the Present* (New York: Palgrave Macmillan, 2012), 150–93.

17. Robin Leaver, "Brahms's Opus 45 and German Protestant Funeral Music," *Journal of Musicology* 19/4 (2002): 636–39.

18. Karsten Blüthgen, "Is there any work capable of replacing Brahms?," liner notes for *Johannes Brahms: Ein deutsches Requiem*, by Vocal Concert Dresden, Dresdner Philharmonie, Dresdner Kreuzchor, Roderich Kreile (Berlin: Berlin Classics, 2014), 20. Blüthgen does not specify a date for the start of this tradition, and publicity for the choir simply notes that this is a long-standing custom. Lott dates the tradition to 1939—a date confirmed by the Kreuzchor scholar Matthias Herrmann. R. Allen Lott, *Brahms's "A German Requiem": Reconsidering Its Biblical, Historical, and Musical Contexts* (Rochester, NY: University of Rochester Press, 2020), 190.

19. Daniel Beller-McKenna, *Brahms and the German Spirit* (Cambridge, MA: Harvard University Press, 2004), 69; Dennis Shrock, "Johannes Brahms—*Ein deutsches Requiem*," in *Choral Monuments: Studies of Eleven Choral Masterworks* (Oxford and New York: Oxford University Press, 2017), 282–87.

20. Adolf Nowak, "'Ein deutsches Requiem' im Traditionszusammenhang," in *Brahms-Analysen*, ed. Friedhelm Krummacher and Wolfram Steinbeck (Kassel: Bärenreiter, 1984), 201–7.

21. Sven Hiemke, *Johannes Brahms: Ein deutsches Requiem* (Kassel: Bärenreiter, 2018), 102–21; Lott, *Brahms's "A German Requiem,"* 168–226; Wolfgang Sandberger, "*Ein deutsches Requiem* als 'offene Kunstwerk'—Aspekte der Aufführungsgeschichte," in *"Ich will euch trösten": Johannes Brahms—ein deutsches Requiem: Symposion—Ausstellung—Katalog* (Munich: Edition Text + Kritik, 2012), 33–38.

22. Scholarship on "the rubble arts" outside of Germany is less common, but we can see analogous examples in musical responses to the aerial destruction of British cities. See, for example, Joanna Bullivant, *Alan Bush, Modern Music and the Cold War: The Cultural Left in Britain and the Communist Bloc* (New York: Cambridge University Press, 2017), 116–38; and Heather Wiebe, *Britten's Unquiet Pasts: Sound and Memory in Postwar Reconstruction* (New York: Cambridge University Press, 2012), 191–225.

23. Celia Applegate, *The Necessity of Music: Variations on a German Theme* (Toronto: University of Toronto Press, 2017), 301.

24. Abby Anderton, *Rubble Music: Occupying the Ruins of Postwar Berlin* (Bloomington: Indiana University Press, 2019).

25. Toby Thacker, *Music after Hitler 1945–1955* (Aldershot: Ashgate, 2007), 75.

26. Thacker, *Music after Hitler*, 29–38.

27. Richard Bessel, *Germany 1945: From War to Peace* (New York: Harper Collins, 2009), 148–68.

28. Pinkert, *Film and Memory in East Germany*, 3.

29. German studies scholars have long challenged the notion of 1945 as a zero hour. For an overview, see Stephen Brockmann, *German Literary Culture at the Zero Hour* (Rochester, NY: Camden House, 2004), 1–20 and 241–62. Brockmann further discusses the zero-hour myth in "The Postwar Restoration in East and West," *New German Critique* 42/3 (2015): 69–90.

30. The oldest boys' choir is the Thomanerchor in Leipzig, which is in the same region of Germany. For a nine-year period the Thomanerchor and the Dresdner Kreuzchor were led by the Mauersberger brothers: Erhard Mauersberger (1903–1982) was the Thomaskantor from 1961 until 1971. For more information about the Mauersberger brothers, consult Helga Mauersberger, ed., *Dresdner Kreuzchor und Thomanerchor Leipzig: Zwei Kantoren und ihre Zeit: Rudolf und Erhard Mauersberger* (Marienberg: Marienberg Druck und Verlagsgesellschaft, 2007).

31. For an English-language study of the Protestant church in the Third Reich, see Matthew D. Hockenos, *A Church Divided: German Protestants Confront the Nazi Past* (Bloomington: Indiana University Press, 2004). The landmark English-language study of the Protestant church in the GDR remains Robert F. Goeckel, *The Lutheran Church and the East German State: Political Conflict and Change under Ulbricht and Honecker* (Ithaca, NY: Cornell University Press, 1990).

32. Jürgen Helfricht, *Dresdner Kreuzchor und Kreuzkirche: Eine Chronik von 1206 bis heute* (Husum: Husum Verlag, 2004), 46.

33. Pamela Potter, "The Arts in Nazi Germany: A Silent Debate," *Contemporary European History* 15/4 (2006): 587.

34. Dieter Härtwig and Matthias Herrmann, *Der Dresdner Kreuzchor: Geschichte und Gegenwart, Wirkungsstätten und Schule* (Leipzig: Evangelische Verlagsanstalt, 2006), 136.

35. Neil Gregor, "Beethoven, Bayreuth, and the Origins of the Federal Republic of Germany," *English Historical Review* 126 (2011): 860.

36. Sonya Winterberg, *Wie keine Andere: Die Dresdner Kreuzschule in der DDR* (Berlin: Bild und Heimat, 2016). I discuss the tension between religious and secular education at the Kreuzschule in *Socialist Laments: Musical Mourning in the German Democratic Republic* (Oxford and New York: Oxford University Press, 2021), 174–78.

37. Along with musicologists and historians already cited in this essay, some of the books examining these institutional histories include: Michael H. Kater, *The Twisted Muse: Musicians and Their Music in the Third Reich* (Oxford and New York: Oxford University Press, 1997); Emily Richmond Pollock, *Opera after the Zero Hour: The Problem of Tradition and the Possibility of Renewal in Postwar West Germany* (Oxford and New York: Oxford University Press, 2019), 12–37; and Fritz Trümpi, *The Political Orchestra: The Vienna and Berlin Philharmonics during the Third Reich*, trans. Kenneth Kronenberg (Chicago: University of Chicago Press, 2016).

38. Pamela Potter, *Most German of the Arts: Musicology and Society from the Weimar Republic to the End of Hitler's Reich* (New Haven, CT: Yale University Press, 1998), and *Art of Suppression: Confronting the Nazi Past in Histories of the Visual and Performing Arts* (Berkeley: University of California Press, 2016).

39. For an example from the Munich Philharmonic, see Neil Gregor, "Siegmund von Hausegger, the Munich Philharmonic Orchestra and Civic Musical Culture in the Third Reich," *German History* 36/4 (2018): 544–73.

40. Helfricht, *Dresdner Kreuzchor und Kreuzkirche*, 47.

41. Programming more contemporary composers was one of Mauersberger's initiatives when he became Kreuzkantor in 1930. Matthias Herrmann, *Kreuzkantor zu Dresden: Rudolf Mauersberger* (Dresden: Mauersberger-Museum, 2004), 45–47.

42. Bettina Varwig, *Histories of Heinrich Schütz* (Cambridge: Cambridge University Press, 2011), 1–7.

43. Varwig, *Histories of Heinrich Schütz*, 161–93; Derek Stauff, "Schütz's *Saul, Saul, was verfolgst du mich?* and the Politics of the Thirty Years War," *Journal of the American Musicological Society* 69/2 (2016): 355–408.

44. Selected programmes of the Dresdner Kreuzchor services and concerts are available through the Sachsen.Digital collections: https://sachsen.digital/sammlungen/bestaende-des-stadtarchivs-dresden (accessed 31 March 2021).

45. Matthias Grün, *Rudolf Mauersberger: Studien zu Leben und Werk* (Regensburg: G. Bosse Verlag, 1986), 104–12; Hermann, *Rudolf Mauersberger: Kreuzkantor zu Dresden*, 40–45.

46. Varwig, *Histories of Heinrich Schütz*, 146.

47. Matthias Herrmann, ed., *Rudolf Mauersberger: Aus der Werkstatt eines Kreuzkantors: Briefe, Texte, Reden* (Marburg: Tectum Verlag, 2014), 86–106. For an example of the choir performing works written with the National Socialist agenda in mind: on 14 November 1936, the choir premiered Bruno Stürmer's Requiem at Vespers. Stürmer wrote several choral works to commemorate Nazi festivals, as mentioned in Karen Painter's work on this topic: "Music and Memory on Volkstrauertag/Heldengedenktag," in *Musik—Kultur—Gedächtnis: Theoretische und analytische Annäherungen an ein Forschungsfeld zwischen den Disziplinen*, ed. Christofer Jost and Gerd Sebald (Wiesbaden: Springer, 2020), 306.

48. Gregor, "Beethoven, Bayreuth, and the Origins of the Federal Republic of Germany"; Neil Gregor, "Music, Memory, Emotion: Richard Strauss and the Legacies of War," *Music and Letters* 96/1 (2015): 55–76; Gregor, "Siegmund von Hausegger, the Munich Philharmonic Orchestra and Civic Musical Culture in the Third Reich."

49. The same can be said of other famous regional boys' choirs, such as the Thomanerchor in Leipzig and the Regensburger Domspatzen in Regensburg.

50. Daniel Härtwig, "Die Kreuzschule im Zeitenwandel," in *Der Dresdner Kreuzchor: Geschichte und Gegenwart*, 331–47.

51. Matthias Grün provides a chronological survey of the choir's concerts in the Third Reich in *Rudolf Mauersberger: Studien zu Leben und Werk*, 65–90. Grün focuses on concerts and does not include Vespers.

52. Herrmann, *Kreuzkantor zu Dresden: Rudolf Mauersberger*, 55. Erik Levi writes about the practical ramifications of the "Konzertverbot" in *Music in the Third Reich* (New York: St. Martin's Press, 1994), 182, 203, 216. In Dresden, the Philharmonie curtailed, but did not entirely stop, performing after August 1944.

53. Programs are available through the Sachsen.Digital collections: https://sachsen.digital/alle-sammlungen/bestaende-des-stadtarchivs-dresden/listenansicht/ (accessed 13 December 2020).

54. *Liederkunde zum Evangelisches Gesangbuch*, No. 518.

55. Bessel, *Germany 1945*, 1–4.

56. Blüthgen, "Is there any work capable of replacing Brahms?," 20.

57. Magirius does not specify which ensemble he heard performing the Requiem at the Sophienkirche in 1944, but according to Herrmann, the Kreuzchor did not perform the Requiem in the final year of the war. I thank Herrmann for taking the time to correspond about piecing together the Kreuzchor's wartime performance history.

58. Heinrich Magirius, *Nachkriegszeit im Dresdner Kreuzchor: Erinnerungen an die Jahre 1945–1952 von Heinrich Magirius* (Beucha and Markleberg: Sax Verlag, 2015).

59. Lott, *Brahms's "A German Requiem,"* 334–41.

60. Lott, *Brahms's "A German Requiem,"* 184–90.

61. Lott, *Brahms's "A German Requiem,"* 218.

62. "Kirchenmusik zum Totensonntag in der Auferstehungskirche am 25. November 1945." From Sachsen Digital collections.

63. Sabine Behrenbeck, *Der Kult um die toten Helden: Nationalsozialistische Mythen, Riten und Symbole, 1923–1945* (Vierow bei Greifswald: SH-Verlag, 1996), 520–32; Neil Gregor, "'Is he still alive, or long since dead?': Loss, Absence and Remembrance in Nuremberg, 1945–1956," *German History* 21 (2003): 184.

64. Süß, *Death from the Skies,* 250–63.

65. Goeckel, *The Lutheran Church and the East German State,* 41.

66. Stadtarchiv Dresden/Kreuzschul-Archiv, Collection: Kreuzchor nach 1945, Signature: 20.1.3, No. 1368. "Wiederbeginn der Tätigkeit des Dresdner Kreuzchores 1945 und seine Mitwirkung während des Jahres 1945."

67. Janette Tilley, "Learning from Lazarus: The Seventeenth-Century Lutheran Art of Dying," *Early Music History* 28 (2009): 139–84.

68. A common myth about the Dresden firebombing of 13–14 February 1945 is that the city had been spared an aerial attack until this one in the final months of the war. But Dresden had been targeted on 7 October 1944, in an air raid that was—in comparison with the attacks on other German cities, and the later raid on Dresden—comparatively light.

69. From: "Betr.: Bei den Angriffen auf Dresdner ums Leben gekommene Kruzianer." Stadtarchiv Dresden/Kreuzschul-Archiv. Collection: Kreuzchor nach 1945. Signature 20.1.3, No. 1079. The works performed were: "Unser Leben ist ein Schatten" (Chronicles 1, 29:15, set as a motet by Johann Bach, 1604–1673), "Siehe, meine Tage" (Psalms 39:5–8, set in Brahms's Requiem), "Gib dich zufrieden" (chorale text by Paul Gerhardt, 1666, music Jakob Hintze, 1670; later set by J. S. Bach), "Mit Fried und Freud" (chorale by Martin Luther, 1527), and "Wie sie so sanft ruhn" (chorale).

70. Craig M. Koslofsky, *The Reformation of the Dead: Death and Ritual in Early Modern Germany, 1450–1700* (New York: St. Martin's Press, 2000), 95.

71. "Betr.: Bei den Angriffen auf Dresdner ums Leben gekommene Kruzianer": "Unserem lieben Mitsänger Herbert Blumstock, der dem Luftangriff am 7.10. zum Opfer fiel, und unserem lieben ehermaligen Kruzianer Lothar Weichhold zum Gedächtnis. Er gab sein Leben zwei Tage nach schwerer Verwundung im Osten am 13. September im Alter von 19 Jahren." This document is an internal memorandum now in the Kreuzschule's archive. I do not know if this memorial notice was included in the public Vespers service, but the Kreuzkirche did print death notices for local residents for their Vespers services during the Second World War.

72. Two of these works are expanded versions of those performed at Blumstock's grave the day earlier. This type of overlap is common in the Kreuzchor's weekly performances, since they choose repertoire to suit the liturgical year and function.

73. Behrenbeck, *Der Kult um die toten Helden,* 65–76.

74. Behrenbeck, *Die Kult um die toten Helden*, 492–532; Painter, "Music and Memory on Volkstrauertag/Heldengedenktag," 298–317.

75. Reinhold Brinkmann, "The Distorted Sublime: Music and National Socialist Ideology—A Sketch," in *Music and Ideology*, ed. Mark Caroll (New York: Routledge, 2012), 225. Katherine FitzGibbon, "Gottfried Müller's *Deutsches Heldenrequiem* (1934): Nazi Ideology Cloaked in Historic Style," in *Composing for the State: Music in Twentieth-Century Dictatorships*, ed. Esteban Buch, Igor Contreras Zubillaga, and Manuel Deniz Silva (Burlington, VT: Ashgate, 2016), 70–82.

76. Black, *Death in Berlin*, 88–91; Behrenbeck, *Der Kult um die toten Helden*, 456–60.

77. Beller-McKenna, *Brahms and the German Spirit*, 165–94; Ulrike Petersen, "The Era of National Socialism," in *Brahms in Context*, ed. Natasha Loges and Katy Hamilton (Cambridge and New York: Cambridge University Press, 2019), 336–46.

78. FitzGibbon, "Gottfried Müller's *Deutsches Heldenrequiem* (1934)," 74; Brinkmann, "The Distorted Sublime," 224–25.

79. Brinkmann, "The Distorted Sublime," 218.

80. In addition to studies cited previously, representative studies of Dresden's memory politics after 1945 include: Matthias Neutzner, "Vom Anklagen zum Erinnern: Die Erzählung vom 13. Februar," in *Das rote Leuchten: Dresden und der Bombenkrieg*, ed. Oliver Reinhard, Matthias Neutzner, and Wolfgang Hesse (Dresden: Edition Sächsische Zeitung, 2005), 129–63; and Susanne Vees-Gulani, "The Politics of New Beginnings: The Continued Exclusion of the Nazi Past in Dresden's Cityscape," in *Beyond Berlin: Twelve German Cities Confront the Nazi Past*, ed. Gavriel D. Rosenfeld and Paul B. Jaskot (Ann Arbor: University of Michigan Press, 2008), 25–47.

81. Herrmann, ed., *Rudolf Mauersberger: Aus der Werkstatt eines Kreuzkantors*, 118–20. Elsewhere I have argued that the choir became a "post-traumatic" community in the wake of the firebombing. Sprigge, *Socialist Laments*, 137–43.

82. Stadtarchiv Dresden/Kreuzschul-Archiv. Collection: Kreuzchor nach 1945, Signature: 20.1.3, No. 1079; Herrmann, ed., *Rudolf Mauersberger: Aus der Werkstatt eines Kreuzkantors*, 113–16.

83. Grün, *Rudolf Mauersberger*, 218; Vitus Froesch, *Die Chormusik von Rudolf Mauersberger: Eine stilkritische Studie* (Marburg: Tectum Verlag, 2013), 128–29.

84. Martha Sprigge, "Dresden's Musical Ruins," *Journal of the Royal Musical Association* 141/1 (2019): 83–121.

85. Sprigge, "Dresden's Musical Ruins," 108–13.

86. Matthias Herrmann and Heinrich Magirius, "Totenklage und Auferstehung: Rudolf Mauersbergers *Dresdner Requiem* und seine Initiativen zum Wiederaufbau der Dresdner Kreuzkirche in den Jahren 1945 bis 1955," in *Dresden und die avancierte Musik im 20. Jahrhundert*, Vol. II: *1933–1966*, ed. Matthias Herrmann and Hanns-Werner Heister (Laaber: Laaber-Verlag, 2002), 337–50.

87. For an overview of the challenges facing Dresden after the Second World War see Fuchs, *After the Dresden Bombing*, 90–95; Thomas Widera, *Dresden*

1945–1948: Politik und Gesellschaft unter sowjetischer Besatzungsherrschaft (Göttingen: Vandenhoeck & Ruprecht, 2004).

88. The Kreuzkirche was reopened on 13 February 1955, on the tenth anniversary of the firebombing. See Hermann and Magirius, "Totenklage und Auferstehung," 337; Sprigge, *Socialist Laments*, 163–74.

89. A document outlining the Kreuzchor's resumption of musical activities, which must have been drawn up by members of the choir's pastoral staff in early May 1945, can be found in the archives of the Kreuzschule. Stadtarchiv Dresden/Kreuzschul-Archiv, Collection: Kreuzchor nach 1945, Signature: 20.1.3, No. 1368. "Wiederbeginn der Tätigkeit des Dresdner Kreuzchores 1945 und seine Mitwirkung während des Jahres 1945." There is a note that the Kreuzchor will not hold their typical Vespers services between 25 December 1945 and 12 February 1946 because of the lack of coal ("Ab Januar zunächst Einstellung der Vespern wegen Kohlenmangel.")

90. *Begegnungen mit Rudolf Mauersberger: Dankesgabe eines Freundenkreises zum 75. Geburtstag des Dresdner Kreuz-Kantors*, ed. Erna Hedwig Hofmann (Berlin: Evangelische Verlagsanstalt, 1968), 131.

91. In his autobiography, Karl Laux estimates that the crowd was 3,000 people: *Nachklang: Autobiographie* (Berlin: Verlag der Nation, 1977), 323.

92. I discuss this service in the article "Dresden's Musical Ruins," 88–94.

93. "Widerbeginn der Tätigkeit." This document does not list the repertoire performed on the first anniversary of the firebombing, but testimonial accounts report that it was Brahms's Requiem. Magirius, *Nachkriegszeit im Dresdner Kreuzchor*, 36.

94. The choir perform Mauersberger's mourning motet *Wie liegt die Stadt so wüst* together with a canonical choral Requiem or Lutheran choral mourning works every year the weekend closest to 13 February. In 2021, the choir planned to give two performances of Brahms's German Requiem on 6 and 7 February 2021, though the entire city's annual commemorative activities—including concerts, church services, and a silent "human chain" (Menschenkette)—ended up taking place virtually due to the Covid-19 pandemic. See "Impressionen vom 13. 2021" https://13februar.dresden.de/de/gedenken/2021/impressionen-2021.php (accessed March 11, 2022). In 2022, the Kreuzchor performed Mauersberger's mourning motet, and two motets by J.S. Bach (*Jesu, meine Freunde*, BWV 227 and *Fürchte dich nicht*, BWV 228). "Gedenkvesper zum 13. February 1945," https://www.kreuzkirche-dresden.de/veranstaltungen/veranstaltung/gedenkvesper-zum-13-februar-1945.html (accessed March 11, 2022).

95. Herrmann, *Rudolf Mauersberger: Aus der Werkstatt eines Kreuzkantors*, 14–16.

96. Matthias Herrmann, ed., *Dresdner Kreuzchor und zeitgenössische Musik: Ur- und Erstaufführungen zwischen Richter und Kreiler* (Marburg: Tectum Verlag, 2017), 308.

97. Stadtarchiv Dresden/Kreuzschul-Archiv. Collection: Kreuzchor nach 1945, Signature: 20.1.3, No. 1368: "Zur Einführung," from the order of service for

the *Dresdner Requiem: Evangelische Totenmesse für drei Chöre a cappella, getrennt aufgestellt, Knabensolostimme, Bläser und Orgel (1. Chor: Hauptchor, 2. Chor: ferngestellt, 3. Chor: Altarchor), nach Worten der Bibel und Gesangbuches.* (13 February 1954 and 1957).

98. Rudolf Mauersberger, *Dresdner Requiem nach Worten der Bibel und des Gesangbuches*, ed. Matthias Herrmann (Stuttgart: Carus Verlag, 1994). The Kreuzchor often performed *Wie liegt die Stadt so wüst* and the *Dresdner Requiem* together. A recording of the two works performed by the Kreuzchor is available through Carus (1995).

99. Nowak, "'Ein deutsches Requiem' im Traditionszusammenhang," 202–3; Froesch, *Die Chormusik von Rudolf Mauersberger*, 39–40.

100. Froesch, *Die Chormusik von Rudolf Mauersberger*, 45.

101. Herrmann, *Rudolf Mauersberger: Kreuzkantor zu Dresden*, 11–17.

102. Mauersberger, *Dresdner Requiem*, xiv–xviii. For further discussion of this section, see Sprigge, *Socialist Laments*, 150–56.

103. Beller-McKenna, *Brahms and the German Spirit*, 75; Nicole Grimes, *Brahms's Elegies: The Poetics of Loss in Nineteenth-Century German Culture* (Cambridge and New York: Cambridge University Press, 2019), 83–95.

104. Vitus Froesch, "Zeitgenössische Chormusik beim Kreuzchor unter Rudolf Mauersberger 1930–1970," in *Dresdner Kreuzchor und zeitgenössische Chormusik: Ur- und Erstaufführungen zwischen Richter und Kreiler*, ed. Matthias Hermann (Marburg: Tectum Verlag, 2017), 76; Herrmann, *Kreuzkantor zu Dresden*, 52.

105. Beller-McKenna, *Brahms and the German Spirit*, 67; Hiemke, *Johannes Brahms*, 10–11.

106. Mauersberger, *Dresdner Requiem*, 20–75.

107. On one note from the Kreuzchor's archive, the distant choir are labeled a "mourning choir" (Trauerchor). Stadtarchiv Dresden/Kreuzschul-Archiv. Collection: Kreuzchor nach 1945, Signature: 20.1.3, No. 1368.

108. Varwig, *Histories of Heinrich Schütz*, 119–23.

109. Gilad Margalit, "Der Luftangriff auf Dresden: Seine Bedeutung für die Erinnerungspolitik der DDR und für die Herauskristallisierung einer historischen Kriegserinnerung im Westen," in *Narrative der Shoah: Repräsentationen der Vergangenheit in Historiographie, Kunst und Politik*, ed. Susanne Düwell and Matthias Schmidt (Paderborn: Schöningh, 2002), 192–93.

110. Bill Niven, "The GDR and Memory of the Bombing of Dresden," in *Germans as Victims: Remembering the Past in Contemporary Germany*, ed. Bill Niven (New York: Palgrave Macmillan, 2006), 109–29. For more discussion about the Kreuzchor's commemoration of the firebombing in the GDR, see Chapter 3 of Sprigge, *Socialist Laments*.

111. Magirius, *Nachkriegszeit im Dresdner Kreuzchor*, 60.

112. Elaine Kelly, *Composing the Canon in the German Democratic Republic: Narratives of Nineteenth-Century Music* (New York: Oxford University Press, 2014), 53.

113. Gilad Margalit, *Guilt, Suffering, and Memory: Germany Remembers Its Dead of World War II*, trans. Haim Watzman (Bloomington: Indiana University Press, 2010), 155–58.
114. Hiemke, *Johannes Brahms*, 115–22.
115. Johannes Behr, "Germany," in *Brahms in Context*, 314–15; Grimes, *Brahms's Elegies*, 1–3.
116. Lott's recent monograph, however, has sought to challenge this secular interpretation of the Requiem's reception history. He asserts that the liturgical context in which Brahms's work would have been heard and understood at the time of its composition. Lott, *Brahms's "A German Requiem."*

Chapter 16

1. Karl Geiringer, "Brahms the Ambivalent," in *Brahms Studies: Analytical and Historical Perspectives*, ed. George Bozarth (Oxford: Clarendon Press, 1990), 1–4; Dillon Parmer, "Brahms the Programmatic?: A Critical Assessment," (PhD diss., Eastman School of Music, 1995); the New York Philharmonic presented "Brahms the Romantic," a six-part concert series from February through June 2007. See the (unflattering) review of the final concert of 2 June (Haydn Variations, Op. 56, and *Ein deutsches Requiem*, Op. 45), Anne Midgette, "Romantic Side of Brahms: So Dark, So Brooding," *New York Times*, 7 June 2007, https://www.nytimes.com/2007/06/07/arts/music/07phil.html (accessed 31 March 2021)
2. Brian MacDonald, choreographer, *Aimez-vous Bach?* (1964); Jean Sanitas, *Aimez-vous Wagner?* (Paris: Éditeurs Français Réunis, 1967); Peter Gay, "Aimez-vous Brahms? Reflections on Modernism," *Salmagundi* 36 (1977): 16–35; Charles Rosen, "Aimez-vous Brahms?," *New York Review of Books*, 22 October 1998, 64–68.
3. *Aimez-vous Brahms "the Progressive"?* ed. Heinz-Klaus Metzger and Rainer Riehn (Munich: Text + Kritik, 1989).
4. "Meinte Sagan . . . in einem Fernsehinterview mit Pierre Dumayet mit, dass der Titel eine einfache und neugierige Frage sei, die man an ein Mädchen richtet, wie zum Beispiel 'Aimez-vous Chopin? Aimez-vous Brahms? Que pensez-vous de Dieu?' Nur 'die Intention der Frage' sei wichtig, nicht aber die Antwort." Nicholas Dufetel, "'Aimez-vous Brahms . . .': Zur Brahms-Rezeption in Frankreich um 1900," in *Konfrontationen: Symposium: Musik im Spannungsfeld des deutsch-französischen Verhältnisses 1871–1918*, ed. Wolfgang Sandberger (Lübeck: Brahms-Institut an der Musikhochschule Lübeck, 2018), 38.
5. Françoise Sagan, *Aimez-vous Brahms . . .*, trans. Peter Wiles (New York: Penguin, 1962), 46.
6. Jim Samson, "Music and Society," in *The Late Romantic Era: From the mid-19th Century to World War I*, ed. Jim Samson (Englewood Cliffs, NJ: Prentice Hall, 1991), 21.

7. Marc Vignal, "Brahms und Frankreich," in *Internationaler Brahms-Kongress Gmunden 1997: Kongress Bericht*, ed. Ingrid Fuchs (Tutzing: Hans Schneider, 2001), 281–88.

8. "Aimez-vous la musique de Brahms?—Je vous répondrai mieux quand je l'aurai tout entière entendue, du moins les vingt-quatre *opera* de sa musique de chambre, puisque l'infatigable Armand Parent nous en réservait, cette année, la primeur à la Schola." Raymond Bouyer, "Quatuor Parent," *Le Guide musical*, 15 March 1908, 228.

9. "Ceci est bien entendu une première à Paris, où Brahms était parcimonieusement diffusé, presque exclusivement auprès de cercles d'initiés germanophiles. Dans un pays où l'éveil à la musique de chambre et à la musique symphonique était encore bien frais, où les musiciens progressistes déployaient des efforts intenses pour oublier que Wagner avait été allemand, Brahms était considéré comme la figure emblématique d'une certaine Germanie pédante, très *Herr Doktor Professor*, artistiquement morte par l'influence dessiccative des ambitions militaires teutonnes." Michel Stockhem, "Armand Parent, Brahms et la France," *Revue belge de Musicologie / Belgisch Tijdschrift voor Muziekwetenschap* 47 (1993): 177–88 (179).

10. "Imbert, critique parmi les plus prolifiques sinon les plus fondamentaux du tourant du siècle." Also in 1894, Hugues Imbert published the pamphlet *Étude sur Johannès Brahms: Avec le catalogue de ses œuvres* (Paris: Fischbacher, 1894). Stockhem, "Parent, Brahms," 180.

11. "Disons vite que l'austère musicien, célébré par la plume enthousiaste de Hugues Imbert et le crayon schumannien de Fantin-Latour, n'a jamais compté, mort ou vivant, parmi les génies contestés, car son œuvre, éminemment orthodoxe, ne parait ni combative ni déroutante; elle est si foncièrement germanique, qu'elle n'attire point, de prime abord, le goût français. . . . Contentons-nous d'écouter la musique de Brahms; . . . L'analyse avant la synthèse! Et gardons-nous des jugements tout faits!" Bouyer, "Quatuor Parent," 228.

12. "[S]eul peut-être parmi les Allemands, il hérita quelque peu du don beethovénien du *développement* des idées, mais au point de vue thématique beaucoup plus qu'au point de vue tonal. Ses idées et ses harmonies ne sont point banales, mais elles sont rarement très caractérisées. Telles qu'elles sont, Brahms les manie avec talent et, pour nous servir de l'image si vulgaire, 'il travaille dans la pâte'; mais cette 'pâte' reste souvent au bout de sa plume, et son style devient alors lourd et indigeste. Comme par ailleurs les rapports de tonalités lui sont trop souvent indifférents, beaucoup de ses œuvres sont embarrassées et fastidieuses à l'audition." Vincent d'Indy, *Cours de composition musicale*, prepared in collaboration with Auguste Sérieyx (Paris: Durand, 1912), 2:415.

13. "Tout être doué de sens artistique doit avoir pour Brahms du *respect*; mais il n'est pas facile de *l'aimer*, car ses œuvres, si honnêtement *composées* qu'elles soient, rayonnent bien rarement de ce charme vrai qui touche notre cœur et le fait vibrer." D'Indy, *Cours de composition musicale*, 2:415–16. This was a familiar criticism in Brahms reception generally, famously lodged by Wolf in Vienna, George Bernard

Shaw in England (a devout Wagnerite), and by American music critic Philip Hale, who is said to have suggested a sign be posted in the newly built Boston Symphony Hall that would read, "Exit Here in Case of Brahms." Shaw later altered his opinion of Brahms, referring to his "hasty (not to say silly) description of Brahms's music." See Nicole Grimes and Angela R. Mace, "Introduction," in *Mendelssohn Perspectives* (Aldershot: Ashgate, 2012), 24, note 1.

14. *La Revue Musicale*, 1908, 80.

15. "Les Sonates pour piano sont intéressantes par la tendance qu'elles manifestent vers la construction cyclique: mais cette conception, encore vague, est bien loin de sa réalisation complète." D'Indy, *Cours de composition musicale*, 2:416.

16. "On voit par ces exemples qu'il y a chez Brahms une tendance assez nette vers la rénovation de la forme Sonate, par le moyen de certaines modifications ou variations thématiques, dont nous ne trouvons nulle trace dans les œuvres de ses contemporains allemands. C'est toujours la conception cyclique latente qui dicte ces tentatives incomplètes, dont la réalisation intégrale était réservée à César Franck et à l'École Française, à peu près exclusivement." D'Indy, *Cours de composition musicale*, 2:418.

17. Marion Schmid, "À bas Wagner!: The French Press Campaign against Wagner during World War I," in *French Music, Culture, and National Identity, 1870–1939*, ed. Barbara L. Kelly (Rochester, NY: University of Rochester Press, 2008), 77–91. See also Carlo Caballero, "Patriotism or Nationalism? Fauré and the Great War," *Journal of the American Musicological Society* 52 (1999): 539–625 (613).

18. Jean Cocteau, "Soyons raisonnable," *Le Mot*, March 1915, as quoted in Schmid, "À bas Wagner!," 86.

19. "Les Français ont tort de considérer Brahms comme un homme de talent moyen. C'est, à la vérité, un très puissant constructeur que l'auteur de cette Sonate en fa mineur.... L'œuvre est empreinte d'une grandeur qui doit se refléter dans l'interprétation qu'on en donne. On a reproché à Brahms son ambition, son désir du sublime: il n'en avait pas seulement le désir, il y atteignait." Alfred Cortot, *Cours d'interprétation*, ed. Jeanne Thieffry (Paris: Legouix, 1934), 158–59. (As cited in Vignal, "Brahms und Frankreich," 285.)

20. "[J]e rencontrais l'autre jour, sur le plan politique, un jeune musicien autrichien; celui-ci, tout heureux de découvrir au bout d'un moment que nous pouvions parler d'autre chose que du statut des immigres, engage aussitôt la conversation. Sa première question: 'Aimez-vous Brahms?' Je réponds aussitôt, bien entendu 'Le premier des raseurs,' et voilà mon Autrichien consterné. L'avez-vous remarqué? Brahms est le réactif spécifique qui sépare musiciens français et musiciens d'Europe Centrale: pour nous, académisme, pour eux le dernier des Trois Grands B, un classique à l'égal de Jean-Sebastian ou de Ludwig.... Il faut sortir de là; parvenir sur le terrain du goût musical, comme sur le terrain politique, à dépasser le culte stérile de la différence incommunicable: ce sera moins, voyons-le bien, un dépassement qu'un approfondissement du nationalisme." Henri Davenson, "Musique française ou musique en France," *Esprit* (new series) 109/5 (April 1945): 742–46 (743).

21. "Nous défendrons donc ici une musique à la française. Position qui arme notre critique d'une parfaite liberté de jugement à l'égard de la musique actuellement réalisée en France. Cette critique, nous avons bien l'intention de la rendre sévère, exigeante,—forte. Il me semble que la musique en France est en ce moment à la veille d'une grande époque de renouveau. L'histoire montre que les grandes renaissances sortent plus souvent d'une influence étrangère assimilée avec ardeur que d'une culture de la pure routine nationale: la Pléiade rompait avec la tradition, elle se mettait servilement à l'école de l'Humanisme italien et c'est pourtant elle qui portait la vraie grandeur française." Davenson, "Musique française," 745.

22. Henri Davenson's books on music are: *Traité de la musique selon l'esprit de saint Augustin* (Paris: Le Seuil, 1942); *Le livre des chansons, ou Introduction à la connaissance de la chanson* (Paris: Le Seuil, 1944); and *Les troubadours* (Paris: Le Seuil, 1961).

23. *Visio pacis* ("vision of peace") is often associated with the city of Jerusalem ("City of peace"), especially the heavenly Jerusalem of the Book of Revelation (Rev. 21:10).

24. "Il y aurait beaucoup de choses à dire sur l'évolution du goût, en France, à l'intérieur d'une seule génération. Rétrospectivement, je suis frappé de constater à quel point l'unité de l'Europe, qui s'achève sous nos yeux, a été longue à se faire. Longtemps, le mot 'musique' n'a pas eu le même sens à Paris, à Milan ou à Londres, pour ne rien dire de l'Allemagne. Il paraît ridicule de le redire, mais la question 'Aimez-vous Brahms?' (avec point d'interrogation, ô Julliard) a bien été, pendant tout ce temps, le schibboleth, le détecteur infaillible au passage du Rhin: j'ai souvent expliqué que le rôle historique du vieux barbu avait été rempli en France par César Franck, d'Indy, la Schola cantorum; les choses d'ailleurs ont-elles vraiment changé?" Davenson, "Un demi-siècle . . .," *Esprit* (new series) 280/1 (January 1960): 12–21 (13). "O Julliard" is a reference to the publisher of Sagan's novel, whose title does not include a question mark.

25. Joseph E. Potts, "Orchestral Concerts in Paris," *Musical Times* 92/1304 (1951): 466–68.

26. "Paris Welcomes Boston Symphony," *New York Times*, 20 September 1956, 29.

27. Gay, "Aimez-vous Brahms?," 19.

28. Historian Pamela Cheek, noting that Scudéry's map, writes, "The *Carte de Tendre* privileged the private amorous contract contingent on women's inclinations for and judgement in favor of a lover; it thus posited an alternative to the official marriage contract of interests controlled and instituted . . . by men." Cheek, *Sexual Antipodes* (Stanford, CA: Stanford University Press, 2003), 45. "[T]he *Carte de Tendre* mapped the different directions that a lover might travel in his attempt to win a woman's love and esteem. Joan DeJean explains that the *Carte de Tendre* was received as a menace to social order long after it originally appeared because it substituted the idea of agency in love and the possibility of 'multiple amorous trajectories' for the "courtly notion of a unique, predestined, irreversible passion"' (citing DeJean, *Tender Geographies*, 89).

29. Lully's *Air des hautbois* dated 1672 in *F-V* 168 is often cited as the first example of the new, French Folia type. Giuseppe Gerbino and Alexander Silbiger, "Folia," *Grove Music Online*, 2001, https://www.oxfordmusiconline.com/grovemusic/view/10.1093/gmo/9781561592630.001.0001/omo-9781561592630-e-0000009929 (accessed 31 March 2021).

30. Louis Malle, *Malle on Malle*, ed. Philip French (London: Faber and Faber, 1993), 21. Malle also made an interesting comment about the *Carte de Tendre* that suggests a connection to Brahms's theme-and-variations second movement at some level. After identifying the map as a product of the literary school around Scudéry, Malle states, "All their writing was about love: what precedes love, love itself, what follows love, all the variations. . . . *La Carte du tendre* is like a map, but the names of the villages and towns are *Passion, Remords, Jalousie*, the rivers and roads go from Passion to Jalousie—it's very bizarre actually, it's a geographic representation of all the variations around the theme of love" (*Malle on Malle*, 24). It is unlikely that Malle was consciously alluding to Brahms's piece. Nevertheless, his references to variations in the *Carte de Tendre* nevertheless accord well with his choice of that movement as the primary one from the Sextet that he employed in *Les Amants*.

31. Françoise Sagan, *Aimez-vous Brahms*, 7.

32. Françoise Sagan, *Aimez-vous Brahms*, 46–47.

33. Françoise Sagan and Anne Borchardt, "Do You Like Flounder? A Talk with Françoise Sagan," *Transatlantic Review* 4 (Summer 1960): 89–90.

34. The concert is mostly presented from Simon's perspective, but reaffirms Paule's response: "It was a concerto which Simon thought he recognized, a trifle sentimental, a trifle too sentimental at times." Sagan, *Aimez-vous Brahms*, 49.

35. Anatole Litvak (director), *Goodbye Again* (Burbank: United Artists, 1961). Although filmed in Paris, the movie was originally released in the United States. When it was released in Europe, it took back the title *Aimez-vous Brahms?* (with the question mark added).

36. Colin Roust, "Reaching a Plus Grand Public: Georges Auric as Populist," *Musical Quarterly* 95/2 (2012): 343–67.

Chapter 17

1. Levit's "Hauskonzert" series ran from mid-March to early May 2020, and most of the live recordings were made in his living room. For a profile of Levit and for further information about his lockdown recitals, see Alex Ross, "Igor Levit Is Like No Other Pianist," *New Yorker*, 18 May 2020, https://www.newyorker.com/magazine/2020/05/18/igor-levit-is-like-no-other-pianist (accessed 15 September 2020).

2. Cited from Anselm Cybinski, "Songs on the Way to an Inner World: Igor Levit's Encounters with Music from Bach to Feldman," liner booklet essay for Levit, *Encounter* (Sony Classical 19439786572, 2020), 10.

3. Press Release, "Prize for Understanding and Tolerance 2020," Website of the Jewish Museum Berlin, https://www.jmberlin.de/en/press-release-27-october-2020 (accessed October 2020).

4. The disc is bookended by Busoni's 1898 transcriptions of ten Bach Chorale Preludes—introspective, chamber-like adaptations of inherently contemplative pieces—and Morton Feldman's *Palais de Mari* (1986), which was written the year before the composer's death and is paradigmatic of his sparse, expansive late style.

5. Nicole Grimes, *Brahms's Elegies: The Poetics of Loss in Nineteenth-Century German Culture* (Cambridge: Cambridge University Press, 2019), 163.

6. Brahms, letter to Max Klinger, 8 May 1896, cited in Styra Avins, *Johannes Brahms: Life and Letters* (Oxford; New York: Oxford University Press, 1997), 734.

7. For a comparison between Brahms's set and Busoni's transcriptions, see Carmen Scialla, *A Study of Ferruccio Busoni's Transcriptions of Six Organ Chorale Preludes by Johannes Brahms* (DMA thesis, Louisiana State University, 1992).

8. Grimes, *Brahms's Elegies*, 3.

9. Levit, cited in Cybinski, liner booklet essay for *Encounter*, 10.

10. David Fanning, "Review: Igor Levit: Encounter," *Gramophone*, October 2020, https://www.gramophone.co.uk/review/igor-levit-encounter (accessed October 2020).

11. Grimes, *Brahms's Elegies*, 202.

12. Igor Levit: Beethoven and Brahms, Wigmore Hall, 8 October 2020. The video stream remained freely available on the Wigmore Hall website for a month afterward.

13. See Anthony L. Weikel III, *Brahms's Four Serious Songs: Arranged for Trombone and String Orchestra* (DMA thesis, Ohio State University, 2015).

14. Lucien Stark, *A Guide to the Solo Songs of Johannes Brahms* (Bloomington: Indiana University Press, 1995), 344.

15. Daniel Beller-McKenna, "Reconsidering the Identity of an Orchestral Sketch by Brahms," *Journal of Musicology* 13/4 (1995): 508–37 (508–9).

16. Kalbeck, cited from Beller-McKenna, "Reconsidering the Identity of an Orchestral Sketch," 209.

17. George Bozarth, "Paths Not Taken: The 'Lost' Works of Johannes Brahms," *Music Review* 50 (1989): 185–205; David Brodbeck, "Review: Margit McCorkle, *Johannes Brahms: Thematisch-bibliographisches Werkverzeichnis*," *Journal of the American Musicological Society* 39 (1989): 418–31. This debate has been reinvigorated recently by Grimes; see *Brahms's Elegies*, 200.

18. Beller-McKenna, "Reconsidering the Identity of an Orchestral Sketch," 253–54.

19. See, for instance, Laura Tunbridge, "Deserted Chambers of the Mind (Schumann Memories)," in *Rethinking Schumann*, ed. Tunbridge and Roe-Min Kok (New York: Oxford University Press, 2011), 395–410.

20. Martin Ennis, "Tumbling in the Godless Deep: Brahms and the Sense of an Ending," *Musicologica Austriaca: Journal for Austrian Musical Studies* (5 February 2020), 5.

21. My list is undoubtedly incomplete, and there are others for which I have been unable to find sufficient information to include in the list, such as a mid-century version by conductor Karl Maria Zwissler.

22. Interview with Leinsdorf in the *San Diego Union*, 1992, cited from Stig Jacobsson, liner booklet essay for *Brahms Transcribed for Orchestra*. Olle Persson, Lü Jia; Norrköping Symphony Orchestra (BIS-CD-1140), 2–6 (6).

23. See Erich Leinsdorf, *The Composer's Advocate: A Radical Orthodoxy for Musicians* (New Haven, CT; London: Yale University Press, 1982), 198ff. The medium-message metaphor is one of the most pervasive in discourse on arrangement: see William J. Drummond, "Arrangement, Listening, and the Music of Gérard Pesson," DPhil thesis, University of Oxford, 2019, especially Chapter 2 ("Approaching Arrangement") and Chapter 3.

24. Malcolm Sargent, "Music and the Interpretive Artist," *Journal of the Royal Society of Arts* 97 (1949): 880–93 (889).

25. According to Jacobsson, he finished the orchestration on 7 July 1944. See liner booklet essay, 6.

26. The "heavy double basses" is borrowed from a comment by A. J. B. Hutchings on Brahms's symphonic writing: "Oh for a respite from heavy double basses! Oh to be rid of the muzzy husking of the wood!" Sargent's orchestration, by chance or design, resonates with this notion of Brahmsian orchestral "heaviness." See Hutchings, "Orchestration and Common Sense," *Musical Times* 72 (1931): 1081–85 (1083).

27. Charles Reid, *Malcolm Sargent: A Biography* (London: Hamish Hamilton, 1968), 304.

28. The translation is lightly adapted from that by Paul England used in Simrock editions from the early 1910s (including the 1914 Reger transcription).

29. With characteristic flair for storytelling, Lutyens recalled: "I had just left my desk by the window to check the drying [of the ink by the fire]. This undoubtedly saved my life for, with an unannounced crash, the windows shattered and the blast, ignominiously, rolled me up in the carpet like jam in a swiss roll. . . . Huge slices of glass were embedded in the desk, which would have been in my head." Cited from Lutyens, *A Goldfish Bowl* (London: Cassell, 1972), 149.

30. Pamela Sargent contracted polio in Portofino in 1937, then at age thirteen. Her difficult return journey was widely reported in the British press in September 1937.

31. Letter from Brahms to Fritz Simrock, 8 May 1896. Cited in Avins, *Johannes Brahms*, 733.

32. An inquiry from Charles Groves (then with the Bournemouth Symphony Orchestra) requesting the hire of the score and parts received the following reply from Sargent's secretary on 10 January 1952: "Sir Malcolm possesses the only score and parts of his arrangement of the 'Four Serious Songs' by Brahms. . . . you will undertake to see that neither score nor parts are marked in any way, even in pencil . . . he stipulates that you perform the arrangement exactly as it stands, and do not make any cuts or alterations." Malcolm Sargent Archive, British Library MS Mus. 1784/1/27.

33. Nancy Evans, interview with Richard Aldous, cited from Aldous, *Tunes of Glory: The Life of Malcolm Sargent* (London: Hutchinson, 2001), 126.

34. Cited from Christopher Fifield, *Letters and Diaries of Kathleen Ferrier* (Woodbridge: Boydell and Brewer, 2011), 245.

35. Max Kalbeck, *Johannes Brahms*, Vol. 4, Band II (Berlin: Deutsche Brahms-Gesellschaft, 1915), Chapter 10.

36. Gustav Ophüls, *Recollections of Johannes Brahms*, cited in Grimes, *Brahms's Elegies*, 204.

37. Data sourced from *Radio Times* and BBC Programme Index, https://genome.ch.bbc.co.uk/.

38. The recording is of a BBC Radio broadcast with the BBC Symphony Orchestra, conducted by Sargent, live from the Royal Albert Hall, 12 January 1949, and has since been re-released multiple times by Decca.

39. Letter to Emmie Tillett, 3 March 1950, cited from Fifield, *Letters and Diaries of Kathleen Ferrier*, 138.

40. Clear parallels here can be drawn with the earlier success of *Ein deutsches Requiem* in translation as an "English Requiem."

41. See, for instance, the tributes gathered in Neville Cardus, ed., *Kathleen Ferrier: A Memoir* (London: Hamish Hamilton, 1954).

42. Jean Stead, "Sir Malcolm's Tribute to 'a perfect artist,'" *Yorkshire Post and Leeds Intelligencer* (9 October 1953), 5.

43. Other Ferrier performances and recordings which carry similar emotional significance include Mahler's "Der Abschied," folksongs such as "Blow the Wind Southerly," and, perhaps most of all, Gluck's "Che Farò." On the last, see Susan Rutherford, "Living, Loving and Dying in Song: Gluck, 'Che farò senza Euridice,'" *Cambridge Opera Journal* 28/2 (2016): 133–36. These examples belong to a broader set of recordings, or even works, that have become inseparable, for many listeners, from the circumstances of performers associated with them—a prominent example would be Jacqueline du Pré's 1965 recording of Elgar's cello concerto.

44. Cited in Stead, "Sir Malcolm's Tribute to 'a perfect artist.'"

45. Aldous, *Tunes of Glory*, 126; Sam Dobson, Repertoire note for the Leicester Symphony Orchestra, undated; Michael Kennedy, *The Hallé Tradition: A Century of Music* (Manchester: Manchester University Press, 1960), 352.

46. James M. Keller, "Brahms-Fantasie: Heliogravure for Orchestra," program note for the New York Philharmonic Orchestra, October 2015.

47. See Glanert, "Zum 175. Geburtstag Johannes Brahms," in *Neugier ist alles. Der Komponist Detlev Glanert*, ed. Stefan Drees (Hofheim: Wolke, 2012), 241–42 (241).

48. In this regard, Glanert draws as much from the tradition of Hans Zender's "composed interpretations" and Aribert Reimann's arrangements as he does from the *neue Einfachheit* sensibilities of his closer contemporaries including Wolfgang Rihm, Manfred Trojahn, and Detlev Müller-Siemens, whose oeuvres, while replete with allusions to, and works inspired by Brahms, Schubert, and Schumann, rarely stray into what is typically considered "arrangement." On the shift in

Notes

German composition in the later 1970s, see Aribert Reimann, "Salut für die junge Avantgarde," *Neue Zeitschrift für Musik* 140/1 (1979): 4–25.

49. On Rihm, see Nicole Grimes's chapter in this volume.

50. Ivan Hewett, "BBC Symphony Orchestra, Barbican, Review: Brahms's Mighty First Symphony glowed magnificently," *Telegraph*, 13 January 2016; Lawrence A. Johnson, "Review: Capuçon's Fiery Playing Sparks Bychkov's Brahms Programme with CSO," *Chicago Classical Review*, 9 October 2015.

51. On Brahms and the historical performance movement, see Michael Musgrave, "Historical Performance," in *Brahms in Context*, ed. Natasha Loges and Katy Hamilton (Cambridge: Cambridge University Press, 2019), 367–75.

52. Doris Hagel, "Johannes Brahms—Betrachtungen zu seinen 'Vier ernsten Gesängen,'" liner booklet note for *Antonín Dvořák, Requiem Op. 89 / Johannes Brahms, Vier ernste Gesänge op. 121*. Klaus Mertens, Doris Hagel; Capella Weilburgensis (Profil Medien, PH06050, 2006), 6–8.

53. Lawrence Venuti, *The Translator's Invisibility: A History of Translation* (London and New York: Routledge, 1995).

54. *Serious Songs—Brahms, Schubert, Barber*. Teddy Tahu Rhodes, Kristian Chong, Sebastian Lang-Lessing, Johannes Fritzsch; Tasmanian Symphony (ABC 4764363, 2014); *Glanert: 4 Präludien und Ernste Gesänge & Weites Land*. Michael Nagy, Kari Kriikku, Olari Elts; Helsinki Philharmonic Orchestra (Ondine 1263, 2017).

55. Jeal, "Review: Brahms-Glanert: Four Serious Songs, etc.," *The Guardian*, 26 January 2017. Guy Rickards, "Time Past, Present, and Future: An Introduction to the Music of Detlev Glanert," Boosey & Hawkes website, https://www.boosey.com/pages/licensing/composer/composer_main?site-lang=en&composerid=2719&langid=1&ttype=INTRODUCTION (accessed 28 March 2021).

56. Rainer Nonnenmann, "Denn es geht dem Menschen wie dem Vieh," *Kölner Anzeiger*, 19 March 2018.

57. Glanert, cited in René Spencer Saller, program booklet essay for the St. Louis Symphony Orchestra, October 2014, 28.

58. "Detlev Glanert on Detlev Glanert," short film directed by Tommy Pearson for Boosey & Hawkes, 2015, https://www.boosey.com/podcast/Detlev-Glanert-on-Detlev-Glanert/100984 (accessed October 2020).

59. Valerie Woodring Goertzen, "Clara Wieck Schumann's Improvisations and Her 'Mosaics' of Small Forms," in *Beyond Notes: Improvisation in Western Music of the Eighteenth and Nineteenth Centuries*, ed. Rudolf Rasch (Turnhout: Brepols, 2011), 153–62.

60. Nicholas Attfield, "'Eine Reihe bunter Zauberbilder': Thomas Mann, Hans Pfitzner, and the Politics of Song Accompaniment," in *German Song Onstage: Lieder Performance in the Nineteenth and Early Twentieth Centuries*, ed. Natasha Loges and Laura Tunbridge (Bloomington: Indiana University Press, 2020), 244–61.

61. Nicholas Attfield, "Thomas Mann, Hans Pfitzner, and the Politics of Song Accompaniment," 249 ff.

62. Habakuk Traber, "Im Raum der Geschichte: Die *Vier Präludien und ernsten Gesänge* (2004–5)," in *Neugier ist alles. Der Komponist Detlev Glanert*, ed. Stefan Drees (Hofheim: Wolke, 2012), 169–77 (169).

63. In *Rendering*, Berio marks the beginning of the nebulous boundary zones between full-Schubert and full-Berio with the entry of the celeste.

64. Although orchestrated for the most part in a Brahmsian style, Kloke's version is interpolated with brief collage-like passages that invoke Mahler, Schoenberg, Messiaen, and others. Kloke also makes the drastic structural change of removing the fourth song, thereby refusing the optimistic turn in Brahms's teleology.

65. Recent arrangements and editions of the Requiem include a chamber orchestration by Iain Farrington, a revised edition of Brahms's piano version undertaken by Joseph Fort and Michael Musgrave, and even a metal arrangement by Selin Schönbeck, which maintains the structural integrity of entire movements.

66. Erica Jeal, *The Guardian*, 31 July 2006; Colin Anderson, *The Classical Source*, 28 July 2006; Rainer Nonnenmann, *Kölner Anzeiger*, 19 March 2018.

67. For an example of an arrangement project by conductor Laurence Equilbey that takes great pains to distance itself from ideas of "infidelity," see Frankie Perry, "CD Review: Franz Schubert, *Nacht & Träume: Lieder with Orchestra*," *Nineteenth-Century Music Review* 17/2 (2020): 293–96.

68. For instance, see the Boosey & Hawkes works page for the *Preludes and Serious Songs*.

69. Traber, "Im Raum der Geschichte," 170.

70. This was claimed in the program booklet essay for WDR Sinfonieorchester Köln (16 March 2018), 8–9 (8).

71. An example of an historically informed approach is found in Glanert's orchestrations of selections of Mahler's *Lieder und Gesänge*, which are closely modeled on Mahler's later orchestral *Wunderhorn* songs and their symphonic intertexts.

72. Traber, "Im Raum der Geschichte," 170–71.

73. Walter Dobner, "Geglückte Probe für Hamburg," *Die Presse*, 15 January 2017, https://www.diepresse.com/5154783/gegluckte-probe-fur-hamburg (accessed September 2020).

74. Dobner, "Geglückte Probe für Hamburg." On Mahler in Hamburg, see Henry-Louis de La Grange, *Gustav Mahler, The Arduous Road to Vienna*, ed. Sybille Werner (Turnhout: Brepols, 2020), Chapters 16–24 ("Mahler in Hamburg" I–IX).

75. Martin Anderson, "Review: Benjamin, Rihm, Brahms-Glanert, Elgar-Payne," *Tempo* 61/239 (2007): 82–86; see also Alexandre Jamar, "Review: Brahms-Glanert: *Vier ernste Gesänge*," *Forum Opera*, 13 March 2017; Colin Anderson, "BBC Symphony Orchestra/Bychkov," *The Classical Source*, 25 March 2011; Anderson, "Review: Serious Songs and Heldenleben," *The Classical Source*, 28 July 2006;

76. Traber, "Im Raum der Geschichte," 177.

77. Kalbeck, "Brahms's Four *Serious Songs*, Op. 121 (1914)," 279, cited in Nicole Grimes, *Brahms's Elegies*, 200.

78. Grimes, *Brahms's Elegies*, 201.

79. Grimes applies to Brahms's Op. 121 Carl Niekerk's suggestion, in *Reading Mahler: German Culture and Jewish Identity in Fin-de-Siècle Vienna* (2010), that Mahler's symphony "question[s] the possibility of a return to a naïve form of religious experience." *Brahms's Elegies*, 201.

80. The four selected are, in order of Glanert's score: 1 ("Mein Jesu, der du mich"), 7 ("O Gott, du frommer Gott"), 9 ("Herzlich tut mich verlangen"), and 3 ("O Welt, ich muss dich lassen"). See Boosey & Hawkes online repertoire note, https://boosey.com/cr/music/Johannes-Brahms-Vier-Choralvorspiele/102774 (accessed October 2020).

81. Virgil Thomson's are published by Boosey & Hawkes; Leinsdorf's by Broude Brothers Ltd; and de Vlieger's by Schott.

82. In her detailed account of Brahms's small body of work for the organ, Barbara Owen suggests that Schumann's worsening health in early 1896 may have motivated Brahms to return to "reminders of their youthful mutual interests—which included the organ—and thus to truly close the circle for good." See Owen, *The Organ Music of Johannes Brahms* (Oxford: Oxford University Press, 2007), 50.

83. Glanert, "Vorwort," in Johannes Brahms/Detlev Glanert, *Vier Choralvorspiele für Orchester* (Berlin: Boosey & Hawkes, 2017).

84. De Vlieger, "Elf Choralvorspiele," program note, https://www.henkdevlieger.nl/choralvorspiele/ (accessed December 2020).

85. In this sense, the later orchestrations continue the work of early transcriptions for piano made by publishers: for an account of these, see Owen, *The Organ Music of Johannes Brahms*, 115–17.

86. De Vlieger, "Elf Choralvorspiele"; Glanert, "Vorwort."

Chapter 18

1. I am grateful to Reuben Phillips for reading this chapter, and for the thoughtful suggestions he offered. For helpful feedback on earlier versions of this material, I thank William Drummond, Paul Harper-Scott, Wolfgang Marx, Frankie Perry, Benedict Taylor, and Edward Venn.
See Nicole Grimes, "Brahms as a Vanishing Point in the Music of Wolfgang Rihm: Reflections on Klavierstück Nr. 6," in *Music Preferred: Essays in Musicology, Cultural History and Analysis, in Honour of Harry White*, ed. Lorraine Byrne-Bodley (Vienna: Hollitzer, 2018), 523–49.

2. *Brahmsliebewalzer* (1985) was orchestrated in 1988 and included in Rihm, *Drei Walzer* (1979–1988), commissioned for the Schleswig-Holstein Musik Festival. In this setting, the *Brahmsliebewalzer* is flanked on either side by the *Sehnsuchtswalzer* (1979–1981), a piece that conjures up Schubert, whose piece of the same name is itself nostalgic for an earlier time, and the *Drängender Walzer* (1979–1986) dedicated to Karsten Witt.

3. Rihm, annotation to the score, *Brahmsliederwalzer* (Vienna: Universal Edition, 1985). Also, see Richard Heuberger, *Erinnerungen an Johannes Brahms* (Tutzing: Schneider, 1976).

4. On these and other Rihm works, see John Warnaby, "Wolfgang Rihm's Recent Music," *Tempo* 213 (2000): 12–19.

5. Thomas Meyer, "Der vollgesogene Komponist. Der vollgesogene Hörer: Antworten auf Brahms; Fragen zu Wolfgang Rihms Orchesterstückchen *Nähe Fern* 1–3," in *Gegen die Diktierte Aktualität: Wolfgang Rihm und die Schweiz. Für Wolfgang Rihm zum 60. Geburtstag*, ed. Antonio Baldasserre (Vienna: Holitzer, 2012), 53.

6. Rihm, on the Universal Edition webpage for *Ernster Gesang*, https://www.universaledition.com/wolfgang-rihm-599/works/ernster-gesang-2335 (accessed 16 December 2020).

7. *Symphonie "Nähe fern"* is scored for 1st flute, 2nd flute (+piccolo); 1st oboe, 2nd oboe (+c.a.); 1st clarinet in A, 2nd clarinet in A (+bass cl (B♭)); 1st and 2nd bassoon, and contrabassoon; 4 horns in F; 1st and 2nd trumpets in C; 3 trombones; bass tuba; timpani; percussion; full string section.

8. Letter from Rihm to Thomas Meyer, as cited in Mark Sattler, "Rihm Plays with Brahms," in the liner notes to Wolfgang Rihm, *Symphonie "Nähe Fern,"* Lucerne Symphonieorchester, James Gaffigan (Harmonia Mundi HMC902153, 2012) 5–6 (5).

9. "Da habe ich mich gar nicht erst vollgesaugt, vielleicht bin ich schon vollgesogen. Da habe ich mich einfach aus meinem Erinnern heraus den Dingen genähert. Ich hatte nur die Partituren der jeweiligen Sinfonien da und habe immer wieder reingeguckt, hatte auch ein anderes Anliegen." Rihm, cited in Meyer, "Der vollgesogene Komponist. Der vollgesogene Hörer," 53.

10. "Ich wollte nicht eine historische Sinfonie in Brahms-Stil schreiben." Meyer, "Der vollgesogene Komponist. Der vollgesogene Hörer," 53.

11. On Rihm and Schumann, see Alastair Williams, "Swaying with Schumann: Subjectivity and Tradition in Wolfgang Rihm's 'Fremde-Szenen' I–III and Related Scores,' *Music & Letters* 87/3 (2006): 379–97. For a description of the seventh scene of *Jakob Lenz*, see Laura Tunbridge, "Deserted Chambers of the Mind (Schumann Memories)," in *Rethinking Schumann*, ed. Roe-Min Kok and Laura Tunbridge (Oxford: Oxford University Press, 2011), 395–410 (403–4).

12. On Rihm and Mahler, see Thomas Schäfer, "Anwesend/abgekehrt: Notizen zu Wolfgang Rihm's Komponieren der 1970er Jahre mit Blick auf Gustav Mahler," in *Wolfgang Rihm*, ed. Ulrich Tadday (Munich: Richard Boorberg Verlag, 2004), 99–108, quoted in Alastair Williams, *Music in Germany since 1968* (Cambridge: Cambridge University Press, 2013).

13. Wolfgang Rihm in conversation with Tom Service, Rihm Composer in Focus Day, Wigmore Hall, 28 February 2015.

14. Rihm had originally composed the song "Dämmrung senkte sich von oben" in 2004 for the cycle *Eins und doppelt*. Three years later he integrated it into his *Goethe Lieder*. See Thomas Seyboldt, "Rihm's Goethe- and Schiller-Lieder: Insights,"

liner notes for the CD *Wolfgang Rihm: Goethe-Lieder* (Bastille Musique, 2016), 19–26 (19).

15. On Wolfgang Rihm's preoccupation with art, see Ulrich Mosch, "Zur Rolle bildnerischer Vorstellugen im musikalischen Denken und Komponieren Wolfgang Rihms," in *Musikwissenschaft zwischen Kunst, Ästhetik und Experiment*, ed. Reinhard Kopiez (Würzburg: Königshausen & Neumann, 1998), 387–92; and Wolfgang Rihm, "Vor Bildern," in *Intermedialität: Studien zur Wechselwirkung zwischen den Künsten*, ed. Günter Schnitzler and Edelgard Spaude (Freiburg im Breisgau: Rombach Verlag, 2004), 95–129, in which Ulrich Mosch has collated excerpts from Rihm's diaries and argues that art became more and more important for Rihm's output from 1980–1981 onward. On Brahms's preoccupation with art, see Grimes, *Brahms's Elegies: The Poetics of Loss in Nineteenth Century German Culture* (Cambridge: Cambridge University Press, 2019); Styra Avins, "Johannes Brahms, Connoisseur of Graphic Arts," in this volume; Reinhold Brinkmann, "Johannes Brahms und die Maler Feuerbach, Böcklin, Klinger und Menzel," in *Vom Pfeifen und von alten Dampfmaschine: Essays zur Musik von Beethoven bis Rihm* (Munich: Paul Szolnay Verlag, 2006), 108–39; and William Vaughan and Natasha Loges, "Visual Arts," in *Brahms in Context*, ed. Natasha Loges and Katy Hamilton (Cambridge: Cambridge University Press, 2019), 286–95.

16. Although Schumann's original title for *Gesänge der Frühe*, Op. 133, *An Diotima*, clearly referred to Hölderlin, he never set any of the writer's poetry. See Laura Tunbridge, *Schumann's Late Style* (Cambridge: Cambridge University Press, 2007), 137–38.

17. See Nicole Grimes, "Brahms's Ascending Circle: Hölderlin, *Schicksalslied*, and the Process of Recollection," *Nineteenth-Century Music Review* 11/1 (2014): 1–36.

18. Also relevant here is the fact that Rihm has reflected in writing on the poetry of the New Humanists, most prominently in an essay that explicitly evokes Goethe's *Iphigenie*. See Wolfgang Rihm, "Verzweifelt human. Neue Musik und Humanismus?," in Rihm, *Offene Enden: Denkbewegung um und durch Musik*, ed. Ulrich Mosch (Munich: Hanser, 2002), 225–44. Rihm is the first composer to have set all twelve stanzas of Goethe's *Harzreise im Winter* to music, unlike Johann Friedrich Reichardt, who set only sixteen lines of the poetry in his *Rhapsodie (Aus der Harzreise)* (1792), and Brahms, who set twenty-two lines in the *Alto Rhapsody*, Op. 53 (1869).

19. Constantin Behler, *Nostalgic Teleology: Friedrich Schiller and the Schemata of Aesthetic Humanism* (Bern and New York: Peter Lang, 1995).

20. See U. C. Fischer, "Goethe's 'Chinese-German Book of Seasons and Hours' and World Literature," *United College Journal* 6 (1967): 27–34.

21. Paul Bishop, "Goethe's 'Chinesisch-deutsche Jahres- und Tageszeiten': An Intercultural Glance," in *Goethe 2000: Intercultural Readings of His Work*, ed. Paul Bishop and R. H. Stephenson (Glasgow: Northern Universities Press, 2000), 93.

22. These translations are taken from Fischer, "Goethe's 'Chinese-German Book of Seasons and Hours,'" 29.

23. This translation is by Richard Stokes in the liner notes of the CD recording *Brahms: The Complete Songs*, Vol. 1 of 10 (Hyperion CDJ33121, London, 2008).

24. Bishop, "Goethe's 'Chinesisch-deutsche Jahres- und Tageszeiten,'" 98.

25. Monika Lemmel, "Der gedichtzyklus 'Chinesisch-Deutsche Jahres- und Tageszeiten' und seine Verortung in Goethes Spätwerk," in *Jahrbuch der deutschen Schillergesellschaft* 36 (1992): 143–66 (164).

26. The allusive web stretches further back if we take into account Brahms's borrowing from Hermann Levi's "Dämmrung senkte sich von oben" (1868). See Frithjof Haas, *Hermann Levi: From Brahms to Wagner*, trans. Cynthia Klohr (Lanham, MA: Scarecrow Press, 2012), 44–45; and Paul Berry, *Brahms among Friends: Listening, Performance, and the Rhetoric of Allusion* (Oxford: Oxford University Press, 2014), 9.

27. A letter from Rihm to Thomas Meyer, as cited in Mark Sattler, "Rihm Plays with Brahms," in the liner notes to Wolfgang Rihm, *Symphonie "Nähe Fern,"* Lucerne Symphonieorchester, James Gaffigan (Harmonia Mundi HMC902153, 2012), 5–6 (6).

28. Writing to Numa Bischoff Ullmann in 2012, Rihm gave the entire composition the title *Lucerne Symphony*. See Sattler, "Rihm Plays with Brahms," 5.

29. Meyer makes a similar observation in "Der vollgesogene Komponist. Der vollgesogene Hörer," 58.

30. This song would find a reminiscence in 1894 in Brahms's Clarinet Sonata No. 2 in E♭ Major, Op. 120, the third movement Andante con moto variations of which are based on the melodic fragment in bars 13–16 heard on the words "doch zuerst emporgehoben / Holdenlichts der Abendstern" ("But there the evening star appears / Shining with its lovely light!").

31. Program booklet of the concert of the Lucerne Symphony Orchestra on 19/20 October 2011, 6. Cited in Meyer, "Der vollgesogene Komponist," 67.

32. Sattler, "Rihm Plays with Brahms," 6.

33. See Fabrice Fitch, "Rihm, *Symphonie 'Nähe Fern,'*" *Gramophone Magazine*, 24 September 2013. If Rihm's intention was to put Brahms equally distant and equally present (if not increasingly distant and increasingly present), then his philosophical point seems to have been lost on Fitch.

34. Falling thirds are a widely commented upon Brahmsian motif, familiar from compositions such as the first movement of the Fourth Symphony, the first of the "Heimweh" lieder, Op. 63, Nos 7–9, and the third of the *Vier ernste Gesänge*, "O Tod, wie bitter bist du," Op. 121, No. 3.

35. Rihm in correspondence with Meyer, as cited in Sattler, "Rihm Plays with Brahms," 6.

36. The word *lontanissimo* is of Rihm's devising and has a clear relationship to Ligeti's composition *Lontano*.

37. Amy Bauer, *Ligeti's Laments: Nostalgia, Exoticism and the Absolute* (Aldershot: Ashgate, 2011), 94.

38. *György Ligeti in Conversation with Péter Várnai, Josef Häusler, Claude Samuel and Himself,* trans. Gabor J. Schabert, Sarah E. Soulsby, Terence Kilmarti, and Geoffrey Skelton (London: Eulenberg, 1983), 98.

39. Andrew Bowie, "Music and the Rise of Aesthetics," in *The Cambridge History of Nineteenth-Century Music,* ed. Jim Samson (Cambridge: Cambridge University Press, 2002), 29–54 (50).

40. Julian Johnson, *Out of Time: Music and the Making of Modernity* (Oxford: Oxford University Press, 2015), 186.

41. Johnson, *Out of Time,* 186.

42. Rihm, as cited in Warnaby, "Wolfgang Rihm's Recent Music," 17. Rihm has written on the subject of tonality in numerous places, giving it most sustained attention in the essay "Neo-Tonalität?" The opening sentence is indicative of the degree of complexity, ambiguity, and intended contradictions in this essay: "Actually there is no tonality. Only harmony. Tonality is an accident, a constellation of harmony." ("Eigentlich gibt es Tonalität nicht. Tonalität ist ein Zufall, eine Konstellation von Harmonik.") See Wolfgang Rihm, *Ausgesprochen 1 & 2,* ed. Ulrich Mosch (Winterthur: Amadeus, 1997), vol. 1, 185–93 (185).

43. Correspondence from Rihm to Meyer, cited in Sattler, "Rihm Plays with Brahms," 6.

44. For a lucid discussion and critique of Hermann Danuser's developing thought on modernism and postmodernism, see Joakim Tillmans, "Postmodernism and Art Music in the German Debate," in *Postmodern Music/Postmodern Thought,* ed. Judy Lochhead and Joseph Auner (New York: Routledge, 2002), 75–91. On Danuser and the distinction between modernism and postmodernism, see Danuser, "Innerlichkeit und Äußerlichkeit in der Musikästhetik der Gegenwart," in *Die Musik der achtziger Jahre,* ed. Ekkehard Jost (Mainz: Schott, 1990) 56–66; Danuser, "Zur Kritik der musikalischen Postmoderne," *Neue Zeitschrift für Musik* 149/12 (1988): 4–9; "Musikalische Zitat—und Collageverfahren im Lichte der (Post) Moderne-Diskussion," in *Jahrbuch 4 der Bayerischen Akademie der Schönen Künste,* ed. Oswald Georg Baur and Sylvia Riedmaier (Schaftlach: Oreos Verlag, 1990), 395–409; and Hermann Danuser, ed., "Postmodernes Musikdenken—Lösung oder Flucht?," in *Neue Musik im politischem Wandel.* Veröffentlichungen des Instituts für Neue Musik und Musikerziehung Darmstadt. Band 32 (Mainz: Schott, 1991).

45. *György Ligeti in Conversation,* 74.

46. Bauer, *Ligeti's Laments,* 104.

47. *György Ligeti in Conversation,* 93. Emphasis added.

48. Rihm in conversation with Service, Rihm Composer in Focus Day, Wigmore Hall, 28 February 2015.

49. Sattler, "Rihm Plays with Brahms," 6

50. Meyer, "Der vollgesogene Komponist. Der vollgesogene Hörer," 54.

51. "'Genauso wenig aber,' fügt Rihm an, 'wie Hitchcocks Vögel ein ornithologischer Fachfilm sind, ist mein Stück musikwissenschaftliche Belegliteratur. Das ist keine Seminararbeit über Brahms. Es ist etwas am lebenden Gegenstand

Erfolgtes.'" Rihm, cited in Meyer, "Der vollgesogene Komponist. Der vollgesogene Hörer," 57.

52. For a discussion of the organicist mindset that gave rise to Schoenberg's concept of developing variation, see Nicole Grimes, "The Schoenberg/Brahms Critical Tradition Reconsidered," *Music Analysis* 31/2-3 (Autumn 2012): 127–75.

53. This quotation is found in Thomas Meyer, "En Passant par Brahms: Zu Wolfgang Rihms Brahms-Zyklus 'Nähe Fern 1–4,'" *Neue Zeitschrift für Musik* 173/5 (2012): 58–61 (59).

54. "Das Präfix 'vor' ist darin wesentlich: Vorfeld, Vorgeschichtlichkeit, es geht um den Zustand vor der Komposition, also auch vor der Dekomposition, es geht um den Zustand des 'noch,' um jenes Vorfeld, wo die Dinge 'noch' ungeordnet herumwirbeln." Meyer, "Der vollgesogene Komponist," 54. The more pedestrian translation of "noch" as "still" fails to capture the sense of that which is "unrealized" that is inherent to the discussion of this musical material.

55. Meyer, "Der vollgesogene Komponist," 63, footnote 36.

56. Meyer, "En Passant par Brahms," 61.

57. Meyer, "Der vollgesogene Komponist," 56.

58. "Man kann wahrnehmen und hören und zu ganz anderen Ergebnissen kommen." Rihm, cited in Meyer, "Der vollgesogene Komponist. Der vollgesogene Hörer," 56.

59. "Brahmsvolle Hörschwämme. *Nähe fern* anhören bedeutet deshalb immer, Brahms mithören, es bedeutet aber auch, den Brahms in uns (nahe bzw. fern) zu hören." Meyer, "Der vollgesogene Komponist. Der vollgesogene Hörer," 56–57.

60. Meyer, "Der vollgesogene Komponist. Der vollgesogene Hörer," 56, footnote 17.

61. In addition to the *Chinesisch-deutsche Jahre- und Tageszeiten*, there is, for instance, the *West-östlicher Divan*, the *Römische Elegien*, and the numerous translations from Greek authors.

62. Peter Szendy, *Listen: A History of Our Ears*, trans. Charlotte Mandell (New York: Fordham University Press, 2008), 52.

63. Szendy, *Listen: A History of Our Ears*, 53.

64. Szendy, *Listen: A History of Our Ears*, 36.

Chapter 19

1. For the most up-to-date list of Finnissy's works, see www.michaelfinnissy.info/works/ (accessed 3 October 2020).

2. I would like to thank Ian Pace for his comments on an early draft of this chapter, and for playing through for me Finnissy's unrecorded *Brahms-Lieder*.

3. For an overview of the range and variety of borrowings in Finnissy's music, including a taxonomy of how they are utilized musically, see Ian Pace, "Negotiating, Borrowing, Genre and Mediation in the Piano Music of Finnissy: Strategies and

Aesthetics," in *Critical Perspectives on Michael Finnissy: Bright Futures, Dark Pasts*, ed. Ian Pace and Nigel McBride (London and New York: Routledge, 2019), 57–103.

4. Christopher Fox, "Michael Finnissy: Modernism with an English Accent," in *Critical Perspectives on Michael Finnissy: Bright Futures, Dark Pasts*, ed. Ian Pace and Nigel McBride (London and New York: Routledge, 2019), 27–38 (33) (emphasis added).

5. Christopher Fox and Ian Pace, "Conversations with Michael Finnissy," in *Uncommon Ground: The Music of Michael Finnissy*, ed. Henrietta Brougham, Christopher Fox, and Ian Pace (Aldershot: Ashgate, 1997), 1–42 (9).

6. Ian Pace, *Michael Finnissy at 70: The Piano Music (6)* (2016), http://openaccess.city.ac.uk/17517/ (accessed 3 October 2020).

7. See Edward Venn, "Thomas Adès and the Spectres of *Brahms*," *Journal of the Royal Musical Association* 140/1 (2015): 163–212. For a more general overview of Brahms's reception as "progressive," see Peter Gay, "Aimez-vous Brahms? On Polarities in Modernism," in Peter Gay, *Freud, Jews and Other Germans: Masters and Victims in Modernist Culture* (Oxford and New York: Oxford University Press, 1978), 231–56.

8. Arnold Schoenberg, "Brahms the Progressive," in *Style and Idea: Selected Writings*, ed. Leonard Stein, trans. Leo Black (Faber: London and Boston, MA, 1975), 398–441. For a discussion of the Brahms-Schoenberg tradition and its nineteenth-century precedents, see Nicole Grimes, "The Schoenberg/Brahms Critical Tradition Reconsidered," *Music Analysis* 31/2 (2012): 127–75. Grimes amply demonstrates that the idea of developing variation has a critical prehistory before Schoenberg. Nevertheless, the discourse around this critical tradition was for Finnissy and his contemporaries indelibly associated with Schoenberg, and so I shall continue to refer to the Brahms-Schoenberg tradition in this chapter.

9. Questions of temporality and teleology are implicated, for instance, in the title of Margaret Notley's *Lateness and Brahms: Music and Culture in the Twilight of Viennese Liberalism* (Oxford and New York: Oxford University Press, 2007). In his "A Photograph of Brahms," the British composer Hugh Wood (who belongs to the generation prior to Finnissy) mulls over the remoteness—the sense of temporal displacement—between today's music and Brahms, but also between Brahms and his contemporaries; in *Staking Out the Territory and Other Writings on Music* (London: Plumbago Books, 2007), 44–63.

10. See Venn, "Thomas Adès and the Spectres of *Brahms*," 192–206.

11. Maarten Beirens, "Archaeology of the Self: Michael Finnissy's 'Folklore,'" *Tempo* 57/223 (2003): 46–56 (47). On Finnissy's critical uses of his sources more generally, see Maarten Beirens, "Questioning the Foreign and the Familiar: Interpreting Michael Finnissy's Use of Traditional and Non-Western Sources," in *Critical Perspectives on Michael Finnissy: Bright Futures, Dark Pasts*, ed. Ian Pace and Nigel McBride (London and New York: Routledge, 2019), 301–15 (308).

12. The key text here is Jacques Derrida, *Specters of Marx: The State of the Debt, the Work of Mourning and the New International*, trans. Peggy Kamuf (New York

and London: Routledge, 1994). I adopt in this chapter a relatively light touch toward the Derridean notion of both the specter and hauntology. For a fuller discussion of musical applications of hauntology, along with a reading of Schoenberg's "Brahms the Progressive" from this perspective, see my "Thomas Adès's and the Spectres of *Brahms*."

13. Derrida's use of spirits and specters within hauntology emerges from his study of Marx and the famous opening line of the Communist Manifesto: "A spectre is haunting Europe—the spectre of communism" (Karl Marx and Friedrich Engels, *The Communist Manifesto* (London: Pluto Press, [1848] 2008), 31). Derrida uses this—interlaced liberally with reflections on the similarly spectral opening to Shakespeare's *Hamlet*—to reflect on the ways in which such summonings collapse temporality (spirits belong to the past; we encounter them in the present as specters; in their eschatological Derridean guise, they point to possible futures). To a greater extent, hauntology is a continuation of the critical practice of deconstruction. I should emphasize that there is no indication that Finnissy thinks of his own critical practice from a Derridean perspective. Nevertheless, such a perspective provides a useful way of framing his relationship with the Brahms-Schoenberg tradition.

14. The strength of this identification resonates in the reception of both composers. For instance, Milton Babbitt, reflecting on the European tradition, exclaimed that he was "delighted to be taken right back to Brahms, because I can go there directly if not by way of Schoenberg." Babbitt, cited in Marie Louise Herzfeld-Schild, "Serialismus aus Tradition: Milton Babbitts Schönberg-Rezeption," *Archiv für Musikwissenschaft* 66/1 (2009): 69–91 (75).

15. Pace, *Michael Finnissy at 70*.

16. Ian Pace, "The Piano Music," in *Uncommon Ground: The Music of Michael Finnissy*, ed. Henrietta Brougham, Christopher Fox, and Ian Pace (Aldershot: Ashgate, 1997), 43–133 (123).

17. "Sehnsucht," Op. 14, No. 8 (1858), the last of the *Lieder und Romanzen*, sets Brahms's own adaptation of the traditional Tyrolese folksong "Mein Schatz ist nicht da." The text of "Sehnsucht," Op. 49, No. 3 (1868) is a translation by the poet Josef Wenzig (1807–1876) of a Bohemian folksong. As I shall discuss in my analyses of *In stiller Nacht* and *Brahms-Lieder*, Brahms's folksong arrangements occupy an important place in Finnissy's response to the Brahms's legacy.

18. Cited in Pace, "The Piano Music," 112.

19. Michael Finnissy, composer's note to *In stiller Nacht*, cited in Jonathan Cross, "Vive la différence," *Musical Times* 137/1837 (March 1996): 7–13 (8).

20. Compare this with Thomas Adès's evocation of, among other pieces, Brahms's Symphony No. 4, Piano Concerto No. 1, "O Tod," and a host of late piano works in his depiction of the composer in *Brahms*. See Venn, "Thomas Adès and the Spectres of *Brahms*."

21. Arnold Whittall, "Recession, Reflation: Skempton, Finnissy and Musical Modernism's Classical Roots," *Musical Times* 159/1943 (Summer 2018): 11–24 (24).

22. Marx and Engels, *The Communist Manifesto*, 38. Finnissy included a visual representation of *The Communist Manifesto* in his 1997 work *False Notions of Progress* for three players.

23. Alan Bass, "Translator's Introduction," to Jacques Derrida, *Writing and Difference*, trans. Alan Bass (London and New York: Routledge, [1967] 1978), ix–xxiii (xviii).

24. While there is a case to be made for treating Finnissy's work as "absolute music" (a high modernist perspective that might be interpreted as an extension of the Brahms-Schoenberg tradition), my sympathies lie with the more open, holistic treatment of the text that recognizes its permeable boundaries and the agency of the performer. For a representative example of the first position, see Richard Beaudoin, "Anonymous Sources: Finnissy Analysis and the Opening of Chapter Eight of *The History of Photography in Sound*," *Perspectives of New Music* 45/2 (Summer 2007): 5–27. For a rebuttal of Beaudoin and an elegant advocacy of the second position, see Pace, "Negotiating, Borrowing, Genre and Mediation in the Piano Music of Finnissy," 57–61.

25. Michael Finnissy, CD liner notes to *In stiller Nacht, Independence Quadrilles* (NMC D107, 2005), 7.

26. Ian Pace, "The Panorama of Michael Finnissy (I)," *Tempo* 196 (April 1996): 25–35 (34).

27. Finnissy, CD notes to *In stiller Nacht*, 7.

28. Cross, "Vive la différence," 8.

29. Fox and Pace, "Conversations with Michael Finnissy," 33. Unlike Schoenberg's "Brahms the Progressive," Finnissy's engagement with the Brahmsian legacy offers little suggestion of a masculinist struggle with grand narratives. For an extended discussion of how such syntheses manifest themselves in Finnissy's music, see Arnold Whittall, "Finnissy and Pantonality: Surface and Inner Necessity," in *Critical Perspectives on the Music of Michael Finnissy: Bright Futures, Dark Pasts*, ed. Ian Pace and Nigel McBride (London and New York: Routledge, 2019), 241–60.

30. Finnissy, CD notes to *In stiller Nacht*, 7.

31. George S. Bozarth, "The Origin of Brahms's *In stiller Nacht*," *Notes* 53/2 (1996): 363–80 (363). Brahms made two arrangements of the song, for four-part unaccompanied choir (WoO 34, No. 8, 1864) and for solo voice and piano (WoO 33, No. 42, 1894).

32. Accidentals within all examples in this chapter reproduce those in Finnissy's scores.

33. Michael Finnissy, Composer's note to score of *In stiller Nacht* (Oxford: Oxford University Press, 1998). Examples 19.1b–19.1d are aligned for visual convenience; there is no complete score, and the published music has separate parts for each player. The use of independent lines in this manner (albeit one in which "the performers should respond to each other by listening, rather than only being aware of their individual parts" (Finnissy, Composer's note to score of *In stiller Nacht*)), can also be found in other works by Finnissy, including *WAM* (1990–1991) which places under critical scrutiny the music of Mozart, a composer

who, like Brahms, sits uneasily within Finnissy's personal pantheon. See Larry Goves, "Michael Finnissy and Wolfgang Amadeus Mozart: The Composer as Anthropologist," *Tempo* 71/280 (2017): 47–55.

34. Finnissy, Composer's note to score of *In stiller Nacht*.

35. Finnissy, CD notes to *In stiller Nacht*, 7.

36. Cited in Cross, "Vive la différence," 8. Roger Redgate notes a similarity between the process of *In stiller Nacht* and that of *Contretänze* (1985; rev. 1986), in which "[t]he source material for this work is indeed the music of Bach, so transformed and integrated into Finnissy's musical language as to be barely recognisable." Roger Redgate, "The Chamber Music," in *Uncommon Ground: The Music of Michael Finnissy*, ed. Henrietta Brougham, Christopher Fox, and Ian Pace (Aldershot: Ashgate, 1997), 134–68 (161; see also 168, footnote 7). The treatment of the melodic line in *In stiller Nacht* is somewhat different to the ways in which folk tunes are arranged in works such as *English Country Tunes* (1977; rev. 1982–1985) and *Folklore* (1993–1994). On *English Country Tunes*, see Pace, "The Piano Music," 65–71. The seventh movement, "My Bonny Boy," is perhaps closest to the violin part of *In stiller Nacht* in its treatment of the given material.

37. Schoenberg, for instance, notes the irregular phrase lengths and overlapping entries in opening of the second movement of Brahms's String Sextet No. 2, Op. 36. Schoenberg, "Brahms the Progressive," 417–18.

38. The Schoenbergian depiction of Brahms, with its emphasis on developing variation, is one that seems in particular to trouble Finnissy. See Pace, *The Piano Music (8)*, 9. It may in this light be significant that Finnissy represents the Schoenbergian Brahms by the cello in his *In stiller Nacht*: Schoenberg used the cello solo from his Serenade, *Pierrot lunaire*, Op. 21/xix, to highlight his affinities with Brahmsian developing variation (see "Brahms the Progressive," 428).

39. Finnissy, CD notes to *In stiller Nacht*, 7.

40. Finnissy, CD notes to *In stiller Nacht*, 7. The context would suggest that Finnissy's use of "actuality," albeit in scare quotes, refers to some sort of objective Brahmsian essence, rather than to Alexander Goehr's use of "Aktualität" that questions Brahms's relevance to contemporary society ("Brahms's *Aktualität*," in Alexander Goehr, *Finding the Key*, ed. Derrick Puffett [London and Boston: Faber & Faber, 1998], 175–88), though in practice Finnissy's musical response to Brahms could be thought to encapsulate both meanings.

41. Even a work such as Cage's *Concert for Piano and Orchestra* (1957–1958), which employs radical notation and generation of material via random (*I-Ching*) procedures, can be shown to owe much to Cage's studies with Schoenberg. See Martin Iddon and Philip Thomas, *John Cage's* Concert for Piano and Orchestra (New York: Oxford University Press, 2020), 40–47. See also Severine Neff, "Point/Counterpoint: John Cage Studies with Arnold Schoenberg," *Contemporary Music Review* 33/5–6 (2014): 451–82 (464–65). Neff argues that Cage's *Second Construction in Metal* (1939) owes much to the Schoenberg and Brahms precedents. See also Brenda Ravenscroft, "Re-construction: Cage and Schoenberg," *Tempo* 60/235 (2006): 2–14, for a similar account of Cage's *First Construction in Metal* (also 1939).

42. Michael Kirby and Richard Schechner, "An Interview with John Cage," *Tulane Drama Review* 10 (1965): 50–72 (53). See also David W. Bernstein, "Techniques of Appropriation in Music of John Cage," *Contemporary Music Review* 20/4 (2001): 71–90. Finnissy, it should be noted, cites Cage's *HPSCHD* as a key influence on his thinking (Anon., "Profile: Michael Finnissy," *Tempo* 70/267 [2016]: 105–7 [106]). Philip Thomas has noted how *HPSCHD* shares with Finnissy's music the "multiple, often simultaneous, uses of material drawn from different sources, even in a solo work." "Post-experimental Survivor: Finnissy the Experimentalist," in *Critical Perspectives on the Music of Michael Finnissy: Bright Futures, Dark Pasts*, ed. Ian Pace and Nigel McBride (London and New York: Routledge, 2019), 39–56 (42).

43. Cage did not, of course, invent such a practice (consider the music of Ives, for instance).

44. Interview with John Palmer, cited in Whittall, "Recession, Reflation," 16. *Conversations* (Vision Edition, 2015), 75. Whittall links Finnissy's avoidance of cadences with Naomi Waltham-Smith's reflections on modernism's rejection of such "communal" devices. Waltham-Smith, *Music and Belonging between Revolution and Restoration* (New York: Oxford University Press, 2017), 5.

45. Bozarth suggests that the quiet night of the text is "the scene of Christ's suffering on the Mount of Olives," transforming the secular lyric into a concealed sacred song. Bozarth, "The Origin of Brahms's 'In stiller Nacht,'" 364.

46. Whittall, "Finnissy and Pantonality," 244.

47. A recording of *In stiller Nacht* by Trio Fibonacci is available on *Independence Quadrilles* (NMC CD D107, 2005).

48. There are only a handful of pianists who have performed *The History of Photography in Sound*; the first, Ian Pace, gave the UK premiere of *Brahms-Lieder* in 2016.

49. Cited in George Grella, "In Arnone's Hand, Finnissy's Piano Music Proves Spellbinding," *New York Classical Review* (24 March 2015), https://newyorkclassicalreview.com/2015/03/in-arnones-hands-finnissys-piano-music-proves-spellbinding/ (accessed 3 October 2020).

50. See, for instance, Fox and Pace, "Conversations with Michael Finnissy," 19–21.

51. Michael Finnissy, "Biting the Hand That Feeds You," *Contemporary Music Review* 21/1 (2002): 71–79 (74).

52. Pace, *Michael Finnissy at 70*.

53. Whittall, "Finnissy and Pantonality," 258.

54. Pace, *Michael Finnissy at 70*. See, for instance, the piano accompaniment to Example 19.1a, bars 4–5, and Example 19.3a for examples of such melodic thickening.

55. See, for instance, Fox and Pace, "Conversations with Michael Finnissy," 5–6. A fuller discussion of Finnissy's approach to form—not least how it deviates from Brahmsian "organic" structures—is beyond the scope of this chapter.

56. Pace, *Michael Finnissy at 70*.
57. Whittall, "Finnissy and Pantonality," 256. A reproduction of the opening of the first movement of *Brahms-Lieder* can be found on this page.
58. See Whittall, "Finnissy and Pantonality," 241–44.
59. Derrida, *Specters of Marx*, xviii–xix (original emphasis).

Bibliography

Aaslestad, Katherine. *Place and Politics: Local Identity, Civic Culture, and German Nationalism in North Germany during the Revolutionary Era*. Leiden and Boston: Brill, 2005.

Abrams, M. H. *Natural Supernaturalism: Tradition and Revolution in Romantic Literature*. New York: W. W. Norton, 1971.

Adorno, Theodor W. *Philosophy of New Music*. Translated by Robert Hullot-Kentor. Minneapolis: University of Minnesota Press, 2006.

Aegidi, Ludwig. "Erinnerung an und von Emanuel Geibel." *Deutsche Revue über das gesamte nationale Leben der Gegenwart* 23/1 (January–March 1898): 6–24.

Aldous, Richard. *Tunes of Glory: The Life of Malcolm Sargent*. London: Hutchinson, 2001.

Almén, Byron. *A Theory of Musical Narrative*. Bloomington: Indiana University Press, 2008.

Anderson, Colin. "BBC Symphony Orchestra/Bychkov." *The Classical Source*, 25 March 2011.

Anderson, Martin. "Review: Benjamin, Rihm, Brahms-Glanert, Elgar-Payne." *Tempo* 61/239 (2007): 82–86.

Anderson, Martin. "Review: *Serious Songs* and *Heldenleben*." *The Classical Source*, 28 July 2006.

Anderton, Abby. *Rubble Music: Occupying the Ruins of Postwar Berlin*. Bloomington: Indiana University Press, 2019.

Anonymous. "Paris Welcomes Boston Symphony." *New York Times*, 20 September 1956.

Anonymous. "Prize for Understanding and Tolerance 2020." Website of the Jewish Museum Berlin, https://www.jmberlin.de/en/press-release-27-october-2020.

Anonymous. "Profile: Michael Finnissy." *Tempo* 70/267 (2016): 105–7.

Anonymous. "A Work for This Moment: 'A German Requiem' by Brahms." *Deutsche Welle*, https://www.dw.com/en/a-work-for-this-moment-a-german-requiem-by-brahms/a-53079994.

Antonicek, Susanne, and Otto Biba, eds. *Brahms-Kongress Wien 1983*. Tutzing: Hans Schneider, 1988.

Appel, Bernhard R., ed. *Robert Schumann in Endenich (1854–1856): Krankenakten, Briefzeugnisse und zeitgenössische Berichte*. Schumann Forschungen 11. Mainz: Schott, 2006.

Appel, Bernhard R., and Inge Hermstrüwer, eds. *Robert Schumann und die Dichter: Ein Musiker als Leser.* Düsseldorf: Droste, 1991.

Applegate, Celia. *The Necessity of Music: Variations on a German Theme.* Toronto: University of Toronto Press, 2017.

Applegate, Celia, and Pamela Potter, eds. *Music and German National Identity.* Chicago and London: University of Chicago Press, 2002.

Arendt, Hannah. *Essays in Understanding, 1930–1954: Formation, Exile, and Totalitarianism.* Edited and translated by Jerome Kohn. New York: Harcourt, Brace, & Co., 1994.

Arnim, Achim von, and Clemens Brentano. *Des Knaben Wunderhorn: Alte deutsche Lieder.* 2 vols. Heidelberg: Mohr & Zimmer, 1806–1808.

Arnold, Friedrich Wilhelm. *Deutsche Lieder aus alter und neuer Zeit gesammelt und mit Clavierbegleitung versehen von F. W. Arnold.* Elberfeld: F. W. Arnold, ca. 1860–1870.

Avins, Styra, ed. *Johannes Brahms: Life and Letters.* Translated by Josef Eisinger and Styra Avins. Oxford and New York: Oxford University Press, 1997.

Badiou, Alain. *L'immanence des vérités: L'être et l'événement.* Paris: Fayard, 2018.

Baldasserre, Antonio, ed. *Gegen die Diktierte Aktualität: Wolfgang Rihm und die Schweiz. Für Wolfgang Rihm zum 60. Geburtstag.* Vienna: Holitzer, 2012.

Ballam-Cross, Paul. "Brahms: Piano Quartet No. 1, Piano Quintet." *Limelight Magazine*, 10 March 2017. www.limelightmagazine.com.au/reviews/brahms-piano-quartet-no-1-piano-quintet-ironwood.

Ballam-Cross, Paul. "Brahms: String Quintets (Takács Quartet, Lawrence Power)." *Limelight Magazine*, 6 January 2015. www.limelightmagazine.com.au/reviews/brahms-string-quintets-takacs-quartet-lawrence-power.

Barth, George. "Effacing Modernism, or How to Perform Less Accurately through Listening." *Historical Performance* 1 (2018): 148–89.

Bass, Alan. "Translator's Introduction." In Jacques Derrida, *Writing and Difference*. Translated by Alan Bass. London and New York: Routledge, [1967] 1978.

Bauer, Amy. *Ligeti's Laments: Nostalgia, Exoticism and the Absolute.* Aldershot: Ashgate, 2011.

Beach, David, and Yosef Goldenberg, eds. *Bach to Brahms: Essays on Musical Design and Structure.* Rochester, NY: University of Rochester Press, 2015.

Beach, David, and Ryan McClelland. *Analysis of 18th- and 19th-Century Works in the Classical Tradition.* New York: Routledge, 2012.

Beattie, Robert. "The Brahms Violin Sonatas Impressively Done by Faust and Melnikov." *Seen and Heard International*, 15 June 2015. https://seenandheard-international.com/2015/06/the-brahms-violin-sonatas-impressively-done-by-faust-and-melnikov.

Beaudoin, Richard. "Anonymous Sources: Finnissy Analysis and the Opening of Chapter Eight of *The History of Photography in Sound*." *Perspectives of New Music* 45/2 (Summer 2007): 5–27.

Becker, Carl. *Lieder und Weisen des vergangenen Jahrhunderte. Worte und Töne von den Originalen entlehnt von C. F. Becker.* Leipzig: Kösling'sche Buchhandlung, 1849.
Beckerath, Heinz von. "Erinnerungen an Johannes Brahms: Brahms und seine Krefelder Freunde." *Die Heimat (Krefeld)* 29/1–4 (1958): 81–93.
Beckerman, Michael. "Dvořák and Brahms: A Question of Influence." *American Brahms Society Newsletter* 4/2 (1986): 6–8.
Beckerman, Michael. *New Worlds of Dvořák: Searching in America for the Composer's Inner Life.* New York: W. W. Norton, 2003.
Beckerman, Michael, ed. *Dvořák and His World.* Princeton, NJ: Princeton University Press, 1993.
Behler, Constantin. *Nostalgic Teleology: Friedrich Schiller and the Schemata of Aesthetic Humanism.* Bern and New York: Peter Lang, 1995.
Behrenbeck, Sabine. *Der Kult um die toten Helden: Nationalsozialistische Mythen, Riten und Symbole, 1923–1945.* Vierow bei Greifswald: SH-Verlag, 1996.
Beirens, Maarten. "Archaeology of the Self: Michael Finnissy's 'Folklore.'" *Tempo* 57/223 (2003): 46–56.
Beller-McKenna, Daniel. *Brahms and the German Spirit.* Cambridge, MA, and London: Harvard University Press, 2004.
Beller-McKenna, Daniel. "Distance and Disembodiment: Harps, Horns, and the Requiem Idea in Schumann and Brahms." *Journal of Musicology* 22/1 (2005): 47–89.
Beller-McKenna, Daniel. "Reconsidering the Identity of an Orchestral Sketch by Brahms." *Journal of Musicology* 13/4 (1995): 508–37.
Bellman, Jonathan, ed. *The Exotic in Western Music.* Boston: Northeastern University Press, 1998.
Bent, Ian, ed. *Music Theory in the Age of Romanticism.* Cambridge: Cambridge University Press, 1996.
Bernstein, David W. "Techniques of Appropriation in Music of John Cage." *Contemporary Music Review* 20/4 (2001): 71–90.
Berry, Paul. *Brahms among Friends: Listening, Performance, and the Rhetoric of Allusion.* Oxford and New York: Oxford University Press, 2014.
Bessel, Richard. *Germany 1945: From War to Peace.* New York: HarperCollins, 2009.
Beuerle, Hans Michael. *Untersuchungen zu den A-cappella-Kompositionen: Ein Beitrag zur Geschichte der Chormusik.* Hamburg: K. D. Wagner, 1987.
Beveridge, David. "Echoes of Dvořák in the Third Symphony of Brahms." *Musik des Ostens* 11 (1989): 221–30.
Beveridge, David. "Romantic Ideas in a Classical Frame: The Sonata Forms of Dvořák." PhD diss., University of California, Berkeley, 1980.
Biba, Otto et al., eds. *Brahms' Schubert-Rezeption im Wiener Kontext. Bericht über das internationale Symposium Wien 2013.* Stuttgart: Franz Steiner Verlag, 2017.
Biba, Otto, and Jürgen Neubacher, eds. *". . . in meinen Tönen spreche ich." Für Johannes Brahms 1833–1897. Ausstellungskatalog Museum für Kunst und Gewerbe Hamburg 1997.* Hamburg: Museum für Kunst und Gewerbe, 1997.

Bishop, Paul, and R. H. Stephenson, eds. *Goethe 2000: Intercultural Readings of His Work*. Glasgow: Northern Universities Press, 2000.

Bismarck, Otto von. Speech to the Prussian Landtag, 30 September 1862 ("Blood and Iron"). Quoted in English translation in https://ghdi.ghi-dc.org/sub_document.cfm?document_id=250.

Black, Monica. *Death in Berlin: From Weimar to Divided Germany*. Cambridge and New York: Cambridge University Press, 2010.

Blackbourn, David. *History of Germany 1780–1918: The Long Nineteenth Century*. 2nd ed. Malden, MA: Blackwell, 2003.

Blum, David. *The Art of Quartet Playing: The Guarneri String Quartet in Conversation with David Blum*. New York: Alfred Knopf, 1986.

Boase, Roger. *The Origin and Meaning of Courtly Love: A Critical Study of European Scholarship*. Manchester: Manchester University Press, 1977.

Böcklin, Arnold. *Ausstellung zum 150. Geburtstag*. Edited by Susanne Bürger. Basel: Kunstmuseum Basel und Basler Kunstverein, 1977.

Böcklin, Arnold, and Heinrich Alfred Schmid. *Arnold Böcklin, eine Auswahl der herforragendsten Werke des Künstlers in Photogravüre*. Munich: Photographische Union, 1894.

Boerner, C. G. *Das radierte Werke des Daniel Chodowiecki: vollständig und durchweg in frühesten Zuständen*. Leipzig: C. G. Boerner, 1919.

Böhme, Franz Magnus. *Altdeutsches Liederbuch: Volkslieder der Deutschen nach Wort und Weise aus dem 12. bis zum 17. Jahrhundert*. Leipzig: Breitkopf & Härtel, 1877.

Bonds, Mark Evan. *After Beethoven: Imperatives of Originality in the Symphony*. Cambridge, MA: Harvard University Press, 1996.

Bonds, Mark Evan. "Idealism and the Aesthetics of Instrumental Music at the Turn of the Nineteenth Century." *Journal of the American Musicological Society* 50/2 (1997): 387–420.

Booth, Wayne C. *The Rhetoric of Fiction*. 2nd ed. Chicago and London: University of California Press, 1983 [1961].

Borchard, Beatrix. *Clara Schumann: Musik als Lebensform*. Hildesheim: Olms, 2019.

Borchard, Beatrix. *Stimme und Geige. Amalie und Joseph Joachim*. Vienna: Böhlau, 2005.

Borchard, Beatrix, and Kerstin Schüssler-Bach, eds. *Brahms Studien*. Vol. 16. Tutzing: Hans Schneider, 2011.

Botstein, Leon. "Brahms and Nineteenth-Century Painting." *19th Century Music* 14/2 (1990): 154–68.

Botstein, Leon, ed. *The Compleat Brahms*. New York: W W. Norton, 1997.

Boyd, Brian. "Shade and Shape in *Pale Fire*." *Nabokov Studies* 4 (1997), libraries.psu.edu/nabokov/boydpf2.htm.

Bouyer, Raymond. "Quatuor Parent." *Le Guide musical*, 15 March 1908, 228.

Bozarth, George. "Johannes Brahms und die Liedersammlungen von David Gregor Corner, Karl Severin Meister und Friedrich Wilhelm Arnold." *Die Musikforschung* 36 (1983): 177–99.

Bibliography

Bozarth, George. "The Origin of Brahms's *In stiller Nacht*." *Notes* 53/2 (1996): 363–80.

Bozarth, George. "Paths Not Taken: The 'Lost' Works of Johannes Brahms." *Music Review* 50 (1989): 185–205.

Bozarth, George, ed. *Brahms Studies: Analytical and Historical Perspectives*. Oxford: Oxford University Press, 1990.

Bozarth, George, and Walter Frisch. "Johannes Brahms." In *The New Grove Dictionary of Music and Musicians*. Edited by Stanley Sadie and John Tyrrell, 120–227. 2nd ed. Vol. 4. London: Macmillan, 2001.

Brachmann, Jan. "Form und Sinn des Buches—Betrachtungen zur *Brahms-Phantasie* von Max Klinger." Essay for the facsimile edition of *Brahms-Phantasie op. XII*. Johannes-Brahms-Gesellschaft. Hamburg: Verlag Ellert & Richter, 2017.

Brachmann, Jan. *"Ins Ungewisse hinauf": Johannes Brahms und Max Klinger im Zwiespalt von Kunst und Kommunikation*. Kassel: Bärenreiter, 1999.

Brachmann, Jan. "Johannes Brahms und Max Klinger—eine Kunstfreundschaft." *Brahms-Studien* 15 (2008): 69–87.

Brachmann, Jan. *Kunst—Religion—Krise. Der Fall Brahms*. Kassel: Bärenreiter, 2003.

Brahms, Johannes. *The Brahms Notebooks: The Little Treasure Chest of the Young Kreisler. Quotations from Poets, Philosophers, and Artists Gathered by Johannes Brahms*. Edited by Carl Krebs; translated by Agnes Eisenberger. Annotations by Siegmund Levarie. Hillsdale, NY: Pendragon Press, 2003.

Brahms, Johannes. *Johannes Brahms Briefwechsel*, 19 vols. to date. 16 orig. vols. Rev. eds., Berlin: Deutsche Brahms-Gesellschaft, 1912–1922; repr., Tutzing: Hans Schneider, 1974. *Neue Folge* consisting of 3 vols. to date. Tutzing: Hans Schneider, 1991–.

Brahms, Johannes. *Johannes Brahms Briefwechsel*, Vols. I and II: *Johannes Brahms im Briefwechsel mit Heinrich und Elisabet von Herzogenberg*. Edited by Max Kalbeck. Berlin: Deutsche Brahms-Gesellschaft, 1906. Reprint, Tutzing: Schneider, 1974.

Brahms, Johannes. *Johannes Brahms Briefwechsel*, Vol. IV: *Johannes Brahms im Briefwechsel mit Julius Otto Grimm*. Edited by Richard Barth. Berlin: Deutsche Brahms-Gesellschaft, 1908. Reprint, Tutzing: Schneider, 1974.

Brahms, Johannes. *Johannes Brahms Briefwechsel*, Vol V: *Johannes Brahms im Briefwechsel mit Joseph Joachim*. Edited by Andreas Moser. 2 Vols, 3rd ed. Berlin: Deutsche Brahms-Gesellschaft, 1908; 1912; 1921; Reprint, Tutzing: Schneider, 1974.

Brahms, Johannes. *Johannes Brahms Briefwechsel*, Vol. VII: *Johannes Brahms im Briefwechsel mit Hermann Levi, Friedrich Gernsheim sowie den Familien Hecht und Fellinger*. Edited by Leopold Schmidt. Berlin: Deutsche Brahms-Gesellschaft, 1910.

Brahms, Johannes. *Johannes Brahms Briefwechsel*, Vol. VIII: *Johannes Brahms an Joseph Victor Widmann, Ellen und Ferdinand Vetter, Adolf Schubring*. Edited by Max Kalbeck. Berlin: Deutsche Brahms-Gesellschaft, 1915.

Brahms, Johannes. *Johannes Brahms Briefwechsel*, Vol. IX: *Johannes Brahms: Briefe an P. J. Simrock and Fritz Simrock*. Edited by Max Kalbeck. Berlin: Deutsche Brahms-Gesellschaft, 1917.

Brahms, Johannes. *Johannes Brahms Briefwechsel*, Vols. XI and XII: *Johannes Brahms Briefe an Fritz Simrock*. Edited by Max Kalbeck. 2 Vols. Berlin: Deutsche Brahms-Gesellschaft, 1919. Reprint, Tutzing: Hans Schneider, 1974.

Brahms, Johannes. *Johannes Brahms Briefwechsel*, Vol. XIII: *Johannes Brahms im Briefwechsel mit Theodor Wilhelm Engelmann*. Edited by Julius Roentgen. Berlin: Deutsche Brahms-Gesellschaft, 1918.

Brahms, Johannes. *Johannes Brahms Briefwechsel*, Vol. XIV: *Johannes Brahms im Briefwechsel mit Breitkopf & Härtel, Bartolf Senff, J. Rieter-Biedermann, C. F. Peters, E. W. Fritzsch und Robert Lienau*. Edited by Wilhelm Altmann. Berlin: Deutsche Brahms-Gesellschaft, 1920.

Brahms, Johannes. *Johannes Brahms Briefwechsel*, Vol. XV: *Johannes Brahms im Briefwechsel mit Franz Wüllner*. Edited by Ernst Wolff. Berlin: Deutsche Brahms-Gesellschaft, 1922. Reprint, Tutzing: Hans Schneider, 1974.

Brahms, Johannes. *Johannes Brahms Briefwechsel*, Vol. XVI: *Johannes Brahms im Briefwechsel mit Philipp Spitta*. Edited by Carl Krebs. Berlin: Deutsche Brahms-Gesellschaft, 1920; repr., Tutzing: Hans Schneider, 1974.

Brahms, Johannes. *Johannes Brahms Briefwechsel*, Vol. XVI: *Johannes Brahms im Briefwechsel mit Philipp Spitta. Briefwechsel mit Otto Dessoff*. Edited by Carl Krebs. Berlin: Deutsche Brahms-Gesellschaft, 1922.

Brahms, Johannes. *Des jungen Kreislers Schatzkästlein: Aussprüche von Dichtern, Philosophen und Künstlern*. Edited by Carl Krebs. Berlin: Deutsche Brahms-Gesellschaft, 1909.

Brahms, Johannes, and Max Klinger. *Briefwechsel*. Edited by Ernst Eggebrecht and Hans Schulz. Leipzig: Verlag Poeschel und Trepte, private printing 1924.

Brednich, Rolf Wilhelm, Lutz Röhrich, and Wolfgang Suppan, eds. *Handbuch des Volksliedes: Historisches und Systematisches. Interethnische Beziehungen, Musikethnologie*. 2 Vols. Munich: W. Fink, 1973–1975.

Bretherton, David. "Review of *A Theory of Musical Narrative*, by Bryon Almén." *Music Analysis* 31/3 (2012): 414–21.

Breuilly, John. *Nineteenth-Century Germany: Politics, Culture and Society, 1780–1918*. 2nd ed. London: Bloomsbury Academic, 2020.

Brill, E. V. K. "The Philistine Concept in German Literature." *European Studies Review* 7 (1977): 77–93.

Brinkmann, Reinhold. *Johannes Brahms. Die zweite Symphonie*. Munich: Edition Text + Kritik, 1990.

Brinkmann, Reinhold. *Vom Pfeifen und von alten Dampfmaschine: Essays zur Musik von Beethoven bis Rihm*. Munich: Paul Szolnay Verlag, 2006.

Brockmann, Stephen. *German Literary Culture at the Zero Hour*. Rochester, NY: Camden House, 2004.

Brockmann, Stephen. "The Postwar Restoration in East and West." *New German Critique* 42/3 (2015): 69–90.

Bibliography

Brodbeck, David. *Brahms and German National Sentiment*. Tentative title, in progress.

Brodbeck, David. *Defining Deutschtum: Political Ideology, German Identity, and Music-Critical Discourse in Liberal Vienna*. New York: Oxford University Pres, 2014.

Brodbeck, David. "Review: Margit McCorkle, *Johannes Brahms: Thematisch-bibliographisches Werkverzeichnis*." *Journal of the American Musicological Society* 39 (1989): 418–31.

Brodbeck, David, ed. *Brahms Studies*. Vol. 1. Lincoln: University of Nebraska Press, 1994.

Brodbeck, David, ed. *Brahms Studies*. Vol. 2. Lincoln: University of Nebraska Press, 1998.

Brodbeck, David, ed. *Brahms Studies*. Vol. 3. Lincoln: University of Nebraska Press, 2001.

Brophy, James M. "The Rhine Crisis of 1840 and German Nationalism: Chauvinism, Skepticism, and Regional Reception." *Journal of Modern History* 85 (2013): 1–35.

Brougham, Henrietta, Christopher Fox, and Ian Pace, eds. *Uncommon Ground: The Music of Michael Finnissy*. Aldershot: Ashgate, 1997.

Brown, Clive. *Classical and Romantic Performing Practice 1750–1900*. Oxford and New York: Oxford University Press, 1999.

Brown, Clive, Neal Peres Da Costa, and Kate Bennett Wadsworth. *Performing Practices in Johannes Brahms's Chamber Music*. Kassel: Bärenreiter, 2015.

Brusniak, Friedhelm, and Dietmar Klenke. " Sängerfeste und die Musikpolitik der deutschen Nationalbewegung." *Die Musikforschung* 52 (1999): 29–54.

Buch, Esteban, Igor Contreras Zubillaga, and Manuel Deniz Silva, eds. *Composing for the State: Music in Twentieth-Century Dictatorships*. Burlington, VT: Ashgate, 2016.

Bullivant, Joanna. *Alan Bush, Modern Music and the Cold War: The Cultural Left in Britain and the Communist Bloc*. New York: Cambridge University Press, 2017.

Bulmahn, Heinz. *Adolf Glassbrenner: His Development from Jungdeutscher to Vormärzler*. Amsterdam: John Benjamins, 1978.

Byrne-Bodley, Lorraine, ed. *Music Preferred: Essays in Musicology, Cultural History and Analysis, in Honour of Harry White*. Vienna: Hollitzer, 2018.

Caballero, Carlo. "Patriotism or Nationalism? Fauré and the Great War." *Journal of the American Musicological Society* 52 (1999): 539–625.

Cadwallader, Allen. "Foreground Motivic Ambiguity: Its Clarification at Middleground Levels in Selected Late Piano Pieces of Johannes Brahms." *Music Analysis* 7/1 (1988): 59–91.

Cadwallader, Allen. "Motivic Unity and Integration of Structural Levels in Brahms's B Minor Intermezzo, Op. 119, No. 1." *Theory and Practice* 8/2 (1983): 5–24.

Caplin, William. *Analyzing Classical Form: An Approach for the Classroom*. New York and Oxford: Oxford University Press, 2013.

Caplin, William. *Classical Form: A Theory of Formal Functions for the Instrumental Music of Haydn, Mozart, and Beethoven.* Oxford and New York: Oxford University Press, 1998.

Cardus, Neville, ed. *Kathleen Ferrier: A Memoir.* London: Hamish Hamilton, 1954.

Caroll, Mark, ed. *Music and Ideology.* New York: Routledge, 2012.

Champa, Kermit Swiler. *Studies in Early Impressionism.* New Haven, CT: Yale University Press, 1973.

Chatman, Seymour. *Story and Discourse: Narrative Structure in Fiction and Film.* Ithaca, NY: Cornell University Press, 1978.

Cheek, Pamela. *Sexual Antipodes.* Stanford, CA: Stanford University Press, 2003.

Christoffel, Ulrich. *Anselm Feuerbach.* Munich: Bruckmann Verlag, 1944.

Clark, Christopher. *Iron Kingdom: The Rise and Fall of Prussia, 1600–1947.* Cambridge, MA: Belknap Press of Harvard University Press, 2006.

Clive, Peter. *Brahms and His World: A Biographical Dictionary.* Latham, MD: Scarecrow Press, 2006).

Cohn, Dorrit. "Discordant Narration." *Style* 34/1 (2000): 307–16.

Cohn, Richard. "Introduction to Neo-Riemannian Theory: A Survey and Historical Perspective." *Journal of Music Theory* 42/2 (1998): 167–80.

Comberiati, Carmelo P., and Matthew C. Steel, eds. *Music from the Middle Ages through the Twentieth Century: Essays in Honor of Gwynn S. McPeek.* New York: Gordon and Breach, 1998.

Comini, Alessandra. "The Visual Brahms: Idols and Images." *Arts Magazine* 54/2 (1979–1980): 123–29.

Cone, Edward T. "Schubert's Promissory Note: An Exercise in Musical Hermeneutics." *19th-Century Music* 5/3 (1982): 233–41.

Cone, Edward T. "Three Ways of Reading a Detective Story—Or a Brahms Intermezzo." *Georgia Review* 31/3 (1977): 554–74.

Cortot, Alfred. *Cours d'interprétation.* Edited by Jeanne Thieffry. Paris: Legouix, 1934.

Cotton, Martin. "Review: *Brahms: Violin Sonatas, Leila Schayegh & Jan Schultz.*" *Classical Music*, 1 March 2020. www.classical-music.com/reviews/chamber/brahms-violin-sonatas-2.

Crispin, Darla, and Bob Gilmore, eds. *Artistic Experimentation in Music.* Leuven: Leuven University Press, 2014.

Cross, Jonathan. "Vive la différence." *Musical Times* 137/1837 (March 1996): 7–13.

Cybinski, Anselm. "Songs on the Way to an Inner World: Igor Levit's Encounters with Music from Bach to Feldman." Liner booklet essay for Levit, *Encounter.* Sony Classical 19439786572, 2020.

Dahlhaus, Carl. *Between Romanticism and Modernism: Four Studies in the Music of the Later Nineteenth Century.* Translated by Mary Whittall. Berkeley: University of California Press, 1980.

Dahlhaus, Carl. *Nineteenth-Century Music.* Translated by J. B. Robinson. Berkeley and Los Angeles: University of California Press, 1989.

Bibliography

Daniel, Harvard, and Jacques Callot. *Callot's Etchings*. New York: Dover Publications, 1974.

Danuser, Hermann. "Zur Kritik der musikalischen Postmoderne." *Neue Zeitschrift für Musik* 149/12 (1988): 4–9.

Danuser, Hermann, ed. *Neue Musik im politischem Wandel*. Veröffentlichungen des Instituts für Neue Musik und Musikerziehung Darmstadt. Mainz: Schott, 1991.

Davenson, Henri. "Un demi-siècle . . ." *Esprit* (new series) 280/1 (January 1960): 12–21.

Davenson, Henri. *Le livre des chansons, ou Introduction à la connaissance de la chanson*. Paris: Le Seuil, 1944.

Davenson, Henri. "Musique française ou musique en France." *Esprit* (new series) 109/5 (April 1945): 742–46.

Davenson, Henri. *Traité de la musique selon l'esprit de saint Augustin*. Paris: Le Seuil, 1942.

Davenson, Henri. *Les troubadours*. Paris: Le Seuil, 1961.

Daverio, John. *Crossing Paths: Schubert, Schumann, and Brahms*. New York: Oxford University Press, 2002.

Daverio, John. *Robert Schumann: Herald of a "New Poetic Age."* New York: Oxford University Press, 1997.

Daverio, John. "Schumann's Ossianic Manner." *19th-Century Music* 21/3 (1998): 247–73.

Daverio, John. "The 'Wechsel der Töne' in Brahms's 'Schicksalslied.'" *Journal of the American Musicological Society* 46/1 (1993): 84–113.

Davis, Andrew. *Sonata Fragments: Romantic Narratives in Chopin, Schumann and Brahms*. Bloomington: Indiana University Press, 2017.

Derrida, Jacques. *Specters of Marx: The State of the Debt, the Work of Mourning and the New International*. Translated by Peggy Kamuf. New York and London: Routledge, 1994.

De Vlieger, Henk. "Elf Choralvorspiele." Program note, https://www.henkdevlieger.nl/choralvorspiele/.

Diergarten, Felix. "Melancholie des Unvermögens: Der Brahmssche Ton und das Intermezzo op. 119, 1." *Musik & Ästhetik* 7/26 (2003): 42–53.

Dietrich, Albert. *Erinnerungen an Johannes Brahms in Briefen besonders aus seiner Jugendzeit*. Leipzig: Otto Wigand, 1898.

d'Indy, Vincent. *Cours de composition musicale*, prepared in collaboration with Auguste Sérieyx. Paris: Durand, 1912.

Distler, Jed. "Brahms: Piano Quintet/Staier." *Classics Today*, www.classicstoday.com/review/review-11464.

Distler, Jed. "Fresh Insights from an Old Master in Brahms Quintet." *Classics Today*, www.classicstoday.com/review/fresh-insights-old-master-brahms-quintet.

Distler, Jed. "Geglückte Probe für Hamburg." *Die Presse*, 15 January 2017. https://www.diepresse.com/5154783/geglückte-probe-fur-hamburg.

Döge, Klaus. "Antonín Dvořák." *Grove Music Online*, 2001. https://www.oxford musiconline.com/grovemusic/view/10.1093/gmo/9781561592630.001.0001/ omo-9781561592630-e-0000051222.

Döhl, Friedhelm. *Brahms-Galerie*. Lübeck: Musikhochschule Lübeck, 2014.

Dowe, Dieter, Heinz-Gerhard Haupt, Dieter Langewiesche, and Jonathan Sperber, eds. *Europe in 1848: Revolution and Reform*. Translated by David Higgins. New York and Oxford: Berghahn Books, 2001.

Draheim, Joachim, Ludwig Finscher, Frithjof Haas, Klaus Häfner, Jeannot Heinen, Brigitte Höft, and Ekkehard Schulz, eds. *Johannes Brahms in Baden-Baden und Karlsruhe, Eine Ausstellung der Badischen Landesbibliothek Karlsruhe und der Brahmsgesellschft Baden-Baden e.V.* Karlsruhe: Badische Landesbibliothek, 1983.

Drees, Stefan, ed. *Neugier ist alles. Der Komponist Detlev Glanert*. Hofheim: Wolke, 2012.

Drinker, Sophie. *Brahms and His Women's Choruses*. Merion, PA: Sophie Drinker, under the auspices of Musurgia Publishers, A. G. Hess, 1952.

Drummond, William J. "Arrangement, Listening, and the Music of Gérard Pesson." DPhil thesis, University of Oxford, 2019.

Dulak Thomson, Michelle. "Astounding Control: Tokyo Quartet on Brahms." *San Francisco Classical Voice*, 14 December 2012. www.sfcv.org/reviews/tone-control-tokyo-takes-on-brahms.

Düwell, Susanne, and Matthias Schmidt, eds. *Narrative der Shoah: Repräsentationen der Vergangenheit in Historiographie, Kunst und Politik*. Paderborn: Schöningh, 2002.

Dyment, Christopher. *Conducting the Brahms Symphonies: From Brahms to Boult*. Woodbridge: The Boydell Press, 2016.

Edwards, David Noel. "Schumann, Brahms Piano Quintets: Truly Titanic Performances at Close Encounters with Music." *The Berkshire Edge*. 4 November 2017. https://theberkshireedge.com/review-schumann-brahms-piano-quintets-truly-titanic-performances-at-close-encounters-with-music.

Einem, Herbert von. "Anselm Feuerbachs 'Orpheus und Eurydike.'" *Wallraf-Richartz-Jahrbuch* 36 (1974): 295–310.

Ellingson, Ter. "Transcription (i)." *Grove Music Online*, 2001. https://www.oxford musiconline.com/grovemusic/view/10.1093/gmo/9781561592630.001.0001/ omo-9781561592630-e-0000028268.

Ellis Benson, Bruce. *The Improvisation of Musical Dialogue: A Phenomenology of Music*. Cambridge: Cambridge University Press, 2003.

Engelmann, Wilhelm. *Daniel Chodowieckis Sämmtlicher Kupferstiche*. Leipzig: Verlag von Wilhelm Engelmann, 1857.

Ennis, Martin. "Tumbling in the Godless Deep: Brahms and the Sense of an Ending." *Musicologica Austriaca: Journal for Austrian Musical Studies* (5 February 2020).

Erk, Ludwig, and Franz Magnus Böhme. *Deutscher Liederhort: Auswahl der vorzüglicheren Deutschen Volkslieder nach Wort und Weise aus der Vorzeit und Gegenwart*. 3 vols. Leipzig: Breitkopf & Härtel, 1893–1894.

Eshbach, Robert. "Digression: The Road to Jewish Emancipation." Blogpost, 2013. https://josephjoachim.com/2013/08/05/digression-the-road-to-jewish-emancipation/.
Eshbach, Robert. "Joachim, Reményi... and Brahms." Paper presented at the 2012 meeting of the American Brahms Society. See https://josephjoachim.com/2014/09/29/remenyi-before-brahms/.
Evangelisches Kirchengesangbuch: Stammausgabe. Kassel: Bärenreiter, 1950.
Evans, Richard J. *Death in Hamburg: Society and Politics in the Cholera Years, 1830–1910*. New York: Penguin, 2005.
Fanning, David. "Review: Igor Levit: Encounter." *Gramophone*, October 2020. https://www.gramophone.co.uk/review/igor-levit-encounter.
Fellinger, Maria. *Johannes Brahms—Bilder*. Leipzig: Breitkopf & Härtel, 1911.
Feurzeig, Lisa, ed. *Deutsche Lieder für Jung und Alt*. Middleton, WI: A-R Editions, 2012.
Fifield, Christopher. *Letters and Diaries of Kathleen Ferrier*. Woodbridge: Boydell and Brewer, 2011.
Finnissy, Michael. "Biting the Hand That Feeds You." *Contemporary Music Review* 21/1 (2002): 71–79.
Finnissy, Michael. CD liner notes to *In stiller Nacht, Independence Quadrilles* (NMC D107, 2005).
Finnissy, Michael. Composer's note to score of *In stiller Nacht*. Oxford: Oxford University Press, 1998.
Finson, Jon W., and R. Larry Todd, eds. *Mendelssohn and Schumann: Essays on Their Music and Its Context*. Durham, NC: Duke University Press, 1984.
Fischer, U. C. "Goethe's 'Chinese-German Book of Seasons and Hours' and World Literature." *United College Journal* 6 (1967): 27–34.
Fiske, Roger. "Brahms and Scotland." *Musical Times* 109 (1968): 1106–7 and 1109–11.
Fitch, Fabrice. "Rihm, *Symphonie 'Nähe Fern.'*" *Gramophone Magazine*, September 2013.
Floros, Constantin. *Brahms und Bruckner: Studien zur musikalischen Exegetik*. Wiesbaden: Breitkopf & Härtel, 1980.
Floros, Constantin, Hans Joachim Marx, and Peter Petersen, eds. *Brahms und seine Zeit. Hamburger Jahrbuch für Musikwissenschaft 7*. Laaber: Laaber Verlag, 1984.
Forster, Georg. *Frische teutsche Liedlein (1539–1556) dritter Teil (1549)*. Edited by Kurt Gudewill and Horst Brunner. Wolfenbüttel: Möseler Verlag, 1966 [1976].
Freiligrath, Ferdinand. *Neuere politische und soziale Gedichte*. 2 vols. Vol. 1: Cologne: Selbstverlag der Verfassers; Düsseldorf: W. H. Scheller, 1849. Vol. 2: Düsseldorf: Selbstverlag der Verfassers, 1851.
Fried, Michael. *Menzel's Realism: Art and Embodiment in Nineteenth-Century Berlin*. New Haven, CT, and London: Yale University Press, 2002.
Friedlaender, Max. *Hundert Deutsche Volkslieder für eine Singstimme mit Begleitung des Klaviers*. Leipzig: Peters, 1886.

Friedlaender, Max. "Zuccalmaglio und das Volkslied: Ein Beitrag zur Stilkritik des deutschen Volksliedes." *Jahrbuch der Musikbibliothek Peters*, 1918.

Frisch, Walter. *Brahms and the Principle of Developing Variation*. Berkeley: University of California Press, 1984.

Frisch, Walter. *German Modernism: Music and the Arts*. Berkeley: University of California Press, 2005.

Frisch, Walter, and Kevin Karnes, eds. *Brahms and His World*. Princeton, NJ: Princeton University Press, 2009.

Froesch, Vitus. *Die Chormusik von Rudolf Mauersberger: Eine stilkritische Studie*. Marburg: Tectum Verlag, 2013.

Fuchs, Anne. *After the Dresden Bombing: Pathways of Memory, 1945 to the Present*. New York: Palgrave Macmillan, 2012.

Fuchs, Ingrid, ed. *Festschrift Otto Biba zum 60. Geburtstag*. Tutzing: Schneider, 2006.

Fuchs, Ingrid, ed. *Internationaler Brahms-Kongress Gmunden 1997: Kongress Bericht*. Tutzing: Hans Schneider, 2001.

Fulbrook, Mary. *A Concise History of Germany*. 3rd ed. Cambridge: Cambridge University Press, 2019.

Furones, Laura. "So Full of Melodies: Kavakos and Wang Play Brahms's Sonatas." *Bachtrack*, 21 October 2014. https://bachtrack.com/review-brahms-kavakos-wang-madrid-october-2014.

Furtwängler, Wilhelm. *Brahms. Bruckner. Mit einem Nachwort über Wilhelm Furtwängler von Dr. W. Riezler*. Leipzig: Reclam, 1942.

Galand, Joel. "Some Eighteenth-Century Ritornello Scripts and Their Nineteenth-Century Revivals." *Music Theory Spectrum* 30/2 (2008): 239–82.

Gay, Peter. "Aimez-vous Brahms? Reflections on Modernism." *Salmagundi* 36 (1977): 16–35.

Gay, Peter. *Freud, Jews and Other Germans: Masters and Victims in Modernist Culture*. Oxford and New York: Oxford University Press, 1978.

Geck, Martin. *Robert Schumann: The Life and Work of a Romantic Composer*. Translated by Stewart Spencer. Chicago: University of Chicago Press, 2013.

Geiringer, Karl. *On Brahms and His Circle: Essays and Documentary Studies by Karl Geiringer*. Revised and enlarged by George S. Bozarth. Sterling Heights, MI: Harmonie Park Press, 2006.

Gellen, Adam. "Eduard Reményis Jugendjahre und seine Beziehung zu Johannes Brahms—Eine biographische Skizze." *Studia Musicologica* 49/3–4 (2008): 295–319.

Georg Baur, Oswald, and Sylvia Riedmaier. *Jahrbuch 4 der Bayerischen Akademie der Schönen Künste*. Schaftlach: Oreos Verlag, 1990.

Gerbino, Giuseppe, and Alexander Silbiger. "Folia." *Grove Music Online*, 2001. https://www.oxfordmusiconline.com/grovemusic/view/10.1093/gmo/978156 1592630.001.0001/omo-9781561592630-e-0000009929.

Gibson, Frank. *The Art of Henri Fantin-Latour: His Life and Work*. London: Dranes Ltd., n.d.

Glanert, Detlev. "Vorwort." In Johannes Brahms/Detlev Glanert. *Vier Choralvorspiele für Orchester*. Berlin: Boosey & Hawkes, 2017.
Goeckel, Robert F. *The Lutheran Church and the East German State: Political Conflict and Change under Ulbricht and Honecker*. Ithaca, NY: Cornell University Press, 1990.
Goehr, Alexander. *Finding the Key*. Edited by Derrick Puffett. London and Boston: Faber & Faber, 1998.
Goltz, Maren, "Feine Unterschiede: Komponisten, Dichter und Interpreten in der Memorialikonographie Meiningens." *Imago Musicae* 25 (2012): 145–86.
Goltz, Maren, Wolfgang Sandberger, and Christiane Wiesenfeldt, eds. *Spätphase(n)? Johannes Brahms' Werke der 1880er und 1890er Jahre. Internationales musikwissenschaftliches Symposium Meiningen 2008*. Munich: Henle, 2010.
Goves, Larry. "Michael Finnissy and Wolfgang Amadeus Mozart: The Composer as Anthropologist." *Tempo* 71/280 (2017): 47–55.
Graf, Max. *Legende einer Musikstadt*. Vienna: Österreichische Buchgemeinschaft, 1949.
Graf, Max. *Legend of a Musical City: The Story of Vienna*. New York: Philosophical Library, 1945. Reprint 1969.
Graybill, Roger. "Brahms' Integration of Traditional and Progressive Tendencies: A Look at Three Sonata Expositions." *Journal of Musicological Research* 8/1–2 (1988): 143–47.
Gregor, Neil. "Beethoven, Bayreuth, and the Origins of the Federal Republic of Germany." *English Historical Review* 126 (2011): 835–77.
Gregor, Neil. "'Is he still alive, or long since dead?': Loss, Absence and Remembrance in Nuremberg, 1945–1956." *German History* 21 (2003): 183–203.
Gregor, Neil. "Music, Memory, Emotion: Richard Strauss and the Legacies of War." *Music and Letters* 96/1 (2015): 55–76.
Gregor, Neil. "Siegmund von Hausegger, the Munich Philharmonic Orchestra and Civic Musical Culture in the Third Reich." *German History* 36/4 (2018): 544–73.
Grella, George. "In Arnone's Hand, Finnissy's Piano Music Proves Spellbinding." *New York Classical Review* (24 March 2015), https://newyorkclassicalreview.com/2015/03/in-arnones-hands-finnissys-piano-music-proves-spellbinding/.
Grenier, Katherine, and Amanda Mushal, eds. *Cultures of Memory in the Nineteenth Century: Consuming Commemoration*. New York: Palgrave Macmillan, 2020.
Grimes, Nicole. "Brahms's Ascending Circle: Hölderlin, *Schicksalslied*, and the Process of Recollection." *Nineteenth-Century Music Review* 11/1 (2014): 1–36.
Grimes, Nicole. *Brahms's Elegies: The Poetics of Loss in Nineteenth-Century German Culture*. Cambridge and New York: Cambridge University Press, 2019.
Grimes, Nicole. "The Schoenberg/Brahms Critical Tradition Reconsidered." *Music Analysis* 31/2 (2012): 127–75.
Grimes, Nicole, and Angela R. Mace. *Mendelssohn Perspectives*. Aldershot: Ashgate, 2012.
Groos, Carl, and Bernhard Klein, eds. *Deutsche Lieder für Jung und Alt*. Berlin: Realschulbuchhandlung, 1818.

Grosch, Nils. "The Old German Folksongs: Tracing a Philological Fake." *Muzikološ kizbornik* 49/2 (2013): 23–32.

Gruber, Gernot, ed. *Die Kammermusik von Johannes Brahms: Tradition und Innovation*. Laaber: Laaber Verlag, 2001.

Grün, Matthias. *Rudolf Mauersberger: Studien zu Leben und Werk*. Regensburg: G. Bosse Verlag, 1986.

Gusick, Barbara I., and Matthew Z. Heintzelman, eds. *Fifteenth-Century Studies 37*. Rochester: Camden House, 2012.

Guttenplan, D. D. *The Holocaust on Trial*. New York: W. W. Norton, 2002.

H . . . . n [pseudonym]. "Kammer und Hausmusik: Lieder für eine Singstimme mit Begleitung des Pianoforte." *Neue Zeitschrift für Musik* 64/18 (24 April 1868): 153–54.

Haas, Frithjof. *Hermann Levi: From Brahms to Wagner*. Translated by Cynthia Klohr. Lanham, MA: Scarecrow Press, 2012.

Habermas, Jürgen. *The Structural Transformation of the Public Sphere: An Inquiry into a Category of Bourgeois Society*. Translated by Thomas Burger. Cambridge, MA: MIT Press, 1989.

Hagel, Doris. "Johannes Brahms—Betrachtungen zu seinen 'Vier ernsten Gesängen.'" Liner booklet note for *Antonín Dvořák, Requiem Op. 89/Johannes Brahms, Vier ernste Gesänge op. 121*. Klaus Mertens, Doris Hagel; Capella Weilburgensis (Profil Medien, PH06050, 2006), 6–8.

Hamilton, John T. *Music, Madness, and the Unworking of Language*. New York: Columbia University Press, 2008.

Hamilton, Katy, and Natasha Loges, eds. *Brahms in the Home and the Concert Hall: Between Private and Public Performance*. Cambridge: Cambridge University Press, 2014.

Harten, Uwe, ed. *Bruckner-Symposion: Bruckner, Vorbilder und Traditionen: im Rahmen des Internationales Brucknerfest Linz 1997*. Vienna: Musikwissenschaftlicher Verlag, 1999.

Härtwig, Dieter, and Matthias Herrmann. *Der Dresdner Kreuzchor: Geschichte und Gegenwart, Wirkungsstätten und Schule*. Leipzig: Evangelische Verlagsanstalt, 2006.

Hastings, Charise. "From Poem to Performance: Brahms's 'Edward' Ballade, Op. 10, No. 1." *College Music Symposium* 48 (2008): 83–97.

Hegel, G. W. F. *Philosophy of Right*. Translated by T. M. Knox. Oxford: Oxford University Press, 1952.

Helfricht, Jürgen. *Dresdner Kreuzchor und Kreuzkirche: Eine Chronik von 1206 bis heute*. Husum: Husum Verlag, 2004.

Helms, Siegmund. "Johannes Brahms und Johann Sebastian Bach." In *Bach-Jahrbuch 57*, 13–81. Berlin: Evangelische Verlagsanstalt, 1971.

Henschel, George. *Personal Recollections of Johannes Brahms*. Boston: R. G. Badger, 1907.

Hepokoski, James. *Sibelius: Symphony No. 5*. Cambridge: Cambridge University Press, 1993.

Hepokoski, James. *A Sonata Theory Handbook.* New York: Oxford University Press, 2020.
Hepokoski, James, and Warren Darcy. *Elements of Sonata Theory: Norms, Types, and Deformations in the Late-Eighteenth-Century Sonata.* New York: Oxford University Press, 2006.
Herrmann, Matthias. *Kreuzkantor zu Dresden: Rudolf Mauersberger.* Dresden: Mauersberger-Museum, 2004.
Hermann, Matthias, ed. *Dresdner Kreuzchor und zeitgenössische Chormusik: Ur- und Erstaufführungen zwischen Richter und Kreiler.* Marburg: Tectum Verlag, 2017.
Herrmann, Matthias, ed. *Rudolf Mauersberger: Aus der Werkstatt eines Kreuzkantors: Briefe, Texte, Reden.* Marburg: Tectum Verlag, 2014.
Herrmann, Matthias, and Hanns-Werner Heister, eds. *Dresden und die avancierte Musik im 20. Jahrhunderti*, Vol. II: *1933–1966.* Laaber: Laaber-Verlag, 2002.
Herwegh, Georg. *Gedichte eines Lebendigen.* 9th printing. Stuttgart: G. J. Göschen, 1871.
Herzfeld-Schild, Marie Louise. "Serialismus aus Tradition: Milton Babbitts Schönberg-Rezeption." *Archiv für Musikwissenschaft* 66/1 (2009): 69–91.
Heuberger, Richard. *Erinnerungen an Johannes Brahms; Tagebuchnotizen aus den Jahren 1875–1897.* Edited by Kurt Hofmann. Tutzing: Hans Schneider, 1971.
Hewett, Ivan. "BBC Symphony Orchestra, Barbican, Review: Brahms's Mighty First Symphony Glowed Magnificently." *Telegraph*, 13 January 2016.
Hewitson, Mark. *Nationalism in Germany, 1848–1866: Revolutionary Nation.* New York: Palgrave Macmillan, 2010.
Hiemke, Sven. *Johannes Brahms: Ein deutsches Requiem.* Kassel: Bärenreiter, 2018.
Hildebrand, Adolf von. *Das Problem der Form in der bildenden Kunst.* Strasbourg: Heitz, 1893.
Hilliard, Kevin. "'Nänie': Critical Reflections on the Sentimental in Poetry." *Publications of the English Goethe Society* 75/1 (2006): 3–13.
Hockenos, Matthew D. *A Church Divided: German Protestants Confront the Nazi Past.* Bloomington: Indiana University Press, 2004.
Hoelscher, Steven. "'Dresden, a Camera Accuses': Rubble Photography and the Politics of Memory in a Divided Germany." *History of Photography* 36 (2012): 288–305.
Høffding, Simon. *A Phenomenology of Musical Absorption.* London: Palgrave Macmillan, 2018.
Hoffmann, E. T. A. *E. T. A. Hoffmann's Musical Writings: "Kreisleriana," "The Poet and the Composer," Music Criticism.* Edited by David Charlton. Translated by Martyn Clarke. Cambridge: Cambridge University Press, 1989.
Hoffmann, E. T. A. *Werke.* 4 Vols. Frankfurt am Main: Insel Verlag, 1967.
Hoffmann von Fallersleben, August Heinrich. *Mein Leben.* 6 vols. Hannover: Carl Rümpler, 1868.
Hofmann, Erna Hedwig, ed. *Begegnungen mit Rudolf Mauersberger: Dankesgabe eines Freundenkreises zum 75. Geburtstag des Dresdner Kreuz-Kantors.* Berlin: Evangelische Verlagsanstalt, 1968.

Hofmann, Kurt. *Die Bibliothek von Johannes Brahms: Bücher- und Musikalienverzeichnis*. Hamburg: Karl Dieter Wagner, 1974.

Hofmann, Renate, and Kurt Hofmann. *Johannes Brahms: Zeittafel zu Leben und Werk*. Tutzing: Hans Schneider, 1983.

Holden, Claire, Eric Clarke, and Cayenna Ponchione-Bailey, eds. *Practice in Context: Perspectives on Historically Informed Practices in Post-Classical Music*. Oxford: Oxford University Press, forthcoming.

Hopkins Porter, Cecilia. "The *Rheinlieder* Critics: A Case of Musical Nationalism." *Musical Quarterly* 63 (1977): 74–98.

Horne, William. "Brahms's Op. 10 Ballades and his *Blätter aus dem Tagebuch eines Musikers*." *Journal of Musicology* 15/1 (1997): 98–115.

Horton, Julian. *Brahms' Second Piano Concerto, Op. 83: Analytical and Contextual Studies*. Leuven: Peeters, 2017.

Horton, Julian. "Criteria for a Theory of Nineteenth-Century Sonata Form." *Music Theory and Analysis* 4/2 (2017): 147–91.

Horton, Julian. "Rethinking Sonata Failure: Mendelssohn's Overture *zum Märchen von der schönen Melusine*." *Music Theory Spectrum* 43/2 (2021): 299–319.

Hotaki, Leander, ed. *Robert Schumanns Mottosammlung: Übertragung, Kommentar, Einführung*. Freiburg: Rombach, 1998.

Howard, Keith. "Euphonic Distortion: Naughty but Nice?" *Stereophile* (30 April 2006). https://www.stereophile.com/reference/406howard/index.html.

Howell, Tim. "Brahms, Kierkegaard, and Repetition: Three Intermezzi." *Nineteenth-Century Music Review* 10 (2013): 101–17.

Hübbe, Walter. *Brahms in Hamburg*. Hamburg: Lütcke & Wulff, 1902.

Hughes, Langston. *The Ways of White Folks*. New York: Vintage, 1933.

Humal, Mart, ed. *A Composition as a Problem III: Proceedings of the 3rd International Conference on Music Theory, Tallinn, March 9–10, 2001*. Tallinn, Estonia: Scripta Musicalia, 2003.

Hurd, Madeleine. *Public Spheres, Public Mores, and Democracy: Hamburg and Stockholm, 1870–1914*. Ann Arbor: University of Michigan Press, 2000.

Hutchings, A. J. B. "Orchestration and Common Sense." *Musical Times* 72 (1931): 1081–85.

Hyun-Su Kim, David. "The Brahmsian Hairpin." *19th-Century Music* 36/1 (2012): 46–57.

Iddon, Martin, and Philip Thomas. *John Cage's "Concert for Piano and Orchestra."* New York: Oxford University Press, 2020.

Imbert, Hugues. *Étude sur Johannès Brahms: Avec le catalogue de ses œuvres*. Paris: Fischbacher, 1894.

Irving, David. *The Destruction of Dresden*. London: W. Kimber, 1963.

Jackson, Timothy L., and Paul Hawkshaw, eds. *Bruckner Studies*. Cambridge: Cambridge University Press, 1997.

Jacobsson, Stig. Liner booklet essay for *Brahms Transcribed for Orchestra*. Olle Persson, Lü Jia; Norrköping Symphony Orchestra. BIS-CD-1140, 2–6.

Jamar, Alexandre. "Review: Brahms-Glanert: *Vier ernste Gesänge*." *Forum Opera*. 13 March 2017.

Janik, Elizabeth. *Recomposing German Music: Politics and Musical Tradition in Cold War Berlin*. Leiden and Boston: Brill, 2005.
Jansen, Gustav F., ed. *Robert Schumann Briefe: Neue Folge*. Leipzig: Breitkopf & Härtel, 1904.
Jaspers, Karl. *The Question of German Guilt*. Translated by E. B. Ashton, with an introduction by Joseph W. Koterski. New York: Fordham University Press, 2001.
Jeal, Erica. "Review: Brahms-Glanert: Four Serious Songs, etc." *The Guardian*, 26 January 2017.
Jenner, Gustav. *Johannes Brahms als Mensch, Lehrer und Künstler*. Marburg: N. G. Elwert'sche Verlagsbuchhandlung, 1905.
Joachim, Joseph. *Festrede zur Enthüllung des Brahms-Denkmals in Meiningen, 7. Oktober 1899*. Diktierte Niederschrift mit autografen Korrekturen und Ergänzungen, Staats- und Universitätsbibliothek Carl von Ossietzky, Hamburg, Signatur: Brahms-Archiv, NL Joseph Joachim.
Joachim, Joseph, and Andreas Moser, eds. *Briefe von und an Joseph Joachim*. 2 vols. Berlin: Julius Bard, 1911.
Jöde, Fritz, ed. *Bicinia Germanica: Deutsche Volkslieder zu zwei gleichen oder gemischten Stimmen. Die deutschen Zwiegesänge aus der Sammlung "Bicinia Gallica, Latina et Germanica ex Praestantissimis Musicorum Monumentis collecta et secundum seriem tonorum disposita" von Georg Rhau, Wittenberg 1545, übertragen von Herman Reichenbach*. Beihefte zum "Musikanten" 10. Wolfenbüttel: Georg Kallmeyer Verlag, 1926.
Joel, Tony. *The Dresden Firebombing: Memory and the Politics of Commemorating Destruction*. London: I. B. Tauris, 2013.
Johnson, Julian. *Out of Time: Music and the Making of Modernity*. Oxford: Oxford University Press, 2015.
Johnson, Lawrence A. "Review: Capuçon's Fiery Playing Sparks Bychkov's Brahms Program with CSO." *Chicago Classical Review*, 9 October 2015.
Jordan, Roland, and Emma Kafalenos. "The Double Trajectory: Ambiguity in Brahms and Henry James." *19th-Century Music* 13/2 (1989): 129–44.
Jost, Christofer, and Gerd Sebald. *Musik—Kultur—Gedächtnis: Theoretische und analytische Annäherungen an ein Forschungsfeld zwischen den Disziplinen*. Wiesbaden: Springer, 2020.
Jost, Ekkehard, ed. *Die Musik der achtziger Jahre*. Mainz: Schott, 1990.
Kaes Long, Megan. *Hearing Homophony: Tonal Expectation at the Turn of the Seventeenth Century*. New York: Oxford University Press, 2020.
Kalbeck, Max. *Johannes Brahms*. 4 Vols. Vienna and Leipzig: Wiener Verlag, 1904; Berlin: Deutsche Brahms-Gesellschaft, 1908–1914.
Kalbeck, Max. *Johannes Brahms*. 4 Vols. in 8. Rev. ed. Berlin: Deutsche Brahms-Gesellschaft, 1915–1921. Repr.; Tutzing: Hans Schneider, 1976.
Kant, Immanuel. *Über Pädagogik*. Königsberg: Friedrich Nicolovius, 1803.
Karnes, Kevin C. *A Kingdom Not of This World: Wagner, the Arts, and Utopian Visions in Fin-de-Siècle Vienna*. New York: Oxford University Press, 2013.
Kastner, Jean-Georges. *Traité général d'instrumentation*. Paris: Prilipp, 1837.

Kater, Michael H. *The Twisted Muse: Musicians and their Music in the Third Reich.* Oxford and New York: Oxford University Press, 1997.
Kedves, Alexandra. "Der Regisseur koppelt Brahms mit Black Lives Matter." *Basler Zeitung,* 29 June 2020, 12.
Keisch, Claude, and Marie Ursula Rieman-Reyer, eds. *Adolph Menzel, 1815–1905: Between Romanticism and Impressionism.* New Haven, CT, and London: Yale University Press in association with the National Gallery of Art, Washington, 1996.
Keller, James M. "Brahms-Fantasie: Heliogravure for Orchestra." Program note for the New York Philharmonic Orchestra, October 2015.
Kelly, Barbara L. *French Music, Culture, and National Identity, 1870–1939.* Rochester, NY: University of Rochester Press, 2008.
Kelly, Elaine. *Composing the Canon in the German Democratic Republic: Narratives of Nineteenth-Century Music.* New York: Oxford University Press, 2014.
Kelley (Hack), Gwendolyn Dunlevy, and George P. Upton. *Edouard Remenyi: Musician, Litterateur and Man.* Chicago: A. C. Mclurg & Co, 1906.
Kennedy, Michael. *The Hallé Tradition: A Century of Music.* Manchester: Manchester University Press, 1960.
Kerry, Gordon. "Brahms: Tones of Romantic Extravagance." *Music Trust,* 2 February 2017. https://musictrust.com.au/loudmouth/brahms-tones-of-romantic-extravagance-piano-quartet-no-1piano-quintet.
Kersten, Ursula. *Max Klinger und die Musik.* 2 vols. Frankfurt am Main: Peter Lang, 1993.
Kinton, Leslie. "A Documentary Study and Schenkerian Analysis of Dvořák's Symphony in D Minor, Op. 70." PhD diss., University of Toronto, 2008.
Kirby, Michael, and Richard Schechner. "An Interview with John Cage." *Tulane Drama Review* 10 (1965): 50–72.
Klein, Michael L., and Nicholas Reyland, eds. *Music and Narrative since 1900.* Bloomington: Indiana University Press, 2013.
Klemperer, Victor. *I Will Bear Witness: A Diary of the Nazi Years, 1942–1945.* Translated by Martin Chalmers. New York: The Modern Library, 2001.
Kok, Roe-Min, and Laura Tunbridge, eds. *Rethinking Schumann.* Oxford: Oxford University Press, 2011.
Kopiez, Reinhard, ed. *Musikwissenschaft zwischen Kunst, Ästhetik und Experiment.* Würzburg: Königshausen & Neumann, 1998.
Köpp, Kai. "Hohe Schule des Portamentos: Violintechnik als Schlüssel für die Gesangspraxis im 19. Jahrhundert." *Dissonance* 132 (2015): 16–25.
Koslofsky, Craig M. *The Reformation of the Dead: Death and Ritual in Early Modern Germany, 1450–1700.* New York: St. Martin's Press, 2000.
Kozinn, Allan. "Sharp Interplay and Melting Lyricism." *New York Times,* 4 July 2011. www.nytimes.com/2011/07/05/arts/music/cassatt-quartet-and-ursula-oppens-at-bargemusic-review.html.
Kraus, Felix von. *Begegnungen mit Anton Bruckner, Johannes Brahms, Cosima Wagner. Aus den Lebenserinnerungen von Dr. Felix Kraus (1870–1937).* Vienna: F. Hain, 1961.

Krebs, Harald. "Third Relation and Dominant in Late 18th- and Early 19th-Century Music." PhD diss., Yale University, 1980.
Kretzschmar, Hermann. *Führer durch den Concertsaal. I. Abtheilung: Sinfonie und Suite.* Leipzig: A. G. Liebeskind, 1887.
Kretszchmer, Andreas, and Anton Wilhelm von Zuccalmaglio. *Deutsche Volkslieder mit ihren Original-Weisen I & II.* Berlin: Vereins-Buchhandlung, 1838–1840.
Krill, Eva. "Die Bibliothek von Johannes Brahms: Zur literarischen Geistigkeit des Komponisten." PhD diss., University of Vienna, 2001.
Kross, Siegfried. "Brahms and E. T. A. Hoffmann." *19th-Century Music* 5/3 (1982): 193–200.
Kross, Siegfried. *Die Chorwerke von Johannes Brahms.* Berlin and Wunsiedel: Max Hesses, 1958.
Krumeich, Gerd, Hartmut Lehmann, eds. *"Gott mit uns": Nation, Religion und Gewalt im 19. und frühen 20. Jahrhundert.* Göttingen: Vandenhoeck & Ruprecht, 2000.
Krummacher, Friedhelm, and Wolfram Steinbeck, eds. *Brahms-Analysen: Referate der Kieler Tagung 1983.* Kassel: Bärenreiter, 1984.
Krummacher, Friedhelm, and Michael Struck, with Constantin Floros and Peter Petersen, eds. *Johannes Brahms: Quellen-Text-Rezeption-Interpretation: Internationaler Brahms-Kongress, Hamburg 1997.* Munich: Henle Verlag 1999.
Kühn, Paul. *Max Klinger.* Leipzig: Breitkopf & Härtel, 1907.
Küntzel, Hans, and Agathe Schütte. *Brahms in Göttingen: Mit Erinnerungen von Agathe Schütte, geboren von Siebold.* Göttingen: Edition Herodot, 1985.
Küthen, Hans-Werner. "Ein verlorener Registerklang: Beethovens Imitation der Aeolsharfe." *Musik & Ästhetik* 34 (2005): 83–92.
Laitz, Steven G. "The Submediant Complex: Its Musical and Poetic Roles in Schubert's Songs." *Theory and Practice* 21 (1996): 123–65.
La Grange, Henry-Louis de. *Gustav Mahler, The Arduous Road to Vienna.* Edited by Sybille Werner. Turnhout: Brepols, 2020.
La Mara (Ida Maria Lipsius). *Briefe hervorragender Zeitgenossen an Franz Liszt: 1824–1854.* Leipzig: Breitkopf & Härtel, 1895.
Laux, Karl. *Nachklang: Autobiographie.* Berlin: Verlag der Nation, 1977.
Leaver, Robin. "Brahms's Opus 45 and German Protestant Funeral Music." *Journal of Musicology* 19/4 (2002): 616–40.
Leinsdorf, Erich. *The Composer's Advocate: A Radical Orthodoxy for Musicians.* New Haven, CT, and London: Yale University Press, 1982.
Leech-Wilkinson, Daniel. *Challenging Performance.* https://challengingperformance.com/the-book-2/.
Leech-Wilkinson, Daniel. *The Changing Sound of Music: Approaches to Studying Recorded Musical Performances* (CHARM, 2009). www.charm.rhul.ac.uk/studies/chapters/intro.html.
Lemcke, Carl. *Lieder und Gedichte.* Hamburg: Hoffmann und Campe, 1861.

Lemmel, Monika. "Der gedichtzyklus 'Chinesisch-Deutsche Jahres-und Tageszeiten' und seine Verortung in Goethes Spätwerk." *Jahrbuch der deutschen Schillergesellschaft* 36 (1992): 143–66.

Lesaffer, Randall. "1864." In *Oxford Public Law International*, https://opil.ouplaw.com/page/545/1864.

Lévêque, Jean-Jacques. *Henri Fantin-Latour*. Paris: ACR Editions Internationale, 1996.

Levi, Erik. *Music in the Third Reich*. New York: St. Martin's Press, 1994.

Lewin, David. "A Formal Theory of Generalized Tonal Functions." *Journal of Music Theory* 26/1 (1982): 43–45.

Lewin, David. *Generalized Musical Intervals and Transformations*. New Haven, CT: Yale University Press, 1987.

Lichtenberg, Georg Christoph. *Hogarth on High Life: The Marriage à la Mode series from Georg Christoph Lichtenberg's Commentaries*. London: Pallas Athene, 2010.

Lieure, Jules, and Jacques Callot. *Jacques Callot: catalogue raisonné de l'oeuvre gravé*. San Francisco: Wofsy, 1989.

Ligeti, György. *György Ligeti in Conversation with Péter Várnai, Josef Häusler, Claude Samuel and Himself*. Translated by Gabor J. Schabert, Sarah E. Soulsby, Terence Kilmarti, and Geoffrey Skelton. London: Eulenberg, 1983.

Liliencron, R. von. *Die historischen Volkslieder der Deutschen vom 13. bis 16. Jahrhundert*. Leipzig: F. C. W. Vogel, 1869.

Lindberg, Morten. "The Nordic Sound." *2L*, www.2l.no.

Linderoth, Ernst, ed. *Bonn im Spiegel der Jahrhunderte: eine Sammlung heimatkundlicher Zeitungsartikel*. Bonn: Bonner Heimat- und Geschichtsverein, 1992.

Lindmayr-Brandl, Andrea. "The Modern Invention of the 'Tenorlied': A Historiography of the Early German Lied Setting." *Early Music History* 32 (2013): 119–77.

Litzmann, Berthold. *Clara Schumann: An Artist's Life, Based on Material Found in Diaries and Letters*. Translated by Grace E. Hadow. 2 vols. London: Macmillan, 1913; repr.: Cambridge: Cambridge University Press, 2013.

Litzmann, Berthold. *Clara Schumann. Ein Künstlerleben. Nach Tagebüchern und Briefen*. 3 vols. Leipzig: Breitkopf & Härtel, 1906.

Litzmann, Berthold, ed. *Clara Schumann–Johannes Brahms: Briefe aus den Jahren 1853–1896*. 2 vols. Leipzig: Brietkopf & Härtel, 1920, 1927.

Lochhead, Judy, and Joseph Auner, eds. *Postmodern Music/Postmodern Thought*. New York: Routledge, 2002.

Lockspeiser, Edward. *Music and Painting: A Study in Comparative Ideas from Turner to Schoenberg*. New York: Harper & Row, 1973.

Loges, Natasha. *Brahms and His Poets: A Handbook*. Woodbridge: Boydell Press, 2017.

Loges, Natasha, and Laura Tunbridge, eds. *German Song Onstage: Lieder Performance in the Nineteenth and Early Twentieth Centuries*. Bloomington: Indiana University Press, 2020.

Loose-Einfalt, Katharina. *Melancholie, Natur, Musik: zum Horntrio von Johannes Brahms*. Mainz: Schott, 2017.

Lorenz, Alfred. *Das Geheimnis der Form bei Richard Wagner*. Berlin: Hesse, 1924–1933.

Lott, R. Allen. *Brahms's "A German Requiem": Reconsidering Its Biblical, Historical, and Musical Contexts*. Rochester, NY: University of Rochester Press, 2020.

Lütteken, Laurenz. *Das Jahr 1868. Musik zwischen Realismus und Gründerzeit. Zürcher Festspiel-Symposium 2018*. Kassel: Bärenreiter, 2019.

Lütteken, Laurenz, ed. *Kunstwerk der Zukunft—Richard Wagner und Zürich (1849–1858)*. Zürich: Verlag Neue Zürcher Zeitung, 2008.

Lutyens, Elisabeth. *A Goldfish Bowl*. London: Cassell, 1972.

MacAuslan, John. *Schumann's Music and E. T. A. Hoffmann's Fiction*. Cambridge: Cambridge University Press, 2016.

MacDonald, Hugh. *Berlioz's Orchestration Treatise: A Translation and Commentary*. New York: Cambridge University Press, 2004.

MacDonald, Hugh. *Music in 1853: The Biography of a Year*. Woodbridge: Boydell & Brewer, 2012.

MacDonald, Malcolm. *Brahms*. Oxford: Oxford University Press, 1990.

Magirius, Heinrich. *Nachkriegszeit im Dresdner Kreuzchor: Erinnerungen an die Jahre 1945–1952 von Heinrich Magirius*. Beucha and Markleberg: Sax Verlag, 2015.

Magnaguagno, Guido, and Juri Steiner. *Arnold Böcklin, Giorgio de Chirico, Max Ernst: eine Reise ins Ungewisse*. Bern: Benteli, 1997.

Malle, Louis. *Malle on Malle*. Edited by Philip French. London: Faber and Faber, 1993.

Mandyczewski, Eusebius. "Die Bibliothek Brahms." *Musikbuch aus Österreich* 1 (1904): 7–17.

Mandyczewski, Eusebius, ed. *28 Deutsche Volkslieder*. Leipzig: Breitkopf & Härtel, 1926.

Manheim, James. "Review of *Brahms: The Violin Sonatas, Leonidas Kavakos & Yuja Wang*." *AllMusic*, www.allmusic.com/album/brahms-the-violin-sonatas-mw0002625014.

Margalit, Gilad. *Guilt, Suffering, and Memory: Germany Remembers Its Dead of World War II*. Translated by Haim Watzman. Bloomington: Indiana University Press, 2010.

Martin, Nathan, Steven Vande Moortele, and Julie Pednault-Deslaurier, eds. *Formal Functions in Perspective*. Rochester, NY: University of Rochester Press, 2017.

Marx, Karl, and Friedrich Engels. *The Communist Manifesto*. London: Pluto Press, [1848] 2008.

Masters, Richard. "Review of *Brahms Violin Sonatas, Alina Ibragimova & Cédric Tiberghien*," 2019. http://www.musicweb-international.com/classrev/2019/Oct/Brahms_violin_CDA68200_RM.htm.

Mattheson, Johann. *Grundlage einer Ehrenpforte*. Hamburg: author's edition, 1740.

Mauersberger, Helga, ed. *Dresdner Kreuzchor und Thomanerchor Leipzig: Zwei Kantoren und ihre Zeit: Rudolf und Erhard Mauersberger.* Marienberg: Marienberg Druck und Verlagsgesellschaft, 2007.
Mauersberger, Rudolf. *Dresdner Requiem nach Worten der Bibel und des Gesangbuches.* Edited by Matthias Herrmann. Stuttgart: Carus Verlag, 1994.
May, Florence. *The Life of Brahms.* 2 vols. London: Edward Arnold, 1905.
Mayer-Pasinski, Karin. *Max Klingers Brahmsphantasie.* Frankfurt am Main: Rita G. Fischer Verlag, 1982.
McClelland, Ryan. "Brahms and the Principle of Destabilised Beginnings." *Music Analysis* 28/1 (2009): 3–61.
McClelland, Ryan. *Brahms and the Scherzo: Studies in Musical Narrative.* Abingdon: Ashgate, 2010.
McColl, Sandra. *Music Criticism in Vienna 1896–1897: Critically Moving Forms.* Oxford: Oxford University Press, 1996.
McCorkle, Margit L. *Johannes Brahms: Thematisch-bibliographisches Werkverzeichnis.* Published following joint preliminary work with Donald McCorkle. Munich: Henle, 1984.
McEwan, Ian. *Atonement.* New York: Nan A. Talese, Doubleday, 2001.
McManus, Laurie. *Brahms in the Priesthood of Art: Gender and Art Religion in the Nineteenth-Century German Musical Imagination.* New York: Oxford University Press, 2021.
McManus, Laurie. "Prostitutes, Trauma, and (Auto)-Biographical Narratives: Revisiting Brahms at the Fin de Siècle." *19th-Century Music* 42/3 (2019): 225–48.
Meissen, Gunter. "Julius Allgeyer." In *Allgemeines Künstlerlexikon,* https://www.degruyter.com/view/mvw/AKL-B.
Metzger, Heinz-Klaus, and Rainer Riehn, eds. *Aimez-vous Brahms "the Progressive"?* Munich: Text+Kritik, 1989.
Meurs, Norbert. *Neue Bahnen? Aspekte der Brahms-Rezeption 1853–1868.* Köln: Studio, 1996.
Meyer, Thomas. "En Passant par Brahms: Zu Wolfgang Rihms Brahms-Zyklus 'Nähe Fern 1–4.'" *Neue Zeitschrift für Musik* 173/5 (2012): 58–61.
Michelmann, Emil. *Agathe von Siebold: Johannes Brahms' Jugendliebe.* Göttingen: Ludwig Hätzschel & Co, 1930.
Midgette, Anne. "Romantic Side of Brahms: So Dark, So Brooding." *New York Times,* 7 June 2007. https://www.nytimes.com/2007/06/07/arts/music/07phil.html.
Mies, Paul. "Herders Edward-Ballade bei Joh. Brahms." *Zeitschrift für Musikwissenschaft* 2 (1919–1920): 225–32.
Miller, Jonathan. *The Afterlife of Plays.* Fifth Distinguished Graduate Research Lecture. San Diego: San Diego State University Press, 1992.
Miller zu Aichholz, Viktor von. *Ein Brahms-Bilderbuch.* Vienna: R. Lechner, 1905.
Milsom, David. "Ironwood: Brahms, Piano Quartet No. 1; Piano Quintet." *The Strad,* 30 October 2017. www.thestrad.com/reviews/ironwood-brahms-piano-quartet-no1-piano-quintet/7240.article.

Milsom, David. *Theory and Practice in Late Nineteenth Century Violin Performance.* Aldershot: Ashgate, 2003.

Minor, Ryan. *Choral Fantasies: Music, Festivity, and Nationhood in Nineteenth-Century Germany.* Cambridge: Cambridge University Press, 2012.

Mitschka, Arno. "Der Sonatensatz in den Werken von Johannes Brahms." PhD diss., Johannes Gutenberg-University of Mainz, 1961.

Moeller, Robert. *War Stories: The Search for a Usable Past in the Federal Republic of Germany.* Berkeley: University of California Press, 2001.

Molleson, Kate. "Brahms: String Quartets, Piano Quintet CD Review—Angst, Ardency and Brilliance." *The Guardian*, 6 October 2016. www.theguardian.com/music/2016/oct/06/brahms-string-quartets-piano-quintet-cd-review-belcea-quartet-till-felner-alpha.

Monahan, Seth. "Action and Agency Revisited." *Journal of Music Theory* 57/2 (2013): 321–71.

Monahan, Seth. "Success and Failure in Mahler's Symphonic Sonatas." *Music Theory Spectrum* 33/1 (2011): 37–58

Monod, David. *Settling Scores: German Music, Denazification, and the Americans, 1945–1953.* Chapel Hill and London: University of North Carolina Press, 2005.

Morik, Werner. *Johannes Brahms und sein Verhältnis zum Deutschen Volkslied.* Tutzing: Hans Schneider, 1965.

Morton, Marsha. *Max Klinger and Wilhelmine Culture: On the Threshold of German Modernism.* London: Routledge, 2014.

Morton, Marsha L., and Peter L. Schumnk, eds. *The Arts Entwined: Music and Painting in the Nineteenth Century.* New York and London: Garland Publishing, 2000.

Moser, Andreas. *Joseph Joachim, Ein Lebensbild.* 2 vols. Berlin: B. Behr, 1898.

Mraz, Sylvia. "Die Bildhauerin Ilse Twardowski-Conrat. Studien zu Leben und Werk." MA diss., University of Vienna, 2003.

Mulligan, Mark, Keith Jopling, and Zach Fuller. "The Classical Music Market: Streaming's Next Genre?" A MIDiA Research White Paper commissioned by IDAGIO. May 2019.

Murphy, Scott. "On Metre in the Rondo of Brahms's Op. 25." *Music Analysis* 26/3 (2007): 323–53.

Murphy, Scott, ed. *Brahms and the Shaping of Time.* Rochester, NY: University of Rochester Press, 2018.

Muscionico, Daniele. "Die neuen Leiden des jungen Virus: Jetzt hat auch das Theater sein Corona-Evangelium." *Neue Zürcher Zeitung*, 28 June 2020.

Musgrave, Michael. *Brahms: A German Requiem.* Cambridge: Cambridge University Press, 1996.

Musgrave, Michael. *A Brahms Reader.* New Haven, CT, and London: Yale University Press, 2000.

Musgrave, Michael. "Frei aber Froh: A Reconsideration." *19th-Century Music* 3/3 (1980): 251–58.

Musgrave, Michael. *The Music of Brahms.* Oxford: Clarendon Press, 1985.

Musgrave, Michael, ed. *Brahms 2: Biographical, Documentary, and Analytical Studies*. Cambridge: Cambridge University Press, 1987.
Musgrave, Michael, ed. *The Cambridge Companion to Brahms*. Cambridge: Cambridge University Press, 1999.
Musgrave, Michael, and Bernhard D. Sherman, eds. *Performing Brahms: Early Evidence of Performance Style*. Cambridge: Cambridge University Press, 2003.
Nabokov, Vladimir. *Pale Fire*. New York: Vintage Books, 1962.
Nagel, Wilibald. *Johannes Brahms als Nachfolger Beethoven's*. Leipzig & Zürich: Gebrüder Hug., 1892.
Nassar, Dalia. *The Romantic Absolute: Being and Knowing in Early German Romantic Philosophy, 1795–1804*. Chicago: University of Chicago Press, 2014.
Nattiez, Jean-Jacques. "Can One Speak of Narrativity in Music?" *Journal of the Royal Musicological Association* 115/2 (1990): 240–57.
Nauhaus, Gerd. "Nachwort" in Robert Schumann, "*Gesammelte Schriften über Musik und Musiker.*" Edited by Gerd Nauhaus and Ingeborg Singer. 2 vols. Wiesbaden: Breitkopf & Härtel, 1985.
Neff, Severine. "Point/Counterpoint: John Cage Studies with Arnold Schoenberg." *Contemporary Music Review* 33/5–6 (2014): 451–82.
Nelson, Thomas K. "Klinger's *Brahmsphantasie* and the Cultural Politics of Absolute Music." *Art History* 19/1 (1996): 26–43.
Neubauer, John. *The Emancipation of Music from Language: Departure from Mimesis in Eighteenth Century Aesthetics*. New Haven, CT: Yale University Press, 1986.
Niecks, Frederick, trans. "Robert Schumann and Bettina von Arnim." *Monthly Musical Record* 53/632 (1 August 1923): 230–32.
Niekerk, Carl. *Reading Mahler: German Culture and Jewish Identity in Fin-de Siècle Vienna*. Rochester, NY: University of Rochester Press, 2010.
Nietzsche, Friedrich. *The Basic Writings of Nietzsche*. Translated and edited by Walter Kaufmann. New York: Random House, 2000.
Nietzsche, Friedrich. *Der Fall Wagner, Götzendämmerung. Nachgelassene Schriften (August 1888–Anfang Januar 1889). Nietzsche Werke. Kritische Gesamtausgabe*. Berlin: Walter de Gruyter, 1969.
Nietzsche, Friedrich. *The Gay Science*. Translated by Walter Kaufmann. New York; Toronto: Random House, 1974.
Niven, Bill, ed. *Germans as Victims: Remembering the Past in Contemporary Germany*. New York: Palgrave Macmillan, 2006.
Nonnenmann, Rainer. "Denn es geht dem Menschen wie dem Vieh." *Kölner Anzeiger*, 19 March 2018.
Notley, Margaret. *Lateness and Brahms: Music and Culture in the Twilight of Viennese Liberalism*. Oxford and New York: Oxford University Press, 2007.
Okina, Risa. "Brahms and the Uncanny." PhD diss., Temple University, 2020.
Olson, Greta. "Reconsidering Unreliability: Fallible and Untrustworthy Narrators." *Narrative* 11/1 (2003): 93–109.
Oltermann, Philip. "Germany's Romantic Literary Revival Built on Blade Runner and Seven Deadly Sins." *The Guardian*, 10 November 2017. www.

theguardian.com/world/2017/nov/10/compromises-compromise-merkel-generation-reinvents-german-romanticism.

Ophüls, Gustav. *Erinnerungen an Johannes Brahms*. Berlin: Deutsche-Brahms Gesellschaft, 1921.

Orel, Alfred. *Johannes Brahms und Julius Allgeyer: Eine Künstlerfreundschaft in Briefen*. Tutzing: Hans Schneider, 1964.

Owen, Barbara. *The Organ Music of Johannes Brahms*. Oxford: Oxford University Press, 2007.

Pace, Ian. *Michael Finnissy at 70: The Piano Music (6)* (2016). http://openaccess.city.ac.uk/17517/.

Pace, Ian. *Michael Finnissy at 70: The Piano Music (8)* (2016). http://openaccess.city.ac.uk/17519/.

Pace, Ian. "The Panorama of Michael Finnissy (I)." *Tempo* 196 (1996): 25–35.

Pace, Ian. "Performing Liszt in the Style Hongroise." *Liszt Society Journal* 32 (2007): 55–90.

Pace, Ian, and Nigel McBride, eds. *Critical Perspectives on Michael Finnissy: Bright Futures, Dark Pasts*. London and New York: Routledge, 2019.

Paine, John Knowles, Theodore Thomas, and Karl Klauser, eds. *Famous Composers and Their Works*. 4 vols. Boston: J. B. Millet, 1891.

Papanikolaou, Eftychia. "Brahms, Böcklin, and the *Gesang der Parzen*." *Music in Art* 30/1–2 (2005): 154–65.

Parakilas, James. *Ballads without Words: Chopin and the Tradition of the Instrumental Ballade*. Portland, OR: Amadeus Press, 1992.

Parmer, Dillon. "Brahms and the Poetic Motto: A Hermeneutic Aid?" *Journal of Musicology* 15/3 (1997): 353–89.

Parmer, Dillon. "Brahms the Programmatic?: A Critical Assessment." PhD diss., Eastman School of Music, 1995.

Partridge, Daniel. "Harmony, Form, and Voice Leading in the Mature Works of Antonín Dvořák." PhD diss., City University of New York, 2012.

Pascall, Robert. "Formal Principles in the Music of Brahms." PhD diss., Oxford University, 1973.

Pascall, Robert. "Some Special Uses of Sonata Form by Brahms." *Soundings* 4 (1974): 58–63.

Pascall, Robert, ed. *Brahms: Biographical, Documentary, and Analytical Studies*. Cambridge: Cambridge University Press, 1983.

Pascall, Robert, ed. *Brahms beyond Mastery: His Sarabande and Gavotte, and Its Recompositions*. Farnham: Ashgate, 2013.

Percy, Bishop Thomas. *Reliques of Ancient English Poetry*. 3 vols. London: Dodsley in Pall-Mall, 1765.

Peres Da Costa, Neal. *Off the Record: Performing Practices in Romantic Piano Playing*. Oxford and New York: Oxford University Press, 2012.

Perry, Frankie. "CD Review: Franz Schubert, *Nacht & Träume: Lieder with Orchestra*." *Nineteenth-Century Music Review* 17/2 (2020): 293–96.

Pethő, Csilla. "'Style Hongrois': Hungarian Elements in the Works of Haydn, Beethoven, Weber and Schubert." *Studia Musicologica Academiae Scientiarum Hungaricae* 41/1-3 (2000): 199-284.

Phelan, James. *Living to Tell about It: A Rhetoric and Ethics of Character Narration*. Ithaca, NY, and London: Cornell University Press, 2005.

Phelan, James, and Peter J. Rabinowitz, eds. *A Companion to Narrative Theory*. Oxford: Blackwell Publishing, 2005.

Philip, Robert. *Early Recordings and Musical Style: Changing Tastes in Instrumental Performance, 1900-1950*. Cambridge: Cambridge University Press, 1992.

Philip, Robert. *Performing Music in the Age of Recording*. New Haven, CT: Yale University Press, 2004.

Phillips, Reuben. "Between Hoffmann and Goethe: The Young Brahms as Reader." *Journal of the Royal Musical Association* 146/2 (2021): 455-89.

Phillips, Reuben. "Brahms as Reader." PhD diss. Princeton University, 2019.

Pietschmann, Klaus, and Melanie Wald-Fuhrmann, eds. *Der Kanon in der Musik. Theorie und Geschichte. Ein Handbuch*. Munich: Edition Text + Kritik, 2013.

Pinkert, Anke. *Film and Memory in East Germany*. Bloomington: Indiana University Press, 2008.

Platt, Heather. *Johannes Brahms: A Research and Information Guide*. New York and London: Taylor and Francis, 2011.

Platt, Heather, and Peter H Smith, eds. *Expressive Intersections in Brahms: Essays in Analysis and Meaning*. Bloomington: Indiana University Press, 2012.

Pollock, Emily Richmond. *Opera after the Zero Hour: The Problem of Tradition and the Possibility of Renewal in Postwar West Germany*. Oxford and New York: Oxford University Press, 2019.

Potter, Pamela. *Art of Suppression: Confronting the Nazi Past in Histories of the Visual and Performing Arts*. Berkeley: University of California Press, 2016.

Potter, Pamela. "The Arts in Nazi Germany: A Silent Debate." *Contemporary European History* 15/4 (2006): 585-99.

Potter, Pamela. *Most German of the Arts: Musicology and Society from the Weimar Republic to the End of Hitler's Reich*. New Haven, CT: Yale University Press, 1998.

Potts, Joseph E. "Orchestral Concerts in Paris." *Musical Times* 92/1304 (1951): 466-68.

Quigley, Thomas. *Johannes Brahms: An Annotated Bibliography of the Literature through 1982*. Metuchen, NJ: Scarecrow Press, 1990.

Quigley, Thomas. *Johannes Brahms: An Annotated Bibliography of the Literature from 1982 to 1996*. Lanham, MD: Scarecrow Press, 1998.

Rapoport, Erez. *Mendelssohn's Instrumental Music: Structure and Style*. Hillsdale, NY: Pendragon Press, 2012.

Rasch, Rudolf, ed. *Beyond Notes: Improvisation in Western Music of the Eighteenth and Nineteenth Centuries*. Turnhout: Brepols, 2011.

Ravenscroft, Brenda. "Re-construction: Cage and Schoenberg." *Tempo* 60/235 (2006): 2-14.

Bibliography

Reddick, Carissa. "Becoming at a Deeper Level: Divisional Overlap in Sonata Forms from the Late Nineteenth Century." *Music Theory Online* 16/2 (2010): 1–5.

Reddick, Carissa. "Formal Fusion and Rotational Overlap in Sonata Forms from the Chamber Music of Brahms, Dvořák, Franck, and Grieg." PhD diss., University of Connecticut, 2009.

Rehding, Alexander. *Music and Monumentality: Commemoration and Wonderment in Nineteenth-Century Germany*. New York: Oxford University Press, 2009.

Reid, Charles. *Malcolm Sargent: A Biography*. London: Hamish Hamilton, 1968.

Reimann, Aribert. "Salut für die junge Avantgarde." *Neue Zeitschrift für Musik* 140/1 (1979): 4–25.

Reinhard, Oliver, Matthias Neutzner, and Wolfgang Hesse, eds. *Das rote Leuchten: Dresden und der Bombenkrieg*. Dresden: Edition Sächsische Zeitung, 2005.

Reinhardt, Carl Phillipp. *Die Heidelberger Liedmeister des 16. Jahrhunderts*. PhD diss., Heidelberg Universität, 1939.

Reyher, Andreas, and Christian Juncker. *Theatrum Latino-Germanico-Graecum sive lexicon linguae latinae*. Leipzig: Klosius, 1712.

Reynolds, Christopher. "Brahms Rhapsodizing: The *Alto Rhapsody* and Its Expressive Double." *Journal of Musicology* 29/2 (2012): 191–238.

Reynolds, Christopher. *Motives for Allusion: Context and Content in Nineteenth-Century Music*. Cambridge, MA: Harvard University Press, 2003.

Reynolds, Christopher. "Review of Daverio, *Crossing Paths*." *Journal of the American Musicological Society* 57 (2004): 664–73.

Rickards, Guy. "Time Past, Present, and Future: An Introduction to the Music of Detlev Glanert." Boosey & Hawkes website, https://www.boosey.com/pages/licensing/composer/composer_main?site-lang=en&composerid=2719&langid=1&ttype=INTRODUCTION.

Rihm, Wolfgang. *Ausgesprochen 1 & 2*. Edited by Ulrich Mosch. Winterthur: Amadeus, 1997.

Rihm, Wolfgang. *Offene Enden: Denkbewegung um und durch Musik*. Edited by Ulrich Mosch. Munich: Hanser, 2002.

Rings, Steven. *Tonality and Transformation*. New York: Oxford University Press, 2011.

Rink, John, and Jim Samson, eds. *Chopin Studies 2*. Cambridge: Cambridge University Press, 1994.

Rosen, Charles. "Aimez-vous Brahms?" *New York Review of Books*, 22 October 1998, 64–68.

Rosen, Charles. *The Romantic Generation*. Cambridge, MA: Harvard University Press, 1995.

Rosenfeld, Gavriel D., and Paul B. Jaskot, eds. *Beyond Berlin: Twelve German Cities Confront the Nazi Past*. Ann Arbor: University of Michigan Press, 2008.

Ross, Alex. "Igor Levit Is Like No Other Pianist." *New Yorker*, 18 May 2020. https://www.newyorker.com/magazine/2020/05/18/igor-levit-is-like-no-other-pianist.

Rothstein, William. *Phrase Rhythm in Tonal Music*. New York: Schirmer, 1989.

Roust, Colin. "Reaching a Plus Grand Public: Georges Auric as Populist." *Musical Quarterly* 95/2 (2012): 343–67.

Rubin, James H., and Olivia Mattis, eds. *Rival Sisters: Art and Music at the Birth of Modernism*. London: Ashgate Lund Humphries, 2014.

Russell, Peter. *Johannes Brahms and Klaus Groth: The Biography of a Friendship*. Aldershot, Hampshire, and Burlington, VT: Ashgate, 2006.

Rutherford, Susan. "Living, Loving and Dying in Song: Gluck, 'Che farò senza Euridice.'" *Cambridge Opera Journal* 28/2 (2016): 133–36.

Sagan, Françoise. *Aimez-vous Brahms . . .* Translated by Peter Wiles. New York: Penguin, 1962.

Sagan, Françoise, and Anne Borchardt. "Do You Like Flounder? A Talk with Françoise Sagan." *Transatlantic Review* 4 (Summer 1960): 89–90.

Saller, René Spencer. Program booklet essay for the St. Louis Symphony Orchestra, October 2014.

Samarotto, Frank. "Fluidities of Phrase and Form in the 'Intermezzo' of Brahms's First Symphony." *Intégral* 22 (2008): 117–143.

Samson, Jim, ed. *Cambridge History of Nineteenth-Century Music*. Cambridge: Cambridge University Press, 2002.

Samson, Jim, ed. *The Late Romantic Era: From the Mid-19th Century to World War I*. Englewood Cliffs, NJ: Prentice Hall, 1991.

Sandberger, Adolf. *Tagebuch meiner Reise nach Wien und Italien. Dezember [18]87– Juni 88*. Handschriftenabteilung of the Bayerische Staatsbibliothek, Ana 431, Schachtel 12a.

Sandberger, Wolfgang. *Imagination und Kanon. Der "Komponistenhimmel" in der Zürcher Tonhalle von 1895*. Winterthur: Amadeus Verlag, 2015.

Sandberger, Wolfgang. "Johannes Brahms in der Walhalla, Rede zum Festakt." *Literatur in Bayern* 61/62 (2000): 2–11.

Sandberger, Wolfgang, ed. *Brahms Handbuch*. Stuttgart: Metzler, 2009.

Sandberger, Wolfgang, ed. *"Ich will euch trösten": Johannes Brahms—ein deutsches Requiem: Symposion—Ausstellung—Katalog*. Munich: Edition Text+Kritik, 2012.

Sandberger, Wolfgang, ed. *Johannes Brahms. Zeichen, Bilder, Phantasien. Katalog zur Ausstellung des Brahms-Instituts an der Musikhochschule Lübeck*. Lübeck: Brahms-Institut an der Musikhochschule Lübeck, 2004.

Sandberger, Wolfgang, ed. *Konfrontationen: Symposium: Musik im Spannungsfeld des deutsch-französischen Verhältnisses 1871–1918*. Lübeck: Brahms-Institut an der Musikhochschule Lübeck, 2018.

Sandberger, Wolfgang, ed. *Konstellationen: Felix Mendelssohn und die deutsche Musikkultur. Felix Mendelssohn und Johannes Brahms*. Lübeck: Brahms-Institut an der Musikhochschule Lübeck, 2015.

Sandberger, Wolfgang, and Stefan Weymar, eds. *Johannes Brahms—Ikone der bürgerlichen Lebenswelt? Ausstellungskatalog des Brahms-Instituts an der Musikhochschule Lübeck*. Lübeck: Brahms-Institut an der Musikhochschule Lübeck, 2008.

Sandberger, Wolfgang, and Christiane Wiesenfeldt. *Brahms-Briefwechsel-Verzeichnis (BBV): chronologisch-systematisches Verzeichnis sämtlicher Briefe von und an Johannes Brahms, gefördert von der Deutschen Forschungsgemeinschaft* with the assistance of Fabian Bergener, Peter Schmitz, and Andreas Hund, www.brahms-institut.de, 2010.

Sanitas, Jean. *Aimez-vous Wagner?* Paris: Éditeurs Français Réunis, 1967.

Sargent, Malcolm. "Music and the Interpretive Artist." *Journal of the Royal Society of Arts* 97 (1949): 880–93.

Sattler, Mark. "Rihm Plays with Brahms." Liner notes to Wolfgang Rihm, *Symphonie "Nähe Fern."* Lucerne Symphonieorchester, James Gaffigan. Harmonia Mundi HMC902153, 2012, 5–6.

Scheffler, Karl. *Adolph Menzel: Der Mensch, das Werk.* Berlin: Cassirer, 1915.

Schenker, Heinrich. *Free Composition.* Translated and edited by Ernst Oster. New York: Longman, 1979.

Schenker, Heinrich. *Der freie Satz,* Vol. III of *Neue musikalische Theorien und Phantasien.* Vienna: Universal Edition, 1935. Second edition edited and revised by Oswald Jonas. Vienna: Universal Edition, 1956.

Schick, Hartmut. *Studien zu Dvořáks Streichquartetten.* Laaber: Laaber-Verlag, 1989.

Schmalfeldt, Janet. "Brahms, again the 'Master of Allusion,' with His Godson in Mind." *Ars Lyrica* 21 (2012): 115–54.

Schmalfeldt, Janet. "From Literary Fiction to Music: Schumann and the Unreliable Narrative." *19th-Century Music* 43/3 (2020): 170–93.

Schmalfeldt, Janet. *In the Process of Becoming: Analytical and Philosophical Perspectives on Form in Early Nineteenth-Century Music.* New York: Oxford University Press, 2011.

Schmidt, Eduard. *Umrisse zur Geschichte der Philosophie.* Berlin: Ferdinand Dümmler, 1839.

Schmidt, Matthias. *Johannes Brahms: Ein Versuch über die musikalische Selbstreflexion.* Wilhelmshaven: F. Noetzel, 2000.

Schnitzler, Günter, and Edelgard Spaude, eds. *Intermedialität: Studien zur Wechselwirkung zwischen den Künsten.* Freiburg im Breisgau: Rombach Verlag, 2004.

Schoenberg, Arnold. *Style and Idea: Selected Writings.* Edited by Leonard Stein. Translated by Leo Black. London and Boston: Faber, 1975.

Schoenberg, Arnold. *Style and Idea.* Edited by Leonard Stein. Berkeley: University of California Press, 1984.

Schorske, Carl E. "Politics in a New Key: An Austrian Triptych." *Journal of Modern History* 39/4 (1967): 343–86.

Schrade, Leo. *Beethoven in France.* New Haven, CT: Yale University Press, 1942.

Schubert, Giselher. "Themes and Double Themes: The Problem of the Symphonic in Brahms." *19th-Century Music* 18/1 (1984): 10–23.

Schubring, Adolf. "Schumanniana Nr. 11: Schumann und Brahms. Brahms' vierhändige Schumann-Variationen." *Allgemeine Musikalische Zeitung* 3/6 (5 February 1868): 41–42.

Schumann, Robert. *Dichtergarten für Musik: eine Anthologie für Freunde der Literatur und Musik*. Edited by Gerd Nauhaus and Ingrid Bodsch. Bonn: Stadt Museum, 2007.

Schumann, Robert. *Gesammelte Schriften*. Leipzig: Georg Wigand, 1854.

Schumann, Robert. "Neue Bahnen." *Neue Zeitschrift für Musik* 39/18 (28 October 1853): 185–86.

Schumann, Robert. *Tagebücher*. Edited by Gerd Nauhaus. 3 vols. Leipzig: VEB Deutscher Verlag für Musik, 1982.

Schüssler-Bach, Kerstin. Program booklet essay for WDR Sinfonieorchester Köln. 16 March 2018, 8–9.

Schütze, George C. *Convergences in Music & Art: A Bibliographic Study*. Detroit Studies in Music Bibliography 86. Warren, MI: Harmonie Park Press, 2005.

Schweitzer, Vivien. "Seeking an Intimate Sound Across a Cavernous Expanse." *New York Times*, 23 November 2014.

Schweitzer, Vivien. "Violin and Piano, in an Evening's Conversation." *New York Times*, 6 May 2011.

Scialla, Carmen. *A Study of Ferruccio Busoni's Transcriptions of Six Organ Chorale Preludes by Johannes Brahms*. DMA thesis, Louisiana State University, 1992.

Scott, Anna. "Romanticizing Brahms: Early Recordings and the Reconstruction of Brahmsian Identity." PhD diss., Leiden University, 2014.

Scott, Darwin F., ed. *For the Love of Music: Festschrift in Honor of Theodore Front on His 90th Birthday*. Lucca: Antigua, 2002.

Seyboldt, Thomas. "Rihm's Goethe- and Schiller-Lieder: Insights." Liner notes for the CD *Wolfgang Rihm: Goethe-Lieder*, 19–26. Bastille Musique, 2016.

Sheehan, James J. *German History 1770–1866*. Oxford: Clarendon Press, 1989.

Sholes, Jacquelyn. *Allusion as Narrative Premise in Brahms's Instrumental Music*. Bloomington: Indiana University Press, 2018.

Shrock, Dennis. *Choral Monuments: Studies of Eleven Choral Masterworks*. Oxford and New York: Oxford University Press, 2017.

Siegel, Robert. "A Ferguson Protest Brings New Meaning to Brahms' Requiem in St. Louis." NPR website, 6 October 2014. https://www.npr.org/sections/deceptivecadence/2014/10/06/354101823/a-ferguson-protest-brings-new-meaning-to-brahms-requiem-in-st-louis.

Simpson, Andrew. "Implications of Nonlinear Distortion in the Ultrasonic Capacitive Microphone: Why Is the Wide-Bandwidth Condenser Microphone a Bad Idea?" Poland: Simpson Microphones, 2009.

Simrock, Karl. *Die deutschen Volkslieder: Gesammelt von Karl Simrock*. Frankfurt am Main: Brönner, 1851.

Slåttebrekk, Sigurd. *Chasing the Butterfly: Recreating Grieg's 1903 Recordings and Beyond* (2010). www.chasingthebutterfly.no.

Smith, Peter H. "Brahms and Schenker: A Mutual Response to Sonata Form." *Music Theory Spectrum* 16/1 (1994): 77–103.

Smith, Peter H. "Brahms and Subject/Answer Rhetoric." *Music Analysis* 20/2 (2001): 193–236.

Smith, Peter H. "Dvořák and Subordinate Theme Closure: 'Positive' Analytic Results from a 'Negative' Approach to Romantic Form." *Journal of Music Theory* 64/2 (2020): 203–40.

Smith, Peter H. "Form and the Large-Scale Connection: Motivic Harmony and the Expanded Type-1 Sonata in Dvořák's Later Chamber Music." *Music Theory Spectrum* 40/2 (2018): 269–75.

Smith, Peter H. "Liquidation, Augmentation, and Brahms's Recapitulatory Overlaps." *19th-Century Music* 17/3 (1994): 237–61.

Smith, Peter H. "New Perspectives on Brahms's Linkage Technique." *Intégral* 21 (2007): 109–54.

Smith, Peter H. "Tonal Pairing and Monotonality in Instrumental Forms of Beethoven, Schubert, Schumann, and Brahms." *Music Theory Spectrum* 35/1 (2013): 77–102.

Smith, Peter H. "The Type 2 Sonata in the Nineteenth Century: Two Case Studies from Mendelssohn and Dvořák." *Journal of Music Theory* 63/1 (2019): 103–38.

Smith, Peter H. "You Reap What You Sow: Some Instances of Rhythmic and Harmonic Ambiguity in Brahms." *Music Theory Spectrum* 28/1 (2006): 57–97.

Sotheby & Co. *Catalogue of Valuable Printed Books, Illuminated and Other Manuscripts, Autograph Letters and Historical Documents, Oriental Miniatures, Etc.* London, 1935.

Sperber, Jonathan, ed. *Germany 1800–1870*. Oxford and New York: Oxford University Press, 2004.

Spitta, Philipp. *Zur Musik. Sechzehn Aufsätze*. Berlin: Gebrüder Paetel, 1892.

Spohr, Louis. *Violinschule*. Translated by C. Rudolphus. London: Wessel & Co. [no date; original edition, 1832]).

Sprigge, Martha. "Dresden's Musical Ruins." *Journal of the Royal Musical Association* 141/1 (2019): 83–121.

Sprigge, Martha. *Socialist Laments: Musical Mourning in the German Democratic Republic*. Oxford and New York: Oxford University Press, 2021.

Stam, Emlyn. "In Search of a Lost Language: Performing in Early-Recorded Style in Viola and String Quartet Repertoires." PhD diss., Leiden University, 2018.

Stark, Lucien. *A Guide to the Solo Songs of Johannes Brahms*. Bloomington: Indiana University Press, 1995.

Stauff, Derek. "Schütz's *Saul, Saul, was verfolgst du mich?* and the Politics of the Thirty Years War." *Journal of the American Musicological Society* 69/2 (2016): 355–408.

Stead, Jean. "Sir Malcolm's Tribute to 'a Perfect Artist.'" *Yorkshire Post and Leeds Intelligencer*, 9 October 1953.

Štědronská, Markéta. *Die Klavierkammermusik von Antonín Dvořák: Studien und Vergleiche mit Werken von Brahms*. Tutzing: Hans Schneider, 2008.

Štědronská, Markéta, ed. *August Wilhelm Ambros Musikaufsätze und -Rezensionen 1872–1876, Historisch-Kritische Ausgabe*. Vienna: Hollitzer Verlag, 2017.

Stekel, Hanns Christian. *Sehnsucht und Distanz: Theologische Aspekte in den wortgebundenen religiösen Kompositionen von Johannes Brahms.* Frankfurt am Main and New York: Peter Lang, 1997.

Stephenson, Kurt. *Johannes Brahms und die Familie von Beckerath.* Hamburg: Christians Verlag, 1979.

Stockhem, Michel. "Armand Parent, Brahms et la France." *Revue belge de Musicologie / Belgisch Tijdschrift voor Muziekwetenschap* 47 (1993): 177–88.

Stokes, Richard. Liner notes of the CD recording *Brahms: The Complete Songs*, Vol. 1 of 10. Hyperion CDJ33121, London, 2008.

Stowell, Robin. "Faust and Melnikov Finish Their Brahms Survey, Eight Years On." *The Strad*, November 2015. www.thestrad.com/brahms-violin-sonatas-no2-in-a-major-op100-no3-in-d-minor-op108-dietrich/schumann/brahms-fae-sonata-schumann-three-romances-op94/1139.article.

Stutte, Sarah. "Dem Virus ins Gesicht lachen." Kirche Schweiz website, 29 July 2020. https://www.kath.ch/newsd/dem-virus-ins-gesicht-lachen/.

Sumner Lott, Marie. *The Social Worlds of Nineteenth-Century Chamber Music: Composers, Consumers, Communities.* Urbana: University of Illinois Press, 2015.

Süß, Dietmar. *Death from the Skies: How the British and Germans Survived Bombing in World War II.* Translated by Lesley Sharpe and Jeremy Noakes. Oxford and New York: Oxford University Press, 2011.

Szendy, Peter. *Listen: A History of Our Ears.* Translated by Charlotte Mandell. New York: Fordham University Press, 2008.

Tadday, Ulrich, ed. *Schumann-Handbuch.* Kassel: Bärenreiter, 2006.

Tadday, Ulrich, ed. *Wolfgang Rihm.* Munich: Richard Boorberg Verlag, 2004.

Tappert, Wilhelm. *12 alte deutsche Lieder für eine Singstimme mit Begleitung des Pianoforte frei bearbeitet von Wilhelm Tappert.* Berlin: Simrock, ca. 1867.

Taylor, Benedict. *Mendelssohn, Time and Memory: The Romantic Conception of Cyclic Form.* Cambridge: Cambridge University Press, 2011.

Taylor, Benedict." Review of Julian Horton, *Brahms's Piano Concerto No. 2, Op. 83*, and Steven Vande Moortele, *The Romantic Overture and Musical Form from Rossini to Wagner.*" *Music Analysis* 37/3 (2018): 415–27.

Taylor, Benedict, ed. *Rethinking Mendelssohn.* New York: Oxford University Press, 2020.

Tenhaef, Peter. "Die Harfe und die absolute Musik." *Die Musikforschung* 46/4 (1993): 391–94.

Thacker, Toby. *Music after Hitler, 1945–1955.* Aldershot: Ashgate, 2007.

Thalmann, Joachim. *Untersuchungen zum Frühwerk von Johannes Brahms.* Kassel: Bärenreiter, 1989.

Thorau, Christian, and Hansjakob Ziemer, eds. *The Oxford Handbook of Musical Listening in the 19th and 20th Centuries.* New York: Oxford University Press, 2019.

Thurman, Kira. "Singing Against the Grain: Playing Beethoven in the #BlackLivesMatter Era." *The Point* 17 (September 28, 2018) https://thepointmag.com/examined-life/singing-against-grain-playing-beethoven-blacklivesmatter-era/.

Tilley, Janette. "Learning from Lazarus: The Seventeenth-Century Lutheran Art of Dying." *Early Music History* 28 (2009): 139–84.

Todd, R. Larry. "Late Brahms, Ancient Modes." *Nineteenth-Century Music Review* 15 (2018): 421–42.

Todd, R. Larry, ed. *Nineteenth-Century Piano Music*. New York: Schirmer Books, 1990.

Tovey, Donald Francis. *Essays and Lectures on Music*. Oxford. Oxford University Press, 1949.

Townsend, Mary Lee. "The Politics of Humor: Adolf Glassbrenner and the Rediscovery of the Prussian *Vormärz* (1815–1848)." *Central European History* 20 (1987): 29–57.

Trentmann, Frank, ed. *Paradoxes of Civil Society: New Perspectives on Modern Germany and British History*. New York: Berghahn Books, 1999.

Trümpi, Fritz. *The Political Orchestra: The Vienna and Berlin Philharmonics during the Third Reich*. Translated by Kenneth Kronenberg. Chicago: University of Chicago Press, 2016.

Truscott, Harold. "Brahms and Sonata Style." *Music Review* 25/3 (1964): 186–201.

Tunbridge, Laura. *Schumann's Late Style*. Cambridge: Cambridge University Press, 2007.

Tunbridge, Laura, and Roe-Min Kok, eds. *Rethinking Schumann*. New York: Oxford University Press, 2011.

Turner, Henry Ashby, Jr. "Victor Klemperer's Holocaust." *German Studies Review* 22/3 (1999): 385–95.

Uhde, Katharina. *The Music of Joseph Joachim*. Rochester, NY: Boydell & Prewer, 2018.

Uhde, Katharina. "Rediscovering Joseph Joachim's 'Hungarian' and 'Irish' [Scottish] Fantasias." *Musical Times* (Winter 2017): 75–99.

Uhde-Bernays, Hermann. *Henriette Feuerbach, Ihr Leben in ihren Briefen*. Berlin: Mayer & Jessen, 1912.

Uhland, Ludwig. *Alte hoch- und niederdeutsche Volkslieder mit Abhandlung und Anmerkungen herausgegeben*. 2 vols. Stuttgart & Tübingen: J. G. Cotta'schen Buchhandlung, 1844–1845.

Vande Moortele, Steven. "In Search of Romantic Form." *Music Analysis* 32/3 (2013): 404–31.

Vande Moortele, Steven. "Review of 'Seth Monahan: *Mahler's Symphonic Sonatas*.'" *Music Theory Spectrum* 40/1 (2018): 166–71.

Vande Moortele, Steven. *The Romantic Overture and Musical Form from Rossini to Wagner*. Cambridge: Cambridge University Press, 2017.

Vandermeulen, A., ed. *Enthüllungen aus der höheren Region der politischen Spionage in Berichten eines ungarischen Judas Ischarioth*. Berlin: Hoffschläger, 1862.

Varwig, Bettina. *Histories of Heinrich Schütz*. Cambridge: Cambridge University Press, 2011.

Venn, Edward. "Thomas Adès and the Spectres of *Brahms*." *Journal of the Royal Musical Association* 140/1 (2015): 163–212.

Venuti, Lawrence. *The Translator's Invisibility: A History of Translation*. London and New York: Routledge, 1995.
Viardot, Louis. "Ut Pictura Musica." *Gazette des Beaux Arts* 1 (January 1859): 19–33.
Vick, Brian E. *The Congress of Vienna: Power and Politics after Napoleon*. Cambridge, MA, and London: Harvard University Press, 2014.
Vick, Brian E. *Defining Germany: The 1848 Frankfurt Parliamentarians and National Identity*. Cambridge, MA, and London: Harvard University Press, 2002.
Vonnegut, Kurt. *Slaughterhouse Five, or The Children's Crusade: A Duty-Dance with Death*. New York: Random House, 1969.
Wackenroder, Wilhelm Heinrich, and Ludwig Tieck. *Phantasien über die Kunst*. Edited by Wolfgang Nehring. Stuttgart: Reclam, 1973.
Wadsworth, Benjamin K. "Directional Tonality in Schumann's Early Works." *Music Theory Online* 18/4 (2012).
Wagner, Günther. *Die Klavierballade um die Mitte des 19. Jahrhunderts*. München: Katzbichler, 1978.
Waltham-Smith, Naomi. *Music and Belonging between Revolution and Restoration*. New York: Oxford University Press, 2017.
Warnaby, John. "Wolfgang Rihm's Recent Music." *Tempo* 213 (2000): 12–19.
Wasielewski, Josef W. von. *Robert Schumann. Eine Biographie*. Dresden: Kunze, 1858.
Webster, James. "Schubert's Sonata Form and Brahms's First Maturity (II)." *19th-Century Music* 3/1 (1979): 52–63.
Weikel, Anthony L., III. *Brahms's Four Serious Songs: Arranged for Trombone and String Orchestra*. DMA thesis, Ohio State University, 2015.
Whittall, Arnold. "Recession, Reflation: Skempton, Finnissy and Musical Modernism's Classical Roots." *Musical Times* 159/1943 (2018): 11–24.
Whitall, Arnold. "Review of *A Theory of Musical Narrative*, by Byron Almén." *Music & Letters* 91/2 (2010): 299–303.
Widera, Thomas. *Dresden 1945–1948: Politik und Gesellschaft unter sowjetischer Besatzungsherrschaft*. Göttingen: Vandenhoeck & Ruprecht, 2004.
Widmann, Joseph Viktor. *Johannes Brahms in Erinnerungen*. Berlin: Gebrüder Patel, 1898. Reprinted as *Erinnerungen an Johannes Brahms*. Zurich and Stuttgart: Rotapfel-Verlag, 1980.
Widmann, Joseph Viktor. *Sizilien und anderer Gegenden Italiens*. Frauenfeld: Verlag J. Huger, 1898.
Wiebe, Heather. *Britten's Unquiet Pasts: Sound and Memory in Postwar Reconstruction*. New York: Cambridge University Press, 2012.
Wierzbicka, Anna. *Understanding Culture through Their Key Words: English, Russian, Polish, German, and Japanese*. New York and Oxford: Oxford University Press, 1997.
Williamon, Aaron, Jane Ginsborg, Rosie Perkins, and George Waddell. *Performing Music Research*. Oxford and New York: Oxford University Press, 2021.

Williams, Alastair. *Music in Germany since 1968*. Cambridge: Cambridge University Press, 2013.
Williams, Alastair. "Swaying with Schumann: Subjectivity and Tradition in Wolfgang Rihm's 'Fremde-Szenen' I–III and Related Scores." *Music & Letters* 87/3 (2006): 379–97.
Willet, John. "The Symmetrical Microphone Capsule and the Quest for the Perfect 'Acoustic Window.'" AES UK 13th Conference (March 1998): "Microphones & Loudspeakers". http://sound-link.co.uk/docs/Acoustic%20Window.pdf.
Winnenberg, Philippen zu. *Christliche Reuter Lieder*. Strasburg: Jobin, 1586.
Winterberg, Sonya. *Wie keine Andere: Die Dresdner Kreuzschule in der DDR*. Berlin: Bild und Heimat, 2016.
Wiora, Walter. *Die rheinischbergischen Melodien bei Zuccalmalgio und Brahms: Alte Liedweisen in romantischer Färbung*. Bad Godesberg: Voggenreiter, 1953.
Wirth, Uwe. *Die Geburt des Autors aus dem Geist der Herausgeberfiktion: Editoriale Rahmung im Roman um 1800*. Munich: Wilhelm Fink, 2008.
Wittgenstein, Ludwig. *Culture and Value*. Edited by G. H. von Wright. Translated by Peter Winch. Oxford: Wiley and Blackwell, 1998.
Wood, Hugh. *Staking Out the Territory and Other Writings on Music*. London: Plumbago Books, 2007.
Wood, James. *How Fiction Works*. New York: Picador; Farrar, Straus and Giroux, 2008.
Zehnder, Carl. *C. Zehnder, Maler—Architekt, 1859–1938: Ideal-Architekturen*. Zürich: ETH, 1981.
Zhang, Xieyi. "Tonicizations, Periods, and Period-Like Structures in the Music of Dvořák." PhD diss., City University of New York, 2019.
Zimmermann, Werner G. *Brahms in der Schweiz. Eine Dokumentation*. Zürich: Atlantis Musikbuch-Verlag, 1983.
Zingel, Hans Joachim. "Die Einführung der Harfe in das romantische Orchester." *Die Musikforschung* 2/2 (1949): 192–204.
Zingel, Hans Joachim. "Die Harfe als Symbol und allegorisches Attribut." *Die Musikforschung* 19/1 (1957): 39–48.

Index of Compositions by Johannes Brahms

Op. 1. *Klaviersonate Nr. 1 C-dur* (Piano Sonata No. 1 in C Major), 158, 160, 163, 175, 195–96, 204, 214, 215, 216, 218, 221, 345

Op. 2. *Klaviersonate Nr. 2 Fis-moll* (Piano Sonata No. 2 in F sharp Minor), 199, 204, 205, 214, 216, 219, 220, 221, 225, 345

Op. 3. *Sechs Gesänge für eine Tenor- oder Sopranstimme und Klavier* (Six Songs for tenor or soprano voice and piano), 159, 163
   No. 1, "Liebestreu" (Robert Reinick), 106, 158, 163
   No. 2, "Liebe und Frühling I" (August Heinrich Hoffmann von Fallersleben), 106
   No. 3, "Liebe und Frühling II" (August Heinrich Hoffmann von Fallersleben), 106
   No. 4, "Lied" (Friedrich Bodenstedt), 175

Op. 4. *Scherzo Es moll für Klavier* (Scherzo in E flat Minor for piano), 158

Op. 5. *Klaviersonate Nr. 3 F moll* (Piano Sonata No. 3 in F Minor), 158, 160, 199, 200, 214, 216, 217, 218, 220, 221, 232, 246, 247, 345, 346

Op. 6. *Sechs Gesänge für eine Tenor- oder Sopranstimme und Klavier* (Six Songs for tenor or soprano voice and piano), 159, 163
   No. 1, "Spanisches Lied" (Paul Heyse), 106

Op. 7. *Sechs Gesänge für eine Singstimme und Klavier* (Six Songs for Voice and Piano)
   No. 2, "Parole" (Joseph von Eichendorff), 106
   No. 3, "Anklänge" (Joseph von Eichendorff), 163

Op. 8. *Klaviertrio Nr. 1 H-dur* (Piano Trio No. 1 in B Major), 183, 199, 210, 214, 216, 217, 218, 219, 221, 239

Op. 9. *Sechzehn Variationen Fis-moll für Klavier über ein Thema von Robert Schumann* (Variations on a Theme of Robert Schumann), 13, 14, 19, 168, 365, 377

Op. 10. *Vier Balladen für Klavier* (Four Ballades for solo piano), 92, 144, 199
   No. 1 in D Minor, Nach der schottischen Ballade "Edward" von Herders "Stimmen der Volker," (From the Scottish Ballad "Edward" from Herder's Stimmen der Volker," 94, 95, 97–105
   No. 4 in B Major, 409

Op. 11. *Serenade Nr. 1 D-dur für großes Orchester* (Serenade No. 1 in D Major), 199, 214, 215, 217, 221, 224

Op. 15. *Klavierkonzert Nr. 1 D-moll* (Piano Concerto No. 1 in D Minor), 198, 199, 214, 215, 217, 221

Op. 16. *Serenade Nr. 2 A-dur für kleines Orchester* (Serenade No. 2 in A Major), 199, 200, 214, 216, 218, 223, 224

Op. 17. *Vier Gesänge für Frauenchor mit Begleitung von zwei Hörnen und Harfe*, 70, 72, 73, 79, 80

Op. 18. *Streichsextett Nr. 1 B-dur* (String Sextet No. 1 in B flat Major), 199, 214, 216, 219, 223, 224, 237, 238, 239, 244, 349, 350

Op. 21. *Variationen für Klavier No. 2. Über ein ungarisches Lied* (Variations on a Hungarian Folksong), 170

Op. 23. *Variationen Es-dur für zwei Klavier zu vier Händen über ein Thema von Robert Schumann* (Variations on a Theme of Schumann), 157

Op. 24. *Variationen und Fuge B-dur über ein Thema von Händel* (Variations and Fugue on a Theme of Handel), 157, 377

Op. 25. *Klavierquartett Nr. 1 G-moll* (Piano Quartet No. 1 in G Minor), 182, 199, 200, 214, 216, 218, 219, 223, 224, 234, 239, 243, 244, 245, 247, 249, 250, 251, 252, 254, 258–62, 270, 276

Op. 26. *Klavierquartett Nr. 2 A-dur* (Piano Quartet No. 2 in A Major), 199, 214, 216, 217, 218, 220, 221, 225, 238, 239, 243, 244, 247

Op. 34. *Klavierquintett F-moll* (Piano Quintet in F Minor), 177, 179, 180, 183, 185–92, 199, 214, 215, 216, 217, 218, 220, 221, 239, 246, 247

Op. 35. *Studien für Klavier A-moll. Variationen über ein Thema von Paganini* (Variations on a Theme of Paganini), 377

Op. 36. *Streichsextett Nr. 2 G-dur* (String Sextet No. 2 in G Major), 199, 200, 207, 214, 216, 217, 218, 219, 222, 225, 227, 245

Op. 38. *Sonate Nr. 1 E-moll für Klavier und Violoncello* (Cello Sonata No. 1 in E Minor), 199, 200, 214, 217, 219, 223, 224

Op. 39. *Walzer für Klavier* (Waltzes for Piano)
 No. 14 in G sharp Minor, 278, 285–89, 36

Op. 40. *Horntrio Es-dur* (Trio for Violin, Horn, and Piano in E flat), 197, 280–82, 391

Op. 41. *Fünf Lieder für vierstimmigen Männerchor* (Five Songs for Four-Part Male Chorus), 61, 62, 63, 64, 66, 68, 69
 No. 1, "Ich schwing mein Horn" (Altdeutsch), 62, 68–69
 No. 2, "Freiwillige her!" (Carl Lemcke), 62–64, 66
 No. 3, "Geleit!" (Carl Lemcke), 62
 No. 4, "Marschieren" (Carl Lemcke), 62
 No. 5, "Gebt Acht!" (Carl Lemcke), 62, 63

Op. 45. *Ein deutsches Requiem* (German Requiem), 2, 70, 73, 74, 75, 79, 80, 82, 83, 84, 85, 289,

Index of Compositions by Johannes Brahms

292–98, 302, 304, 313, 319, 320, 321, 322, 332, 333, 334, 336, 338, 339, 341, 367, 368, 369, 375

Op. 49 *Fünf Lieder für eine Singstimme und Klavier* (Five Songs for Voice and Piano)
  No. 1, "Am Sonntag Morgen" (Paul Heyse), 48, 85
  No. 3, "Sehnsucht" (Joseph Wenzig), 48, 85
  No. 4, "Wiegenlied" (From *Des Knaben Wunderhorn*), 183, 233

Op. 50. Rinaldo (Goethe), 36

Op. 51. *Zwei Streichquartette* (Two String Quartets), 195, 270
  No. 1 in C Minor, 199, 200, 214, 216, 219, 220, 221, 237, 241–2, 398
  No. 2 in A Minor, 199, 214, 216, 219, 221, 243

Op. 52. *Liebeslieder Walzer für Gesang und Klavier zu vier Händen* (Liebeslieder Waltzes for Voices and Piano), 375

Op. 53. *Alt Rhapsodie* (Alto Rhapsody), 75, 79, 378

Op. 54. *Schicksalslied von Friedrich Hölderlin für Chor und Orchester*, 75, 78, 79, 80, 81, 82, 86, 88, 142, 378

Op. 55. *Triumphlied für achtstimmigen Chor und Orchester*, 61, 75, 77, 310, 312

Op. 59. *Acht Lieder und Gesänge für eine Singstimme und Klavier* (Eight Songs for Voice and Piano), Op. 59, 381
  No. 1, "Dämmrung senkte sich von oben," 379, 382, 395

Op. 60. *Klavierquartett Nr. 3 C-moll* (Piano Quartet No. 3 in C Minor), 199, 202–3, 204, 214, 215, 216, 218, 220, 221, 231, 239

Op. 67. *Streichquartett Nr. 3 B-dur* (String Quartet No. 3 in B flat Major), 199, 214, 216, 219, 222, 243

Op. 68. *Symphonie Nr. 1 C-moll* (Symphony No. 1 in C Minor), 199, 210, 213, 214, 216, 217, 218, 219, 223, 224, 247, 354, 365, 381, 382

Op. 72. *Fünf Gesänge für eine Singstimme und Klavier*
  No. 1, "Alte Liebe" (Karl Candidus), 48, 50, 85

Op. 73. *Symphonie Nr. 2 D-dur* (Symphony No. 2 in D Major), 199, 214, 216, 219, 222, 365, 382, 384, 385

Op. 74. *Zwei Motetten für gemischten Chor a cappella* (Two Motets), No. 1, "Warum ist das Licht gegeben," 334, 335

Op. 77. *Violinkonzert D-dur* (Violin Concerto in D Major), 156, 198, 199, 200, 201, 214, 216, 217, 218, 219, 223, 224

Op. 78. *Violinsonate Nr. 1 G-dur* (Violin Sonata No. 1 in G Major), 199, 200, 214, 217, 219, 221, 242, 243, 250, 262, 267, 270, 272–76

Op. 79 *Zwei Rhapsodien für Klavier* (Two Rhapsodies for Piano) No. 1 in B Minor, 285, 287, 290–93

Op. 80. *Akademische Festouvertüre C-moll für großes Orchester* (Academic Festival Overture), 197

Op. 81. *Tragische Ouvertüre (Tragic Overture)*, 199, 210–13, 214, 216, 217, 218, 221

Op. 82. *Nänie von Friedrich Schiller für Chor und Orchester*, 70, 73, 74, 75, 76, 78, 80, 82, 83, 84, 378

Op. 83. *Klavierkonzert Nr. 2 B-dur* (Piano Concerto No. 2 in B flat Major), 198, 199, 214, 215, 217, 221

Op. 86. *Sechs Lieder für eine tiefere Stimme und Klavier* (Six Songs for Low Voice and Piano) No. 2, "Feldeinsamkeit" (Hermann Allmers), 48, 85

Op. 87. *Klaviertrio Nr. 2 C-dur* (Piano Trio No. 2 in C Major), 199, 200, 208–10, 214, 216, 217, 219, 220, 221, 241

Op. 88. *Streichquintett Nr. 1 F-dur* (String Quintet No. 1 in F Major), 199, 200, 207, 214, 216, 217, 218, 223, 224

Op. 89. *Gesang der Parzen von Goethe für sechsstimmigen Chor und Orchester*, 78

Op. 90. *Symphonie Nr. 3 F-dur* (Symphony No. 3 in F Major), 199, 200, 201, 214, 216, 218, 221, 247, 385, 394

Op. 94. *Fünf Lieder für eine tiefe Stimme und Klavier* (Five Songs for Low Voice and Piano)
No. 1, "Mit vierzig Jahren" (Friedrich Rückert), 153
No. 5, "Kein Haus, Keine Heimat" (Friedrich Halm), 48, 85

Op. 98. *Symphonie Nr. 4 E-moll* (Symphony No. 4 in E Minor), 197, 199, 210–11, 214, 216, 218, 222, 224, 227, 237, 270, 365, 369, 385

Op. 99. *Cellosonate Nr. 2 F-dur* (Cello Sonata No. 2 in F Major), 199, 214, 216, 219, 220, 222, 235, 237, 244

Op. 100. *Violinsonate Nr. 2 A-dur* (Sonata for Violin and Piano in A Major), 177, 179, 180, 183, 185–92, 214, 215, 217, 218, 220, 222

Op. 101. *Klaviertrio Nr. 3 C-moll* (Piano Trio No. 3 in C Minor), 183, 199, 214, 216, 219, 222, 225, 239, 270

Op. 102. *Konzert A-moll (Doppelkonzert) für Violine und Violoncello mit Orchester* (Concerto for Violin and Violoncello in A Minor (Double Concerto)), 198, 199, 214, 215, 216, 217, 218, 221, 222

Op. 104. *Fünf Gesänge für gemischten Chor a cappella* (Five Songs for Mixed Choir a cappella)
No. 1, "Nachtwache I" (Friedrich Rückert), 315
No. 2, "Nachtwache II" (Friedrich Rückert), 315

Op. 105. *Fünf Lieder für eine tiefere Stimme und Klavier* (Five Songs for Low Voice and Piano)
No. 1, "Wie Melodien zieht es mir" (Klaus Groth), 183
No. 2, "Immer leiser wird mein Schlummer" (Hermann Lingg), 183

Op. 108. *Violinsonate Nr. 3 D-moll* (Violin Sonata No. 3 in D Minor), 199, 214, 217, 218, 220, 221

Index of Compositions by Johannes Brahms

Op. 111. *Streichquintett Nr. 2 G-dur* (String Quintet No. 2 in G Major), 199, 214, 216, 218, 222, 233, 239
Op. 114. *Klarinettentrio A-moll* (Clarinet Trio in A Minor), 199, 210, 214, 217, 219, 222, 243
Op. 115. *Klarinettenquintett H-moll* (Clarinet Quintet in B Minor), 43, 199, 205–6, 214, 216, 217, 219, 221, 222, 239, 243
Op. 117. *Drei Intermezzi für Klavier* (Three Intermezzi for Piano), 142
Op. 118. *Sechs Klavierstücke* (Six Piano Pieces), 142, 143, 149, 155
　No. 1, Intermezzo, 145–146
　No. 2, Intermezzo, 147
　No. 6, Intermezzo, 148, 149, 375
Op. 119. *Vier Klavierstücke* (Four Piano Pieces), 142, 143, 155, 365
　No. 1, Intermezzo, 151, 152, 153, 184
　No. 2, Intermezzo, 184
Op. 120. *Zwei Sonaten für Klavier und Klarinette (oder Bratsche)*, Two Sonatas for Piano and Clarinet (or Viola)
　No. 1 in F Minor, 199, 200, 214, 217, 218, 220, 221, 241, 250, 262–67, 270–74, 276, 282–85
　No. 2 in E flat Major, 196, 199, 214, 217, 219, 220, 221, 270
Op. 121. *Vier ernste Gesänge für eine Baßstimme und Klavier* (Four Serious Songs for Bass and Piano), 309, 316, 333, 357–74, 375
Op. 122. *Elf Choralvorspiele für Orgel* (Eleven Chorale Preludes for Organ), 357, 358, 373, 374

Compositions without Opus Numbers

WoO 3. *Zwei Gavotten für Klavier* (Two Gavottes for Piano), 377
WoO 6. *51 Übungen für Klavier* (Fifty-one Exercises for Piano), 168
WoO 32. *28 Deutsche Volkslieder für eine Singstimme und Klavier*, 118
　No. 16, "Scheiden," 118, 121, 122
WoO 33. *49 Deutsche Volkslieder, 42 für eine Singstimme mit Klavierbegleitung; 7 für vierstimmigen Chor und Vorsänger*, 110, 137, 399, 406
　No. 17, "Ach Gott, wie weh tut Scheiden," 112–118, 122, 123, 124
　No. 24, "Mir ist schöns brauns Maidelein," 134–6
　No. 29, "Es war ein Markgraf überm Rhein," 409
　No. 30, "All mein Gedanken," 408, 409
　No. 35, "Soll sich der Mond nicht heller scheinen," 407, 408
　No. 42, "In stiller Nacht," 398, 400, 402, 403, 404, 405

Works of other composers arranged by Brahms

Anh. 1a No. 2, Christoph Willibald Gluck, Gavotte A-dur aus der Oper *"Iphigénie en Aulide," Bearbeitung für Klavier*, 377

Varia, fragments, and sketches

Anh. 3 No. 13, "Die Müllerin," *Lied für eine Singstimme und Klavier*, fragment, 159, 163

Uncatalogued works

Hymne zur Verherrlichung des großen Joachim ("Hymn in Adulation of the Great Joachim"), 157, 159, 163–69, 176

Works now lost
String Quartet (inspired by Hoffmann's *Prinzessin Brambilla*), 10, 19

Leaves from the Diary of a Musician, Edited by the Young Kreisler, 19
Violin Sonata in A Minor (written before 1853), 159

General Index

Abrams, M. H. (1912–2015), 2
Achilles, 84
Adonis, 84
Adorno, Theodor W. (1903–
    1969), 225
Aegidi, Ludwig (1825–1901), 60
Aeschylus, 17
Akademie der bildenden Künste,
    Wien, 315
Aldous, Richard, 363
Allgeyer, Julius (1829–1900), 27, 30,
    31, 34, 106, 107
    Portrait of Anselm Feuerbach,
        1865, 35
    Portrait of Brahms, 1866, 34
Allied attack on Dresden, 1945. *See*
    Dresden firebombing
Almén, Byron, 105
    A Theory of Music Narrative, 105
Ambros, August Wilhelm (1817–
    1876), 75, 77
Anderson, Colin, 368
AnyTune app, 184
Aphrodite, 84
Applegate, Celia, 321
Arendt, Hannah (1906–1975), 319
Ariosto, Ludovico (1474–1533), 13
Aristotle, 175
Arnim, Achim von (1781–1831), 19,
    115–116
    See also *Knaben Wunderhorn, Des*

Arnim, Bettina von (1785–1859), 10,
    18, 160
Arnim, Gisela von (1827–1889),
    160, 165–66
Arnold, Friedrich Wilhelm (1810–
    1864), 111, 112, 113, 118, 119–
    20, 122
Arnone, Augustus, 405, 409
Attfield, Nicholas, 368
Auric, Georges (1899–1983), 352,
    353, 354
Avé-Lallement, Theodor (1806–
    1890), 59, 60
Avins, Styra, 157

Bach-Gesellschaft Edition, 13
Bach, Carl Philipp Emanuel
    (1714–1788), 46
Bach, Johann (1604–1672), 334
    Unser Leben ist ein Schatten, 334
Bach, Johann Sebastian (1685–1750),
    19, 159, 184, 302, 310, 311, 321,
    332, 343, 346, 347, 377, 396
    "Gib dich zufrieden und sei
        stille," 334
    St. Matthew Passion, 333
Badiou, Alain (b. 1937), 151
Balakirev, Mily (1837–1910), 72
    Symphony No. 1, 72
Balzac, Honoré de (1799–1850), 302
    Comédie humaine, 302

Barbi, Alice (1858–1948), 183
Barenboim, Daniel, 377
Baudelaire, Charles (1821–1867), 36
Bauer, Amy, 388, 391, 392
Becker, Carl (1804–1877), 125, 126, 128, 129, 130, 133, 141
Becker, Nikolaus (1809–1845), 64
  "Rheinlied," 64
Beethoven, Ludwig van (1770–1827), 1, 19, 53, 159, 162, 181, 196, 229, 230, 235, 236, 246, 247, 302, 305, 310, 311, 312, 342, 343, 345, 346, 347, 382, 396
  Piano Sonata No. 17 in D Minor, Op. 31 No. 2, "Tempest," 225
  Piano Sonata No. 23 in F Minor, Op. 57, "Appassionata," 245, 246
  Piano Sonata No. 26 in E flat Major, "Lebewohl," Op. 81a, 75
  String Quartet No. 12 in E flat Major, Op. 127
  Symphony No. 3 in E flat Major, Op. 55, 210
  Symphony No. 5 in C Minor, Op. 67, 79
  Symphony No. 7 in A Major, Op. 92, 210
  Symphony No. 9 in D Minor, Op. 125, 12, 245
  Violin Sonata No. 7 in C Minor, Op. 30 No. 2
Behler, Constantin, 378
  Nostalgic teleology, 378, 387, 394, 395
Bekova Sisters, 399
Belcea Quartet, 179
Beller-McKenna, Daniel, 61, 75, 360
Bellman, Jonathan, 169, 175
Bendemann, Eduard (1811–1889), 307
Benson, Bruce Ellis, 181
Berio, Luciano (1925–2003), 368, 396
  Rendering, 368

Berkhemer, Joan, 185
Berlin Singakademie, 321
Berlioz, Hector (1803–1869), 36, 71, 306
  Grand traité d'instrumentation et d'orchestration modernes, 71, 72
  Lélio, ou Le retour à la vie Op. 14b, 71
  Symphonie fantastique, 71
Berry, Paul, 137, 150
Beuerle, Hans Michael, 61
Bible, The, 18
Bildung, 23, 60, 161, 176, 395
  performance-based *Bildung*, 176
  performative *Bildung*, 176
Bishop, Paul, 381
Bismarck, Otto von (1815–1898), 53, 55, 60, 61, 67, 428n25, 429n27, 512
Bizet, Georges (1838–1875), 304
  Carmen, 304
Blackbourn, David, 57
Black Lives Matter, 2
Blumstock, Herbert, 333, 334, 335, 483n71, 483n72
Böcklin, Arnold (1827–1901), 33, 37, 38, 39, 40, 41, 42, 50, 55, 317, 421n1, 424n23, 424n24, 435n40, 499n15, 512
  Arnold Böcklin: eine Auswahl der hervorragendsten Werke des Künstlers in Photogravüre, 41
  Bergruine, ca. 1886, 42
  Die Toteninsel (The Isle of the Dead), 40, 42, 50, 317
  Flora, 1875, 39
  Ruine am Meer (Ruin by the Sea), 1880, 41
  Selbstbildnis mit fiedelndem Tod (Self-Portrait with Death Fiddling) 1872, 39–40

Bodsch, Ingrid, 17, 419, 537
Böhler, Otto (1847–1913), 301
   Brahms's Arrival in Heaven (Die Ankunft Brahms' im Himmel), 301
Böhme, Franz Magnus (1827–1898), 110, 111, 113, 114, 115, 125, 126, 127, 128, 441n2, 442n7, 443n13, 443n14, 443n17, 443n23, 445n36, 445n37, 445n38, 512, 518
Boosey & Hawkes, 361, 365, 495, 496, 497, 521, 535
Booth, Wayne C., 92, 93, 436n1, 437n5, 512
   The Rhetoric of Fiction, 92
Borchard, Beatrix, 174, 418n27, 430n37, 455n72, 512
Boston Symphony Orchestra, 348
Bouyer, Raymond (1862–1935), 343–46, 350, 351, 488n8, 488n811, 512
Bowie, Andrew, 389, 501n39
Bozarth, George, 159, 170, 172, 359, 400, 512–13
Brahms, Johann Jakob (1806–1872), 34, 160
Brahms, Johannes (1833–1897)
   as an arranger, 161
   busts of, 310, 315
   canonization of, 301, 302, 310, 312
   as a collector of folk melodies, 161
   in "Composer's Heaven," 301, 310–313
   counterpoint exchange with Joseph Joachim, 156
   death of, 1
   Des jungen Kreislers Schatzkästlein (The Young Kreisler's Treasure Chest), 9, 11, 13, 17, 18, 19, 20, 22, 24, 58, 107
   Hamburg Women's Choir, 60, 68
   Kreisler persona, 8, 12, 13, 19, 20, 25, 168, 305
   and lateness, 304
   and melancholy, 304
   performative identity, 174
Brahms, Johannes and Ede Reményi, *Magyar dalok*, 158, 163, 170–72
Brasch, C., 309
Breitkopf & Härtel, 68, 305, 316
Brentano, Clemens (1778–1842), 19, 116, 510
   See also *Knaben Wundernhorn, Des*
Brinkmann, Reinhold, 334, 421, 465, 514
Britten, Benjamin (1913–1976), 378, 543
Brodbeck, David, 359, 515
Brontë, Emily, 93
   Wuthering Heights (1847), 93
Bruch, Max, 247
Bruckner, Anton (1824–1896), 72, 196, 207, 301, 302, 304
   Symphony No. 8, 72
Bruneau, Alfred (1857–1934), 342
Busoni, Ferrucio (1866–1924), 357, 374
   transcription of Brahms, *Eleven Chorale Preludes*, 357, 358
Bußtag. See *Totensonntag*

Cadwallader, Allen, 143, 515
Cage, John (1912–1992), 403
Calamatta, Luigi (1801–1869), 54
Callot, Jacques (1592–1635), 25–28, 55
   A Few Gobbi, 28
   The Temptation of St. Anthony, 26–27
Camus, Albert (1913–1960), 92
Caplin, William, 196, 198, 200, 202, 203, 210, 215, 220, 230, 515, 516
Cassatt Quartet, 179

Cervantes, Miguel de (1547–1616), 93
    Don Quixote, 93
Cherubini, Luigi (1760–1842), 53, 54
Chodowiecki, Daniel (1726–1801), 41, 43, 44, 54, 55
    Coriolanus Greeting His Mother at the Gate, 43, 44
    Kitchen Work, 43
    Ziethen sitzend vor seinem Königen (Ziethen sitting before his King), 54
Christie, Agatha (1890–1976), 92
Cocteau, Jean (1889–1963), 346, 353
Cohn, Richard, 278
Cone, Edward T. (1917–2004), 143, 145, 150, 516
Conrat, Ilse. *See* Ilse Twardowski-Conrat
Cornelius, Peter von (1783–1867), 54
Coronavirus, 2, 357, 373, 394
"Corps Saxonia" fraternity, 162
Cortot, Alfred (1877–1962), 346, 516

Daguerre, Louis (1787–1851), 34
Dahlhaus, Carl (1928–1989), 200, 225, 247, 516
Dante Alighieri (1265–1321), 13
Danuser, Hermann, 391, 517
Darcy, Warren, 196, 210, 230, 247, 523
Dauerhafte Musik (enduring music), 155, 302
Daumer, Georg Friedrich (1800–1875), 30
Davenson, Henri (1904–1977), 346–48, 352, 354, 517
Daverio, John (1954–2003), 19, 78, 230, 247, 517
Davies, Fanny (1861–1934), 183, 184
Da Vinci, Leonardo (1452–1519), 35
    Il paragone delle arti (Comparison of the Arts), 35
    Mona Lisa, 36, 54
Davis, Andrew, 196, 517

DeJean, Joan, 349
De Lara, Adelina (1872–1961), 184
Denazification, 319, 320, 322
Dessoff, Otto (1835–1892), 233
Deutsche Demokratische Republik (DDR). *See* German Democratic Republic
Deutsche Lieder für Jung und Alt (Groos-Klein), 115, 116, 118, 125
Deutsches Symphonie-Orchester Berlin, 368
Developing variation, 225, 227, 249, 258, 262, 273, 393, 396, 399, 402, 406, 407, 408, 410, 411, 520
Diaghilev, Sergei (1872–1929), 353
Dietrich, Albert (1829–1908), 7, 18, 59, 160, 164
D'Indy, Vincent (1851–1931), 343, 345, 348, 353, 517
    Cours de composition, 345
    Symphony No. 2 in B flat Major, Op. 57, 345
Distler, Hugo (1908–1942), 323
Dobson, Sam, 364
Dostoevsky, Fyodor (1821–1881), 93
Dresden firebombing, 319, 320, 321, 324, 325, 333, 334–39
Dresdner Kreuzchor, 319–40
Dresdner Kreuzkirche, 322, 324, 333, 335, 336
Dresdner Kreuzschule, 325, 335
Dresdner Philharmonie, 320
Dufetel, Nicolas, 341, 342, 352
Dukas, Paul (1865–1935), 343
Dumayet, Pierre (1923–2011), 341
Dunsby, Jonathan, 147, 155
Dürer, Albrecht (1471–1528), 48
Dussek, Jan Ladislav (1760–1812), 144
Dvořák, Antonin (1841–1904), 3, 249–77, 367
    American works, 251, 277
    Piano Quartet No. 2 in E flat Major, Op. 87

General Index

Requiem in B flat Minor,
   Op. 89, 367
String Quartet No. 8 in E Major,
   Op. 80, 262, 265, 267–73, 276
String Quartet No. 9 in D
   Minor, Op. 34
String Quartet No. 14 in A flat
   Major, Op. 105
String Quintet No. 3 in E flat
   Major, Op. 97, 249, 250, 251, 253,
   254–8, 262
Symphony No. 8 in G Major,
   Op. 88, 270, 276

East Germany. *See* German
   Democratic Republic (GDR)
Eibenschütz, Ilona
   (1872–1967), 184
Eich, Katrin, 143
Eichendorff, Joseph von (1788–1857),
   7, 12, 19, 22, 106
   Dichter und ihre Gesellen, 22
Elbphilharmonie Hamburg, 369
Engelmann, Theodor
   (1843–1909), 43
Engelmann, Wilhelm
   (1808–1878), 41, 43
Érard, Sébastien (1752–1831), 71
Erk, Ludwig (1807–1883), 114
Ernst, Heinrich Wilhelm
   (1812–1865), 158
   Elegy and Carnaval, 158
   Erlkönig, 159
Eshbach, Robert, 174, 519
Eurydice, 75, 78, 84
Evangelisches Kreuzgymnasium. *See*
   Dresdner Kreuzschule
Evans, Nancy (1915–2000), 362, 363

F.A.E. ["Frei aber Einsam"] Sonata
   (Johannes Brahms, Albert
   Dietrich, Robert Schumann),
   160, 164, 165, 168, 172

Fantin-Latour, Henri (1836–1904),
   36, 37, 38, 50, 344
   Four Truths: Schumann, Berlioz,
   Wagner, and Brahms (1881), 36
   Hommage à Brahms, 1900, 38
   J. Brahms, Rinaldo, 1877, 37
Fauré, Gabriel (1845–1924),
   342, 347
Faust, Isabelle, 180, 181
Fellinger, Maria (1849–1925), 302
Fellner, Till, 179
Ferrier, Kathleen (1912–1953), 362,
   363, 364, 373
Feuerbach, Anselm (1829–1880), 30,
   31, 32, 33, 34, 38, 55, 75
   Amazonenschlacht (The Battle of
   the Amazonians), 33
   Musikalische Poesie (Musical
   Poetry), 32
   Orpheus and Euridike, 31
   Symposium, The, 32, 33
Feuerbach, Henriette, 31, 33, 34
Finnissy, Michael (b. 1946), 3,
   396–411
   Brahms-Lieder, 398, 399,
   405–411
   Folklore 3, 398
   Gershwin, 396
   Gershwin Arrangements, 396
   History of Photography in Sound,
   The, 405, 406
   In stiller Nacht, 398, 399–405,
   406, 409–11
   Mit Arnold Schoenberg, 398
   Piano Quartet in A Major
   (1861–62), 398
   Piano Quartet in C Minor
   (1861), 398
   Romance (with Intermezzo) for
   piano, 396
   Second Political Agenda, 398
   Sehnsucht, 398
   Verdi Transcriptions, 396

Finscher, Ludwig (1930–2020), 305
First World War. *See* World War I
Fischer-Dieskau, Dietrich (1925–2012), 318
Fitch, Fabrice, 385
Ford, Ford Madox (1873–1939), 93
Formenlehre, 195, 196, 229, 230, 235
  New *Formenlehre*, 195, 235
  Romantic *Formenlehre*, 196, 229
Forster, Georg (1510–1568), 111, 112, 113, 115, 116, 125, 126, 128, 139
Franck, César (1822–1890), 345, 348
Franco-Prussian War (1870), 341, 342
Frankfurt National Assembly (18 May 1848–31 May 1849), 56, 57
Freiligrath, Fredinand (1810–1876), 58
Freund, Etelka (1879–1977), 184
Friedberg, Carl (1872–1955), 184
Frisch, Walter, 95, 198, 225, 520
Fritz, Gunther, 318
Frye, Northrop (1912–1991), 105
Furtwängler, Wilhelm (1886–1954), 346

Gade, Niels (1817–1890), 247
  Symphony No. 4 in B flat Major, Op. 20, 247
  Violin Sonata No. 2 in D Minor Op. 21, 247
Gänsbacher, Josef (1829–1911), 308
Garcia Viardot, Pauline (1821–1910), 36
Gastein Convention (1865), 67
Gastgeb, Peregrin von, 310
Gautier, Théophile (1811–1872), 36
Gay, Peter, 341, 348, 349
  "Aimez-vous Brahms? Reflections on Modernism," 348
Geck, Martin, 14, 520
Gellen, Adam, 157, 158, 520

German Democratic Republic (GDR), 322, 323
German Symbolist School, 39
Gershwin, George (1898–1937), 396
Gesualdo, Carlo (1566–1613), 377
Gjerdingen, Robert, 224
Glanert, Detlev (b. 1960), 3, 360, 361, 365–74
  Brahms-Fantasie (Heliogravure für Orchester), 365, 366
  Idyllium (Metamorphosen nach Brahms für Orchester), 365, 366
  Variationen über ein Thema von Schumann, Op. 9, 366
  Vier Choralvorspiele, 366
  Vier ernste Gesänge, Op. 121, 366
  Vier Klavierstücke, Op. 119, 366
  Vier Präludien und ernste Gesänge, 366–73
  Walzer, Op. 39, 366
  Weites Land (Musik mit Brahms für Orchester), 365, 366
Glassbrenner, Adolf (1810–1876), 56, 58
Gluck, Christoph Willibald (1714–1787), 302, 310, 311, 363, 377
Goebbels, Joseph (1897–1945), 325, 334
Goethe, Johann Wolfgang von (1749–1832), 22, 23, 53, 79, 161, 376, 378–82, 391, 394
  Chinesisch-deutsche Jahre- und Tageszeiten (Chinese German Collection of Seasons and Hours), 379, 380 (No. 8, "Dämmrung senkte sich von oben," 376, 379, 380)
  Harzreise im Winter, 79, 378
  Italienische Reise, 161
  Die Leiden des jungen Werthers, 22

Wilhelm Meisters Lehrjahre, 23
Grädener, Carl Georg Peter (1812–1883), 59
Graf, Max (1873–1958), 183, 308, 309
Gramsci, Antonio (1891–1937), 398
Green, Abigail, 66
Gregor, Neil, 323, 324, 521
Grimes, Nicole, 23, 78, 79, 142, 358, 373, 521
Grimm, Hermann (1828–1901), 54
Grimm, Julius Otto (1827–1903), 25, 59, 72, 73, 108
Groos, Carl (1861–1946), 113, 115, 118
　See also *Deutsche Lieder für Jung und Alt*
Groth, Klaus (1819–1899), 33
Grützke, Johannes (1937–2017), 318
Guarneri String Quartet, 181
Gypsy music, 156, 169, 172, 175

Habermas, Jürgen (b. 1929), 59, 522
Hafis, 30
Hallé Orchestra, 364
Hamilton, John T., 143
Hamilton, Katy, 156
Handel, Georg Friedrich, 28, 29, 53, 157, 302, 310, 311, 377
Hanslick, Eduard (1825–1904), 82, 143, 155
Hastings, Charise, 98, 99
Hatten, Robert, 105
Hausmann, Robert (1852–1909), 183, 185
Haussmann, Elias, 53
Haydn, Joseph (1732–1809), 52, 78, 79, 164, 196, 230, 235, 302, 310, 311, 312, 342, 396
　Symphony No. 60 in C Major, Hob I/60, 164
　The Creation, 78–79
Hecht, Felix (1894–1917), 56

Hegel, Georg Wilhelm Friedrich (1770–1831), 144
Heldengedenktag (Nazi heroes' day of mourning), 334
Helst, Bartholomeus van der (1613–1670), 54
Henze, Hans Werner (1926–2012), 378
Hepokoski, James, 196, 197, 210, 230, 247
　"Brahmsian deformation," 197, 232, 243
Herder, Gottfried (1744–1803), 93, 96, 107
　"Edward" Ballad, 96, 97, 98, 99
　Stimmen der Völker, 93, 106, 107
Herwegh, Georg (1817–1875), 58
Herzogenberg, Elisabeth von (1847–1892), 304
Heuberger, Richard (1850–1914), 303, 375, 523
Heyse, Paul (1830–1914), 38, 39
Hildebrand, Adolf von (1847–1921), 313, 314
Hitchcock, Alfred (1899–1980), 392
Hitler Youth, 323
Hobday, Ethel (1872–1947), 183
Høffding, Simon, 180, 181
Hofmann, Kurt, 107, 523
Hofmann, Kurt and Renate, 157, 158, 159, 524
Hoffmann, E. T. A. (1776–1822), 7, 10, 12, 19, 20, 22, 25, 27, 35, 156, 168, 305
　"Beethoven's Instrumental Music," 20
　Fantasiestücke in Callots Manier (*Fantasy Pieces in Callot's Manner*), 12, 21, 25, 168
　Kater Murr, 12
　Kreisleriana, 12, 25

Hoffmann, E. T. A. (1776–1822) (*cont.*)
  Prinzessin Brambilla, 10, 19
  Rath Krespel, 11
  Die Serapionsbrüder, 11
Hoffmann von Fallersleben, August Heinrich (1798–1874), 58, 63, 64, 106, 159, 164
Hogarth, William (1697–1764), 25, 27, 28, 29, 41, 53, 55
  Marriage à la Mode—Betrothal, 28
  Portrait of George Friedrich Handel, 28, 53
Hölderlin, Friedrich (1770–1843), 10, 79, 80, 85, 86, 378, 391
  Hyperion, 79, 80, 86, 378
Holocaust, The, 319
Holtzmann, Adolf (1810–1870), 13
Holy Scriptures, 18
Homer, 18, 72, 85, 86
Horne, William, 106, 108
Hughes, Langston (1901–1967), 2, 524
Hungarian style, 175. See also *style hongrois*
Hurd, Madeleine, 59, 524

Ibragimova, Alina, 179
Imbert, Hugues (1842–1905), 344
Ingres, Jean-Auguste-Dominique (1780–1867), 53, 54
Ironwood, 182
Ives, Charles (1874–1954), 398

Jacques Derrida (1930–2004), 397, 399, 407, 410, 517
  hauntology, 397, 400
  spectrality, 397
Japtha, Louise, 10
Japtha, Minna, 10
Järvi, Paavi, 2

Jeal, Erica, 367, 368
Jean Paul. *See* Jean Paul Richter
Jenner, Gustav (1865–1920), 155, 264, 302
Joachim, Joseph (1831–1907), 11–12, 17–18, 20, 25, 27, 59, 60, 144, 156–76, 183, 185, 313
  Hamlet Overture, 158, 163, 168
  Hungarian Fantasy, 158, 172, 173, 174
  as "Magyarember" (Magyar), 174
  Overture to *Heinrich IV*, 163
  Romance for Violin and Piano, 159
  3 *Stücke*, Op. 2, 164, 166, 167, 168
  Three Pieces, Op. 5, 163, 164, 165, 166, 167, 168
  Violin Concerto No. 1 in G Minor, Op. 3
Johann, Archduke of Habsburg, 57
Johnson, Julian, 390
Jones, Kimberly, 2
Jordan, Max (1837–1906), 46

Kalbeck, Max (1850–1921), 9, 10, 18, 19, 58, 98, 144, 156, 157, 158, 160, 161, 162, 172, 173, 175, 315, 359, 360, 363, 373, 525
Kant, Immanuel (1724–1804), 23
Kavakos, Leonidas, 180, 181
Kawohl, Friedemann, 156, 157, 168
Kelly, Elaine, 338, 526
Kennedy, Michael, 364, 526
Kerner, Justinus (1786–1862), 11
Kimura, Ben, 180
Kinderman, William, 144
Kinkel, Gottfried (1815–1882), 22
Klein, Bernhard (1793–1832), 113, 115
  See also *Deutsche Lieder für Jung und Alt*

General Index

Klein, Franz (1779–1840), 53
Klein, Michael, 105
Klenze, Leo von (1784–1864), 302
Klemperer, Victor (1881–1960), 320
Klinger, Max (1857–1920), 33, 37–40, 47, 48, 50, 51, 52, 54, 55, 71, 83, 85–88, 313, 316, 317
  Amor und Psyche Op. V, 50
  Brahms Monument in Hamburg Musikhalle, 316, 317
  Brahms-Phantasie, 47, 48, 50, 71, 83, 85, 86, 87, 316, 317
  Brahms-Phantasie, "Alte Liebe," 51
  Brahms-Phantasie, "Accorde," 57, 317
  Brahms-Phantasie, "Evocation," 57
  12 Intermezzi, 51
  Radierung Op. IV, 12 Compositions, 51–52
  Radierung Op. IV, "Intermezzo No. 4," 53
  Rettungen Ovidische Opfer ("Rescues of Ovid's Victims"), 86
Klingler Quartet, 185
Kloke, Eberhard (b. 1948), 361, 368
Klopstock, Friedrich Gottlieb (1724–1803), 373
Knaben Wunderhorn, Des, 116, 140, 373
Knobloch, Milan, 313
Komma, Karl Michael (1913–2012), 361
Körner, Theodor (1791–1813), 63
Kraus, Felix (1870–1937), 309
Krebs, Carl (1857–1937), 19
Krefeld Festival, 183
Kross, Siegfried, 61, 195, 527
Küchler, Rudolf (1867–1954), 310
Kugler, Franz (1808–1858), 30

Kühn, Paul, 86, 88, 527
Kulmann, Elisabeth, 19

Lalo, Édouard (1823–1892), 342
Lamoureux, Charles (1834–1899), 343
Laurens, Jean-Joseph Bonaventura (1801–1890), 305
Laux, Karl (1896–1978), 319, 320, 322, 527
Leaver, Robin, 321, 332, 527
Leech-Wilkinson, Daniel, 178, 179
Leinsdorf, Erich (1912–1993), 360, 361, 364, 365, 374
Leipzig Quartet, 180
Leistra-Jones, Karen, 162
Lemcke, Carl (1831–1913), 62, 63, 64, 66, 68
Lessing, Karl Friedrich (1808–1880), 30
Les Six, 346, 352
Levi, Hermann (1839–1900), 30, 38
Levit, Igor, 357, 358, 373, 374
Lewin, David, 280–81, 528
Lichtenberg, Georg Christoph (1742–1799), 27, 28
Ligeti, György (1923–2006), 388, 391, 392, 528
Lindberg, Morten, 186, 528
Liszka, James Jacób, 105
Liszt, Franz (1811–1886), 12, 36, 156, 159, 172, 174, 196, 278, 306, 341
Litvak, Anatole (1902–1974), 352, 354
Liverpool Philharmonic Orchestra, 362
Loewe, Carl (1796–1869), 104
Loges, Natasha, 156, 528
London Philharmonic Orchestra, 185
London Protocol (1952), 65, 66
Lott, R. Allen, 332
Löwe, Ferdinand (1865–1925), 315
Lucerne Festival, 375, 377, 393

Lucerne Symphony, 381. See also
  Wolfgang Rihm, *Symphonie*
  "Nähe Fern"
Lully, Jean-Baptiste (1632–1687), 349
Luther, Martin (1483–1546), 18, 325
Lutheran *ars moriendi*, 333–35
Lutheran church, 324, 332
Lutheran musical traditions, 321,
  322, 325, 332, 333, 335, 336, 337,
  339, 358
Lutyens, Elisabeth (1906–1983),
  362, 529
Luzerner Sinfonieorchester, 375

Macpherson, James. *See* Ossian
Magirius, Heinrich (1934–2021), 332
Mahler, Gustav (1860–1911), 72, 196,
  363, 367, 368, 369, 373, 377, 378,
  392, 529
  Symphony No. 1 in D Major,
    "Titan", 72
  Symphony No. 2 in C Minor,
    "Resurrection", 373
  Symphony No. 5, 373
  Symphony No. 7, 373
Makart, Hans (1840–1884), 310, 315
Malle, Louis (1932–1995), 349, 350, 529
Marrou, Henri-Irénée (1904–
  1977), 347
Marx, Karl (1818–1883), 399, 529
Marxsen, Eduard (1806–1887),
  11, 106
Matthews, David (b. 1943), 361
Mauersberger, Rudolf (1889–1971),
  322, 323, 324, 335–39
  Dresdner Requiem, 336, 337,
    338, 339
  Wie liegt die Stadt so wüst, 335, 336
May, Florence (1845–1923), 28, 108,
  156, 157, 529
McClelland, Ryan, 148, 195, 198, 227,
  228, 530

McEwan, Ian, 92
McManus, Laurie, 150
Melnikov, Alexander, 180, 181
Mendelssohn, Felix (1809–1847), 3,
  53, 144, 196, 229–48, 276, 342
  Cello Sonata No. 1 in B flat Major,
    Op. 45, 235, 236, 238, 242
  Midsummer Night's Dream, A,
    overture, 239
  Octet in E flat Major, Op. 20, 234,
    236, 238
  Piano Quartet No. 1 in C Minor,
    Op. 1, 237
  Piano Quartet No. 2 in F Minor,
    Op. 2, 144
  Piano Trio No. 1 in D Minor,
    Op. 49, 236, 242
  Piano Trio No. 2 in C Minor,
    Op. 66, 231, 236, 238, 232, 243
  String Quartet No. 2 in A Minor,
    Op. 13, 144, 238
  String Quartet No. 3 in D Major,
    Op. 44 No. 1, 241, 244
  String Quartet No. 4 in E Minor,
    Op. 44, No. 2, 241–2
  String Quartet No. 5 in E flat
    Major, Op. 44 No. 3, 242
  String Quintet No. 1 in A Major,
    Op. 18, 144
  String Quintet No. 2 in B flat
    Major, Op. 87, 233, 237
  Symphony No. 3 in A Minor,
    "Scottish," Op. 56, 232
Menzel, Adolph (1815–1905), 19, 33,
  43–49, 55
  *Emilie am Klavier stehend (Emilie
    Standing at the Piano)*, 1866, 48
  Flötenkonzert (Flute Concert),
    ca. 1848, 46
  Iron Rolling Mill, 1872–1875, 45
  Krönung (Coronation),
    1861–865, 49

General Index

Leipziger Volksszenen (Leipzig Folk Scenes), 1831, 47
Meyer, Thomas, 377, 382, 392, 393, 394, 530
Micznik, Vera, 105
Mies, Paul, 95, 98, 104, 530
Miles, Geoff, 185, 186, 187
Miller, Jonathan, 3, 530
Miller, Patrick, 148
Misch, Ludwig (1887–1967), 361
Monahan, Seth, 105, 196, 531
Montand, Yves (1921–1991), 352
Moreau, Jeanne (1928–2017), 349
Morghen, Raphael (1758–1833), 54
Moser, Andreas (1859–1925), 156, 157, 158, 160, 161, 162, 173, 175, 531
Mozart, Wolfgang Amadeus (1756–1791), 19, 54, 185, 196, 230, 235, 278, 302, 310, 311, 312, 342, 396
   Piano Sonata No. 1, K. 279, 239
   Sinfonia Concertante, K. 364, 185
   Symphony No. 40 in G Minor, K. 550, 210
   Symphony No. 41 in C Major, K. 551, 210
Mueller-Stahl, Arnim, 318
Mühlfeld, Richard (1856–1907), 43
Munch, Charles (1891–1968), 348
Musgrave, Michael, 95, 98, 160, 531
Mussorgsky, Modest (1839–1881), 347

Nabokov, Vladimir (1899–1977), 91
Nagano, Kent, 368
Nagel, Wilibald (1870–1911), 1
Nakamastsu, Jon, 179
Napoleon Bonaparte (1769–1821), 57, 64
National Socialist German Workers' Party. *See* Nazis
National Socialist sublime, 334
Nattiez, Jean-Jacques, 105, 532

Nauhaus, Gerd, 17, 532
Nazis, 61, 319, 323, 325, 334, 335, 346
Neo-Riemannian theory, 278, 279
New *Formenlehre*, 19, 235
Nézet-Séguin, Yannick, 373
Nietzsche, Friedrich (1844–1900), 304, 352, 373, 532
Nonnenmann, Rainer, 367, 368
Nono, Luigi (1924–1990), 378
Notley, Margaret, 23, 532
Novalis (Friedrich von Hardenberg, 1772–1801), 19, 24, 389, 391

Onslow, George (1784–1853), 230
Ossian (James Macpherson), 13, 72
Othmayr, Caspar (1515–1553), 114–16, 125–28
Otten, Georg Dietrich (1806–1890), 59
Ovid (Pūblius Ovidius Nāsō, 43BC–17/18AD), 86

Pace, Ian, 174, 398, 399, 406, 407, 408, 533
Palestrina, Giovanni Pierluigi da (ca. 1525–1594), 19
Parakilas, James, 95, 105
Parent, Armand, 343, 344
Parmer, Dillon, 93–96, 98, 533
Pasdeloup, Jules, 343
Peace of Prague (1866), 67
Percy, Thomas (1729–1811), 93, 107
Peres Da Costa, Neal, 178, 182
Petersen, Peter, 249
Peyfuss, Karl Johann (1865–1932), 310
Pfitzner, Hans (1869–1949), 368
Phelan, James, 92
Philadelphia Orchestra, 373, 375
Philip, Robert, 178
Pinkert, Anke, 322, 534
Plato, 18, 32

Pléiade, the, 347
Poe, Edgar Allan (1809–1849), 93
Pohl, Carl Ferdinand (1819–1887), 52
Potter, Pamela, 323, 534
Poulenc, Francis (1899–1963), 343
Power, Lawrence, 179
Prometheus, 83, 85, 86, 88
Prussian Order *Pour le Mérite*, 44

Rachmaninoff, Sergei (1873–1943), 40
Ranke, Leopold von (1795–1886), 302
Raphael (Raffaello Sanzio da Urbino, 1483–1520), 54
Raphael, Günter (1903–1960), 361
Reddick, Carissa, 207, 534
Reger, Max (1873–1916), 302, 332, 357, 358, 359, 373
Reinick, Robert (1805–1852), 106
Reményi, Ede (1828–1898), 156–64, 169, 170–76, 305
Reni, Guido (1575–1642), 54
Revolutions of 1848, 34, 56, 60
Reyland, Nicholas, 105, 526
Reynolds, Christopher, 79, 535
Rhau, Georg (1488–1548), 126
Richter, Jean Paul (1763–1825), 8, 10, 13, 18–22
Rickards, Guy, 367
Rihm, Wolfgang (b. 1952), 3, 365, 375–95
  Brahmsliebewalzer, 373, 375
  Das Lesen der Schrift, 368, 375
  Dis-Kontur, 378
  Ernster Gesang, 375, 377, 381
  Erscheinung: Skizze über Schubert, 377
  Fremde Szenen I–III, 378
  Goethe Lieder, 376, 378
    ("Dämmrung senkte sich von oben," 376, 378, 379, 395)
  Harzreise im Winter, 378
  Hölderlin Fragmente, 378
  Jakob Lenz, 378
  Klavierstück Nr 6, 375
  Ländler, 378
  Morphonie, Sektor IV, 378
  Sub-Kontur, 378
  Symphonie "Nähe Fern," 365, 375–95 ("Nähe Fern 1,"381–84; "Nähe Fern 2," 382, 385–87; "Nähe Fern 3," 385; "Nähe Fern 4," 385, 388–90, 391
  Symphony No. 2, 378
  Symphony No. 3, 378
Rings, Steven, 151, 154, 535
Rink, John, 148, 150, 535
Robbe-Grillet, Alain (1922–2008), 93
Rodin, Auguste (1840–1917), 314
Romantic *Formenlehre*, 196, 229
Romanticism, 10, 23, 346, 348, 391, 392, 394
Rosen, Charles (1927–2012), 341, 535
Rosovsky, Zoia, 185
Rossini, Gioachino (1792–1868), 75, 77
Rubinstein, Anton (1829–1894), 247
Rückert, Friedrich (1788–1866), 18, 23, 152

Sagan, Françoise (1935–2004), 341, 342, 349, 350
Saint-Saëns, Camille (1835–1921), 342, 346
Salinger, J. D. (1919–2010), 93
Salomon, Hedwig (1900–1942), 305
Sammons, Albert (1886–1957), 185
Samson, Jim, 342, 535, 536
Sandberger, Adolf (1864–1943), 308
Sargent, Malcolm (1895–1967), 360–64, 365, 373

General Index

Sargent, Pamela (1924–1944), 362, 363, 364
Satie, Erik (1866–1925), 346, 405
Sattler, Carlo (1877–1966), 313
Sattler, Michael, 385, 537
Sawallisch, Wolfgang (1923–2012), 375
Schayegh, Leila, 182
Schenker, Heinrich (1868–1935), 237, 278, 279, 280, 537
Schiller, Friedrich (1759–1805), 13, 23, 33, 75, 84, 85, 147, 148, 378, 379
Schirmer, Johann Wilhelm (1807–1863), 30
Schmalfeldt, Janet, 137, 154, 155, 196, 197, 198, 225, 537
Schneckenburger, Max (1819–1849), 64
Schoenberg, Arnold (1874–1951), 262, 276, 341, 342, 349, 392, 396–99, 402, 403, 406, 408, 410, 411, 537
   "Brahms the Progressive," 276, 341, 396, 397, 398, 402, 410, 411
Schopenhauer, Arthur (1788–1860), 35, 373
Schubert, Franz (1797–1827), 83, 169, 174, 196, 230, 235, 238, 245, 247, 276, 278, 302, 346, 368, 377, 378, 398
   Piano Sonata in B flat, D. 960, 238
Schubert, Giselher, 227
Schubring, Adolf (1817–1893), 9, 537
Schultz, Jan, 182
Schumann, Clara (1819–1896), 7, 11, 12, 17, 18, 24, 25, 27, 28, 30, 36, 44, 59, 84, 107, 137, 149, 151, 183, 184, 273, 305, 307, 310, 363, 368, 374
Schumann, Clara and Robert, 7, 12, 30, 34, 53, 72, 107, 108
Schumann, Felix (1854–1879), 273
Schumann, Georg (1866–1952), 321
Schumann, Robert (1810–1856), 7, 9, 11, 12, 17, 18, 19, 20, 22, 59, 70, 75, 107, 165, 229, 230, 235, 276, 302, 305, 306, 307, 341, 360, 368, 377
   Bunte Blätter, Op. 99
   Davidsbündler, 22, 24
   Davidsbündlertänze, Op. 6, 388
   Dichtergarten für Musik, 17, 18, 19, 20, 21
   Dichterliebe, Op. 48, 368
   Gesammelte Schriften, 13, 17
   Gesänge der Frühe, Op. 133, 10
   Kinderszenen, Op. 15, 378
   Liederkreis, Op. 39, 368
   and mental illness, 360
   "Neue Bahnen," 1, 10, 305
   Six Intermezzi, Op. 4
   Symphony No. 3, 247
   Szenen aus Goethes Faust (*Scenes from Goethe's Faust*), 70, 77
Schütz, Carl (1745–1800), 54
Schütz, Heinrich (1585–1672), 321, 323, 324, 325, 332, 333, 337, 338
Schütz-Tage (Schütz festival), 324
Scriabin, Alexander (1872–1915), 398
Scudéry, Madeleine de (1607–1701), 349
Second Viennese School, 367, 402
Second World War. *See* World War II
Shakespeare, William (ca. 1564–1616), 17, 18, 19, 43, 53, 55, 60, 73, 364
Sheehan, James J., 64, 538
Sholes, Jacquelyn, 164, 166, 169, 172, 538
Simrock, Fritz (1837–1901), 137, 250, 270, 362

Simrock, Karl (1802–1876), 112, 116–18, 128
Simrock, Peter Joseph (1792–1868), 68
Singverein of the Gesellschaft der Musikfreunde, 315
Smith, Peter H., 143, 150, 195, 196, 198, 207, 237, 538–39
Sophocles, 13, 107
Sotheby's, 19
Spies, Hermine (1857–1893), 183
Spitta, Philipp (1841–1894), 1, 110, 112, 137, 142, 143, 145, 304, 539
Spohr, Louis (1784–1859), 182, 184, 230, 539
Staatskapelle Berlin, 377
Stäger, Friedrich Wilhelm Georg, 107
Staier, Andreas, 180
Stam, Emlyn, 184, 185
Stam, Willem, 185
Stark, Lucien, 359
Stemann, Nicolas, 2
  Coronavirus Passion Play, 2
Sternau, C. O. (Otto Julius Inkermann, 1823–1862), 144
Sterne, Laurence (1713–1768), 56, 93
Stockhausen, Karlheinz (1928–2007), 377
Stockhem, Michel, 344
Stowell, Robin, 181
Strauss, Joseph (1827–1870), 304
Strauss, Richard (1864–1949), 196, 302
Stravinsky, Igor (1882–1971), 346, 392
Style hongrois, 157, 164, 167, 169, 170, 172–76, 251
Sumner Lott, Marie, 230
Szendy, Peter, 394, 540

Tappert, Wilhelm (1830–1907), 110, 111, 112, 125, 126, 128, 129, 130, 131–3, 136, 137, 540
Tarasti, Eero, 105
Taylor, Benedict, 196, 540
Taylor, Samuel A (1912–2000), 352
Tchaikovsky, Pyotr Ilyich (1840–1893), 185, 229
Tertis, Lionel, 184, 185
Thalmann, Joachim, 157, 540
Thibaut, Anton Friedrich (1772–1840), 22
Third Reich, Germany, 319, 320, 321–24, 339
Thirty Years' War (1618–1648), 324, 334
Thomson, Virgil (1896–1989), 374
Thousand and One Nights, 13, 108
Thuringian *Residenzstadt* Meiningen, 313
Tiberghien, Cédric, 179
Tieck, Ludwig (1773–1853), 19, 20, 24, 27, 35, 36
Tilgner, Viktor (1844–1896), 310, 315
Tokyo Quartet, 179
Totensonntag (Sunday of the Dead), 320, 321, 322, 324–333, 336, 337
Tovey, Donald Francis (1875–1940), 230, 541
Townsend, Mary Lee, 56, 541
Traber, Habakuk (b. 1948), 368, 369, 373
Treaty of Vienna (1864), 66
Trümmerkünste (rubble arts), 322
Twain, Mark (1835–1910), 91, 93
Twardowski-Conrat, Ilse (1880–1942), 313, 314, 315

Uecker, Günther (b. 1930), 318
Uhland, Ludwig (1787–1862), 112, 116, 117, 118, 128, 541

General Index

Ullmann, Numa Bischof, 375
Ullmann, Viktor (1898–1944), 391

Vande Moortele, Steven, 196, 197, 198, 200, 529, 541
Varwig, Bettina, 324, 541
Venuti, Lawrence, 367
Viardot, Louis (1800–1883), 35
Viardot, Pauline. *See* Pauline Garcia Viardot
Vienna
   Akademie der bildenden Künste, 315
   Beethovenplatz, 83
   Brahms-Denkmal in the Karlsplatz, 83
   Central Cemetery, 314
   Ringstraße, 315
   Schubert-Denkmal, 83
Vieuxtemps, Henri (1820–1881), 158
Vignal, Marc, 343, 346
Vlieger, Henk de (b. 1953), 361, 374
Volkmann, Robert (1815–1883), 247
Völlner, Johann Anton, 307

Wackenroder, Wilhelm Heinrich (1773–1798), 20, 78, 82
Wagner, Günther, 98
Wagner, Richard (1813–1883), 34, 36, 126, 264, 278, 302, 304, 310, 311, 312, 341, 343–46, 351, 352
Wang, Yuja, 180, 181
Wasielewski, Josef W. von (1822–1896), 9, 17
Weber, Carl Maria von (1786–1826), 13, 158, 169, 196, 302, 342

Webster, James, 79, 195, 196, 198, 228, 229, 230, 247, 542
Wehner, Arnold (1820–1880), 58, 159, 166
Wehnert-Beckmann, Berta (1815–1901), 305
Weichhold, Lothar, 334, 335
Wendt, Gustav (1827–1912), 107
Weyr, Rudolf (1847–1914), 83, 313, 315
Whittall, Arnold, 399, 405, 406, 409, 542
Widmann, Joseph Viktor, (1842–1911), 33, 51, 55, 308, 312, 542
Wigand, Georg (1808–1858), 17
Wood, James, 105, 106
World War I, 346
World War II, 319, 321, 322, 324, 325, 332, 335, 336, 337, 338, 346, 347, 350
Wüllner, Franz (1832–1902), 38, 70, 73, 77, 160

Zedlitz, J. C. von (1790–1862), 19
Zehnder, Carl (1859–1938), 3
Zender, Hans (1936–2019), 367
Ziethen, Hans Joachim von (1699–1786), 54
Zimmermann, Bernd Alois (1918–1970), 396
Zuccalmaglio, Anton Wilhelm von (1803–1869), 111, 115
Zumbusch, Caspar von (1830–1915), 53
Zurich Tonhalle, 301, 310, 311, 312